HOW TO GO DIRECTLY INTO YOUR OWN SOLO LAW PRACTICE AND SUCCEED

INTO THE NEW MILLENNIUM AND BEYOND

By Gerald M. Singer, Esq.
of the California Bar

Complete Revision of How to Go Directly Into and Manage Your Own Solo Law Practice Without Missing a Meal (1993 Edition)

WEST GROUP

Bancroft-Whitney • Clark Boardman Callaghan
Lawyers Cooperative Publishing • WESTLAW® • West Publishing

For Customer Assistance Call 1-800-328-4880

"This publication is designed to provide accurate and authoritative information in regard to the subject matter covered. It is sold with the understanding that the publisher is not engaged in rendering legal, accounting, or other professional service. If legal advice or other expert assistance is required, the services of a competent professional person should be sought."—From a Declaration of Principles jointly adopted by a Committee of the American Bar Association and a Committee of Publishers and Associations.

The paper used in this publication meets the minimum requirements of American National Standard for Information Sciences—Permanence of Paper for Printed Library Materials, ANSI Z92.48-1984.

TM

WEST GROUP is a trademark used herein under license.

Library of Congress Catalog Card Number 93-77905

DEDICATION

To Lillian, who, after more than fifty-five years, still puts up with me, is still my best friend and is more than ever the most desirable woman there is for me.

PREFATORY REMARKS

I suppose it's a lot to say that any single volume book provides all of the information needed to "go directly into, manage *and* succeed in your own solo law practice."

Well **this** one does and it *is* a lot.

That statement was made and supported in each of "*Solo*'s" preceding three editions, 1975, 1986 and 1993. It is renewed in this fourth edition for the Millennium--2000 and beyond.

Everything you need to know about going solo, from deciding whether to go solo or to find a job, through opening, managing and succeeding in your solo law practice is right here in this book, including:

Making the decision to go solo or find a job;

Finding the office you want, (at the location you want,) **and furnishing it** (free if you want);

Getting the equipment you need (free if you want);

Getting enough legal work to live on from the start, (or more if you want);

Getting case and client referrals (as much as you want);

Getting all the experience you need (faster and better than "on-the-job-training"); and

Learning the finer nuances of being a better, more productive and more successful lawyer.

There's also point-by-point guidance on how to find your best employment and get rapid advancement, if that's your decision.

There is no hedging about your part in this bargain. You must have a license to practice law and the willingness and ability to tenaciously execute the steps laid out in the text.

That was true in the first edition, 1975, in the second edition, 1986, the third edition, 1993, and it is true in this new 25th Anniversary edition for the Millennium, year 2000.

This book cannot do the job for you. No written words can. But when you read it and follow it like a road map, it will lead you through each phase from passing the Bar into your own solo law practice.

This book can be a powerful tool for you even if you decide that employment is your better choice. Many of the factors involved in a successful solo practice also make the difference between a potential law firm partner and just another associate.

Take a look at the Table of Contents and you'll see your route to a successful solo law practice laid out in spoon-feeding simplicity. Follow these steps diligently and you'll be there sooner than you thought possible.

What's happened since publication of *SOLO*-III in 1993?

Annual supplements covered some of the twists and turns along the way. Add them all up and lots of changes occurred in our law practices and, not in the least, in the technology we use. This edition covers the remaining gap.

What does it take?

Advertisements for this book have contained the proposal:

WHAT DO YOU NEED TO OPEN A SOLO LAW PRACTICE? NOTHING! *BESIDES YOUR BAR CARD and***THIS BOOK!**

That statement, unlike most commercial ads, suffers from only a minimum of excluded facts. No special attributes are required. You don't need any special kind of personality or special business acumen.

You don't need training in accounting, business administration, marketing, merchandising, or any of the other dozens of accomplishments that might serve you well in most other kinds of business enterprises.

Uh oh! I can see the sneers on the ranks of solo practice "experts" as they sniff, "of course one needs training in those things if one is to survive as a solo lawyer." Books and articles are stacked up, each specifically proclaiming this need.

Well, my written word came *first*. More importantly, **my** written word is right and theirs is wrong. What nerve! What colossal temerity.

This is a minor transgression. Read on to learn many really outrageous contradictions of "truths" that "everyone knows." No. You certainly do not need training in any of those professions for success in solo law practice.

If you happen to have such training you won't be hurt by it, but you don't need it. You **do** need to be dedicated to success. But, you'd need that dedication to be a good lawyer, wouldn't you? Of course.

You really can open your new solo law office without any training or experience.

During most of my classes, groups or seminars on "Solo," someone will interrupt with, "are you saying to open a solo law office without outside financing?" And, "do you mean to go solo without training or experience?" I've answered both of these questions up one side and down the other.

Yes, yes, to both questions. Yes, go solo without outside financing and without any prior training or experience. You could as well ask, "can you really seek a job as a lawyer without any training or experience?"

It's a wonderment to me that as many solos try it as do in the face of the many negative, even hopeless, articles and statements by the purveyors of doom. Those inaccurate prognostications--much as they are wrong--have one powerful support. They are deadly *logical*.

What I say here defies that logic with an even more powerful support: Truth! You have already demonstrated your disdain for their logic and your search for the truth in reading this book.

You get all of the training and experience you need from your association with your assigning attorneys. Aside from college, law school and this book, no other prior training or experience is needed. In my view, this is the most comprehensive and useful experience and training you can get.

These answers are clearly and unequivocally stated throughout each previous edition of *Solo* and restated in every supplement. Why these persistent doubts exist has always puzzled me.

You don't need further assurances. Just read the parts of the text dealing with soliciting as many assigning lawyers as you can and then go to work. All financing and needed training will come from your fifteen, twenty or more enthusiastic tutors.

Those attorneys will see to it that you're properly prepared before they send you out into the cruel world. They don't want you messing up their clients' cases any more than you want to fall on your face. While you are cogitating on your inadequacies, think about this: No attorney is ever sufficiently trained to handle a new case with unfamiliar issues. Add this to your fears: Almost every new case poses new unfamiliar issues.

Then why aren't all lawyers in psychotherapy? Because they know, as you will learn, that all that separates the beginner from the veteran is confidence.

Your college education and your training in law school have given you the basics for finding the information you need. Your work with your assigning lawyers will give you sufficient practical competence to help shape your confidence.

Your first few cases will complete your elevation to the level of professionalism. Without noticing when or where you've crossed that line, you've become a lawyer.

I was just 17, facing my first solo flight in a Fleet open cockpit biplane. The instructor got out of the front cockpit and said, "O.K. Jerry, take off." I didn't know whether to pee, vomit or shove the throttle forward. I did the latter. Rules required eight hours of dual flight instruction before flying solo. I'd had about twelve hours. If I wasn't ready then, when?

I made a sloppy take off and a worse landing. I did better the next time. Then, without my noticing, I was a pilot. Flying forever with an instructor wouldn't have done that for me. I had to do it alone. So will you.

Before you find your own first client, you will have garnered sufficient training and experience. And you're earning a reasonable income along the way.

Why does it happen this way? It just does. I have been waiting twenty-five years since the first edition of *Solo* for the other shoe to drop. No one has ever called or written to complain that he or she followed the book and starved. Not one irate solo ever reported he/she lacked whatever training or experience was needed to operate a solo law practice. Neither will you.

But not starving or missing meals isn't all you want from your practice, is it? You want financial and personal success, don't you? That takes something more than following the road to your solo law practice. That something extra is summed up in one word: "Salesmanship."

Selling is a common thread running through every phase of your law practice. Negotiating for an office is selling. Negotiating with other attorneys for work assignments is selling. Interviewing prospective clients is selling. Dealing with other lawyers during the course of litigation is selling. Getting the highest dollar figures from insurance adjusters is selling.

Getting judges to buy your positions on issues is selling. Persuading juries to find for your clients is selling. These things just scratch the surface of your practice. You are selling from the moment you enter your office until you go home for the night. Then, if you sell well enough, you'll get rich.

Learning to become a professional salesman requires much, much more information than will be given to you in this book. However, the parts not included are unnecessary for the selling you'll be doing in your law practice. You won't be less skilled than the professional in what you must do.

Salesmanship is simply the giving of information that is valued by the listener.

Obviously, much more than this simple fact must be learned. That is why the subject is covered in a whole chapter and in other information scattered throughout this book.

You must learn how to derive that information and by what technique you determine that the listener will be interested.

You'll learn how to avoid contaminating the valued information with other information. You must also keep the getting and giving information phases scrupulously separated.

You will be conditioned for solo practice by the material in this book. You will, figuratively be held by the hand as you take the preliminary steps, find your office, set up your office, manage your office and practice, and make sufficient amounts of money all the while. You will literally "go directly into solo law practice without missing a meal."

Anyone can become a solo lawyer, but not everyone is made for solo law practice.

For reasons I have never really understood, some folks just cannot be on their own. These exceptions to the solo practice crowd simply must have direction or they just cannot function. They need to be told where to go, when, why and what to do when they get there.

Not everyone recognizes that need in himself or herself. Some folks do not believe they have it, though others near and dear to them often know they do. This book makes it clear for you. You will know whether you are, or are not, solo practice material.

Just be honest with yourself as you read the tests for the solo lawyer. Those tests will be like a mirror you must hold up to yourself. Look closely. If you see someone you recognize in the analyses, and that person is you, don't fight it. You may do well in employment but not as a solo lawyer.

There's something for everyone in this book whether solo lawyer or employee.

Much of what's in this book is common to both solo practice and successful career employment. If you're pre-directed toward employment rather than operating your own law office, read the whole book. You will then be better prepared for making a successful career of employment rather than just a job.

You will learn what makes the difference between employees who are dropped by the firms and those who are retained, and even promoted, in tough times.

My belief is that solo law practice is the only way to fly. So, in this book you will never see a discouraging word. It will be your decision, based on your own self- recognition that you will form. If you must be employed, be the best, dammed employee you can possibly be. This book will help you do just that.

But, if, like me, you cannot see any other road for yourself but the solo practice of law, then pay close attention and follow the words as though lines on a road map. Keep one thing in mind at all times. The subject of going solo is not just one person's opinion over another's.

This subject is as much a body of knowledge to be learned as the study of mathematics, electronics or even the study of law itself. It is not "common sense," "logic" or anything of the kind.

These facts are not open to debate. Is that dogmatic? Perhaps. But trust in this. If you want to open your own solo law practice, directly from law school, you will be shown how to do that, step-by-step. Can you learn that from any other book? You'll know why you cannot after you've read the first quarter of this book.

You may jump to a conclusion here and there, believing that you grasp a particular topic without reading it fully. Don't do that. This book is intended to show you the way to a **successful** solo law practice, not just how to make a few bucks working for other lawyers.

You are NOT a "contract attorney" or anything of that sort.

A "contract attorney" is just another form of employee. He/she may be an independent contractor instead of pay-rolled help, but it is still essentially employment. This is inversely proportional to what this book is preparing you to do.

You want your own practice with your own clientele.

You want to practice law *your way,* not as someone else dictates. You want the independence that comes with being a solo law practitioner.

Beyond that, a successful law practice is much more than earning however much or even having a yard full of good-paying clients. You'll learn from this book what some lawyers have failed to learn in a practice lifetime.

You are not ready to go solo until you have finished this book, completely. Read it, line-by-line, chapter-by-chapter. It takes just a few hours of your time. It's not too much to give in exchange for an enviable career. It's easy to get sidetracked.

Many clever attorneys who have tried solo practice the wrong way have found that out. This book will show you how to start earning money in your solo practice right from the start.

But earning money, even lots of money, is not all there is to a solid law practice. This book is about building something more than an income of so many dollars per year. A job will do that.

You'll want an entity with a secure future and some personal satisfaction. Financial reward is a start. You'll learn how to gain that fast. The rest takes a bit longer. You'll learn it all right here in this book. Be patient and read it all, carefully.

GERALD M. SINGER

WHO IS GERALD M. SINGER AND WHAT BUSINESS DOES HE HAVE WRITING THIS BOOK?

Before discussing my background and qualifications to teach and write on this subject, I'd like to explain how this book came to be. Thoughts about writing a book on this subject began forming while I was an adjunct professor of law at Loyola Law School, Los Angeles, in 1974.

I was asked to teach a course on the nuts and bolts of practicing law. I shaped the course within the vehicle of opening a new law office.

I discovered that learning to start and operate a solo law office includes basic information for success in any phase of law practice. A lawyer should know all about the functions of running a law office even as an employee. You can't do a topnotch job as an associate lawyer without understanding the concerns of your employer.

Over the next eleven years I innovated and taught Lawyering Skills and the Practicalities of Legal Practice. I also taught several semesters of Legal Ethics.

Each of these subjects dealt directly with methods, functions, concerns and problems involved in a law office operation. Where do the employee lawyer's duties and solo practitioner's duties separate?

I've lectured on this subject in many prominent law schools and before bar association conventions and a large number of other lawyers' gatherings for more than twenty-five years. In 1991 and 1992, I was commissioned to teach a series of classes at Loyola Law School for the California State Bar Minimum Continuing Legal Education Program.

Why was I selected to establish and teach these subjects?

My business background was uniquely shaped to provide the precise information needed to start and run a solo law practice. I have had two highly successful and satisfying careers.

First, as a "hands-on" chief executive officer of a large electronics manufacturing, distribution and retailing firm. The second as a successful solo lawyer. Both careers have spanned more than fifty years.

As president of Bigg of California, Inc., a California corporation, I conceived and developed methods for the opening of seven profitable company-owned retail electronic, audio-video showrooms. I was also directly involved in the implementation of over 250 national franchised retail stores.

The trick is to start the business "in the black," fast. I have no patience with the idea that you must starve for a year or two while waiting for business.

What made that "trick" possible was my constant experimentation with diversified marketing, merchandising, advertising and general promotional activities. Not the least important was the highly acclaimed, tested sales training program that I conceived, designed, wrote and produced for my firm and its franchise operations.

This was the very first sales training program to reduce the course to a specific body of knowledge. The program's substance could be learned by anyone willing to apply the required effort without any personality or background requisites.

Training salespeople, like training in other fields, required learnable information and not just demonstration. I had long since concluded something that was not then widely accepted.

Selling is the giving of valued information rather than trying to persuade. But the method by which such information is transacted remained to be developed.

The majority of all salespeople then firmly believed that the task in selling is persuading the customer to buy the product. One just could not differ with this view. So ingrained was this common belief that to suggest an opposing view was tantamount to challenging one's religious belief.

When we consider the fact that the majority of salespeople then, as now, failed to earn more than a bare living, it's a lesser stretch to accept this opposing view.

To say that we do not attempt to persuade anyone to do, or not do, anything was then almost blasphemy. "How can you sell something to someone without persuading that person to buy it?" A logical and seemingly impenetrable contention.

Yet, as you will learn, this is one of several fallacies that have perpetuated mediocrity in the sales force ranks. We will expand on this subject, dissect it and analyze it painstakingly.

It's necessary that you know the basics of selling to succeed as a lawyer. This is so whether as a law firm associate, partner or a solo practitioner. Without a basic understanding of this vital subject, the lawyer is limited to picking up practice scraps.

The top earning lawyers are the best lawyers. Right? **Wrong!** The top earning lawyers are the best attorney salesmen. You don't believe this? Of course you don't. How could you when you haven't yet learned what selling is all about.

What is the basic difference between an attorney who charges $250 per hour from one charging $600 per hour? What does the client who engages the $600 per hour lawyer know about that lawyer? One fact that's known is that he/she knows how to get a fee of $600 per hour.

Is that lawyer worth $600 per hour? How can a prospective client make that judgment? Veteran attorneys will disagree in discussions about the qualities of other attorneys with almost as many diverse opinions as there are attorneys. Pity the poor client left to his/her own devices for that decision. What's it all about? Salesmanship.

I started with structuring the sales interview and then developed a worktable on the dynamics of selling. From this, the total selling transaction was built upon four basic phases:

1) Getting information,
2) Giving information,
3) The demonstration (or the "show"), and
4) The close.

The result, finally achieved in 1955, was a course and teaching method that had little or nothing to do with the style or special ability of the student. The course was taught to teachers by the same method.

I've held sales symposia in almost every major city on behalf of my company, as well as other firms over a period of many years. My conclusion on the need to maintain precise separation of the four phases to achieve the highest "close" percentage was totally justified.

At age 45, I decided to leave business for a new venture. Some of my friends and business associates questioned my mental state in leaving a well established, lucrative business at its peak. Not Lillian, my wife. She totally supported me in whatever I chose to do. [Oddly, that's still her view.]

I felt the need for something more, perhaps more personal, from my efforts. There were many jabs of personal satisfaction in the business but I was feeling more and more detached as the business grew.

I wanted to study medicine, but at my age I was not admissible. They wanted live doctors. The same demand was not made of lawyers so I opted out for law school. I became a candidate for the California Bar as a student at Loyola Law School in 1965.

In June 1968, upon graduation and before taking the Bar exam, I opened my new office on a legal services in exchange for space arrangement. At that time, little was known of such arrangements. The term "time-for-space" was yet to be coined by me for use in my classes at Loyola and later in *Solo*-I.

My first try at finding a new office was a phone call to a lawyer who had advertised for an employee. I convinced the advertiser that my services would benefit him more per dollar than an employee.

I showed him how my work would more than equal the rent and overhead for the use of an office. We agreed on terms despite my not yet having been admitted to practice.

I could afford to pay rent, but I wanted fast experience through concentrated exercises of law work. A time-for-space arrangement seemed like the best way of getting rapid, diversified assignments. It worked out fine.

Two weeks after being sworn in, I had my first jury trial. It took little time and effort to garner about fifteen lawyers who would provide me with work projects to fill my days. I was confident that the training I would get from those lawyers would surpass what I might gain working in a large law firm.

I knew that the business experience that I used to start my law practice was translatable to a course for aspiring solo practitioners. My first task was to adapt this subject to the substance test as I did in developing my selling course.

It was then commonly believed among lawyers that starting a law practice would take lots of money and experience. Teaching the subject mandated diametrical opposition to that belief. This required that the course content and materials be simple and irrefutable.

Most law students have had little or no practical experience in business. Their traditional training and experience was limited to academics and only a theoretical understanding of business. To make matters worse, lawyers are predisposed to disparage opposing views.

I had seen lawyers trying to make it on their own, chasing circular pathways. Even more pitiable were the trapped lawyers, who believed that the only way to private practice was years chained in large firm apprenticeships, holding little prospect of escape.

"Where do you get your experience? Who's going to finance the years of 'red ink' before you start earning a living?" These and other such questions had to be answered. Most important, the new practitioner student must be assured of a living while building the practice.

The finalized course offered something for everyone. The more venturesome could start by plunging right in. Those with nagging doubts could step in toes first until accustomed to the water. In either case, the charts were clearly marked.

I began lecturing on the subject at Loyola Law School, and elsewhere. With a fist full of lecture syllabus pages, thoughts about writing a book began to stir. Thus appeared the first edition of *How to Go Directly into Your Own Solo Law Practice (Without Missing a Meal)* (1975, LCP/BW).

Then the personal computer thundered upon the scene. I had been using a computer for my practice and personal affairs almost from its inception but with little real expertise.

The 1986 revision of *Solo* required inclusion of computers for lawyers. Knowing that the computer would be indispensable as a lawyer's tool, I had to "crash" learn all about it for use in my book and my teachings.

That was easier said than done. I faced the same obstructions that kept me from developing extensive computer skills for my own use. There were few reliable and **readable** sources of information on hardware, software or methodologies. A scant, few well-informed sales people or technical experts existed then (even as today).

So, it was necessary for me to do my own research to find the right equipment and programs. I was in the same boat as my students and readers. Computer texts offered no comfort.

Each book started, almost stereotypically, with the assurance of simple, plain English, easily understood by neophytes. Then, suddenly, those "simple" words and phrases changed, line by line, into an abyss of inscrutable hyper-technical "computerese." The turn of a page and you knew you weren't in Kansas anymore.

I had to spend countless hours deciphering the gibberish and gobbledygook of the written and spoken words. Expressions and smirks of pseudo "experts" made it clear that my failure to understand them was tantamount to low grade idiocy.

I established my own computer "primer" from an elementary restructuring of hardware and software data. From that as a source, I composed what was then to be a computer guidebook for solo lawyers.

Solo-I, *Solo*-II, *Solo*-III and now into the Millennium, *Solo*-IV 2000, remains the only authoritative source on starting, managing and succeeding in your own solo practice.

Apply your best efforts in following the material in this book and use your good judgment in making decisions along the way and you may say, in the twilight of your career, as the author now says, *"the game was worth the candle."*

PUBLISHER'S FORWARD

This "millennium and beyond" edition of *How to Go Directly into Your Solo Law Practice and Succeed* builds on the past efforts of Gerald M. Singer and blazes the trail for a solo law practitioner into the third millennium. Importantly, this new edition addresses the astonishing technological advances that have occurred since the third edition of *Solo* published in 1993.

Ahead of his time, Mr. Singer featured the value of computers in the second edition of *Solo*, in 1986, and now continues to stress the value that technology provides to the solo practitioner; especially in the way that it can "level the playing field" with larger firms and attorneys that have greater resources.

Still, many of the same principles that appeared in the first *Solo* edition of 1975 maintain their importance in this version. One of the most important of these principles is "Salesmanship," which Mr. Singer identifies as a key factor to any successful law practice. As he emphasizes throughout this book, "salesmanship" means the giving of information that is valued by the listener.

This book, of course, provides much more and addresses all aspects of a solo law practice, from the initial groundwork required to establish the practice to the final goal of a successful and enriching professional experience. Mr. Singer provides the road map to show the way, though it is up to the practitioner to carry out the plan. However, as Mr. Singer continually states, he has the confidence that his methods will serve as the proper guide.

How to Solo shows the way for a new lawyer to start a practice without many resources nor much practical training. As Mr. Singer states, "all you need is your bar card and this book." In accomplishing this, the book also raises thoughtful matters that help a new lawyer decide whether he or she is "solo material" or whether employment is the wiser path.

The book also stresses the value of professionalism, hard work and confidence as key traits a solo lawyer must have. Mr. Singer explains how these traits can develop and flourish. With the "Seven Basic Rules for Solo Practice Survival," Mr. Singer highlights the essential habits required to not just survive but succeed as a "solo."

Of course, this book also addresses the day-to-day aspects of a successful solo law practice. It illustrates how to find and start an office and identifies the resources a solo practice requires. As indicated above, the importance and great value of computer technology serves as a cornerstone of any successful law practice. This book reviews a variety of hardware and software options from computer specifications to word processing and billing software, as well as the usefulness of electronic legal research materials.

In addition, the issues of law practice administration and management, billing, ethical matters, professional liability insurance, and even tax and investment considerations for the solo practitioner all receive the attention of Mr. Singer. Moreover, the book discusses the eventual expansion of a solo law practice and specific areas or specialties for a solo practitioner.

As Mr. Singer proclaims, after bar admission, this book provides what the novice attorney requires for a successful and worthwhile solo law practice. One final thing, this book will be fun to read. With his informal and witty style of writing, Mr. Singer educates and amuses the reader at the same time. Importantly, however, in this 25th Anniversary edition, Mr. Singer expresses in a sincere manner *How to Go Directly into Your Solo Law Practice and Succeed.*

George M. Gullo
West Group

CONTENTS OF THIS VOLUME

Chapter 1

An Outline of the Dynamics of a Successful Solo Practice

§ 1:1 Generally

The Singer Method.

What is the "Singer Method?" This is a two-part question: (1) How can you go directly into a solo law practice with no financial backing? and (2) How do you do this with no previous experience?

These subjects are dealt with from all different angles throughout this book. However, the following information may cause some to conclude that the answers to this question and its two sub-parts are simple. They are not.

At the risk of impatience overtaking better judgment, a sketchy approach and generalized view to the answers follow. Please read all parts of this book for full and complete answers to these important matters.

The first thing you must understand about the following information is that you are NOT operating as a "contract attorney" or anything of the sort. As you read further into this book you will see clearly that what you'll be doing is as far from what "contract attorneys" do as the earth is from the sun.

At the outset you'll recognize that "contract attorneys" are in business to get work from other attorneys. They work at a low price because that price is all they're worth. You are in business to develop your own solo law practice. That is your goal and your only goal. You work at a low price, perhaps lower than the contract attorney's price solely to attract more assignments and thus more experience. That price is not a measure of your worth.

You should charge as little as you can consistent with your living costs because you want experience, the training the assigning lawyers can give, and their client and case referrals. The contract attorney wants only the fee they charge. See the difference?

To start with, here is the basic proposition:

How can you go directly into a solo law practice with no financial backing?

During the first phase of your solo practice development, you'll receive work assignments from a whole gallery of other lawyers at your own selected hourly rate. You'll be paid for the work you do each day. Your fee for work from other lawyers will be much lower than your charges to new clients but sufficient to finance your practice and your life. (How you get those new clients is fully explained later.)

How can you do this with no previous experience?

These assigning lawyers will train you as you progress in your work assignments. All along the way, you'll collect a steady flow of your own clients and cases referred to you by these attorneys. (Why and how these referrals will occur is also explained in full detail.)

When you have accrued sufficient training, experience, clients and cases you will methodically withdraw from these assignments and build on your own law practice. This whole first phase shouldn't take longer than a few months.

This method has been tested and proven by thousands of attorneys who have read the previous three editions of this book over the past twenty-five years. In all this time, I've not received a single report of failure from any reader nor any student of classes that I have taught on this subject for twelve years.

Well, actually, there was one negative report. Several years ago I received a phone call from an irate woman. She complained that I was remiss in failing to warn women of the dangers of sex discrimination in law practice. She related a couple of stories to support her complaint. I asked her how long she had been in practice. She said she was admitted to the bar of her state "three weeks ago."

I agreed with her that women were not being treated fairly in many instances but that overall she should do quite well as a solo practitioner. At that time there weren't many women in solo practice and there was virtually an open field for them. Although women in law practice continue to grow in numbers and proportion, they still are a small minority as solo lawyers.

I suggested that she give it a few months following the book's methods. She agreed to do that. I invited her to call me then and share her experiences with me. I received a very laudatory letter from her some time later. Apparently her solo practice had become quite active and she was able to cope with the inequities.

You should be aware of the possibility of premature conclusions. Don't be hasty in deciding that you understand all of the phases in preparing for your solo practice. Some of the points may seem simpler than they really are. Do both of us the favor of completing the whole book before you jump the gun.

§ 1:2 A first approach

Charge as LITTLE, not as much, as you can get by with.

I have been preaching for over twenty-five years that brand new lawyers should charge not as much, but as little, as possible. That is, fees charged to assigning attorneys, not clients. Of course, we're not usually dealing with that many clients at first, are we?

Do the mathematics. Compute how much you need to support your family. Divide that by the hours you anticipate your workdays will be. My recommendation is to charge that much only. More will come later.

Remember the reason that you're in business during those first few months. You're not trying to build a practice based on what other attorneys pay you. You have two goals: first, to receive the necessary training and experience from them (being paid a living stipend along the way) and second, to build a practice through their client referrals, since, the hourly fees paid you for your work is only a means to this end.

Essentially, you will be starting your solo practice through accepting work assignments on an hourly fee arrangement. Your hourly fee to other lawyers will be substantially less than the fees you will be charging clients. This first stage will last only a few short months after which you will be up and running as a solo lawyer with a clientele of your own.

Many questions will occur to you. Don't waste your time trying to find the answers at this point. Everything will fall into place at the proper time as you read through the book.

You are not operating as a "contract attorney."

This will be repeated a few times throughout this book. There have been some misconceptions about the work assignments method. None more irritating to me than the totally fallacious comparison to the notion of a "contract attorney."

This is not what you are. You are NOT in the "business" of contracting out your services. Your goal is NOT to establish a practice on a wholesale hourly basis. You are trying to build a law practice of your own, not to spend your life working for other lawyers. Those who've perpetuated these erroneous conclusions seem not to have read any of the editions of this book. Still, there are usually one or two members of the audience attending my lectures who refer to that foolish notion.

You will inform the lawyers whom you contact that you are only temporarily offering your services to them until you establish your own solo law practice. How this is done will be fully explained and detailed in the following chapters. All of your questions will be answered, and all of your fears and doubts dispelled.

§ 1:3 Compare your services with cost of hiring employee

You'll discover that you can get immediate work assignments from other lawyers at decent fees. Let's call these assigning lawyers "Assignors." You will quickly show prospective employers how they will profit from being "Assignors" instead of employers. It will be easy for the Assignors to see how letting you do their work on an assignment basis will save them loads of money over the cost of hiring a lawyer employee.

Invite the Assignor to make these comparisons:

COST OF EMPLOYEE:

1. WAGES: Wages are only a part of the employee's pay cost, including:
   a) Social Security and Unemployment Insurance
   b) Workers' Compensation Insurance Premiums
   c) Sick Leave
   d) Vacation Pay
   e) Pension Plan
   f) Medical Insurance
2. HIDDEN COSTS: Hidden employment costs amount to even more:
   a) Absenteeism
   b) Mistakes and do-overs
   c) Idle time
   d) Teaching and orientation time
   e) Palavering
   f) Severance pay
3. COST OF OFFICE, EQUIPMENT AND FURNISHINGS: This is the most substantial of all of the added costs of hiring an employee:
   a) Office. An employee must have a place to work.
   b) Furniture. An employee's office must be furnished. A desk is needed, chairs, tables, etc.

c) Equipment. An employee needs such equipment as is necessary to accomplish the assigned work; including computers and software.

COMPARE ALL OF THE ABOVE TO COST OF WORK ASSIGNMENT TO YOU:

1. YOUR FEE. Make them an offer they can't refuse.
2. THAT'S IT!! NO CONTRIBUTIONS, NO EXTRAS, NOTHING HIDDEN.
3. WAIT! THAT'S NOT ALL!
   a) THE OFFICE. You will need only one office and ask only one Assignor for an office. HOWEVER, if you use that office, they don't pay for it. You do. HOW? You pay by contributing a given number of your work hours in exchange.
   b) REMEMBER, when they *hire* a lawyer, they get nothing for that office. It's the employer's normal expense. BUT YOU are willing to pay for the office in value-given work hours. If they have no extra office, that's fine. You'll get your office elsewhere. But they won't have the expense of finding an office somewhere for their unnecessary lawyer employee.
4. TIME WASTE. It won't cost them for wasted time because you won't waste either their time or yours. You charge only for completed work at the reasonably interpreted time based on the agreed fee.

Other ways of saving your assigning lawyers money: Payroll costs, absenteeism, health care, child care, etc.

More and more employment costs are being heaped upon employers, including attorney employers. Some of these nouveau costs are not mandatory, but are bargaining points when negotiating with the more desirable employee candidates.

Health care and child care are two important additions to the "Cost of Employee" list. An important reason for the stagnation of President Clinton's proposed Health Care bill was the sizable added payroll cost imposed on smaller employers.

Despite that objection, many businesses, including the smaller ones, are voluntarily offering private health care coverage to enhance the quality of their personnel rolls. More recently, the larger firms are beginning to include child care arrangements to encourage newer mothers to join the firm or to stay on the job.

Whether or not the firm you are soliciting has entered that part of the arena, you should include these added employment costs. This helps to demonstrate the savings you offer whether in a "Time For Space" approach or seeking work assignments.

You will stress that failing to offer these benefits limits them to the second string employee prospects. You would be a first string addition to the firm without any employee payroll costs, contributions, salary leakages or inducements of any kind or at all.

Point out that whether they now offer such benefits, sooner or later these voluntary perks will become mandatory. History has taught us that employee benefits starting as "good ideas" ultimately become statutory requisites. It would profit the firm to engage a work assistance program that avoids all of the present, as well as future, costs and entanglements. **You!**

§ 1:4 Your first exercise

Consider the following:

1. An average starting fee for a new lawyer in your town.

2. An average work week of eight hours per day, five days per week.

3. Now, let's take an arbitrary $30 per hour as your "offer they can't refuse." If you are given five hours per day at $30 per hour, that's $150 daily or $750 per week. At that rate, you're paid $36,750 per year based on a forty-nine week year. No employee will produce anywhere near that many work weeks per year. Plus, an employee will be paid for vacation periods. *Not you.* Where in the U.S. will a good employee like yourself be obtained for $36,750? Of course, they won't need you for five hours a day; you're too productive for that. Hence, their cost will be substantially less to obtain the same work quotient that an employee would put out working the theoretical eight hours per day.

4. Now, consider that you will be working eight hours per day for your collective assignors (you'll be deriving work assignments from several would-be "employers"). That totals $240 per day or $1,200 per week. At that rate, your yearly income would be $58,800 based on the same 49 workweek year. That's only about $20,000 per year more than the displaced employee.

BUT LOOK!! That's just the base number. You'll be getting client referrals constantly along the way. How? You'll be shown how to do this, step-by-step, point-by-point on a road map of "how to."

You have, of course, silently asked how you will find time to accommodate these many new client referrals when your work weeks are filled, top to bottom, by work assignments. Right? Good question. The answer is so simple you'll wonder why you thought the question was a good one. You start cutting down your work assignments as your client referrals begin.

As your clientele develops, you phase out your work assignments. Of course, you're way ahead of me. You obviously do not charge your clients $30 or $40 per hour (nor do you necessarily even charge your work assignors that low a fee). Remember, that was "an offer they cannot refuse." Do a bit more canvassing and use a smidgen more *chutzpah,* and you can get $40, $50, even $60 per hour from your assigning attorneys. After all, haven't you saved them thousands of dollars in squandered, unproductive employee costs. You can surely show them in black and white how $50, maybe $60 per hour can be a bargain compared to the costs of employment. Right?

BUT WAIT! That's a good idea ONLY if you can get that much without losing an assignor who can contribute to your education, give you lots of work of a better class and provide you with client referrals. Don't be too quick to sell out such opportunities for a few bucks more. Bear in mind that the assignment process is designed to be temporary. This is a technique to get you into your own solo law practice (without missing a meal) and not a permanent way of life.

§ 1:5 You're beginning to see the light

You haven't grasped the whole picture yet. You have bushels of questions, doubts and fears, of course. You've been promised that all the questions will be answered and the haze and cobwebs will be cleared up. It's far too soon for you to see the whole scenario.

It's all here for you within the following pages. By the time you've turned the last page you'll see it all vividly clear. But even now you have a glimpse of your future. You know now that you aren't working for the bucks you're getting while working for other lawyers. The experience gained while doing these jobs is one goal. The other goal is the building of your own roster of clients and cases.

Think of it this way: You're being trained to fly solo while being paid. That's a switch from law school where you paid for your education. Right?

You're learning while you're earning.

The practical experience you get is worth far more than what misguided employees get after enduring personal servitude for years. As you pick up good paying clients, you phase out your work assignments. Of course you don't charge your new clients the few bucks an hour paid to you by the other lawyers.

You must keep firmly in mind that the assignment process is only temporary. This is used solely to stay alive while you're getting your experience and developing your own clientele. Keep in mind also that you're being trained not just by one employer but by ten, twelve, fifteen or more lawyers or law firms. You'll be learning different slants on a multitude of ways of doing things. You'll see how easy it is to slip into your own practice using the leverage and efficiency of computerized law office and practice management.

This book presents only those programs and techniques suitable for small offices. These are easy to learn and operate. If you're really computer shy, you'll learn how to get by without one. But don't. You'll also be aware of the solo lawyer's ethical problems and stress, usually caused by organizational confusions. Simplified methods are shown on how to prevent these and other "solo syndromes."

§ 1:6 Solo practice: The choice for all seasons

Economic conditions and your solo law practice.

Solo practice can be a better, more lucrative, choice than employment, in *any* economic climate, especially in a recession. Here are some thoughts about the economic facts that may influence the dynamics of legal life. Economic factors, like the weather, may change faster than any warning signs can signal. Economic conditions will directly influence the income and profit picture of law. As you'll learn, the solo lawyer whose practice has been established on a sound footing can mount a variety of methods to cope with a fast changing financial environment.

Let's take a quick look at some general aspects of the economy. Then we'll explore a few daring and innovative ventures that can turn a staid law practice into an adventure.

Who's kidding whom about inflation?

Mr. Greenspan, the Federal Reserve Board ("FED") Chairman, apparently thinks there's only a slight indication of inflation justifying only a very modest increase in interest rates. Why then has the minimum wage accelerated? Everywhere you look costs are rising. Take another look at your book of accounts. Has your income been rising?

That is, rising in excess of your natural growth pattern. A new lawyer is expected to earn more and more income as his or her practice develops from its starting point.

Your hourly rate should also accelerate as your experience merits the increase. Beyond these guidelines, if the curve shows an incongruous burst, that may signify an inflationary thrust.

But there's another crazy situation formulating in the wings. The Asian financial collapse has affected many things in the U.S. besides the stock market. Prices for Asian goods have been steadily falling. This seems to have stemmed from the conversion of Hong Kong back to China ownership, although Thailand has been carrying the blame.

Whatever the cause, it has spread throughout Asia and now has even tarnished the untarnishable, Japan, where banks have been failing, reminiscent of U.S. bank failures in the 1980's. Still, there are unmistakable signs of a coming inflation here.

Well, inflation, deflation, prosperity, depression are just words. Whatever the fiscal situation, you simply roll up your sleeves and shift gears. There's always a road to take that's good for you regardless of what happens around you.

When things are good we don't ask questions we just have fun. But while our income builds what's happening to our expenses? It can be deceiving. Money comes rolling in like the tide.

Is that good? Good, yeah, if your practice is "robust" or "hot." If not, your expenses could be running away from your income. But, isn't it nice that the economy, "as a whole," is doing so well. Still, the word is that salaries have not gone up that much for the past couple of years. But you and I aren't on salaries, are we.

I've had little success in getting a reliable cross-sectional reading on just where solo law practices fit into this "hot" economy, "no inflation" picture. The higher hourly rates of the late 1980's have not since been generally exceeded in the regions I've canvassed.

When the first edition of this book was published in 1975, new lawyers were charging their own clients about $40 or $50 per hour. During the best years since then, an average solo lawyer in his or her first or second year of practice could charge, and get, as much as $150 per hour. I've not seen many newer attorneys billing much over $100 per hour these days. How does that fit this "no inflation" but "hot" economy we're experiencing? Well, rents have not been zooming up as happened back in the 80's. In fact, in some areas, rents have been relatively stable. That's possibly due to the real property foreclosure crunches that have happened since.

That's not the state of things in general. Food prices are higher. Cars have edged up. Entertainment is a bit more expensive. Other day-to-day costs have risen. But, as the records indicate, salaries have remained relatively level in some fields while inching up in others.

Still, unemployment is decreasing. Remember, the culprit in the 70's was, and could be again, oil. If, for whatever reason, oil prices zoom upward, we could be riding another rocket. Oil escalations may only be a diversion. The real villain could be real estate.

If property prices continue their upward spiral that could be the focal point for inflation. That could be even worse than the oil elevator. The collapse of real estate in the 80's created the most horrific calamity in banking in recent U.S. economic history. Banks went broke faster than the FDIC could even catalog them. Billions were lost in bank savings and holdings.

More businesses have failed within the past few years than in similar time frames of so-called "robust" economic conditions. Mortgage failures and foreclosures have subsided somewhat but are still above normal.

Shrinking profit margins have been steadily squeezing smaller businesses, and even larger discount chains, out of the retail scene. Nonetheless, housing prices are rising. Logical? Who says that logic is a necessary ingredient in any situation.

The 1980's mortgage crash was the result of overpriced realty, overeager lenders offering low-down, long-term payments, high salaried borrowers with eyes on false horizons, and a government spending rug pulled out from under all the above. Banks were taken over by a hair-triggered FDIC leaving the public holding the bag. "That can't happen again," say the banking experts. They don't explain why not.

The 1929 stock market crash was the result of a market rising faster than a bullet. Overeager brokers offering tiny margin for overpriced no-name stocks. Everyone, I mean everyone, from ditch diggers and janitors to and through corporation presidents, wanted riches and more than riches-more! Banks failed and so did the confidence of a nation. That can't happen again, say the government and market experts. Can it?

In the late 1980's, life savings were drowned by a double digit inflation. Some banks and S&L's were paying as much as 20% annual interest rates on large CD's. Businesses, unable to get workable loans, were going belly up faster than the corpses could be dragged off.

Not so long ago, $100,000 was more than enough for a comfortable retirement. $20,000 could buy a rather luxurious home purchased on a workable payment schedule. A new 1963 Cadillac cost less than $4,000. $20,000 per year was considered a fine, executive salary. Everything seemed going along smoothly. What was there to worry about? Apparently not a thing.

What about now? The administration says things are fine. Good economy, low unemployment, little inflation, everything checks out, just like 1929, 1985—Oops!

Again, the realtors are looking at real property as "wonderful security." Home owners are deluged with letters and brochures from lenders offering to throw money at their feet. Down payments? Naw. Just sign here, we trust you. Payments? Well, sure there are payments, but they don't amount to much and besides we won't bother you with them until next year. Use the money for whatever you want. Modernize the kitchen? Of course. Take the vacation now instead of next year when you can better afford it? Why not. We'll give you the money.

How about paying my bills that are way past due: Heck yes. That's what loans are for. How about to buy stocks? Well, sure. Stocks always go up, don't they?

Want to buy some stocks? Sure. Isn't there a law against buying stocks without legal margin requirements? Naw. Not when you use your very own cash that we'll give you. Pay off your overdue credit card balances. Then you can rush out and load them up again.

What has this to do with the economy indexes? Well, the most reliable index is retail sales. People don't buy things when things are tough. 1997 showed a substantial gain in retail sales. 1998 and 1999 haven't been bad either. Isn't that a real good sign? What could be better? Well, people have been fooling themselves right along about good things lasting forever. So, maybe this time they could be right.

This could be the age of the grasshopper. Down with the ants. Look at those nutty squirrels storing up for the winter.

The American Bankers Association had something to say about that. Their reports show that credit card delinquencies rose to a record level at the same time. What does that mean? It means that lots of people who couldn't pay their bills before taking out those "easy loans" are being even more strapped. That could mean a reversal toward employment shrinking, together with a more jolting stock market "adjustment." Not like 1929, certainly. Stocks can't be purchased on that old thin margin. Can they?

How does the weather vane of economy affect your practice?

Good times and bad times are not necessary adjuncts to the frivolities of economics. Things can be good for you either way. The old time sexy actress Mae West put it this way: "When I'm good, I'm great, but when I'm bad, I'm better."

As President Franklin D. Roosevelt so correctly observed when he first took office: *"The only thing we have to fear is fear itself."* Good times can be good for your practice but bad times can be even better. The problem is that people become fearful when the economic tide turns toward a recession. Would it be dangerous for you to start your new solo law practice during a recession?

Not if you've been paying attention.

Well, it IS true. All you need to do is:

1. **Open your new office early on.**
2. **Start immediately to line up a bevy of assigning lawyers.**
3. **Get the assignments done quickly and accurately.**
4. **Pester all assigning lawyers for case and client referrals. Follow the book instructions on building your clientele fast.**

Guess what? The economy is GREAT!

What do the big firms do when times get rough? They stop hiring. Some even start firing people in a panic. The result is insufficient help to get the work done. A clientele is like a big steam locomotive. It's hard to stop even when the engine stops turning.

Never fear, you are here. You're ready to do whatever they need to have done. You're not asking for anything but your meager $30, $40 or $50 per work hour. They pay you only for what you do, not for you just being there. Paradoxically, they don't need you nearly as much when things are good. Then they can hire all the help they need. Not really though. They will always need you to pick up the slack with things to be done. So, either way, it's always a good time to start.

Your time will come. Keep working the program. Before you know it, your own clientele will develop and you'll be on your way. Money is important. But to me, even more important than making more money is INDEPENDENCE! Isn't that what being a lawyer is all about? The four "B's" of legal practice:

Be healthy;
Be confident;
Be financially successful;
Be independent.

Now let's peek at vistas open to the independent solo lawyer that are closed to the workaday associate of a large law firm. Some of these ideas were crazy, some were weird and some maybe seemed that way but actually operated to change our laws and even our mores. What's more, they made millionaires of lawyers.

§ 1:7 Doorways open in solo practice: New lucrative case ideas

Being a solo practitioner affords opportunities to explore avenues of the law as the spirit may move you. Employees must perform services as directed by employers. Employees may be fascinated by new, exciting legal ideas but frustrated by the staid conservatism of the firm that pays their salary. Sure, you'll be putting in longer hours and perhaps working a bit harder at first than some employees but look what you have in your future. You're your own boss and you chart your own course. But there's even more!

Being an employee means doing what you're told to do. As a solo lawyer you can practice law as you believe you should. The following novel case ideas were innovated by independent attorneys not by associates of big law firms.

These ideas aren't included for you to rush to try out. These matters are included only to illustrate how the independent lawyer can reach out for a star and touch it. Could the attorneys who sponsored these ambitious cases have done it as associates in big law firms? Hah!

Believe it or not, most of these novel case theories were developed by solo practitioners, not by the large law firms. They didn't all fly but most of them resulted in "name appeal" for the enterprising lawyers who launched them.

Not everyone who reads and follows this book will touch a star. What is important is that the stars are out there and they are touchable and by YOU! You are a solo lawyer and you are at the helm of your own ship. You can be as creative as you dare.

Here are some thoughts to chew on. Don't get carried away, but consider some of these ideas. The first reaction to a novel situation is "The law doesn't cover it." Take note that some enterprising young attorneys have stretched that cover to carve out new, viable legal theories. You'll be too busy for the next few months, but review these recent innovations. Maybe you might find some inspiration for your own future inventions.

Some lawyers do become millionaires. Why not you? The articles reporting attorneys' million dollar fees in newspapers and on television throughout the country have not dwindled. However, many of the "new legal case theorems" that had made obscure attorneys overnight sensations and millionaires, have burst into illusory bubbles for those who elected the same pathways.

But never fear because new legal ideas are popping up all around you. New things have been happening, and *ARE STILL* happening, in the law. The frustrated courts and legislators are trying to keep pace with rapidly changing social mores, leaving fewer and fewer comforting certainties.

No one has said, with a straight face, that the law is predictable. Let's take the example of the Internet.

"Cyberspace" law: Wide open for fees. Is it for real?

There's little question that an unplumbed depth of filth is transmitted through the Internet at all times, readable by minds sharp enough to operate it but too young to deal with it. Whether or not such input will injure those tender minds, there's enough outcry to influence the prosecutorial forces.

This may be the proverbial irresistible force meeting the immovable object. The global computer network is blind to terrestrial boundaries. Legal scholars, libertarians, crypto-anarchists and ordinary Internet users are predicting failure to meaningfully legislate anything by any one country. The very nature of cyberspace will render any present nation or state's laws irrelevant.

Law is and, under its existing structure, must be, rooted in proprietary geographical control. Treaties and comity aside, all countries will treat Internet content as they please within their own concepts of propriety.

This is not to say that it must always be thus. While cyberspace does spell the ultimate doom to present methods of national controls, it is just as predictable that there will, and must, be some form of international unity.

Whose jurisdiction? Where? What parameters, etc. Perhaps the World Court at The Hague will be our new "supreme court." It does test one's powers of prognostication to envision anyone in the Netherlands seriously adjudicating the American concepts of "obscenity." We'll have to just wait and see.

Why must we wait until then? Why? Haven't lawyers moved their own boundaries from time to time? Well, they certainly have done so lately. If the instant obscenity matters are being heard by, no less than, the U.S. Supreme Court, then what's to stop enterprising attorneys from opening the can a bit more.

Don't laugh; remember *Marvin vs. Marvin.* Many "laughable" legal theories have become viable tools even though the originator may have failed in the prototype case. Recall Marvin Michelson's strategy of "Palimony" in the Lee Marvin case.

A more immediate concern is the continued viability of encryption as a means of privacy protection by individuals. So far the U.S. government's attempts to launch a global enforcement allowing warrants for access to code keys has failed.

This isn't just an academic idea of privacy. Encryption would permit movement of money through networks away from the prying eyes of the IRS. Not only would tax evasion prosecutions become virtually extinct, but money laundering would be as simple as conventional banking. Think of the test challenge for lawyers. The right to privacy versus the government's interest in controlling income tax and drug money circulation.

Regardless of how we view this sleeping monster, it's clear that Internet and cyberspace will, in fact, be an enormous factor, if not total control, of our future. I would say, not MY future, at my age, but the way things are moving I'm afraid my life span, at least actuarially, won't escape it.

Think novel defense strategy before you cop out. More and more novel legal theories at work. (But some are falling along the wayside.) Criminal verdict, "not guilty." Never mind, sue civilly.

The stunning "not guilty" verdict for O.J. Simpson has opened the way for a whole new concept in "Wrongful Death" actions. Never mind that the defendant was acquitted in the murder trial. Look at the prospects. Sue the guy anyway.

"Justice" may be served in spite of the jury's will. With a judgment against him for more than $32,000,000, it could be that Simpson may have been better off with a criminal verdict of "guilty." If anything like that sum is upheld, think of the fees.

Great, isn't it. You serve not only justice, but you get filthy rich in the bargain. What did it all prove? According to pollsters, the same division of opinions in Simpson's guilt or innocence exists after the civil verdict as did after the criminal verdict.

Child abuse, new dimensions.

"Honor Thy Father and Thy Mother" is now a diminishing reverberation on the theme, "Sue Thy Father and Thy Mother." Daddies and mommies who were exposed daily as somewhat less than that revered haven of song and story. Visions of child abuse were "recalled" in hypnosis.

Statutes of Limitations? No matter that these things happened twenty, thirty or more, years ago. Everything starts when the long past dastardly deeds are brought into present focus.

Such charges are not just grounds for lucrative civil lawsuits. Potential defense theories lie in the ashes of failed tests in some prominent cases. Sure Lyle and Eric Menendez were finally convicted, but the infamous "abuse excuse" defense lingers on.

Do these anomalous defense methods herald a new era in strategy? It seems clear that "Nothing ventured, nothing gained" has renewed efficacy. And, to the audacious goes the prize. That idiotic *Marvin* "Palimony" idea has since flown and is alive and well. The idea is to be innovative. The future apparently belongs to the most audacious "creative" attorney.

A while back, when you learned that your client did the dastardly deed, you sought out the prosecutor to cut a deal. Nowadays, you just shift gears into a different defense posture. Are you skittish about defending someone who did the bad act? You shouldn't be.

Remember the first legal tenet of criminal defense. Everyone has the right to a legal defense. Nothing is said about did he do it or not. If your delicacies would deny that right, are you really dedicated to the principles of criminal defense?

Besides, these innovative defense theories are now proving to be the brass rings of criminal law. You don't read about fees paid to lawyers who dump a deuce for a cop-out, nor about a garden variety defense to a narcotics charge.

Evidence ain't evidence unless it's "authenticated."

Talking about "dead to rights" defense theories here's one for your everyday stuff. Your client was not drunk; he was embalmed. He blew over .350. He couldn't walk much less a straight line. What do you do? You don't cop one.

The U.S. Supreme Court, no less, gives you the strategy. The new ("new" at this time) *Kumho* decision forces prosecutors to *"validate"* their scientific evidence. This means everything, including blood tests, field sobriety tests, laser gun reports, everything.

It's not just the validation, which is bad enough, it's the time constraints to comply. Most prosecutors are amenable to a reduction rather than face that burden. In fact, if you play hard ball you could even get it kicked, or maybe win at trial for failure to produce timely validation.

Highest fees earned by solos and small firms.

The O.J. and Menendez fees were front page stuff everywhere. Those lawyers could probably retire on their fees, let alone their multi-million dollar book deals. Are these successful lawyers all in large firms? Are the big money earners exclusively large firms? Not at all. Some of the biggest fee earners in the country are solos or very small firms.

In fact **ten of the highest paid attorneys are solos or work at small firms.** This proves only that it can be done. But making money, as you've learned from this book, is a profession unto itself.

And that's just the front line troops. Dozens of lawyers, law professors, law school deans, judges, ex-judges and other self-styled "experts" on the subject, are handsomely paid as TV "commentators" on the case. So, stand in line. You can't tell one expert from another without a program. Why not you? Why not, indeed.

With all of these things happening, why trudge along for a few measly dollars an hour making your way as a solo lawyer? You're as good a lawyer as most of those "experts" making headlines and millions. Maybe you, too, can devise some bizarre case theory to collect an obscene fee. You could also play Lotto.

During the terrible thirties, movie stars were collecting six figure salaries, driving Rolls Royces and living in mansions. All of this while "One-third of a nation was ill-fed, ill-clothed and ill-housed." (Franklin Delano Roosevelt, 1932).

Despite the eye-popping fees reputedly paid to legal superstars, fees in general, are still down from a few years ago. Call it an inflationless "hot" economy, or a gilded recession, a buck still comes with a struggle out on the street.

Clienteles for most general practitioners are still sparser than back in the early eighties. Some economic improvements have occurred, but we're not much farther from square one than we were when this third edition was published.

Of course, most general practitioners haven't received your training. They know nothing of salesmanship or the other information you're getting from this book.

Pick the right plaintiff, if you drive in California.

California voters supported Proposition 213, codified in Civil Code 3333.4, which prevents an injured plaintiff from recovering "noneconomic losses" by way of damages if that plaintiff is uninsured. So, no "pain and suffering" for the plaintiff who drives without insurance.

The most that plaintiff can receive, if he or she prevails in a lawsuit, is reimbursement for the medical services reasonably necessary for treatment of injuries. The moral of this story is that it's no longer sufficient to know whether the defendant is insured, but whether your own client, the plaintiff, is insured.

Cases are presently in the appellate courts testing that law. Perhaps by the time you read this, there will be a new slant on uninsured motorists. California, like several other states, has been trying in various ways over the past few years to limit the growth of uninsured drivers. If successful, it is likely that most other states will follow California's lead. The fly in the appeal ointment is the cast of characters. The insurance company lobbyists have been all too visible. Nobody loves insurance companies.

Another new idea never got off the ground, (but did it?).

Y2K. Seemed like fertile ground until someone looked at the back of the book. The predictions were that lots of repercussions would be felt from hardware and software noncompliant with Y2K. Tons of lawsuits were filed, some in anticipation, others with claimed evidence of harm due to noncompliance. Not surprisingly, many of the claims were filed as class actions.

Rashes of lawsuits smacking of Y2K failures created an atmosphere of terror among businesses of all sizes and kinds. Predictions of stalled elevators, hospital surgery power losses, critical functions in a wide variety of institutions offered fertile ground for potential law suits should there be any relationship to computers.

As a result, over a hundred bills have been introduced in states around the country. The U.S. Senate and House are already considering measures of limitation. At this point, it looks like Congress will limit suits down to a roar on this issue.

All of those great new case theories that looked so good in 1998, started to shrivel in 1999 and seem headed to the scrap heap as 2000 approached. Like the old chain letter idea, the ones at the top of the pyramid made it big while the next in line had to scrounge for fees. So what's to be learned? Dream up a new case theory and get your case to court fast. Maybe you'll be one of the lucky ones. It's got to be somebody, right? Why not you?

Elderly abuse law.

Here's another old law breathing with new life. An old California statute dormant for years, has arisen as though from the grave. It was called *"Elderly Abuse and Dependent Adult Civil Protection Act."* Why now?

Geriatric medicine has been stretching the seniors' life span to older years. Law enforcement agencies and legislators have become more and more alert to this burgeoning voting power block. That old law has not only been dusted off, it has been completely refurbished with fangs of treble damages and attorneys fees. Active applications of this law have been financial as well physical abuse of seniors.

A recent case involved a young woman who befriended a senior widower, inducing him to sign over financial documents through which she embezzled almost half a million dollars. The result of the suit was a judgment restoring to the senior the full amount misappropriated.

Other cases involve abuse by insurance firms charging unconscionably high "reverse mortgages" fees, one resulting in a $5 million class action settlement. Look to this fast growing area for legal fertility. The seniors are not only the faster growing but wealthier parts of the country's population. They are more vulnerable because of age related susceptibilities.

A variation on an old theme. A new twist on a personal injury verdict.

P.I. lawsuits are divided into two parts, liability and damages. Experience proves that one can affect the other. If the defendant's conduct causing the accident is extremely reprehensible, the sum of damages will climb.

Likewise, if the damages are especially severe, liability will more likely be found. A recent case exposes yet another exercise in splicing.

Plaintiffs severely burned in a rear end collision awarded a jury verdict of $4.5 *billion*. **You read that right.** ***Billion,*** **not million. The defendant was not the driver of the rear-ending vehicle. It was the manufacturer of the burned car, General Motors.**

Why? Because the evidence shows the fuel tank was behind the rear axel and more vulnerable to the collision impact. The plaintiffs claimed had the tank been mounted in front of the axel, the gasoline might not have exploded.

Ah but wait. The judge saw the folly of so huge a verdict. After all, despite the severity of the damages resulting from the blaze, there must be some rational nexus to the amount of the damages award. If a brain surgeon's hands are irreparably injured one can reasonably calculate the loss.

Here was a family driving a twenty year old Chevrolet Malibu. Not to say that the financial standing of the defendants should dictate the verdict limits, but $4.5 billion?

So the judge dutifully reduced the sum down to a mere $1.2 billion. Well, we do need to punish these reckless auto manufacturers for so ill-designing their products, right?

Moral: Damn the limiting ratios; go for the sky!

The central lesson to be learned from these sprouting sources is to keep an open mind as to the possibilities. Precedents are fine but look to new uncharted territories.

Is this in your future?

Apparently no one is so big or powerful as to be immune to the courts' jurisdiction. The rich, the influential, the powerful and the mighty have all felt the sting of being on the receiving end of lawsuits lately.

Who would of thought that the president of the United States could be sued while still in office. Whatever happened to the separation of powers doctrine? It used to be that the only way to breach that separation was through impeachment.

How far can this go? An action for high crimes against humanity, invidious discrimination, tortuous conduct, intentional infliction of emotional distress, breach of fiduciary duty, gross negligence, and a host of other legal theories, against—are you ready?—The **ALMIGHTY.**

Blasphemous! Sacrilegious! Yes of course. Based on the present trend, is it out of the realm of extreme possibilities? Indubitably.

Could some heretical attorney agree to take such a case? Could some deviant, atheistic, renegade lawyer agree that the Lord has misused the faith of His flocks? What kind of disreputable client would seek to hold God liable for breaching His fiduciary duty to act reasonably upon that faith?

Utterly unthinkable. No one would dare. Certainly not. There is a limit, isn't there, to how far the law's tentacles can encroach. Still, who would have predicted just a few years ago the case theories that have unfolded recently?

Am I serious? No, of course not. How could I be?

Chapter 2

An Overview of the Solo Practice of Law

§ 2:1 Generally

What Is Solo Practice All About?

It's mainly about opportunity. Career employment is only a job regardless of its wrappings. But opportunity is a challenge not a gift. If you're up to the challenge, solo practice is the vehicle for success.

Some want the umbilical "security" of a job. That "security" may be as illusory as a guarantee of good health and long life. Law firm employees are being discharged every day. Your future as an employee is only as secure as the firm's commitment to retain you as their employee. Sometimes that decision is made by economic conditions.

This outline will give you some idea of the relative values and decisions that you must make. Each and every point in this outline will be given full treatment in the relevant sections ahead. This outline is intended more to provoke your thought processes on some preliminary factors.

The first decision, of course, is whether you really want to be, or should be, a solo lawyer. That big question should not be answered by an appraisal of your competence, but by a candid and perhaps painful awareness of your personality, habits, bents and temperament.

There's no question of your ability to do anything and everything needed to succeed in solo law practice. But there may be a question, and only you know the answer, of your willingness to do these things. "Willingness" may be an oversimplification. Call it personality trait, predisposition, devotion, self-application, or any other descriptive term that fits.

This outline will help you to form a predetermination of your fitness for solo practice. Whichever direction your thoughts take you, reserve a final decision until after you've read all of the material on these subjects in later chapters.

Fairness-Unfairness: Sometimes the toughest of all issues.

Fairness vs. Unfairness: Give some thought to how you react to unfairness. This is a relevant part of what makes a solo lawyer function well.

We all learned long before taking up the study of law that life is not always fair. Most of the time in our earlier life, we were able to handle unfair treatment because it did not encroach very far into our lives. Unfair grading, or other discriminatory treatment by schoolteachers or college professors, gave many people their first experience with pain from unfairness, rather than the familiar confusion suffered in childhood. For others, law school traumas may have been their baptism in the fires of unfairness.

No unfairness that happened prior to law practice can equal the hurt resulting from an unfair decision from the bench. Who can philosophically deal with an adverse judicial ruling after having meticulously prepared and presented a position totally consonant with the law?

The unkindest cut is the lack of even a spark of legal support to the judge's mockery. You stand there facing the bench. You don't know whether to laugh, cry or spit. You do not believe you heard correctly. You feel dizzy, nauseated and faint. You believe you'll wake up from this crazy dream.

Unfairness comes in many forms and faces.

You have a good case, a great case. You know positively that when it ends, you will score a major victory. The stage is set for a big win. All that stands in the way is a client with limited funds and an opposing party with unlimited funds represented by a large, aggressive law firm.

Somewhere down the line your client runs out of money. The other side has accelerated the procedures. Your financing is gone. Your client hasn't paid you in weeks, and your services have run miles ahead of fee payments.

Your opposing attorney has offered a settlement. Not a bad settlement if your side of the case were in the slightest doubt. But you know, and you know the other lawyer knows, it's his case that is the loser, not yours. The offer grates at the fabric of your being.

To compound the hurt, your client is a sweetheart of a person. You'd love to continue the case without payment. You know, you just **know**, you can't lose. The case is a business matter. It's not one that chafes at either civil rights or personal jeopardy. You cannot justify continuing on a pro bono basis or even on contingency. You couldn't afford to carry it anyway.

You're offered a settlement that denies your client a right you know you'd win if you could complete the case. You have been literally "muscled" into submission because of financing superiority.

Nice person that your client is, the decision is strictly up to you. There'd be no second-guessing or remonstrations. You have the ball. Do you punt? What do you do? To continue would exhaust your client's funds. Your client is fully aware of the situation and offers no resistance or resentment towards you. He/she recognizes the stone wall you face. Continuing with the case would also exhaust your own funds and your ability to serve other clients. You have no choice but to go ahead with the humiliating settlement.

Can you do that? If this sticks in your craw, you're a good lawyer. If this mortifies you to the quick, you still may be a good lawyer, but perhaps not as a solo lawyer. If you just cannot throw in the towel, don't even think about going solo. Solo practice will either bankrupt you or kill you, whichever comes first.

Fair is nice, and something everyone should be and expect others to be. Not infrequently in law practice, there is a total failure of fairness. It does not always affect the people who you think should be subjected to unfairness. More often, it hits the nicest and most deserving people.

Some people are not made for solo practice. Are you?

A quick test to help you decide:

The alternative is employment by others. For many, the biggest advantage sought, and sometimes found in employment is "job security." Solo practice, like any business, is often seen as chancy or hazardous. In a job you have X dollars coming each payday. You can plan your budget and foresee your future, or so you believe. You needn't concern yourself with time lost in illness or medical expenses since that is arranged for in your fringe benefit program. You will have a profit sharing and pension plan, no doubt, and other benefits to accommodate most of life's uncertainties. Of course, a portion of the costs of these programs is extracted from your salary but you must have these assurances and are willing to pay for them.

For those who see this as an absolute requirement, consider

this book as an aid in getting the most suitable employment for you. It will also highlight methods and pathways to your career success. The fact that such assurance is misplaced is beside the point. Your *belief* is what will determine your law practice future.

DO NOT, however, even think of pursuing a career in your own law office. But DO read ahead because there's big stuff ahead to make your life as an associate much more promising.

Advantages-disadvantages in solo practice and employment.

Going solo is not being cast adrift in an open boat on the high seas. There are as many benefit plans available to the solo as there are for the employee. The only difference is that the solo pays for these benefits from income instead of salary.

No one dictates which plans you'll get or how much you must pay. As a solo, you make all the choices yourself. It's true that you must make your own arrangements for substitutions during any illnesses as well as vacations.

It's not my intent to squander my sales ability on those who cannot, or will not, see the preference for being your own master. Of course, the successful solo will realize more income than the employee. This is not, in my opinion, the ultimate target. If it isn't crystal clear to you that having freedom to practice law your way and not someone else's is an advantage, the rest of it shouldn't count.

The solo practice work ethic.

Some people need to be prodded to do their day's work. Some need to be told where to go, when to go and what to do when you get there. Some don't need such proctoring. Which are you? If you doubt your ability to do what you must do without supervision, forget solo practice.

The learning process and experience gained from solo practice compared with the learning and experience gained in employment.

Some people need to know that someone will be there to tell them what to do each step of the way. They fear that will not be the case in solo practice. Of course, it will. But lack of self confidence will interfere with the judgment needed to make the choice. If you doubt that the various assigning lawyers who provide the work projects will instruct you properly in each matter, your doubts will be an enduring impediment to entering solo practice.

Fringe benefits in employment: paid vacations; medical; sick pay; profit sharing; pension plans; workers' compensation; unemployment insurance; paid malpractice insurance; secretarial assistance, etc.

What fringe benefits does solo practice offer?

These are huge enticements. For some reason, there are those who place getting such benefits above the methods for payment. Taking the costs from your paycheck doesn't seem so painful as buying such programs with your hard-earned cash.

§ 2:2 Not a book for hard times

I'm loath to believe that anyone considers private practice a default in a poor job market, instead of an intelligent career choice.

Are things tough out there? Forget about that. Things have always been tough on new admittees in the job market. Do tough times mean one cannot succeed? Not at all. Nothing will prevent an informed and determined person from reaching success. Even in the bad 1930's, some people were earning money. Certainly, unemployment was rampant then, as it is in some areas now. But those times, like all times, were made for some, not everyone.

Actually, in some ways, hard times paradoxically present some unusual opportunities. But opportunities are not like stones scattered on the ground for anyone to pick up and recognize.

In many areas, some of the largest law firms are trimming their sails. In some instances, even good, productive associates are being discharged. In the past, some firms used two or three associates to do the work of a single skilled lawyer. Now, they've sifted down to that one lawyer to do the work of two or three. But, even the best and most able attorney cannot do it all.

That's where you come in. You want an office to start your own practice. You also do not want to pay for that office, nor do you want to pay for the other costs of a law practice.

You know that firms are cutting their personnel but also feeling the squeeze of insufficient and inadequate legal help. So, what do you do? It's a natural. You will simply trade your capable legal services for an office plus the office accouterments. So, you have *your* consent; all you need is the consent of someone who has a vacant office.

How do you know who has a vacant office? Simple. Almost every law firm, large or small, has at least one vacant office. This becomes more and more true as the economy becomes more and more grim. So, you just assume that whichever firm you pick for your office has one waiting for you.

Put yourself in the position of a harassed senior partner in charge of work dispatch. You are pulling your hair out (if you have any left) wondering how you will get the work done. You know that policy will not permit any more hiring. Then you get a letter that reads:

Dear [Lawyer]:

You have an empty office, and you need a lawyer to help you get your work done. **Don't hire another lawyer.** I've got a better idea.

I'll get your work done faster and less expensively than your least salaried associate. No cost for payroll expenses, employee benefits, idle or lost time, sick-outs, do-overs or other waste. I cost you none of that.

I am NOT a "contract attorney" or anything like that. I am what you are looking for but at far less cost than an employee.

You pay me only for completed, satisfactory work. I'll show you, **in black and white**, to the penny, how I can do your work better, faster and at lower cost to you than adding a salaried associate to your payroll.

Sincerely,

GERALD M. SINGER

Would that letter get your attention? I think yes.

This is just one of several suggested letters you'll see further along.

§ 2:3 Who wants to hire a new lawyer?

There have always been job opportunities for new lawyers, just as there are right now. But where, what firms? What conditions, and why? These are not just questions, they're employment issues, part of your dilemma in deciding whether to be employed or employ yourself.

You'll discover that private practice, whether as a solo lawyer or a member of a small law firm, can be the career of choice. A lawyer should be independent. But how independent are you as an employee? You are at the beck and call of your superior, who probably couldn't match your abilities in any department. You are herded into a corner of the law whether or not that is your choice, and it probably isn't. Worst of all, you are told to do things their way, which is not infrequently the wrong way. Moreover, the beginning period, often longer than reasonable, is merely an excuse for your superior to keep you subordinated (another name for slave).

Don't make the mistake of believing that displaying your stellar qualities will move you to the top ranks like a shot. It rarely works that way. There are ways to make your talent known to those in the firm's hierarchy who care. If employment is what you want, you'll see how that's done later in the book. But bear in mind that getting ahead as an employee is the result of abilities to be learned, just like learning solo practice.

For some people, and such people are rare, employment is certainly the proper route. For others, it's frustrating, inhibiting, demeaning and soul-dampening. Private practice can be, and should be, better than employment, even in the best of times. So, to best assess this choice, let's begin with this hypothesis: *There is a good job waiting out there for you.*

§ 2:4 Whether solo or an employee, you must do your job

To do your job, you must be a good lawyer, among other things. But just being a good lawyer is not enough.

As a private practitioner you must:

1. **Open an office;**
2. **Be a good lawyer;**
3. **Do a good job;**
4. **Get clients and;**
5. **Make money.**

For successful prospects as an employee, you must:

1. **Find a good job;**
2. **Be a good lawyer;**
3. **Do a good job;**
4. **Please your boss. (If you succeed with 4, never mind 2 and 3.)**

Does a "HOT" economy mean smooth sailing to start your new solo law practice? Can a new lawyer be blamed for believing the road to success is a fast track certainty? Law school is a tough, tough, grind. Not everyone can even get into law school, much less survive with a law degree. Then, the ultimate achievement, passing the Bar. What else can they do to you? Of course you deserve that pot of gold.

Then you discover that half the world consists of attorneys, each of whom ran the gamut and survived, just like you. The world owes you something, but collecting is something else you still have yet to learn about. What a bummer!

It'll be O.K. All that good stuff will come your way. After what you've been through, the rest is a cinch. All you need to do is know what there is for you to do and do it. There have always been more lawyers being churned out by law schools than there are job berths. Some grads use their law degrees to improve their resumes for a crack at higher level career employment. Some simply attended law school under parental pressure, for lack of any other motivation. The majority of lawyer dropouts sincerely wanted law, but just couldn't find a job equal to their expectations.

This situation contrasts with the general economy, which experts say is now "robust" or "hot." Still, nobody is pounding on your door to hire you. Does this mean too many lawyers rather than too few jobs? Well, as they say, whether the rock hits the vase or the vase hits the rock, it has to be bad for the vase.

The reduction in applications to ABA-approved law schools over the last six years hasn't diminished the high ratio of new lawyers to satisfactory employment targets. Even with the continual drop of applicants, more than 67,000 eager candidates applied for 1995 admission to ABA accredited law schools, with more than 85,000 applying to all law schools. These statistics are useful for demographic studies, but they don't distinguish between those who've learned how to get what they want and those who haven't.

Accurate statistics exist on the progress of neophytes in most professions because they are registered and proctored. We know how many apply for training, how many are certified, and what percentages succeed within their chosen disciplines. Accurate logs don't exist in the bulk of the nonprofessional fields. No one knows how many salespeople try and fail in that occupation. Still, competent salespeople even now are among the nation's highest paid wage earners with expert sales closers occupying the crest. Those who can't sell are low salaried sales clerks where selling expertise isn't a requisite.

What is different about lawyers? A salesman is a good salesman if he or she sells lots of his or her products. When is a lawyer a good lawyer? Making money is the criterion for salespeople as with most people in the market.

Should the same measure be used for lawyers? Of course not. Many marginally capable lawyers are earning top dollars while some of the top echelon of legal scholars have trouble making a living.

If that "top legal scholar" graduated from the top law schools, all bets are off. There are certain exceptions to the general rule. 1996 statistics show that more than 99% of the grads from Yale, Harvard, Stanford and Columbia, were employed soon after being admitted. Of course, about 97% of those same grads passed their respective Bars the first time out of the box.

Most of those aristocrats who gained employment so readily, were placed in top berths with the highest rated law firms. Have these placements given them all the personal validation and satisfaction that the law has to offer? The answer to this must come from each of those individuals.

An employed attorney experiences only a part of the law's

excitement and rewards. That employee may be doing good work, but his or her own assessment of that work doesn't count. Someone else must judge that quality. At least a part of that effort must be directed toward pleasing that person. Sometimes what that person expects may be contrary to what you know is good lawyering.

Sometimes the person placed as your superior doesn't have your best interests in mind. It's hard to accept that not all persons placed in charge of others are interested in the best performance by those others. Not so infrequently, supervisors are more interested in the homage paid to them by underlings rather than their best work.

I want ALL of my efforts directed toward doing the best job possible as a lawyer. This is what I've done for thirty years as an attorney and what I shall continue to strive for. This is what you will do in your own solo law practice. Whether you are a solo lawyer and work for yourself, or you're an employee and work for someone else, you gotta do your job.

Any top salesman will laugh if you warn of diminishing opportunities. He or she knows what it takes for selling success. The more dismal it is for the sales crowd, the easier and better for the expert.

So, lawyers have a double duty task. You must not just learn how to be a good lawyer, you must also learn what is necessary to make your practice financially successful. You're up to that.

If you're hesitant about which way to go, solo or employment, bear this in mind: You can't escape what you have to do by hiding in law firm employment. If you can't be financially successful for yourself as a solo attorney, no firm will want you to work for them. You may get hired, but you won't make it past the entry level, if you can even remain there.

Well, who said becoming a financially successful attorney either way would be a snap? Not me.

No. 4 in the list above dictates that you must please your boss (if you succeed with number 4, never mind 2 and 3). We've known many employees who keep their jobs and even advance over others who are better trained and better equipped to do the job. Alas, too many employers, or those in charge of personnel, fancy those who please them rather than those who are more capable.

In fact, some employees who fail in that department not only don't advance, they may even find themselves on the disposable list. So, it's vital that you do find the method of pleasing, or at least not displeasing, that person in charge. We will deal with "selling the boss" further along.

But there's something else, isn't there.

There's another most crucial element for success in any employment career. **You must please yourself.** You must be satisfied with the kind of work you are doing. Pleasing your boss may not always be consistent with pleasing yourself. In fact, sometimes, even quite often, these are two diametrically opposed efforts. Worse, in some law firms, you have not just one boss, you have several. And, compounding this, you may find yourself in a balancing act, trying to please everybody.

Notice I don't say be "happy" in your work in either case. "Happy" is quite another thing. I say you need satisfaction and self-esteem. We'll talk about "happy" later.

For now, let's talk about satisfaction and self-esteem. As an employee, you cannot always pick and choose your area of practice. And even if you are successful in having this prerogative, you may find employment, like the "golden chariot," only thinly gold plated.

Private practice is not the only way that you can be satisfied with your work. But, as a solo lawyer, you have more control over what you do in your day-to-day practice. You can gear yourself toward work that satisfies you.

No matter which kind of career you choose, solo practice or employment, you will gain from what you learn in the following material. You will learn things to make you a better, more successful and productive employee as well as how to successfully start and manage your own solo or small law office.

What's the competition?

Analysts had projected that by the year 2000, more than one million lawyers would be practicing in the United States. Even with diminished applications, tens of thousands are becoming lawyers each year. Lawyers are pouring into practice constantly, saturating the job market.

Authorities are in fundamental agreement with the conclusion that this overpopulation of lawyers is not expected to improve much during the first years of the twenty-first century in this new millennium. Big firms are increasingly trimming their staffs. Corporate clients are seeking more and better services for their legal dollars.

Larger firms are less and less willing to accept young attorneys viewed as "too inexperienced" for the job. Many experts opine that this overhauling of the legal market would have happened with, or without, a recession. The market is simply unable to absorb the large number of lawyers overflowing into the legal stream. The bottom line is there are simply too many attorneys.

Despite this, large numbers of candidates are crowding into law schools as this book is written. Reports show that over one hundred thousand applicants sought to enter the 175 A.B.A. accredited law schools in the fall of 1998. This large number was only slightly less than the record year of 1995 when about 105,000 attempted admission.

Should that make a difference to you? Should the overcrowding of the marketplace be a factor in your decision to practice law? Should it alter your resolve to be a solo lawyer? What, if anything, do these numbers mean and how should they affect you?

First, let's examine the reasons for the failure of the bulk of new employees to make the grade with the better law firms. We start with those top students who came to their new jobs with the very best academic credentials but failed to survive their probationary employment period.

Why? What did these academic high achievers lack? Let me start by giving you this bit of information. Everyone who runs a business, and make no mistake, a law office is a business, expects every employee to make a profit for the firm. This may come as a shock to people who seek a law degree only to do good deeds.

To know and understand the business entrepreneur, whether the marketable product or service they provide, one must know and understand the business of cost, expense, income and profit. Every successful business person is first, last and always, a skillful buyer. Not the least on the list of things a business person must buy are the people who will, in one or another way, cause the business to flourish. Highest on that list, in the business of making movies, are the actors whose names appear on theater marquees.

Does the word "buy" bother you when applied to people? You say, people are not chattels, they're human beings and are not bought and sold. That kind of transaction went out with the Emancipation Proclamation.

Abraham Lincoln said "An attorney's advice is his (or her) only stock in trade." So maybe only the "advice" of an attorney is what the employer "buys." Before we get into a superficial debate, let's examine what the employing law firm seeks to gain by employing you or anyone else.

What does your prospective employer want from you?

No one, *but **no one***, pays a penny for talent when that talent is used commercially. What is paid for is the ability of that person to cause customers to put their money down to view the talent. That ability is sometimes, but alas not always, an accompaniment to the talent.

There are, in the movie business, certain stars who are identified as "bankable." This means that money lenders, usually banks, will lend money strictly on the basis that one or more of those "bankable" stars will appear in the film for which the loan is taken.

The great, ultra-gifted actor, Laurence Olivier, considered by many the finest actor then alive, was never among those called "bankable." Many "bankable" movie actors are not rated as especially talented.

Orson Welles, great actor though he was, never was counted among the big box office stars. His "Citizen Kane"—contained within every list of the greatest films of all time—made no money until its subsequent releases. Welles may have also understandably complained about the choice roles and high salaries denied him in later years.

The one factor, and the only factor, important in listing an actor as "bankable" is the appeal of that actor, called "box office." This means that when that actor's name is on the theater marquee, customers will come, and the film will predictably make money.

When it comes to negotiations for contract salaries in the movie business, as in any other business, the market rules. In the region of making a profit, the one who can reach the highest plateau will reap the highest bid for compensation.

Lawyers, like actors and any other persons in business or in an occupation or profession, must be "bankable," if not literally, then in effect. You must have, in addition to talent, that certain something, that ability to cause "customers" to pay money at the box office for the exhibition of that talent.

You'll see more of this important ingredient as you read along further in this book. However, the most important part of that revelation will emphasize the difference in that ability between an actor and a lawyer.

The actor lacking "box office" can rarely acquire it. The lawyer who lacks that ability can acquire it by simply learning how. Actors cannot literally fill theaters with patrons. Lawyers can, and indeed do, bring clients into their firms. How is this done?

You'll find the answer to this and other questions. You'll also learn how to be among those who stick with the firm, if that's what you want to do with your life.

§ 2:5 Law school success vs. career success

Comparative analysis: Law school examination results and law practice achievements. What correlatives? Is there a relationship between grades and practice success?

Elements of law school exam success

1. Assiduous notes taken in class.
2. Study, research, reading comprehension.
3. Classroom discussions, participation. (Test your ideas in the market place.)
4. Testing issue approach in factual matters.
5. Analytical development.
6. Relevancy discrimination: Ability to separate issues from dicta.
7. Writing ability. Can't get credit for what you can't write.
8. Speed. Ability to find issues and form thoughts for expression fast to beat the clock.

Elements of job success

1. Certainly, you must have the ability to take meaningful notes in client interviews.
2. You must be excellent at legal research.
3. While you won't have a classroom, you should be able to engage other lawyers in a rap session about your case to test your own ideas about the facts and the law.
4. You must be highly proficient in analytical abilities.
5. You must, of course, be able to distinguish a case holding from the case dicta.
6. You must be able to write well and with the early punch necessary to grab the judge's rapt attention.
7. Speed will certainly be an ingredient in getting your act together, so you can stay out in front of the group.

Is that all? If so, why are so many new lawyers who've demonstrated these skills terminated after their trial period? Obviously there's more. Much, much more. Or, more to the point, something much different.

Be ready for some surprises. Keep in mind the comparatives between law school teachings, textbook and casebook studies and examination grade results on the one hand, and what is required of you to succeed in your law practice, whether employed or self-employed.

§ 2:6 Let's take a look at going solo

Recessions can swarm into the economy like a dense fog.

What if one hits while you are preparing your new office?

Bad times are perfect for the new solo. What!? Am I crazy?

Why did I say that? Seriously. That would be the time for the new solo to hop on the rocket and get a better, faster start than ever before.

It's true. Small firms and large firms alike will feel the pinch in a wide spread recession. What is also certainly true is that the courts' fast track is piling it high on the backs of all firms, large and small. Pressures would be such that law firms would need to scramble to just keep abreast of changes in law and procedure.

Why does this augur well for the new solo?

Simple. It's easier than ever to find new work assignments. From whom? Of course, from those very small firms and solos, as well as the Biggies, that would be having it so rough. They'd be in the biggest pickle of all. They wouldn't be hiring help but at the same time they also couldn't afford to be without help. So, where would they get the help? **GUESS!**

What else will solo practice do for you? Aside from being given the opportunity of choosing your own way, whatever that may be, your profits will be made for you, not some employer. But these things you know about. Here are some things you may not, have thought about.

Speaking of solo practice "fringe benefits."

You can make elections as a solo lawyer not possible as an employee:

1. You can select your own fiscal course, involving:

   a) Your tax year selection.

   b) Whether to incorporate or remain private.

   c) Your own accounting method, whether "cash" or "accrual" or otherwise.

2. You may schedule your own trust fund deposits and withdrawals based on whatever fiscal persuasion you choose.

3. You can elect a customized retirement plan:

   a) Defined Contributions Plan (if you have employees; plan is limited to a finite percentage, including all).

   b) Defined Benefits Plan, permitting tax deferred deposits based on your own actuarial schedule for your own targeted retirement date.

   [Note: Either of these plans allow you to deduct all contributions from income tax. This would be impractical if you have employees, since they would be entitled to share in your declaration. Defined benefits plans wouldn't be offered to associates of large firms.]

4. You schedule your own vacations and time off when, where and how. You decide which trips are business and might be tax

deductible (if the IRS is agreeable), and how often they may be taken.

5. You decide which days and hours you wish to devote to your office and whatever else.

6. You decide which cases to take and which to leave alone. You make your own decisions on the directions your practice will take.

7. You make all decisions on how much to charge clients and which clients should not be charged a fee at all.

8. It all boils down to dollars and cents. Somebody's got to earn the bucks from which your benefits, fringe or otherwise, will flow. If an employer is willing to fork out the money to buy your vacations, medical premiums, sick pay, etc., that means you, not somebody else, is paying the freight for those things.

You are worth the GROSS of the salary paid to you, INCLUDING costs of all job benefits, or your employer wouldn't be paying that amount to you, or for your benefit. It's doubtful that you know, or ever will know, the extent of all of the costs of an employee. This doesn't mean you will never be an employer yourself. The sad truth is that most employers really do not understand or appreciate the full cost of employing other people. Employers do ultimately learn whether their business is or is not earning a profit.

You'll not be knowingly paid one red cent by an employer for anything that your efforts on the job have not earned for your employer, plus a healthy profit. Does this thought confound you?

But it ain't all beer and skittles, as they say.

§ 2:7 Solo lawyers: Errors and omissions; discipline

There are some potholes along the merry solo practice road. All of these hazards are avoidable if you just know about them. A big one, and I won't minimize its importance, is the **Ethics Pitfall.**

I have been asked many times for the reason that so many solo lawyers are disciplined whereas big firms seem not to be. Discipline sometimes results even in being disbarred.

Statistics show that members of big firms are rarely disbarred. The fundamental reasons for these calamities are:

1. Solos are often not properly trained in office and case management.

2. Priorities of solos are sometimes mis-scheduled or vague.

3. Solos sometimes fail to recognize their time limitations and are overworked. Some lawyers (both employees and solos) cannot judge when a job is done.

4. Some solos just cannot get up to speed each day.
5. Sometimes a solo may just not be solo material.
6. Sometimes all of the above.

Does it have to happen to you? It does not, and should not. All you need are a few basic facts that are easy to understand and just as easy to put into operation.

You may not believe that this subject holds any importance for you now but it does. Forewarned is, indeed, forearmed. You'll be shocked to know of the large percentage of successful solo lawyers who have fallen into those traps and pitfalls. It will surprise you even more to learn how easily they could have avoided those debacles simply by knowing about them.

I am proud of the many thousands of new lawyers who were introduced to solo practice through my books, classes, lectures and general advice. I am most proud of their fine records of success, but no less proud that they avoided those ethics pitfalls. I am just as proud, even more so, when I meet some of them in court and they pin my ears back. Well, they had a good teacher.

Chapter 3

The Decision: Solo Practice or Employment, and What To Do About It

§ 3:1 Generally

Whatever your reasons for choosing either solo practice or employment, let it not be on the basis of challenge. If you really want success as a lawyer, whether in a job or in your own office, you've got to be prepared for a challenge. If your purpose is only to hide from the tumult of competition by seeking employment, you'll not only be disappointed, you'll be jobless. No one wants an employee who is content to be second best.

You must fight your way up the ladder in whichever format you've chosen. Very few attorneys keep their jobs by just hanging on. Just as professors must "publish or perish," so must employees move toward partnership or perish.

I have faith in you because you are reading this book. Much as I feel this is a good book, even the very best of its kind, I must assume you didn't buy it for entertainment literature. I will further assume that you are considering solo practice over job seeking.

What will it be like for new solo lawyers in the coming millennium? One thing can be predicted for absolute certain. There will be undulations in economy cycles. Some will be good, some bad. What will that mean to you?

The three previous editions of this book covered an enormous range of challenges to the solo law practitioner. Fluctuations in the economy, the law, and mounting pressures on lawyers, have made it necessary for the solo to shift operational gears many times. Paradoxically, many of these changes have been beneficial to the solo lawyer. In the old days of typewriters, keeping up with the large firms and their phalanxes of associates, paralegals, secretaries, runners, investigators, etc., kept the solo hopping.

I advised then, "Do your own typing." But in litigating against the biggies, that was often easier said than done. Although I did employ secretaries from time to time, I proved as you will that one can earn more, do more and recreate more, without hiring a full or even a part-time secretary. Now, with a modern computer, staying abreast of the largest adversary is doable without drawing a deep breath. Even with my clumsy, all thumbs typing, my computer can churn out stacks of papers equal to the best efforts of the biggest of them.

Thousands of successful solo lawyers have dared to go directly into solo law practice through the inspiration of the first three editions of this book. Each of those fine lawyers has proved the truth of the opening statement of that first edition, published over twenty-five years ago:

> "Most anyone with the brains and perspicacity to survive the rigors of law school and the bar exam has what it takes to go directly from law school into the solo practice of law. This is so, even though the new lawyer has little or no financial staying power."

Just as in 1975, a great many law students and lawyers, new or experienced, are still convinced that starting a solo practice is a dangerous course for the new admittee. Many still cling to the erroneous conviction that seeking employment offers financial security plus opportunity for further development of basic legal skills. When you have read a bit further you will probably agree that it is quite the other way around.

The greater gamble is in the quest for suitable and satisfying employment. And the gamble is not only a financial one. As you will discover, your solo practice will offer a far superior training ground for the practicalities of legal practice to most employment situations.

Many changes and events in the past twenty-five years have emphasized and re-emphasized the truth of these statements. More and more of the most prestigious and imposing law firms, targeted by graduating students as the most desirable employers, have completely disintegrated or fallen from contention.

The "security" sought by new attorneys in ivory employment towers has proved in many instances to be the farthest reach from that kind of haven. Some of the more fortunate partners in such ill-fated law firms were able to relocate successfully in the wake of the debacles, a few even finding copartners with whom to start new firms.

Alas, transitions were not so comfortable in many instances. Somehow, the indignity of discharge, when accompanied by the usual notice and severance pay, would seem to be joyful compared to being suddenly cast adrift with no warning and no buffer of any kind, as sometimes happened.

The general state of the economy in law firm circles has not been its best for much of the period since 1975. Further aggravating the economic pressures was the debacle of the 80's and early 90's. These and other factors have created a squeeze in the overall employment picture.

Even more pressing has been the continuing "revolution" by the junior partners of these firms, who have long resented the milking techniques employed by some senior partners in certain of the larger firms. In other times, when business for law firms was lush, it didn't matter quite so much that the "name" partners took such large chunks of the firms' incomes. With the encroachment of tougher economic conditions, and with the advent of a more sophisticated level of partner-associate, much more scrutiny has been cast toward these "prerogatives."

Partners with larger quotients of client responsibilities began to hold caucuses, ultimately realizing that they, not the golfing, vacationing, clubbing "name" partners, held the firms' reins. They believed that they could spin off from the firm and take many of the firm's more lucrative clients.

In some instances they were right and sometimes they were wrong. Right or wrong, the vast majority of employees, even partners, did not have such options. The result, in cases where the exodus caused the firm's dissolution, was simply unemployment. Re-employment has not always been timely enough to prevent grave financial problems.

On a more positive note, solo practice has been steadily improving in its stature and financial rewards for those properly trained to practice alone. A major reason for this improvement has been the tremendous jump in the efficiency of both practice and office management produced by the personal computer.

The previous limitation on work output by solos has been raised by multiples. The computer has single-handedly reduced the distinction in caseload processing between large firms and solos to a workable one. In earlier days, the "paper mill" technique of large firms litigating against small firms proved devastating. Then, a phalanx of secretaries was needed to grind out documents, with painstaking editing and corrections. Copying machines and paper were expensive. The entire process was prohibitively costly for smaller firms.

Not so today. Now with the computer's versatility and workhorse printers available to solo lawyers as well as the biggest firms, the gap has narrowed considerably. While operating against a secretarial onslaught by the biggies may not be the most fun you can have, it's not frightening anymore. The enormous capacities and speed of modern computers, the automation and flexibility of programs and other advancements make document work simplicity itself. Most of the court forms, such as Legal Solutions Plus, now are computer operated and take only minutes to complete instead of the hours as in the past.

Most states have followed the procedure of such court forms. Even done manually, filling in the blanks of a document form beats the older method of pleading composition. Here again, the computer narrows the gap.

Some courts are now allowing filing and even motions by fax and phone, minimizing the costly court appearances. The procedures have become so mechanized lately that much of the work force of larger firms has been cut by gobs. These reductions and equalizations have not only narrowed the margin between big and small firms but have contributed to the profits earnable by solo lawyers. Efficiency, the leveler, works for everybody.

You will clearly see the truth of the following further along but for the moment accept it: You will begin to earn about as much money in your solo practice within the same approximate time period as you would expect upon taking one of the better jobs for new attorneys.

I said that entering solo practice is, more than ever, and in more ways than one, less of a gamble than job seeking. As in other studies, it is essential to compare terms before analysis. Hence, in order to weigh the advantages and disadvantages of each of these paths, we must start at the beginning of both.

§ 3:2 The alternative: Employment bondage

If your decision is to get a job rather than to set up solo practice, make sure of your true motive. You may somehow have concluded that being an employee is safer or easier than striking out on your own. As you've seen, and will see more plainly further along, it's at least as "safe" to go solo as in employment. "Easier" is a bad word. Neither is "easy." Neither is harder than the other.

No offense is intended toward those who choose employment. For some, that's the correct choice. This doesn't imply that being a jobholder has less merit than those who prefer operating their own law practices. It's just that I find it very difficult to appreciate that choice. In my view, a job is a job whether in business or law practice. Either way, the employee is at the beck and call of the person calling the shots.

I rankle at the thought of someone deciding for me what course I must follow each day. I've said this so often that it must seem like a broken record to you. Maybe my repetition is a reflection of my confusion as to the reason for anyone making this choice of their own free will.

I've always looked upon employees as people who started out that way and for whatever reason were not able to break free. I've attributed this situation to circumstances that conspired against volition. It's easy to say give up the security of an income to venture into something new. Many people have expressed admiration for my having given up a going business with an assured income to gamble on a law career, particularly at age 45. That admiration was misplaced of course. I did what I wanted to do. I'd had enough of business and wanted something more personal from my work.

Most readers of this book will not be in that kind of situation. In fact, most will not have had an occupation of any kind prior to making this choice. So the only thing "given up" will be an alternative choice. You must decide what it is you want.

The employment choice offers no greater assurance of ultimate success than solo practice. In fact, for reasons expressed below, the obstacles are greater in employment. Those who've read this book, followed its guidelines into solo law practice, and succeeded, doubtlessly would have been equally successful as associate attorneys if that was their choice. To be in solo practice should be based upon style and bent, and the result of frustration or discouragement in the job market.

Being one's own boss offers no refuge from mundane workaday duties. The same brand of monotony confronts the new solo practitioner as it does the job applicant who distributes resumes, makes phone calls, trudges from interview to interview, then when hired faces mounds of mundane duties shunned by senior employees.

The difference is that the solo knows what he or she wants and is on the way toward that goal. The job aspirant may know what he or she wants but needs the assent of someone else to find the road toward that goal. The job seeker's fortunes are, in a manner of speaking, in the hands of that third party. If a wrong guess is made, the unraveling process can be lengthy and expensive. The solo lawyer can switch circuits with a simple twist.

Of course there are tradeoffs. There always are. This book is written expressly for those whose object is choice but not alternatives to hard work. The information that follows is included to demonstrate the similarities of qualifications for success in solo practice and in employment.

To be successful in law practice, a lawyer must make a profit from his or her work for someone. In solo law practice, the lawyer must make a profit for himself or herself. As an employee, the lawyer must make a profit for the employer. Even as a public servant, the lawyer's work must be efficiently dispatched to be valued as one who does not waste the taxpayer's taxes.

Profit in a law practice is computed in the same manner as in any other field. The gain directly produced by the lawyer's work minus all of the lawyer's employment costs, of which salary is just a part, must leave the employer a percentage of that gain as that profit.

All you need to find and keep a good job is academic excellence, keen knowledge of the law, and capable crafts in the legal disciplines. RIGHT? **WRONG!** If you have those things be happy because they could serve you well after you've acquired that "something extra" needed for success.

If you fall a bit short of "excellent" in academics, are you out of the picture? What about a short supply of some of the other attributes? Getting a good job and keeping that job are part of the same mechanics.

It's difficult to understand, much less to accept, that the best qualified candidates are not always the most successful employees. There's another ingredient besides those that fall within the framework of the conventional term, "best qualified." There is a gap between being educated and learning. This book attempts to bridge that gap by providing information that can not only make up for a less prodigious academic standing but could place you way above many stellar scholars.

That "something extra," you're learning about now, can help you get the job you want. More important, it can help you keep your job during times when other competent lawyers, with perhaps better qualification than yours, are being discharged.

There are some possible qualifications to the above. Public agencies, such as District Attorneys offices, City Attorneys, U.S. Attorneys, County Counsels, Public Defenders, etc., may have a different appraisal of your credentials. But that distinction might be more hyper-technical than practical.

Although public agencies may not be as directly concerned with the profit idea as are private firms, you would usually be expected to produce satisfactory work with efficiency. Notwithstanding that distinction, or its lack, the information in this book and its supplements is more closely attuned to lawyers and law firms more directly concerned with profit and loss.

Whether solo or employed, you need the same abilities.

It's difficult to convince some law students and new lawyers that success in employment, and in solo practice, requires similar abilities. If you cannot make a profit for yourself in solo practice, you will fail to make a profit for your boss as an employee. Failing that you will not find success in career employment.

Why some high achiever grads fail in the job market. It can be confounding to a new lawyer with an upper 3% law school standing, a four plus college G.P.A. and straight A high school record to be unable to find or keep a good job. Students are simply not informed that academic achievement may not necessarily signal a well-oiled path to commercial success.

Why are some academically brilliant new associates discarded after a trial period while others of inferior scholastic standing are ushered to the partnership ladder? Is it comparative legal talent? Is it personality attributes? What is the "certain something" that augurs well for employment success and security that some new lawyers have and some haven't?

Recall what was said about legal knowledge and competence. Being a good lawyer is fine but is it enough? Why shouldn't it be? What else does a client want? If you do a good job and win cases wouldn't that be the criterion for professional success? Well, of course it isn't. What else is needed? That's part of what you're learning in this book. Hopefully, these chapters and your good sense will complete your preparation for a productive practice.

What was said about this earlier has caused such consternation among students taking my classes and attending my lectures that I repeat it.

> *"No one, but no one, pays a penny for talent when that talent is used commercially. What is paid for is the ability of that person to cause customers to put their money down to view the talent."*

That ability is sometimes, but alas not always, an accompaniment to the talent. There is an obvious problem with that paragraph. Most people will not, and some cannot, accept it.

Substituting "academic excellence" for "talent," the confusion is even exacerbated. It has been so ingrained within us since childhood that being a high achiever will ensure all of our goals that anything to the contrary offends. Why do so few lawyers understand the economic realities of private law practice, whether in solo practice or large firms?

The confusion lies in the statement that you are viewed as you are perceived, not as you are. It's not whether you are a good lawyer; it is whether clients and prospective clients *believe* you are a good lawyer.

That belief is based on the wrong criteria, you say? Yes, of course. A better lawyer will do a better job and get a better result. After all, that's what the client is paying for, isn't it?

The process of translating that perception into the *illusion* of reality is a problem we grapple with. The term "illusion" can cause some indignation without an understanding of this problem. We say "illusion" because we are really dealing with ideas that are conjured up in the minds of others with whom the lawyer deals. Many marginally skilled attorneys are successful, some even enormously successful, in their practices.

There may, or may not, be some consistency in what is conjured up, or conceived, and what is factual about you and your legal skills. Let's say that your clients all believe you are the most skillful attorney there is. Hopefully you are all of that. If you are less than that, will your clients leave you for another attorney? No. They'll stay with you because they see you as that conceived attorney.

What's the difference between you and that attorney whose talents may be greater than yours? Bankability. You are like the actor whom the public will pay to see. You aren't right now of course. You will be though after you've read and followed this entire book. You'll begin to understand and will feel the excitement of that difference as you read.

Think about it. How can the public know a good lawyer from a bad one? Even lawyers stumble over that distinction. How can a client say, with a straight face, "My attorney is the best one in the city." What basis is there for that kind of statement? Does that mean it's all a ridiculous hoax? Are there no attorneys who live up to their billing? Is everybody being bilked?

The answer could be yes but not solely because of the illusion. No lawyer is the equal of that conceived attorney. On the other hand only a very few lawyers are as bad as the losses of cases they're charged with.

Litigation is largely a crapshoot. So many variables cross over the performances of the attorneys that few can legitimately take the credit for wins or justifiably be blamed for their losses.

You'll do your job as an attorney. You are properly trained and will learn your craft and develop your professional skills with the help of those attorneys in whose charges you are placed. From that point it's up to you to establish yourself as what we've called the "bankable" star. You know now that to reach that lofty plateau, you have some selling to do.

The foregoing shouldn't leave you in the dark. Whether you are a "bankable" star or just run-of-the-mill or even a "loser" lawyer, depends on having that one distinguishing accomplishment. Let's give it a name. For now let's call it *salesmanship!*

We could call it something else. Other names may be more palatable for some folks. Salesmanship sounds like a "bill of goods." How can a lawyer who lacks every basic essential still succeed if the singular quality of "salesmanship" is present?

The answer to that one is simple: he/she can't. Let's be clear about this. You must have the basic skills of a lawyer. That must be assumed since you are a lawyer. We must also assume that you didn't merely "escape" from law school, though we know some lawyers who apparently did.

So let's start with the proposition that you do have those elemental abilities. Where do we go from here? We need to push you through another level of training that will add that one additional element we are temporarily calling "salesmanship."

The employment interview is a selling job.

O.K. Let's say you don't want to be your own boss. You don't want solo practice. You want employment. Keep in mind always that your business during an employment interview is to SELL! You'll learn in the salesmanship chapter that selling is *the giving of information valued by the listener*. You will find also that giving valued information requires knowledge of what information is valued.

This first important information you should have for all interview situations is that a law firm is a business. So somewhere down the line, look for an opportunity to express that information. Express understanding that your services should add to the firm's profits. You have learned from this book that every employee must in some way make a profit for the employer. That is, whatever the employee costs, his or her work must return to the boss more income than those costs. Remember that salary is only a part, often the lesser part, of an employee's total employment costs.

Most employers haven't a clue on how to make money from employees' services. Some bosses know about giving orders and getting things done. Few know anything about the priorities of services or how to organize the day's work. Fewer still are able to expedite and systematize the work "product" toward a profit goal.

Anyone can hire and fire, but it takes a true executive to use employees efficiently. In law firms, as in most businesses, the employer resorts to the game of hire and fire. If the combination of work force and profit is coincidentally stumbled upon before bankruptcy, the business may survive and even show a profit.

The employee, therefore, cannot rely upon being trained in such things. If the law firm had competent business people instead of just lucky lawyers to train new lawyers, it could bypass the firing process. Every lawyer hired could be trained and wouldn't need to fear job loss. Alas, such is not the case with most law firms, even the best ones.

The employee must just find his or her own way to that form of competency. Such information is often acquired through environmental influences. Families in business are fortuitous environments in which to be born. Some business experience before law school could do the trick if one is perceptive enough.

Happily, you have this book. If you are perspicacious, you will find more than enough information in the text to supply the missing qualities and demonstrate your profitability to your employer. Knowing something about employment costs and the general costs of operating a business is a good start.

The law firm interviewer never tells the candidate that the firm is a business and it must make a profit to survive. But it is, and it must. Most often, even the interviewer isn't quite clear on that concept. Interviews do not usually include questions along that line, nor do they expect any information on that subject.

Most people who conduct interviews wouldn't recognize many of the correct answers if given. But everyone is presumed to know that income must exceed expense in any business, including law firms. Some indication by you during the interview that you understand and respect that basic arithmetical point should give you some momentum. Just saying something like, "Of course, I'm a good lawyer, but I also know that my work must be profitable for the firm," can be a startling revelation to the interviewer. So many attorneys find it more difficult to understand this than any subject in law school.

There are some key scoring points that could tip the scale for the candidate. These have to do with the day-to-day detailed functions of the particular interviewing firm. What do you, the candidate, know of these details?

Knowing some particulars about your target law firm can put you way out in front. If, for instance, you are interviewing with a tax law firm, you should know something about tax law, of course. You would have doubtlessly taken some optional tax law courses in law school. Besides the generalized functions of that law firm's business, what disciplines in the tax arena is this firm's forte? What specific range of jobs would the newer associates be expected to deal with? Knowing such facts gives you a powerful advantage.

This knowledge must be generated from a bit of pre-interview investigation. You might start by reading about the firm in whatever published sources available. Martindale-Hubbell publishes sketches on many of the higher profile law firms. Speaking with some of the firm's associates if you know any or can wangle a way to get to them, can be productive. "Grapevine" information might serve as a starting point. Just make sure you verify any such "information" before you quote it in your application.

Look for an early opening to expand on your familiarity with the firm's particulars. This will emphasize your efficiency and express an understanding of a profit component. Such an opportunity could arise when the interviewer asks the expected question, "Why do you want to associate with this firm?" This would invite your narrative answer. From then on, the stage is all yours.

You would express your confidence that you could best contribute your services most profitably for this firm. This places you miles above the star law school graduate who relies mainly on his or her GPA or other law school successes.

Obtaining an interview is also a selling job.

Remember that your writing is just another form of selling? This is especially so in submitting your employment resume. Whether your resume is read, discarded, considered, or whether after consideration, you are invited to an interview, all depend on your written salesmanship.

What does your resume say that is not said in the several dozen other resumes sent to that firm? Why should yours be given greater consideration than the others? Were you the best student of all? Is your background training or experience so compelling? Read it again. Put yourself in the place of the prospective interviewer. Are your stated facts so much better than, or even that much different from, the rest?

So what can you do? You can't change your class standing or other law school achievements. What can you state that might raise the interest of whoever will glance at the paper? Without these verbal condiments, you won't be heard.

First, instead of sending out tons of mailings to every law firm in town, select all of those firms that you believe you might fit into, or would like to fit into. Then, spend some time with the same preliminary investigation suggested above for use in the drafting of your resume.

In many ways, your resume will be the same for all recipients. It is only in a few areas that it will be customized. Those areas will of course be more prominent than the others. So, you will draft a resume with all the usual standard stuff on your computer. Then use the "copy" command of your word processor to copy that standard form. It will be in the copy that you draft the customized information to fit a certain application to a certain law firm. Make as many copies as you have selected specific firms for applications. Each of those customized applications will be addressed to each of the particular firms selected.

Each will recite very customized facts pertaining to the information you have gleaned concerning each firm you have researched. You are in this way writing the same kind of selling information that you would be orally telling the interviewer. Your resume is in effect conveying to the firm your understanding that you need to be, and will be, a profitable addition to that firm.

It's not so time-consuming to customize your applications to individual firms. Whatever the time spent, the exercise will generate spectacular results. Logic should tell you that the more specifically an application is directed to a selected firm, the better the chance it will be read and perhaps considered.

Your word processor will prepare the document to make it appear singular rather than as a group specimen. Even though every sophisticated reader today knows that such applications are sent en masse, the personalized approach is still not the norm and will attract his or her attention.

Stress in your resume the particulars you've learned about that firm and how you can fit into their operation better than other applicants. Include all of the other wonderful self-appraised accolades about yourself that you are sending out generally, but emphasize the specifics and insert them toward the top of your paper.

Remember, like the judge reading your motion briefs, the reader has received dozens of other papers. He or she will not have time to scrutinize each and every one. So, get your main points out fast with sufficient detail (but not boringly) to convey the salient facts. If just one thought grabs the reader, the rest will be read also. If you've done your job, an interview will follow.

How to keep the job and advance.

Your final chore will be to demonstrate to your employer that you deserve consideration as a potential partner. Most of the better firms view associates in one of two ways. Either the candidate is partnership material or destined for the junkyard. Your value to your employer is no greater than your appraised value to the clients you service. If an appreciable number of those clients request your replacement with other associates to handle their work, you'll be left at the dock when the partner "ship" sails.

No matter how much you are liked by the clients, you will fall along the wayside if you forget the formula for employment success. You must adhere to the basics for commercial success. Your value to the firm must be substantially greater than your costs of employment. This means you must know how to budget your time on assigned tasks, knowing also what essential parts must be completed and which parts may be skimmed.

Make sure your total time spent is recorded on your drafts and other records of your work. In this way, information about your efficiency will drift over to firm members who are concerned with your economic value as well as your legal expertise.

Keep in mind the requirement that your superior must approve of you or nothing else will matter.

Rainmakers: The stars of the law firms.

A "rainmaker" is a lawyer who makes it his or her business to attract clients to the firm. As with salesmanship, this is a cultivated ability, but with some reservations. If you lack the adaptive personality, cultivating this attribute may be a bit more challenging. Perhaps my next book will be entitled "How To Be a Law Firm Rainmaker." If you've guessed that this subject is large, you've guessed right. We can only touch on it here. Some points on rainmaking are expanded further in Chapter 6.

Rainmakers are the rarest and highest paid members of any law firm. Getting clients is where the big money lies. If you avoid losing clients you are quite a ways up the ladder. But, if you can GET clients, you're all the way up.

It may seem too simple merely to say that an employee who knows the value of getting and keeping clients is more than half way there. That, in fact, is truly the case. Many new lawyers mistakenly believe that clients simply come to the firm without anyone's special effort.

Some lawyers, losers, of course, believe that clients are expendable and can be dispensed with if there is a personality clash. Thin skinned, impatient lawyers can sometimes be inflamed by a client with the result that the client takes his or her law business elsewhere. These hopeless, hapless misplaced attorneys will ultimately learn that the law is no business for them. But then, what business would be?

If you are one of those and cannot fight your way out of that whirlpool, employment is no better refuge than solo practice. Even more disturbing is that few other places exist for your kind of temperament. But, as you've found in reading this book, there is little chiseled in stone. Whatever your Achilles heel, once you know about it, you can change it.

The more you know about solo practice, the better your employment odds.

All of the information written here directed to potential solo lawyers is useful to potential employees as well. Some of the points require some interpolation, so use your common sense while reading the book.

Most law students begin preparations for job seeking in their final year of law school. Resumes are drafted, geographic areas and job opportunities are researched, consultations with counselors and placement officers (either on staff or available through law schools) are had, and, in general, a fair amount of groundwork is covered prior to law school graduation.

Most seniors know (or *think* they know) at least the general nature of the job they will seek before throwing their hats into the ring. The job applicant completes many phases essential to the well-planned job search long before the first interview is even contemplated. Like fighter planes in echelon, each peels off into a separate pursuit curve designed (or so each hopes) to attack and conquer a target especially suited to the talents of each. In many cases, the blueprint for the search and capture of a job is the best bit of planning and organization that the fledgling lawyer will ever execute.

Yet, with all of this precision, the job applicant is at the mercy of a multitude of factors over which there is little or no control. For example, your resume offers some flexibility in rhetoric, but facts are facts, and there is little you can do to change them. If you have been a stellar student throughout your academic career, and are graduating at the top of your class, you will be content with the immutability of such facts.

If you attended the best schools. If you found time to law clerk with an eminent judge during your senior year. If you were Moot Court champion. If you were Editor-In-Chief of your Law Review. If you won a raft of Am Jur awards for high grades in classes. If you were Order of the Coif, if, if, if . . . All of these facts will speak well and loudly for you.

But, to the extent that you need euphemisms in place of facts and evasive responses instead of direct statements, you are faced with an inflexibility that could confound and distress you. Logic should say that none of these things ought to be important. What business is it of anyone's which law school you went to? Isn't the bar examination the only qualifying criterion?

In California, as in most states, no grades are revealed to the successful bar exam candidates, so that no admittee will be deemed a second class lawyer. If these grades are confidential, why is the same not so with all of these other factors?

The study of law is a personal and individual effort that frequently leads to crossroads offering a choice between the chase for grades and the quest for knowledge. Often times a grade-oriented study plan is inimical to the most profound learning of the law.

It is not always the case that the top ten percent of the graduates of the best law schools are the best or most successful lawyers. Can you think of more arguments to emphasize the point? Of course you can. But save your breath. If you are not in the top percentiles from the "right" schools, you can forget the top job berths. O.K., there are still plenty of good jobs for the second string.

Every year there are rumors that the more prestigious law firms are going to institute progressive plans to help homogenize the legal profession. You hear poetically high sounding phrases to the effect that the aristocracy of law academicians has dominated the leading law firms long enough (ho hum).

All right. You are realistic. You know where you fit, and you have no delusions of grandeur. You are Mr. or Ms. typical American law student, not at the top and not at the bottom. You have nothing to be ashamed of, but neither can you find too much to brag about. You strain your head to find things to put into your resume to impress. Let's see. You won an Am Jur award for the highest grade in Labor Law. You belong to a legal fraternity. Actually, there are some nice things to add, when you start thinking back.

You've given this job thing plenty of thought, and you know just what you want to do. You've researched the geography, and you know where you want to situate. You have looked into the various firms that offer services of the kind in which you would like to specialize. You know which of the firms can offer the best opportunities for you, so you're all set for your campaign of siege.

Now you start interviewing. It doesn't take you long to learn that the firms you want are not proselytizing for your kind of "specialist." All right, so you lower your sights, and then you lower your sights some more.

You finally realize that you must forage and not choose. The job market is definitely not a seeker's one, and there's little evidence of much change, except perhaps for the worse.

You also come face-to-face with another disturbing fact. You found exam writing much easier than the test of a real life job interview. But you are an old hand at competitive pressure. So you bear up under the strain and forge ahead through interview after interview. You don't complain, because you know that many applicants don't even get the chance to interview that much.

How are you doing? You don't know. Nobody tells you. You get a bit discouraged because none of the interviewers will ask the kind of questions that will let you show off your strong points. Very little is said to you that will clue you in on where you stand. It's as though the interviewer is merely taking a survey and has nothing to do with anyone getting a job. But the interviewers are always very polite and thank you for the interview.

You trudge along and then you wait. And then you wait some more. Nothing happens. You wonder what to do, and you ask what to do, but no one gives you anything constructive. You can't see straight or think straight, but you continue sending out your resumes. Your hopes are not high, to say the least. Finally, you get a couple of responses, but they are from insurance companies offering what amounts to clerkships in a field far removed from your lowest expectation. You are also offered an office in a collection agency, provided that you allow them to use your stationery to send out "dun" letters. You can't believe that this is all there is after three long hard years of the law school grind. They can't do this to you!

Just when you are about to give up and join your father in the family drugstore business, an offer comes from a law firm. Not exactly the firm you would prefer or the kind of assignment you get excited about but, with your expanded parameters of acceptance, not so bad. You accept it. You have a job.

You look back, and you realize that more time has gone by than you ever thought it would take even to get your "dream" job. But you are philosophical, and you know that you were lucky to get the job you have. Time, as you will learn in the big cruel world, is money. But you have a job now, and you can start catching up.

After a few weeks (or months) roll by, certain questions begin to form in your mind. You assess your job for challenge, intellectually. Sure, it requires all of your time, and then some. But is it, or will it ever be, up to the level of your ability and imagination?

Even as a beginner, you were able to meet every demand almost from the start. You don't care that no one has mentioned more money. Goodness knows you need money, but more important you need fulfillment and personal satisfaction.

You look at your superiors, and you know that they know you are as competent to do their jobs as they are. Is this the kind of job you will be content to stay with, even with your reduced demands? How long will you have to endure duties, conditions and a salary, inimical to your style and spirit?

It begins to dawn on you that this job is not just an unacceptable substitute for what you really wanted, it is completely wrong for you. The hours are ridiculous, the load is inhuman, and the intellectual level of the work would insult an enterprising first year law student. You've tried for a while to convince yourself that you are getting "experience." After two, or maybe three or more, wasted years, you ultimately get wise that the only experience you have been getting deals with how to pull in your belt another notch.

What's a nice, energetic and capable young lawyer like you doing in a place like this? The answer to this question causes you to quit the job and leave like a flash. Even the drugstore business looks good by comparison.

You start the trek all over again, thinking that now, with at least some experience under your belt, you can find something closer to what you want. But, alas, you find that the market is thin for lawyers limited to what you have been doing. You find it difficult to believe, but it appears that you have gone backwards in acceptability. You have spent two, three, or four years working in a field that has made you fit for doing only what you've been doing.

And you still don't know where the courthouse is.

Looking back, the picture is not very inspiring, is it? Of course, it doesn't have to be this way. You could luck out and get a great job with all kinds of challenges and satisfying assignments, and even lots of money. So, before we take a look at the other path, the one toward solo practice, let's find out whether you were born to be an employee.

For some people, employment is not only preferable but inescapable. In such instances, marriage between them and good jobs offers bliss. For them, employment can be beautiful. For instance, if you are the country club type, a great career as a full partner with Snob, Piffle, Whitetie and Tayle is waiting for you with a rosy future. If this is you, don't even think about solo practice because your future has already been computerized and gold-plated.

Others, though not of that pedigree, are lost unless told constantly what to do, how to do it, and where to go to do it. If you are this type, forget about being your own boss. Having to make decisions for yourself will drive you up the wall, out the door, and into the booby hatch. But, if you believe, as I do, that to be a lawyer is a wondrous thing, that among other facts you are by nature independent in mind and spirit, and that you will need to go your own way, then you are solo practice material.

§ 3:3 Preparing yourself for solo practice

I know that you believe it takes months, perhaps even years, for a solo practice to earn a living for you. Of course, you would be absolutely correct if you were to follow the usual fuzzy, uncharted course. If, for example, you were to open an office, furnish it, hire a secretary, get all of the trappings you've been told you need, and then sit back and wait for clients, you probably wouldn't live long enough to see the practice thrive.

I've said that you can start earning as much money from the start of your solo practice as in the average job available to you, as an average or better-than-average student. When I say from the start, I mean from the point at which you would have started preparations for your job campaign.

Just as you start your job campaign preparations before graduation, you also start the ball rolling for your solo practice early. The difference is that once you elect to go out on your own, both your timetable and progress rate are controllable by you alone. As you have seen, this is far from true in job hunting.

You've seen how you, as a job hunter, can be led down a garden path so far distant that it's difficult and hazardous to retrace your steps. Logic further tells you that, even when you regroup your forces and try again, you may be no more successful.

But, while you may not like it, and may be in misery, you have a job, and are eating. That is true. But if all you wanted out of law school was a job and to be earning money, you have cheated your parents (and/or whoever else helped put you through law school) and yourself. You didn't need to go through all that trouble and pain just to get a job.

So that you won't think there are any "catches" to what I have been saying, I will lay my cards on the table right now. I am not saying that you will make money in your solo practice if this or if that. There is one condition that you might call an "if," but I don't think you will consider it a "catch." You need no special talents, insight, business acumen, or anything of the sort. However, I'm not going to kid you about the "if" I spoke of—it's an important one.

The condition, and the only one, is the kind that you can be assured you can meet. You are an average or better-than-average student, and you have passed the bar exam. Hence you are the stuff of which this condition is made.

The condition is merely this: You *must give yourself the same* full measure of employment time, effort, energy, and enthusiasm as you would give the most exciting and challenging job you could hope to find.

When you open your practice, you will be, so to speak, your own employer. So, as your own boss, you must give yourself the same zing, relentless push, and stamina as you would give to any other boss who would hire you. That's not too tough, is it?

Although that condition is reasonably clear and concise, I suppose there are some necessarily included parts that could use further expansion. One such part is your willingness and ability to suffer a certain amount of what you might think is embarrassment. The combination of this willingness and your ability with a bit of aggressiveness, or brazenness, thrown in, will serve as your own private insurance policy to guarantee success. No road map will get you anywhere unless you follow it.

As you will see, the development of the early stages of your solo practice will entail a bit of bravado. You will ask other lawyers for work assignments of the kind that they neither want nor have time for. You could even be assigned work of the nature involved in that job that was so degrading.

So, what's the difference? Ah, but there's an enormous difference. This is your business, not someone else's. More important is the fact that this is a temporary condition that will last only a very few months at most. Your need to be brazen occurs when you are told that such work exists, but to come back at another time. What you say at this point is designed to get the assignment then and there, and requires just a bit of extra "push."

How to get past the secretary to get to the lawyer.

The instant you start your solo practice you begin selling. When you negotiate for your office, whether time for space or pay your way, you're selling. When you canvass attorneys to get work assignments, you're selling. You've learned that much. What may have escaped you is that getting past the secretary also requires selling. Secretaries were born to prevent as many people as possible from seeing the lawyer/employer. Most of them take that duty quite seriously. Some of them even make a fetish of it. The most dedicated secretaries in this latter class will be stone walls. You'll recognize this type by the automated "no" that rolls off the tongue instantly on cue. Don't fight that battle. You're outclassed. Move on to the next one.

Since selling means to cause someone to do, or not do, something that would not have occurred without the sale, you must sell to avoid being rejected. We know that the selling "key" is to give information of value to the listener. But how do we identify that information? If we say we want to talk to Mr. Jones to get some work assignments, we'll be told he's busy now, write a letter. If we say we're here in response to an employment ad, we'll be shuffled off to some hireling interviewer. Or, maybe we'll be given an employment application to fill out. But we won't get to see Mr. Jones.

What information do we have that could do the trick? We say,

"I'm a lawyer. My name is Jerry Singer. I need to speak with Mr. Jones **about making money for him."** [Point to your watch.] "I've got to be somewhere in just a few minutes, so I won't be taking up much of his/her time."

Those tidings should place the secretary in a quandary.

Few secretaries would gamble on debating the subject. Secretaries often handle the day-to-day book entries. Many of them know about meeting payrolls and other office expenses. "Making money" are words that could press the switch. More times than not you should be ushered in to Mr. Jones' office.

Good salespeople do not lie. To sell, one must simply adjust the priorities in interviews. You are truthful in stating that you have information that will serve to make money for Jones. It's just that the money making part might be a bit further along in the script. You are merely advancing that phrase a bit ahead of other planned explanations.

To refresh yourself on how he/she will be saving all those employee costs by dealing with you. Remember to stress that the firm must pay for the employee's office space, furniture, equipment and supplies, whereas you will PAY THE FIRM for the use of those things. Your services exchanged for that space makes that office an asset rather than an employment liability.

Don't get carried away like a sideshow pitchman. Keep your tone low and reserved. Use your fingers as gestures to index all the employee savings the firm will realize. If you keep in mind that you're bringing something to the firm rather than asking for something, you will avoid overplaying your hand.

When you turn on that new lawyer charm, all resistance will melt away, and you'll be whisked into Mr. Jones' office. So, how do you get your point across within the "very few minutes" you promised? You will say something like:

"I know you're busy, so I can get started right away. You'll make more money working on the big stuff. I can take care of the other stuff for you. I'm fast and good at research, collections, drafting, or anything at all."

Of course, you will tailor your little speech to suit your own personality, but you must force yourself just a bit to get the words out of your mouth. I must caution you on this point that it may be somewhat more difficult for certain types of people than for others.

When the time comes to open your mouth, you could experience some embarrassment. You might feel shy about taking someone's time for what then will seem like asking for something.

So, this is a good time to remind you that you are a professional and competent journeyman lawyer. You are not asking for something *from* someone; you are offering to do something *for* someone. Think about that difference.

What you are really doing is making that person the best offer he or she has had all week. You are offering that person some help that is sorely needed. The problem is that the other person may have put that need for help out of his/her mind.

Your job is to remind him/her with gentle but firm persuasion. The further back into the recesses of the mind that the other person has put this need, the more you must prod and prod.

We will be dealing with the particular subject of the "monster" embarrassment further along in Chapter 13. You'll learn how to not only diminish your own problem of embarrassment but to instead place that monster right into the hands of your interviewer. You might add a subtle thought: There will be no emotional involvement as there often is in the employer/employee situation. No one likes to fire employees. Restate that you're NOT an employee, so there's no hiring or firing to it. This is a mutually profitable arrangement. When it's over, and that goes for both sides, it's over.

Of course, you needn't dwell on the greater probability that you will outgrow your need for the firm. When your own clientele and practice expands toward your full time capacity, you will, like the Arab, strike your tent and move silently into the night. Each firm that you must leave behind, will be the sadder for losing you, but the richer for having learned the benefit of the arrangement you taught them.

If you've already obtained your home-base office, you will skip the part of the office asset/liability. Instead you will emphasize that your use of that office, when your assignments require office work, will cost the firm only a fraction of that of a full time employee. Add that your needs are only that of a Trappist monk. You won't be bothering the firm with the luxuries that employees usually demand. Still, you'll turn out superior work in a fraction of the usual employee's time.

You might end your pitch with:

> "Well, Mr./Ms. Jones, if you have some questions about how I'll be saving the firm lots of money and bringing in a better work product, I'd be pleased to hear and answer them."

To the extent that you may, or may not, have difficulties confronting embarrassing interviews head-on, you may suffer some discomfort in avoiding being put off. This book is not being written for the paragon of all abilities, so I'm going to assume that making speeches like these are not your favorite pastime.

Well, this little prologue may give you some idea of the quantum of vinegar you will need in beginning your new practice. Naturally, there are other things you will need to do, as covered throughout this book that will take a certain amount of determination. Any of the things to be done can be done by you just as well as by anyone else. All that is necessary is for you to resolve to do them.

You're the boss.

For some people, being your own boss may be a problem. When you enter your own law practice, you will be your own boss. No one will tell you what time to come to work or when to go home at night. No one will fire you if you take a few days off once in a while. You will be absolutely free to make your own decisions day by day.

You can put off until tomorrow what you know should be done today, or you may do what you wish. Such complete power and freedom can be either a blessing or a horrible burden, depending upon what you are made of. This is the only variable that will be mentioned in this book for which a solution is not suggested

I shall not distinguish between the brand new lawyer and the veteran who, at long last, has decided to go it alone. Veterans will enjoy certain advantages over the neophyte, such as, for example, a probable nucleus of clientele to start with. But the veterans will also suffer certain disadvantages that will shortly become apparent. Either way, though, your new practice will be both satisfying and remunerative right from the start.

Chapter 4

The Importance of the "Pro" in Professionalism

§ 4:1 Some economic realities of solo practice

Know your capabilities.

Do you know what your capabilities are? Do you know what you need to do to expand them? Do you know the limitations of your abilities? Have you set any goals for yourself? Are your self-assessments realistic? Are your goals attainable?

If you haven't done so already, you'll need to decide the question of going solo or seeking employment. To do this effectively, you should be able to answer these questions with reasonable certitude. This means to know yourself. Not everyone does. Many people go through their entire lives knowing very little about themselves. That may work fine for those who are never put to the test. Lawyers are tested almost daily. Some pass with good grades while others come up wanting.

Those who don't know themselves will blame others for their frustrated hopes and aspirations. Lawyers who fail their tests will blame judges, other lawyers and even their own clients. Some people will complain about their burden, in the job, at home, even in play. How many times have you seen golfers cursing and even throwing their clubs in disgust or anger. Those angry golfers usually share a common belief that they play better than they really do. Listen to their lament, "If only I could play my normal game *just once!*"

Complainers abound everywhere. Some complain at parties about the food, the drinks, the company, just about all that's supposed to be fun. Life has its foibles, trials and tribulations. The chronic complainer will see only the negatives. The good things in life belong to the visionaries. Those successful solo lawyers I've seen are the visionaries. They knew from the start that their careers would be successful.

Law practice for the serious lawyer isn't fun, it's work! You've not seen one word in this book that law practice is fun. I've heard some say it is, but I've never seen the fun in it. What I do see, and saw from the start, is personal satisfaction, self-esteem and a sense of accomplishment and achievement. If you invite me to a party, I will expect to have fun. I expect to have fun in entertainment or in playing games. To me, practicing law is hard work. Everything I've experienced that is worthwhile required effort to do well, at least for me.

Tough as times may be, or ever will be, going solo as charted by this book will give you your fair share of law practice. Whether that share is an envious one, or something less than that, depends upon what you will do with your practice. Opportunities do not make successes. People who take full advantage of opportunities become successes. You hear some folks say, "I've never had the opportunity" to do this or that. Malarkey! Opportunities do not shout: "Here I am. Come and get me!"

Opportunities are there, everywhere. No one is so blind as those who will not see. Plenty of lawyers have spent their whole lives in mediocrity. If you ask, they'll say they're doing just fine. If this is all they want, who's to argue. If mediocrity satisfies you, then that's what you'll get and no more.

Going solo, as I have charted it, is an opportunity. You have seen that in buying this book. That's a start. Following this book into your solo law practice is the next phase of your adventure. You'll start to earn money almost from day one. You can either rest there or go on to the next phase. Some folks would call that first level enough for them. After all, they're earning a living, perhaps a good living. Is that enough for you? Not if you are a real "pro."

So, before we plunge into the nuts and bolts of how to become a successful solo lawyer, there's another term that we should define and deal with. Your bar examination has qualified you as a professional. But are you a "pro"? The term "pro" is supposed to be an abbreviation for "professional." But in my view these terms are *not* synonymous. Merriam-Webster's New Collegiate Dictionary defines a professional as:

"One engaged in one of the learned professions, characterized by or conforming to the technical or ethical standards of a profession."

This certainly fits the description of an attorney. But, to me, it takes much more than that to fill the bill as a "pro." How do you differentiate a run-of-the-mill attorney from a lawyer who is highly skilled and qualified in his or her profession? Isn't it about the highest form of compliment to say of any professional that he or she is a "*real pro.*"

More than that, a "pro" is one who has a broader knowledge than just about the law. He or she knows something about human nature and many facts about the real world. In my definition of the word "pro," it takes more than a legal education to make one.

I am hopeful that the material in this book will stimulate your interests toward broader boundaries than those of the attorney at law. I believe your mind should contemplate more than merely how to practice law or even how to go directly into solo law practice with some success.

A lawyer, in analyzing a contract, gives a client short shrift if the lawyer merely comments on the legal aspects. A "pro" will extend that analysis to the economic realities of the contract. Before the lawyer can do that, the lawyer must know something about economic realities. If you are the typical law student or new attorney, you probably lack both practical training and experience in conducting ongoing business transactions.

Yet, as a lawyer, you advise your business clients on legal matters concerning the client's business. Before you start to grapple with this thought, read on a bit. You do not need to know every little detail concerning your client's business in order to give legal advice concerning that business. To be concerned with economic realities only requires that you perceive some basic and elemental business facts.

§ 4:2 What is your "Commercial" I.Q?

Bear with me in a little experiment. Just off the top of your head, try to list all items of operational overhead and administrative costs and expenses in the operation of a solo law office such as you might enter directly, taking no more than five minutes.

Now compare that list with the references to those items after you've completed the recommended research and as they appear throughout the text of this book. Did you cover those items? If you did, you get an "A" in "Promanship." If you covered even more than the listed items, you get an "A+."

Now, consider some other economic facts that may be outside of your life's experiences, but part of the real world of law business. In answering the following questions, state whatever you know or what you guess. Then, compare your answers or guesses with the information given further along in this book.

1. Approximate the average cost of office space per square foot in the district of your city where you'd like to practice? (Insert the current cost after you've researched this.)

2. Approximate the average range of salaries for legal secretaries in your part of the city? (Place the current sum here after researching.)

3. What qualities would distinguish highly competent secretaries from others?

4. What is the approximate range of fees for lawyers practicing in the city or district where you would practice? (Insert the actual range of fees here when ascertained.)

5. Define "gross income," "gross profit" and "net profit" in a business.

6. Define "gross income" and "net profit" in a law practice.

7. Why is there no "gross profit" structure in a law practice?

8. What is the approximate ratio of net profit to gross income for the average solo or small law office in your city or district?

9. State the difference between net profit and "true" net profit in a business or profession.

10. State some examples of tax advantages and consequences of operating a law office as opposed to salaried employment.

11. Define "raw space" as it applies to an office building.

12. List a typical employer's payroll costs and taxes.

13. State all factors comprising office overhead for the solo lawyer operating in a medium-sized city office.

These are bits of information you should know about even if you elect to find a job rather than open your own law office.

It isn't necessary to provide accurate dollars and cents in each answer. I would not even suggest that the figures I've given are within striking distance of accurate values at the time of this book's publication.

What's important is that you understand the existence of these items. If your mind goes to such things as costs, depreciation, capital investments, fees, gross income and profit ratios, etc., you start some jumps ahead.

If you gave reasonably correct answers to eight or more of the above questions without referring to any of the other materials in this book, you own a high place on the list of real "pros." If you had to resort to sheer guesswork, or honestly admit you hadn't an inkling as to the answers to a majority of the questions, you are about average among your fledgling peers.

If you drew more or less a blank on these questions, but you at least thought about them, don't despair. If you reacted with unconcern, you may have a problem operating your own law office.

Just thinking about these things, recognizing that they do exist is enough for now. Obviously you'll need to be concerned with such things as profit and loss in your law office just as any business person would.

§ 4:3 Your latent knowledge quotient

You'll be given relative value answers to those general questions and your research will fill you in on local numbers. More important, this will stir a latent ability within you that will enable you to find answers with no further help from me or anyone else.

Your law school education, excellent as it was, could not possibly fortify you with every fact of law required of a lawyer. Your present inventory of legal knowledge will not even scratch the surface of what your attorney experience will produce for you in your first year or two of practice. I know something that you don't yet know. You've got it in you. Let it out.

Despite any present limitations, your law school and the bar examiners of your state qualified you as a lawyer. You have established your competence to seek and find once you have been pointed in the right direction. All that this exercise is designed to do is alert you to the "pro" challenge.

I'll trust that brain of yours to do the rest. Just as with legal analysis, you have powers of economic analysis. Just remember to go that extra mile for your clients. You are not afraid of what you do not know about the law, because you have been trained to research the law as needed. The processes are the same. Take a look at the practical and economic factors that must concern your client. Then, use those same skills.

Don't worry about labels.

Obviously, I can't provide answers to questions applicable to each and every state and city of your interest. But, good lawyer that you are, you don't need that specific information.

§ 4:4 A few basic commercial facts

Gross profit vs. Net profit.

Let me point out a few facts, however.

Businesses generally sell products purchased at a distributor's or wholesaler's cost price. The products are sold at retail. The difference is "gross profit." From that figure, costs of operation, personnel, rent, utilities, insurance, and general and administration expenses are deducted. The figure remaining, if any, is "net profit."

Lawyers have no products to sell, thus, no cost of goods sold and no "gross profit." What we sell is *time*. That is the most expensive product of all, but has no assessable cost factor.

Our time cost is computed upon a demand for our time at a rate acceptable to our clients. If our clientele is equal to time demands that would fill our days, then each hour lost or misspent would effectively represent a loss of that hourly rate.

All we have is income from fees derived at that given rate from which we deduct our cost of operation leaving, hopefully, a "net profit." Any hourly number taken from anywhere other than that given rate, often an imaginary one, is fictitious.

The cost per square foot of office space anywhere in the world will be subject to certain variables. For instance, "raw" space in an office building is space that is taken without any appurtenances such as decoration, fixtures, furniture, or even sometimes, partitioning. Sometimes "raw" space comes as merely a large area, with four bare walls and a bare concrete floor. In other instances, "raw" space could include partitions, and even some wall covering or paint, and perhaps floor covering of some sort.

In any case, if you were to rent such space, you would be all alone. No one would be there to answer your phones, assuming phones were installed. No receptionist would greet your clients, assuming you had clients.

There is another way in which office space is made available. This is called an office "complex." In this situation, the office is fully decorated. Each office is separated by partitions from other offices and from open space areas.

Various levels of services are provided, depending upon the kind of complex operated. Some are so complete as to comprise "turnkey" office plans. These services often include complete on-the-premises telephone answering, a central receptionist, a law library, conference rooms, photocopying facilities, legal secretarial pools, and other such amenities.

In the more complete complex operations, mail services are provided, and your mail is sorted and placed in your own mail slots. Messages are taken by the phone personnel and/or the receptionist, and are directed to you wherever you are, vacationing or otherwise.

If you are without a legal secretary, you may "rent" one whenever needed. The same is true of paralegals or even lawyers on a "pay-as-you-go" basis.

You see, you can engage a solo aspirant almost from the start, if the need arises. Stay away from "contract lawyers." They haven't the hunger for success you, and those like you, have.

I cannot give you a dollars and cents figure for office space wherever you are, but I can provide you with some useful comparatives. Present space in the general Los Angeles area, where I practice, may serve as a sort of pedestal, or an introduction to the subject for your preliminary analysis.

"Raw" space, at this writing, generally will lease for anywhere between $1.26 per square foot to about $2.50 per square foot. The latter number would apply perhaps to a penthouse suite in prestigious Beverly Hills, or in some comparable area.

For $2.50 or maybe $2.75 per square foot, you can presently lease an office in a very complete complex located in such a prestigious area. A complex office in a very respectable but not so prestigious area could be rented for less than $2 per square foot.

Taking the above general approach, one can rent a reasonably complete office suite of approximately 15 feet x 15 feet, totaling 225 square feet, for about $450 per month, including all of the above services. Sometimes even some furniture may be thrown in, if you're not too fussy.

I have information from cities and districts all over the United States, that office space, whether "raw" or "complex," is available at figures more than reasonably commensurate with the client "pulling power" of each such area.

In the general Los Angeles area, legal secretaries are very, very expensive. An experienced and skilled secretary will demand, and get, somewhere between $25 and $35, and in some instances even $50 per hour. That's about $35,000 and $41,000, and more than $65,000 per year, respectively, depending on his/her hourly workday.

Trainees, with superior basic secretarial skills, will get at least $10 per hour, and, depending upon the degree of skill and ingenuity, as much as $20 per hour. This means that for the privilege of training a secretary, you can expect to pay anywhere from about $20,000 to about $30,000 per year.

You can "rent" a secretary from the complex pool or elsewhere, but again, in Los Angeles, you can expect to pay at least $20, and maybe as much as $35 per hour for anyone with the level of skills to help you on a moment's notice.

Another "out" is through the use of the so-called secretarial services. This requires that you deliver your work to the secretary's office. The secretary will not come to you. Then you must retrieve the work when you are notified that it is done. This isn't too bad. The work is usually completed overnight. But this too is expensive.

The real virtue of this service is that you pay for work done "net." When a secretary is rented, you must pay for all of the time consumed whether or not productive work is accomplished. A service will only charge you for actual time spent for work completed.

If you lease "raw" space, you have no alternative to the hiring of phone-answering and receptionist personnel. These are virtually indispensable services if you are at all busy, and you can bet that in following this book you will be busy!

Hence, even though it costs more money per square foot, the complex route is almost mandatory for a new lawyer. This leaves you with only the contemplation of hiring a secretary.

So, if parting with at least $20,000 to $30,000 or more per year (or comparable figures in your area) of your hard-earned money offends you, as it does me, you should take a look at yet another alternative.

For something in the neighborhood of $800, you can be the proud owner of a modern efficient computer, together with a monitor, printer and all-necessary software programs and accessories (but see my discussion of the best all-around systems, in Chapter 12). With a minimum of time consumed, you can use your "Typing Tutor" program to teach yourself the art of "all thumbs" typing.

No matter how clumsy your typing, you will do your work at least as fast as it would be done with a reasonably talented secretary at your elbow. You don't believe this? Please do. It's true.

What is more, that's all you will spend for your "secretarial" needs.

A secretary's salary is not his/her only expense. You can add about 20% to 30% more for all payroll contributions and other salary add-ons. Further, you'll be paying plenty for time lost. Even the best secretaries will need time off at your expense. More on this later.

The actual employee cost depends upon many variables. The most costly is for inefficiency. Even at best, you'd need to factor in about double the gross salary. This would include your time waste in supervision, administration and work repeats.

Some prior experience handling personnel might limit the inefficiency factor to a degree. Predictably, you have none. You'll learn that deriving the maximum benefits from employees is a business in itself.

When do you issue an order as opposed to asking an employee to do something? How do you get an employee to do a work-over without offense or embarrassment? How do you plan an employee's day? How do you change the day's schedule and keep it within the normal scope of the day's events? How do you develop the appearance of a "friendly" relationship and at once maintain discipline? When and how do you correct or chastise an employee?

Some employees take to discharging duties readily and need little direction. Others need constant proctoring. Sometimes a "natural" like the former can deteriorate into the latter by lack of proper employer control. How do you prevent this from occurring?

While you may have no need for direct application of employer supervisory skills, some knowledge of these facts is valuable to complete your "pro" status. Having such information in your lawyer's inventory makes you more valuable to your business client.

All of the above figures and computations apply as of the time of this writing. I have not yet perfected the skill of accurate prognostication. But, I'm working on it! So, you'll have to compensate somewhat for additions and subtractions necessitated by the predicted, unpredictable inflations, deflations, depressions, recessions, and prosperities of the future.

"Net profit" is a derivation of accounting procedures. Therefore, the actual resultant figure is in essence a product of such "creative" bookkeeping as may be employed. "True" profit is computed by a much more direct route of arithmetic.

This gets complicated to the extent that figures are added such as reserves for depreciation and other deductions. While the final "profit" numbers may pass muster with the IRS, the actual "spendable" figure may be considerably higher.

The court may, and should, disregard the "paper" expenses when computing the amount available for spousal or child support. In other words, even though deductions are appropriate for determining tax applications, they do not affect the percentage of funds left for spending.

You'll learn this distinction in one way the first time you try a marital dissolution or divorce case.

Example of "Net profit" and "True profit."

You represent the husband or wife, who is a self-employed business person, like yourself. You'll want to introduce a very impressive bit of evidence; his or her book of accounts showing all income, expenses, profits, losses, and balance sheets.

You won't be shocked by the judge's skepticism of this very artistic and creative set of documents, because you've read this book. Not a word of it is untrue, so why is the judge dubious? Tax returns show deductions for such things as equipment and property depreciation, income averaging, tax shelter treatment, tax credits, and other "book" type "losses."

Then there is the question of how the profit is derived. Is the business on the "cash" or "accrual" basis. In the former, gross profits are what remains after expenses paid from cash received. Costs and expenses are simply those that are paid by checks issued. "Net" profit is another level.

If on the cash basis, how much is left unstated that is due and owing from clients? No entries are made until the fees have been paid. The accrual system will show all sums due by way of accounts receivable. All expenses are listed as sums owed though yet unpaid.

It gets even better. How do you quantify the profits in a personal injury practice? This is an unknown whether working on cash or accrual. Even the client-attorney contracts can't reveal how much, if any, will be collected whether by judgment or settlement.

Of course, an actuarial anticipation can estimate yearly income based on previous year's receipts. Some experts believe that years' accounting totals don't vary too much. If a practice has grossed about $300,000, give or take a percentage, for the previous two or three years, it'll follow approximately this same trend.

However, if such theories are suggested, this opens the doorway to speculation that may work the other way. See, creative accounting can be done whichever way a particular case is best served.

These things, while perfectly legal and unchallenged by the IRS, do not actually impinge upon your true "spendable" net profit. These unsympathetic judges just do not appreciate the depreciables.

Your client will have to pay child support with part of the "take home" dollars, not those contrived "stated profits." What this really means is that what may be relevant to tax advantages may not be relevant to your actual business "true profits" barometer.

The term "stated" profit, as your accountant will advise you, is the number you will consider for tax and statistical matters, is not really a determination of the dollars you have earned for purposes of enjoyment, living needs, and investment capabilities.

If your client is the business person husband or wife involved in a divorce, you might, just might, find a judge who will accept the tax return's stated profit concept. Or, if your client is the wife or husband of the business person, defending such a contention, you can nip it in the bud.

You can see how an intermix of legal analysis with economic realities can auger well for your client, and for you as the attorney. So open up your mind to the practice peripheries. Look around. Ask questions. Don't be afraid to use your instincts and your intuition. You'll be surprised at how much more you know than you think you know.

Here's something for you to chew on as you develop that certain something that makes you bankable. This isn't any kind of bromide or hokus pokus. Belief in yourself is as important as anything you have learned, are learning, or will ever learn. ***YOU ARE WHAT YOU BELIEVE YOU ARE.***

Chapter 5

The Threshold to Entering Your Solo Law Practice

§ 5:1 Generally

It seems to me that beneath the many precautions usually stated in books on going into solo practice is ***FEAR***. New lawyers are fearful of going into solo law practice. Authors capitalize on that fear. My books have eschewed such fear.

Put all trepidations out of your mind. Enter solo practice with the confidence that your basic education and legal training should justify. Follow the guidelines in this book and keep your eyes firmly ahead to your successful practice.

Your income and training are included in the plan.

From the moment you take your first step toward solo practice, keep two things solidly in mind:

(1) The work assigned by other attorneys should provide a living for you within a matter of days. Thus, any form of outside financing shouldn't be necessary.

You make it clear to all assigning attorneys that you are NOT a "contract attorney," nor anything of the kind. You are doing this work only until you gather enough referred clients as a nucleus for your new solo practice. You explain that you are very serious about perfecting your skills, so they can be sure you will strive to do the best work possible.

How and why you can expect to receive enough new clients from these assignors to form that nucleus is fully explained throughout this text. It's important that you fully understand this not only to reassure yourself but to explain it to prospective assignors.

The "Contract Attorney" concept is contrary to everything you want to accomplish. He or she is in the business they've elected to pursue. They presumably are satisfied with whatever they can collect on a pay-as-you-go basis. In most cases, development of skills would probably not be on their agendas.

You have your eyes set on a much higher goal. You will work cheaper and produce a much higher quality product. Your development of skills, techniques and your learning process are much more valuable to you than any hourly fee you will collect.

You're working to establish an independent private practice. Your target is to develop your own clientele. You do not, absolutely do NOT want to subordinate yourself to a career of working for other attorneys. This phase is designedly temporary. You are in fact using those assigning attorneys strictly as a means to that goal.

(2) You will no doubt be fully trained by each of the respective assigning lawyers on how to properly perform the work assigned.

The reason you can expect adequate training from your 15 or 20 "professors" is that they want your best performance and you are as concerned about their clients as they are.

You accomplish nothing from your work unless you have done the job with professional skill. You need this for yourself as well as for your assignors. The contract lawyer is interested only in payment. You are eager to learn and to please. This much must be explained to your assignors. They gain in two ways: Your fee is lower and your efforts will be much greater.

These two facts are stressed because of the skepticism of new lawyers. Despite my repetition on the subject, I'm constantly asked during seminars, "How can a lawyer open an office without thousands of dollars to support himself/herself while building a practice?" and "How can a new lawyer open an office without any practical experience?"

The estimated 3, 4 or 5 months training session has been shown to be sufficient in most instances, but if you need further assurance, by all means take as much umbilical time as comforts you. But don't get too comfortable in your legal fetal position. Remember you are a visionary, looking ahead to a much greater day.

Your learning curve should be more concentrated and instructive than anything you would get in an employment situation and far more diversified. These two factors should answer your nagging questions on how you get "on the job training and payment."

Something to bear in mind as you build your roster of assigning attorneys is the kind of attorneys you want to include. In general, you should seek lawyers who specialize. It's not so important as to their specialty disciplines as that they are not too deep into general practice.

A general practitioner should not be expected to refer higher quality cases or clients to you. Oh, you'll get clients, but with few exceptions they will be clients you don't need. General practice means generally all clients and cases of all kinds.

Personal injury attorneys are probably the assignors of choice. A high activity P.I. mill attorney will normally avoid court like the plague. He or she needs to be in the office as much as possible, signing new clients and discussing settlement with opposing attorneys and insurance adjusters.

§ 5:2 The velvet trap

You'll not only get tons of court experience but virtually every client other than a P.I. matter will be yours. In fact, many P.I. lawyers won't even take tort matters other than traffic. Other specialists can be good sources as well.

Tax attorneys would not usually be open to matters other than tax. Criminal lawyers are ripe subjects for civil case referrals. If you have enough diversity of assigning lawyer specialties, you will quickly absorb sufficient procedural experience to handle your own clientele as it develops. The nature of things is that you won't get in over your head asynchronous with a naturally paced learning process.

There's more to the difference between pay your way and time-for-space than the "umbilical security." That security some find in the time-for-space route can be addictive. It could be far too comfortable in your cozy little office knowing that your work assignments will come without lifting a finger.

Your landlord lawyer will doubtlessly give you enough extra work to live on as well as pay the rent. This isn't where you intend to end up in solo practice. But it's so restful not needing to even think about trudging along getting added work assignments. Like Scarlet, you'll think about those extra work assignments tomorrow.

Of course, that's not you, is it? You're too dedicated and energetic, right? Still, that kind of velvet trap can be mighty magnetic. Keep in mind always, you want more.

If you were the other type, more on the laid-back side, that could be a problem. Well, maybe you should give this pay your way method a bit more thought. Think hard about the advantages of being free of any kind of obligations other than doing a good job on assignments and getting your share of case and client referrals.

Think about it. Either way you're paying for that office. You start out by overpaying for the office if you're in a time-for-space deal. Your hourly rate will be low and the office price, even after skilled negotiation, will be high.

At first that's no big deal. You have the time so what's a few bucks more of that time. As your time gets spread thinner and thinner, the office becomes more and more expensive. If you've been following the book steadfastly, that time comes faster than you might contemplate.

Starting out on a pay-as-you-go program, you might feel a bit skittish about laying out rent money before the dough comes rolling in. Staying on top of the method will get you work assignments faster than your anxiety will cause you any real sleepless nights. However, if you are too nervous about rent payment, make a deal with the landlord to defer payment (not the rental, just the payment) for a few weeks. This will give you time for your income to pay the rent.

§ 5:3 Are you really alone in your solo law practice?

I don't advise starting your solo law practice alone. Does that sound contradictory? It's not. If you should open your office in your home or in a place where no other lawyers are nearby, you'll need lots of luck to make it to your next meal. You do not open your office alone.

Look for an office either in a law suite complex or in a busy multi-lawyer law firm within a law suite complex. If in a firm, you won't be a part of that firm. You'll only be occupying an extra office within that firm.

A "law suite complex" is a group of offices leased by an operator as part of an office building. This can be a subdivision of a floor, an entire floor or even multiple floors. The complex usually includes a reception area, a telephone switchboard, a mail room, a conference room, areas for photocopying, a law library, and sundry other common area facilities.

This is more fully explored in the sections following. Your selection may be narrowed somewhat by the range of alternatives available in your town. In any case, you will need the reception area, phone answering service, conference room, photocopy facility and, most certainly, a law library.

If your town does not contain a law office complex, you'll have to find your spot in an existing law firm. For reasons later explained, select the largest firm available for your new office.

Next, decide whether your law office will be "time-for-space" or "pay-as-you-go." As you will learn, this choice will be more of a nerve pacifier than a meaningful business decision.

Now, let's get your law practice started.

§ 5:4 The first decision: Time-for-space or pay your way

You have two options. You may seek a law firm that will trade an office and certain facilities in exchange for your services, or you can rent an office and pay your own way with your hourly fees.

Taking the first choice first, let's examine the ways in which you might find a "time-for-space" office. You can follow the easy route, research the legal newspaper advertisements for time-for-space offers and simply apply. Or, you can work a bit harder, with more flexibility, potentially greater rewards, and solicit the "attorney wanted" ads.

An advantage in following the attorney help wanted ads is that it expands the choices. You'll find many more ads for employment than for office/services exchanges. More important, the conversion of a prospective employer to a prospective landlord probably gives you a wider scope of goodies to bargain for.

The "time-for-space" advertiser is probably better educated on the time-for-space market deal points than the employer. An advertiser for time-for-space has no doubt lots of experience bargaining with TFS applicants.

The prospective employer would normally be oriented toward employee benefits. You'd have a greater probability of more concessions granted without adding substantial hours of your service. You could get lucky and "inherit" many benefits from the firm's "employer/employee" orientation.

Extras like paid parking, courtesy photocopying, use of the firm's attorney service, and other perks that you might have to pay for under the usual time-for-space agreement could add comfort to you during this first phase.

The larger executive-suite type firms don't usually advertise for employees. This is what you need for more effective gathering of assigning lawyers. If the firm is located within a building occupied by lots of other attorneys, whether solo or otherwise, it's size is unimportant.

If the employment offer is from a small firm tucked away somewhere, pass on it. Your main objective, whichever way you choose, is to have the most convenient access to lots of attorneys.

Although getting a time-for-space slot is easier, you would still need to negotiate for as many of the comforts as the traffic will bear. We'll go into that next, but first, how do you convert the advertising employer to a willing time-for-space landlord?

You will respond to the advertisement, but in a way different from a hopeful employment applicant. You will telephone, if, and ONLY if, the ad invites telephone inquiries. Otherwise, and this will usually be the case, you will send your application by letter.

Since fax has become so commonplace it might also be an acceptable method of transmission. This way you'll get the benefit of speed and directness. Fax messages seem to find their way to the right desk more promptly than regular mail.

Your letter can follow the suggestion appearing in Chapter 2, or you can devise your own letter according to your style and temperament. However it's done, the letter should emphasize the economic advantages of your time-for-space offer vs. hiring an employee.

You could, I suppose, overstate the low cost element in your pitch. Most always, "You get what you pay for." My experience is that most people like a bargain so well that they more often lose sight of the correlative quality.

So, if you tend to overstate either dollars or quality, err on the side of the dollar. Never underestimate a lawyer's frugality. Frugality, that is, on everything but golf, skiing or whatever the sporting choice.

You needn't state everything contained in the previous pages on this subject, but you should reread all of those points and be sure that you have them clearly in your mind when you phone or write the letter. Reread them again before you go for your interviews.

The key words are:

"I'll do a better job and save you tons of money over the cost of an employee."

Those key words need to be subtly supported by casual reminders of all that an employee costs.

You might not believe that a successful law firm lacks a handy reference to what their employees cost the firm, but that is most often the case. In fact, very few, if any, law firm interviewers really have any idea about the peripheral costs of employment.

That doesn't mean that the points you raise will not be familiar to them or that they will not appreciate the compelling logic in your approach. If the interviewer is close enough to the profit and loss picture of the firm, you might detect some curiosity if not a direct interest in your calculations.

Of course, the odds for scoring an interview will stem directly from your first approach, be it by phone, fax or letter. So, your pitch, oral or written, must be short and carry a dynamite punch. I invite you to improve on my specimen letter, but keep it short.

Don't make the reader hunt for your point. Lawyers have a tendency to do that. You'll see more of what I mean by that when we get to the subject of "salesmanship."

Remember that whoever is assigned to hold the interview is

still a lawyer, and his or her time is valuable. Don't pad your part. Say it and get off the stage.

If your application is by letter, make sure everything is said in one page, short and sweet but sufficient. Use wide margins, short paragraphs, but get the point made.

The difference is only academic.

The "pay-your-way" route only means you rent an office with *money*, not with services. Before you hold your head in your hands, I can assure you both ways are relatively the same. The main advantage in TFS over PYW is its pacifying influence and perhaps some "employee" perks.

Paying your way has big advantages. You aren't obligated to anyone for work priorities. You can pick and choose your office and location.

You are free even of the suggestion of being an "employee." You can locate within a massive "executive suite" among many other lawyers for greater potential work assignments.

Although you won't have the illusory "security" of no rent to pay, your work assignment program will be just the same. Having no rent to pay means little if you aren't actively obtaining a full work schedule to cover all your needs. After the first few days of meeting with other lawyers and assessing your assignments, you'll see that there's no need for such umbilical cradling.

You could, if it would give you more comfort, ask your landlord attorney if you could defray some rent for a few weeks. If necessary, agree to make up the deficit later on.

Actually, since we're making comparisons to employment, you don't get money up front from an employer either. Consider all the time taken to locate a suitable job and then having to work for some time period, usually two or more weeks, before your first pay check. So, a solo venture would probably get you your starting money quicker than a job.

Chapter 6

The Roadmap Into Your Own Solo Law Practice (Without Missing A Meal)

§ 6:1 Generally

It may seem to a nervous new lawyer that a time-for-space rental deal is a haven. Actually, the only difference between the time-for-space deal and paying your way is your state of mind. Your office overhead will be paid either way. Whether you're paid with rent and other concessions or with money really makes no difference.

Either way, you'll be allocating a given number of work hours for rent and overhead. The lawyer who provides the office would probably be just as willing to pay your hourly fee if you have an office elsewhere.

Your fears are understandable, although not justified. Law practice, as with any business, experiences the feast or famine cycles. Every lawyer faces times when he or she will not know when, if ever, another client will come through the door.

You will face the same quandary. However, never again will you feel the same security as you do when you are working assignments from other lawyers. Lawyers cannot solicit clients the way other businesses solicit customers. Neither can the big firms so don't feel sorry for yourself. When your practice reaches the independent stage, which shouldn't take more than just a few months, the integrated income will be more than enough to smooth out the dry periods.

If it salves your worried brow, lawyers are free to solicit work assignments from other lawyers as much as they wish. You will have all the work you want. If that is all you want, your days will be jam-packed until you retire.

That may be fine for some people. Not for you. Maybe $60,000, $80,000, or so, per year sounds O.K. to you now. But if that is really all you want, you'd be better off getting a job. That is not what solo practice is all about. Remember independence.

Consider also that if you follow the guidelines set for you here, your income should be several times the salary you'd expect to receive at any stage of the game. You want your own practice, not merely the cast-offs of others.

Getting assignments will be no problem. You can safely choose either plan so long as you follow the method. For the moment, let's stick with the time-for-space plan.

Set up your interviews geographically. Review every spot offered in the legal newspapers under the time-for-space column. Use the process of elimination, reducing the eligible suites to preferable suites as your negotiations progress.

Ads for employment are far more numerous than time-for-space ads. Don't make any office deals until you've explored all of those employment ads. Use the technique you've learned. Convince them of what you're learning here; that your time-for-space offer will be better and more economical for them than hiring an employee.

When you have narrowed down your choices, you should have several prospects offering small to moderate-sized offices at no more than prevailing rates. They should include an adequate library, good reception service, efficient telephone answering, a conference room, a photocopier or facilities for duplicating, plus a few extra comforts previously described.

Your preferred office should be located within a large master suite or floor containing many lawyers other than those of the firm you're interviewing. Ease of contact and your familiar appearance is important. You won't have that advantage if your solicitations are too spread out.

Office prices vary from place to place and from time to time. At this writing, an adequate office for your purposes with all of the above should not be more than about $450 to $600 per month, even in Beverly Hills, California. Rents elsewhere should be substantially less and will be controlled by the prevailing market and economy.

Don't be afraid to ask for whatever sum you've decided upon. But try to induce the other person to name the figure first. Don't be cagey, but be a good listener. There's an old saying: "The first person doesn't have a chance." This means that whatever the first person says, will be attacked by the second person's parry. If you say $50, you may be offered $30, or maybe only $25. It's basic human nature. Let the other person make the offer, and then you say your piece.

If their quoted price is satisfactory and you like the office, no need to start auction bidding. Keep in mind that your goal is really a varied work experience and referrals, not the highest hourly fee.

You may have some trouble accepting my advice in taking the lowest fee you can live with. The more palatable your fee, the more work you'll get and the sooner you'll get it. Along with that work will be your much-needed experience.

Another thing to remember is that one of you will "upstage" the other because of the psychology of giving something other than money as a consideration. We are so used to trading dollars for what we want that we tend to undervalue things in exchange for things. Use your "horse trading" sense.

With some reservations, it could be a questionable bargain for you to be offered a generous hourly rate in exchange for a grossly overpriced office. You will find that rentals vary from area to area, but you will quickly develop an ability to estimate the approximate worth of space.

There is another side to the "grossly overpriced office." If your fee is that generous, think about it before you say no. Remember that you are entitled to a *guarantee* of at least as many hours as it takes to pay the rent. Rarely will it be possible to schedule your assignments precisely equal to the rental requirement. Most often your assignor will be taking full advantage of your position by tossing you more and more work.

If the hourly fee is so "generous" to be at least proportionately disproportionate to the overpriced office, you could gain a net profit from the deal. The overage of fees at the higher hourly rate could more than make up for the excess of rental charge.

In order to assess this kind of windfall, you must use every means of calculating the probable assessment hours. Use your head in making this evaluation. If you find that the deal doesn't live up to your expectations, you can invoke the termination clause in your contract and seek your fortunes elsewhere.

Any bargaining you do would be more productively spent in getting "extras" in your arrangement. Get the use of equipment such as a computer, printer, copier, etc., rather than a buck or two more.

Maybe you can even wangle a parking space as an included "extra." You'll need some services for your work outside of that office. Get all you can by way of services and equipment to help you with your developing practice aside from the assignments your landlord attorney gives you.

Even if you know what area you want to settle in, it will be advantageous for you to get the feel of rental values in surrounding areas. Look at lots of offices and get lots of rent quotes. Of course, in this research you will not be concerned with time-for-space, only rental figures.

Since rental values vary all over the map as well as with the economy, just as do most market prices, it means little to give any specifics for rental space costs. But it may serve as some sort of subjective guideline to quote certain figures applicable, at this writing, in the greater Los Angeles area.

§ 6:2 Raw or decorated space

Distinctions between the two general rental configuration types, "raw space" and "decorated space," sometimes take subtle forms. The "raw space" we've discussed is most often space in new buildings.

Often no partitioning is even completed. Such space is usually contracted by massive space users. The small or even moderate-sized law firm negotiator can rarely finance a basic configuration or even know how to utilize it.

The smaller partitioned "raw space" user would normally be a moderate-sized law firm. The sublease would not be for an entire floor, but only for a small part. Offices would be apportioned in various sizes. The library would be considerably smaller than that of the larger operator, there being fewer subscribing lawyers.

The reception lobby and conference room would likewise be much smaller. After decorating the total space, including offices, one or more offices would be offered to users such as you and me as "decorated space," is the second level configuration.

There are many variations to both of these terms that would apply to each in different levels of scarcity or completion. "Raw space" might be offered in an existing building that a previous tenant had vacated.

In such a case, the "raw space" would still have its original "decoration" left by the previous tenant. Still, the prospective tenant would be offered the entire space, not just the preferred part. In such cases, the term "raw space" is a misnomer.

"Decorated space" is also offered under varying conditions. In some cases, the offer is for the particular office space but with no facility other than the office itself. This means that there would be no library, no telephone answering, no receptionist, etc., but the office would be the net space desired by the prospective tenant.

Offered in the smaller setting, as in the above-described operating law firm, an office may seem comfortable and cozy, but usually has serious limitations. Besides the restricted library and reception service, one usually would find marginal or inadequate phone answering. It would not only be expensive but inconvenient to arrange for all the peripherals from your income. Don't do it. Keep looking.

"Raw space" will presently rent for approximately $1.30 per square foot, to about $2.50 per square foot in the better areas such as Westwood, Beverly Hills, Century City, Encino, etc. Of course, in individual negotiations, many concessions may be had, such as new decoration, some "free" months of rental, etc.

Space completely barren should be of no interest to us. The reason for discussing it is to acquaint you with the evolution of finished office space. If the thought of utilizing raw space has crept into your head, perhaps with the idea of amalgamating with other new admittees, forget it! That's a quick, but not painless, death.

§ 6:3 Don't insulate yourself

This is a classic example of "the blind leading the blind." You need to be surrounded by a homogenized group of attorneys. Remember that your prime purpose, besides getting lucrative assignments, is to acquire needed practical training.

There are too many disadvantages in developing your own space. First, your costs and overhead would kill you. Not least, you need as much advisory input as you can get. The most effective source of your practical education is right in your home office. Also, having an abundant source of client referrals right down the hall offers much more fluidity to your efforts than having to work at long range.

"Solo" practice does not mean *absolutely* solo. You must have a receptionist, telephone service, library maintenance people, and others. Before you decide to ignore my advice against leasing space with your new lawyer colleagues, consider that you each would have to share the costs of that personnel. Also shared would be the substantial cost of a library and so much more.

"Raw" or "decorated," you would need to share the space costs of all of the common areas. And you would need to maintain all of that space and its facilities as well. These costs are borne by the executive suite operator.

Normally, in leasing "raw space," further concessions are given by way of "builders' allowances." A given sum is included as a concession to the lessee to decorate the suite. Normally, the allowance is somewhere around $17 to about $19.50 per square foot. In the usual space size sought by such lawyer combines, those sums are far from sufficient. The result is that an additional substantial investment is required by each participant.

Large, multiple suite operators are usually able to negotiate for a lease price far beneath the sum per foot that small users of say 2,000 to 10,000 square feet would get. This is simply the well established "volume user" vs. the "little guy" who wants to get into the act. The latter just hasn't a chance.

"Decorated space," as of this writing, will vary from about $2.50 to $3.50 per foot, again depending upon the degree of services and facilities afforded. An average rental in a suite offered by such an entrepreneur might be as little as $2.70 per foot in a luxury area. However, it must be appreciated that the size computation will include the tenant's fair portion of the totality of the leased premises.

This means that to compute the area leased, you must include the proper ratio of all space you will be utilizing, including the telephone rooms, reception lobby, library, conference rooms, etc. However, this would not include the customary building common area or the areas taken up by bathrooms, etc.

Certainly, the net space of the individual offices will cost considerably more. But one must consider that, as a tenant with undivided facilities and service privileges, your actual uses are far greater than the confines of your individual office alone. The cost of the library and its monthly maintenance alone would be more than you could afford at the start.

So, for all practical purposes, at least for the solo practitioner, the first choice is to seek space in a fully maintained complex operated by such an entrepreneur. You don't need to confine your time for space search to the multiple attorney firms. A successful solo lawyer operating a large suite within a larger law complex could be looking for you.

For these reasons, as well as dozens of other reasons, you should not dwell on the idea of setting up shop in an isolated office apart from other attorneys. No matter what the proposition, even if rent-free, you simply cannot practice law in total, or even partial isolation. Any plan to use a remote library would be a dismal one, no matter how well organized you are. Just as important is the need to be within a lawyers' atmosphere.

To practice law productively one must be in the "swim" of things, so to speak. You just have to bounce ideas off of other attorneys whose knowledge and experience surpasses yours from time to time. The interplay in large law firms provides this kind of advantage. But being in any surrounding of practicing attorneys might offer the same thing.

Like red wine that must splash around and aerate for a while before drinking, so must a lawyer mingle and converse with other lawyers before settling into any legal theory contemplated for a case.

This warning especially applies to any thoughts of practicing from one's home. Absence of the law suite hallway dynamism will result in lethargy and stagnation. Though often irritating and distracting, the buzz-buzz of hallway chatter by your colleagues can be regenerating to the mind. You need these things. Don't minimize them. Practice from the home results in almost certain stagnation. From there, it's dead city. That is, unless you intend to practice hermit law.

There is a way to beat the "floor space" mathematics. It's easy to see that the entrepreneur pays "X" dollars for the total space, including toilets, hallways and all common areas.

Added to this is the cost to completely decorate and prepare the suites for occupancy. Such preparation will include full library installations, furniture and furnishings for common area facilities such as reception, library, conference rooms, etc.

Each tenant's rental must be proportionately greater than the entrepreneur's gross monthly rental, as well as the monthly cost for reception and phone answering personnel, and all other help in the library, etc. That gross monthly rental owed by the suite operator includes all of the space housing these facilities and the space needed for the hallways, foyers, lobbies, etc.

Space is space no matter how it is used. The division must be normally integrated throughout the entire tenancy. Therein lies the basis for defeating the floor space mathematics.

Window offices are normally more expensive than inside offices. Also, certain locations within the suite are more desirable than others. Strange as it seems, the most expensive locations are normally gobbled up faster than the better bargains.

Oddly enough, the best space bargain in the entire suite is the little, out-of-the-way, inside "closet" type office. If you can suppress your glamour instinct, your bargaining position will be greatly enhanced. The landlord knows that such space is not easily rented. You're not alone in preferring fancy trappings.

Therefore, the landlord may be very willing to throw away the calculator and talk "turkey" with you. Don't be afraid to make an "offer that he or she can't refuse." You'll find you have an eager audience for negotiation.

§ 6:4 Facilities which should be "Standard Equipment" in all office deals

Standard facilities normally offered in time-for-space setups are library, secretarial space with desk, space for filing cabinets (usually about three), reception area, conference room and phone answering services. Added extras to be bargained for are parking spaces, part-time secretarial service, attorney's court service, and access to forms.

If the actual office itself is very small, you will need to use a conference room on occasion. Whether you occupy on a time-for-space or pay-as-you-go basis, you must have the right to use the conference room. Even a larger office will not suffice for the occasional multiparity office conference.

§ 6:5 Minimum basics, especially telephone answering

Assuming that you have spent some missionary time in learning about general rental figures, you are ready to approach some prospective landlords. Your preliminary research work has also no doubt taught you to distinguish the various suite qualities and the differing values of extra facilities offered. You should also have decided on what minimal extra services and facilities you will require and what things you can do without.

There are some basics you are going to need whether you get them included in the deal or whether you must pay for them from your practice proceeds. You *must have telephone answering, both in your suite during office hours and remotely through a service after hours.*

The phone operators, employed by your landlord, will answer your extension with whatever greeting you instruct. You will then be buzzed through an intercom line and informed as to the identity of the caller. When you are absent from the office, a message will be taken.

The remote answering service is not suite-connected and will not be a part of your rental plan. However, this service is usually not expensive. Normally it will pay for itself in new clients and the saving of a client here and there who could drift away because of an unanswered phone.

The service is arranged through a nearby company so that phone line charges may be minimized. The service also answers through an extension with your desired greeting. This service varies from miserable to barely satisfactory, but it is indispensable during your first few phases.

You may also need parking for your automobile on a monthly basis. The landlord normally arranges for a number of spaces in the master lease. Most of these spaces have been assigned to regular members of the law firm. If there are any left unassigned, you should try to get one included in your deal.

§ 6:6 Securing a "Time-For-Space" arrangement

Resist your natural enthusiasm to start talking. Let the other person do all of the talking at first, and most of the talking throughout the entire interview. If there are any alternatives in what is being offered, let the other person describe each fully without any comment on your part. You'll learn more about this technique in Chapter 13 on Salesmanship in Solo Practice.

The other person will usually inflate the value of facility for obvious reasons. This tactic is, and always has been, built into the barter system. If the only office available is a large and expensive one requiring a mammoth amount of your time, pass it up.

You cannot start out with too much of your time taken for more office than you need. But, if the cost of rent is greater because of the extra services and higher potential income from expected assignments or your hourly fee is more, you might have a start for negotiations.

Reception service is rarely a problem in negotiation. Since there must be a receptionist anyway, it is little extra trouble to add the slight load of your new practice. The telephone is another matter. Law office phones are always busy, and the operators are hopping just to care for those of the firm members.

Telephone operators in a law office are among the most harried of all people. If their answering load is so great that to add your calls would diminish their efficiency substantially, or require the hiring of another person, you can forget getting on the board. Look elsewhere for your office.

Unless you are starting your practice with a full-time secretary, forget trying to get by without phone service. Don't confuse my reference to "phone service" with the kind that answers your phone remotely after office hours. Don't try to use that kind of service for your regular daytime answering. It never works out. You must have in-suite phone answering during the day.

You cannot successfully substitute one of those answering contraptions for in-suite telephone service. Such a "robot" might suffice for your personal calls at home, but not for your professional office calls. Such use, even temporarily, will earmark you as second rate with prospective clients and other lawyers. Clients may view your spartan office trappings as prudential economy. Your use of a mechanical phone answerer will be looked upon as "tacky."

At best, people are not enamored of such devices, and are often intimidated by them. At worst, they will simply hang up and move on to the next available attorney. Your loss of just one good client as a result of this form of economy will cost you more than any alleged "savings."

When you think you've gone as far as you can on your price per hour, work on getting a reduction in the amount of time exchanged for your office rental. Don't get stubborn on either point.

Keep your mind clicking on the bottom line. All things considered, a usable guideline is an office with the described facilities and services for approximately 8 to 12 hours of your time per month.

O.K., so you're offered a nice office worth about $450 to maybe $650 per month (or the equivalent wherever you are), including all above-described extras, for say 8 to 12 hours per month. Not bad.

Not so fast! Your mommy didn't send you through law school by taking in floors to scrub so that you could bury yourself. She wouldn't want you in some cockamamie, two- or three-member, struggling law partnership.

What are you offered *besides* the office and facilities? A most important consideration is the prospect of additional overflow work. An even more important consideration is client referrals.

§ 6:7 Work overflow

Through all of your negotiations, bear one thing in mind. Everybody is trying to sell something to somebody. They want your services (or somebody's services) just as much as you want an office. That's fine, but there's more for you to consider.

To be sure, you will be getting work assignments, and client referrals, from many other lawyers. You also want experience fast. There's no better source for assignments and experience than within your office suite.

You may be *told* that there will be plenty of overflow work just to induce you to take the deal. You should look for signs other than their promises. Look for the signs of a thriving law practice. Others cannot give you any overflow unless they are up to their eyebrows with work.

Some pretty reliable indications of a busy office are things like secretaries frantically banging on their computers, telephones constantly ringing, scads of filing cabinets with trays full of case files waiting to be filed, and at least a few clients waiting out in the reception room.

Another sure sign of success is the presence of bottles of antacid stomach medicines on the partners' desks. If they are nearly empty, so much the better. Of course, if you see an oxygen tank over in the corner, that should be a clincher.

Seriously, you must be convinced that your prospective office is so overloaded with work that there's no way to avoid assigning extra work to you. If not, remember, your rental hours are *guaranteed.* If they assign less, any rent deficit is offset for that month. The next month starts with a new slate. But any hours exceeding your agreed time-for-space must be paid to you in cash. Naturally, it is to your advantage to have as much excess momentum going for you as possible right from the start.

You should also discover what, if any, other such arrangements may have been made with solo lawyers. If there are competing time-for-space lawyers, you will only be getting a part of any available extra work.

If it is divided among too many or if favoritism exists, there can be a possibility of only scraps for you. Check it out. But don't be concerned if there is some competition. Remember, you've been trained. Can your competition equal that?

Overflow work can be in the form of additional hourly work, or it may be in the form of outright case or client referrals. In the beginning, you should bend more toward the hourly deal. This is because you will need the training that goes with the assignments.

As you develop momentum, you should curry as much referral business as you can. This is where your future success lies. Although the hourly basis eliminates risk and delay, your topside gain factor is limited to the hourly amount. With referrals, the sky may be the only limit.

Most cases that are referred to you will ultimately generate some income to you. Since the vast majority of cases are settled rather than tried, your risk is mainly one of time rather than event. Hearken unto one of the *seven basic rules for survival* that will be detailed for you in Chapter 7: "Settle the case."

You will not be committed to accept any overflow work or referrals. If you just take all that are offered to you without quibbling, and the firm you are with is a jumping one, you'll no doubt do just fine. Don't ever complain about any client or case that's given to you, even in jest. That would be a capital error.

If the client given to you turns out to be the dud of the century, or the case an impossible mess, don't complain to the referring lawyer. Keep all of these troubles to yourself. Your assigning lawyers could react negatively to this information. They may feel personally responsible for having given you a bad referral. So, contrary to what you might think, instead of getting another and probably a better case, you'll get no more cases from that lawyer.

The referring lawyer could feel self-conscious, so your name could be strickened from the referral list. No matter how much you try to convince the referring lawyer that you understand about such things, your case with him or her is lost. Your reward for relating your sad experience will be silence.

So, keep your little troubles to yourself. When you're asked about how things are going with "what's his name," say "Fine, just fine." If circumstances force you to explain later, that negative reaction won't occur. But don't look for an opportunity to explain. It doesn't work that way.

In addition to whatever assessment you have made as to the probabilities of getting overflow work, you should get further assurance. Even though all signs show that this office is the world's busiest, that is no guarantee that you will get any substantial quantity of work assignments or referrals.

All of the tests suggested by which you may assess such probabilities will only broaden the odds for you. What you should search for is reasonable certainty. You should make it clear to the referring lawyer that you need the additional work and will be relying upon a substantial amount of it.

Even with that assurance, and all signs indicating that you will be getting lots of work, you must follow through with a "nudging" campaign. You must keep the assignments coming. It is important, particularly at the beginning, to work very hard and put in heavy hours so that you can handle as big a workload as possible.

This is so that you will demonstrate your need for more and more work. If you show a large capacity for work, you will train your referring lawyers to scrounge around to find lots of things for you to do. You'll be surprised at the work he or she can scrounge up if pushed.

You will also be making a better impression by showing that you can get the work out fast. This is the most important thing for you to prove. Any lawyer can get the job done if there is forever to do it. If you are given a job of some consequence, say on Friday, and you finish it by Monday, you will be a hero.

If you perform in this fashion consistently, you won't have to worry about bugging lawyers to get work. They'll be looking for you. Strangely enough, even though the lawyer doesn't need the product until next month, you will have made an impression, and he or she will want to use you again real soon.

But, at the start, before you've had a chance to show your mettle, you will need to resort to "pest" tactics. Call on each contributing lawyer often and aggressively. Remind him or her of your insatiable work appetite.

A strange twist regarding your pushing for more work is that you'll get more work. You'd think there would be a kind of "take your turn" limit on assignments. If your work is fast and good, you'll get more and more heaped on you.

If you're just starting or you have to press a bit harder for work, remember that your mission is to resist the embarrassment syndrome. Let the referring lawyer wrestle with that little problem. Just as you will feel like folding when you aren't being given a tumble and you're being put off with a "See me later," make the referring lawyer wilt with your persistence. Remember your little "pitch" and hang in there.

Bargain for all you can get in your time-for-space deal.

Your responsibility to pay for all facilities and services included in your program is limited to your commitment to give service. The time to negotiate for everything you need or want is before you make the deal. Once you are located in the office, you can forget about getting any additional benefits included.

Obviously, the more services you get included, the more business your referring lawyer will be committed to give you. If the referring lawyer fails to give you sufficient business in any given month to offset all that's included, any excess in your favor is exonerated. So, the more the merrier. But don't be confused. By this logic, you should not necessarily go for a bigger or more luxurious office.

All of the "extras" described above are needed in your practice, but a big beautiful luxury office you don't need. On the other hand, should you be given more than you have bargained for in business, the referring lawyer must pay for the excess in cash at the end of the month. This is one form of "overflow" and, as I have said, is important for you to look for.

The best form of "overflow" is client and case referral business given to you in a raw state by another lawyer. Either cases will be turned over to you on some agreed basis, or clients will be referred to you. These will usually be matters that are outside of the referring lawyer's practice limitations. Normally, if a client is referred to you, you will be free to set up your own file and bill at your own fees. This will be discussed in depth later.

The hourly fee you will be paid under your time-for-space deal will depend upon two things. Your built-in talent as a lawyer is, of course, a big consideration. But perhaps even more important will be your selling ability.

That ability, like everything else you need to know about solo practice, is canned, right here in this book. Read the material but, more important, absorb it. Have no concern. You'll do just fine.

As a beginning lawyer, you have no track record, so no one knows whether you are solid gold or just gold-plated brass. You didn't allow yourself to be abused for years in law school and then tormented at the bar exam with the idea that you would be a second-class lawyer, so you've got to be as good as they come.

You are alert, sharp, hard working, and thorough. You can produce. Don't just tell all of that to yourself, proclaim it! Let your prospect know about it. Lawyers are like Presidents of the United States. We all rise to the challenges of our offices.

The time-for-space deal has been examined in detail, but one more preliminary fact should be considered. I spoke of the "guarantee" that your referring attorney owes you on his or her business commitment as your landlord. This guarantee is actually a two-way street.

You are also committed to the referring lawyer for the number of hours you must give him or her. Your commitment in this regard is on a preferential basis. This means that you must be available to the referring lawyer on first call.

You cannot refuse an assignment, even for an important appointment with a client of your own. This agreement may be no problem for you at the beginning, but as your clientele develops, there are bound to be collisions. As these collisions increase in frequency, the arrangement becomes less and less desirable to your referring lawyer as well as to you.

Naturally, you'll have some flexibility in organizing your own workday. But if doing that compromises your obligation to your assignor, you'll not only possibly lose your office deal but you may even face Bar problems.

The time-for-space deal has a limited life. Of course, the shorter its life span, the better for you. This means that your own practice is rapidly flourishing.

Let's expand a bit on the subject of the high fee and office rental inflation. A successful negotiation on this plane involves certain natural propensities inherent in such an arrangement.

A somewhat inflated rental could conceivably put you ahead of the game. Although speculative, your acceptance of what might at first appear to be an unfair proposition could pay dividends. This isn't necessarily a recommendation, but just a thought.

This requires some apple barrel pounding on your part. It also depends upon your refraining from quoting your fee until after the rental number has been tentatively agreed upon. One would suspect that in quoting a higher than market value rental, the referring lawyer is almost expecting that you will do likewise with your fee.

Logically, the higher the "nut" that your referring lawyer is obligated to offset with work "assignments," the greater the probability of substantial overflow work additionally assigned to you. Strangely, the more you are entitled to get in assignments, the more difficult it will be to tidily customize that number to the monthly total of work assigned.

The happy result of this strange compromise is that you will be getting a lion's share of work from your "landlord" lawyer for which you will be receiving a paycheck, not a credit for rent. See how nicely this works? You would have been quite willing to work for less money per hour, but the landlord's greed has forced you to accept more. Doesn't this scenario sound familiar?

In every successful law office, there are certain cases either turned away or are taken as a matter of obligation only. For various reasons, certain kinds of cases are undesirable to certain lawyers. Some matters are shunned by lawyers because of marginal financial return.

Ordinarily, disinterest in handling certain matters is due to being outside of the firm's practice specialty. A tax attorney who is offered a family law matter will refer it to another attorney. That aside, the new lawyer can expect most of the referrals to be of marginal fees.

The term "marginal," like most terms, is relative. The question of a case or client being desirable or undesirable is a subjective one. If a lawyer's practice involves lucrative and interesting matters, one less interesting or lucrative may be unattractive to that lawyer. But for you, such cases can be both rewarding financially and interesting. To the new lawyer, all cases and fees are exciting.

The object of the referral system is to have these "less desirable" matters siphoned off to you. It will be a rare law office or lawyer who will have sufficient business to fill your day. To follow this system, you must form and maintain relationships with a number of lawyers and law firms.

§ 6:8 The *Right Choice* can enhance referrals

You may be so anxious to get started in your new office that your over-enthusiasm can block better judgment. Choosing the right office setting sometimes requires some self-restraint.

The firm you select as your time-for-space berth can enhance your opportunities for client referrals. The choice I made for my first law office was with a personal injury specialist. At that time, there were no classified specialties in law as there are today. Still, certain kinds of practices by their nature led to exclusivity.

Then, as now, personal injury attorneys largely preferred to not try cases. They're usually busy interviewing new clients and negotiating settlements. Trials are a waste of their time. Courtrooms merely keep them from greeting new clients and getting their cases settled.

It was true then, and has not since changed. Two things would be gained from working with a thriving P.I. firm. First, there would be an opportunity to get fast trial experience. The P.I. lawyer could concentrate on the lucrative part of the practice, while you do all the courtroom chores. Second, the firm's specializing on P.I. cases would mean being heir to all cases other than personal injuries. This conclusion depended upon the success of the P.I. firm.

The firm I selected for my law practice baptism had all the earmarks of a thriving P.I. mill. The entire office was oriented toward a very narrow channel of personal injury matters, automobile only. This was confirmed through some snooping at the secretarial output and other office functions.

I was correct on all counts. In a very few months, I had gained heavy experience in trials, motions and all forms of court hearings. Most important, I became virtually glutted with client referrals.

I was assigned my first jury trial within two weeks after joining the firm, which meant two weeks after being admitted to the California Bar. I won that trial. It could be argued whether P.I. may, or may not, be the best choice of practices. There's no argument about the prolificacy of clients in that field.

It isn't necessary to follow in those footsteps. Any firm with an active, aggressive practice within a confined specialty could provide the same advantages to you. A criminal lawyer, for instance, would not normally be interested in any cases outside of that specialty. Often the criminal lawyer, like the P.I. lawyer, specializes in a particular discipline within that area, such as drugs, drunks, prostitution, rape, child or sexual harassment or molestation.

You may even get referrals of criminal matters outside of that phase of the practice. You should be in line for all such nonspecialized referrals. Of course, your work assignments may not be as frequent or as hectic as those in the frenetic P.I. business.

You may be starting to see now why the need for as many assignors as you can muster. Normally, each work assignment won't be that time consuming. Your average work time shouldn't exceed much over two or three hours. Drafting, research and other such chores can be scheduled by you. Court dates, depositions, etc., are calendared and must conform to times and dates given.

There'll be date and time conflicts, of course. Sometimes your choices will be difficult. Obviously, the more assignments you get the more such conflicts will arise. Ain't it grand?

§ 6:9 The "Pay-As-You-Go" office lease plan: Your highest priority: The multi-lawyer suite

Now, let's take a closer look at the entrepreneur's law office complex. More and more attorneys, not just the newer variety but even older, fully established and successful practitioners, are finding the advantage in such trappings.

Lawyers of all levels have found that the single, double, or triple lawyer office is just too inefficient to operate profitably. Costs of personnel, libraries, etc., have risen beyond the scope of income for most smaller law combines.

Law school "study buddies" still talk and dream of forming partnerships after graduation. Some of them foolishly do actually go this route. But there is nothing so pathetic as the sight of two or three silly and frightened tenderfoot lawyers huddling together, staring at each other, wondering how they are going to pay their rent.

Most of the larger cities have law office complexes. There's just no way to beat the rental price, which includes just about everything you need in office facilities. Even if you could group up with five or six other lawyers who have the liquidity to underwrite overhead, you could not compete with these subleases. It takes guts (and resources) to lease whole floors of prestigious high-rise buildings.

The rental figures are far below anything comparable on an independent basis. Because of the nature and scope of the operation, even that low rent should be profitable for the entrepreneur. This is a happy coincidence since you want to be in that complex.

It is not unusual these days to find as many as 25, 30 or even 50 or more lawyers in one extended suite. Each office has its own separate solo or two- or three-member practice. They all share the general overhead, and generate some profit to the suite master.

It is within such an arrangement that you will find the greatest potential for spillover business, whether instead of, or in addition to, the "time-for-space" arrangement. Very few of the participants resent the profits earned by the suite operator, even though he or she may be (or appears to be) living like a millionaire.

Not everyone has either the temperament or the talent to put such an operation together or to maintain it. It takes a great deal of know-how, patience, courage, and diplomacy, plus lots of luck and even some clairvoyance, to put it together and keep it together.

Some of the more successful operators have capitalized on this special talent and have opened a string of such suites. In some instances, the combination of talents permits success in both the suite operations and the practice of law.

Such an operator is usually made of the stuff of success. This person is the kind who would succeed in just about any venture. It is only with this kind of operator that you can get all of the amenities you need, at a price you can afford with assurance that it won't melt away just as you are relying on it most.

With all of this luxury, rentals are usually even lower than you will find in more austere surroundings. The operator offers a choice of office sizes from tiny to immense. But whether you choose the smallest or the largest, you will share in the abundant common areas and facilities.

Anomalously, the deal gets better as the choice goes to the smaller offices. The price escalation is directly proportional to the size of the office. An office half the size is half the price. And yet, you get exactly the same share in all of the common areas, facilities, and services.

So, for the beginner, it would seem best to take the smallest office. You still get the full treatment in reception service, deluxe telephone answering (as you like it), library use, conference room, and maybe even a sauna bath, no matter how small your rent.

Other suite operators follow this same rent scale. The thinking is simple, but logical. If you can afford the luxury of a large opulent office, why should you resent the new lawyer who shares the same services?

This "share-the-wealth" concept may fall hard upon the more

cavalier types, but it works and everyone seems to like it. Although the deal is best in the tiniest office, the occupier of the largest office also has an unbeatable deal.

§ 6:10 Take the smallest office

Of course, for you the choice is a simple one. You will take the very smallest office available. You don't need the extra space, and since most of your time at first will be spent either in the library or out making new contacts, the smallest office will be just fine.

If you're not convinced, look at it arithmetically. Let us say that an office 9' x 12', perhaps not in the choicest suite location, rents for $395 per month, including all of the extras. This office will have an area of 108 square feet.

Another office 12 'x 18', in a preferred location, has an area of 216 square feet, just twice the size, and might rent for as much as $1,600. That added $1,205 gives you no additional extras except space and maybe a little view.

Considering that the package consists of the common areas, facilities and services, as well as the actual office itself, it would be silly to pay over three times the price and get only double the office space, with or without the "view." Silly, that is, unless you are willing to pay handsomely for your pleasures. And, I do mean "pleasures."

In any event, whether you want to swing with the biggies, away from the common folk, or take the smallest office and laugh all the way to the bank, this is where you will find enough spillover work to get you started with a vengeance.

It also seems likely that lawyers will be more enthusiastic about assigning work to you in a "cubby hole" than seeing you living it up. Part of your appeal will be your need for help to get started. You lose that appeal if you appear not to need that help.

If you insist, and you should, you can often squeeze the suite operator into the following deal. Let us take the $395 office, for example. You are negotiating a lease for three years. That will come to $4,740 per year, or a total of $14,220. Your offer now takes a different tack. You are just starting out and need the break of a little better rent deal.

You offer to pay $250 per month the first year totaling $3,000 for the year. This leaves a deficit of $1,740 for the first year. The second year you agree to pay an increase to $350 or $4,200 for that year, adding an additional $540 to that deficit.

The third year you would agree to absorb the entire deficit by increasing the monthly rental to $585 per month. The total number on this sliding scale rental is the same $14,220 the landlord would realize under the conventional plan. There would, of course, be a revenue loss during the first and second years for the landlord, but it all evens out in the end. Besides, it allows him to get tenants he'd otherwise lose.

Many of these otherwise hardheaded entrepreneurs are in the habit of considering such rent deferments or kindred arrangements when offered by relatively new admittees.

This permits you to start less painfully and defer some of the cost to later, when you will be better able to afford it. The clinker of this deal is the sourness often felt by tenants in the last year of "excessive rent." Memories, being what they are, will often fail in the recall of sorely needed past favors.

Notice the lease provides that the while tenant may elect any term length, only the landlord is locked in. The tenant may terminate at any time upon giving notice. In essence, the lease is a one-way street, benefiting the lessee.

The number of lease years is determined by the number of security deposits given. The deposit consists of one month's rent. If you deposit two months' rent, you have a two-year lease, and so on. At the back end, there may be a "last month's rent" deposit. So, if you opt for a five-year lease, you'd actually be depositing six months' rental sums.

That kind of provision is not found in your run-of-the-mill lease. However, a lengthy lease of that genre would require a heavy dose of deposit funding. This fund is kept and used by the landlord. Still, there's much to be said for having your cake and eating it too.

There is a potential downside to the heavy deposit method. The risk of bankruptcy by the operator is an always present negative. You won't be allowed a secured trust fund deal because the whole idea is to provide the operator with working capital. In effect, you are trading this one-way lease for that capital risk.

In case you would feel better with some confirmation of what I tell you, you can run a very simple test before you start the program. Select a suite that you think you would like, and canvass the lawyers there on a "dry run." Tell them that you are considering starting your practice there, but you want to assure yourself that you will be able to pay your way.

Ask each of them whether they would be willing and able to pass some work along to you, either on a modest hourly basis or by referral. Tell them specifically that you are interested in taking any kind of case or client no matter how "doggy." Tell them that you are a hard worker and will conscientiously discharge any assignments that they give you.

So that you won't feel you have been given a stall if they say yes, ask whether they have anything to give you at the moment. The chances are that after canvassing all of the 20 or 30 lawyers in the suite, you will have collected enough new business to start you off.

You'll be collecting for your work at the end of each day. You can see that this system will provide income starting from day one. To be sure, the figures used as examples are subject to variation, depending upon where you are located. Other things will likewise vary, such as the availability of large law complexes.

If you are in a smaller city where there are no such suites, you will still follow the same procedure. You'll just consider your whole neighborhood or town your "complex," and you will do your soliciting from office to office throughout the neighborhood or entire town.

The only significance to the large suite or law complex idea is the relationship between you and your fellow lawyer-tenants. Lawyers in smaller communities will have an even closer camaraderie though perhaps city blocks or even a mile or two apart.

It is strange, but it is very difficult to compress neighborliness. Residents of small towns, with rare exception, know each other. For the most part, they consider each other neighbors though on opposite sides of the town. Consider the fact that farmers are often "neighbors" with the next farm "up the road," although that "next" farm is ten, twenty, or more miles away.

Yet, in a large city, a lawyer may not know, or recognize, another lawyer on the floor beneath or above him or her in the same office building. So, for the purpose of establishing a basis for some familiarity, we are using the larger city law complex concept.

One thing is reasonably certain wherever you are, everything remaining equal, the larger and more plush the office, the more expensive per square foot. You can go for a larger and nicer office if you wish, but don't kid yourself about it. You are not making this selection for business reasons, but because of your ego.

It is a fallacy to believe that, if you have a fancier office, you will attract a higher class of clientele. Anybody smart enough to afford a high-priced lawyer is smart enough to look beyond the lawyer's trappings. You will only accomplish having a higher "nut" or monthly expense to meet, if you have more and prettier space and facilities.

It seems to be human nature to want to justify the spending of money for luxuries and other nonnecessaries. If it serves such a purpose for you to believe that you will do better in plusher surroundings than in a simpler framework, go ahead and sell yourself that program. But don't look to this book or any other reasonable criterion for justification.

Then, there are those who just cannot flourish in anything but the "big-shot" trappings. Just as some must have the most expensive clothes and the fanciest imported sports cars, there seems to be an absolute necessity with certain people to have luxury all around wherever they are. If this is you, what can I say but "be my guest."

A bit more of Time-For-Space: The office contract.

Confusion abounds, and memories tend to dim. *Whatever the terms of your time-for-space agreement, reduce them to a written document.* Even though both parties are completely honorable, there could be an honest disparity as to the precise agreement. There could have been a number of offers and counteroffers prior to the final basis for agreement, and a resulting confusion.

When you finally reach an accord, set all of the terms down on paper. State the exact amount to be charged for office rent, inclusive of reception service, library, common facilities, etc., and all other services, such as telephone answering, to be included at whatever charge is agreed upon. Set forth also any arrangement for pro rata charges for use of common facilities such as photocopying, etc.

The agreement must also state that any services by you in excess of the amount needed to defray your overhead must be paid to you each month in cash. On the other hand, any deficiency caused by your landlord's failure to give you enough work in any month is forgiven at the end of any such month. Of course, the rate at which you will be compensated is an essential term.

Let the landlord lawyer draft the agreement. Remember the basic legal tenet that a document is construed most strictly against the drafter. However, the writing should be as simple as possible. It's a mistake to make the terms too detailed. It's enough that each term is commemorated.

As with all written documents, your time-for-space agreement depends upon its spirit, rather than its letter. Anyone more interested in finding "loopholes" than cooperating will undoubtedly succeed. Courts increasingly frown upon such manipulations, but why buy into a lawsuit.

There was an interesting scene in a W C. Fields movie. Fields played the captain of a showboat, and Bing Crosby was his new singing star. After signing their contract, Fields said: "Well, that's fine. If either of us is ever unhappy, we'll just tear the contract up." So saying, he tore up the contract, and they had a drink on it.

The scene was meant to be funny, and it was, but it offers much to think about. The essence of any agreement is that both parties get what they want and want what they get. If either party is really unhappy, the other will have a rough time keeping the unhappy one bound. It's no answer to say that the courts will enforce it.

You must devote sufficient time and thought to exactly what you want and what you believe you can get. Then, and only then, you can start thinking of an agreement. Consider an agreement the way a furniture maker treats glue. The pieces are fitted together with dowels, pins, screws or whatever, so that the joint is almost secure enough to use without any glue at all. Then, the furniture maker applies the glue.

The furniture maker never considers the glue to be the binding element. An agreement is much the same. If the pieces fit tight and secure, you needn't worry that much about the farthest meaning of the printed word.

It's to be presumed that you as a lawyer can read and understand a contract. Yet, it's perplexing to know how many veteran attorneys have been confounded by certain clauses in contracts they've signed. Perhaps it's because we attorneys don't always read things as carefully as we advise our clients to do. Or, perhaps we suffer from the same faults of our clients, too close to the picture and too eager.

The trait of wanting something enough to disregard a cautious restraint is not an unusual human blemish. One of my clients once explained the reason for not showing me an agreement before signing it, "I knew you wouldn't let me sign it."

Fixations of this type also distort reason in preparing contracts. It isn't always dishonesty that drives one to seek an unfair advantage. It's often the same over-enthusiasm blinding one to his or her better nature.

A client once asked me to include a clause in a contract that would give her some additional rights. She asked that it be done in such a way that the other party wouldn't realize it was there. She knew that if the other party was aware of it, he would never agree to it. It was necessary not only to explain that I could not and would not do such a thing, but why I wouldn't and couldn't do it.

No one, and certainly not a lawyer, would have trouble seeing the wrongfulness of such a plan for cheating. The particular client was an unsophisticated woman who was the widow of an old friend and client. She had been sheltered throughout the many years of their marriage, and suddenly found herself thrust upon the controls of a complicated business. Naiveté rather than dishonesty caused her difficulty in distinguishing keenness from craftiness, and shrewdness from dishonesty.

The client referred to had a great deal of respect for me. However, she chose an unfortunate expression to convey her admiration. She said, "You can do it, you are a sharp lawyer." She had known of situations where I had demonstrated an ability to deal with obscure (at least to her) provisions during the course of representing her and her husband. It was difficult to explain to her the difference between careful concern and outright deception.

In the unlikely event that you may be dealing with such a person in your time-for-space plan, you should carefully analyze the agreement before signing it. Then, if there's reason to distrust that person, don't sign but run for cover.

It is for such an unlikely possibility that you must stress both in the agreement and in your oral negotiations that you are a solo *practitioner* and not an employee. You should particularize that all clients referred to you, whether by the referring lawyer or by anyone else, are your clients to take with you when you leave that office.

A dentist client, involved in a time-for-space deal in a dental suite, engaged me to defend a suit. The arrangement was similar to the usual law office agreement. He had terminated his tenancy, taking his patients and files. The suite operators sued for, among other things, restoration of all charts, files, etc., on all patients he had treated while in their suite.

They had contacted each patient and instructed each to send all future checks for treatment during the said period to them, made payable to them. We cross-complained. In that case, there was only an oral agreement. No doubt the result would have been the same had there been a written contract. My client was a young, naive, newly-admitted dentist, with virtually no business acumen.

The patients that my client took with him when he left the complex were at all times his own patients. He was entitled to continue the "doctor-patient" relationship no matter where he located his office. He was likewise entitled to remove all of the charts, files, and other data referring to his patients.

The same will be true of your clients and all of the material referable to your clients. There will be no right in your referring lawyer to have these clients, or the files related to them, remain with him. They are yours. And you are not only entitled to keep them, but even duty-bound to do so.

Needless to say, this does not apply to clients of your referring lawyer. Assignments to perform tasks for his or her clients give you no right to these clients or their files. Neither has the referring lawyer any right to any of your clients or files.

Your clients are yours, and the others belong to the assigning lawyer. There should never be any complication in keeping them separate.

But, as in the case of my young and naive dentist client, you can buy yourself a whole lot of trouble if you are not cautious in analyzing the character of anyone you deal with. Just as "An oral contract isn't worth the paper it's written on" (courtesy of Samuel Goldwyn, movie producer), neither is a written contract worth much more if the other party is not sincere and you are unwary.

Unfortunately, there are those who have never learned that the shortest distance between two points is—in the law, as elsewhere—a straight line. There are people, some, regrettably, lawyers, that believe that whatever can be gotten away with is fair game.

These are unfortunate people who must live with a nagging problem. The need to constantly play "one-upmanship" can be tiresome. But, their problem is not theirs alone. It is also the problem of just about everyone with whom they come in contact. As a lawyer, it becomes your problem whenever you cross such a person's path.

Sample form of "Time-For-Space" office agreement

The following is an example, from which you may extract some ideas to serve as a basis for your contract:

PETER PIPER ("LANDLORD") and JOHN JONES ("TENANT") agree:

1. Landlord holds a lease (a copy attached), to the entire ________ *[tenth floor]* of the office building known as ________, located at ________ *[address]*, in the City of ________, State of ________.

2. Landlord operates therein a complex of law offices subleased by lawyer/tenants and for which landlord provides the following services and facilities, appropriately furnished: (a) a reasonably complete law library; (b) a conference room; (c) reception area and receptionist; (d) switchboard and constant duty telephone service during normal working hours; (e) copying service at fair competitive rates; (f) mail sorting; and (g) common passways, comfort areas, and lavatories.

3. Tenant agrees to rent Office No. ________ inclusive of said facilities and services plus such other services as may from time to time be provided to all tenants therein, on a month-to-month

basis, commencing on ________ *[date]* upon the following terms and conditions.

4. Tenant will provide to Landlord, upon a preferential basis, services as a lawyer for ________ *[seven hours]* per month, promptly upon assignment by Landlord, as payment for said rental. Said services shall be the full extent of Tenant's obligation for payment of rent.

5. Tenant further agrees to maintain reasonably regular office hours during the normal workday, i.e., Monday through Friday, with holidays excepted. The parties will use their best efforts to work around Tenant's days off, other work commitments, and vacations.

6. It is understood that Tenant will be concerned with the development of tenant's own practice. However, so long as it is practicable, Tenant will devote his/her time preferentially to Landlord. At such time as this is no longer practicable, i.e., as the demands of Tenant's own practice increase, the parties will attempt to modify the time allocations within reason. When such modifications are no longer feasible, it will be expected of the dissatisfied party to give notice of termination of this agreement, as herein provided.

7. The value of said space, facilities, and services is agreed by the parties to be $________ per month.

8. The value of said legal services is agreed by the parties to be $________ per hour. The aggregate of ________ hours per month is agreed to equal the office rental value.

9. Tenant shall be responsible for performance of his/her services only upon the assignment thereof by Landlord. Should Landlord fail to assign the agreed number of hours of work during any given month, any time deficiency shall be waived and forgiven.

10. Tenant may, at his option, utilize one space for the parking of one automobile in the lot adjoining said building, as provided in said master lease, for which Tenant will pay as per terms of the master lease.

11. This agreement is subject to termination by either party upon thirty (30) days' written notice, deemed "served" when placed upon the desk or in the mail cubicle of the party being served.

12. Should Landlord assign more than the agreed number of hours in any given month to Tenant for services to be performed, Landlord agrees to pay to Tenant, as an hourly fee for Tenant's legal services, the sum of $________ per hour for each such hour of excess to be paid no later than on the tenth of the following month.

13. In the event of termination of this agreement, Tenant may remove from said premises any and all property belonging to him. The parties will cooperate in facilitating such removal.

14. The parties further agree that Tenant is an independent contractor and is not an employee of Landlord's for any purpose, including, but not limited to taxation, insurance, or laws governing employee/employer relations. All acts or conduct by either party are acts of parties independent of each other and it is agreed that the manner and method of performing legal services by Tenant as contracted by Landlord shall be determined solely by Tenant and in no way controlled or supervised by Landlord.

Dated: ________.

[Signature of Landlord]
[Signature of Tenant]

Wherever you are, you'll find a master suite in some form or other. High rise buildings containing one or more lawyer complexes are prevalent in larger cities. Master suites exist in smaller towns as well although in smaller buildings.

The advantages of the master suite, whether large or small, are similar in concept, if not in design or extensiveness. It is not so important that you have lavish surroundings as that you have access to the basic services and facilities discussed above. A small library may not be equipped with every publication and yet be quite sufficient.

Your job is to find the place closest to your preferred location and start negotiating. Don't accept the statement that, "These lease provisions are standard for all tenants." Persistence on your part can reduce any "standard" provision to a customization reasonably fitting your requirements.

Needless to say that you won't be arguing points for the sake of demonstrating your legal ability. Your purpose will be to get the deal done and start your practice. Read the entire lease carefully and thoroughly. Often times what appears to be an objectionable provision is seen in a subsequent clause to be acceptable.

§ 6:12 Keep client lists current

Keep good notes, updated frequently and filed appropriately.

Like they say, "You can't go home again." The only thing for sure is change. As you get older, you go home to visit occasionally. You don't notice the subtle changes; the house shows age, Mom and Dad are grayer, the dog can barely move around. Still, it's home.

A few more years pass. The folks have moved to smaller quarters. You don't even recognize the old neighborhood. Then, like a thunderbolt, it's all gone. Nothing is left for you in the old hometown. Even the friends' list has shrunk. Visiting becomes a chore.

You're in a town full of strangers and empty lots where family, relatives and friends dwelt. The old hometown, family, friends, aren't the only things that change. The law changes. We know that so we keep abreast by reading advance sheets, squibs, news reports, etc. Everything changes, even you and I.

One of the comforts of life is the illusion of stability. We leave home to make our own way in life, happy in the knowledge that we can return anytime to find things unchanged. But, alas, we do not find it so. Things change, as do people.

Nothing mentioned in this book is designed to comfort you with permanence. Products, places, brand names, operations and people identified are intended only to demonstrate the qualities and varieties of such things available to aid the solo lawyer.

Don't wait too long to send mailings out to your clients. If you do, you'll find a startlingly high rate of returns marked, "No longer at this address, left no forwarding address," or some such other remark.

I moved from suite 400 to suite 500 at the same street address a few years ago. My name was clearly printed on the lobby board. I had been in that same building for over 12 years. Although I filed change of address cards repeatedly, some mail addressed to suite 400 was marked, "Return to sender." One recent return was even noted, "Left no forwarding address." Why? Who knows?

So, don't take a chance. Send out mailings to all of your clients, even if it's just to remind them that you're still alive and perching at the same post. This technique not only keeps your list up-to-date but also churns up some good thoughts for your P.R. processes. Try to make whatever thoughts you express in your mailings of general interest.

Redundant mailings are fine. Your clients won't be conscious of having received the same information even if more than once before. Just add a few new things each time.

Find some excuse to send such a letter even if you haven't moved. Maybe something has changed. Perhaps you want to make sure everyone has your present address. Maybe your phone area code had been changed a while back. They'll need to know about that.

Mailouts are your best means of keeping your client list current. Don't hesitate to send out such letters. Make it a strict routine to do this at specific and regular intervals. Find some excuse for the letter and then include any information that you can think of to juice the letter up a bit.

If indeed you have moved, you might send a letter something like this:

Dear Mr. and Mrs. Abernathy:

I've moved my office from ______ *[old address]* to ______ *[new address]*. My phone number hasn't changed. [Or if it has, give the new number. Don't refer to either the address or phone number in your letterhead. Repeat them both in the body of the letter. You can't overdo this.]

If I'm in court, in the library, or anywhere away from my office, please leave a message with my secretary or my voice mail and I'll get back to you right away. [You have no "secretary" but a good phone answering crew will give that impression.]

[Then you might mention some past matter with an inquiry as to any possible loose ends. Or, you could use this opportunity to announce some general legal point of interest.]

To keep my records current, I would appreciate knowing about any possible changes.

Sincerely,

GERALD M. SINGER

Even if you have no earthshaking information to share, a contact letter should be sent from time to time anyway. It's also expedient, as well as nice, to include a return, self-addressed, stamped envelope. Doing this is important enough to calendar the mailings at planned intervals.

There are benefits to memory limits as well as detriments. Unhappy events may also be forgotten. Maybe the last matter for Ms. Jones wasn't resolved to her satisfaction. She hasn't called for a long time. You concluded that she's lost to you.

Include her in your mailing list. The first few mailings produce no results. Then, along the way, a phone call from her and a new matter. Why is this? You may have misjudged her attitude. Maybe she felt you were unhappy with her. Maybe it was nothing at all, just the usual inertia.

Perhaps she was at the time miffed over your supposed mishandling of her matter. Time can dim such thoughts and she may recall more vividly all the good things you had done.

What can you lose by including all such past clients in your mailings? I can guarantee that a portion of those old clients you are sure are gone forever will slip back to you if you make the needed contact. At a few cents a pop, you can afford it.

§ 6:13 Other referral sources: Joining clubs and organizations

It doesn't take any particular kind of personality to succeed as a solo lawyer. That's been repeated in all three of the preceding versions of *Solo* as well as this one. There are certain ways of developing a client list that do require special characteristics in people.

Some people exude a certain something that draws others to them. A charm of some sort surrounds them for some reason that says convincingly, "You can trust me to handle your life." Sometimes, that "charm" is toxic and results in victims being swindled.

This talent is not only indescribable it's almost indiscernible. It's a little like trying to describe the taste of an oyster. If it were otherwise, I guess it wouldn't work. The very nature of its being so subtle is its genius. If it were more finite, people would be more wary of it.

This doesn't mean that everyone with that certain something is dishonest. I suppose those who do misuse that charm do so because it comes so easy to them. People who get what they want with little more than a smile sometimes find it a bore to do more than that.

At any rate, that "certain something" is a requisite of those who get substantial business from club groups. If this is you, you don't need my suggestion to go for it. You're already out the door and half way there.

Club joining can be profitable if worked correctly.

In each of the previous editions of *Solo*, I cautioned against overdoing the club-joining syndrome. More harm than good is accomplished by pseudo "experts" advising multi-club memberships. If you aren't one of those special charmers, cool your joining urges.

This isn't to say that no business can result from club activities if you lack that charm. There are methods that can be learned to use club memberships as business getters.

Still, you must have the mind and spirit that's needed to support those efforts. You should also have the necessary extra drive. This will become more apparent after you've read more on how to be an artificial "pied piper."

Spend a certain amount of time cultivating groups, clubs and organizations but be wary of overdoing this. You can waste much valuable time, money and energy chasing down dead-end streets as a chronic "joiner."

Prudence and good judgment should be your guide in choosing

which of the many clubs can source business for you. Be especially cynical of glowing promises, or even suggestions by membership hawkers, that your membership can "pay big dividends" in building your clientele.

Resist the idea that your membership fee may be deductible as a business expense. It probably would not be. Social club membership fees normally wouldn't qualify as a business expense much less tax deductible.

You know, of course, that "nonprofit corporations" do not mean tax-exempt corporations. Even if you legitimately list your membership fee and other contributions as charitable tax deductibles, it does you no good if the income generated isn't justified by the tax break.

Don't be swayed by the impressive statistics you'll be given on the number of doctors, industrialists, entertainers and other "juicy prospects" who are club members anxiously waiting to be your clients. You won't be told about the equal, or greater, number of lawyer members who've been swarming all over those "easy pickings." Those "easy pickings" aren't that "easy" anyway.

Joining *can* be profitable, if you know the ropes.

Some lawyers, though, are quite successful in cultivating a significant number of clients from social clubs even without that special "certain something," described. You might be able to do this also. Without that natural something we've discussed, you need to follow a pretty rigid program.

If every member in your club knew you were an attorney, you might get a client or two out of it. But it would hardly be worth your time, trouble and membership costs. Other ingredients must be added.

Chances are you wouldn't think of following the moves outlined below, but you will nod your head as you read along, thinking, "of course." So much of it follows common logic but so little of it comes with built-in automation.

Knowing what you do for a living is hardly enough to start a stampede to your clientele list. Making known some other facts about you can add positive ingredients, if they're good things. Something of your background, academics, achievements in law or politics, or that you do nice things for people, are all good, positive bits of information that could lead to some client siphoning.

How do you get that information to the membership at large? Can you pass out a resume? Can you corner people and announce all of your qualifications from time to time? Yes, you can do these things. Aside from the time, effort and self-serving nature of such a method, will it get you business? Probably not.

Get someone else to blow your horn for you.

Have you ever seen a guest speaker stand up and list all of his or her sterling qualities? No. And you never will. Someone else must do that for the speaker. Notice also how shy and even a bit embarrassed the speaker will appear as all of his or her attributes unfold.

This is the pseudo-humble bit that must precede acceptance of the speaker's expertise. The more flowery and flattering the praise, the more the speaker will appear to blush. It doesn't matter much who broadcasts the flattery as long as it's not the speaker.

How do you place yourself in a position to have your trumpets blare out all that good stuff? You can volunteer to speak at meetings or special events. Of course, you can't do that many times or frequently. It's better to find some method to keep all of those marvelous qualifications fresh before the membership on a relatively constant basis.

What do you know all about other than the law? Are you an accountant? Are you a good organizer? Can you write, produce or direct a show? How are you at administration? Pick something the club can use and offer your services. But, be sure you're an expert at whatever post you accept. If your volunteer work is poor, you will lose, not gain, points.

Get some project going as soon as you start your duties to attract attention your way. Every time your name appears in the club news, on bulletins, in announcements, whatever, see to it a few lines are added about your stellar legal background.

Make sure that important issues are brought up at each club meeting involving your post. Develop opportunities for others to ask for your legal opinion about as many of these issues as possible. Get known as the legal eagle of the club.

Take care that none of these accolades originate with you or through your obvious inspiration. Never overlook effecting the humble and modest attitude each time. You know, "Aw shucks, folks, t'weren't nothin'."

Your written profile for club use should be extravagant.

If your club has a newspaper or bulletin, suggest that it include a member profile in each issue. Wait for some other member profiles to be published, then work yours in. Cite every citation you've received. List all publications of yours or those with which you've had any involvement. Insert every honor given you including military decorations.

Incorporate every license you've ever had, legal certifications and boards, if any. Your judge pro tem and arbitrator experiences, if any, are valuable additions.

Listings of prominence in any field, every award for excellence anywhere, whether in high school, college law school or wherever, should be included. All lectures you've given anywhere on any subject, preferably in law, are catchy additions. Shove in every damned other thing you can think of.

Be sure that every item you include is absolutely true. It won't do at all to have you exposed as a fraud even on the simplest unimportant point. People love to expose frauds. It makes them feel, oh, so big to bring someone crashing down. "How hath the mighty fallen," is a gleeful shout, not a lament.

If you can do all that, and do it right, you can get lots of business from each such membership you hold. But, all of this takes time. You'll feel the pinch practicing law or working other methods of getting work assignments or client referrals while you're laying all this groundwork.

You've got to be ready, willing and able to grab the new clients.

Unlike succeeding in solo practice generally, it takes a special kind of person to make the club thing work. The shyness, modesty, the humble bit, must not actually be you. It must only *appear* to be you, and only when you're on the receiving end of the praise. If you are really quite shy, you just won't do what's necessary to work yourself into that position.

You've got to be bold. What's more, you've got to snap up every opportunity that comes your way to sign up club member clients. That's tougher than it sounds. People tend to get club "patriotism." This leads to giving your "fellow" members the benefit of your legal talent for free.

Once the member approaches you to ask "just one little question." Treat him or her just like the phone caller. Immediately turn the conversation to your little handy pocket calendar and say, "Hey, I'm going to be in the office later today. Can you slip by at say 4:00 P.M.?"

You must do this before any thoughts of extending the discussion further into the member's legal problem. Remember the narcotic of phone discussions. The same thing happens face-to-face.

GET THE PROSPECTIVE CLIENT OUT OF THE CLUB ENVIRONS AND INTO YOUR OFFICE.

Your ability to perform as outlined above, separates you from ordinary lawyers and places you among the RAINMAKERS. You are a client getter. This is the most valuable member of any law firm, yours or anyone's. Remember your salesmanship at all times. None of this does you a bit of good if you don't sell at each stage

If you lack that ability, forget club joining. It won't do you, or your pocketbook, the slightest good. Now that you've read this, can you honestly answer that this is you? You've learned enough in reading this book not to kid yourself. Don't.

§ 6:14 Bar Association lawyer referral services

An important suggestion included in *Solo*-I and *Solo*-II was to join every Bar Lawyer Referral Service you can. That suggestion is as valid now as it ever was. Don't fret about being deluged with "pro bono" clients. Those are not routed to you unless you volunteer to accept them. You are free to discuss fees up front with Bar referred clients just as with any other prospect.

Most Bar referrals won't make your day, but good ones outweigh the bad.

It is true that many, perhaps even most, of these referrals will lead to minimal fees, or sometimes even no fee at all. This isn't because of any "pro bono" or legal aid thing, it's the same as with any prospect. You don't score with every referral.

Most bar referral services require that you charge a minimal initial interview fee. That fee generally goes to the bar association. Then, there is an additional charge in the form of a percentage of the fees ultimately collected by you.

There will be that big one here and there to make up for the piddlers. This method of client trolling is no different from the rest of the methods and groundwork necessary to build your practice. It requires patience and hard work.

Keep in mind that these referrals were steered to you by a bar association. The prospect called that organization because he or she felt that such an organization would recommend only the highest qualified lawyer for his or her needs.

When you greet that client, keep that momentum going. You are everything that the prospect hoped and expected you would be. Use the collective "we" when referring to your services. "We," meaning that bar association, of which you are a part.

The prospect is unsure. That is the reason for having called the bar association instead of resorting to the telephone directory or other source. Reassurance was, and is, needed. You must provide that reassurance right from the start.

When you canvass the various bar associations, ask for written information on their rules and requirements for joining and operation. They differ in many respects but are reasonably consistent in certain areas.

I would dare say that if you affiliated with three or four bar associations for a year, you would look back on some very satisfactory experiences. You won't remember the flakes, no-shows and losers, but you will the outstanding cases and clients you collected.

The bar referral method, like the hourly assignment phase, should be relatively short-lived. Within a time period so short your head will swim, you'll have outgrown those and the other pump priming exercises. You'll soon develop a first-class clientele filling every day with satisfying, lucrative work.

§ 6:15 Family, friends, employees, business acquaintances, etc.

Referrals move in mysterious ways and even may come from unlikely sources. Referrals will come from all kinds of sources. The trick is to recognize and act upon the information that comes your way. Don't fear being "too pushy."

A friend may tell you that he can't keep the golf date with you because his aunt was rushed to the hospital. You might just sympathize with him and then suggest golf for another day. You might, but you won't. Instead you ask why his aunt is in the hospital. Who knows, perhaps there was an accident or some other reason for possible legal assistance. At the very least, your concern will be appreciated. On the other hand, you might have a lead to a new client.

A friend tells you his uncle is having some problems with his insurance policy. Why is the uncle concerned with his insurance policy? If you don't ask, you won't know. Ask! Be concerned. You're there to help, if help is needed. But you can't be of help if you don't know the facts and that help is needed.

Sometimes the reference is not so subtle. Sometimes your help is requested "as a favor." So, what do you do? You do a favor. You give off the top of your head opinions. Two things will usually be true:

That opinion will be given free, and that opinion will usually be wrong. Why? You got off the professional track. Professionals don't blurt out rash opinions. If legal advice is requested, then give it. But give it in a professional manner, meaning in your office and for a fee.

NEVER suggest any possible solution to ANY legal situation without having interviewed the person directly involved. First, you do run the risk of some possible malpractice involvement somewhere down the line. Second, you haven't helped anyone despite your good intentions, and a "free" advice. Third, you have cheated yourself out of a fee and the object of your opinion out of decent legal service.

CAVEAT!! Beware of ethics violations; solicitation.

Everything contained in this book should be considered only in consonance with the laws in your state and your local Bar Rules. The advertising liberality championed in California a few years ago and since followed has been scrutinized. The number of detractors who would limit attorney advertising to the handing out of business cards, and then under certain restrictions, has been steadily growing.

That group has been bolstered by a staunch alliance. Attorneys who have construed the term "freedom of speech" so literally as to engage in outright huckstering are the censoring advocates' best friend. The next logical step for these hotshot lawyers is telemarketing.

How's this for a phone pitch: "Hello Mrs. Jones. How are you today? The reason I'm calling is that we are running a special on divorces this week. How are you and Mr. Jones getting along?"

Far fetched? Yes, but not awfully. Read some of the ads run by attorneys in your local newspapers. Are they that much less offensive than my example? Next case!

You don't need to go that far to step over bounds. You can't initiate the subject of legal representation, but to avoid the trouble spots requires adequate training in legal ethics. Your local Bar MCLE courses should give you the information you need.

The information you give to the member may constitute solicitation. What if that member's aunt was indeed rear-ended in a traffic accident. Can you then say, "Where can I sign her up? I specialize in personal injury cases, especially those involving automobile rear-enders." You can, but your shouldn't. Besides the solicitation infection, it's bad salesmanship.

If you've done your preliminary work adequately, that member will already know you're a lawyer and even probably will know about what areas of the law are yours. Your reputation will work for you. Predictably, your asking about the aunt will be enough to trigger the member's thoughts toward you and your qualifications. Very little more will need to be said.

Now if the member asks whether you do that kind of work, you can say, "As a matter of fact, that happens to be one of my specialties." (Or, however you wish to indicate that, yes, you certainly do that kind of work.) When he or she asks if you'd be willing to see his or her aunt, you can be as eager as you wish. "Yes, of course. I'd be happy to do that. After you've spoken with your aunt about me and she'd like me to represent her, find out from her doctor or the staff when I can come."

This is an easy situation. More often you'd need to dig harder for the kind of information that would give you a legitimate opening.

All of the above within this chapter falls under the "getting information" phase of salesmanship. If your selling antenna is properly tuned in, you will zero in on this signal as from a prospective client. When you do that, you will ask for information, more information, even more information and then, you will ask for even more information.

The measure of success in pursuing these avenues of business is equal to the product of your ability to recognize opportunities and to extract the maximum from each. Remember what was said about "opportunities." They don't all come wrapped in pretty colored paper tied with nice pink ribbon.

Someone had to recognize the goodness of coconuts enough to persevere chopping away at the resistant, stubborn outer shell. Then, a second challenging barrier was in the shell covering the fruit itself. Those of us who like coconut and its products should drink an occasional toast to that indomitable pioneer. Coconut juice, of course.

How many would prevail under such a challenge? Would you? That's just a coconut. No embarrassment, pride or ego involved. How far are you prepared to press against odds in a professional matter?

You've learned to subordinate those tender sensitivities enough to open your office and get sufficient work assignments to pay bills and live a little. Then, you learned to persist far enough to get some case and client referrals to live a little better.

Building your practice further through social interfacing takes a different kind of, and much more, adeptness. Even more important is that working this wrinkle requires something of a different kind of person. I'm not sure that this difference can be seen and learned about as readily as all the other information in this book.

The biggest problem is your own recognition of yourself. We can see others clearly but it gets fuzzy when we focus on ourselves. In some cases, it's like using different languages. The words are heard and believed understood, but they are not.

People are different and that difference isn't always translated by words. Certain characteristics can't be taught nor learned. The best we can do is learn to use what we have to its best advantage.

Some people have a naturally fetching personality. People seem to gravitate around them to seek their advice or simply to engage in conversation. Such people would be more prone towards cultivating the kind of club relationships described above.

Still, even those special attributes would be inadequate without development of the methods and purposes discussed in this section. This is kind of a departure from the principles discussed in the chapter on Salesmanship.

Recall that special personalities, wit, charm, style, appearance, etc., were said to be irrelevant in selling. Selling is vital and a major part in cultivating business from social club membership. But maneuvering yourself into a position from which you can sell requires something else.

If you have a natural magnetism to draw people, you can reach that position easier and faster. But what you do with that position requires the knowledge and abilities derived from the information given here. The crucial attribute is your willingness to employ that degree of "chutzpah" necessary to score.

Your brass must be tempered with ethical restraints. Don't confuse the quality of "chutzpah" you should use in canvassing other lawyers with what you may do with potential clients. I leave that considerable distinction to your tender sensitivities and good judgment.

Chapter 7

Seven Basic Rules for Solo Practice Survival

§ 7:1 Generally

The point of optimal conclusion.

The "Six" Rules contained in all three previous editions of *Solo* have been referred to, quoted and the topic of discussion more times than any other part of the book. I can't say which part of the book is most important but I can state that failure to follow these rules (now seven) will be as effective a way to leave solo practice as any other.

Imposing a rule on a lawyer is like telling a cat to let the mouse go. Ordinarily, a rule is seen as an obstacle. The lawyer will study the rule carefully, play around with it awhile, and then seek to circumvent it. Rules to a lawyer are not meant to be followed, but to be evaded. These rules are different.

These aren't just "more rules." These SEVEN RULES are pals of yours, though you may not see it that way at first. Following or not following these rules could make the difference between a successful or unsuccessful practice.

These seven basic rules are a must for the solo practitioner, but should be honored by every attorney. You'll writhe and wriggle on the hook, but don't fight it. Read the following carefully. Learn how to follow each rule, not how to evade any of them.

RULE No. 7. ORGANIZE YOUR PRACTICE AND YOUR LIFE.

Why is Rule No. 7 listed here at the top where Rule No. 1 should be? Good question. Read on.

The original Six Rules for Survival in Solo Law Practice," reprised in this Fourth Edition, omitted an essential rule that should have been labeled "Rule #1." This vitally important rule is Organize Your Practice. Why No.1? Is it the most important of all seven rules?

In a way, yes. Your practice might, just might, survive if you fail in any one of the other six admonitions. If you fail in this one, neglect sufficient organization, your practice will ultimately fail. Most important, you could face disastrous malpractice lawsuits and very probably Bar problems.

The regrettable omission of the rule from the list of basic rules for solo practice survival may have been due to my business training and experience. Perhaps it was instinctive to assume that work organization is basic in the makeup of all lawyers. My research has since proved this assumption wrong.

A more stinging realization is that the disorganized attorney is not a rarity. In fact, lack of organization is a major contributor to ethical problems for inveterate, as well as new, lawyers.

As a prologue to this rule it should be said that disorganization can sprout from organization. Someone once said, ***"don't file it, throw it away."*** Or, put another way, the cure can be worse than the illness.

Too many cabinets, filing trays, card boxes, "organizer slots" and other devices for sorting things can lead to confusion more than help. This virus comes from just too many stored items.

Before you file a document, ask yourself whether you need it. If you don't, toss it. There's only one thing in a filing system worse than looking for something without it being indexed in a recognized way. It's worse to look for something that you don't have.

So, the prudence in filing selection is your judgment in making that selection. Don't play with a "scared buck" when making the decision to keep or toss. Yet, make that decision intelligently. The author of that saying says be ruthless. Toss it even if there's a doubt.

Many documents are either cumulative or of moot significance. Notices of Motions, Court Orders on strictly procedural matters and other papers that had only temporary uses, should be tossed.

The most cursory examination of case files will reveal some duplicated documents. Why were both filed? Who knows. Anyway, toss it. Your good judgment is the key. Don't be afraid to use it.

To start with, pending work should not be listed under "Things-

To-Do." Each and every job should be calendared with a date and time, the same as a court appearance. Each selected date should permit ample time to complete the task before it's due.

If there is no due date, more the reason to calendar it. You may have a brain buzzer that reminds you of things to be done on "D Day," but less time-sensitive stuff is often placed outside the inventory of "things-to-do." Don't rely on that "brain buzzer." It's overrated. Calendar everything.

Your client wants a will drafted. You write that down. You'll do it as soon as you get around to it. When will that be? Meanwhile, your client, believing the will is important (silly client) goes elsewhere to get it done. You lose that job and the fee. Worse, you'll also lose the client to another attorney who calendared the work.

So, instead of just writing it down somewhere for your later consideration, which may, or may not, occur, calendar it. Don't just mark it for execution sometime next Tuesday. You've got the time. You might just be failing to equate the job with the importance of other assignments.

It's just as important to complete jobs for existing clients as it is to make appointments for new clients. That "new client" may never materialize, but your existing client is a solid fact. Don't let it vaporize. Your calendared matters are the surest generator of income producing activity you have.

It's more than a good thing to generate a work calendar. It can be prophylactic. In the past, such oversight meant lost income and possible lost clients. In these litigious days, it can mean a major malpractice claim.

Can a lawyer be held liable for failure to complete a job even though no specific time for completion was scheduled? Worse, can a lawyer be held to answer for failure to recommend an alternative plan? For instance, should a lawyer be targeted because he or she didn't suggest a living will or an inter vivos trust?

Keep your eyes peeled to current malpractice matters. Don't be surprised to find successful suits by disgruntled clients claiming damages for things undone that were not specifically requested. Do we need to be mind readers? Not exactly. We need to calendar things for "CYA" letters at least, if not to execute proposed work.

It's good for you, really. The worst that can happen is that you'll do a bit more work and earn more money. Write everything down. Leave nothing to memory. Don't just write notes, write directly in your calendar and then copy the notes in the client's file. You'll love the result. You'll get everything done, make more clients happy, and make you happy in the bargain.

Calendaring things can be extended to sharpen your practice in many ways. We don't think of our calendars other than to schedule court and appointment dates or other commitments that are time sensitive. That's a mistake. It may crowd your calendar a bit, but everything to be done, regardless of how tentative, should be included in your calendar. If it clutters your calendar too much, get a bigger calendar. Most computer calendars can handle extensive data.

If, for some reason, you can't find a calendar date to complete the work within a reasonable time, send out a CYA letter so informing your client. Ask for his/her understanding and patience.

Advise him/her that if expedience is important, you have another lawyer to do the job. Explain the problem and estimate the time lapse that you anticipate. If time can be stretched somehow, reset the work for a later date, with his/her agreement, of course.

Organizing your practice involves much more than just calendaring work. But if you do at least this much, you'll be miles ahead. Other important facets of organization are treated in various parts of this book. Read it all.

§ 7:2 Rule #1: Get the caller off the phone and into your office

Famous last words: "I only want to ask you one simple question." Sooner than you think, your phone will start ringing, and you will hear something like, "I want to come in to see you, but let me ask you a question in the meantime." These are what are known as "famous *last words*."

Your caller will ask questions; he'll talk and talk and talk. Then you'll talk, and talk and talk. Wasting time is bad enough, but that's not all. You will never see that caller in your office.

You don't think that such a thing could happen to you? Picture this: You've been working on assignments for other lawyers for several weeks, on *their* client's matters. You love it, but these are not *your* clients.

Suddenly the phone rings and behold! A client (or so you think) is on the phone. The caller was referred by a friend, a lawyer or a bar association. He/she wants you as his/her legal representative.

You are going to be given the awesome, frightening and marvelous opportunity of counseling, protecting and enforcing the rights and interests of another person. In all the world, you have been chosen to do this. You are flattered. You are ecstatic. You are thrilled. You are beside yourself with sheer delight and excitement.

In such a state of mind, will you be objective, calm, and collected? Yes. You will remain cool because you've read these rules, you'll know what to do, and you'll do it.

You will not become engrossed in the client's problem on the telephone. You will resist the urge to create a "good impression" by following the "talk" pattern, and you will instead get the client off the phone and into your office.

You will thrust aside the feelings of excitement, thrill, flattery, or whatever. You will ignore the initial stages of embarrassment welling up. You will take steps **right now** to get the caller off the phone and into your office.

You know that if you do not do this, you'll let your "fish off the line." The conversation will stretch to a point beyond recall, and you will never see the client in your office.

It may seem strange to you that being nice and cooperative on the phone will cause you to lose the prospective client. I know that you believe it to be quite the opposite.

It's logical that a nice, congenial manner and pleasant tone of voice should be the start of a long "client-attorney" relationship. It is logical, but it just ain't so. What did I tell you about "logic" and cleansing your mind of things you are positively sure are true.

Didn't I warn you of these traps? Sure I did. Later in this book, and even after you've been in practice for awhile, you'll wonder at the reason, or lack of reason, that you ever doubted this strange bit of human nature.

There are many, many reasons for this twist of logic. I suppose that psychologists and other experts on the subject of human behavioral patterns can offer some opinions on the subject.

I don't doubt that there are many deep and profound analyses which could satisfy the human behavioral scientists. My experience, and such analysis as I am qualified to make, lead me to the following explanations.

First, there is a great possibility that you gave the client what appears to be all of the information needed, and therefore there is no further need for your services. Whether the client is right or wrong in this conclusion is irrelevant, since you will not be at the client's side to correct his or her thinking.

Second, you may have given the client exactly the opposite impression of your ability from that which you strove to give in your "niceness." In your understandable zeal to answer questions and give information, you may have misunderstood some of the facts, and your advice may have been patently misdirected.

Telephone conversations can play such strange tricks, particularly when you are talking to someone whose manner and mode of speaking are strange to you. So much crucial information is transmitted between people when engaged in a face-to-face discussion that cannot be translated by voice alone.

Third, and possibly the most difficult to understand of the reasons, is the strange phenomenon which occurs to most people, having something to do with quitting while ahead. Your caller may well have decided, after your lengthy and productive talk, that he or she got a wealth of legal information from you for free, and that he or she will be far ahead of the game if yet another lawyer is consulted.

Or your caller may deduce that if an appointment is made, and kept, with you, somehow there will be a charge for the time spent on the phone. Your caller got away with something. A return visit may mean ultimately paying for that something. W.C Fields said that everyone has a bit of larceny in their heart.

Whatever the reason, whether one of those I suggest or some other, you can be sure that in the dominant percentage of phone calls, the result will be as predicted, unless you take steps to change the course of things.

You must stop your caller just as the conversation gets past the *barest* description of the problem. As soon as you have ascertained the general nature of the case, you must divert the conversation, into something like this:

"This seems like a simple matter. Drop by the office and let's kick it around. Why don't you gather all of your letters, documents, and everything having to do with this matter, and bring them along. Tell you what. My office is not too far. I'll see you at 3:00 this afternoon. How's that with you?"

Note "3:00 this afternoon" instead of 3:00 next Thursday afternoon. This is again contrary to the popular belief. It's a misconception that a more favorable impression is made if you string out the time for appointments. That's supposed to create the impression that you have a very busy schedule.

This is not only incorrect, it's often counter-productive. At best, you will have caused some question about your interest in the matter. At worst, you could lose the prospective client. In any event, you'd permit a delay that could result in a drifting client.

During the course of the delay, your disappearing "client" may well stumble into the hands of another lawyer. There are other lawyers out there, you know. Or the prospect may fall by the wayside for some other reason.

If you tighten up the time of waiting to as short a period as possible, your odds that the appointment will be kept will be infinitely better. There's little chance that you could impress the caller with your "heavy schedule" anyway. Most likely, the caller would have told by the referrer that you're a relatively new attorney.

Don't be afraid of sounding too eager. Even if that is how you may seem, nothing will be lost by it. Most likely, though, your routing the client to your office in the shortest possible time will merely demonstrate your efficiency and interest in the client's problem.

On this same subject, it is not a good idea to let the telephone ring extra rings just to impress the caller that you are busy. It is irritating to the caller, and proves nothing except the inefficiency of your office. Answer the phone as quickly as you can get to it.

In my business days, my employees knew if the phone rang three times someone would be "skinned." You'd be surprised at how many fourth rings never occur because impatient callers won't wait. Don't count on prospective clients being patient. Your colleagues down the hall have a corner on the patient client market.

Of the various tidbits which I hope you will gather from this book, you should focus on how elusive clients can be. Know that one little point will help make you a winner. I could not afford employees in my business who took unnecessary chances with my potential customers.

Allowing the phone to ring past twice was taking such a chance. "Allowing" is a bad word. You do not "allow" any ring, or any part of any ring.

My business rules were simple. Whoever was close to a phone grabbed it at the first instant possible. Only a broken leg could excuse even the shortest delay. My law practice rules are precisely the same. There are no excuses for tardiness in phone answering.

These days it seems good phone answering people are hard to get. Call most anywhere. You'll hear long rings and then a "please hold," and an even longer wait on pause.

Oh, there's music. But doesn't that add to the irritation? Sometimes you don't even get the "please hold," just the pause and music. Maybe not even the music.

Being in a large suite, you will be at the mercy of the telephone board people hired by your landlord. You will not be at liberty to discipline them. All you can do is complain.

Of course, being an old hand at employing people, I can empathize with employers these days. Good help is hard to get nowadays. So, I don't complain. I pick up the phone myself when it passes the third ring.

If instead, you do complain, that complaint is relayed to the culpable answerer. Does that cure the situation? Probably not. Resentment may creep in, and you're on an even longer ring and hold.

Don't compound the problem by making your caller wait even longer. Stop whatever you're doing and take the call, post haste.

If your caller insists on asking questions, tell the caller to write them down along with other notes, and to bring them to you at the time of the interview. You'll be better able to analyze the questions and, if necessary, research for more cogent answers.

You might say, "I've got a good idea of what this case is, and I can do some preliminary research on the most recent cases and legislation. By the time you get here, I'll have further thoughts on the law to discuss with you."

Say as little as possible to the caller on the phone. Get the caller into your office. Far from being a turn-off, your tactic will be viewed not as evasiveness but as thoroughness.

You will be much more admired for your professionalism than for any loose knit phone dallying.

Following this rule meticulously will accomplish several things for you. First, it gets the prospective client into your office where you can arrange to get paid. Second, it gets the caller into your office and out of harm's way. Third, it limits your wasted telephone time, which I assure you would otherwise amount to many hours and dollars per month.

If you don't like my reasons, construct a few of your own. **But for whatever reason, get the caller off the phone and into your office, along with the caller's checkbook.**

§ 7:3 Rule #2: Get your retainer early

A strange paradox is the fact that sharp business people rely so much upon the advice of their lawyers as to money matters. Lawyers, generally, are perhaps the least sophisticated people on this subject.

Lawyers, who can draft ironclad contracts, collect past-due accounts from deadbeats, and do all manner of difficult things, cannot find the courage to ask a client for a retainer. A lack of sophistication is not the only reason for this failing.

It is much easier to be firm for someone else than for yourself. You can be a real tough guy for your client, but you are a pussycat when it comes to pulling your own chestnuts out of the fire. There is good reason for this reluctance.

You can be very demanding, even petty, when it comes to

protecting a client's interests. But being a brute for yourself offers no such redemption. This is just another indication of the workings of that monster "embarrassment" that we will be looking at throughout this book.

You'll find a million excuses for not asking for a retainer. You know the client is "good for it." You think it's *declasseé* to ask for money in advance. You're not quite ready for that stage. You don't want to insult the potential client by implying he or she may not pay fees as agreed. How many such excuses can you think of?

Those are logical thoughts, but you know what? They are, each and all, plus all you can dream up, escapes. Escapes from what? **EMBARRASSMENT!** All those other reasons are just baloney. You are too embarrassed to ask for the retainer. Don't protest on this point. Accept it. If you can't ask for the money, right there and then, as you should, you have succumbed to ***embarrassment***.

You've had a million-dollar education. You are fully trained and completely able to identify and classify the problems posed to you. You have the ability to estimate the number of hours to be consumed during the first few stages of the matter at hand. There is no valid reason for your inability to request that your client pay you a reasonable sum for your retainer.

If it is a case of higher trial court jurisdiction, you must add time for certain procedures which are necessarily required over those of the lower justice or municipal courts. You should be able to estimate the time in drafting the pleadings, including the research.

If it is an involved matter, you should include substantial time for discovery. Expect much of it to be accomplished within the first few weeks. In some cases, there will be some motions or other procedures requiring court appearances.

In estimating the time required for these procedures, you should not be unduly conservative. Don't let your fear or hesitation rob you of your right to a retainer. Don't concern yourself with losing the client. The right time to get the retainer is NOW!

A little bravery at the start will prevent much lamentation on your part later on. Remember that you are earning your living from your other assignments so you can afford to be forthright about it. You cannot afford not to be.

Fear of losing the client is, in this situation, an unjustified fear. As with terminating a potentially lengthy phone conversation, asking for a retainer will not result in losing a client.

More accurately, any client you would lose in such a situation is better lost. You don't need clients who resist paying your fee, whether in advance or not. So, your risk of loss is, at worst, a minor one, if any at all.

Does this frighten you even more? It shouldn't. I know the sensitive, albeit misplaced, fears of untutored people can be terribly distressing. I warned you, didn't I, that the most difficult part of following this pattern of solo practice is simply accepting the rules. That difficulty, whether you can admit it now or not, comes from only one obstacle. That is embarrassment!

I could be less dogmatic and support everything that I say more fully. But then this book would be several times as large and would have cost you many times its price. Besides, there are enough words between these covers. So, for the sake of expedience and economy, accept the rules.

You must impress upon your client that the retainer is a minimum fee. If the case ends in settlement, long before the time that you have estimated you retain it all. If the case goes on to trial, then you apply the retainer to the actual time spent at your regular hourly rate.

To a large extent, your client controls the extent of your time and duty obligations. Presumably, your client will benefit from an early case termination and should be happy to pay your fee in the settlement figure.

Basic arithmetic is all that's required to estimate the probable number of hours and to multiply that number by $150, or whatever your hourly rate. Amounts will vary from case to case and time to time, but a retainer of $3,750 to $6,000 (at this writing), paid up front, should not be out of line for the average court matter. This amount is based upon an average case that would entail about 25 to 40 hours of preparation and discovery procedure during the early stages.

Cover the time you expect to spend in the initial phases with an adequate retainer. Otherwise, you are likely to find yourself on the "hook." Your work throughout the first phases could be rewarded with no compensation for your efforts.

An attorney cannot simply refuse to proceed on behalf of a client solely for nonpayment of fees. You may move the court to be relieved as counsel. Usually, that motion will be granted, but it could be denied.

Your only really free option is to not take the case when it is first offered to you. At this point, you can say "no" to the client without apology or guilt. The client has that prerogative at all times, not you.

The monster "embarrassment" rears its ugly head in this

situation, as it often will throughout your practice. You will be involved in the case. That alone can minimize your objectivity.

It becomes even more compelling as you drift into more involvement with your client. The client and the case can be so appealing that you just can't walk away.

Why do you need these complications? Why subject yourself to even the probability of making such a motion. Your client must pay you eventually, why not now? If the client cannot pay you now, don't depend upon being paid ever.

There is also the matter of the client's motivation to pay you. Your client is under the greatest pressure of need at the moment of the first interview. There will probably never be that much pressure again in a given matter.

Once you've taken the case, the pressure is relieved. Your client's problems have now become your problems. Don't let the problem of fees payment become your problem as well.

A wise old jurist once said, "Get the money while the tears are still flowing." The same may be said of adrenaline. When your client first comes to you to report the dastardly thing done to him or her, he/she is often livid with rage. "Sue the bastard to the ends of the earth," the client cries.

The client doesn't care if it costs every dime he or she has in the world. It's "not the money, it's the principle of the thing." The client isn't at all concerned about recovering any money. He/she just wants to teach the no good so and so a lesson.

Of course, you will have a duty to attempt a "cooling off" and get the client to view the facts objectively, but if this doesn't work, and it rarely will, *that's when you ask for the money!*

Explain that these first procedures develop rapidly, and there is no time for intermittent billing. Hence, you'll need to have these services covered by retainer. Also, don't forget the court costs. Filing fees and process are very expensive.

It is advisable to get at least $500 as an advance against court costs to cover these costs plus service of process, copy service, etc. Your attorney-client agreement should also provide that any excess paid against costs will be credited to the general retainer, but that any shortage will be billed and that payment must be made promptly regardless of any unused general retainer.

If your client tries to stall you on payment of the retainer, the client is probably only as good as the party he or she wants to sue. Explain the enormity of responsibility in taking the case and the obligations imposed by the court upon attorneys of record. Insist upon the retainer to help offset the demanding time and responsibility commitments.

There can be some ticklish decisions. What if the client can only come up with part of the retainer? If the client offers only a small fraction, pass. However, if the client is able to pay a more substantial part, say at least 50% or so, make this deal, *in writing*, as part of your attorney/client agreement.

Agree to write demand letters, etc., but withhold filing of the complaint until the client pays the balance. If the client is a defendant, insist on the entire amount on the table.

In any case, have a full and complete understanding with your client. If you are going to start on the case with part payment, make sure that your client fully understands that you will not go beyond a certain point until you have been paid the full retainer. Make it clear to your client that you will go only so far as to draft and send a demand letter. You will also do some preliminary research, but you will not actually file the complaint.

We are all lawyers. It should not be necessary to even mention this point. Yet I emphasize it. Why? The answer is simple. Remember what I said about being better able to do for others what you find exceedingly difficult to do for yourself?

For some unfathomable reason, and I have erred in this myself. Lawyers very often neglect this important part of self-preservation. I say that I have never sued a client for fees, and that is the truth. Why, then, is a contract important? Simply because if it's there, it's there.

The client who might trouble you about fees often will base the dispute on a difference of memory. The presence of a written agreement will dispel this dispute. The flaky client will ignore the contract, but, with some discretion, you can minimize the flakes in your practice.

Make certain, also, that you have your client sign an "Attorney-Client" contract before the client leaves your office on the first interview. Include in the agreement all such matters as the payment schedule for your retainer. See the sample retainer agreement in Chapter 11.

If there is a deferred payment plan, include in your agreement that you are not obligated to continue beyond the agreed stage if the client fails to pay as agreed. Include also that you will be held free and harmless from any prejudices that the client may suffer as a result of your withdrawal. Such a clause may not hold up in many jurisdictions, but it could possibly eliminate, or minimize, disputes.

Even in jurisdictions where such escape provisions are supportable, they are frowned upon. As a general proposition, a lawyer is expected to go forward with full representation of any client, irrespective of the lawyer's fees. This is why, no matter where you practice law, it is always important to get the full retainer up front.

Your contract should also set forth the continuing basis for fees, after the retainer is consumed by your services. For example, if you are billing at the rate of $100 per hour, the contract should state that, upon exhaustion of the time covered by the amount of the retainer, all additional time will be billed at that rate.

Be all the more cautious about taking partial payments where your client is a defendant in a lawsuit. As a plaintiff, you can at least control when, or if, the complaint will be filed and the matter started. In addition, as plaintiff, you will have some control, theoretically at least, over the progress of the case. Defendants are usually content to have cases delayed or especially dismissed.

Although not really to be counted upon, defendants will usually allow the plaintiff to set the pace for a lawsuit. As a defendant, you are often at the mercy of the plaintiff's election of procedures and the ensuing time frames. Of course, there are sometimes special circumstances that displace dollars and cents.

But in the usual case, I can think of no logical reason for assuming the defense of any substantial matter without being paid a reasonable retainer fee *up-front*. If you fail to do this, and the case gets out of hand (and usually the unpaid ones do), you'll rue not having heeded this advice. Get the money, and rue not.

Be a bit wary of checks. Make sure that you verify accounts and balances before relying upon a check for a retainer on a litigated matter. If there is the slightest question of the check's rubber content, and no time to get the bank's O.K., put the burden on your client to get the cash, or a certified or cashier's check.

Rule #2 is a hard one, I'll admit. It's going to take some firm intestinal fortitude to stand by what I've laid down as your retainer rules. But, you'll need to develop such hardness fast in order to make your way as a solo practitioner during the first few months.

Remember the monster *embarrassment*. Who is the embarrassed one if you are fearful of getting your retainer, and in cash, if needed? You, that's who. Who *should* the embarrassed one be? Your client, not you.

Later, when you have become a roaring success, you can afford to be as much of a jellyfish as you wish. If you're afraid of the criticism that you are too mercenary and that lawyers should be more concerned with their clients' welfare, ask if your critic would be willing to indemnify your living and practice expenses. You'll hear silence.

You owe your first charity to your family, present or future, and if there's any excess, to your grandchildren, present or future. If there's any excess, save some for yourself.

§ 7:4 Rule #3: Say "NO" to contingency fees cases . . . Except

You will see some examples of the very few types of cases when it's O.K., and sometimes even preferable, to take contingency fee arrangements. Except for such cases, you should be avoid any kind of litigation without a full retainer.

I've made it a hard and fast rule to say absolutely "no" to any case in which I am restricted to a contingency fee *and* the answers to the following three questions cannot be answered emphatically in the affirmative:

(a) **Is the defendant's liability unequivocally established?**

(b) **Are damages conventional and substantial?**

(c) **Is the defendant collectible?**

There may be some modification of these questions. For instance in automobile personal injury cases, damages needn't be so substantial. The usual time spent on auto PI cases is relatively minimal and stereotyped.

Further, the "defendant" will be, in most instances, an insurance company. Collectability would then not be a problem. But, in other cases, the rules should be followed, and the questions asked with unrelenting regularity.

You'll be tempted to deviate from this pattern, but if you do, you'll be sorry. You'll find there is one thing worse than not being paid for your services. That is not being able to pay your bills because you're not being paid.

You'll be offered a "pat" million dollar lawsuit. Your eager client will assure you that the facts are all on his or her side. You'll be told there is no room for doubt. This will be the "case of the century."

You will be so impressed with the prospective client's glowing report of the case and the millions which you'll win that you'll hesitate to ask this question: Why is this client willing to give a third, forty percent or even fifty percent of the proceeds away for fees?

So who is the salesman and who is being sold? Guess who? Your client is spinning the wheel and you, you dope, are placing the bet. Who loses if the case is lost? Not your client, you!

There is another test you can make. Ask your client for a mere

$1,500 as a partial fee, to be deducted from the millions you are going to win. Will the prospective client do it? Don't be silly.

Even better, ask the prospective client to advance only the costs. Watch him or her bluster all about what lack of vision you have. Why can't you see all the glory, fame, and fortune that this case will certainly bring you. What an ingrate you are, and shame on you for your lack of vision.

It is quite natural, under the circumstances, that you will be expected to put out all of the risk capital, do all the work, and stall your bill collectors, while your client assumes the great burden of being your cheering section. You are not only the lawyer, you are also the client's banker.

You'll even see ads in the legal papers for lawyers to handle such great opportunity cases. Any lawyer will do. Any lawyer, that is, who left his or her brains in the bar examiner's room.

I don't know if I can save you from the pitfalls of taking imprudent contingency cases by merely warning you. For some strange reason, it is a disease with new lawyers to fall for such traps. I suppose it's part of the "get rich quick" syndrome.

Tell your would-be million dollar case benefactor that you have no wish to deprive him or her of so large a percentage of the "certain" million dollar judgment. Tell the benefactor that you will be very happy to take the case upon payment of your modest retainer and fees.

You might suggest this proposition: after payment of your retainer, and your exposure to the first blush of the case, you may assess the case as a good contingency fee type case, though perhaps not as optimistically as the prospective client has represented it.

In such an event, you will forego the balance of your fee, keeping the retainer of course, and go forward on a contingency basis. Upon your success, you will deduct the retainer from your share of the "spoils."

If this is not acceptable, or practicable, tell your client that you cannot afford to take such cases on retainer because your apartment landlord, your grocer, your butcher, and all others who depend upon your income for their income, will not agree to contingency arrangements.

Tell your client that you are a simple person with simple needs that a regular fee will satisfy. Say that you are not interested in becoming a millionaire, but that you only want to live like one. Resist the temptation to get rich overnight.

Remember, above all, that the cardinal rule in any contingency fee case is the certainty of collectability. Don't follow a rainbow without a gold pot at its end.

Most lawyers with any length of practice have drawers filled with judgments that are uncollectable and on which they had contingency interests. It's one thing to take the risk of winning a case. It is quite another thing to risk not being able to collect your judgment amount after you've endured the rigors and trauma of trial, and won.

§ 7:5 Rule #4: Bill your friends

This is perhaps the toughest rule of all. If you think that Rule #3 will be tough to follow, then, as Al Jolson said, "You ain't heard nothin' yet." Rule #4 is a killer. But, if you fail to follow it, you can be in worse trouble than if you goof up on the other rules.

If you fail to set a hard line on billing your friends right from the start, you'll be carrying them gratis to the end of your practicing days, or their lives, whichever comes first.

One thing may save you. If you are naturally as nasty as some lawyers that I know, you won't have any problem at all. You won't have that many friends to worry about.

Being a new attorney, right out of the box, you possibly have not yet had that many bumps and grinds of life to make you miserable. What's worse, you may even be prompted to start making new friends to show off your new lawyerness.

Even one friend, with a penchant for problems, can be far too many to subsidize. Just follow this rule, and bill your friends regardless of how many, how few, or what the problems.

A friendly way to handle the billing of friends is to start out with light billings. You can then graduate from step to step with fee increases. This way, they will appreciate the special courtesy at the beginning and will consider the same as fully compatible with friendship.

Good friends will realize that your time is all that you have to sell. It is all that exists between you and the bankruptcy courts. You only have so much time in a day, and only so many days in a week in which to earn what you need to live on.

A friend in the retail business may give you one of the items at wholesale. But giving you this item does not deprive the friend of selling another such item to another customer.

The time that you give to your friend cannot be used for your other clients. It is forever gone. Those of your "friends" who cannot see things this way are better disposed of anyway. With "friends" like these, you don't need any enemies.

With relatives you have a different problem. If you have many, you may need to dump them all into the "friend" category. If there are just a few, and they are not trouble oriented, apply *noblesse oblige* and be a good Samaritan.

The "freebie fee" idea is that, like cancer, it has a tendency to spread. You will remember from the rationale in Rule #2 that there is a strange reluctance in lawyers to ask for the money anyway.

It is so much more comfortable to find a reason not to charge for your services. "Oh, you know good ol' Bill. He's done so much for me. How can I charge him?" "Good ol' Bill" has probably not done that much for you, and, even if he has, when does your obligation to repay him cease? Once you start not charging "good ol' Bill," you might as well forget ever doing anything different.

If you resolve to charge everyone, it will be slightly painful at first, but pretty soon the pain will go away, and you'll be paying your bills. If you don't immediately start charging and avoiding "freebie" service to your ol' buddies, the pain will go on and on forever. Better a quick pain.

There are other explanations for reluctance to charge. You feel a natural and understandable pride in the awareness of the power of your opinion. You are very gratified when people who are meaningful to you seek your advice and dote on it.

It is important to one's self esteem that one's ideas and opinions are valued by others. Older people for whom you have always had the greatest respect will now be coming to you for advice.

But for training in the law, there are many who might never know the satisfying feeling that comes with having so many diversified types of people hang on every word as though it were the Scriptures. Strangely, this feeling does not dim with time.

Few are so blasé that such responses are not extremely important to their egos. These gratifications are important to be sure. In most instances, the praise received will be very flattering. But, to coin a phrase, *their* flattery will get you nowhere.

The purpose of this book is not to develop means of inflating your ego, but to build your bank account. Of course, if your ego builds along with your bank account, that's O.K. with me.

Thank each of your friends and all of the kind people for their nice compliments and send them, each and every one, a bill for your services. Remember a basic fact of life. People value services received according to cost. For that reason, as well as any other, people have to be constantly reminded that "the best things in life are [not always] free."

§ 7:6 Rule #5: Send bills promptly and regularly

It is not only hazardous and costly to delay sending bills to your clients, but it is grossly unfair to them. If you wait, you run the danger of never getting paid at all, or only getting a portion of what you have earned.

When long periods go by between billings, certain of your clients might conclude, justifiably in some cases, that some of your services were not billable. Once such an idea has formed, it becomes, in the minds of some people, an absolute justification to ignore all subsequent billings for those services.

The danger then is of that idea becoming solidified. Later, when you start to dun them, they assume the attitude of a victim. They will even "remember" when you said that you would not charge for the service. You will dispute this, but you will succeed only in taking part in a verbal sparring match.

In the end you will be faced with two alternatives: either forget ever collecting the fee, or sue for it. To put much faith in the latter alternative is to fail to understand a basic legal truism.

Judges do not like lawyers who sue their clients for unpaid fees. Besides, there is nothing so unproductive as having to do the same kind of job twice for only possibly being paid once.

It is also a simple matter of courtesy to let your client know the status of the client account with you at regular intervals. It just isn't fair to let charges run up and then to spring a large accrued balance upon any client.

No matter how nominal your charges, or even how favorable the results which you have obtained through your services, it will be difficult for your client to understand or evaluate the reasonableness of a large and protracted balance which covers a long period of multiple services. Bill all clients regularly, in small doses. The clients will appreciate it, and you'll benefit from the habit.

The use of your computer, with a program like Tussman, Gryphon99, ProLaw, ST Software Tech., Inc., TimeSlips, TreeBased, or whatever other billing program you select, can make time and charges tracking so simple that the chore part of billing will be completely removed. All that it takes with any of these programs is a few clicks or key touches.

Your printer begins chirping, and the statement flips out. You'll have window envelopes, and the statements are pre-addressed. All you need to do is fold, stamp, lick and mail.

More than simple, this little twist is even enjoyable to do. I don't know how long it will take before the fun part ends. I've been computing for many years, and I still get the same kick that I did at the start. Read more about this in the relevant chapters.

§ 7:7 Rule #6: Settle the case

Settlement target: Find the "point of optimal conclusion."

You alone can't settle cases. You can't settle a damned thing without the other guy, whomever he or she is. What does it take to get the case settled? Salesmanship. Negotiation is just another word for a selling interview. (Please see Chapter 13 for a full treatment on selling the settlement.)

Almost on the heels of opening your law office, you'll be faced with crossroads towards litigation or alternatively, other means of resolving disputes. My experiences have taught me, as it will you, that a case settled is usually a case won. That is, settled through salesmanship.

The most obstinate lawyer would, if pressed, admit that a reasonable settlement is always preferable to the courtroom. Yet, many more cases than necessary follow the long, wasteful, expensive, and often unsatisfying pathway toward trial.

It's hard to say which of the Rules for Solo Practice Survival is most important; getting the case settled, getting paid and getting on with your practice are top contenders. Words that can be said to expedite case settlement shouldn't be withheld. Everyone knows that. Why then do so many cases get tried?

The magic words to settlement.

Inertia is perhaps the biggest cause of cases going to trial. Two lawyers simply lay back and allow a case to lumber slowly on to trial. I have found that perhaps the most tenacious factor in this inexorable migration toward the courthouse is ignorance of how to stop it.

The magic words to open the doorway toward settlement are complicated and require much learning. Study them hard. It may take you several hours to learn them well enough to negotiate a case settlement. Remember, these are magic words and must be said in the exact phrasing stated.

They are:

> ***"What do I have to do to get you to talk settlement with me?"***

Those words, for some unknown reason, are often the most difficult for an attorney to utter. More often than not, settlement talk is restrained far too distant upon that silly road to the courthouse. Why is this so?

There are several possibilities. Both lawyers may be too thick-headed to see the right choice. One may be stubborn and the other too confused to know how to open the subject. Both might like to settle but each may feel that to open the subject would indicate case frailty.

Another possibility I hate to accept is ***greed***. One lawyer simply may want to keep the case alive to earn more fees. It's so easy to justify going on with case. All the hours of preparation, discovery, pretrial and then trial are lucrative. Settlement ends all of those luscious fees.

One can talk oneself into trial without thinking too much about it. No explanation is needed for the client. The case just goes on as it's supposed to do. Right?

If it is greed, the solution is difficult but not hopeless. The answer lies in human nature. Greed is not necessarily a vice. It's natural for people to want what's best for them.

You can often find the solution here as elsewhere in salesmanship. Try to remain objective and keep argument out of the discussions. We'll look at the "defective merchandise" idea in Chapter 13.

Briefly, the idea is to expose some vulnerability in your case. Don't clutch your head. You're not surrendering the family jewels. Read the part about the scratched cabinet. You'll understand how this approach can work wonders.

Attorneys want fees. Judges want a scanty docket. You cannot force a lawyer to forgo fees to expedite settlement. If all else fails, you might be able to find an ally in the court. Request a voluntary settlement conference. You can count on the judge to help get the case off the court docket.

Once the recalcitrant lawyer is on the spot, you can use the monster *embarrassment*. Most judges lean heavily toward settlement. With a little push from you, the judge just might take it from there.

There are some valuable computer software programs expressly designed for difficult situations in getting negotiations underway. One such program is called "Negotiator Pro." The cost of $189 plus $49 for appropriate modules to fit your particular case (sometimes multiples are needed) isn't cheap. The program develops the values and probabilities as applied to each issue as sort of branches on a decision tree. Call (800) 448-3308 for more information.

The advantage in using the computerized method is its avoidance of personalities and personal opinions. Opinions expressed by attorneys regarding relative case strengths are about as gripping as weather reports.

But a one-on-one discussion isn't useless. You might not think so, but sometimes a single participant can get a settlement talk going despite no help from the others.

Whether a computer program or direct method is used, present the appearance of nonpartisanship. The trick is to use the objective means of keeping adversarial tones out of the conference.

"Trick" is the right word. And it's a neat trick if you can do it. One of the toughest chores for any lawyer is to remain objective and avoid slipping into argument. This becomes especially demanding when certain points in the series of values and probabilities appear to favor his or her side.

For this reason, as well as many others, independent mediation or negotiation may be preferable. You must concentrate hard on the business of staying objective and impersonal.

Once you open the polemic can of worms, it's hard, sometimes even impossible, to close it. Don't let this happen. All cases, no matter how complex or aggressively disputed, have a point of reasonable determination. Sometimes the flies in the ointment are the parties, either or both

If a judge or jury can render a decision, why can't the parties and their counsel do the same? Mediation and negotiation are means of reaching that point of reasonable determination through careful exploration of values and probabilities.

The point of optimal conclusion.

Only in a very few cases is one party absolutely right and the other wrong. Though to hear lawyers tell it, both parties are absolutely right.

In most cases, both parties have some weight. One side has more weight than the other, though the difference may be small. Finding that point of weight disparity is difficult for third parties whether judges or juries. For parties, that task is usually overwhelming.

The clinker in case settlement is facing the reduction of expectations. The plaintiff expects it all. The defendant expects to give nothing.

Judges and juries have nothing but their good conscience to lose either way. Parties are the winners and losers. How can the translation of "nothing to lose" be imparted to the parties?

A mediator can find this point of optimal conclusion if he/she can overcome just one potential obstacle, prejudice. This assumes that the mediator has sufficient intellect and has listened carefully to the opposing positions.

Prejudice doesn't necessarily relate to the parties' identities, natures, race, or whatever. It may be in the attitude of the mediator. Is he/she pro- or anti-business, or whatever the nature of the dispute?

The case may involve breach of contract. The mediator may be predisposed toward upholding a contract despite whatever claimed failure may be claimed by the defendant.

That aside, the mediator is in a position of making an impartial value judgment of the issues to find that point of optimal conclusion. In general, that conclusion will not be enthusiastically greeted by either party.

The lawyer who truly represents his/her client will strive to find that point though it may appear to disserve the client. Wiping his/her mind of the negative side of client loyalty, the lawyer may be able to see that point as well as a mediator.

The problem then is to sell the conclusion to the client. Once that position is attained, the rest is salesmanship.

Litigation has never been cheap. More and more it has become too expensive even to contemplate. Judges do not like trials. That much has become crystal clear over the years.

Judges are now routinely sending motions out to referees, at the expense of parties. Referees, arbitrators, mediators, conciliators, and other court adjunct services have become commonplace, and all at the parties' expense. You won't like it, your opponent won't like it and the clients won't like it.

Where costs used to be a minimal part of litigation expenses, they are fast becoming a major portion. And with these added costs, the quality and reliability of results have degraded. The old reliance on legal support, which used to buoy the skilled courtroom lawyer, has crumbled under the "off-the-wall" rulings of these temporary "judges."

Fast track procedures are playing havoc with adequate preparation. Lawyers are sometimes subject to sanctions for failures that may be unavoidable.

Most of all, trials are no longer fun. In many states, the quality of recently appointed (or elected) judges has greatly deteriorated. Relations between attorneys in aggressively contested matters have become more and more hostile. Judges these days think little of belittling lawyers in open court in the presence of their clients.

Cases are being tried throughout the country at an expanding rate. The increase of judge seats has not been viewed as necessary despite the inadequate number of judges to hear pending cases.

People are looking more and more to their attorneys to get the problem solved with the least time waste and expense. Judges consider it an imposition for you to set foot in their courtroom.

The recent televising of trials, most prominently the O.J. Simpson case, has done much to sour the public on the whole litigation process. You do no one a favor by dragging him or her into the court morass.

Recall in the texts of each of the three previous editions of *Solo* the urging to "give when it costs little or nothing to give." That philosophy is as applicable to settlement as in responding to a stipulation request by your opponent.

Often times, an issue may conceal a sub-issue of little value to one side but important to the other side. For example, a business buyer breached a contract to buy a quantity of model M units. Seller sued and the parties' anger prevented their ability to further communicate.

Through mediation and negotiation, a simple fact was disclosed. Buyer didn't want model M units but did want the older model L's. Buyer's anger impeded his ability to disclose that preference to Seller. Buyer instead stuck to his original version to justify the breach.

Once that issue was revealed, Seller, happy to dispose of the older models, revised the contract. Both parties were totally satisfied. Seller sold products at a greater profit and Buyer got the preferred model L's.

This demonstrates a strange thing. It's possible in meaningful negotiations that both parties can emerge with actually more than they could have won in the most favorable litigation. Seller "gave" on an issue that cost nothing yet gained for Seller. Buyer also "gave" a point that served Buyer far better than simply getting out of the contract.

A key point to remember in negotiation, mediation or basic settlement discussion: hearken back to the Salesmanship rules. Most important, get information.

Getting information is the biggest part of selling. Once you know enough of the background facts, you can start delving in and around the issues for settlement.

The information you've gleaned will enable you to ask questions the answers to which you already know. You can therefore ask questions to induce "yes" answers. Remember that your goal is to produce a "win-win" condition.

The hypothetical L and M shipment is not really unique. Many surface differences have such situations concealed somewhere in the woodwork of the case. Your job in negotiating is to dig that information out.

As in selling, stay away from contentious statements and argument. You cannot settle a case by proving the other fellow wrong. Try any tactic that may give the illusion of both sides being right. Sound tough? Well, it is and it isn't.

If you can get emotions out of the way, it isn't. If you can't, it is. Negotiation does not always win better prizes for both sides. But with all considerations factored into the case, the result will usually be better than trial.

Lawyers don't talk to each other; they argue.

Before thinking about mediation, negotiation or any other methodology of settlement, consider your thought processes on the subject. Remember selling basics. The most important phase of the sales interview is the "Listening" phase. This doesn't just mean hearing the other person. It means listening. Quite another thing.

Lawyers don't talk to each other. They argue, or make speeches, but they don't converse. It isn't so much that lawyers don't talk. Actually, they do pretty well as talkers. It's that they just can't seem to listen.

They may give the appearance of listening but they're only waiting for a pause in the conversation so they can resume their verbal assault. Lawyers fear most being convinced of something. Lawyers believe that if they talk long and loud enough, they, not the other fellow, will do the convincing.

Much of a lawyer's entire career is spent attempting to convince the other lawyer that his or her case is hopeless. The lawyer who will admit a case weakness has yet to leave the womb.

Most any judge can decide which side carries the superior evidence weight in a minute. That decision is customarily withheld for days, weeks, even months. Why?

Well, that's part of the judicial fiction. But lawyers will carry on endlessly, arguing and bulldozing as though their tenuous side were impregnable.

Think about this: To settle a case through negotiation, the object is to obtain a result favorable to your client. Can you argue another attorney into accepting such a reason to settle? What is the alternative?

You must somehow find a line of logic upon which your adversary may conclude that this settlement basis should have an appeal to his/her client. You must simply persuade the other person that the settlement will be as much to his/her favor as yours.

Hearing is easy; LISTENING is hard to do.

As we've learned early on in school, acquiring knowledge can be done through two senses, sight and hearing. We read material, contemplate it and assimilate it through our mental processes. Hopefully, that material will be to some extent filed in our mental inventory of facts.

That is hard work. Reading fiction is easy. But reading text material for learning is hard work. We recall how stressful studying for an exam or the bar was. Getting that diverse and complex matter from the printed page to our brains and storing it for such demanding use was exhausting.

Listening, whether to a professor's lectures or discussing settlement with an adversary, should be just as painstaking if we really are examining what's said for specific application. If we listen as glibly as we often talk, no such usefulness can occur.

If we do not listen intently, we do not persuade anyone of anything for any purpose. If we do listen with the analysis of study, we are preparing for meaningful negotiations and a possible settlement.

What is that process? Salesmanship. What does salesmanship consist of? Again. The main, and most time consuming, phase of the sales interview is ***listening***. Listen to the other person, carefully. Then construct your approach in accordance with as much of the "yes-yes" or "win-win" techniques as your scrupulous listening and research may have revealed to you. Then, SETTLE THE CASE. PERIOD.

As a lawyer, your duty will often lie in diverse paths. One such duty is to negotiate with the adversary for the best possible settlement. Another such duty is to assess the case properly so that you will understand how to recognize an acceptable settlement figure.

Yet another such duty is to acquaint your client with some economic realities. You must condition your client to consider that a figure in the light of the probabilities and hazards of a lawsuit is preferable to an uncertain verdict.

The course that leads to concluding a case through settlement is often a serpentine one. You will understand later what I mean by this.

But you should start as early as possible to think settlement for your client's benefit as well as yours. Discuss this with your client early on. You are practicing law at a high level when you can orchestrate a good settlement rather than subject the client to the rigors of trial and its uncertain end.

So, whether you handle it beautifully or just bumble your way through it, you must convince your client at the appropriate time to settle the case. Whether or not you earn the client's gratitude, you will have done the best thing, and you will make another bank deposit.

Alternative dispute resolution (ADR): The newest and best method for case settlement.

Alternative dispute resolution (ADR) has become an increasingly important tool in settling disputes. A valuable aid in understanding the many approaches to ADR is a handbook on the subject written by Bette J. Roth, entitled, The Alternative Dispute Resolution Practice Guide (West Group). This is a loose-leaf book, regularly supplemented. It lists eight ADR options, contractual arbitration, judicial arbitration, mediation, dispute review boards, med-arb, mini-trials, partnering and private judging. Arbitration, both commercial and judicial, is treated in the main Solo Practice text. Mini-trials and private judging are, like arbitration, merely a different form of litigation, albeit more efficient.

ADR formats run the cost gamut from too expensive for solos and small firms to cost productive and economical. I would urge you to concentrate more on Mediation from the view point of the negotiative stance. This process, as a precursor to the settlement process, offers the most direct and productive means of resolving the dispute.

Of course, any procedure requiring the lawyers or parties to get together presupposes that somehow they want to engage in some form of settlement. Actually, the methodologies contained in both The Alternative Dispute Resolution Practice Guide and the software program, "Negotiator Pro-4.5 for Windows" (discussed above) demonstrate ways in which recalcitrant parties, or attorneys, can be inspired to join in the process. This takes considerable patience on the part of the one who is forwarding the Mediation idea.

§ 7:8 Rule #7: ORGANIZE!! Organize your practice, your life AND yourself

The essences of this SEVENTH RULE are at the head of the list, as they should be. Please re-read them before you continue on.

Conclusion: The legally trained mind seems to operate best under sets of rules. There are as many rules on how to run a law practice as there are rules of law. If you get nothing else from this book, remember the above seven rules and you will get by in your law practice. I shall expect much more from you than merely this, however. So read on carefully and concentrate.

Chapter 8

How To Administer Your Office and Practice

§ 8:1 Generally

Starting out with work assignments from other lawyers can be a two-edged sword. Without your dedication to starting your *own* practice instead of just doing work projects for other lawyers, not "someday" but right now, you can get on the wrong track. Poor office and practice habits are easy to start and difficult to correct.

A wrong attitude can be generated by an "employee" fixation. The more routine duties done by each of your assignor offices the less effective initiating your own practice will be.

The longer and deeper that attitude abides, the more solidified will be your acceptance of an "employee" syndrome. You are NOT an employee, a "contract attorney," a "work for hire lawyer" or anything of that sort. You are an independent law practitioner.

Do the routine work yourself at a nominal charge to each assignor. This way you're starting good productive habits that will develop for you as your own practice progresses. It may take a bit more self-starting push but it will pay dividends in the not to distant future.

Keep duplicate files and records of every single chore you do under the heading of the assigning firm but subheaded under the name of each client served. This is a nothing job for your computer and printer.

This not only gives you a complete record of what you've done and for whom it was done but it starts you on the road to a healthy practice management and an attitude of *independence*.

Ethics failures related.

Good management is essential for a successful law practice but even more important for your physical and emotional health. Research and experience has taught me that most ethical problems follow deterioration of, or ineffectiveness in, office and practice routines.

Management failures start with decisional equivocation. This is followed by frustration and then resignation. Where and how to file this or that are questions that plague the solo lawyer. The answer is pile it in a stack for later decision.

The "later" decision is either wrong or never made. Frustrations begin when you are looking for a document in a file that was never filed. Resignation sets in when you either wipe the concern from your mind or start calculating the method for doing without that paper.

The most common reason for these dilemmas is the lack of simplified methods for document control and management. More than simplified, the methods should be automated. Prior to computers, automation was accomplished by a sort of mental autopilot. One became so grooved in the routine that the action was done almost without thought.

That method is dangerous for all but the most regimented type of person. Some people lack the ability to relegate matters to repetitive routine. Others rebel at regimentation. Both apply to me. I hate imperative routine. I did it, but hated it.

Most ethics failures due to mismanagement.

Decisional equivocation is often directly or indirectly the cause of some form of ethics failure. Most ethics violations are unintentional but that doesn't relieve the onus. Knowing the rules of professional conduct is imperative but good management discipline will avoid most ethics problems.

Filing involves constant decisions. Should it be filed under this or that heading? So much of the time and headaches in filing relates to that one equivocation.

A grocer needed a new manager. One of his clerks seemed a likely prospect. He was young, bright and energetic. He offered the job to him at a substantial salary increase. He told him his first job was to go downstairs and price the potatoes according to size and quality.

After two hours, he hadn't come upstairs. The owner went downstairs to see his new manager in tears. "Please sir," he said, "give me back my old job. I'll take the lower salary. I'll do anything but save me from these decisions."

Computer programs are made to solve these quandaries. The filing is done automatically but, more important, the retrieval is automatic. If for no other reason than to "save you from these decisions," computers were born.

Computers automate file control and "detoxify."

Computerization hasn't made me love filing, but the chores have been somewhat detoxified by the computer's automating qualities. For one thing, filing errors have been substantially reduced through electronic copies. All documents are computer drafted and kept intact on floppy disks, filed under each client's name and case.

Each floppy is labeled with an abbreviated title of each document recorded. In that way, if any document is misplaced, a copy can be quickly duplicated.

§ 8:2 Computer management of your office and practice

By now, most lawyers are familiar with computers at least in theory if not in practical use. Some lawyers contemplating solo practice may not have had actual hands on experience with keyboards.

Your computer will permit you to accomplish your routines, such as accounting, client time and charges, billing, checkbook management, reconciliation and balancing, check printing and full client file document retrieval, drafting of pleadings, contracts, correspondence, full-scale research, litigation support and almost everything else comprising your office and practice chores.

You'll be able to conduct almost all of your legal research "on-line" through services like Westlaw and Lexis. Your CD-ROM reader will permit legal research closely equivalent to these massive libraries without the enormous expense of the on-line charges.

You can easily develop the ability to do word processing such as WordPerfect, Word, and other prominent programs. This will permit you to do absolutely all of your drafting of pleadings, briefs, memoranda, correspondence, wills, corporation documents, contracts, and other written material of any and all kinds.

While some of you may whine, "But gee, I don't type," you will forget that nonsense because you do know how to type. You may not be a whiz at the keys, but even a hunt-and-peck talent will serve your needs.

Your old typewriters will be useless, even for such mundane work as addressing envelopes. Even those chores will be done on your computer and printer.

Computers: Are they controlling your office and practice or are YOU?

Computers will indeed control your practice as they should, but not to the exclusion of your supervision. You're still the boss. Your computer is your employee and the only employee you should have for quite some time. Human employees have been known to take over the employer's businesses often with disastrous results. It can be the same with mechanical "employees."

The movie "2001" demonstrates the point to ridiculum. In that film, "Hal," the highly sophisticated computer, moved to confiscate control of the project spacecraft. Fiction? Yes, but only as of 2000. Wait for 2001.

It's important to bear in mind that computers, marvels they are, have limitations. Work within those limitations and your private "Hal" will perform wonders for you. That's "Hal," spelled H-a-l.

Microsoft's Office 2000, what does it do, and why?

Microsoft Word in Office 2000, is released in standard, small business, professional and premium versions. All versions include Microsoft Excel and the PowerPoint® presentation graphics program.

A hard copy manual doesn't come with the CD-ROM set. You must resort to the screen written, and sometimes spoken, word for your instructions. I am an enthusiastic fan of CD-ROM, and an arch enemy of hard copy manuals.

A hands-down supporter of the "on-line" method of instruction, I hate conventionally printed indexes. Somehow the particular reference sought seems to be never indexed although present in the text.

A mere clicking of your mouse on the on-line documentation icon produces virtually the entire manual documentation with the added convenience of a simplified search facility. But, for those who would prefer scanning through actual printed pages, the omission of the printed manual could provide some frustration. You can, if you wish, print out any part, or all, of the manual. That would take lots of pages but it's there if you want it.

The accompanying programs of both Office 97 and 2000 are also very good and useful for us solos. Excel is the best of the "user friendly" spreadsheet programs that I've seen.

While spreadsheets are not the most facile of classification methods, they can provide more versatility than other systems. If you use graphs, spreadsheets are almost a necessity. If wrestling with a spreadsheet program isn't a turn-off to you, take a look at Microsoft Excel.

PowerPoint gives you, among other things, an easy approach to composing colorful slides for use in court and elsewhere. Slides of graphs, like poignant pictures, can drive home a point to a judge or jury where eloquent argument may fail.

Somehow, a graph seems to validate numerical references or calculations. You simply point to the graph and invite your audience to "see for yourself." Excel offers relatively simple methods of creating various chart and graph formats.

While most Windows-based word processing programs are WYSIWYG, Word's icon "Zoom," brings up the screen font size without affecting the hard copy result. The Professional set includes the additional program, Microsoft Access. Access is a database program. This enables composition of related tables.

For example, tables may consist of clients and cases. This would provide an immediate correlation of all matters in which each of your clients may be involved. Another table could list all documents which can be linked to both each client and all associated matters.

Another valuable addition to Office is "Schedule." This program will handle lots of processes advantageous for your office and for your client control as well as any club or other organization rosters that you may need to proctor.

Office 2000 "Premium" version has lots more on board. It includes an elaborate photo program to facilitate photograph insertion as well as other graphics. It also updates Microsoft Publisher to Publisher 2000.

Premium not only costs bundles more, about $800, it consumes mega space on your hard drive. I've not seen anything in this luxury version to warrant putting that much of my money in it. You may differ.

§ 8:3 The Internet: Don't let the "Net" part take over

The first thing to know about Internet is that you can't get on it. Well, not exactly "can't," but it sometimes takes patience. Since increasing competition among software companies has resulted in "all you can eat" deals, at monthly prices from about $20, greedy surfers have all but consumed the highway space.

It seems that because of a few discourteous users who log on and stay logged on continuously for days at a time, all available toll free lines are busy, end-to-end. Some of the hosts are trying to combat that time holding, by notifying its clients that unused connections will be summarily disconnected.

You might think that your activity registers as busy on the Internet, but you may be wrong. For instance, while you're reading your mail on the screen, there's no activity registered. Hence, your host may conclude that you've wandered off leaving the computer running on Internet. So, a window appears asking if you want to remain connected.

That seems like a fair method of handling the situation. However, that window might appear way over to the side or under another window where you don't see it. Suddenly, you hear the voice say "goodbye." That's NOT fair, you think.

Sometimes even that class of "fairness" breaks down and you'll be shut down frivolously. It can be disconcerting to hear that "goodbye" in the middle or, worse, towards the end, of a lengthy download. But it happens.

If you're not on an "all you can eat" deal with your Internet host, don't waste your on-line time reading mail. Save the mail on your word processor or notebook file or print it out. Then you can read the mail at leisure without incurring time charges.

It's a good idea to do that anyway. Why consume internet time inconveniencing others. Wouldn't it be nice if everyone suddenly got the consideration bug.

Competition among internet hosts has provided the motive for improvement in their services. Bad service as well as price has been the cause of subscribers moving to a competitive carrier.

I haven't tried all of them. I am on AOL because so many of my friends and colleagues use AOL. A good reason? Perhaps not. Try a few and take your choice. They all offer about a month of free trial time.

High speed internet connect is here but at a price.

Lots of people are scurrying to the DSL method of Internet contact. DSL is offered by several firms, such as TelePacific Communications. This new system has fractionated the time for logging on, downloading and all other time-consuming uses of the Internet. In fact, it's speed is about 100 times that of using your modem.

TelePacific offers service free for a month, free installation and equipment, free fax to e-mail number, free web hosting and its promise to "beat any competitor's price." What's that mean? TelePacific, providing SDSL, or Symmetrical Digital Subscriber Lines, claims price leadership, but that class of DSL, though superior, is expensive.

It's cost is $119 per month. That's cheap compared with other SDSL firms' charges. So, if you're satisfied with the "asymmetrical" class, with speeds about 60 or 70 times faster than regular modem contact, the cost would be about half.

Being that as it may, the cost upwards of $50 or $60 monthly may be enough to give pause. But it is a solution to most of the Internet's ills. You can contact TelePacific on Internet at http://www.telepacific.com.

There is a bonus advantage to DSL. It doesn't occupy a phone line as modem access does. This means that the cost of an extra line is avoided. Or, avoiding the inconvenience of waiting while someone else in your house is off the phone before you can share that single line.

Even though you may not want Telepacific's services, you might learn some interesting facts about DSL from them. Give them a call. What can it cost you.

Another cure on the horizon is satellite contact by means of cellular connection. However it's done, the people in charge must find a way to keep the operation flowing for the good of all users and profitability for the highway businesses.

If you think that getting on is a drag, wait 'til you try to get OFF.

If you decide that you've had enough of your valuable time wasted, trying to squeeze onto a local, or 800 phone number, and want to stop the merry-go-round, you may find that chore tougher than logging on.

Contracting for limitless usage at say, $20 per month, is about as easy as subscribing to a magazine. Now you want to unwind the deal. You've had enough of the clowns hogging all the access phone lines. So, you call the same number that got you the deal in the first place. Your credit card was fine to open your account. Now you want someone to credit the card and remove your membership.

You're given an address to write to. Can't you reach anyone by phone? No phone number is available for cancellations. You call your credit card company. You're told that this particular month's $19.95 can be credited, but there'll be new charges each and every month. You're outraged. How can this happen to you! The credit card people tell you that since you gave the number by phone, they can continue to enter it as a charge against you until you get it canceled.

All right. So you haven't had these troubles. You opened your account, got the local or 800 phone line, got logged on and have been merrily surfing and having dialogue helter skelter across the Internet sky. You're having a great time, meeting new Internet buddies, passing time with other surfers, etc.

So what about your law practice? Time enough for everything? O.K. Getting enough sleep, or are you whiling away time into the wee morning hours? Eyes bloodshot? Hey, a bit of red goes well with your pallid complexion. Find yourself drifting off as you type the rushed memo or brief?

Time is time, whether nighttime or daytime. You need time to get your work done, time to play, and time to sleep. The penalty for stealing time in any of these categories is severe. Play means to get out, away from your office and your computer.

Get out in the sun. Play golf, swim, or go for a walk. Switching computer use from work to games isn't the relief you need. A bit of Internet can be worked into the "play" sector, but only a bit. Control it.

Internet, the new integrated communication method for computerists, has come a long way over the past two years. The topical coverage is too gargantuan to attempt any form of itemization. More and more subjects of interest to lawyers are added, day-by-day. Patents, Supreme Court Reports, legal news articles, important intermediate court decisions, as well as thousands of items of general interest are there for your perusal.

What is Internet?

Internet is a network formed by the cooperative interconnection of computing networks. The word, "internet," is a composite of "interconnection" and "network." The word "network" could be a bit off-putting to some people. Actually, Internet really has nothing to do with technical computer networking on a local basis.

At present, there are an approximate 10,000,000 hosts on the Internet highway. There are figures indicating some 10,000 hosts being added daily. It's difficult to estimate the number of users either in total or per host. It has been guessed that somewhere between 60 million and 80 million people are using the Internet.

All one needs to join the Internet is a modem, connected to a computer and a telephone number accessible to the Internet. There are so many entry phone numbers, you're bound to find a local number in your area. Just dial one of those numbers through your modem and you're on the highway. A more simplified method is the procure software of one of the several host companies which will guide you through the maze of material.

Who "owns" the Internet? Just as it is cooperatively interconnected, so is it cooperatively assembled and maintained. Each participant owns its own network. The user may not be conscious of the multiplicity of interconnections when seeking information. All of this is silent and unseen much like the network of various organizations within the complex of telephone systems.

You'll see a menu of various topics. You can even have a mailbox to receive messages from interested persons using the Internet. The subscription costs vary from cheap to inexpensive. At first it's only intriguing. After you've gotten into it, you should find some uses to justify the small monthly cost if you decide you'd like to subscribe.

You can browse through it to see the huge spectrum of connecting facilities without charge. For example, check out this nice site: http://lawschool.westlaw.com. In addition to other materials geared toward the law student, the site provides an online newsletter called "Beyond the Bar" that offers advice to newly admitted attorneys. In particular its features include "Ask the Reference Attorney," which gives hands-on guidance through Westlaw resources, and "Build Your Own Practice," which is intended to help new attorneys establish themselves in the legal community. Check it out as well as many of the other resources—but don't get too carried away.

Internet's mailbox facilities may be more practical than you might believe. You'll be surprised by the number of individuals and companies who subscribe to mailboxes as well as to other Internet services.

For those who would enjoy less complexity involved in the UNIX based interfaces or in memorizing certain of the cryptic commands to perform simple tasks such as voicemail, there is Net Cruiser, a PC Windows based package. It's inexpensive and even a fun way to cruise Internet.

Once the program is installed in Windows by way of simple menued instructions, you are spoon fed your way through the myriad of selections. Click on the icon and cruise along. I've not yet used Net Cruiser, but I'm informed that it's the method of choice for Internet operations.

Not to add further confusion, but one can engage in Internet functions through the use of a local or "LAN" network. As with your other computer operations, the network permits Internet inquiries to be accomplished more speedily and less downtime.

I wouldn't suggest installing a network in your office merely to accommodate Internet. If you have use for the other purposes mentioned in this book, I would recommend that you think about a network. Standard Microsystems Corporation "SMC" offers a variety of network card packages to fit most any office setup for LAN.

There are many other brands of cards, but I was impressed by the favorable pricing of complete packages offered by SMC. SMC can be reached by telephone at (800) 762-4968 or by mail at 80 Arkay Drive, Hauppauge, New York 11788.

§ 8:4 Systemize and computerize your scheduling

Learn to love your office. Regard it more as a mistress than as a spouse away from your spouse. Going home to your family should also be fun and not be neglected. But your office should not be a drudge.

Look forward to going to the office each day. Keep regular office hours to the extent possible. Hopefully, you'll be spending a good deal of time out soliciting work, but spend as much of your early morning and late afternoon hours in office routine as you are able. For some unknown reason, many clients will call either in the early morning or late afternoon. If you are not in, you may miss the call and the client.

If you must be a "golfaholic," forage into the crowds on weekends only, or wait until you have made it big enough not to mind losing the extra business. The main thing is not to squander your weekday time on your hobbies and other diversions until you are way ahead of the money game.

Even then, don't. The more successful you become, the more fun you'll have being successful. Fun from golf is overrated. Being in the office affords more than just the opportunity to answer the phone and greet new clients. There's always more to do than just sit and wait.

Look around. There's a will to draw. There's a letter or two to get out. What about that collection matter? No job will ever get done unless you start working on it.

If you must play, play with your computer. Playing around with your computer is not wasted time. The more familiar you get with its functions, the more you can use it productively. It takes office time to do that. Bills need paying. Then there's some billing to do. You cannot collect fees without first sending the statements.

Straighten up those files. What about the case? Lots of work is needed to get all those evidence ducks in a row. There's a lot to be done. You've pushed these things to the back of your mind to justify some play. There'll be time for that later.

Use the computer for making notes of things to do. You know how notes can get misplaced. Where did you put that note you made yesterday? Is it in the client file? Is it under the desk blotter? Who knows!

If it's in your "Note" file, it can never get lost. All you do is type the key and there it is, voila! These and other excellent little note file programs are available at very low prices. Windows has several such note keeping files. Pick any one of them and use it.

It's just as simple and convenient as looking through piled papers for a scratch pad. You won't lose the notes or have trouble accessing them. You'll find the program so simple that you'll discover more and more uses for this gem of a helpmate.

Use the notepad as a document index file. Microsoft Works offers a useful note taking function. In fact there is a variety of such programs contained in Office 2000. Take your pick.

§ 8:5 Download to floppies for each client

The documents served by opponents are scanned and recorded on the respective client's floppy. Discovery documents are scanned to eliminate the need to re-type questions or other demands in preparing responses. Hence, both demands and responses are archived together.

Only one file of each genre per client is kept on the hard drive. Everything else is deleted after downloading to the client's floppy disk. The file retained, such as a pleading form, correspondence, etc., is used only to copy for the form or attorney's address, or whatever.

All billing, statements, checks, deposits and everything else related to accounting are kept in floppy archives. In that way, any question regarding payment of a bill, an item related to fees, deposits or whatever, can quickly be verified by resort to the relevant floppy disk. Duplicates of each are kept.

Keeping the respective floppies in logical storage places not only provides that convenience but serves to permit regular removal of data that would otherwise clutter my hard drive. Minimizing files and data on the hard disk speeds the computer substantially and reduces the possibility of data-related disk problems.

Two floppies: One in client file, other in storage.

What about the possibility of floppy disk failure? Experience, a merciless teacher, has convinced me that duplicate back-up for everything is not just prudent but imperative. So, one copy goes into the client file. The other, a safety copy, is filed under the client's name in a floppy storage case.

Keep several floppy cases for each category, i.e., client material, billing, accounting and miscellaneous. Maintain separate disks for each account, such as general accounts, trust accounts, investment accounts, etc.

Although all accounting disks are filed in the case marked

"Accounting," they are tucked in separate categories within the case.

Floppy disks are cheap. They once cost as much as $4 or $5 per disk. Now, fine, guaranteed disks can be found for as little as 10 cents each.

If you believe the fetching "rebate" offers, you can get the disks free, after receiving the "rebate. "Take my advice, pay the 10 cents and forget that nonsense.

Download each client's documents on separate disks. Store one disk in a common storage case under that client's alphabetical place, and insert the other in the client's general file. Where a separate billing involves the same client, for example, billed to an insurance company, download to a third disk for the carrier's file.

Where there are construable distinctions from a client's other regular business, keep those records on a separate disk. Client backup disks kept in a storage case are grouped within each client's alphabetical space in the case.

The disks related to different matters pertaining to a given client are kept within the respective file for that client. Where there are many different matters for one client, you may experience some confusion as to which matter a certain issue is related to. Simply review the several disks stored together in the storage case by reading the label list.

This system may seem to you to involve thousands of disks, each leading to successive volumes. Not so. Each floppy holds hundreds of pages of data. In most situations, one single disk for correspondence, contracts, etc., and one for pleadings, if applicable, are usually ample for each client.

§ 8:6 Archived material on floppy disks

The storage capacity of each disk is so voluminous that it's not cumbersome to keep the disks readily available involving cases that are closed and perhaps even archived. If the need arises to refer to an archived document, you can usually find it within minutes and at arm's reach.

The same is true of archived billing and accounting records. I have complete accounts for years dating back to 1983 right at my fingertips. That same claim could be made for another twenty years.

A high volume of stuff can be kept on disks in a relatively small storage space. The ways and means will be detailed for you on law office and practice management further along.

The foregoing should give you a glimmer as to how good management can comfort the solo lawyer. If you haven't been responsible for office and practice management in the past, you may not fully appreciate the monsters lurking in an untidy law office.

The other side of that coin is the great amount of confidence a well managed office and practice can contribute to you and your well being. Good management may not in itself ensure a happy and successful practice nor prevent all kinds of disciplinary problems.

But bad management will ensure an unhappy, unsuccessful practice. Most common varieties of solo practice failure as well as ethical violations are directly attributable to inadequate management.

§ 8:7 Your computer and your law practice

Admittedly, ease of operation is a desirable ingredient to the control of personal habits. If you have a tendency toward superficiality or avoiding a chore, complications or drudgeries will not be strong allies in your office management.

It's true that learning to use a computer is a task requiring a measure of diligence. This may not be entirely conducive to enticing you to either start the learning process or to stick with it.

Think of it rather as an admission price to a place where life will be easier for you a bit later. Chores are often on-going, repetitive tasks, boring and unpleasant. Such chores, like bookkeeping, filing, etc., are there waiting to be done daily.

Learning to use a computer is a chore, and I won't minimize it's requirements for concentration, self-application and diligence. However, once learned, the chore of learning ends. Once you've learned the basics of computering, the problem is licked for all time.

Then, the other chores, bookkeeping, filing, etc., become simple and even fun. All of the drudgery and boredom of finding this, entering that, replacing this and recovering that are all ended. The computer does all of these complicated and boring things for you. Your part in the process is simply pressing a few keys.

§ 8:8 An office diary is a mandatory must

The first step in the approach to administration of your office is to get a good daybook or diary program. Your computer calendar program can and should serve as your diary far better than any you may keep on your desk. For this to work well, you must print out a "hard copy" at least daily.

Your hard copy, together with the "saved" software version,

provides the duplicate method required by most professional responsibility insurance carriers, as well as by the dictates of sound business practice.

Your calendar should have a summary of each month's business, as well as separate pages for entries during each month on a day-to-day basis. Your calendar should be opened first thing each day.

These programs automatically open to the current month, day and date so you can see at a glance what your commitments are for that whole month. Make **absolutely sure** that both the monthly and daily entries are up to the minute.

You should always have your schedule right at your finger tips. Never, but *never*, permit yourself to look away from your work and appearance schedule. More claims are made against lawyers for missed dates than for almost any other failure.

§ 8:9 Of books and bookkeeping, including how to avoid inadvertent commingling

There are some things you need to know to operate an accounting program. You would have to know how to make out a check and make out a deposit to your bank account.

You'd also need to know why you are making out that check, to whom and for what purpose. Then, you also need to know why you are making out a deposit, the source of the money and the reason it was paid to you.

If you are paying your office rent, "rent" is the "why." You would make the check out for, say, $395 to Leechy Landlord. Mr. Landlord is the "whom." The "purpose" is to prevent being evicted.

When you make a deposit for $1,500 received from a client, "Richard Greene," for fees, your deposit would read $1,500 from Richard Greene for "Fees." The "Fees" part would be the category. If you are paying an electric bill, the category would be "Utilities."

If you are paying an installment to West Group for one of their sets (or for this book), the category would be "Library Maintenance." Each deposit and check is so categorized as part of your program daily input.

Unless you want your office routine housekeeping to be more complicated than need be, I'd suggest the simplest accounting and billing programs and the "cash" system. The "cash" system, rather than the "accrual" system, means that you do not keep a book entry accounts receivable. Of course, you will keep adequate records of your time and to whom that time was devoted. But you don't necessarily record these transactions in your books of account as a "receivable."

In reality, most simple accounting systems will record payments made by each individual client. However, it's your billing program that will show the balance of payments and time billed.

You will necessarily need more than one account. You'll need to keep a trust account and most likely a personal, or home, and as many others as you'd like.

You must distinguish these accounts from each other. This is particularly so of your trust accounts. Failure to do this could result in some real trouble called "commingling." That specter will be treated in great depth later.

Individual labeling of accounts could also provide a means of securitizing your accounts from any possible prying eyes. You can name each such account with an esoteric name that only you would know.

Identify your office name where indicated, and then state an opening balance. Approximate your opening balance as accurately as possible, but don't worry if you're a bit off. You can always adjust this balance later. When you do, all of your totals will be likewise adjusted, with absolutely no harm done or inconvenience to you.

There is another handy thing about most of these programs. You can correct any mistake in any entry or total at any time, no matter what the function, and that corrective entry will follow all the way through your accounts and re-total and re-calculate everything within a split second.

Most all of these accounting programs make counter-entries wherever appropriate. When you make out a deposit for "Fees," for instance, that sum will automatically be added to the "Fees" account as well as any other account that may be relevant according to your chart of accounts or categories selections.

Thus, if you make any corrective entry regarding "Fees," that correction will automatically carry through to every posting of the particular sum corrected, wherever it may have been entered. If you made a mistake and deleted an entry for "Fees," the deletion will remove a like sum everywhere else appropriately.

This is also true of your category selections. If you wish to change any of them at any time, you may do so and the re-identification will carry through the entire program to all functions of that category. So make your category selections as tentative as you wish.

Some programs ask for re-identity of the selection. This only requires a simple key touch or response of "yes." While certain of these accounting systems may be more involved than others, the only imposition is a slight bit more self-training time.

No matter how many mistakes like that you make, you can always correct them at your leisure. No mistake is ever fatal, and no mistake is ever buried. Each time you ask to total all accounts, you will see everything you've done, including any and all "mistakes." You merely correct each such "mistake" as you spot it.

Your law business account is called your "GENERAL ACCOUNT." You may have as many such accounts as you wish, and you may intermix them for any reason best suiting your purposes. But no client's money may be recorded there, and no client's funds may be deposited in any bank account in common with any other of your funds. Of course, the opposite is also true.

You certainly know this well, or your law school would never have let you get past your legal ethics course. If you've had some accounting experience or training, your understanding of the above may be better than mine. If not, your mind could be boggled with the simplest examples of bookkeeping procedures.

Of course, if you want to be a coward about all of this, you can hire a bookkeeper and let the bookkeeper do all of this nasty work. You'll probably need an accountant around tax time anyway, so you might get the accountant to set up your book system for you for a fee. Still, you'll have to work the system yourself, or have someone on the payroll to make these daily entries for you.

My guess is that, if a professional accountant sets your books up for you, you won't be able to do the work yourself. For some unknown reason, most accountants just do not speak simple bookkeeping. At least, this has been my experience.

Be assured that however good your memory may be, you will forget some things unless you write everything down as you go along. Your calendar "memo" entry is the proper place for reminders. Unless you are willing to work for nothing, and it won't always be for the people that you like, I urge you to be very serious about this procedure.

§ 8:10 Your attorney/client trust account

Commingling: you're sure you understand it, and yet . . .. You've heard so much about "commingling" that I'm sure you've wondered why this sin was not considered among the original Commandments.

I would dare say that, in a poll of law students asked to state offenses for which lawyers could be disciplined, commingling would be blurted out first among the majority. And yet, strangely enough, probably less is known about this transgression than about many more complicated and heinous crimes.

I would venture a guess that at least one-third of all practicing lawyers are guilty of commingling to a greater or lesser extent. This is because the lawyer's mind is just not finely attuned to the intricacies of sophisticated accounting.

Would you believe that many violations of commingling occur as a result of excessive caution? Here is a typical example: Lawyer Jones wants no problems with commingling. He wants to make absolutely certain that all client funds are kept completely isolated from his general funds.

He knows that a common source of trouble is the court cost payment. When a client gives his lawyer the money for a filing fee, this amount must be deposited immediately into the client's trust account. This, Lawyer Jones knows. He wants there to be no mistake.

So what does he do? He pays all court costs from the trust account. That way he can't have any trouble. All court costs are beautifully insulated from all other funds. Logical, beautiful and pure.

The only trouble with this is that not all of the disbursements made by Jones from the account had a corresponding entry for a deposit by the respective client for whose benefit the court cost was paid. Jones did not always wait until the client had given him the money before drafting the check.

A complaint or an answer had to be filed. The cost must be posted with the filing or no filing. Clerks are funny that way. So, to the shock, chagrin, and bewilderment of Lawyer Jones, he is overdrawn on his Client's Trust Account by several hundred dollars.

He checks his records, and finds that this overdraft consists of many payments of filing fees for which there were no counter deposits. In other words, he was hung out to dry by umpteen deadbeat clients who are just as adept at not paying for court costs as they are at not paying lawyer's fees.

All right, so you are smart. That sort of thing could never happen to you. Never will you make payment from your Trust Account unless a credit entry is first made from the client's funds. Fine. You are audited by the Bar Association. You are smug. What can they find? Nothing at all.

But wait. You are $173.14 short and there is an imbalance. Why? What could have happened? Calamity, the bank erred. No way. You made the error, you bum.

A very common error. Your trust account is relatively inactive. So, there are bank charges. You forgot to instruct the bank to assess all bank charges to your general account. What do bank charges debit against? Client funds.

But that doesn't account for all of the $173.14. Oh yes, there were several check books, deposit stamps, and other paraphernalia ordered by you and they were all debited. Guess where? Right. What else?

Despite your constant reminder to your bank never to debit any bank charges to the trust account, what did they do? You got it. A debit for these items associated with the trust account, right where banks normally debit such things, the trust account.

You should have known about this. Oh, you did. So what happened? You made out a check to be deposited in your Trust Account but where did it go? Wow. Right into your General Account.

How did this happen? Simple. Your secretary used the wrong deposit slip. It can happen. Say what?? You have no secretary? So, it was you then.

O.K. And all banks are now computerized so that the only entry instruction is on the deposit slip by electronic designation. All of your careful concern and diligent work notwithstanding, the deposit was made to your General Account and not to the Trust Account.

Will you go to jail? Will you be disbarred? Are you to end up in disgrace after all you've gone through to be a lawyer? Promise not to do it again, and you may get probation. You'll promise, but can you keep that promise?

Yes. But you must take the most meticulous pains to prevent even these silly, inadvertent comminglings. You must direct your bank, in writing, to make all debits of all bank charges and bank services to your General Account.

Make certain that there are distinctive colors and designs separating your Trust Account from your General Account. Mark your Trust Account deposit card with great big red letters, "TRUST ACCOUNT." Make all of your deposits yourself.

Here's another test for you. You have just settled a case in a personal injury matter. You have 40% of the settlement. The check is for a big $5,000. Your Attorney/Client Contract provides that you may take your share, without notice, from the proceeds. The check, conveniently enough, is made out to you and you alone.

You deposit the five grand in your General Account. But you are fully conscious of your duty to your client, *so you simulta-*

neously make out a check to your client for his share. Everything is hotsy-totsy. You get $2,000, which is 40% and your client gets $3,000, or his 60%.

Perfect? Not so perfect. Not even legal. In fact, you have committed a classical act of commingling.

You may never commingle the client's funds with yours for even one single second. When you made the deposit, you commingled the funds. True, your intent was to pay your client back. Oh, I know, that's what they all say. San Quentin is filled with the nice fellows who insist that they intended to "put the money back."

The *entire* amount received in settlement must be deposited in the Client's Trust Fund Account. Then, you may make such distribution and in such manner as your contract dictates.

You are not authorized to negotiate the check for your own purposes. Your computation in the previous example was mathematically correct, but ethically incorrect.

The example giving you $2,000 for your 40% cut was a little oversimplified. Actually, in most cases there will be other disbursements besides those to you and to your client.

There will usually be doctor's bills, pharmaceuticals, and other costs. Perhaps there will be court costs, if the case was filed. Usually, though, settlements precede the need to file.

Let's take a typical example and apply it to a sample trust fund deposit and disbursement. Using the same settlement figure and the same ratio of distribution, we will add medical fees of $1,000, a drug bill of $125, and sundry costs of $35. The account entries will appear as follows:

DEPOSIT	CLIENT	MED.	PHARM	COSTS	CLIENT	ATT.
$5,000	Smith	$1,000	$125	$35	$1,840	$2000

The above indicates what the distribution would be under a "gross distribution" agreement. This means that your fee is taken off the top, before any deductions are taken. This arrangement should be spelled out in your contract, if this is to be the division. As you can see, the figures would vary depending on your Attorney/Client Agreement.

Your Trust Account is kept just as you keep your General Account. Balances are struck after each entry, and a running balance is kept, showing the state of the account.

Since nothing is paid from the trust account, nor are any deductions made without a corresponding entry of deposit in equal sum, the account should remain in balance and should stand at no less than zero at all times.

Another important precaution to be taken is never to make a disbursement from the Trust Account against a check or draft received until you have ascertained that the check or draft has cleared the bank. Otherwise, you run the risk of the check that you received bouncing, and your client, having received his share, not being willing to return the check to you.

If it happens that the amount is more than you are capable of raising immediately, you will be in imbalance. Don't let this sort of thing happen.

Bear in mind that drafts are different from checks. A check is honored forthwith upon presentation to the maker bank. This means that, within the time allotted for such clearance, you can assume that the check has cleared. Not so with a draft.

A draft is a horse of a different color. Drafts must be approved at the pleasure of the maker. For instance, in drafts issued by insurance companies, as in settlements in personal injury cases, the insurance company has the ability to disapprove the draft at anytime within the policy period.

This means that the draft may be bounced as long as two or three months later, and in some instances, even longer. Get the facts concerning each draft that you accept before you set about to make distribution.

On the subject of separating the bank accounts, some lawyers even prefer to use separate banks to further ensure that no bank errors can cause problems. This is inconvenient, but not a bad idea.

The second part of your account system is the "Disbursement" section. Here, all of your checks are broken down, showing the amount, the name of the payee, and the purpose for which the expenditure was made. These divisions are essential for many purposes, including the preparation of your income tax returns.

Your accountant will need to know which amounts may be deducted as a business expense and which may only be depreciated as a capital asset. Your accountant will also need to know the nature of the deduction, such as whether it is a charitable contribution, determined after computation of your adjusted gross income.

Such information is also useful in guiding your operation. An analysis might show that spending in one or another area is excessive. You may not have realized this, and a reflection from your accounts could be the only tip-off to you as to why you may be having trouble getting out in front financially.

You will need to make regular entries in your general income account in order to prepare your bank deposits. But you won't have to make such regular check disbursement entries. Therefore, you will need to remind yourself to bring these entries up-to-date from time to time so that you won't find yourself at the end of the year with an entire year's work to do to prepare for your accountant.

If you must do this manually, the best system is a card file.

All of this information on manual bookkeeping procedures will be important only if you are keeping your books manually, instead of with a computer accounting program. I sincerely hope that is not your choice. You wouldn't do that. Would you?

These manual entries are demonstrated only to show the gross time wasted by those who still fight the losing battle against using computers. One simply cannot justify that choice.

In addition to the other account books, etc., mentioned, you will need some form of accounting records for time charges not collected whether or not billed. Call it an "accounts receivable register" or whatever. The simplest and best system for keeping a record of what each client owes you is a conventional card file, about 5" x 9".

Inscribe the name of each client on a separate card, along with the client's office and home address and the phone numbers at home and at the office. The left hand vertical column should show the number of hours performed on the date indicated in the next column.

These entries should be a direct copy of the items tracked in your calendar or diary. When the work is transposed, it should be either crossed out or checked off.

In the center, under "services performed," you should state, in a very brief form, the nature of the services performed on that date. The next column to the right shows the sum charged for the work performed. This should be a direct multiple of the hours at the rate which you charge.

The next column records the payments or credits to the accounts. This consists of payments made by the client to you or sums received for the client's benefit. All other credits for whatever reason, which would reduce the amount that the client owes you, should also be in this column.

The last right hand column shows the balance of the amount owed on any given date. This amount, of course, will reflect the difference between what you charge for your services and all of the credits (mainly payments by the client) against the charges.

These cards should be placed in a container tall enough to keep them intact, but short enough so that about half the height of the cards will be exposed. This is so that you can flip through the cards and view the state of the accounts with ease.

Another fun procedure to brighten your day is called, for want of a more exciting name, "posting and billing." Here is where all of the information you've been storing up in your daily diary, such as cash receipts, trust accounts, check disbursements, etc., gets transferred onto the account cards of your clients.

This process is followed so that every once in a while you will be able to look at some record and know who owes you what. Then you can send statements, so that you will be paid (you hope) and you can eat.

So that the job doesn't take on astronomical proportions, I suggest that this be done at least once a week. This not only makes the job easier, if not a sheer delight, but it also is conducive to more frequent billing. This, as you now know, is a distinct advantage.

To do this job properly, you should have all of your records arrayed before you. This will include your daily diary, your cash receipts, check disbursements, and the accounts receivable file.

Start with your daily diary. Look at the first entry, and record the name of the client on one of your account cards. Then transcribe the number of hours and the services performed, in very brief language, and compute the charge, based on your hourly rate, for insertion in the appropriate column. Repeat this process for each diary entry.

Next, refer to your receipts book. Wherever you find entry of a payment by a client, find the account card for that client, and mark the date when received and the word "payment" in the "services performed" column, and mark the amount which was paid in the next to the last column on the right, identified as "credits."

Don't become alarmed if you find a payment from a client for whom there is no account card. This means that you have not been keeping the job up properly, you have not been posting in the right order, or you have gotten a "retainer" for work that had not yet been performed. It's probably the latter situation. Prepare a card, and enter the retainer amount.

Then, refer to the check disbursement account. Go through the list of entries of payees until you find a payee of the type that would indicate a payment made was on behalf of a client. Such a payee would be, for example, a court clerk.

For instance, if you had advanced payment of a court filing fee on behalf of a client, such an entry should be recorded as follows: In the column for "hours," you insert the word "costs."

Next, indicate the date of the check and repeat the word "costs" under "services performed," with the description next to it, i.e., "costs-filing fee." Then, mark the amount of the costs in the charge column and add this expenditure to the balance.

The reverse side of the accounts receivable card is reserved for Trust Account entries. Here, you would record such entries as advancements paid to you by the client to be held as a "costs fund."

For instance, where you expect to have a number of outlays in a case, it is customary for the client to merely advance an approximate amount to cover the cost expectations. The amount is, of course, deposited in your trust account, and each disbursement is recorded on this reverse side of the account card.

Eventually, the amount of the client's advancement will or should be exhausted. On any given day, you can bill any client by merely referring to the outstanding balance on his or her account card.

§ 8:11 Law office chores using your secretarial service

You can efficiently and effectively gross $100,000, $200,000 or even more per year, without the use of a secretary, hired or rented. Still, for one or another reason, you may need, or think you need, some secretarial help. You know enough now to avoid hiring a part-time secretary. So, you'll resort to the "rent-a-sec" method.

After you've thought about it until your head hurts, think about it some more. Do you absolutely, positively, without a question of a doubt, need, can't live without, and are desperate for, a secretary? Really?

Each of the secretarial services operates on its own set of rules and methods. Most of them will pick up dictated tapes, and deliver completed work each afternoon. Some work with a variety of dictating machines, and others use only the most popular makes.

Many will loan or rent machines for a nominal charge. So, before you think of buying a dictating machine, investigate which service you intend to use.

All dictating machines have some form of indicator showing the length of each paper dictated. You will make life easier for the service, and get a better work product out of it, if you note the length of each dictation on a note pad accompanying the tape. This information will permit the service to space the papers intelligently.

For example, if they know in advance that a particular letter is to consist only of a single paragraph, they will start typing at an appropriate place on your letterhead stationery. A letter with everything grouped at the top looks amateurish.

This is what will happen if you don't give advance information with your tapes. They don't have time to preview each document and still give you your best price per page.

Finish your tapes well in advance of the scheduled pickup time. The services hate customers who cause their delivery people to wait while tapes are being completed. You'll get better service if you can be relied upon not to cause this problem.

Invest in a low cost portable tape machine that you can carry around with you. If your service uses machines of the standard cassette type, so much the better. Small cassette machines can be purchased for as little as $20 or $30.

Digital tapeless hand-held recorders are now available from about $25 to $100. They're very handy for several reasons. No need to shuttle back and forth to find the point needed. No bothering with tapes. The recording is done on a chip. Your work remains recorded even if the battery fails or is replaced.

The recordings are allocated to separate "folders" much as on your computer. To find a particular entry you can flip to the subject folder and click to the particular file.

Back at the office, you upload your field work into your dictating machine and get it typed onto a hard copy. In fact, some of these newer digital models have a simplified method for transition to typed pages.

This will allow you to do some dictating at home, at the library, in the car, or wherever you are. If you have your machine wherever you are, you will function much better, since you won't need to rely on scribbly notes.

Develop the habit of dictating everything. You can have the service prepare your billing statements, memos, "things to do," in fact, anything that involves information to be given to another. If you discipline yourself to do so, you can utilize the service as fully as a secretary located right in your own office. Within reasonable bounds, of course.

Keep copies of work submitted by the service in a "monthly" folder. When you receive your bill for the month's service, compare the lineage charges with the lineage on the copies. You can make a quick, approximate check by counting the average number of words in each line and multiplying these by the average number of lines on the pages times the number of pages.

If there is a reasonable consistency, file the bill for payment. If the bill seems excessive upon this comparison, ask the service for a breakdown. They, like everyone else, make mistakes, and should be willing to review the computation.

After completing this check, distribute the copies into the various files appropriate to each document. This procedure will serve as a forced review of each active matter monthly, as well as the above-described check.

Many services offer the extra convenience of a special phone number to an answer machine. Your dictation is received at any time of the day or night. If you have forgotten a letter that must be sent out immediately, or if you get a thought in the middle of the night, you can dial the number and start dictating.

All such material is collected and added to the day's work, delivered that afternoon. This special service avoids the delay to the next day's work. There are some limitations to the use of this telephone dictation. You cannot backspace and make corrections, as you are able to do with your dictating machine.

Further, you cannot stop the machine and wait for thoughts to occur to you, as you may do with your own machine.

This system may be used effectively only if you have fully prepared the text of your dictation. If you make a mistake, you must identify the words or lines to be changed or deleted with precision.

With these shortcomings, and others that you will discover for yourself. This feature is still a very valuable one. You should discipline yourself to accommodate its capabilities.

One other problem inherent in the phone dictation method is the compounded distortion added by the telephone equipment to the residual distortion of the recording equipment itself. Telephone answering tape recorders are not famous for great fidelity. Telephone sound, likewise, will not win any special awards for purity. Either of these devices alone would succeed in reducing the quality of Sir Laurence Olivier's voice to that of Porky Pig's.

When you combine the two, there is a result that will challenge even your dulcet tones. The antidote to this audio pathology is to speak ever so much more plainly.

§ 8:12 Cassette recorders, beepers, copiers, and other office equipment

New mini-disc "MD" writeable recorder/player.

Although it is not technically a "CD" unit, and it doesn't "burn" the information onto the disk, it operates much the same way. The device is about the size of a moderately sized mini cassette recorder/player and slightly heavier. I have a Sony midi record/

player. The discs can be recorded over and over an infinite number of times. The sound quality seems to be as good as conventional CDs and the discs come in two lengths: 60 and 74 minutes.

The advantages of the MD over the conventional cassette are obvious. No wear or tear no matter how many times played or re-recorded. But most important, the seek time, as with CD-ROM, is instantaneous.

If you are making notes, you may separate notes by track numbers. Thus, in addition to the usual search methods you can reach any track needed at any time without delay. This is especially valuable in recording depositions. Also, the insert capability allows you to insert page numbers after the transcript is available.

The MD unit is more expensive than a cassette recorder, certainly. So are the discs more expensive than tape cassettes. But the many advantages of its search facility make this handy little cutie worth that difference. This is especially so when you're working on a tight schedule. Also, the sound quality is not to be believed.

At present, the MD prices have been steadily falling. MD players without the record facility are becoming commonplace. Because of the much greater flexibility of the MD over the tape cassettes, it shouldn't be long before they, or something similar, completely replace tape.

Pagers are becoming more and more necessary.

Whether in court, at appointments, at lunch or driving your car, you need to be in touch. The cellular phone is fine, but sometimes an inconvenient annoyance. Lawyers are increasingly finding pagers a better solution when used along with your cellular phone.

Beeper installation and subscription costs have been coming down to practicality. Initial costs vary with the companies and geographics but hover somewhere between $12 to $20. Subscriptions run anywhere from $6 to $10 per month.

Fax or copier; which, or both in one?

You need a fax machine and also a copier. If your needs for both are not too heavy, you can get one machine to do double duty. Several manufacturers are offering combination "do everything" machines. Hewlett Packard and Brother market units that combine fax, scanner, copier, printer, modem and possibly even the kitchen sink.

Prices are attractive for machines using the Ink Jet method of inking. The Brother is a laser-jet type and does reasonably well in all categories, costing around $250 to $350 or so.

§ 8:13 Stationery and other office needs and supplies

You will immediately need stationery, legal paper, and other such things. All of your letterhead, statements, envelopes, business cards, pleading paper, will and will envelope materials, and the like, should be imprinted with your name, office address, phone number, etc., styled in the manner most suitable for your taste and personality.

All of these items can be printed by you on your trusty laser printer. Your word processor will give you an ample choice of fonts to make them distinctively your own. Most word processors, like Microsoft Word and Corel Corporation's WordPerfect, offer several attractive templates for both business and personal stationary. Pick one and then customize it to suit your taste.

There are many things that can be done to give these otherwise dull and drab papers a sparkling lift. And, it makes a big difference, when it is done with a bit of style and class.

Your stationery and most important your business cards, should not only identify who you are, but what kind of who you are. It doesn't take much in the way of stylization; often the material of the card or paper alone is sufficient. A classical typeface, placed a bit off center, may create an effect to set your material apart from the next person's.

Your preference might be for a parchment card, a special watermark bond, or whatever. You might like a card similar to mine, with all of the printing over to one side instead of the conventional center style.

The effect of this is to permit your printed material to be fully exposed when you hand it to a person, instead of your thumb covering a portion of it. A little thought applied to these items will be a small imposition upon you and might add a little touch of class to your identity.

If you have an email address don't forget to include that on all your printing, including business cards, letterheads, everything.

Even your pleading forms, document covers, and other such things can reflect some of this stylizing. Some lawyers prefer their name and firm at the bottom left, in the conventional manner, and others, like myself, rebel at this stereotype and instead place such information along the side. Here again, the typeface needn't be in the orthodox pica style, but may instead have a more modern flair.

Again, your word processor will doubtlessly have a variety of court pleading forms, ruled and numbered or otherwise. Choose one that fits your jurisdiction and fancy.

These forms are mechanized to the correct margins, spacing

and caption spaces. Your job is simply to fill in the requisite information.

Unless your correspondent is really sneaky and goes so far as to "feel" the imprint, there will be little detectable difference. Aw, but who the heck really cares. Besides, I'll let you in on an open "secret": Everybody's doing it.

So long as your letters and pleadings look nice and reasonably professional, who's counting? Save the loot and do your own. Your laser printer will soon pay for itself.

Composing your own stationery profits you in more ways than saving the printing costs. You are assured of a constant supply and are not at the mercy of printing company delays. A variety of stationery styles are available on both Microsoft Word and Corel WordPerfect.

Moreover, during these beginning stages, you may find yourself changing locations quite often. Having the ability to change your letterhead, envelopes, etc., at a moment's notice can be a big relief. Most all word processors have envelope design and printing that you can customize easily.

Even remaining at the same address, changes in stationery design can be interesting. People like to move furniture around, change their clothing, automobiles, whatever, why not stationery.

You may see someone's stationery design that you admire and would like to copy it. Voila! There it is! The why's and how's of using your computer for these purposes will be detailed just ahead.

Customized Pleading and Judicial Council Pleading Forms.

Word 2000 has a "Wizard" of a customizing program for legal documents. It takes you step-by-step through the formulation of any style of pleading acceptable in your state.

Use some ingenuity. Try your name over to the left and the address to the right. Use larger type size, say Times 15, for the first letters of your name, including initial, and smaller for the rest of your name. Use petite universal, say size 8, for your address, phone number, etc.

Try a different style. Type your name at top left with "Lawyer," "Attorney" or whatever, just beneath that, or even over to the right. Now, at the page bottom, type the rest of your letterhead information; address, phone number, etc. Hey, cute, huh?

No law office management system, whether or not computerized, can succeed without your having completed the basics properly in setting up your office. The foregoing is not intended to cover absolutely everything in law office and practice management. But it should get you into the spirit of things.

Next, consider what you need to do to automate your practice activities, including research, litigation support, drafting and everything necessary for your full practice of law.

§ 8:14 Don't use engraved cards to announce office opening

Type a simple letter on your law office letterhead to announce the opening of your office, instead of using the much more expensive engraved announcement card. You can address each such letter with a computer stroke. The rest is just stuffing, stamping, and mailing.

Those fancy, expensively engraved announcement cards may do something for your own ego, but they'll not impress the recipients. The fond father is convinced that the whole world stops in celebration of the new baby. So the new attorney cannot believe that anyone would be indifferent to his or her grand entrance into the world of law.

The world of law does not stop. Busy lawyers go on about their business completely unmindful of your ecstasy. If you can capture the interest of even a small part of that world, it will not be by way of that beautiful, expensive epistle.

Almost every attorney receives those fancy tidings very frequently. I know this must sound to you like blasphemy, but the great likelihood is that your proud and extravagantly prepared announcements will get tossed unopened and unread.

On the other hand, a letter from you, on your nice, lawyer-like stationery, enclosed in your nice, lawyer-like envelope, will certainly be opened and read. Then maybe tossed, but it first will have been read. No one, but no one, will toss a letter from an attorney without first opening and then carefully reading it.

Give this your fullest consideration. I know how you feel. You are mighty proud of your achievement, and you should be. But the announcement message, not ego, is what's important. Getting it read, not appraised, is your target.

Do have some of those expensive, impressive announcement cards made if you like. But use them only for your closest friends and relatives. They'll care about your noteworthy achievement, and they'll read and savor every line.

Chapter 9

Law Practice Management

§ 9:1 Generally

Rule 7 of the Seven Rules Of Solo Practice Survival—"Organization"— is the keystone of management (see Chapter 7). This applies to both your office routine and law practice. Waiting for your practice to build before instituting an efficient organizational plan is a big mistake.

Start with a practical method of handling files, clientele, accounting, document management and retrieval, and all other aspects of your office and practice management. You'll be thankful that you did this when you had the time rather than be harassed into it by urgent necessity.

Organizing your practice the old manual way was inefficient, unreliable, time consuming and confusing. Some people still prefer it that way though I don't know why. In the old days, there was no choice. That was the only game in town.

I recall wishing I could just snap my fingers and a genie would swoop down, gather up all my files and documents and place them neatly under an organized plan. POOF! Here's your magic genie. It's called a computer.

It still takes more than a fingers' snap, but not much more. A few key touches and it's all done for you, like magic. Now even document filing takes only a few key touches. Paper documents can be stored chronologically so that no time is wasted in finding their proper places.

Every document is filed correctly on your computer. Any file needed for editing or print out is available with a few key strokes. No more clutter up or piles of paper waiting for the tedious job of filing. No more finger paper cuts. No more frustration.

A few document management programs are reviewed here with some recommendations for your consideration. Whether you choose one of these or some other available method, get it going now. Don't wait until you "need it." You need it now.

Things can be tough or easy. Disorganization makes it tough. Organization makes it easy. If your practice is disorganized, you must remember things and search for things. If you're organized, everything is laid out for you in apple pie order.

The bridge to an organized practice is a calendar chronologizing every appointment, scheduled work project, memorandum, and procedure. A filing system is set up enabling rapid location and retrieval of any document related to any case or client.

Each case and client is identifiable through a cross sectional indexing method whether by name, case, description case type or date. An infallible method of locating anything by any key word, index identification or phrase, is established.

§ 9:2 Document management and retrieval programs

Dedicated programs.

Computerized document management systems until recently were priced out of range for new lawyers. Some of them still are. There are a few good systems available at a reasonable price now. One that I personally like is PageKeeper.

"PageKeeper 3.0" by Caere Corporation is a program designed to file paper documents electronically and/or to organize computer documents into PageKeeper's folder system. Documents can then be organized into related groups, previewed, annotated, retrieved, or applied in any other way desired.

You can set up a "Folder Watch" in PageKeeper to detect when documents are added to specified folders in Windows Explorer. Detected documents will automatically be added to specified PageKeeper folder.

Documents may be opened directly in Windows applications. Find documents easily by content, keyword search, relevancy ranking and similar document cross searching.

It's much less expensive than other document management and retrieval systems and my opinion is that it's as good as any of them. The retail price is $29, which is about a tenth or less of the cost of others I've seen with little more to offer.

Some offices still keep that old relic typewriter just to do block forms that don't come in programs such as Legal Solutions Plus, etc. Now they can finally be donated to your favorite charity.

Caere's Logical Form Recognition ("LFR") OmniForm 4.0.1 offers a way to convert any kind of paper form to electronic form. This ingenious operation lets you scan any kind of form and then fill it out on the screen by using "tab and type" as in standard forms seen in judicial council forms programs. If your use is to simply scan a form for "tab and fill," the first option, "scan a form or image file," is pressed. The result is the exact copy described.

This LFR permits the use of any kind of form, insurance, medical, legal, or any other type, regardless of color, style or format. You can even create a form from scratch.

There's no need to proof read, correct or alter anything. Just scan, tab and fill. The scanned image follows the scanned paper just like a copier. What appears on your monitor is an exact reproduction of the document scanned. After you've tabbed and filled, the completed form from your printer is even more perfect that anything your typewriter could do.

Generic document management.

If $29 is too rich for your ultra-conservative style, there are other systems for document management that come with the territory. There's no reason for any lawyer to use the archaic stuff and seek "come out wherever you are" means of storing and finding your crucial papers.

There are a variety of methods both electronically and manually to store and retrieve documents whether categorized under clients or preferred headings. The method of choice is electronic.

While the filing is done according to case and client, a general index is set up for reference to any document in your office. If all documents related to any particular case are downloaded into separately stored disks such as floppies or zip disks, the general index would still refer to them, identifying their respective cases or clients. This would obviate the need to keep all documents on your hard drive.

An elephant, they say, never forgets. If true, it would be for a very good reason. An elephant never forgets because he has so little to remember.

You are a lawyer. Unlike an elephant you've got lots of things to remember. Your reputation, your practice, in fact, your whole life depends on your remembering things.

That's not just a whole big bundle heaped on your head, that's impossible. No human memory is so competent that it can remember each and every detail impressed upon a law practice, even a new one. You may believe yours is but it's not.

If you try proving your memory is so omnipotent that it needs no help, you won't just be proven wrong, you'll be in serious trouble. Don't be a hero. Respect your clients, your practice and yourself enough to adopt an organized management plan right now.

Being in an executive office complex offers you a giant step towards tidying your office routine. Many of the things done for you by your suite management would otherwise occupy a great deal of your management time and processes.

Your executive suite has built-in reception and telephone answering services, an adequate library, a photocopy facility, a conference room and even a coffee and snack hideaway. That's a start. Preparation for your new law practice includes a well thought-out plan for managing that practice.

Search and find; mini-retrieval systems.

As you've already seen, the computer can find and correct words, sort them, and rearrange them in any fashion desired. It can also find anything stored anywhere on your hard drives and bring it to your attention for use within a matter of seconds.

If cost is no object to you, there are gobs of fancy search and retrieval programs, some of which have been reviewed elsewhere in this text. What they will do for you consistent with their lofty prices I have yet to discover.

If you've selected WordPerfect as your word processor, you have an efficient file finding function found under the "Insert" bar "file" button. Clicking on this will take you to any file on your computer. New for the millennium is WordPerfect "Law Office 2000." Perhaps this new program will have even more useful features especially for us.

Taking best advantage of this feature, you should file your documents under folders that best describe the filing order. This can be done under a "Clients" folder or better yet cross-filed under type as well as client.

This can also be accomplished with Word by clicking on "file" and then on "open." You can then select any drive or folder on your computer and view all files in each. Retrieval under this method is meant for editing but the file may instead simply be printed out to a hard copy.

Whichever file finding method you choose, you'd need a scanner to scan the document. Then each document scanned should be placed in the appropriate folder. If none of the existing folders suit the purpose, you may make new folders by selecting "New" under the file button located at the top of your word processor.

A folder appears called "folder." Your computer data consists of files, the documents or other material prepared for storage in your hard drive, and folders, the means of grouping those files in a methodical manner. You'd need a folder for each group of documents, such as for each client and for the category into which each such document belongs.

Click the right button (left if you're left-handed) and then select "rename." Name the folder appropriately. You can create and name folders with whatever heading you choose for ease in locating and retrieving documents.

Windows includes a simplified "Find" function to locate documents whose titles you've forgotten. See this on the start bar. It's a cumbersome operation but when all else fails it can possibly save the day.

Touch "Find" on the Start bar and select files and folders. When the Find window appears, type in any phrase specific to the document sought. The more exclusive that phrase is to that document, the less selections would need to be culled.

Chances are that however specific your phrase to the document sought may be, you will be indexed to a variety of files which appear to be wholly irrelevant. This is one of the drawbacks of the "Find" feature of Windows. But then you paid nothing extra for it anyway and the inconvenience is slight.

The ultimate result is finding the particular document sought. By double clicking on that file identification, the needed document appears on your word processor. You can review it, edit it, print it, delete it or do whatever you wish with it. By all means, rename it with a title you will remember. I can't see resorting to this when programs like PageKeeper are available for as little as $29.

Programs such as Microsoft "Works," and several of the programs under Microsoft Office also have search and find methods.

I can't see struggling to manage and retrieve documents when a program to do all this automatically is available for $29.99 by Caere in its PageKeeper 3.0.

§ 9:3 Computerized legal forms

Virtually all legal forms now on computer.

Most every form needed for normal law practice is now available on computer programs. Some are provided on the usual computer floppy disks; others, more voluminous, need the higher capacity of CD-ROM disks. Whatever the form, the convenience and relative low cost of computerized forms makes the conventional paper form prehistoric.

The latest release of Legal Solutions Plus provides bankruptcy forms. New features include the ability to create common creditors' list, citations statute list. Legal Solutions' new "context sensitive" help screen is reportedly a first in computerized forms. What is unique about this feature is the attorney's option to create customized help. You can write in special notes which will attach to the help screen for reference to either L.S. help line, or your later research.

L.S. also offers an Immigration package. The bankruptcy package remains at $350. The entire Judicial Council set now sells for about $500. The set includes all civil, family law, probate and juvenile law. Not a bad price when you consider it practically covers the range of your practice. Call L.S. about special pricing.

West Group provides CD-ROM versions of two comprehensive and well-regarded legal form publications: Am Jur Legal Forms 2d on LawDesk and Am Jur Pleading and Practice Forms on LawDesk. Call 1-800-328-4880 for more information.

Modern computer technology has virtually extinguished the need for a paper form file. Methods for developing and maintaining pleading and other form files as efficient as they may have been in past years would now be considered unwieldy and superfluous.

Every form needed for the practice of law in most states can now be generated with a few key strokes of your computer. Legal Solutions, now published by West Group, has produced all of the California Judicial Council forms, supplied on a series of floppies for simple downloading into your computer.

Once that's done, it's simpler to call up and complete one of the forms than you can imagine. Just summon the form your need from the forms list, get the form you want and just fill in the blanks.

All of this takes no more time than to read the above two paragraphs. Actually, if you use the preprinted form, the time taken to load it into the typewriter, then to flip the carriage from space to space, line to line, is far greater than the zip, zip of pressing the tab key of your computer.

What about mistakes and typos? Using white-out or correctable type is O.K. but not invisible. Making corrections on your computer shows nothing. Moreover, the time to make the correction is not even worth thinking about.

I got rid of my typewriters years ago. The last remaining Selectric was kept only for those few forms then not computerized and envelope addressing. Now that OmniForm 4.0 is here and all kinds of envelope addressing programs abound, why do you need another dust catcher?

Then, when you print the form on your Hewlett-Packard LaserJet printer, the form is precisely the same, identical, to the regularly printed Judicial Council form, with the proper numbers and other identification. You even print on both sides just like the forms you buy.

The fonts used by Legal Solutions are the same fonts as used in the regular forms. You cannot tell the difference. There is none.

Legal Solutions Plus (Version 2.5) has a new and improved menu system, a bit easier to use than the former menu. One of the complaints I had with the older program was the enormous amount of space consumed on the hard drive. The new Legal Solutions program uses only a fraction of that space.

Don't ask me how that is done. It's not through economy of fewer forms. Quite the opposite. More forms are included than ever before. Still, by some technological magic, this was accomplished by economy of space consumption only. Whew! The things they do with electrons.

Certain forms related but collateral to law practice, such as insurance and real estate forms, are available free of charge from various banks and title companies. A few phone calls will yield gobs of great material, most of which you'll find extremely useful in your practice. Don't put this off. No need to groan if the forms are the "tab and fill" variety. Right?

CD-ROM research programs, like the "LawDesk," or "Authority," will provide all pleading material to further simplify your practice management.

Document storage and indexing on CD-ROM.

These concentrated 5" metal disks hold about 680MB of data. A CD-RW drive can quickly store all of your case and client documents on CD-ROM. Unless your practice is enormous, it will take very few disks to store everything in your office. Once stored, indexing can be easy.

For forms not in electronic format, Caere Corporation's OmniPage Pro, version 10.0, offers a new engine and other enhancements to improve this venerable OCR product. An important feature in 10.0 is a new recognition engine to provide a much higher level of accuracy. I tried some very complex documents and was surprised at the result. No errors. We can't always expect 100% perfection, but it's safe to predict an end to endless spell checks.

§ 9:4 Legal research on CD-ROM

These days CD-ROM drives are standard equipment on virtually all computers. So is the floppy drive though I don't know for how much longer.

An attempt was made to market a floppy drive with 1.5MB storage space but it hasn't really gone over. It's not a bad device but for whatever reason the ZIP drive seems to be pushing it off the road.

Things are moving along so fast now that we can see the trail's end for the CD-ROM. Sooner than you think, the DVD drive will overtake the CD-ROM. So many programs even now occupy more space than CD's can accommodate.

Microsoft's new Office 2000 Premium is loaded through four CD's. Programs have gotten so bulky that CD's are getting too cumbersome, let alone the floppy.

Treatises such as the famous Bernard Witkin sets on California law and practice have been included in West Group's "LawDesk," along with all of the California Supreme Court and appellate cases as far back as you'd want to search.

Dozens of other files will soon join those sets, still encompassed on that tiny disk. You'll find similar works recorded in various formats for your state.

What has not yet been converted from the printed publications is no doubt being converted now, or will be by the time you read this book. This technique is not just a space saver, although miles of bookshelf space have been freed thereby.

Its development and usefulness have just begun. I wish I were your age, if for no other reason than to see the electronic marvels you'll be seeing and using.

CD-ROM means "compact disk read only memory." Tons of material are contained in that little 5" disk. The newer DVD disk holds many times more. Look for those multiple CD disks being replaced with a single DVD disk in the very near future.

The Matthew Bender Search Master that contained all of the California Pleading and Practice set is now called "Authority." In essence, it retains the general flavor of the old Search Master but is greatly enhanced and augmented by many more applications.

The complete Practice and Procedure forms set, Jury Instructions, BAJI and CALJIC, Legal forms, California Codes, California cases, both Supreme Court and appellate, Points and Authorities, Wills and Trusts, Corporation Law, plus many, many other sets are all contained in that little disk.

The CD-ROM or DVD are available in either internal or external models. If internal, it would occupy one of those "drive bays" along with your floppy drives and tape drive, described previously.

If you select an external drive, it would fit somewhere along side or on top of your computer. As with other peripherals, the drive may be operated through your parallel port or USB. The USB is preferable.

Computers normally are outfitted with eight slots for cards and five bays for various drives. If you prefer an internal CD, mount it in one of the computer bays. You may, or may not, need a card installation as well.

The CD-ROM or DVD must also have a software program that will instruct your computer on the reader's existence, as well as the method of interfacing. That program, as with all programs, will be menu-driven and easy to install.

Once installed, your CD or DVD will be identified as an additional "drive" in your computer. As you recall, your floppy drive is "drive A." Your hard drives start with "drive C" and continue through the alphabet depending on how many drives or partitions you have.

Your CD or DVD drive would be identified as the letter following your last hard drive. If you have one hard drive, that letter would be "C" and the CD drive would be "D." The drive letter assignments are automatically done by Windows.

If your computer was packaged with everything you need installed, none of the above should interest you except academically.

Research on CD-ROM is in many ways simpler than using the usual library procedures. After starting the program, you will be asked for your search information. This can be given as a direct case or statute citation, just as you would need to go to the cases or statute books.

If you don't know the citation, you can type words and phrases as you would need in a library search. There are prescribed easy to learn methods for doing this in the program instructions.

The name of a plaintiff or defendant may be enough to find your case. Try that one in your library! If you know the judge's name, you can access all cases decided by him or her. That won't be as many as you may think. The case listings are limited to appellate decisions.

You can also access all cases in which a particular attorney was involved. You can type his or her name, and each such case will appear. If the first case is not what you seek, you can order up the next and the next, until your case appears. There won't be that many.

There are many other methods for finding what you want with CD-ROM that you cannot use in a conventional library. What's more, all of this is done without ever leaving your desk and chair. Watch your beam and waistline!

Word 2000 offers a "time-out" provision which can be set for your choice of time intervals. A bell rings and a message appears, "You've been working for 30 minutes (or whatever)." Another message advises, "Take a breather."

There are, of course, some limitations to CD-ROM. At the moment, cases do not cover all the years that you'll find in a full-scale library. However, if the case you want is of moment, it will be cited throughout the years your CD-ROM program covers.

The big advantage in having as many programs as possible, all on one disk, is the convenience of inter-access to cited authorities. For instance, after bringing up your selected case, you note another case cited, you can access that cited case by simply tabbing over to the cite and pressing return. You are now in the cited case. The same can be done with statutes or any other cite within a case.

CD-ROM research lets you "copy and paste" any part of a form or case decision into your brief. While drafting a brief on your computer, you will find the need to cite a case or statute. Access the CD-ROM disk containing your state's cases and statutes. There you find the relevant citation.

You then use the menu driven method of marking the portions of the relevant cases and statutes for transfer to your brief. In seconds, those cited parts are written to your brief.

Consider also the verity of your transcription. When copying the cited portion from a casebook, there is always the possibility of some transposition or other error. When you invoke the material directly from CD-ROM, it is copied letter for letter. No mistake is possible, unless it is in the original transfer to CD-ROM. That is extremely unlikely if you are using products of leading publishers.

Your CD-ROM disks will also provide all of the documents for corporations you'll form. It will contain your "buy and sell" contracts, your Uniform Commercial Code filings and publications, partnership formations and dissolutions, and all other business-type or commercial documentations.

They are all there, waiting for you to press the few chosen keys. All of this is at your finger tips. You never have to leave your desk. Instead of trotting up to your library, finding the right books, lugging them down to your office and thumbing through page after page, you simply type in the cites and there they are.

Finding the cases and statutes is not just easier, it's more complete and more reliable. Those "words and phrases," or encyclopedias we've been taught to use at law school, are all part of the CD-ROM method. But, you don't need to go from book to book. The computer does all of that for you.

All of the above may be done using Westlaw or Lexis but you pay for this service while you're daydreaming or thinking of what you will type next. The same is true of cutting and pasting. The clock is ticking all the while.

The on-line method is much more comprehensive but costlier. Later when your practice merits the added expense, one of these fine on-line services would be a very valuable addition to your research methods.

Don't over rely on any canned legal form.

Keep in mind that prepared documents are just "canned" drafts, whether you get them from files, books or drafting services. There is, as always, a danger in placing too much reliance upon such preparations, whether from your own files or from the form books.

Used properly, such material can be a valuable tool. In fact, in the competitive legal world, it is a must. Drafts prepared by such reliable publishers as those described above can be of inestimable aid. Such firms keep well abreast of legal changes.

Issues resolved in cases that may have escaped your attention are incorporated in the material sent to you regularly under your subscriptions. Legislative changes are incorporated in those prepared documents that you would not have thought to research. Using such material can be an assurance that your work will not contain a legal misstep.

Start with the prepared draft and then take it in whatever direction that your particular use requires. No form or prepared draft, however derived, can precisely serve your special purpose.

An unmistakable earmark of a "canned" form is "boilerplate." Added to this is the lawyer's common syndrome of computer diarrhea. This drives the infected lawyer to write like Mickey Spillane under a publishing deadline.

Drafting on the computer provides dozens of ways to edit your work. You can delete words, sentences, and even whole paragraphs, as you need to sharpen up your work. Trying to do that with a typewriter, dictating machine, or yellow tablet can put you in a bad frame of mind.

Adding words, phrases, sentences or whole paragraphs is as easy as thinking of doing it. Changing positions of words, sentences, phrases or whole paragraphs is just a flick of your mouse. Move things around, rearrange, scramble or anything you want is right there for you.

The term "cut and paste" is just click, click. Cutting and pasting from multiple typed, hard copy drafts is a whole different can of peanuts. The former is done without even thinking. The latter can be a script for a horror movie.

Drafting interrogatories, notices to produce, requests for admissions, and outlines for deposition examinations are all tailor-made for your computer and the many discovery forms programs available. If you prepare these documents in the same file, you can interpose materials from, say, interrogatories to requests for admissions or depositions.

Using the "find" feature of Word or WordPerfect, you can seek components of any particular pattern of questions from or to alternate documents. This can be done by either searching for particular question numbers, by words used, or by asterisks placed strategically next to sensitive questions.

§ 9:5 Purchase of law books

As with other matters, analyze your needs before you plunge ahead with law book purchases. Using a computer will narrow your need for hard copy books. If you still insist you can live without a computer, there are some books you should strongly consider.

For Californians, indispensable tools are the Witkin practice book published by West Group. There isn't a better catalyst to shift your mind from nebulous legal theories to some earthbound, practical causes of action.

Most such sets are available on the "never, never" plan, and you really will find them worth their cost. You'll find many of your "unusual" case fact situations in the text material and case citations in Witkin, for example.

If your executive suite includes such sets in the library, you could do without your own private set. But some books are used so often that you may find the particular volume that you need missing from the shelf more often than not.

You will eventually (sooner than you think) be getting most, if not all, of these essential books and sets included as software for your computer. So, I wouldn't be too anxious to become obligated for long-term book debts.

You won't believe this, but your law school case and text books can be surprisingly useful as research aids in your practice. There will be times when no other source will be better to get you on the right path, especially when you are way out in left field on a problem. When you are faced with a strange fact situation, don't panic. Hearken back to your classroom lectures and class material.

I know you've been told so often that there is no relationship between law school and law practice. This is simply not true. That nonsense must have been dreamed up by some borderline student who learned about cases from canned briefs.

If you did your homework and read and briefed all of the assigned cases, you will be well prepared for most of those "strange" situations. You will be amazed, over and over again, at the similarity of the matters you will be handling to cases that you studied in school.

Sure, the law changes, and you always have your work cut out for you as a lawyer, but many of the essences remain intact. You'll find so many of your clients' problems reminiscent of your text book case to justify a review of those old casebooks. So, don't discard your schoolbooks. Place them all on a prominent shelf in your office library. They'll look good there anyway.

Litigation support.

Litigation support is a valuable tool for the trial attorney. We'll be looking at some programs which offer a great deal of help in this regard, but true litigation support programs are a bit too sophisticated for lawyers not dedicated to litigation.

More to the point, such programs would not be cost productive unless the user is engaged in multiple and very heavyweight actions.

One such program that I have briefly viewed is called "Evidence Master, A Litigation Management and Support Program." This is produced by San Francisco Legal Systems, and was coauthored by Chris Visher.

This program appears to be quite comprehensive, and yet is not overpriced when compared with similar works. Still, even at a bargain, this program is certainly not cheap. If this kind of program interests you, you might give Mr. Visher a call.

In addition to the usual need to retrieve documents, Evidence Master will facilitate making a record of all documents from each side in the file; cross-reference your case records; help to analyze the strengths and weaknesses of your case; index exhibits; set up a work product index; provide a schedule and coordinate case work; and much more.

Litigation support information is given limited treatment in this book. Until the scope of your trial practice is so large that manual retrieval is no longer practical, I would not advise a full-fledged retrieval program.

This is not just because of the high cost of such programs. More forbidding is the time and effort needed to learn to use it. I'd recommend some index functions such as the client list and business list in Microsoft Works or in Excel. A bit of ingenuity can change them into very operational selection indexing.

§ 9:6 On-line research

There are, at this writing, two major computer "on-line" research operations.

Westlaw offers a comprehensive, word-searchable legal research service, as does Lexis. Either of these fine on-line services will serve you as well as the most complete library. They're easier to use as well.

The problem generally with on-line services is mainly the cost. Unless your office is brimming over with cases, these are probably too rich for your budget. They both require substantial monthly subscription fees plus a use cost that ticks away by the minute.

These on-line services offer access to the full text of hundreds of thousands of state and federal cases and administrative decisions, and to the thousands of annotations in West Group's American Law Reports (ALR). Westlaw also contains the KeyCite case validation service, which provides title, year of decision, court, jurisdiction, official and parallel references (including topical looseleaf reporters), and prior and later history for requested citations.

Westlaw permits attorneys to begin their research by first consulting such familiar research tools as encyclopedias, textbooks, digests, and the like, to identify at least one case on or close to the point being researched. The citation to a single case thus discovered is all that is needed to begin a research session.

Once in Westlaw, the researcher is dealing with familiar research materials—cases, annotations and citators, all interconnected by the common element of a citation.

In a less expensive manner, your more immediate needs in legal research can probably be satisfied by using your CD-ROM. Each disk holds as much as 680MB of case and other research materials.

§ 9:7 A recommended filing system

A very common hazard is the misfiling of documents, particularly where there are several matters being handled for the same client. Even when you start doing well enough to hire some help, you should still continue to do your own filing.

A single misfiled paper can be the source of great embarrassment at trial. You will not only be without the paper you need, but you will waste much time, both yours and the court's, looking for the document that you are positive is there, but isn't.

As the seconds tick off and become minutes, your panic

increases. The judge is glaring at you with increasing ominousness, and the opposition counsel's smirks are becoming more and more obnoxious.

The upshot of it all is a lesson teaching you the value of preciseness in filing. Learn it now, and spare yourself the agony of learning it the hard way.

Keep an envelope in each file for the storing of small notes and phone messages. There is no better way of convincing the court that a certain agreement was reached with opposing counsel during a phone conversation than to attach the very phone message to your declaration.

All of your chicken scratches accumulated during the case that have any bearing on the matter, should be slipped into that envelope. Other small items, such as check stubs, receipts, and other papers too small to fit on the file clasps, can also go into the envelope. The envelope can then be hole-punched and affixed to the file clasps.

Another way of handling these small items is to staple or scotch tape them to larger sheets of paper, and then to hole punch and clasp them in the files. But this gets to be a cumbersome job, particularly where there are lots of such little pieces and bits.

The journals print case notes from current cases, summarizing the holdings. Add any of these articles related to the case to your file. You never know how these bits and pieces may somehow fit into your position.

Every document received in your office should be date stamped. All letters, pleadings, and papers of all kinds should indicate the date upon which each was received. There will be more of office routine and administration in later pages.

A separate file for each case, not just for each client.

All material relevant to each particular matter should be kept separated from each other matter handled for each client. A common error among lawyers is the grouping of all matters within a single file designation under the client's name. Logic should warn that such a practice must ultimately lead to gross confusion, as the number of diverse cases arises with regard to certain clients.

Although you will have some clients involved in just one matter, others will have case after case. There is no way of knowing which of your new clients you will be seeing again nor how involved their matters may become.

Each file that you set up for a new client must be prepared as though a landmark case. Admittedly, a single sheet of yellow paper, inscribed with a name, phone number, address, a few scribbles of facts, may seem superfluous standing all alone in a big case file. Don't be surprised at how often such fragments blow up to huge proportions.

All documents, notes, correspondence, and any material with reference to the matter which you are handling for each of your clients must be placed in a sturdy file folder and entitled by the case name. This is your case file.

There are many different styles of file folders. Some having divisions for various categories. Some come with compartments for notes and paper scraps. Some are large, some small, some thin, some bulky, some very expensive, and some cost only a few cents each. Each has its own range of usefulness and its inherent limitations.

I suggest that you start with the least expensive type so that you will be less reluctant to use a separate one for each little matter at the start of your practice. Besides, you will need a large quantity of folders right away, so price will probably be an issue.

Check with some of the cut-rate office supply houses. Some of them quite often have a quantity on hand of a certain kind of folder obtained from a manufacturer as an "overrun." After termination of an order by a large user, the supplier is often left with a surplus quantity too small for a stock item, and yet large enough to interest one of these discount house operators.

It's also a good idea to check these places out for other of your office supply needs. Be careful, though, since all items there may not be bargains. Spend some time shopping the regular supply stores first so you will know something of prices.

It isn't necessary that your files be uniform, either in style or bulk, so the fact that an "overrun" cannot be reordered is no disadvantage. Even though there is a trend by many courts toward letter-sized documents, your file folders should all be legal size. This will not only accommodate the leftovers from legal size, but will handle more bulk and keep the letter-sized papers more tidy.

There are almost as many kinds of systems for filing as there are lawyers. Each lawyer you meet will enthusiastically tout his or her particular system. Since I have your attention first, I'll tout mine.

Get a couple of 4 drawer legal sized steel cabinets even though most required court forms are now letter sized. They're inexpensive if you're not too fussy. Place the file folders in the cabinet in numerical order, not alphabetical order.

You will also need a card file for small index cards. You can start with something like a recipe card file. You will later need a more elaborate system like the Rolodex index.

Each file number will have a corresponding number on a card, and each card will be filed alphabetically. Thus, when you wish to get a file from the cabinet, you will first need to check the number by looking up the client's index card.

You won't need to bother going through this routine at first. You will be very familiar with each file number until your case load gets really big.

In addition to the number and client's name, each index card will also show the client's address, phone number, court case number, opposing attorney's phone number, brief case description, and other information valuable to have handy.

You'll need a separate index card for each separate matter handled for each client. Thus, you will have several cards for certain clients. This is preferred for several reasons.

First, you can keep the index file locked up in a desk drawer. Without an index, no one can tell whose file is whose unless they want to go through each and every folder. You can also lock the cabinets.

This becomes a nuisance as your practice grows and so do your filing cabinets. Your index case will always remain relatively small and easy to lock away.

Security is not the only advantage to the numerical system. There will always be a positive check for missing folders. You will never discard a number upon closing a case file because you will reuse the number for a new matter.

There will never be a gap in the numerical sequence. At the end of each day, when all files have been returned to the cabinet, there should once again be an absolute unbroken sequence.

No matter how strictly you alphabetize your folders, you can never be sure a folder isn't missing. You should have no concern for a missing alphabetical index card since no reason exists for ever removing any of them.

Use a locking storage box for index cards of the type that make cards difficult to remove. Start with the number 100. Number about 200 cards so that you will be ready for a reasonable starting volume of case files.

§ 9:8 How to set up your case file folders

To set up the folder, place all pleading and other court documents on the right. Place all correspondence and "evidence" type material on the left. The first item on the left will be your "Attorney/Client Contract."

In this document will be contained all of the provisions of your agreement with the client. It will include your retainer amount, hourly fee, and the particulars of the matter involved. It is mandatory that your client sign the document before you begin service of any kind. In many states, as in California, this is a legal requirement.

The next document on the left will be the "Attorney Interview" sheet. On this paper will be scribbled all of the facts of the case which the client told you during your first interview.

This happens after you have received the retainer and your client has signed the agreement. From this sheet, you should have enough information to construct the complaint, answer, or such other pleading as the matter requires.

The first document on the right side will be the complaint or answer depending upon whether your client is the plaintiff or defendant. Then, in succeeding chronological order, all court papers related to that case, such as motions, orders, stipulations, applications, summons, etc., face up.

The most recent document will face you as you open the file, looking at either side. On the left, you will see the most recent correspondence. A glance at the right side should tell you what stage the case is in with regard to court procedures.

Court documents may be reviewed from back to front in order of filing. The most recent document will face you as you open the folder.

If the case becomes voluminous, you will need two, three, or even four or more folders. All succeeding folders dealing with the same case will bear the same file number with sub "A," "B," "C," etc.

Although others may argue for other systems, I consider this one the best, especially for a solo practitioner. It's simple, neat, and positive. The sequence of filing, as well as the fact of documents inclusions, are vital. This is the reason that you must do this monotonous job yourself.

When a matter terminates, you simply remove the papers from the numbered folder, place them in an alphabetically identified folder of the cheapest kind, and place it alphabetically in the dead file.

No matter how extensive your practice becomes, you will use cheap folders for your dead files. The chances of repeated handling of a dead file are unlikely.

The matter then becomes ended, and you will most likely only resort to that material for reference to a pleading form or some such thing. You need good quality folders only for your active files to withstand constant handling. Any appreciable amount of handling will wear through a poor quality folder.

I won't mention the other unlikely event, a client's later claim or malpractice action. Forget it. That won't happen to you. You're learning all of the good methods of avoiding such icky things.

If you're not computering, which of course you are, you must also have a court calendar book. This is a date book containing all of your court appointments, deposition schedules, client conferences, luncheons, etc. The most practical way to keep your calendar is to have it as an integral part of your daily diary. Such a combination is available in various forms and at a variety of styles and prices. This book is your bible.

You must be meticulous in its upkeep. You will have the impact of this admonition fall down upon your head and come home like thunder if you ever miss a court date because you failed to inscribe the date in your calendar.

Keep a separate calendar for your "statute of limitations" references. Keep this separate and apart from the daily calendar. This will be another date book where you will note all dates with regard to each of your cases that have any relationship to the termination of a legal right.

For instance, a client consults you on a personal injury automobile accident. Note the date of the accident in your statute book. Make a corresponding entry on the date when the right of action will lapse. This is vital information.

The client's right to pursue a remedy for personal injury expires after that crucial statutory date. Make a notation about ninety days prior to the expiration date to remind you of the expiration. Take steps to file the complaint, with further reminders along the way.

If, for whatever reason, you elect to pass on the case, send an immediate letter to the client explaining your election and advising to seek representation elsewhere mindful of the statute date. Even though your options were explained during the interview, you could still be held responsible for failure to timely file.

The term "client" is appropriate despite your repeated disclaimer during the interview that the consultation is only to decide whether you will or won't take the case. The most casual discussion about an actionable matter can, under many jurisdictions, create a "client/attorney" relationship whatever you may have decided.

The interim period prior to filing is to facilitate negotiations for settlement among other things. You are more likely to get a prompt and possibly better settlement with an insurance adjuster than with an opposing attorney.

Usually, as soon as you have filed and served a complaint, the matter will pass from the adjuster's hands to a defense lawyer. An unfortunate, but not unusual, fact of life is that some defense attorneys are not amenable to dispose of cases. Could this be an economic rather than a professional state of mind?

Although there is a good reason for delaying the complaint, the delay could extend into the danger zone. There are some defaults that can be cured by resort to the court's compassion. Unfortunately, in most states, a filing beyond the statute date is a default beyond the court's compassion.

If you are a 'fraidy cat, a member of which society I must admit to being, you will make several notations throughout the year. My tender timidity says you can't have too many reminders to keep you from disaster.

As you know, failure to take timely legal procedural steps could subject you to malpractice charges. Once a client dumps problems on your desk, many legal duties are dumped with them.

Failure to timely bring a matter to trial, failure to amend a complaint as ordered, failure to respond to discovery, failure to do this, or failure to do that, can lead to serious embarrassment for you. As if losing a client isn't enough, being thrust into a malpractice suit is the ultimate indignity. So the most compounded prophylaxis may be well worth whatever bit of extra trouble it might be.

All of the foregoing routines will be simplified, as well as expedited, with your computer. All of your calendaring needs can be adequately handled in the Calendar accessory to Microsoft's Works. You can install as many kinds of calendars in this program as you need.

Your "pop-up" calendar reminder can be orchestrated to remind you of any important dates, crucial or otherwise. So in addition to the ease of entry and maintenance, you have an additional reliable system to guard you against failure.

Most billing programs have some form of docket control that will include a calendaring system. It is not so important that you choose one or another program to do any of these important jobs as it is to religiously use them. The best choice in programs will be woefully inadequate if you install them and expect them to enter data by themselves.

Both Word and WordPerfect have adjunct indexing programs for entering all information concerning all of your clients, cases, documents, correspondence and notes. To call up a category, you only need to type the first two or three letters of any key, and the information you seek appears on screen. This applies to statute dates as well as to case issues, documents or anything else you care to review.

The foregoing is not intended to cover every detail involved in setting up your practice management. Other suggestions are given in other chapters on systematizing your practice as well as your office. Do read each chapter and section of this book carefully. After you have digested everything offered, you should have a good picture of what you must do.

Now that you've seen just a bit of the complications of the physical, manual method of office and practice management, don't you agree that the push-button means of computer management is better? Get a computer and get your practice started right.

I don't advise spending money freely for new lawyers. Certain things are so cost-productive that doing without them is more costly than buying them. A computer heads that list. The best computers cost about $2000. Suitable machines, though not the best, range from $300 to $600. If you can't go for better, get the cheapest but get one.

Chapter 10

How You'll Get Things Done

§ 10:1 Generally

There's more than economy to be gained by doing everything yourself in the first phases of your practice. There's also a learning process that you'll find invaluable as your practice progresses. Knowing enough about every part of your practice to do it yourself can produce more dividends later on than the cash you save.

Keep in mind the first order of business is to learn all you can about operating your office as well as your practice. This means learning from the ground up. A hands-on computer use is the best way to learn and understand not just computer operation but the functions of all of the programs designed to run your office and practice.

Whatever your ultimate idea may be about office help, you should know all there is to know about the whats and whys of your accounting and billing system, the legal research methods and all other parts that make your office and practice run. This would be so whether you operate manually or by computer.

A successful restaurateur told me that his success was largely due to being personally able to do every job necessary in his business. He could cook, wait tables, cashier, take reservations, tend bar, janitor, wash pots, pans and dishes, park cars, or do anything else that any emergency required.

These abilities insulated him from the threat of any last minute help "walkouts." If any of his employees didn't appear on a busy Saturday night, he would don the proper garb and perform those duties. He was confident he could do as well or better than the absent employee. He did not wait to acquire these capabilities until after becoming successful. He learned how to do all of these things during the training stages of his trade.

During the first days of your solo law practice, you can take the time to apply this same principle.

Don't hire anything to be done that you can do yourself until your practice demands that your time be spent on other things.

Happily, You can't afford such hired help anyway. So enjoy the bonus received in this training.

§ 10:2 Don't be too proud to use the keyboard!

Your good sense should overcome ego. Be content with the smallest available office. You won't need a secretary at first, even if you're all thumbs at your computer keyboard.

All needed secretarial work can be adequately done by you. If you can type, you'll be way ahead of the game. Don't be too proud to sit in front of a computer. Be grateful that you can do it. If you can use a typewriter, however so stumbling, you can use a computer.

Even if you've never learned to type, you can do it easily. It takes very little training to get your work done on a keyboard light-years faster than any other method. For a thousand other reasons, don't slave any more than you must just to support another dependent.

I don't knock the value of a first class secretary. Such a one is pure gold in every sense of the word, not excluding the word "cost." For those who really need and can afford one, a qualified secretary can be truly a blessing.

But at your stage of the game, you neither need nor can afford one. Moreover, you don't know nearly enough to properly utilize a good secretary. I'll explain something about this special knowledge, but the facts alone won't be enough. This is another talent that needs more than book learning.

You'll be told that your time is worth $150 per hour (or whatever) and a secretary's time is worth only $50 per hour (or whatever). Thus, you cannot afford to sit and type at your rate when you can hire a secretary for so much less.

There are two basic flaws in this argument. First, your time is worth $150 per hour only when there is someone waiting to pay that much for your time. Second, any time that may, or may not, be misused by your typing is not so simply assessed.

If you do your own typing on a computer, you will, as they say, kill two birds with one stone. You will be composing as you type. Chances are, the first draft out of the computer will not be the final draft.

If a secretary does the typing, you will need to draft the material on a dictating machine. This requires some of your $150 time. If you dictate directly to the secretary, you will be using both your $150 rate and the secretary's $50 rate. You'll no doubt need to correct you secretary's first draft. There will be more $150 time, plus some more $50 time.

It sounds silly, but think about this. Run a time check on some typing costs both ways. If you are *reasonably* handy at typing, don't be surprised to find that it costs you less when you do your own typing than when it is done by a secretary. The only penalty will be injury to your ego and pride. No one is looking. The patsies playing big boss and secretary will secretly envy you.

I'll share an "open secret" with you. I've had a reasonably substantial practice over the past 30 years. For more years than not, I've managed rather well without a secretary.

I've also done the office routine work myself. This wasn't for economic reasons or to prove a point. Nor is it that I didn't have confidence in others to do the work properly. I could do all of that within so short a time period that it didn't prevent completion of my lawyering commitments.

During the first months of my practice development, I had time for those chores. Later, as my time constraints became more pressing, those routines became so automated that they didn't intrude significantly upon my legal duties.

I have the greatest respect for competent professionals in all disciplines. I had the great pleasure of working with some fine people as my employees during the years I spent in the business arena. My business, as most businesses, was diversified.

My office help was not organized simply to make my life more pleasurable. Each employee did work that circumstances prevented me from doing, not that I chose not to do. Those conditions are not true in my law office or in most small law offices.

There are times when professional help, including secretaries, would be warranted. I do not minimize the indispensable aid that such employees can provide in appropriate circumstances.

In a high volume practice of largely perfunctory duties, as in probate or debt collections, such routine would be an inefficient use of an attorney's time. In fact, skilled secretaries in such fields are usually more competent in the routine work than are most employer-lawyers. Those secretaries do that kind of work repeatedly and know all of the slips and slides.

In the varied environment of the solo's usual practice, that would not be the scenario. This is particularly so during the beginning years when you'll be touching virtually every area of the law.

It is difficult, perhaps even impossible, to establish any predictable routine. As a new attorney, you will be feeling your way around. You will be busy pumping out your duties through a pipeline directly to your hands from your brain.

There may come a time when you'll need such an employee. I've had secretaries during my law practice years. But, I'm not sure that it was "need" as much as a luxury for me. In candor, I can't recall a time when such employment was indispensable.

There's something else. I was not only adequately financed to see me through law school, but throughout my practice as well. I could afford to indulge myself with full time secretaries. My business bent wouldn't permit that.

One must analyze the circumstances of the individual practice so that an intelligent decision may be made as to such a need. The major problem is that too often such help is engaged merely from "want to believe," rather than belief.

As clumsy and painstaking as my typing is, I have proved logistically that my output through computer operation is more efficient and more economical than with a secretary. This is so even though my hourly rate is perhaps more than twice what yours is, or will be, during the first years. I know this is difficult to accept, but you will see the mechanics of computer operation and will be convinced before you finish this book.

The laborious task of combining your brain processes with your drafting chores just works better when you are doing your own complete composition. You will find the need to make changes in text on the spot.

It's much easier to see the text as it unfolds on the screen. The changes may be made instantaneously rather than waiting for a draft from a secretary. Besides, the creative brain of the productive lawyer is not necessarily a totally retentive one.

We can remember everything of major importance in each matter. But ideas on phrasing or on how to better express thoughts may slip away if we wait for a secretary's draft.

When we sit right at the computer, these ideas and thoughts zip right from our brains, through our fingers, to the keyboard. Lawyers who use secretaries don't fully appreciate that.

The trick is to see the original thought on the screen as it's being composed. Then, ideas for revisions, additions and improvements come flowing out. Later, it's just patchwork.

§ 10:3 Some problems with becoming an employer too soon

There may come a time when you find it too pressing to do it all, even with a computer. However, even with an excess of typing work to be done, you won't actually need a secretary.

You will merely contract with an outside secretarial service. Such services are offered wherever lawyers practice. There are dozens of such services to choose from in almost every town of any size.

Though secretarial services charge more than the usual hourly wage of a full- or part-time secretary, the cost will be only a fraction of the total expense of salaried help. Put that calculator down. There are other things to consider besides salary.

If you add one-third more to the salary cost of any employee, you'll be only at the threshold of the cost of hired help. Most small business employers, and this includes people having probably far more personnel experience than you, simply do not realize the true extent of the cost of employees. Neither do most employees.

Employees complain about their "take-home pay." They grouse about how much is taken out of their salary. Actually, *nothing is* taken out of their salary. Every penny that is not paid directly to the employee, plus the employer's contribution, is invested for his or her direct, if not immediate, benefit.

Income tax must be paid, whether by the employee or the employer. Medical benefits, unemployment insurance, workers' compensation, and, where applicable, pension and other retirement plans are all credited to the employee's account strictly for his or her own use and benefit.

If employees were paid 100% gross, they, not the employer, would be the losers. It would cost them far more for these extra benefits if they were purchased outside of employment. Moreover, most employees wouldn't have the foresight to allocate sufficient funds for those probable future needs.

Employers, on the other hand, bear the brutal brunt of those "deductions." Employers must contribute substantial sums to each employee's account for these withholding deductions. Ask almost any employee whether he or she would prefer to receive the full gross salary amount or suffer the deductions. They would not hesitate: "Give me the loot. Never mind any deductions."

Many people wanted to work for Bigg of California as "independent contractors." In those days, the rules on independent contractors were much more lax than they are today. But even then, there were dangers. Not for the employees. Penalties imposed upon employers by both state and federal agencies were even then very severe.

Employer/employee laws are made to protect the gullible employee. I've always felt the word "gullible" should be changed to "greedy." I've seen cases, both in business and as a lawyer, where it is the ex-employee who blows the whistle on the ex-employer who agreed to the "independent contractor" status of that employee.

Later on, when that employee could not get unemployment benefits, workers' compensation or medical benefits, or when income tax is due which the employee cannot pay, who complains?

The employee goes to the respective agency and complains. The complaint goes: "Hey, I didn't know about those things. The employer wanted things that way, not me. I'm entitled to all of those benefits." Think not? Think again.

Is there any doubt by the authorities as to who's telling the truth? Don't be silly. Employees never lie. Only employers lie. Who pays no matter which way the cookie crumbles? Guess who. And pays, and pays and pays.

Whether you are in one of those borderline positions between needing or not needing a secretary, it might be wise to discuss the philosophies involved in the employer/employee relationship.

Most states have special laws treating the respective rights and duties of employers and employees. The trend in most of such states has been toward steady enhancement of the rights of employees and diminution of the rights of employers.

In California, for example, the Labor Law requires that payment be made of all salary owed to the employee no later than seventy two hours after termination, even though the employee may have quit without notice and in the middle of some crucial duty.

It doesn't matter that the unfinished work resulted in losses to the employer many times the salary owed. Nor does it matter that some valuable property of the employer coincidentally left when the employee left. Nor does it even matter that the value of this property is much more than the wages owed.

The salary must be paid within that time period *without deduction or offset*. Even the employee's gross incompetence cannot relieve the employer of the legal requirement of paying the full amount of the agreed salary, including salary for the day of departure.

If there happens to be any kind of writing (a letter, memo or even a note on a scratch pad) which remotely suggests anything over and above that salary, such as vacations, sick pay, profit or pension plan entitlements, special working conditions, etc., you could be liable for such trimmings in addition to salary. Don't bet on winning that point, even though oral, if you're the employer.

An even worse problem could arise if there is any basis (or maybe even no basis) for a claim of employment duration. For instance, you may have indicated that the employment could be for a particular period of time if the employee "works out," or something of that nature. You could be stuck for that period of time, even though the employee didn't "work out" and is no longer working for you.

Paying a salary week after week, maybe month after month, long after the employee has been terminated, can be very distressing. Like alimony, it's painful to pay for what you used to have and can't get anymore.

That one is easy to see. More difficult to envision is the waste of your output in trying to make the secretary thing work. A skilled employer can most often predict the suitability of an employee candidate. The novice employer must pay through the nose for the lengthy, and unsatisfactory, trial period.

It's not only difficult for the amateur employer to know when the trial period should end, but even more difficult to end the employment relationship. Hiring is difficult, but firing can be, for some people, far, far, more difficult.

A common syndrome, disabling for a would-be employer is malaise. This is simply the inertia that consumes the employer when the realization of the employee's incompetence sets in. It's even worse than being unable to recognize the issue. It's simply the "I'll think about that tomorrow" sickness.

There's another side to that coin. The veteran employer can see the possibilities in a struggling employee. Sometimes what looks like a total washout can be due to some curable glitch in the setting or situation. The true executive can perhaps see that glitch and understand what to do about it. It's not so easy for the amateur employer.

Anyone can hire and fire but it takes a good executive to see usefulness in what appears to be a useless employee. That is not a thought that you should take into your employer portfolio.

Don't mistake what is being said here. Giving you some information about the employer's armory is not intended to make a competent employer out of you. While good employers are made, not born, it takes years to make one.

Unlike becoming a salesman or a solo lawyer, employers do not become good employers from reading books or attending lectures. And, unlike learning solo practice or salesmanship, being a competent employer ***does*** require a certain kind of personality.

Almost anyone can be taught to be a successful salesman or solo lawyer. Not just anyone can be taught to be a successful employer. Making money through employment is as much an art as running a business profitably.

I will predict that certain readers of this book will label me a fascistic, slave-driving tyrant after reading the following material. I can only repeat: *"He jests at scars that never felt a wound."*

There are many myths concerning the employee-employer relationship. One concerns the legendary employee "loyalty." Few battlefield lines are ever drawn more often than in the arena of "capital and labor." The minute you hire someone for any kind of duty, you could become a sort of "capitalist" in the eyes of your employee.

It doesn't matter that you may even be paying your employee more money than you are taking home. You are often viewed as the rich "boss," trying to squeeze more dollar juice out of the overworked help.

Multiply that disparity many times over if your office is located in one of the luxury areas. You are not just an ordinary businessperson. You are worse. You are a member of a certain kind of aristocracy. You are an attorney "plutocrat" and fair game.

Do these sound like words of sour grapes cynicism? Maybe so. But, this you can bank on. Personnel operation is unquestionably a profession in itself. I know that game very well. My company maintained a rather large and diversified employee roster.

This feeling is not always true, nor in every instance so. Although it's been more than thirty-five years since my business days, I still receive Christmas and birthday cards from some of my former employees. Sadly, many of my employees have passed on.

But, for the most part, employment is a business within a business and demands a special kind of ability. I had, and have, that ability, but I wasn't born with it. It took years of painful experience and many costly mistakes to hone it.

Because I am an expert on that subject, I could successfully operate in that field today. That does not mean that it would be my choice or my pleasure. Not the least of the reasons for being totally independent of personnel is the ecstatic joy of being relieved of those demands. I leave all of those little joys to my successors.

Not everyone has the training, talent, or temperament for dealing with hired help. Contrary to uninformed belief, it is at least as difficult to handle one employee as a hundred employees. In many ways, a single employee is even more of a challenge.

If your only employee is a secretary, that person will also be responsible for tasks that may, arguably, not fall within that work discipline. Secretaries do not enjoy filing work, as a general rule.

I haven't done research on documents being stashed in drawers, way, way back out of sight "until later." I can assure you that such a thing is not unusual.

Often, those sequestered items are not discovered until after the secretary has been replaced. Unhappily, that also may be after you have been in court with the missing paper being the subject of the hearing (your fault for not prechecking the file the day before).

Law offices, just like any other small business, are subject to "feast or famine" vacillations. Work does not come so evenly that tasks can be organized neatly and routinely. There will be days with seemingly nothing to do.

Then, there are those days when the ceiling caves in. It could be on those days when your secretary might rebel and say: "I'm not a horse. I only have two hands." Recollection of the days of end-to-end personal phone calls, and doing personal correspondence for lack of anything else to do, might be dimmed.

Don't expect words of gratitude for the days when you were paying for the secretary just "being there," or willingness to take what comes for the "common good." After all, this is your business. You're the one who's getting "rich."

These statements aren't made through expressions of cynicism. I make them objectively as part of your training process. The employer/employee relationship is not a tale for children. It's a hard business if one is to succeed hiring people.

§ 10:4 Hiring out standard support services

Yet, there will come a time when you will need the help of a secretary, just as you will need persons offering other kinds of services. Employment is not the manner by which a solo practitioner obtains such services. One can hire the needed labor, pay the freight, and then get back to the serene independence of solo practice. You have not bought the chickens, just the eggs.

Some of these services offer a base rate for a given threshold of words per month. Others charge by the hour, and still others will charge by the page. No matter how you slice it, the cost-per-page runs about the same.

My preference would be to slash through the complications to the price-per-page method. That's not only simpler to calculate but cheaper than an hourly rate. You know how much pages cost per job but integrating an hourly rate into each case folder takes more accounting brains than I've got.

The rates for secretaries are as varied across the country, and indeed within any large city, as any other market price. In the greater Los Angeles area, the average secretarial service will charge anywhere from \$1.50 to \$3 per page for double-spaced pleading pages and \$2.75 to \$4.75 per page for single-spaced pages, such as for correspondence, contracts, leases, or whatever. Don't expect those prices to hold when you read this.

Local secretaries charge from $20 to $40 per hour. It wasn't so long ago that lawyers charged no more than that amount. As a matter of fact, that's about what you may be charging other lawyers at first.

A doctor called a plumber to fix a minor plumbing leak. The charge was **$150** for less than an hour call. The doctor whistled. "My God," he complained, "that's over $150 an hour. I'm a physician and I don't charge that much!" The plumber took a couple of puffs on his pipe and said, "Yes, I know. When I was a doctor, I didn't charge that much either."

As bad as this seems, even a mild inflation, if it continues, may cause today's prices to seem bargain basement. But rest assured that inflation is a natural ingredient of our economy. Just pray that a coming inflation will not accompany an economic depression.

For those who haven't read of the German Republic economy following World War I, it took a bushel of marks to buy a loaf of bread. And unemployment was rampant. The fallout of that period was the spawning of Adolf Hitler.

Remember that while these prices may seem out of whack when compared with the cheapest hourly rate for a hired secretary, you are only paying for precisely what you need. You are not paying for a secretary's idle time, absenteeism, or other wastes. And unless your practice skyrockets in volume immediately, such a service will suffice for your needs and will be comparatively economical.

Now you can re-read the material on how to convince a prospective employer that your time-for-space offer is superior to employment. See how it is when the shoe is on the other foot?

There are some fringe benefits to the use of these secretarial services over any other form of secretarial help. This is not to say that I would endorse any such help at all, whether an outside service or otherwise. You should be able to handle all work to be done with your trusty computer. Those fringe benefits can be obtained from other sources without paying fees.

However, many of these services do excellent typing work. They also offer additional "know how" benefits regarding form and format of legal documents. Some of the crackerjack secretaries in those services have been known to give lawyers inferiority complexes.

The people who work in these services are mostly semi-retired legal secretaries who've spent many years involved with the court system and procedures. They can often save you some time and effort in pointing you in the right direction.

Of course, you are the lawyer and must instruct them on the content. Further, even this added advantage would not justify subscribing to such a service unless the particulars of your practice could absorb the costs with a reasonable ratio to profits.

Do not consider a "shared secretary."

Hiring a secretary on a shared basis is foolish at any time. The chances are that you will get a secretary who is just a notch above barely adequate. Any secretary with skills equal to those in the secretarial service would demand much more salary than a beginning attorney could pay.

If you're thinking of sharing a secretary so that you can get a talented one, forget it. The better secretaries normally wouldn't consider a shared basis. They know how difficult trying to please diverse temperaments can be.

It is extremely unlikely that you'd succeed in convincing a really talented secretary to work for your combine, no matter how strenuous your attempted persuasion. Most experienced secretaries have been through that gamut and don't need it to get employment.

Then, as indicated before, there are other problems with hiring your own secretary. Salary is only one of the costs. There are many other costs, some obvious and some not so obvious. There are payroll contributions, workers' compensation insurance (which is mandatory unless you can self-insure), health insurance, vacation pay, sick leave, buying lunches once in a while, and others.

There is also the cost of lost days when the secretary just can't make it into the office. Then there are the usual "add-ons," such as for holidays, special bonuses, the Christmas gift, etc.

The secretarial service gets paid only for what is done. No extras, no headaches. When the sky falls in and the work load overwhelms your office (which will periodically happen in every lawyer's office), your average hired secretary could panic with a "Gee, I've only got two hands." A secretarial service has as many "hands" as it takes to get the work out that day.

You'll be given details on how to get the most out of your secretarial service later on. So, if you simply cannot do without some secretarial help, you'll find it to be the best method for filling the gap. When, as and if you reach the point in your practice where money is no object and you just want the prestige of a human coffee serving machine, by all means get a "secretary." That is, if you can find a good secretary who'll "do coffee."

§ 10:5 Other ways to get things done

Another service that is available on an outside labor contract is the "Attorneys' Court Service." Again, you'll find a great number of such services to choose from in most cities. This service, if properly run, will provide a multitude of operations for you.

The present problem of inefficient help has diminished the value of this service, as has happened in many other industries. Still, for many, it's the "only game in town." If you are fortunate enough in your area to have an efficient attorneys' service available, it could be of inestimable aid in your practice.

For a monthly fee, this service will, on a daily basis, pick up your court documents to be filed, serve your process, circulate documents for multiple signatures, and, in some jurisdictions, obtain court dates, get certain court orders signed ex-parte, and perform a multitude of functions to save you time and energy.

For the new practitioner, there is more than a time savings. Such services make a wealth of information available to you that you would otherwise spin your wheels attempting to get.

Attorneys' services, like gas stations, earned reputations in past years for giving services "above and beyond" normal duties. Sure, they filed your court documents in daily court runs and served process. But their real value was in the "extra" services performed that literally kept your office running like a well-oiled machine.

There was little about the entire court system unknown to the service personnel. If you needed to know the particular procedure in some remote small town to avoid antagonizing the judge, you simply called the service. If you weren't sure about which form was appropriate for some little known procedure, you simply called the service.

Filing fees for virtually every area and/or state could be learned with a phone call to your service. That was the way it was. And, no doubt there are still some services, somewhere, which will provide those old fashioned "extra" services.

Like the "Shadow," the competent attorneys' service operator knew many things that lurked in the heart of the court system. If you wanted to know some of these secrets, you didn't need to be shy. You only had to ask.

One of your tasks in starting solo practice will be to search the field for a really competent attorneys' service. Don't just grab the first one that's offered. Many of them, you'll find, like the old gray mare, ain't what they used to be.

The old cliché that "you can't get decent help anymore" appears as appropriate in this field as in any other. This does not mean that the old values are not still alive and well. It only means that you must learn what the different services offer and set about to find the best you can get for your dollar.

The unkindest cut of all is that the quality and quantity of the services have eroded, while the prices have risen almost inversely proportionately.

What used to be a rather standard $20 or $25 per month fee, which included filings in courts for many miles around, has now become a $150 to $250 per month fee for service that only touches the nearby courts.

Unless you have searched for, and found, a competent service, you cannot even be certain that the document put out for filing will be filed on the day required. Pointing the finger at the service in court won't save you. It may even increase the sanctions.

Process service has likewise plummeted in reliability in many of the operations. In some cases, unless the defendant is sitting outside waiting for the server, and is willing to yell "Here I am," the report could be returned marked "unable to locate" or some such nonsense.

Nonetheless, before you turn to alternatives, I would suggest that you attempt to find a good service, which may mean trying a few on a temporary basis, in the hope that you might strike it lucky and find the kind that used to be, or at least find one with the ability to get things done correctly.

Happily, there are alternatives. Not as convenient or as efficient as was the case with the old attorneys' service system, but alternatives. And, as a booby prize, there will be a considerable savings to you, since you won't be paying a monthly fee.

Mail the document directly to the particular court or relevant branch.

Unless there is a statute problem, the mail can be just as effective as attorneys' services. However, you must be very certain to enclose the correct sum for the filing fee and apply the proper amount of postage to the envelope.

Many of the court clerks will not accept anything with even a cent of postage due on it. Further, if there is anything at all wrong with the document, or with the sum enclosed for the filing fee, back it might go to you.

Even worse, it could be held and not filed or otherwise disposed of. Nice feeling, expecting that the papers were filed, only to learn that you are in default.

To minimize this kind of calamity, always include an extra copy of the document (or at least a caption sheet) with a self-addressed and stamped envelope enclosing a "to be returned" cover letter to the clerk of the relevant court department requesting a confirmed copy.

Before you run to the expected protective skirts of the attorneys' service, let me warn you that much of the ingenuity that used to be there is gone. No longer will many of the service operators supply an extra $.50 or so to make up the inadvertent deficiency.

No longer will many of the operators spend the time to correct a minor problem in a pleading, such as an unchecked box. Back it may come, with an inscrutable "explanation" that will not really inform you of the problem at all.

If you have filings in branch courts, they may be filed in the main court. This can routinely be done except in cases of special hearings or other matters where expedience is needed in the filing. Then, those are cases for the messenger service.

Filing by a colleague.

Just as you may do a colleague a favor when you are attending court by filing something, you may ask the same favor. Obviously, timing and circumstances will not make this suggestion a regular alternative, but it can be used occasionally as an adjunct alternative.

These alternatives were not the greatest back in the days of the super efficient attorneys' services, but these days they are quite good by comparison. You can even establish a credit account with certain public agencies. Their charges are far less than the attorneys' services, and they will often perform at least as well by today's standards.

In minor league cases, you can explain to your client about the savings if he/she makes the drop. Perhaps the client has a friend who would be willing to do this favor. With minimal instruction from you, most anyone can run this kind of errand. You might even suggest some token payment.

Your local law school could be a good source of runner power for process serving and even court filings. The odds are that some of the students would be quite willing to get some experience in these activities and earn some sorely needed funds in the bargain. It wouldn't hurt to inquire.

The point of these alternatives is to illustrate that you do not need to be chained to a service that only has its hand out, but is not willing or able to provide the performance for which it asks such disproportionate fees. Think about the varied other ways to get the job done.

More to the point is that you can be quite self-sufficient in this part of the practice as well as in all other functions of your office. Do not "sweat the small stuff," as they say.

The "negatives" attributed to these outside services should not depress you. They should only make you more alert to their failings and foibles, so that you can engage in more monitoring for your own protection.

You may not be as fussy as I am. I do know many lawyers who appear to be more or less satisfied with services I have found to be totally unacceptable.

Most important, it should make you even more aware of the value of going solo. You'll find that "help," in the general sense, is not all that reliable. Your best "help" is yourself. You, you can always rely on. Whichever your choice on these subjects, you'll do just fine in your solo practice.

Chapter 11

Billing Your Clients and Paying Your Bills

§ 11:1 Generally

Are you a commercialist or an altruist?

Getting money from clients often confounds even the more sophisticated attorneys. For some reason, many lawyers find a huge gap between law practice and law business. Among your first chores in going solo will be to narrow that gap to a thin, thin slot.

Being paid for what you do is nothing more than a fair exchange for services rendered. There is nothing degrading about asking a client for your fee. Not asking for a fee is degrading to yourself.

Some attorneys believe that getting paid for legal services is a secondary concern. Others place payment over everything else. To address the gap between those two views, some self-searching must be done. Are you a commercialist or an altruist?

As an altruist, you may truly believe that getting paid for what you do should not be important. Some believe that the lawyer's every act must be for the betterment of society and that fees play no part in the transaction. At the other extreme, some commercialists believe that being a lawyer is just a way to make lots of money.

Louis B. Mayer, one of the originators and longtime head of the film studio, Metro-Goldwyn-Mayer, said to a director who wanted to make a "prestige," noncommercial movie: "You want to be an artist, but you want other people to starve for your art."

Conversely, he said, "Life without service isn't worth living." Can it be both? Can you be a humanitarian and still make lots of money? Whether you're one or the other, it's more important that you understand the relationship between commercialism and humanitarianism.

You've learned in your early practice days that all work is welcome if done free. It's only when there's a charge for the service that people become concerned with the quality of work. As with most everything in life, a practical balance would be ideal.

It would be nice if all lawyers were to do their best to benefit clients, provide a reasonable quotient of pro bono publico contribution, and without minimizing its importance, make lots of money. Unfortunately, the drive for bucks in some people places pro bono a poor third. The opposite is just as unfortunate. Losing sight of fiscal needs can be financially devastating.

Unless you send bills regularly and promptly, you may be contributing unintended and untoward gratis work. The more time passing between your work done and billing dates, the less collectible your fees will be.

It's the nature of things.

Walk from room to room carrying a brim full glass of water and not spill a drop. Iron won't float. Still, lay a plain pin on top of that water and it floats. Ships made of iron, even of concrete, sail the seas regularly. Some people explain these phenomena scientifically with words like, surface tension, viscosity, water volume displacement, etc. Others shrug it off with a simple, "Well, it's the nature of things."

Your neighbor borrows your pet wrench. You don't need it so you don't ask for its return for several months, then you ask for it. "What wrench?" You lend a friend $5. You don't need it so months pass before you ask for it. "What $5?" It's the nature of things. Time goes by and memory becomes selectively less of indebtedness and more proprietary.

You do lots of things for clients and get good results. You send a statement after a few months of accrued services. The bill is relatively large. "What's all this for? Why is this bill so big? Hey! I paid for all this stuff before. Why are you including all this old stuff now? It's the nature of things.

Are these people dishonest? Some, perhaps. It's usually more a matter of subliminal memory rejection or selection. Your recollection of the loan is vivid. Theirs may well present a quite different picture. If these people aren't trying to cheat you, what's the answer? "It's the nature of things."

§ 11:2 Timing it right: Billing to insure cash flow

Accrued fee debts. How to recognize collection trouble signs and what to do about them.

Doing excellent work is fine. Billing for your fees is also fine. But none of that, or anything else you do, other than intended pro bono publico, is worth scrap unless you can collect what is owed to you.

This part should be printed in bright red ink. If you do not understand what is stated here, red ink is what you'll need to total your net profit or loss column. This part cannot be overstated.

Some fee debts are in the bag despite being large and perhaps even a bit delinquent. Other fee collections are less certain, and still others are virtually uncollectable without legal process. Then, there are debt collections that are best described with two words: "IM-POSSIBLE!"

These four categories offer different collection probabilities depending upon your attitude towards collection.

There are two sides to these probabilities. Side one covers fee debts to attorneys who do not sue clients. That's the side I am on. I not only do not sue clients, I let my clients know that I do not sue clients. They know that if they do not pay me, they will not be legally forced to do so.

Side two covers fee debts that are subject to debt collection suits. Collection successes through lawsuits depend upon:

1. **Collectability after judgment;**
2. **Enforcement tenacity;**
3. **Regularity of your records; and**
4. **Vulnerability to cross-action.**

Obviously, the last of these offers the greatest negative. This involves a return action for malpractice. Often, that result is accompanied by a report to your state bar association on a claimed attorney's error or omission.

Item "4)" states "vulnerability to cross-action," but that oversimplifies the point. "Vulnerability" does not necessarily mean the existence of a genuine error or omission. It often depends only upon some vague, arguably disputable, issue.

Clients who sue their attorneys do not need the degree of probable cause that must preface other kinds of lawsuits. Don't look for this as a classification for probable cause formally.

Before getting into the melange of pros and cons concerning when, whether or if clients should be sued, consider some of the following generalities about fee debts and how they should be viewed.

How to know when fees are still collectible.

Fees usually collectible are those owed by clients using your services on an ongoing basis. If your services are vital to the client, the fees owed are practically in your bank account.

Collection is questionable when the services rendered are not vital. Where a client can dispense with your services, even though this may be inconvenient to the client, expect some balance owed that will not be paid without enforcement. Bill frequently in smaller amounts. The larger and more accrued the balance, the more difficult it is to collect when services discontinue.

This is a circuitous development. The more dispensable your services, the higher the fees balance, the more likely fees will not be paid. If your services are not essential, keep the balance low.

If services are expected where fees are not paid within customary periods, send statement duplicates frequently. If indications are that fees are not forthcoming within the usual payment time, inquire as to: a) the time expected to receive payment; and b) confirmation of services requested to be performed.

If your services have been reasonably necessary for the maintenance of a business, and the business is still functioning, it would indicate the intrusion of another attorney. If your services have been not necessary on a day-to-day operation, as in corporations work, contract review, etc., it's probable that your client considered your work displaceable and has decided to eliminate it in an economy move.

Keep your clients happy (or you won't be happy).

This topic really deserved a separate chapter in the book marked "IMPORTANT." So much can be said about happy clients and their loyalties that cement them to you seemingly forever, and then suddenly, forever ends.

This commentary is part of the "Timing it right: Billing to insure cash flow" because billing and client contentment are intimately intertwined. So much of your client relationships relate to how you bill, when you bill, and for what, that it is dizzying.

Sometimes this connection is made violently clear to you. When your client flies into a rage because of your charge for a particular service, you'll have no doubt about the reason for his or her discontent. That clarity, unfortunately, occurs only in a tiny percentage of your clientele attrition.

Unquestionably, other factors are involved in client disenchantment. Although you won't always be privileged to know of it, fees are usually, if not always, somewhere down there, perhaps near, or at, the root.

Keeping clients, and keeping clients happy, are synonymous. If your client is unhappy, you will keep him or her only so long as your client absolutely needs you. This is where many lawyers fail in the prediction business.

We lawyers tend to over estimate our clients' need for our services. We base our value to a client upon our review of past results. We've done well for the client through the years. We've gotten good results on all cases or most of them. That should be enough to keep the client happy. Not quite. We look at history. Our client looks at our present fee statement. The client doesn't ask "What have you done for me lately," the question is "What are you doing for me right now?" The worst part of this is not just losing a client, but maybe not even getting paid for services performed.

Even if the client could bring to mind all the wonderful things we've done, which is asking far too much, this still wouldn't make the difference. Lawyers are supposed to win cases, aren't they? We're supposed to do good things all the time, not so? So what. How does that make up for a fee statement to choke a horse?

Whether or not a horse is choked, the client is viewing your fees as too high for what you're worth. Don't waste your time trying to prove that your services were well worth your fees. Winning that argument will push the client further away. Something else is missing.

So, what does make the difference? An attorney/client relationship that is attractive to the client. What does that mean? Think back. Remember those accolades. Recall the many times the client told you how wonderful you are. How long has it been since you were told, "What would I do without you."

Sure, those were days of jeopardy. But you were there for the client. You reassured him or her. Somehow you provided a buffer between the client and the threat, whatever it was. You were a safety zone, a protector.

Why has that changed? Do you have value only during days of jeopardy? That can't be right. Why doesn't the client understand that you are there for the client now and will be there in the future, just as you were there during those past bad days.

For some reason, that reassurance felt in the past has evaporated. Logic will not tell you why. You could mount an excellent argument to persuade that you are the perfect lawyer for the client. Haven't you represented the client for years successfully? Aren't you more familiar with his or her business than anyone else? Don't you have the client's best interests at heart? What else can anyone say?

That's a bit like a spouse facing divorce asking the other, "Why don't you love me anymore?" A million good arguments could be powerfully presented. Would any of them do any good? Well, love between spouses is different from attorney/client relations, isn't it? But is it?

Can you always put your finger on why a client no longer values the attorney? Not even most of the time. Why not? There are differences between spouses and attorney/clients, of course. But there are also some things in common. The attraction held by a client for his or her attorney is not altogether different from a love affair.

What client can truly evaluate an attorney's ability? Even lawyers fail in the appraisal of other lawyers. A lawyer makes a mistake so he or she is a lousy lawyer. Not so? Maybe not. So what then? Lawyers make lots of mistakes.

A lawyer loses a case. Another lousy lawyer? Hey, you can't win 'em all, right? Don't try that line on your client. Clients don't like losers. Lawyers are divided into two parts, winners and losers. Well, you never lose so you're on the right side.

Point out the mistakes and losses to another lawyer and the cross is set up for a crucifixion. Clients in the throws of a good attorney/client relationship will not always be so eager to condemn. Yet, in a different setting, no mistakes, no failings, nothing is wrong and the client is drifting away. Why?

Schedule visits with your clients. A matter of housekeeping.

Ask the client, "Don't you love me anymore?" Will you get an answer? Sure. "Of course I love you." That question put to the estranged spouse could well get that same answer. So will the client rethink and stay with the attorney? About the same chance as the spouse rethinking and staying in the marriage. None, to less-than-none.

Isn't this a job for SUPER SALESMAN?

What can a salesman do when his or her spouse announces a breakup? Probably nothing. Why not? Simple. Salesmen, like everyone else, do not always give valued information. Objectivity, an essential of information given in the sales interview, is rarely present during emotional discussions.

Recall we agreed that the desperate salesman will fail. Emotions displace training and knowledge of the subject. Concern will swamp the brain's selectivity and the information given will register that concern instead of the proper data.

Not being a lonely hearts expert, I can't advise on how to save a foundering marriage. Despite our fifty-five years of marriage, Lillian would doubtlessly volunteer to list the 20 million or so totally wrong things I've said to her at countless wrong times.

I can't recall having ever solved any of our major marital problems through the giving of any information, valued or otherwise. Our marriage has persisted mainly because Lillian has a sense of humor. While I don't claim an abundance of that virtue, I value it in Lillian.

Third parties have been notoriously unsuccessful in patching up failing marriages. Dismal as that seems, the parties themselves have even a worse track record. The toxic ingredient is the emotional barrier.

Selling a prospect where there's some interest in the product is one thing. Selling against emotional resistance is quite another. The usual pitch involves advice that impinges upon the sensitized issue.

Theoretically, there is a way to solve marital break-ups. The method is not that complicated to understand. It's difficult to do only because of the strange attraction to the sore spot. People just can't seem to avoid giving bromide "cures."

The approach must be a circumvention of that trouble area. One must innocuously discover the nature and focal point of the dangerous subject and then find the particular information to give without treading upon the injury.

I have rehabilitated more than a few discontented clients, however. This only means that the emotional impact of a dissonant attorney/client relationship is not as severe as a threatened marital situation.

Remember the example about the house you've seen that your friend might like. Apply that principle to the disenchanted client matter. Keep your objectivity. Try to effect the posture of one whose only intent is to convey information of interest to the listener.

Before you start, think about this. There may be a brick wall between you and patching up the discord with your client. That wall may be something you perceive as an ethical obligation.

The contention between you may rest upon your view of what your client wants. Perhaps you feel that satisfying your client could compromise your integrity. Maybe a breach of legal ethics could be the result of making the client happy.

Or, it might be that this is the way you see it, but, in actuality, that problem may not exist. Regardless of whether that wall is solid or vaporous, its importance is your appraisal of it. If you believe that you cannot satisfy your client without violating your own principles, and you are a person of principles, it matters not whether your concern is real or imagined. You won't do it.

No mule has ever dug its heels in the dirt as immovably as a lawyer who has elected to obstruct a pathway with a principle. God help the one who argues against it regardless of whether that lawyer has correctly assessed that principle.

That brick wall aside, assume that we don't know the nature of the problem, or indeed even if there is a problem at all. All we do know is that the client has not been calling as often of late, and when we do talk, there just doesn't seem to be that old chumminess.

We need to find out if there is a problem, and if so, its nature. To do so, we must develop a sales interview requiring first that we get information.

Of course, the first task is to identify what that information would be. Whoa! Don't judge that too quickly. You can be just as guilty in tainting your selection of information as in giving it. Keep your objectivity. Try to determine what has fallen out of the relationship.

Make certain you distill out every little contaminant that could reveal the slightest personal interest in that information. Remember the house situation. You couldn't care less whether your friend actually buys that house or not. You only want to serve your client and not keep him/her as a client for any selfish purpose. Right?

You've got to reflect that same personal disinterest in both selecting the information and giving information to your client. That is difficult to do if you do not retain your objectivity. Recall that salesmanship requires keeping the phases separate. That can be difficult as well. We will explore some examples but each situation requires customization.

Remember the basics. In order to give valued information, you must know what information will be valued. How do you obtain that knowledge? You ask for it. Meet with your client. Then ask questions.

Set up a meeting preferably at your client's place of business. You want the least possible intrusive negatives. If workable, meet for lunch, coffee, or whatever. Then, start asking questions away from the point. Get your client to talk. Trigger his or her vocality on any subject that will produce a flow.

Then, move on to significant stuff. Do not, repeat, do NOT ask anything like "Why don't you love me anymore?" Don't ask whether there is a problem, or whether the client is unhappy about anything.

If you ask enough questions of the right kind, the conversation will drift around to subjects that will answer your questions without your ever having to broach them. You must avoid making any statement or asking any question that would reveal your concern about the relationship.

This is to validate your objectivity in giving valued information. If your client senses that concern, your motive of self-interest will overwhelm the entire agenda and you will lose credibility instantly.

This conversation should be a general housekeeping one. It's the kind of meeting every lawyer should have with every client at least once and probably every so often. Accordingly, your opening gambit should be along that tack. Address any subject related to any extant matter. Where you go from there will depend upon the assortment of material at hand.

Ask questions like, "What do you think of that?" or some other such trolling cast at every opportune point. Sooner or later, the conversation will turn productive. You must be attuned to sensitive issues. As soon as you hear something, anything, that could be revealing, ask more questions within that central area.

Be aware at this point that you could easily convert your innocent questions into argument. Obviously, that would be dumb and even perhaps fatal to your purpose. You must be able to discern the difference between an *argumentative* question and an *exploratory* one.

For instance, if your client complains about some particular act of yours, your question, "Well, why do you suppose I did that?" would be argumentative, not exploratory. Don't do this.

Don't be afraid to ask more and more questions. You simply cannot know too much. The more you know, the more you can sort out for the business of information giving. When your inventory of facts is adequate, wait for a conversational lull and then start your sale. Remember to be objective and never self-vindicating.

Most important, never, NEVER, suggest by word or innuendo, that anything between you is amiss. Everything is fine. This meeting is simply housekeeping you decided is overdue.

Another problem. Even getting the meeting set up requires selling. If the client is unhappy, why should he/she agree to meet with you? The basis for the meeting must not be telegraphic.

Little by little, you will find your way into the target subject.

That subject may not be what you might expect. Most often it is not a "sore" point. Usually, the problem is one of simple apathy. The analogy to marriage can be startling. More marriages break up because of boredom than from any other cause.

Don't be surprised at the conclusion that you may just have lost your client's interest. That alone is no pathology. But when coupled with a fees statement, the trigger could be pulled.

Sometimes, a festering process sets in. The longer the apathetic condition continues, the greater the possibility that some little irritant between you can become a focal point for inflammation. This is another reason to tend to these matters early on.

So, a bit of attention, a little TLC or whatever you call it, and your love affair could be rekindled. Laugh if you want to. But these are the things that can make the difference.

Have I indicated that this mission is a tough one? Of course it is. But it's doable. It not only can be done but it MUST be done and you, only you, must do it.

Prophylaxis; Some preventative medicine steps.

Take some preventative medicine steps. Go through your client list. Set up meetings on a staggered basis. You don't need to do this with each client. You only need to do it with clients you want to keep. The bottom line is, keep your clients happy and you'll be happy.

Written questionnaires to clients; Is this a practical method?

Can this be done in writing? I've read many articles and attended seminars in which the idea of sending out survey questionnaires to clients is suggested. Some specifics, not many, are given, such as questions, "What am I doing right?" and "What am I doing wrong?" "How can I improve upon my services to you?"

Some of the sample questions even intrude upon the touchy subject of "fees." "Do you consider my fees to be reasonable for my services to you?" Other such questions poke and probe at the nerve centers of the attorney/client relationship.

No client has yet been born who will agree that lawyers' fees are "reasonable." That's not the important point. The relationship is tenuous enough without jabbing it with a sharp stick.

If there are any questions that can effectively be written to produce helpful information, I have yet to find one. If answers to the sample questions I've seen all come back positively answered, "Yes, your fees are reasonable; yes, your services are great, etc.," what will that prove? Will that assure a continued relationship? Don't be silly.

First of all, it is a gross imposition upon your client to ask for the time and effort to even think about those questions, much less to frame suitable answers. The entire purpose of the interview is to slyly ease the helpful information from your client with more than a bit of subterfuge.

Never ask a direct question about anything concerning you, your fees, your services or your practice. It's vital to hear answers to those indirect questions without taint, so you can evaluate them and carefully decide what information can be inventoried for your ultimate use.

So much depends upon attitude. You may have to shift gears several times to finally find the right formula. This simply cannot be done through any kind of remote control method.

A prominent Los Angeles lightweight boxer of the 1950's ran up an early string of sensational knockout victories. Most impressive were his speed and graceful movements. He had textbook form and the perfect fighter's physique, trim, sleek and powerful. He had everything except one thing. In his later fights, he became a loser.

It wasn't until years later that, in retrospect, his problem became clear to me. He just couldn't put it all together. Everything that he did was an independent act, having little or nothing to do with anything else he did.

In his younger years, his hand speed was so fast that he reached his opponent before there was time to set up a defense. Speed is power and he had that, big time.

He had no plan of operation. But he didn't need one when speed and youth were on his side. Without a doubt, he never knew what he was going to do from move to move. As he aged, his hand speed slowed just enough for his opponent to get to him.

Had he learned about planning in his earlier years, he could have added some time to his career. His problem was his ability to win without a plan.

Most prizefighters in the early days were not well educated. Unscrupulous managers and promoters made a practice of paying fighters with huge rolls of $1 bills. Getting this impressive roll of dollar bills, the fighters believed they had been well paid for their frightful services.

Just as a fighter must have his mind fixed on objectives, so must a lawyer. It isn't enough that a fighter has a good punch arsenal and defense talent, if he lacks two other essential abilities. He must be able to put all of his physical skills together in a unified package. He must also be able to distinguish dollar bills from tens, twenties and hundreds, and understand which and how many of them should be his.

These days, fighters are better protected from unscrupulous managers, for the most part. Generally speaking, the main objective for a modern day fighter is a singular one: to score points and win the fight.

Alas, the lawyer's objective is not so simplistic. While most lawyers can tell the difference between dollar bills and other denominations, more than this is needed. Even though the lawyer puts combinations together and scores points, this is not enough. Even though the lawyer wins cases, this is not enough. The lawyer must also score a financial victory.

You may milk all sources for legal business, and in spite of a bustling and active office, get nowhere. This would be simply because you don't know when, and how, to ask for the money.

Although you will be told all about how to schedule your time and set up your billing procedure in Chapter 12, such information is not enough. Unless you learn how to get retainer fees up front in most cases and you bill unflaggingly, you will be fighting a sorry battle as a solo practitioner.

Taking a case, whether on behalf of a defendant or plaintiff, is a great responsibility. The most important services you will render for your client will come during the first stages of the suit. Much of what you do in those first weeks will influence the direction that the case takes. Many of your early decisions will affect probabilities as to whether the matter will settle and the amount of settlement, or the alternative of sending it on the road toward trial.

For these and other reasons, it is proper that a nonrefundable retainer be taken to assume these responsibilities and time priorities. You must explain very carefully and thoroughly that no refund will be given.

This is so, even though settlement or other termination may occur to end the case before you would have earned that retainer on an hourly basis. On the other hand, should the case move on past those first important procedures, the time spent during the subsequent phases will continue to generate an hourly fee.

For example, if you take a retainer of, say $3,000 to cover those important initial services, and you expend only ten hours prior to settlement, you will be entitled to keep that entire retainer. This is so even though you may have only earned $1,000 based on your regular fee of $100 per hour. [See sample form of retainer agreement below in this Chapter.]

Your right to keep the retainer even though you haven't worked all hours for the fee charged is based on the contract language. It must be stated, clearly and in bold type; it is specifically bargained for in exchange for your willingness to assume those particular duties.

If you don't see it that way, draft the contract to reflect your preference. In that event, you must place the entire retainer in your attorney/client trust account and draw out sums equal to the particular services performed on the hourly fee agreed upon.

Under the proprietary retainer arrangement, if the case doesn't settle and you go on to trial, you will merely credit your client with the remaining $2,000 against the services yet to be performed.

If you had billed your client in the conventional manner, you would have received (if your billing is effective and you are lucky at collection) only the $1,000 time charges. This is neither fair nor properly compensatory to you.

The energy and commitment involved in the representation of a client in a trial can't be compared with drafting a will or a "buy and sell" agreement. The stress and demands of litigation will justify a retainer as a minimum fee.

In addition to the possibility of early settlement, you will benefit from the use of the money in advance. You will find, to your consternation, that lawyers are not far up on the list of you clients' payment priorities.

Among the many facts that you had lacked before reading this book is the one common to most clients concerning payment of their legal bills. Billing for your services ain't the same as getting paid.

Another strange fact is the correlative to suing a client for fees. That is being sued by the client for malpractice. Of course, it doesn't happen every time, but it is happening more and more often.

The client who is reluctant to pay for legal services, and there are more of them now than ever, is the same breed of cat who'll look for any out, even a claim that you fumbled the ball. I just never sue anyone for fees. For one thing, I abhor doing a job twice for the same fee.

§ 11:3 Fee differentials

Determining fee differentials is an exercise in which the use of your computer and a billing program will be of great help to you. Such a program can identify, quantify and segregate earnings at different hourly rates. The use of billing programs (which will be explored below in this Chapter) permits you to state the hours of service at a given rate, and to make entries for each hourly rate at which you work. The computer does the rest.

Thus, if you are working for different lawyers at various rates, i.e., lawyer A at $40 per hour, lawyer B at $50 per hour and lawyer C at $60 per hour, and for client D at $150 per hour, your computer will meticulously track and calculate all time spent. It will also include a detailed description of the work, and print out statements for each lawyer showing totals of fees due to you.

This exercise is by way of example only. Remember that work done for other lawyers is collected for each evening. Your cheap "wholesale" fee arrangements for lawyers don't include the luxury of billing.

As you will see, all of this will be done without any other operation on your part or knowledge of any of the bookkeeping or mathematical procedures used. Even with my electronics background, I still view these programs and computers as miraculous.

You've been taught how to separate issues and points of law. But you're going to have trouble separating your services to your neighbor lawyer for one figure and another figure to your clients.

At the time of the writing of this book, fees in and around the Los Angeles area averaged from about $100 to about $400 per hour. These figures like everything else vary in different areas. These "average" fees do not represent the full range of fees.

There are Beverly Hills and Century City attorneys who command, and get, well over $450 per hour. There may be some lawyers in these regions getting less than $100 per hour, but I haven't discovered many lately.

If you are starting your practice in Beverly Hills, California, you might offer your services to other lawyers anywhere from $40 to $60 per hour. This depends upon your qualifications and your "chutzpah," maybe more upon your "chutzpah."

I'll repeat that you don't try for the highest fee you can get. You are more interested in keeping your stable of feeding lawyers content to keep you in work and continuing client referrals.

Should an unwary client stumble into your office, you will charge that client whatever the appropriate rate may be. At the time of writing, a fee of about $100 to $150 per hour in the general Los Angeles area was reasonably a threshold rate. You do not charge that client the $40 or $60 per hour you charge other lawyers.

Remember, you are hoping to build your own clientele, while you are doing the so-called "garbage" work for other lawyers. It would not serve you very well to be building one "garbage" practice while you are trying to phase out another one.

It may be difficult for you to think in terms of $100 or more per hour for your new client, while charging perhaps $30, $40 or $50 per hour to the lawyers. You know, of course, that the lawyer is not passing your $50 fee to his client. He will be charging the going attorney's rate. Either way, the client gets billed professional rates.

Consider this: if you charged only $20 per hour and kept busy all day only five days a week, you would have a gross income of $800 per week. That comes to $40,000 annually with a vacation.

If you are in doubt that you could be kept busy all day at that figure, just ask a few lawyers how much time you can count on from each at that rate. Be careful or you'll start a stampede.

I don't say that $40,000 a year is a bonanza. But, it is a start, and it's *net* to you, less rent, since the assigning lawyers pay all of your expenses on such assignments. Lots of jobs will not pay more than that sum as a starting salary.

If that were your only income for the year, solo practice would leave something to be desired. But consider this: all the while that you are accepting those $30, $40, $50 or whatever per hour assignments, you are receiving case referrals from those assigning lawyers.

It's not necessary to offer your lawyer work for only $30 per hour. I only want to illustrate how small hourly sums calculate to startlingly high yearly incomes. Now try out $40 per hour, $50 per hour, and so forth.

If you're wondering why you cannot charge that rate for your own clientele, take a look at the difference in overhead. When you do work for another attorney at $30 per hour or more, the other attorney covers all outside expenses.

The other attorney's secretary does all required typing. The other attorney pays for duplicating all materials. The other attorney advances all court fees, service of process costs, etc. When you work for your own client, you incur all of these expenses and up-front costs.

He/she is the attorney "of record," not you. That means that he or she must pay the professional responsibility insurance premiums and bear responsibility for any problems arising from errors and omissions, even those made by you.

Of course, your client is expected to reimburse you for your advancement of court costs and process serving expenses, etc. But there are many expenses absorbed by you that must be a part of your total hourly fee. In unsuccessful cases, count the clients who reimburse you for those costs, fees, etc. You won't need your toes.

So, when you look at that $50,000 or $60,000 income, based on only your hourly fee to other lawyers, as being *net*, not gross, it isn't that bad. Certainly, you won't be satisfied with such a sum, but you can see how it adds up.

If you are thinking that $50,000 or even $60,000 a year will be no big fortune, you are right, of course. In addition, you will be working very hard, and much of the work assigned to you will not be intellectually stimulating, to say the least. But you would have to be awfully dense not to see that, from this humble start, will come the lovely, prestigious practice that you studied so hard in law school to get.

Don't forget that you have been paying for your education in law school. Now, you're not paying but being paid and still being educated. If you do not think that your interplay with the assigning lawyers will be an education for you equal or superior to what you got in law school, you haven't been paying attention.

Follow this book as it reads, and you will get the income that you want from the very first year in practice. I say the income that you "want." This is the amount that you set as a goal and the amount that you will work toward getting. Of course, this means hard work, and work that may not be precisely what you would carve out for yourself.

What does it take to grow big and beautiful roses? Fertilizer! There are other names for it, and that's the kind of practice you will have at first, but it's from such acorns that big oaks grow. And, in the meantime, you are eating regularly and paying your bills. You will even have a few bucks left over for some fun, if you watch your expenses.

Another thing. You won't have to look only toward your own clientele for income increases. As time goes by, and you pick up speed and experience, you will be able to command bigger fees from your lawyers.

Soon, you will become a plutocrat and will be charging $75 per hour or more to other lawyers. Finally, you will discard the lawyer work altogether. As your gross grows, you start moving into a different echelon.

Then, you will be expected to provide your own secretarial work, duplicating, and the other expenses of a law office. This doesn't mean that you will hire a secretary or even use a secretarial service. You'll be doing your own typing at your trusty old computer. Still, you will be netting considerably more income.

Strangely, even though your fees to other lawyers will double, or even triple, you will not be charging that much more to your own clients for quite some time. If you started at $100 per hour, you will perhaps raise your fees to $125 or $135 per hour, as you gain in knowledge, experience, and reputation.

Suddenly, you will realize that you are right along side of the "biggies" you used to admire so. Then, without me or anyone else to guide you, you'll be charging $175, $200 and up per hour with your clients loving it.

As time passes, you will have to divert from one plan to another, or phase into certain channels of practice, but such choices will be left to you at the proper time. The main thing is that your risk is hedged when you follow the plans in this book.

The choices that you will make as you develop your practice will be towards the kind of practice that makes you most comfortable and satisfied. That is where your patience then pays off. Taking all those junk work assignments has paved the way to your nice, satisfying practice.

§ 11:4 Regular monthly retainer

Clients for whom you are performing frequent or continuing services could be put on a regular monthly retainer basis. Analyze the general run of services over the period of your representation and strike a monthly time average.

This is a sort of "flat fee" and falls within the category of a "true retainer agreement" discussed below. This retainer should cover a range of specific ongoing services in the nature of those previously and regularly performed. It is designed to cover any and all such services whether or not they would exceed the regular hourly fee normally charged.

The agreement for this arrangement must carefully spell out the services included in that range. Conversely, the agreement must specifically state which services would be excluded, such as court and other "out-of-office" work or appearances.

The term "out-of-office" would mean anything that would keep you away from the phone, from greeting new clients or accepting work assignments. All court related matters, such as attending depositions or outside conferences, etc., would be charged at an additional hourly rate.

If you haven't had a long enough history to arrive at a computed average, estimate one based on your predictions. Then, multiply the monthly average of time by the hourly rate you charge. This will be the monthly retainer opener. The term "opener" is used because this figure is subject to modification depending upon the weight of use.

This is an advantageous arrangement for you since it brings you *prepaid* fees, i.e., fees for which payment is automatic and on a regular basis. You do not start such an arrangement until all outstanding charges have been paid. You then start the coming month with an advance payment from your client. You also train the client to get the fee in on or before the first day of each month.

This retainer would normally cover office work only, including research, drafting, in-office and phone conferences. Any court or other outside appearances would be billed separately on your usual hourly basis.

Naturally, this kind of arrangement will not relieve you of the necessity of keeping accurate time logs. You must still keep regular diary entries of all work done for your clients on retainer just as for those on a time-bill basis. This is the only way you will have of assessing the equitability of the arrangement.

A retainer agreement essentially permits your client to receive your services however and whenever needed, by either a phone call or office visit without extra-billed costs. This means that your client can make as many calls as desired.

Some of your clients will forget prudence when you put them on retainer and start accelerating demands for your time. You will need to remind them that the retainer basis is only a convenience and should not be abused. The idea is not to give the client substantially more time per dollar than the billed method, but to cut the costs and time wasted in billing.

For some reason, this abuse does not seem to extend to office visits. Still, the waste in phone time can be quite substantial. If your client cannot be controlled in phone abuses, the regular billing status should be reinstated. Remember, though, you can afford to be more lenient with time for the retainer-basis client because of the advantage of prepayment plus the regularity of income.

If time exceeds the exact hourly equivalent, don't make a big thing of it. If it goes beyond 15% or so, you should re-evaluate the retainer or revert to the hourly fee.

Another advantage to the retainer basis is that it serves to keep clients with you. The client gets used to the regularity of it, and it becomes habit like club membership. The "piece work" client has more of a tendency to examine the day-by-day relationship.

The billed-fee client relationship is more volatile. That type of client is more likely to look toward other pastures than the retainer client. Your practice becomes more solid and dependable as you develop more retainer clients.

One of the frustrations of law practice, as in any business, is the "feast or famine" cycle. One day you may score with a big fee, and then you see nothing at all for several days. The worry about where the next dollar will come from during the "famine" days unnerves the beginner.

It will be difficult for you to retain your faith and confidence in the upside of business until you have been in practice for a few years. Suddenly one day, you'll realize that you have lost that fear. You will begin to relax and accept the ups and downs without anxiety.

There is nothing that I can say that will prevent your shakes except to assure you that they will go away after awhile. You are not alone. Every business has this "feast or famine" cyclical machination.

But you can see that having a few reliable retainer clients will do much to calm your fears. Either way, though, you will get your share of business, and you will do just fine. Some weeks will be great, some only good, and some not so good. But each year, you will give your accountant income figures that somehow will top the year before.

I have predicted unequivocally that you will earn your living as a solo practitioner if you follow the pattern outlined. I can also predict that the business will flow irregularly. It is a strange thing.

You can have days, even weeks, of lousy action, and then bingo, you hit jackpot after jackpot. I don't know the reason for this, but then I have lived long enough to know that it doesn't matter in the long run. Someday perhaps, a study will be made of this phenomenon, and some genius will tell us why this is so.

§ 11:5 Sample retainer form

A sample of a customized Attorney/Client Retainer Agreement follows. Adaptations to the boilerplate clauses are obviously encouraged. Putting your favorite version (or versions) on word processing means quick and easy generation of copy ready for signature(s), and confines your proofreading to the variables.

PLEASE READ THIS SAMPLE FORM CAREFULLY. There are several parts of this agreement varying considerably from the standard form. You can get dozens of variations of these forms. The main difference here is that the retainer sum received on contracting with the client for representation is kept by the attorney regardless of whether the matter is settled prior to the use of all the hours equivalent to the retainer sum.

Thus, a $5,000 retainer in a matter for which you are charging **$200** per hour should cover 25 hours. This would be a rather nominal fee even for a municipal court matter that might consume that amount of time within the first few weeks of a litigated case.

However, should that matter be settled prior to the use of the

25 hours, you would still be entitled to retain the entire $5,000. This is your fee for your willingness to undertake the rigors of litigation. This also contemplates that should you succeed in an early settlement, your client will be extra-specially happy.

On the other hand, in the event that the case consumes more than the 25 hours, as it would be expected to do, your client would be obligated to pay any additional fees, as would be the case with the ordinary retainer. The ordinary retainer, without this clause, would need to be placed in a trust account with you withdrawing sums only as they are earned by services performed.

This particular contract will entitle you to place the entire $5,000 in your general account for any use to which you may put it at any time. Consult your local bar rules and state laws for the legality of any attorney/client agreement drawn.

(Sample Form of Retainer Agreement)

ATTORNEY-CLIENT FEE AGREEMENT

________ *[Client's name]*, ("Client"), and GERALD M. SINGER, Lawyer ("Attorney") agree:

1. **Services to be Provided by Attorney.** Client engages Attorney to provide all legal services reasonably required to represent Client in connection with the matter described below, subject to the division of this matter into parts, portions of which may be covered by a nonrefundable retainer and remaining portions of which may be subject to the hourly and daily fee schedule in the addenda attached to this agreement: (Preliminary headings as causes, subject to factual support later supplied).

(a) Client represents that he/she has made a full, fair and complete disclosure of all facts to Attorney appearing to support the action described below. Client agrees to supply Attorney with all other documentation and other material and information in his or her possession or under Client's care, custody or control, or in the possession of anyone else, to which Client may have access, which relate in any way, directly or indirectly, to the subject matter of this action which Client may still have in his or her possession or may later discover. Attorney has explained to Client that the filing of any cause of action which is not supported by sufficiently provable facts may entitle the opposing side to sanctions against Client and Attorney, or to bring a subsequent lawsuit in the event of a termination favoring the opposing side ("Favorable Termination").

(b) The nature of the action that appears to be supported by facts as revealed by Client to Attorney may tentatively cover, without limitation, the following potential cause or causes of action:

[Here, the particular part of the case covered by the retainer is stated briefly but fully enough to distinguish it from any portion not so covered. For example, the matter covered may be the first phase of litigation, the fact-finding, investigatory and negotiation stage. Or it might be the first and second phase, which is the stage immediately following filing of pleadings. This would be precisely delineated and separated from the third phase, the actual time in court.

The second phase might involve certain court appearances, such as demurrers, motions of various kinds including summary judgment, motions to quash, changes of venue, etc. Any such court appearances should be excluded from the covered matter and should be subject to the fee schedule attached by addendum.

The third phase, trial, is definitely excluded from the retainer coverage and is subject to the hourly, daily, and portions of daily fees as provided in the Fees Schedule.]

In order to enable Attorney to effectively render such services, Client agrees to be truthful with Attorney in discussing the matter and shall keep attorney apprised of all developments in the matter promptly. Client shall cooperate with Attorney in all ways pertinent to the matter and shall be reasonably available to promptly attend meetings, office conferences in Attorney's offices or elsewhere at Attorney's direction, court appearances and all other proceedings related to the matter. Client acknowledges that Attorney is not Client's general counsel and that acceptance of this engagement by Attorney does not in any way obligate Attorney to represent Client, or Client's business interests in any matter other than the matter described in this Agreement.

2. **Fees**

(a) Except as provided below in this agreement as a "non-refundable" retainer, described as a "true retainer," and deemed to be earned immediately upon payment, any and all further or additional services shall be subject to payment as follows:

As compensation for the services to be performed by Attorney as described above, Client agrees to pay fees to Attorney at the basic hourly rate set forth on the Fees Schedule (Schedule) attached to this agreement as Exhibit A, subject to periodic changes as provided in this Agreement and subject to adjustment as provided in paragraph 2(b) below. The basic hourly rates contained in the Schedule are subject to review and change by Attorney on a periodic basis. In the event of such change, Attorney shall give Client thirty (30) days notice prior to invoking such change, and Client shall be presumed to have agreed to the new basic hourly rates if Client does not discharge Attorney within the 30-day period before the new rates take effect.

(b) Time for legal personnel is charged in the minimum increments set forth on the Schedule, except as may otherwise be noted on the fees schedule with respect to a specific task. Any minimum time charges for a specific task noted on the Fees Schedule are subject to periodic change in the same manner provided for the basic hourly rates as set forth in 2(a) above.

(c) Client acknowledges that although Attorney may, from time to time for Client's convenience, furnish Client with estimates of the amount of fees which Attorney may anticipate will be charged with respect to services to be performed under this agreement, such estimates are by their nature inexact and are not binding on either Attorney or Client.

(d) Client agrees that Attorney may engage an associate attorney at any time to discharge duties which Attorney may not at the relevant time be in a position to attend to, provided that Client will not be charged a fee for such service in excess of the fees provided for in this agreement. Such services may include any and all court appearances or other services, except that research assistance are separately charged as provided in paragraph 3 below.

3. **Costs and Expenses**. Client agrees to pay Attorney all costs and expenses incurred in performing legal services in connection with the matter. Such costs and expenses may include, without limitation, long-distance telephone calls, messenger and other delivery fees, postage, computer research, outside assists in research, travel expenses, parking, meals and hotel accommodations, plus hourly fees during travel time, photocopying and other means of reproduction, word processing charges, computer time, process server fees, filing fees and other court and public agency charges, court reporters' fees, jury fees, witness fees, investigators' fees, experts' and consultants' fees, and other similar items. Except as may be listed on the Schedule, all such items will be charged to Client at Attorney's cost. The charges for any items listed on an attachment to this agreement are subject to periodic change in the same manner provided for the basic hourly rates as set forth in 2(a) above.

[CAVEAT! IMPORTANT: RESEARCH THE ADVISABILITY OF THE NEXT PROVISION UNDER YOUR STATE LAWS ON PROFESSIONAL RESPONSIBILITY AND

OTHER CANONS OF ETHICS AS WELL AS YOUR STATE BAR RULES REGARDING ATTORNEY/CLIENT AGREEMENTS. IT IS MY VIEW THAT THE FOLLOWING PROVISION SHOULD BE PERMISSIBLE IF, AND ONLY IF, YOU CLARIFY THIS PROVISION, USING PLAIN AND SIMPLE LANGUAGE AND REPEAT IT AT LEAST TWICE WITHIN THE AGREEMENT. REQUIRE YOUR CLIENT'S SIGNATURE OR INITIALS ADJACENT TO THIS PARAGRAPH INDICATING THAT IT HAS BEEN READ AND UNDERSTOOD.]

NOTICE—NOTICE—NOTICE—NOTICE

THE RETAINER SUM, DESCRIBED BELOW, IS KNOWN AS A "TRUE RETAINER," AND IS NOT REFUNDABLE. READ THIS PARAGRAPH CAREFULLY AND ASK TO HAVE IT EXPLAINED IF YOU FAIL TO UNDERSTAND IT.

4. **True Retainer**. Client agrees to pay, upon execution of this Agreement, a retainer in the sum of $________. This Agreement shall not become effective until Attorney receives the retainer. The retainer is paid by Client, and accepted by Attorney, as compensation to Attorney for Attorney's willingness to assume the responsibilities of the particular matter, or portion, or portions of the matter, as described below, and no part of the retainer sum is subject to refund regardless of whether a settlement, or other basis for termination of Client's case is consummated prior to Attorney's services at Attorney's hourly rate having reached a sum equal to the retainer sum.

In other words, even though fewer hours of Attorney's time are spent than the number of hours to equal the amount represented by the retainer at the time of such settlement or other event which terminates Client's case, Attorney shall be, and is, entitled to the entire retainer sum as an earned fee in exchange for Attorney's willingness and agreement to assume the burden and responsibilities involved in representing Client's interest in Client's case.

In the event that further or other services may be required, provided that such further or other services are reasonably and directly related to the matter, or portions of the matter, client shall pay to attorney any additional sums for fees based upon the number of hours, days or parts of days, as set forth in the fees addendum attached to this agreement.

No part of the retainer shall apply to any of the further or other services and Client agrees that the full amount of the retainer is deemed earned when paid.

All costs and expenses as per paragraph 3 above will at all times be the separate responsibility of Client to either pay as directed by Attorney, or to reimburse Attorney should Attorney advance any such costs and expenses.

5. **Billing**. Attorney will send Client a statement for fees and costs from time to time. Client agrees to pay each such statement within 15 days of its date. Attorney's statements shall clearly state the basis of the fees and charges, including the amount, rate and basis for calculation (or other method of computation) of Attorney's fees.

6. **Grant of Lien**. Client grants Attorney a lien on any and all causes of action Client may assert in any court action brought by Attorney on Client's behalf under this Agreement. The lien shall be in addition to all other rights of Attorney to receive sums owing from Client under this Agreement.

7. **Disclaimer**. Attorney has made no promise, prediction or guarantee to Client concerning the outcome of this Matter, and nothing in this Agreement shall be construed as such a promise, prediction or guarantee, despite any statement Attorney may, or may not, have made.

8. **Termination of Services**.

(a) Client shall have the right at any time to terminate Attorney's services upon written notice to Attorney, and Attorney shall immediately after receiving the notice cease to render additional services. The termination shall not, however, relieve Client of the obligation to pay the fees due for services rendered and costs incurred prior to the termination.

(b) If Client fails to meet any of Client's obligations under this Agreement, Attorney shall have the right to terminate this Agreement, and Client shall take all steps necessary to free Attorney of any obligation to perform further, including without limitation, the execution of any documents necessary to complete Attorney's discharge or withdrawal. The right of Attorney under this agreement is in addition to those created by statute or recognized by rules of professional conduct.

9. **Binding Arbitration**. Both Client and Attorney agree that any dispute under this Agreement shall be submitted to binding arbitration by [identify arbiter]. Subject to applicable bar rules, the prevailing party in any such arbitration shall be awarded its reasonable costs and attorneys' fees incurred in connection with the dispute.

<u>PLEASE RE-READ PARAGRAPH 4. "RETAINER" AGAIN TO BE SURE YOU UNDERSTAND ITS TERMS. THE RETAINER THAT YOU MUST PAY UNDER PARAGRAPH 4 IS NOT</u>

REFUNDABLE REGARDLESS OF WHETHER THIS MATTER IS TERMINATED BEFORE THAT SUM IS CONSUMED IN THE NUMBER OF HOURS WHICH IT REPRESENTS AT THE STATED HOURLY FEE. ALTHOUGH THIS RETAINER RESEMBLES A FLAT LEGAL FEE IN SOME RESPECTS, IT IS NOT A FLAT FEE. YOU WILL STILL BE CHARGED THE ATTORNEY'S REGULAR HOURLY FEE IF AND WHEN ANY FURTHER OR ADDITIONAL SERVICES ARE REQUIRED BEYOND THE MATTER OR PORTIONS OF THE MATTER WHICH IS OR ARE THE SUBJECT OR SUBJECTS OF THE "TRUE RETAINER."

HOWEVER, IN THE EVENT THAT THIS MATTER IS TERMINATED BY WAY OF SETTLEMENT OR FOR WHATEVER REASON, OR TO COMPLETION OF THE ENTIRE MATTER, NO PART OR PORTION OF THE RETAINER SHALL BE REFUNDED SINCE THE RETAINER IS DEEMED TO BE EARNED IMMEDIATELY UPON PAYMENT BY CLIENT TO ATTORNEY AND IT SHALL BE NONETHELESS RETAINED BY THE ATTORNEY AS CONSIDERATION FOR THE UNDERTAKING IN WHOLE OR OF A PORTION OR PORTIONS OF SAID MATTER.

The parties have witnessed and executed this Agreement on the date below.

DATED: ________.

[Signature of "Client"]

GERALD M. SINGER, "Attorney"

DESCRIPTION OF MATTER AND SCHEDULE OF RATES

Matter:

(See description of matter in paragraph 1 (a) and (b) above.)

Fees.

Rates per hour:

Attorney $275.00

Law Clerks $100.00

Paralegals $75.00

Computer CD-ROM Research: $350.00

Computer Library Services: billed as needed.

ALL HOURLY RATES ARE BILLED IN MINIMUM INCREMENTS OF.25

Per diem rates, Office: $2,000.00

Court rates: Per day: $2,750.00 Half day: $1,500.00

HALF DAY CHARGES FOR ANY PART OF HALF DAY TIME SPENT.

FULL DAY CHARGES FOR ANY PART SECOND HALF-DAY SPENT.

HALF DAY HOURS ARE FROM 8:30 TO 12:00 NOON OR 1:30 P.M. TO 5:00 PM.

Retainer. $10,000.00

Once again, the above rates are used as examples only. Fees and rates have always varied geographically plus substantial swings plus and minus from time to time. No doubt by the time you read this, rates will have changed considerably. Substitute up-to-date and geographic area numbers for these examples.

Many states, including California, now require a statement in your attorney/client contracts of coverage for errors and omissions. If you are not so insured, the statement must declare your financial ability to protect clients from your misdeeds.

Some believe, as I do, that this requirement is a precursor to mandatory professional responsibility coverage. While this advent has engendered some expressed fears, it may not be all that bad.

A larger segment of the legal population is bare than popularly believed. If those lawyers were to subscribe to E & O insurance, the increased premium spread could very likely result in the mass premium reduction predicted by carriers. [See Chapter 15, Liability Insurance.]

Review the above agreement and note that the provision entitling you to the proprietary right to the entire retainer upon execution of the agreement is recited twice. That is to clarify its content. You are also advised to read that paragraph aloud to the client and explain its terms fully.

As with all terms and conditions in this or any other agreement to which you are a party, the above provision is certainly optional. If you feel uncomfortable using it, then by all means do not use it. My personal belief tracks the language of that provision. You are undertaking much responsibility for any litigated matter, and a firm retainer agreement such as this one is not inappropriate.

You may find, as I have found, after some years of experience through courtroom traumas, that the undertaking of any litigation is an exhausting ordeal. Even more wrenching is the gamut of salvos through which you must run during the first few weeks of the case.

Many state courts are adopting the breakneck pace that has traditionally been imposed by federal courts. In California, half of the cases filed fall within what is called the "fast track" category. This not only accelerates the time schedule of procedures but imposes severe penalties for any delays, even sometimes when justified.

Failure to comply, however innocent, falls upon your head, not your client's. It would be a mistake to view this phase of litigation, or indeed any part of the litigated case, as similar to other legal services. Think about this before you conclude that the proprietary retainer provision is inappropriate.

§ 11:6 Cash flow related to prompt billing

The following describes the **manual** (not computerized) recordation of time and billing. Hopefully, you will computerize these steps to avoid the laborious input associated with the pen and paper. The time you save avoiding these tiresome steps can provide some R & R or maybe more work output. For whatever reason, GO COMPUTER!

You have recorded the time you have spent each hour, meticulously, in your diary. You have religiously done this immediately upon completion of each service performed, then and there. Each entry will show the name of the client for whose benefit the work was done, the time of beginning, the time of completion, and a description of all services performed.

If you have an uncontrollable bent toward philanthropy, don't manifest it by failing to make such entries into your diary. Give instead to the charity or law school of your choice, after making the money derived through proper charging and billing.

Even if you are doggedly determined to give some time away, enter it anyway. At the very least, you will then have a record of your philanthropy. It's important to look back at your past workdays to know what your work output was for any given period of time.

At the end of each week, at the latest (during the weekends, preferably), transcribe the diary entries onto the various accounts receivable cards. Each card will show the client's name, address, and phone number. Each entry will show the date, the hours spent on that date, an abbreviated description of the services, and the expanded fee derived through the hours times the hourly rate.

Then, on a selected day each and every month, you will transcribe the entries from the accounts receivable cards to a statement form to be sent to your client.

Use the same abbreviated form in referring to the work performed when making out the statements. Your client will want to know what he or she is being billed for, but will not want to be treated to a diatribe in legalese.

Let us assume that you have shown several entries in your diary on behalf of John Jones during the months of October,

November, and December. On October 23rd, he conferred with you in your office for 1-1/2 hours.

You set up a client file, and advised him as to his position in a breach of contract matter. On the 28th of October, you spent four hours in the library researching his legal problem, and you spent the next half-day drafting papers needed to start his court matter.

During the month of October, you spent a total of about 3 hours in sundry phone conversations with your client, with others having information concerning the matter, and with the attorney representing your client's adversary. On November 8th, you drafted a memorandum outlining the issues and facts of the case upon which to predicate a complaint. You prepared and drafted the complaint incorporating the issues that you deemed relevant and useful, stating them in their respective separate causes of action.

You then prepared all of the associated court documents, such as summons, cover sheet, assignment, etc., plus the needed documents for service of process. All documents were then collated and prepared for filing and service. The total time spent was 6-1/2 hours.

Then, on November 11th, you received service of a demurrer to the complaint. You spent four hours researching the legal grounds stated by your opponent in support of the demurrer and in outlining your opposition to it. You then spent two hours preparing and drafting the opposition.

On December 14th, you appeared in court to oppose the demurrer and won an order overruling it. Although the actual hearing took only 10 or 15 minutes, the calendar was heavy and you spent most of the morning in court. There was also travel time to and from court.

There is also the fact that while you are in court, you are away from your office, and therefore cannot take calls from prospective new clients or from other attorneys who may want your services. You are also denied the convenience of tending to matters that arise constantly in a law office.

For these and other reasons, time in court is more expensive than time in the office. It would be unwieldy to merely increase your hourly charge since you'd need to include travel time, court delays and other time uses clients may not understand or appreciate.

The solution customarily applied is to charge by the day or half day in, to or from, court. This charge, substantially more than your usual hourly fee, would be calculated to include all such extra time periods and delays.

A reasonable court day charge for a reasonably new attorney, based upon a $100 per hour office fee, is $1,000. Half days would be $650. It would not be unreasonable to bill these figures as minimums for half or full days. After you have fully developed your practice, you will probably be charging multiple of these sums for court appearances.

A computer billing system also protects you from your failure to include all of your services. The same register records both the work description and billing charges at once. Add to this advantage a time saving of several hours per month plus unwavering accuracy. For these advantages alone, your computer should be considered a mandatory investment. The almost certain result of a more timely billing will be faster income and more reliable cash flow.

That last point is worth repeating. Whether you bill by computer or manually, do not delay in billing. It is a disservice to both your client and yourself to delay this important function. It would be grossly unfair to your client to send a bill covering several months at one time.

First, you will catch the client with his checkbook down. Most people simply do not keep excessive bank balances. This is the reason that many people who earn good money prefer to pay their bills with outrageous interest over a time period rather than by cash lump sum.

Second, your client will never remember all of those wonderful things you've done over the months, if he or she is first apprised of the cost at that later time. Your statement won't help his or her memory one bit.

Third, they will feel justifiably "sandbagged" by what they will interpret as a form of deception. If they are billed on a regular basis, and believe your fees to be high, they could elect to seek other counsel. Your withholding that information until the fees have accrued to a huge sum will have been denied that right.

Lastly, you will suffer for the lack of use of that income. You may indulge in the fiction that the client should be grateful for free use of your fee money, but that won't fly. So bill regularly.

Of course, such numbers will vary in accordance with your particular geography and other considerations. But the theory would remain the same. The value of your services away from your office may be difficult for you to appreciate at first, just as you might have trouble assessing the value of your services period.

Examples of computer generated billing statements follow. Whether done longhand or by computer, these entries would be sufficient. There is no virtue to writing lengthy narratives concerning the work done. On the other hand, much more abbreviation could underplay your work value.

If you have a flair for prose, you might tend to embellish your statement of services. But the average lay person might not be able to relate time spent to each specific procedure, nor understand the legal jargon you use to "enlighten." So some lawyers find it simpler to state their services with a bit less detail. I leave such decisions to your tendencies.

The more that you "explain," the more trouble it seems that you may brew. This is not to say that you should evade the issue or deceive your client. On the contrary, you must keep your client absolutely informed of all that you are doing every step of the way.

This is not a suggestion. It's a caveat. Remember the ethical pitfalls by a failure to keep the client adequately informed.

Letters to your client will have detailed your researched legal points favoring your client's side of the case. You will have also pointed out the problems you must overcome and what steps you must take to do this. You will have described the hearing on the demurrer that you won, blow-by-blow.

The client will have had so much information by the time he receives your statement that he will be relieved at how cheap your fee is. But that same client might not feel this way if you give him hour-by-hour reports in your statement.

§ 11:7 Computer-generated billing

Your computer billing program will reduce the time and effort to accomplish all of the above to a very few minutes. There are many excellent billing and accounting programs presently available to make your practice easier and more productive than using the manual method. [See Chapter 12, Computers and Programs.]

As readers of previous editions of *Solo* will know, I had used Legal Tender, ACS Software, for many years and became quite fond, even perhaps addicted, to it. It's gone now, perhaps for the best since it wasn't Y2K compliant. I found it simple, expedient and comprehensive. I'm sorry to lose it, and so, I believe, will those readers whom have followed my suggestions to use it.

One of the billing and accounting programs I found useful though perhaps more complicated than you or I need, is called TABS-III by Software Technology, Inc. ("STI"). More of this is seen in Chapter 12. Another is Tussman, also reviewed in Chapter 8 along with several other such programs.

STI also includes besides billing and accounting, trust accounts, client and case management, document management and retrieval, calendaring, general ledger and other accounts. The accounting features include check writing.

The particular examples used are only meant to show you how these billing programs work and what they will do for you. As with all competitive programs, the advantages and disadvantages between them are usually trade-offs in one way or another.

These are tricky times, Y2K being what it is. You'll have to resort to your own ingenuity and perspicacity to locate a billing program to suit your fancies. Some of my students and readers have done well with programs like Microsoft Works, selecting data screens that will fill their billing needs. The "Works" program offers a simple but workable billing setup for those who need only an invoicing or statement generating method.

Microsoft Works provides a handy spreadsheet that can be manipulated in any fashion you might choose. Each column can be sized to accommodate whatever class of entry you prefer. Narrow columns would be for dates, hourly charges, time spent, etc. Columns could be a bit wider for hourly fees and balances. The widest column would contain the descriptions of the work done.

Some expenses are business deductible, some tax deductible and some are personal. All legitimate business expenses incurred in your practice are deductible whether they pass technical muster as a tax deduction or not. To distinguish these disbursements, different categories are set up.

Look for a tab identifying categories, chart of accounts or some other similar term. Most of the category divisions selected by the software company will not be useful in a law practice. You'll need to customize those that apply. There'll be a means to do that plainly seen.

The Chart of Accounts is the backbone of any accounting system. It includes accounts that are maintained primarily for the business side of your law practice. These items chart the categories to describe the nature of each income or expenditure entry.

Each account is classified as an asset, liability, income, expense or retained earnings account. If you aren't disposed toward donating additional dollars to the IRS as taxes, I heartily recommend that you label all categories with the proper identification as "tax related" or not so related.

Select as many as you can think of to start the program. You can expect to add some as you find the need. It's not necessary to divide categories into the smallest possible subdivision. Gas, electric and water can all be lumped under "utilities." The fewer divisions the better, so long as they may be understood by your accountant.

Before you start churning out an unending flow of rhetorical headings, study those that come with your accounting program. Quicken has a rather complete list of common categories. Listings like legal fees, law library, attorney's services, etc. will need to be added as a "new" or "custom" entry.

STI's General Ledger Chart of Accounts is an advanced method of selecting and categorizing each item. Each entry is identified by account number, description, account type and other qualifications.

After reviewing many billing programs, I have found that most of them offer similar basic functions. Some have better or faster ways of doing some things; others offer innovative methods of categorizing accounts. The examples are therefore not meant to show any uniqueness in any particular software but to show what billing programs in general can accomplish for you.

More detailed examples and information on bookkeeping and office routine follow further along. You will have entered your services for John Jones, including all phone calls. This procedure requires only a single entry. Counter entries are done automatically.

The procedures for billing in TABS-III are adaptable to any sized firm large or small. You can expand the program as your practice grows. STI's software produces good-looking documents. That, as much as anything else, makes TABS-III a reasonably good choice.

Now, when you are ready to bill, one single entry, and your statement is rendered with a flick of finger. Your printer ticks out a highly professional looking statement.

STI's Case Master-III program, included in the bundle, covers a reasonably wide assortment of case file and client categories. For example, it includes fields to note case notes, the time of entry, all related parties, a calendar file and a document history of the matter.

Other fields any potential "Conflicts of Interest," a calendar of "due dates," case time summary and the all important "Statute of Limitations." Moreover, the program provides a Document Assembly of the case and optionally other matters concerning this client. Another field permits the editing of the document history and a provision applies to Document Cross Reference Files.

My personal preference is not to print out the hourly charge or the dollar amount per entry. My clients know my hourly rate. That is made clear at several intervals, and in the Attorney/Client contract. That choice is up to you.

I just do not see the virtue in the entry-by-entry repetition. Some firms do not even separate the entries by date, but merely lump all monthly services together. You can customize the statements as you wish. Use the samples here only as a generalization as to what they will show.

As a solo lawyer, you may also have selected rates for different kinds of matters or for different clients depending upon ability to pay or whatever criteria. These are matters left strictly up to your own discretion.

All of your arithmetic is done for you. You needn't sit with a calculator in one hand and an accounts receivable file in the other, punching away, trying to arrive at a final number. You say you don't use a calculator? Oh, your fingers and toes. Well, that's another way. One press of your computer key and the work is all done for you in a few seconds. Better than fingers and toes, right?

Your program knows how to do the math. You've told it what your hourly fee is. You also tell it how much time you've taken to do each service. All the rest is computer operation.

You can have as many different rates as you wish. For your mother, if you're an old softy, you can work out a discount or even log time without any billing rate at all.

You'll be shocked at the detail composition of your Summary Balance Sheet composed by most all of these accounting programs whether the cheaper simple kind or the more deluxe programs.

As in other such programs, the Balance is taken from the Chart of Accounts for the Asset and Liability accounts. The program calculates the percentage of change for the same period of the preceding year as well as the differential dollar change.

Most computer calendar or docketing programs are made for larger firms with many potential conflict situations. As you've seen, the STI program has a provision for that. You and I don't have such complications. Still, we need a selective calendar program that will alert us to the functions important to our practice

Microsoft Works contains a calendar that should accomplish that for us. It has a reminder pop-up window to give you advance notice up to one week. Any and all appointments may be so scheduled reminding you what you must do during the coming week each time you open your computer.

STI's calendar plan in its Case Master III provides for entries "TO DO." This comports with my urging to calendar all of your pending projects in the "Seven Basic Rules." [See Chapter 7.]

The reminder pop-up screen appears immediately following the boot up to desktop showing whatever you have scheduled within the period selected. The pop-up window does just that; pops up. It announces itself with a musical tone and appears in the midst of your desktop icons.

I find this a positive, reliable method of triggering my schedules of appointments whether in office or in court. I've had some strange effects with older calendar programs, such as loss of data. This was disconcerting as well as inconvenient, requiring all data to be re-entered. Frightening, since some data may not be all that available for recovery.

The "Works" Calendar, as will most all calendars, offers daily, weekly, monthly or whatever display on the screen upon access. I use the monthly system. Each day on the month's page of dates on which you have an engagement displays the first few words of your engagement.

When you access the calendar by double clicking the Calendar icon, the current month page will appear on screen. Today's date will be highlighted.

No setup is required for this calendar. It's not necessary to do anything to save your entries. This is done automatically when you exit.

Your billing program, whatever you choose, will probably have a choice of different statement formats. You can choose the full format, including the name of each attorney involved in each service, the hourly rate charged, the price per hour, and the subtotaled fee for each individual service performed. Or, you can choose one of several more succinct versions.

Most programs provide for client lists searchable by both code number and alphabetically. If you file by number, as I do and recommend, each client's code will be the file number. If you file alphabetically, the client code would be in reference to the alphabet.

A disadvantage of the alphabetical system is in adding or deleting a client file you've disrupted the alphabetical order. When you add a client you simply add to the numerical sequence. When you delete a file, you merely replace that number with the next client's file.

You always know when a folder is out of file because the number sequence is disrupted. You have no such signal in the alphabetical system. If folder numbers aren't replenished with new clients, the empty file folder is in its proper numerical place although empty.

In addition to this listing automatically addressing the statements, it can also serve as a client list for mail merging or other uses. A printout of this list, done at the flick of a finger, can also serve as your card file index.

Another plus of the computerized method of billing is that its simplicity removes most of the drudgery of that process when done manually. The computerization process also assures reliability. It removes inaccuracy and possible duplication.

Information given on this program, as well as on the other programs used for demonstration, is not intended to serve as an operator's manual. Specific information on how to use any of these programs must be taken from the individual program manuals.

However, this overview should provide a general concept by which you might understand the approach to the computerized law office. With this background, you should find the specifics more familiar and less intimidating than if viewed from a "cold start."

I haven't tried all legal billing systems, nor even a high percentage of them. Most billing programs are overkills for solos. My conclusion after trying a reasonable cross sectional number of programs is that they suffer from sameness rather any claim to distinction.

Timeslips (Timeslips® is a registered trademark of the Timeslips Corporation) an economical, "do much" program, has, as expected, released a much improved program. This allows a virtually instantaneous application of the services performed to the billing program.

Timeslips 5.5 economy "Personal Plus," version is offered at a greatly reduced price (only $99.90). The only difference between the programs is the number of timekeeping lawyers on track. The $99.90 "Personal Plus" version limits use to just two timekeepers. There are other limitations, as you'll see in comparing it with the deluxe version below. As I see it, this $99.90 version should be reasonably acceptable for a solo lawyer or a two-lawyer firm. This program has several upgrades over the 5.1 version reported in last year's supplement. Plus, it's "Year 2000" compliant.

Timeslips 8.5 Personal Plus Deluxe is customizable, it has text search, and is much faster than the 5.5 version. 8.5 is Windows 98 and Y2K compliant. It's a bit pricier at $179.90. If you can float the bucks difference, you might find 8.5, or whatever the updated version number, more satisfactory.

Bear in mind that all prices quoted should be whittled away in discount stores or at what we call "street" prices. You'll be busy lining up referring attorneys and working your assignments for the first few months so getting prices and buying products won't be your first concerns. However, when time permits, do some shopping.

The money you save will be money you earn. The troublesome part of producing an inexpensive, simplified billing program is defining the functions that specifically apply to a legal practice. It seems more practical to use an existing complex system and ignore the parts that are surplus to the solo lawyer. That way, the program would be available in two versions, the simple one for newer lawyers and the more deluxe system for well established firms.

Most any billing program could be trimmed down to parameters useful for new solo practitioners. Just cut out all of the needless complicated reporting files that would only apply to a larger multi-attorney firm. Then, reduce its span to accommodate one or two lawyers instead of the virtually limitless number covered by the high powered systems.

Other excesses are the interlocking functions from billing to accounting systems, complicated means of updating statements, end-of-month procedures, aggregate input and balances and other reports of no interest to solo and small firms.

Unfortunately, most producers of inexpensive, "simplified" billing, and even accounting, programs just cannot let go of that tiger they hold by the tail. Even Timeslips 5.5, "simple" by comparison, and the accounting system Quicken are more complicated than is needed for our use.

The problem is the procedure needed to operate the program. The more steps necessary, the greater the frustration and potential for error even though those steps may be relatively simple.

If you are tuned into a particular client's record, you can shuttle back and forth between whatever program is generating the input, such as your CD-ROM research disk, your word processor, or whatever, and the billing information directly to that client's statement.

Timeslips has enhanced the customization method for customized billing and statements. The program has speeded up somewhat and can interface with many different accounting programs. Timeslips is well worth looking into. So far as I can see, it's as much as you'll need and far cheaper than strict legal billing programs.

As we get into the computers for solos Chapter, we'll explore possible construction of billing programs from data or spread sheet operations. Although one needn't be a computer "hacker" to do this, it requires more than a basic knowledge of computers.

Whatever billing program you choose, its functions should include your schedule of projects and planned time; triggers for important due dates; record of expenditure of time; record of income; preparation of the clients' statements; monitoring receivables; preparation of management reports; and maintenance of your client trust fund.

The multi-tasking operations in Microsoft Windows 98 (or perhaps you'll have Windows 2000 by now), will permit making entries into billing and accounting systems in simultaneous screens. To change from one account to another can be done in several different ways.

I find it convenient to simply move the current window over to a side to view the second window. Accessing either doesn't require leaving either program. Hence, there's no big chore in keeping all accounting business done within minutes each day.

I suggest use of a simple accounting program along with a more sophisticated billing program. You might consider Quicken, QuickBooks, Microsoft Money, or any of the several good accounting programs found everywhere.

There is the advantage of automation. Entries made though the ledger accounts will post to the respective client accounts.

Most accounting programs these days are grossly over-involved. Who needs budgets in a business? If you don't know your financial status on a minute-by-minute basis constantly, you should give more thought to whether you ought to own your own business. Other "nice" facilities to those programs may seem handy but, chances are, you'll not use half of them.

I'm presently using Microsoft Money. Not that this program isn't as unwieldy as the rest, but it's no worse. I found it a bit complicated to learn, but not more so than the others. Once learned, however, it's operation is at least workable and it does offer much more facility than my old Checks & Balances.

For instance, when you prepare a check for a new payee, a window will pop up asking you to insert the address. In C&B, you needed to enter the address under a function called "Names." If you failed to do this, the check would print with the payee's name only.

C&B also demanded that you entered the name word precisely as you phrased in under "names" or the reference wouldn't work. Even after years using C&B, I often needed to look up names to get them right.

Once the relevant information is entered in Money, all of this information, full name, category, etc., will appear to complete the entry for you. Forgiveness is far-ranging on most modern accounting programs.

Checkbook balancing is also a snap. All that is asked is the statement's opening and closing balances, any bank charges or interest accrued, and then a mouse click on each check issued and deposit reported in your statement. A comforting musical cord is sounded and the pronouncement that you've balanced the accounts.

Sometime either just before or just after the turn of the Millennium, I will switch from Money to Quicken. Then I can report on a comparison check between these two programs in the 2001 supplement.

I describe the useful features of the selected programs to demonstrate what such programs can do for you. I don't claim that any one of these programs is superior to any other similar type. I have seen some marvelous accounting and billing programs that I feel may be either too expensive or too confusing.

My complaint about all of them stems from their overambitiousness to accomplish entirely too much. It appears much of the confusion comes from an over eagerness to do complicated things and then finding the method to do them as afterthoughts.

Test all the programs carefully. Choose what you like, can afford and can use. By the time you read this, most any program you choose will be Y2K compliant. Still, it wouldn't hurt to check it out.

I hope the information given helps you to decide on what's best for you. There are great programs that can do lots of startling things. You should just decide whether the expense or complications are worth it.

My selections are the results of both my experiences and research. Your preferences may be quite different. My purpose in referencing the features of each is to give you a general idea of what these programs can do for you.

These same facilities will be true, more or less, of other available programs. Trade-offs are to be expected in making your selections, whether by price or special attributes. This is not to say that you'll get the best by paying more.

If you don't purposely try for needless complications, you'll do best at the lowest prices. This does not mean that in some cases more expensive or more intricate programs do not offer advantages you might appreciate that I do not.

Be forewarned. If you are not really well-informed on computer technologies and do not understand programming principles, you can easily be deceived by computer "hype" vagueness. You may be oversold on what you "need" in a program.

I learned the hard way that simplicity and economy were not only virtues in themselves, but the way to better computer use by solo lawyers. Unless you are one of a kind, your solo practice will not benefit by overly sophisticated and costly programs.

You'll find most, or all, of these macros and other software shortcuts in most of the better billing programs mentioned and in dozens of others on the market. You won't find a program with the precise offerings of the particular ones I've selected, but what you don't get you probably don't need anyhow.

Where one program offers this or that advantage, there is this or that disadvantage. Where one program has a particularly desirable feature, another program has a different feature just as good.

Getting started.

Most sizable programs these days are packaged with CD disks. The first step will be to install the program from those CD's onto your computer hard drive. Installation procedures will vary in some ways from program to program. In the main, however, they all follow a more or less generalized format.

In most instances, inserting the CD in the drive will bring up the installation process automatically. The company window logo will appear after which you'll follow a menued instruction.

Other systems will need to be installed by accessing your control panel and choosing "Add New Programs." In some cases installation is done through the "RUN" provision on your start list and stating the drive letter, path and program command.

If things go well, the term "install" or "setup" would start the installation procedure. From that point, you would be instructed, step-by-step on the monitor to install the program.

You may, or may not, be told to "reboot" your computer. After that, it might be necessary to customize the program according to the particular computer and printer you own. Usually, though, Windows will automate through the rest of the installation process.

Every part of this "installation" session is what is called "menu-driven." This means that you are taken from one schedule of options to the next. You are never left to your own devices. If you are distracted somehow and follow the wrong pathway, you'll soon recognize it and retrace your steps without difficulty.

You will need to decide how you want the program to work for you. You will need to tell it about your billing setup, the manner of applying charges, whether to add late fees, how you want your statement formed, and as many other things as it's complications demand.

"Free" warranty services are not really free.

Most of these program manufacturers offer a phone number to

a service called "Tech Support." These lines are tended by qualified technicians able to answer the questions you might ask.

These days, many program manufacturers are requiring a toll number to call tech support even though services are "free" during warranty periods. Toll-free numbers are provided but only for automated methods, often not satisfactory. After expiration of your warranty, you will be charged so much per service call.

Don't underestimate the cost of phoning long distance. The term "free" appeals to massive callers. You can be held on hold, listening to the producers' sales pitches or nauseating music. Or even silence, for seemingly ages. Even worse, they can pull you through endless recorded instructions to press this or that number for this or that department. That's not only boring but requires your rapt attention.

There are a number of more-or-less generic billing programs on the market. Some follow logical formulas and some do not. I would skip those that offer confusing or ambiguous instructions. Among things left to your own creativity in almost all billing programs is the closing line to your statements. I selected

"THANK YOU FOR ALLOWING ME TO BE OF SERVICE TO YOU."

You can use this or any other such statement that you prefer. You are confined only to the number of spaces available.

You might then be required to make a brief phone call to have your program or parts of it "unlocked." This process involves following simple instructions to type five or six symbols on your keyboard. Without this being done, you would not be able to enter that portion.

An infinite number of billing arrangements are offered. This is convenient for applications to an array of charges for several assigning attorneys.

In case you've forgotten, you will establish different work fee schedule for each of your several assigning attorneys if for no other reason than your charges increase as you develop your practice. You will also have an assortment of time charges for your clients depending on the kinds of matters handled.

You will have followed the set of questions for installation of your client list. Each client would be identified with a code, either alphabetical or numerical. I use the numerical system in this as well as for client files.

Your screen should then show a form to the client code and the attorney hourly rate, and type the date, the number of hours (or fractions of hours), and the description of your services. You should be able to change the rate at any entry. Thereafter, if you have several entries for that same client, the same information would be transferred from form to form until changed by you.

When you have made all current entries for that client, you simply show the next client code in the form and continue with that client, and so on.

Payments on account by clients are entered in much the same fashion with a menu identifying the amount and so on. You are also given a menu for costs advanced and other pertinent information.

All of the computation is done for you, fully and completely, without your help (or hindrance).

There are many, many more options available with most billing programs. I predict that you will use only a small part of the power offered by these billing programs. Unfortunately, good programs containing only the functions you or I need are not available.

Many solos and small firms find the generic program "Timeslips" adequate. Although this program is not made specifically for lawyers, it has the essentials and is not overly complicated to use. Take a look at it.

Lots of articles have been written on the subject of what and how to buy computer programs. Some offer interesting ideas, but mostly they lack practical approaches to the problems of the new lawyer. One article in particular dealt strictly with contracting for the purchase of customized programs.

To the new lawyer, this approach suffers from fatal flaws. The cost of program customization is enormous. You might pay several thousand dollars for a billing program custom-designed for you and still not be assured that you would get any kind of satisfactory result.

Each of the programs used as illustrators in this book has undergone several revisions. By the time you read this book, each will no doubt have had several more. Moreover, such revisions usually result from, and incorporate, multiple and diverse views.

Expert reviewers help shape the program format. Users add their criticisms and suggestions to the input of the programmers. The version that you load into your computer is most likely such a compilation. Your purchase price of a marketed program buys you the right to update to the newest and highest state of that art whenever it is offered.

Most producers will regularly contact their subscribers with current news of new versions. When, as, and if you find that a newer version will serve a substantial purpose, you can usually get it for far less than new subscribers Thus, you figuratively have a whole team of experts working on your behalf to assure the highest and best applications consistent with the capabilities of the program.

When you contract for a custom program, it is just you and your programmer. You alone are responsible for submitting your proposed program functions and operation. You are charged with not only knowing what you want the program to accomplish but with foreseeing the limitations and inadequacies of your plan.

Designing computer programs requires not just computer programming skills. One must also be an expert in the subject matter of the program. Few programmers have any such skills. They are geniuses, to be sure, but in their own expertise, programming, not necessarily in accounting, word processing, billing, etc.

To produce a competent accounting program, for instance, a highly skilled accountant must work with the programmer. But even this is not enough. Even persons skilled within a given discipline will suffer to some extent from "tunnel vision."

You may think you know what you want a given program to do for you, but think again. If these professional programming firms, with all of their help and guidance from programming and subject matter experts, need all of this manifold preparation, what would your chances be?

In my research on this subject, I have learned that some of the simplest programs have cost more than $100,000 to develop, and are still undergoing constant revisions. Programs for much simpler uses than billing and accounting are festooned with glitches and inadequacies. Even after several revisions, you can't be sure of getting what you want.

Programmers marketing their products expect their products to be sold to thousands and thousands of users, so that their costs will be amortized and profits earned on each sale. More often than not, those programs won't meet the anticipated sales level, or even the "break-even" point. Happily, that is not your gamble.

There is no program to perform every function that one could think of. But, not every function you might dream up would have the usefulness you might envision in actual practice anyway. Until you have had the idea subjected to the torture tests of computer adaptability and field practicality, you would have no way of knowing about its suitability or failings.

If you contract for a program individually and the programmer delivers it to you as per the contract terms, it's your baby. What you get will be a prototype for your thousands of dollars in cost. This is just the threshold.

You would then face the same revision processes that confound professional programming firms. But you do not have their resources, background, experience, or facilities. You would pay out lots of money in your chase for the utility you sought. But the overwhelming chances are that your product would fall far short of an acceptable standard of quality and usefulness.

So, even though these professionally designed programs are not all the perfection that you'd dream of, they're often mighty close. This would deny you the fun of the many hours of frustrated failures and aggravation. You would also be burdened with the price difference remaining in your bank account.

§ 11:8 Computer-generated bill paying

This is the other side of the coin in the accounting procedure consisting of income and disbursements. You should decide whether you will operate this accounting program on the "cash" or "accrual" method.

Cash or accrual accounting system.

The cash system records money received as income and money paid out as costs, expenses, investments or whatever other purposes you use your money. The accrual system is more complicated.

Money earned but still owed to you, as under a delayed payment schedule, are shown as assets. Money owed to others, as in installment purchases, are shown as liabilities.

Income recorded under the accrual method is subject to modifications dependent upon whether, for one or another reason, the money will not be paid to you. This requires attention on your part and can lead to problems if not regularly proctored.

Money owed to you recorded under the accrual method is entered in an account called accounts receivable. Money you owe you will enter in an accounts payable account.

If you choose the accrual method and your accounts receivable shows much more money than your accounts payable, your financial status may possibly be artificially inflated. The reverse may also be true. Your debts may exceed your prospective income.

For these reasons as well as my general dislike for unnecessary complications, I have operated under the cash basis from the start of my practice. I've never found a good reason to consider the accrual method.

The cash basis is relatively simple. A client pays your fee entered as cash received under "fees." Your rent is entered as a disbursement under "rent." Any bills you owe won't be visible in your accounting system until you choose to pay them. No future obligation of that client is identified in your ledger.

Each service you perform is recorded on each client's account for whom you did the work. You will access those accounts when you bill for your services but the amounts owed to you aren't recorded as assets until paid.

Time for payment of bills.

There comes a dreary day, once a month, when you must pay your bills. In the business world, this is called "the 10th of the month blues." This won't be your song because you won't be spending that much for quite a while. But paying bills isn't your favorite pastime.

Your bill payment scenario should follow something like this. You get a shipping slip with the goods. Place the shipping slip in a tray marked "goods received."

When the invoice comes, check the price and other information with the order form you used, or whatever other method you have to determine that you are being charged the agreed upon or anticipated price.

Staple the shipping slip to the invoice and move them to the next tray marked "O.K. for payment." But this tray is not for bills to be paid, regardless of what is said on the invoice.

When the statement finally comes, staple the invoice and shipping slip to the statement. Place them in the last tray marked "Bills to be paid."

Some business people divide this last tray into two parts. The first is marked "Preferred Creditors, Drop Dead Immediately." The others must wait six months. These are filed in the second part of the tray.

If you follow the above routine, all reference to the goods received will have been removed from the trays. They will have been stamped or marked "Paid" by you, with the date of payment and the check number noted.

This will be elaborated on in the computer's Chapter, but you should consider using your printer to print checks. Since you must do all the work necessary anyway, why not print the check with the touch of your mouse.

This not only makes life easier for you but it eliminates the possibility of transposition of numbers. So many mistakes can be made in the simple matter of transcribing information from your accounts sheet to your manual checkbook.

If you have a laser printer, you'd use automated 8-1/2 x 11 laser paper for checks as well as everything else you print. This will give you a check and two vouchers. One voucher goes with the check and the other you staple to the combination invoice, shipping slip and statement.

You cannot pay twice for the same goods, because there will be no opportunity for you to do so. That is unless you make the mistake of paying on the invoice instead of the statement. Then, you might stumble over the subsequent statement and pay a second time.

Filing paid bills in some sort of order to enable locating any particular one is very difficult if done manually. If done by computer, your program makes finding things a simple matter of a keystroke or two. It also virtually eliminates the possibility of double payment.

Difficulties in filing paid bills manually.

File the packet of papers evidencing the payment into a file identified as "Paid Bills." This file is composed of a series of file folders, each marked with a letter of the alphabet. The paid bill is deposited into the envelope of the letter best identifying the company from which the goods were purchased.

For example, if the company is the Stuart F. Cooper Co., you will select the folder marked "S" for "Stuart," or possibly "C" for "Cooper." Compound company names like that do present filing problems. The difficulty is that without a computer you would have no reliable way of remembering what initial you've used in any of these situations.

The only thing you can be sure of is the occasional frustration you'll experience in trying to locate a paid bill when you need it. There really is no foolproof way of filing the hard copies of paid bills so that they may be easily found in future days.

No matter what letter is selected for the filing of a given bill, you will be sure to look under some other letter when trying to find it later. Be consoled with the knowledge that you will find it sooner or later.

Simplicity of filing paid bills by computer.

You can always find the company description on your computer accounting system by typing any word in the name. Poof, the correct name will appear. Matter of fact, when you write the check, you need only type the first two or three letters of the name and the entire company name appears ready to go.

The "correct name" will be the one you label on the file folder. This assures you will always be ushered to the proper place for filing or finding a document. The computer, in effect, "rides herd" on your name fragments to group them all under the correct heading.

In addition to the correct name, the check number will also be seen. Since you've filed the invoices and statements numerically per check number as well as by date, retrieval is a picnic.

Forget that "drop dead" joke. Pay your bills on time. Don't be a wise lawyer who thinks that it's cute to roust a merchant around on payment. I have no respect for any lawyer who uses his professional knowledge to escape his proper financial or other obligations.

I have known many such "cutie" attorneys. But I have never known one who gained anything by these tactics. Even in the largest cities, the legal community is a small one where reputations are concerned. Your reputation will precede you.

Then, the practical manifestation is the loss of credit rating. Deadbeats in other vocations can change their names and residences. They can find jobs in other places. Lawyers are on a sort of leash.

Your bar affiliation is a tracer that cannot be avoided. As the great champion, Joe Louis, once said, "You can run, but you can't hide."

The time to use your head in the saving of money is not when bill paying time comes along, but at the time of the decision "to buy or not to buy." If you're in doubt, don't buy. The trick in any business to making money is to spend less than you earn.

Don't collect a bunch of garbage that you will never use or, even if you can use it, that you can do without. When you have the urge to buy something, wait a few minutes before pulling out your checkbook. Like a headache, the urge to buy will usually go away if you relax.

Many modern accounting programs come with CD software. Besides containing the program itself, it also has an indexed operator's manual. If you wish, you can print out the entire manual or part of it, or you can refer to any subject on screen by clicking on the reference bar.

There are many accounting programs available now that will serve your purposes just dandy. The one I've been using lately is Microsoft Money 99. There's also Quicken, QuickBooks and many others.

Unless you opt for one of the specifically applied legal accounting programs, several of which are fully explored in Chapter 12, most of the general systems are pretty much alike. One has this or that feature and the other emphasizes a different approach. Whichever one you select will be just fine if you take the time to learn it.

As with all descriptions of the various programs referred to in this book, no attempt is made to offer complete instructions or to substitute for the respective instruction manuals. The information given is merely to illustrate the general methods one might follow in a computerized law office.

No matter which kind of computer you choose, or which particular programs you may prefer, the object will be to systematize and expedite your office and practice chores. Even the slowest and least efficient of these will speed your practice and office administration to a fraction of the time taken in manual methods.

Most accounting programs can accommodate as many accounts as you wish. You will have at least two accounts, one being your Attorney General Account and the other your Client Trust Account.

The identification of these accounts can be kept secret as a security measure, or you can use a generic designation such as "GERALD SINGER GENERAL ACCOUNT" for the general account and "TRUST ACCOUNT" for the trust account. Isn't that convenient?

You may have a third account recording your personal or home accounts. Any transactions not of a business nature can be tracked in this account.

These accounts have both been "installed," as we previously noted, and are ready for operation. Since the bills to be paid are general operational expenses, the funds must come from the general, not the trust, account. We will deal with the trust account a bit later.

Setting up such a program is time-consuming and sometimes fraught with ambiguities. Expect to spend some hours doing this and contain your impatience.

Windows will do much of your work for you. Your printer will be found and identified. You'll need to select the format for your checks. Some programs will permit use of any blank you want. Some require proprietary blanks but the cost isn't a lot different from those purchased elsewhere.

As you enter names of clients and payees, you'll be asked to provide addresses, phone numbers, etc. Then, each time you type in a few letters of a subject, the program will find the entry and automatically fill in the rest of the name.

If you're writing a check, a few key touches and all information will be ready for printing. Click on "print" and the check will print out showing the full payee's name and address. Now all you need to do is slip the printed check into a window envelope for quick mailing.

Whether you print your checks or manually write them, the check sums will be processed and posted automatically to the correct category application. There will also be an automatic recalculation of your check balance. This will occur with each deposit and check entered. The resulting balance will reflect all entries and will correctly track your check statement.

You needn't follow any separate ritual for either making deposits or writing checks. For instance, while you are in the middle of writing checks, you can suddenly switch to recording income deposits. The same account sheet is used for both. You can click on either "checks" or "deposits" depending on which you want to enter.

The account sheet covers many entries on one screen page. You can see at a glance what checks you've written and deposits made. Some programs require a multiple check deposit to be entered as a "split."

Although this seems cumbersome to me, it's necessary to accumulate those multiple checks to constitute a single deposit instead of separate deposits for each check. No doubt some programs have a simpler way than the "split" method to do this, but those I've seen require this or something as complicated. Oh, where or where is Checks & Balances?

Then, after recording the deposit, with its breakdown of the different sources of income to comprise that deposit, you would resume your bill paying or whatever else you want to do.

Using our previous accounting example, see how easy and quick it would be to apply those same entries to a computer computation.

Your first check will be for rent, $350, payable to Flint Blackhart, your landlord. On your next check number in view, you show "Flint Blackhart" as the name on the "Pay To" line. Press return, and the cursor appears in the area where you register the amount.

You type "350". You don't need the zeros. If the amount were $3.50, you would designate that sum by typing the decimal point. Otherwise, the program assumes all whole numbers. Could it be simpler?

Then, in the memo box you will type the category as "RENT." This has already been defined under your Categories. That simple entry has already been distributed to the "RENT" account.

After you pay your rent for the first month's entry, the program will remember the amount paid as well as all other input information. The rent will probably be the same from month to month, but other regular bills will change in amounts. Disregard the presumed amount from the last entry and override with the correct sum.

There'll be a tab called "reports" that will permit a running report on any part of your accounts. This will allow you to review totals on any expense. After ten months you'll see an accumulated rent total of $3,500. The same will be true of each of the other expense categories, such as "LIBRARY MAINTENANCE, TRAVEL, ENTERTAINMENT, ATTORNEY SERVICE, SECRETARIAL SERVICE, OFFICE EXPENSE, AUTO EXPENSE, TAXES, LICENSES, POSTAGE, COURT COSTS," etc. Each of these categories will automatically track each check entry and will total up as each entry is made.

Any of these reports may be printed out at any time. You will, of course, want a complete report for your tax accountant. Variations on these reports are almost limitless. You can show totals on any selected category for any period, monthly, quarterly, semiannually or whatever.

It's just not possible to do all these things manually, much less in the time taken by these wonder programs. While I may criticize one program or another for some complication or whatever, I would have given a lot for even the worst of them just a few years ago.

Any of these programs will also help you to budget your income and expense accounts if you want this function. They include a function called "Budget" for just that purpose.

Just because you prepare checks doesn't mean you must print them. You can print them later or you can schedule them for payment on a selected regimen. All of these "can do" functions demand more time and effort in setting the program up. Is it worth it? Well, now that Checks & Balances is gone, what choice is there?

You can have as many accounts as you wish. Just press the tab, "accounts," then press "new account" and follow the menu. Set up your trust account just as you did the general account. You can also have a personal account or a home account.

Lillian, who prides herself on being non-technical, also prides herself on being expert in using her own accounting program. Since having to change from Checks & Balances, I feared that Lillian would rebel. After all she went through to learn one program, she's got to learn another one.

She just shrugged and said "Get over here and show me how to use this dang thing." I did and now she's as expert using the new program as she was using C&B. Though she hasn't been using the new one for long, she even now sees the huge advantages it offers.

As delighted as she was with C&B's fast, accurate method of check balancing, she seems ecstatic with the simplicity of this one. It even informs you as to any cause of imbalance.

Lillian still believes that these computer programs will slip up one day so she can say, "You're not so smart." That satisfaction has eluded her. So far, all errors have been human ones. Sometimes even mine (NAW!).

Lillian normally has little patience with what she calls "contraptions." She will not operate a VCR. She will deign to use the TV remote control but only to the extent of finding her favorite morning TV show and CNN. How or why she agreed to learn Checks & Balances and now even this more complex one is a mystery to me.

Another important bonus in automatic check writing is the elimination of transposition errors. How often have you had to spend hours tracking down a checkbook error to find a transposition between your check amount and the check stub entry (i.e., $289.14 on the check and $298.41 on the stub)?

As you can appreciate, this cannot happen in the automatic system since only one entry is made and that entry is what is imprinted on both the check and in your check register. If you've made any mistakes, they are at least consistent in both the checks and the register as well as elsewhere.

Because of the nature of the entries, mistakes are unlikely and very easy to detect. Moreover, any mistake can be simply corrected at the instant of detection. Then, upon correction, all totals and balances are automatically and instantaneously readjusted.

Corrections and readjustments in other programs I've reviewed require much more effort. In some cases, certain kinds of corrections are not even possible, requiring cumbersome counter-entries. I've found no error that cannot be immediately corrected, at whatever stage detected, in this or other programs of the same genre.

Filling out a check is about as simple as making a check from that same personal checkbook. If you want the check to show the payee's full address, you merely fill it out on the blank. The next time you send a check to that same payee, all that will be done for you automatically.

You don't have to enter that information in the check register as you must with your personal checkbook. That too is done for you automatically.

This automation is not only a great convenience and time saver, it's a protection against mistakes that we all make once-in-a-while. Transpositions are made between the bill and the check and the check and the register. Here, it's all automatic.

I urge that you strongly consider this kind of program for your accounting system. The same applies to each of the programs used as examples in this book. Make the routines of your practice as simple as possible. These programs were selected for just that purpose.

Computer hardware and software are undergoing changes almost as speedily as you read this book. No doubt by the time you obtain this copy, other computers and programs will have surfaced that might make these routines even simpler and yet more effective.

Being the first kid on the block, or having the fastest, best computer is not the only reason to keep abreast of changes. Programs that seemed to do everything are now doing even more for more things.

Such programs require more speed, more memory and more storage space. You shouldn't be left short on your tools. Computers are not luxuries; they're necessities. And, it's necessary that you keep up with your competition.

QuickBooks Pro may, in fact, supply most or possibly all of your needs for both billing and accounting. This product includes billing charts, invoicing and statements. A customized version is available specifically for lawyers. It's conveniently called QuickBooks Pro Legal.

The "Legal" version includes a timing feature you could learn to love. At the start of any procedure, such as research, drafting, conferencing or whatever, the timer is clicked and the time used will be addressed to your assigned hourly charge. The accrued time charges for each such procedure is amalgamated into the statement ultimately billed to the client for whom the work was done.

You say you want more for your money? The Legal version also has an assortment of legal documents such as wills, trusts, law dictionary and a variety of other legal documents.

The price for this handy program is now only $149.99 for a single user, that's you. When you get big enough for more users in your practice and you're still satisfied with what this system will do, you can upgrade to a multi-user version at a higher cost.

I haven't yet had an opportunity to inspect the QuickBooks Legal version, but I expect to have done that before the next supplement is issued. Meanwhile, check it out.

I don't mean for the terms "simple" and "complicated" to be either/or. Simple or complicated would be for each user to judge. For instance, the accounting program TreeBased, may be viewed as a step beyond the parameters of Money or Quicken, although I'm not sure that it exceeds the scope of QuickBooks Pro Legal. Much of the "complexity" of a program seen in the approach may be quite simple when learned.

The billing part is devoted to preparation of generic "invoices" not specifically applicable to legal billing. But it also generates statements. So, if we ignore the invoicing and utilize the statement portion only, it could be used as a complete package, accounting and billing.

TreeBased puts out two versions. The one I reviewed awhile back is version 2.5E Trigo sells at a nominal price. The other version is a "free" program dedicated to the public domain. You could take a look at the free version, and if you like it, order version 2.5E.

I suspect that the "free," or public domain, version lacks many of the refinements of the protected version. I suppose that this belongs to the "free lunch" kind of thing, of which they say there is none.

If a bit more learning work doesn't turn you off, take a look at TreeBased to perhaps satisfy your bookkeeping needs. Before you make any decision, check out QuickBooks Pro Legal and all other accounting and billing programs you can find.

Whatever system you get, be sure to go for any updates provided. You might avoid some headaches. I wanted to use the same specimen data for both Quicken and Money. When I tried to convert the data, as advertised, the program announced that Quicken 99 will not convert Money 99 data.

A call to Quicken's tech support people and I downloaded the new Quicken convert patch enabling me to make that switch. A simple matter but I could ill afford the time wasted in learning about it. If you don't see the message about upgrades on the program, call their tech support or customer relations department.

§ 11:9 Sample of billing statement

LAW OFFICES OF ________

[address]
[city, state, zip]

Phone: ________
Fax: ________

[Client Name]
[address]
[city, state, zip]

Billing Date: ________

Account ID: ________
Previous Balance: ________

CHARGES

DATE	INVOICE NO.	DESCRIPTION	REFERENCE	CHARGES
		Office conference on failure of lateral land support.	2.00 Hrs.	$300.00
		Research issue of adjacent land excavation.	1.00 Hrs.	$150.00
			TOTAL CHARGES:	**$450.00**

PAYMENTS

DATE	CHECK NO.	DESCRIPTION	REFERENCE	AMOUNT
			TOTAL CREDITS:	
			BALANCE FORWARD:	$445.00
			PLEASE PAY THIS AMOUNT:	**$895.00**

Terms: ________ days

When sending payment, include the invoice number on the check.
Thank you.

§ 11:10 Sample of billing spreadsheet

Page: ________
Date: ________
Account No: ________
Statement No: ________

[Client Name]
[address]
[city, state, zip]

________ *[Divorce]*
[Case Name]

Interim Statement

Fees

DATE	TIMEKEEPER	DESCRIPTION	RATE	HOURS	TOTAL
______	______	Open file/initial conference with client			n/c
______	______	Letter to accountant requesting tax returns	125.00	0.40	50.00
______	______	Letter to (name) requesting financial net worth of spouse	125.00	0.40	50.00
______	______	Letters to bank and brokerage firms requesting status of account	125.00	1.25	156.25
		For Current Services Rendered		2.05	256.25
		Total Nonbillable Hours		1.00	

Recapitulation

______	______		2.05	$125.00	$256.25

Expenses

______	Photocopy Charges	4.50
______	Postage	3.48
	Total Expenses	7.98
	Total Current Work	264.23

Payments

______	Payment to firm to cover outstanding costs	−7.98
______	Payment	−256.25
	Total Payments	−264.23
	Balance Due	$0.00

Billing History

FEES	HOURS	EXPENSES	ADVANCES	FINANCE CHARGE	PAYMENTS
256.25	2.05	7.98	0.00	0.00	264.23

Client Funds

Beginning Client Funds	$0.00

§ 11:11 Sample of summary balance sheet

Date: ________ Page: ________

Summary Balance Sheet

________ P.C.

Reporting Period: ________

Department: ________

	CURRENT	LAST MONTH			LAST YEAR		
	BALANCE	BALANCE	$ CHANGE	%	BALANCE	$ CHANGE	%
ASSETS							
Total Cash	____	____	____	____	____	____	____
Total Current Assets	____	____	____	____	____	____	____
Total Fixed Assets	____	____	____	____	____	____	____
Miscellaneous Assets	____	____	____	____	____	____	____
Total Assets	____	____	____	____	____	____	____
LIABILITIES							
Total Payables	____	____	____	____	____	____	____
Total Employer Tax Liability	____	____	____	____	____	____	____
Miscellaneous Liabilities	____	____	____	____	____	____	____
Total Liabilities	____	____	____	____	____	____	____
OWNER EQUITY							
Total Partner's Accounts	____	____	____	____	____	____	____
Retained Earnings	____	____	____	____	____	____	____
Total Owner Equity	____	____	____	____	____	____	____
Total Liability & Owner Equity	____	____	____	____	____	____	____

§ 11:12 Sample of detailed balance sheet

Date: ________ Page: ________

Detail Balance Sheet

STI Demonstration Client

Reporting Period: ________

Department: ________

	CURRENT	LAST MONTH			LAST YEAR		
DESCRIPTION	BALANCE	BALANCE	$ CHANGE	%	BALANCE	$ CHANGE	%
ASSETS							
Cash							
Bank Account #1							
Bank Account #2							
Total Cash							
Total Current Assets							
Fixed Assets							
Furniture & Fixtures (FMV $2000)							
Equipment (FMV $5150)							
Accum. Depr.–Furn & Fixtures							
Accum. Depr.–Equipment							
Total Fixed Assets							
Miscellaneous Assets							
Total Assets							
LIABILITIES							
Payables							
Bank Loans Payable							
Notes Payable							
Total Payables							
Employer Tax Liability							
Fed Income Tax Withheld							
State Income Tax Withheld							
Employee FICA Withheld							
Employer FICA Payable							
FUTA Payable							
SUTA Payable							
Total Employer Tax Liability							
Total Liabilities							
OWNER EQUITY							
Partner's Accounts							
Partner's Capital Account							
Partner's							
Drawing Account							
Total Partner's Accounts							
Retained Earnings							
Total Owner Equity							
Total Liability & Owner Equity							

Chapter 12

Computers and Programs Especially for Solo Lawyers

§ 12:1 Generally

Vi a duck? Vi not a chicken?

Groucho Marx told Chico to meet him at the viaduct.

Chico asked,

"Vi a duck? Vi not a chicken?"

That makes as much sense as lawyers who ask,

"Vi a computer? Vi not a typewriter?"

Before we get further involved in how your computer can manage your practice and office, we should explore some of the basics of computers and computering, costs, financing; the where and how of obtaining computers.

How to use a computer and other equipment free!

You can get everything you need to operate your practice for nothing. How is this done? The use of a computer with all needed peripherals as well as a copier, scanner and the rest, can be part of your original negotiations on your time for space deal.

I use the term "free," and it might be just that. This depends upon your virtuosity as a salesman. Toss in the issue of equipment usage AFTER you've made your hourly fee deal. If you're successful, the equipment use is free.

It may or may not mean a slight reduction on your hourly fee but this is also a deal point. Your success in getting what you want on this subject as well as any other will be the product of your success in salesmanship.

"O.K. Mr. Johnson, I'll do all your work for $50 an hour but I'm going to need the use of one of your computers, a printer, scanner (etc.) So, will you arrange for these?"

If this is stated in a matter-of-fact tone, the issue may be settled then and there. It may require one or two more interviews, but you'll get everything you want through persistent selling. Obviously, the limit line will be whether that office can muster up some spare equipment.

Most offices have older machines around that have been upgraded. You can't expect the latest and best models, but then you won't need the best for the next couple of months.

By the time your practice blossoms to where speed and output is essential, you will have become financially healthier. Then, you can shop for better quality stuff. Patience is a needed accouterment in starting your practice in everything but getting your assignors and filling your workdays.

Sooner or later everything comes your way. When finances are thin, you'll need to put up with a few inconveniences. Whichever direction you can travel, you'll reach the point of your destined practice at about the same time.

If you have some bucks to start with, you'll follow the charts further along in this book to buy what you need. Still, there's no need to be more extravagant than necessary.

I started on my time-for-space sojourn using equipment provided by my assignor-landlord. This was before computers, but I received a Selectric typewriter, copier, filing cabinet and most of my expendable office supplies were supplied for me while I remained in that office. I could afford to buy everything needed but salesmanship was one of my better commodities. I suggest that exercising your sales ability would be good for you too. Why spend more than you need to.

BEWARE the great "REBATE" caper.

To paraphrase,

"Money delayed is money denied."

An essential in starting your new solo law practice is getting your cash flow without delay. This is the reason for arranging with your work assignors to pay you each evening for that day's work.

If the issue arises, your response is that you have an arrangement with the banks. They don't practice law and you don't make loans. Payment later for work done today is equivalent to making a loan to the assigning lawyer. You need the dough more than he/she does.

Admittedly, payment nightly is an inconvenience but you need the dough fast to handle your daily expenses. You have no back-up financing. Your only income is payment for your work assignments.

This is part of the cost to the assigning lawyer for getting first class work from you at bargain basement prices. Getting that arrangement is also part of your salesmanship project. [See Chapter 13 on "Salesmanship In Your Law Practice.] Payments or rental on your home, groceries, installment payments, childcare, etc., won't wait, neither should you.

Expense prudence is as vital as expediting income in setting up your first office. Buying equipment with expectations of "rebates" by mail can severely restrict your cash flow, sometimes indefinitely.

The whole rebate scenario could possibly become moot by the time you read this. Some recent ads are showing some improvement in clarifying "rebate" offers. Ads are even beginning to appear on sale items stating "NO REBATE HASSLES."

This expression at least admits to the inequities of the rebate scam. The heart of the rip-off is in the advertising. Any ad that leads to belief of one thing but results in delivery of another is, to one degree or another, false and fraudulent.

In my opinion to be ethical, the nature of, and method of obtaining, the rebate should be clear, bold and unequivocal. That qualifying language should also be as prominent as the price.

Further complications lurk in the required application for the rebate. Usually, unless you ask for the application, often none is offered. The form is often very small with the type instructing how to obtain the rebate even tinier.

At the present state of "clarification," it's still not obvious that you must buy something, contract for something, subscribe to something, wait interminably or follow some complicated esoteric instructions before you see a dime of the "rebate." So long as there remains any need to scrutinize the ad or the application to find the clinker, the program remains a scam.

As an expert in merchandising, I can sniff out fast pitches about as fast as they throw them. In this case, get set for the fast ball but watch for the curve.

The grabber of this dodge is that almost every legitimate retail business is involved in its practice. Well, if the Shmohawk Company offers rebates, they must be O.K. In my view, a business that takes any part in a scam—any kind of scam—should reassess its business principles.

If you don't already know, you should know about the asterisk"*" slight of hand in advertising. Now you see it, now you don't. The big advertised low, low price and the asterisk that mysteriously refers to some small print down, way down at the bottom.

You don't need to be a lawyer to recognize a "switch-pitch" or "lowball" tactic. The store price for an item is not the same as the advertised price. We've all experienced the "wudjatake" tactic by car salesmen, dealing on your trade-in. The "rebate" con can be even slicker. You buy at the retail price expecting that the advertised "rebate" will be mailed to you in due course. But will it?

The "rebate" dodge as presently practiced is as smooth a swindle as has ever been practiced in merchandising since the "SEW-VAC" scam. The advertised price in large print is NOT the price you pay for the item.

In one instance, the large type price read $150. Somewhere down at the bottom in the smallest print (if you can read it), **mail in rebate, $300, in store price $450."*

That means you actually pay the store price of $450. The $300 rebate will be mailed, they say.

Sometimes the "price" may even be a big type **"FREE."** *Subject of course to a rebate of perhaps $500. This means you pay the* *store $500 and then you follow the "simple" process of filling out the form, complying with the most exacting, esoteric instructions and of course, beating the date deadline.*

Recently, $400 rebates have been coupled with requirements to contract for Internet hosts. The usual condition is a three-year contract. If the contract is canceled, the rebate sum and often other penalties, are back charged.

The biggest laugh is that at least one of these Internet hosts offers the same $400 "gift" if you order the 3 year subscription at $21.95 per month directly. You get the $400 mailed to you without the need for any other purchase. Of course, the same penalties apply for early cancellation.

Sometimes the rebate requires subscriptions to a few magazines you don't need. If you don't subscribe, you don't get the rebate. Almost every conceivable gimmick has been attached to magazine subscription offers, including the infamous "You've already won," multi-million dollar Publisher's Clearing House mailings.

Information I've received, and believe, is that less than twenty (20%) of the purchasers ever receive a rebate of any sum. Why? They don't follow the instructions *exactly* or just don't bother.

Those "simple" instructions are anything but. You must include a specific part of the shipping carton. They don't say how you remove it but it actually requires cutting away a chunk of the carton.

You must then enclose the original receipt, (not a copy) which must contain a description of the product and other varied requirements. Where to mail it? Oh, the address is there, but try to find it. Use a magnifying glass. It might help.

Many folks who do attempt compliance are either ignored or everything is sent back for failure to touch some elusive base. For whichever of these, or other, reasons, over eighty (80%) percent of the buyers end up paying the "in store" price.

Retailers have been prosecuted for operating the "bait and switch," "lowball," "switch-pitch" or other such scams. They were child's play compared to this new, slick rip-off.

At least those old tactics gave you a sporting chance. You were in the store, face-to-face with the salesperson. He'd look you in the eye and blithely ask $250 for the sewing machine instead of the $9.95 advertised model. Well, at least you'd get one that would sew.

There was a real, live person to debate it with. This new wrinkle doesn't even give you a chance to argue. You complain to the store, "It's been six months and no rebate." You're told, "Oh, it sometimes takes longer than that." Or, "Well, we don't handle that; talk to the rebate company." Never mind you've tried that.

It's as though the "rebate company" is just a fiction. You get an answering machine that instructs you to press every number known to arithmetic, and then start over. But you seldom get to talk to anyone. Or, if you do, they offer to send you a new blank form. Maybe it's too late anyway by this time.

Oh yes, you may eventually get your rebate. Congratulations! You're one of the lucky fewer than twenty percent. What this really means is that the retailer gets its money, the distributor is paid in full and the manufacturer also receives payment.

The whole deception is based on probabilities. The statistical factors make this a predictable less than 20% discount sale. You can get better than that at any decent discount store. In the meantime, you're financing the operation. You can't afford that.

If you can't do better than the rebate item, go for it. But only if you consider the "in-store" price fair without the rebate. Then, if you never get the rebate, you're still not too unhappy. Funny, it seems that's the time you do finally get the rebate.

Hopefully, by the time you read this, there'll be a law prohibiting this kind of scam. If not, you're forewarned. Don't fall for it.

§ 12:2 So, what's a computer all about?

For those who don't know, would like a quick review or have some tepid curiosity, here's some basic information on how these technicalities interact with the mechanics of computerizing your law practice.

The computer itself is a dummy. Until an operating system such as Windows is installed, it can do nothing. Even then, a program, such as Microsoft Word or Corel WordPerfect, must be loaded to do word processing.

Other programs for billing and accounting, legal research, forms applications, calendaring, document management, etc., are needed to bring your computer to competency to handle your office and practice.

The computer needs immediate memory to temporarily facilitate the access of data for you to work on, and then a storage medium (hard drive) to permanently store that data when you've completed your work.

It needs much, much more to bring all of the factors of computer operation together so that all the work needed to be done can be done with minimal effort by you.

You really don't need to know all that your computer consists of other than to know something of what is needed to accommodate the width, breadth and depth of your office and practice needs. The bigger and more demanding your practice, the more capacity and speed your computer should have.

The hard drive.

Your computer hard drive stores all of the software necessary to operate the computer. All of those powerful programs that operate to make your law practice and your law office routine more expedient and fun are on that hard drive.

In addition to space consumed by those hungry programs, the hard drive will store many thousands of data sheets, such as pleadings, contracts, correspondence, etc. Don't think of this as a constantly accruing storage of archival material.

Actually, once prepared, most data files will be copied from the hard drive onto floppies, zip disks or other removables for filing in each respective client's file. Second back-ups will be copied and filed elsewhere for security. That data should then be deleted from the hard drive.

This is not simply to make room for more data but to keep the hard drive from needing to work harder to sift through many multiple ranks of folders and files. It will also protect that data from possible accidents, erroneously called "crashes," that could, in some drastic circumstances, erase files.

Your word processor and the "source code."

A word processor is a conglomeration of separately programmed information in a particular computer language, composed and identified by what is termed a "source code." The "source code" is as revealing to a computer programmer as a safe combination to Jimmy Valentine. Knowing the source code, any competent programmer, or even a well-informed computer amateur "hacker," can duplicate almost any program.

Each word processor such as WordPerfect or Word has its own structure and, even though programmed with similar computer language, is indifferent to the data written with another word processor. Data written under WordPerfect, cannot be fully used by Word, with all of its attributes unless first "converted" into Word's own language and vice versa.

Corel WordPerfect and Microsoft Word are close computer language cousins. Still, each should be converted to the other's language to be processed to its best use. An attempt to view such data by another host program might sometimes be interspersed with "hieroglyphics."

Most word processors now have such conversion programs included in their portfolios. However, "converted" data is not always successfully interpreted by a foreign word processor.

Some clean up work might need to be done within the host word processor before data can be relied upon. Features like spell check, grammar check, hyphenation, page breaks, etc., may not work properly from one to the other.

Nowadays, the major difference between word processors is in operational methods. All of the leading programs have been brought to within fractional qualities of each other. Each "big feature" of one program is equaled by a countering "big feature" of its competitor.

Source codes and programming.

All programs must follow a rigid foundational pattern. This is true of your billing, accounting, indexing, document retrieval, calendaring, and all other programs you will use in your practice. Each is composed under a "source code," and programmed with whichever language is preferred, so long as it all falls within the rules of the operating system, be it Windows, DOS, Macintosh, or whatever.

A keyboard is not a typewriter.

The transfer of information from your keyboard is not related in any way to that of a typewriter, whether mechanical or electronic. Each typewriter key is dedicated to a specific thrusting apparatus, whether directly in a mechanical typewriter, or indirectly in an electronic typewriter.

The typewriter key is a lever, or activates a lever, upon which the font facing is attached. The force, whether mechanical or electrical, causes the lever to impress the font upon the paper.

No such interconnection exists in a computer. The letter appearing on your monitor, and ultimately on the paper in your printer, is formed by an extremely complicated interpretation of the binary digital system of the zero/one combinations.

None of this information is necessary to your ability to use a computer. It's included to let you know something of what happens in that amazing box. It also might avoid some perplexity when you are trying to do things the computer just cannot accommodate.

Differentiate RAM as "MEMORY" from hard drive storage.

After all of those miraculous gyrations, manipulations and manifestations are completed, you have, if you've done your job right, some intelligible material temporarily occupying the RAM (random access memory) capacity of your computer and viewable on your monitor. This material is NOT STORED.

Every few minutes, or hopefully at some point prior to an electrical failure or other interruption, you will have saved that material permanently to your hard drive. At that point, the material is stored.

The major proportion of permanently recorded hard drive material is not what you would be printing. That part consists of the various programs that permit you to enter the data in preparation for printing on paper.

Again, the word "permanently" is provisional. Anything stored on the hard drive can be deleted or erased, whether intentionally or accidentally. If your hard drive becomes loaded near capacity, selected data may be copied over to a storage device such as a floppy, zip or other sort of removable disk or tape cassette and then erased from the hard drive.

There are dozens of programs stored on your computer with plenty of room left to store your data or for printing. For some inexplicable reason, the printed copy on paper is called "hard copy," while the program disk is called "software."

A will or pleading that is typed out on your printer is "hard copy" instead of typed copy or printed copy. Other descriptive words, whether or not better choices, are useless since the computer lexicon die is apparently cast.

Most programs are designed for ultimate disposition to printed pages. You will be able to produce pleadings, briefs, wills, correspondence, contracts, corporation materials, memos, research outlines, etc., through your word processing program.

Your accounting program will help you render and print balance sheets, check registers, checks, category totals, profit and loss statements, etc. The billing and calendar program is designed to prepare client statements, reports, calendar printouts, and other relevant papers.

Once these renderings are done, you can either copy the data to some form of alternate storage media, i.e. floppy disks, zip disks, tapes, etc., or leave on the hard drive for future reference.

These days hard drives are available in such enormous capacities that keeping voluminous files stored there is not a problem. Older, less efficient drives became bogged down with file surplusage.

Present day hard drives not only have high storage capacity but the access and transfer rates even under heaviest burdens far exceed the speed of drives just a few years old. Still, a certain amount of loading economy is highly recommended.

Document drafting and research consumes the bulk of a lawyer's day. Added to this is the time for housekeeping chores, such as record keeping, accounting, filing, time keeping, calendaring, billing, and other reporting. Each such chore may be done manually, in the same manner as it has been since lawyering began. That statement is meant only academically.

Even if you've never used a computer, you can't have escaped seeing them wherever you've looked. The keyboard may have intimidated you because of the strange key labels.

Mainly, the differences in operation between a typewriter keyboard and a computer keyboard lie in the multiple uses for the keys. The "return" key of the typewriter is labeled "enter" on the keyboard.

It operates as a "return" but does much more. The same is true of the "shift," "tab," "space bar" and other keys. They all serve many purposes. It will do little good to try explanations at this time. Just be assured that you will learn far more than enough to use the keyboard within a very short time.

The daunting "F" keys are macro customizable for many purposes. They are not essential for the elementary uses to which you'll put the computer at first. There are default values that we'll take up later.

There are many different computer configurations, different styles of housings, keyboards, monitors and whatever. The PC type using Windows and the Macintosh are different basically.

Each system has its own idiosyncrasies, foibles, advantages and disadvantages. Like almost everything else, it's a trade-off arrangement. Unfortunately, many of the so-called advantages to some of the other systems are esoteric and not at all applicable to your use or mine.

Computer demonstration for novices.

Now, let's go through some demonstrations of the computer, the printer, and various programs that lawyers use and that you should use in your office and practice.

Aside from the keyboard being different from a typewriter, neither the keyboard nor the computer itself has a life of its own. Pressing a key produces no effect until a program conveys an instruction to the computer system.

All programs will respect the integrity of keyboard letters and numbers. Regardless of which program is accessed, letters and numbers will appear as they are identified on the keys. This is true only because the programs will have it so. Accounting programs require alpha input just as word processing does. Numbers are likewise universal.

Let's start with your word processor, say, Microsoft Word of Microsoft Office 2000. We access this program by pressing the "start" button and then "programs" and then "Microsoft Word." We are in a sort of home base window titled "Microsoft Word."

Type a key. Any key. The letter you struck appears and the cursor moves one space to the right. The cursor occupies the place where any letter you select will appear. Now, type several words.

Each letter struck will cause the cursor to move one space to the right until it reaches the end of the line, when it will automatically drop one line, return, and be ready to type the second line of your document. The same will be true of spaces between letters.

This happens because the program will select the "wrap around" style of typing. Typewriters require a carriage return whether automatic or manual. This wrap around feature may be defeated if some purpose prefers a continual line.

The automatic carriage return ("word wrap") is just one of the many functions of a word processor program. Now, press the "up" arrow. Note the cursor moves up one line. Press the right arrow, and the cursor will move one space right.

The left arrow will move the cursor one space to the left. The down arrow will move the cursor one line down. This arrow movement is a simplified way to perform editing features that word processors offer.

You can move the cursor to a particular letter to correct a misspelling, (now done automatically in modern spell-checking word processors), to add space between words, to add words, or even to add complete sentences or paragraphs. As you make these additions or deletions, all of the sentences and paragraphs will be reformed automatically to restore your document as though the changes had been there all the time.

It will even automatically re-page the sheets if the changes caused extensions beyond the parameters of the original sheets. Notice also that the document had reformed itself as though you had restructured the whole thing yourself. Marvelous.

You can bold type, underline, italicize, invert, do whatever delights you for emphasis. You can change fonts, font sizes or slant type, and so many other things, if distinctiveness is your aim.

You can move paragraphs around, delete words, phrases, whole paragraphs or even the whole damned thing, if you like. If you are unhappy with the indentation or paragraphing, you can redo those things with a keystroke. Editing can truly be fun. But don't get carried away.

That's just a teeny sample of the wonders of word processing. All of these typing treatments are common to all word processors. It's only in the more sophisticated usages that one word processor differs from another.

Whatever your choice of word processors, you'll learn how sentences and entire paragraphs can be changed, increased, decreased, or even totally deleted without interfering with the general composition of your document. You'll also see how paragraphs can be moved and inserted into previous pages, into later pages, or anywhere within the document, or into an entirely different document, at anytime.

One thing is very certain: Change. Each program will be jockeyed around either to get even with its competitors or ahead of them. Both Word and WordPerfect have gone through so many mutations one wouldn't recognize earlier generations of either.

While it's a nuisance to keep changing versions, we are the beneficiaries of that competition. Word processors currently do so much more than past versions making our work so much more simplified.

The previous version of Word provided a "cut or copy and paste" facility limited to a single pass. If we needed several portions of other documents cut and pasted to the document being created, we had to return to the well, so to speak for each pass.

The current version, Word 2000, allows a dozen cuts or copies at a time, saving the extra time and effort of repeated passes. Changing fonts in the previous Word generation, required knowledge of the font style. Word 2000 shows each font's style as you review the list.

Eeeekk. A mouse in the house.

If you've never used a computer, you'll probably find some minor frustration at first learning to use your mouse. The mouse was used to some extent even before Windows, but with Windows, it's an absolute necessity.

There are basically three types of mouses or mice. The conventional mouse you move along a surface causing a pointer to scurry about on your screen. The second type, the trackball, consists of a ball set in a case. You roll the ball with your fingers or thumb causing the pointer to move. The pointer moves consistently with the direction and speed of your hand or fingers.

The third type is called a "touch plate." These are generally found on laptops or notebook computers. Some of the newer keyboards have touch plates built in. The pointer is activated symmetrically with your finger movement along the plate surface.

All three have two or three buttons. For right-handers, the left button is the operator. If you're left-handed, it's the right button. The process is to coordinate your hand or finger movement with the button that you need to press at certain positions to access whatever function is desired.

Using a conventional mouse, lay your hand over the top of the mouse with your finger resting on, but not pressing, the relevant right or left button. Your hand should be comfortable resting lightly on the mouse.

Move the mouse while watching the pointer flip all around the screen. Notice how the pointer follows the movement of your hand, or fingers, if a trackball or touch plate.

For familiarity, fit the pointer to an icon on the desktop screen and press the relevant button twice in rhythmic sequence. A program window will appear on the screen awaiting your command.

You don't want this program now so look for the "x" at the top right of that window. Move the pointer to that "x" and press the button, once. The window disappears. Try a few more exercises like this. The same general procedure is followed using the track ball or touch plate.

I prefer the trackball or the touch plate which, for some reason, I can coordinate easier and faster. Both are stationary. The movement is limited to the ball or the plate.

The conventional mouse needs to be moved around to accommodate the pointer area selection. The trackball and touch plate take less desk room of which I have none to spare. You're a citizen take your choice.

All mice come with software permitting various adjustments including the speed of the pointer movements. You may wish to slow it down at first to get the hang of it.

Actually, there is a fourth type of mouse. This is Toshiba's "pointer" system. It exists on all Toshiba laptops and notebooks. A very few other makers follow this kind of "mouse."

A kind of nub or protrusion extends somewhere within the keyboard. You apply your fingertip to that pointer and tilt it in any direction you wish. The harder you push, the faster the arrow goes. The longer you hold the position, the more continued the arrow movement. I've tried this system for an extended period. I'm not a "pointer" enthusiast.

I find it tiring and a bit awkward to control. After relatively short intervals, the tip of my finger begins to ache. I also found the protrusion somewhat clumsy.

My finger would sometimes hit that button instead of the key. You may find it useful, but I'd recommend an extended tryout before buying. Happily, my present Compaq notebook utilizes the more conventional touch-plate.

Operating systems; Windows, DOS and Macintosh.

Most lawyers use computers with the Windows processing systems. While Windows is indeed the processor, the basis of operation is still DOS, meaning Disk Operating System. There is a sprinkling of Macintosh or Apple systems here and there.

The term originally associated with DOS is PC, meaning

Personal Computer. Then, there is MS DOS, meaning Microsoft Disk Operating System. A cursory scan of PC and MS and DOS development and applications might be a logical start. Even among lawyers familiar with computers, there is much misinformation and confusion.

Bugs, glitches, chaos and Y2K fables.

Horror stories abound of lost client and case data, entire offices and practices paralyzed, chaos and catastrophe everywhere. Fear of computer "crashes," "bugs," "viruses," and other maladies, have caused some reluctance step into the computer age.

Consider the horrific nightmare stories spread around concerning the Y2K Godzilla. It may come as a surprise to Windows users, but Macintosh systems have not had the Y2K threat. I guess they've always used four digits in their dating.

Hopefully, this material will offer a step toward overcoming any such reservations. With all of the startling innovations in computer technology in the part few years, reliability hasn't been an issue. Computer reliability has not been a serious problem since its earliest generations.

There have been, and are, from time to time, certain computer defects. But most of these have been, and are, in the programs, the "software," not the actual computer equipment, the "hardware." Most problems occur when trying to adapt older programs to newer operating systems. Some glitches stem from uses of "Beta," or pre-release testing software or software released before adequate testing has been completed.

When I first heard the term "virus" in connection with computers, I got set for the tag line. Many computer hackers are infected more with dry humor than viruses. Then I saw assortments of "anti-virus" software, some priced at lofty tickets. I still reserve judgment on the humor aspect. I have yet to experience anything related to a mysterious cause, virus or other.

The so-called "viruses" infect mostly when downloading files from unknown Internet sources. These aren't normally within lawyers' activities. Warnings are published repeatedly to avoid downloading anything from any unfamiliar source. If you don't know with whom you're dealing, don't download anything offered.

Viruses are actually programs composed by deranged but competent and probably highly intelligent hackers. These unique products are prepared solely for the purpose of causing chaos and even possible destruction of computers at random.

These evil persons incorporate the infected programs within host programs. The Trojan Horse "gift" packages are usually offered "free" on the Internet in interesting or provocative wrappings.

It may confound the legal mind to contemplate whatever incentive may stimulate these otherwise creative, perhaps genius, programmers to devote their efforts to negative rather than positive purpose. You will learn as you progress, particularly if you do criminal work, that some logic simply works counter rather than clockwise.

There are prophylactic programs designed to protect computers from viruses. Subscriptions include updates to accommodate new or more innovative versions of viruses.

Unfortunately, these scum renegades are ever ready to keep a jump ahead of the anti-virus programmers. No matter how pervasive the protective programs may be, the danger of infection is always present for those who venture into the Internet uncharted regions.

Don't fall prey to these enchanters. Just say "no." Take their word for their promised exciting and thrilling experiences and get on with your work.

Pioneering in any field often brings unexpected surprises. Many of them are not positive. In these "frontier" operations, "bugs" often are found. Normally, the tested, developed and distributed programs are user-safe.

Even these problems are hardly more than inconveniences. There are preventative measures that can and should be taken to avoid such surprises. Where more extensive problems occur, there are usually painless effective cures.

The important thing is to avoid panic. Be confident that you will not lose your data and your office will not be "paralyzed." Your computer, whatever brand, type or style you have chosen, or will choose, should serve you faithfully and reliably.

Whether or not you now believe it, your computer will be the most important part of your practice. We're going to explore some programs as examples to manage your office and practice needs.

Computer technologies have been burgeoning at a rate faster than print drying time. Even supplements to this book cannot keep on the leading edge of hardware, firmware and software progress.

Use what is written here as a helpful guide to your own research resources. When, not "if," newer and better systems and programs are offered, this information can be a cornerstone to your selections.

The programs that we will examine are offered solely as examples. You'll be expected to select your own preferences from what's available when you're ready.

The programs featured in this book were selected because they were especially suitable for solo or small offices. In some instances, the programs' growth potential impressed me. Software is particularly appealing when it runs the gamut of simplicity through adaptability to greater demands. As you go through the process of selecting programs you prefer, hearken back to these suggestions.

§ 12:3 The solo and small law offices computer operating system

Computer programs made for large complex firms are useless for smaller firms. That statement should not be shocking. Programs are not routinely made for solo or small law firms, even though they make up the majority of law practices. Compounding this anomaly is that programs for large firms require expensive and complicated hardware for their adaptation.

Not surprisingly, the cost of those programs is high, often running into thousands of dollars. The right programs at the right price for small firms are as illusive as a winning lottery ticket.

The solo or small law firm often accepts expensive overkill programs by default. That is disturbing enough. But the real tragedy is that the high priced "do everything" program is ultimately thrust on the shelf in disgust because it "does nothing" for the small law firm.

Why aren't there inexpensive, good, simple programs for solos and small firms? There used to be back in the DOS days. For some reason, most of them disappeared along with the DOS system. Still, we'll look at some Windows programs for you that are the least complicated and costly.

Advertising space rates have moved out of range for the producers of those inexpensive, good, simple programs. Moreover, most of the productive distributors and dealers simply won't market programs with small ticket prices. The small ticket sell is just as hard as for big price tag items, with profit dollars just too soft.

Computer distributors and dealers mercilessly tout overly sophisticated, expensive computers, other hardware and software to small firms. Sometimes this misdirection is profit motivated. Often it's lack of knowledge of the small law firm's needs. Since many solo lawyers know little or nothing about what hardware and software are best suited to their practice, the result is a catch-22.

So, the small office lawyer often settles for universal or generic programs made for a variety of applications. Because such programs have higher marketability, prices can be kept relatively low.

§ 12:4 DOS. Once over lightly

DOS, you've heard of it, but what is it? DOS, as some of you know, means Disc Operating System. There is "PC-DOS," which is the original IBM system for its first PC (meaning "personal computer") in 1981. This archaic, hopelessly inefficient machine stored its data on single-sided floppy disks. Yes, I had one of those pioneering units, but I'm not bragging about it.

Then there is "MS-DOS" which indicates the DOS program developed by the firm Microsoft under a cooperative agreement with IBM. While they share the same basic program technologies, there are some differences.

Many scientific marvels, marvels though they are, suffer through endless, cumbersome revisions, from one primitive, clumsy generation after another, bearing the albatross of their premature birth.

If we humans were smarter than we are, we could see the folly of regenerating obsolescence. This insight might, if we had it, enable us to avoid the regenerative defects by starting with the perfect scientific germination.

But ineptness alone is not always enough to doom a product. Persuasive marketing can forge a pathway through the forest of obstacles, if there is an ultimate compensative clearing.

In the beginning, it was difficult to find that DOS "clearing" for lack of software useful to small businesses. As a result, few smaller users were even curious about the "Rube Goldberg" mishmash that offered only theoretically potential purposes.

But DOS has retained some glory, albeit tarnished. No longer an operating system, DOS still is the system "behind the throne." At the root of Windows, we find DOS alive, though maybe not so well. Some will complain that Windows' shortcomings stem from its reliance upon some of the basic principles of DOS.

§ 12:5 Then came CP/M. But now, who cares?

Then CP/M (meaning Control Program for Microcomputers) was born. Originally, CP/M accommodated only a floppy disk drive attended by an IMSAI 8080 "Intel-Chip," licensed by Digital Research.

CP/M stole the thunder from DOS because of its rash of programs which small business and professions needed. It was also easier to use and more facilitative then DOS. Somewhere along the way, DOS sped up and CP/M slowed down and lost the battle.

Even to this day, there are CP/M diehards who will insist that their choice was the better of the two. Your author was among them for a while. DOS did come a long way relatively quickly, realizing it was in a race for life.

Though CP/M is now just a memory, DOS owed much of its success to the "flash that sputtered and died." Most of the successful CP/M programs could be easily translated to DOS. Moreover, many of the basics of both systems were intertransmutable.

CP/M's command interpreter, CCP (meaning Console Command Processor) and its system files BDOS and BIOS were cousins, if not siblings, of DOS's "Command.Com, IBMDOS and IBMBIO.COM" system files.

(I still get a shiver when I reread the chapter on CP/M in the second edition of this book. My unrequited love affair with CP/M was as futile as it was an inaccurate prognostication. It is for that reason, as well as a few hundred others, that the third edition was, and this Millennium 2000 4th edition will be, regularly supplemented.)

§ 12:6 A quick look at Macintosh

The "APPLE," and its progeny "MACINTOSH," is not just a different form of operating system from Windows. This system is a complete departure from the functionality of Windows and its basic DOS. Macintosh and DOS have little in common except that they are both disc operating systems (the generic term).

There are pro and con arguments for each of these operating systems, but the important fact is that to follow one method is almost an irreversible choice. One can, if motivated, learn either method well enough to operate the other if demands are relatively simple.

Getting proficient enough to excel in either method is quite another matter. The time taken would virtually preclude developing an equal skill in the other. Macintosh proponents would argue that mastering their choice is much easier than with DOS. DOS enthusiasts say: "So what? Easier is not necessarily better."

This is precisely the reason that Windows was born and continues to grow with each generation. In truth, Macintosh did offer graphics operational skills in a fractional time period compared with DOS.

Even Windows is hard pressed to keep pace with Macintosh in the learning process. Arguments really are useless. Those in the Macintosh camp can't be argued into Windows any more than vice versa.

In some instances, no method exists in Windows to accomplish exactly the same graphics result as in Macintosh without multiple entries. Again, the Windows experts will answer: "So what? Nothing like that is needed in computering except for children playing tricky games."

I can't comment on that. Perhaps some of you with Macintosh experience will smirk and say: "What does Singer know." And you'd be absolutely right.

For four reasons, I will stick with Windows in reviewing the computer part of this book. First, this is because I have never used Macintosh other than toyingly. Second, more attorneys use Windows than Mac. Third, as with hardware and peripherals, the software is often more expensive than for Windows. Lastly, there are many important legal programs designed expressly for Windows.

I will accept the claim by Macintoshers that their way is easier to learn for beginners. That being as it may, there seems to be little virtue in an easy learn for something that you might find less useful in your practice.

§ 12:7 Computers for solos and small law offices

Computers for solos or small law offices are not that much different from those for larger offices. Whether a small office or a large one the computer should be equally capable.

However, the programs that are loaded into the computer should be much different. Needs of a large operation are much more demanding. Scheduling, tasking, reporting, calendaring and so many other functions in a multi-lawyer office require highly sophisticated and more complicated and expensive than for a small office.

Paradoxically, the difficulties in finding suitable computer programs for solos and small offices are far greater than for a larger office. Silly, isn't it. This will become clearer to you as we progress in this chapter.

§ 12:8 The quest for computer hardware and software information

Trying to get information about computers is like being in a large dark room with sharp sticks all around you. You ask for help and are told, "This is the way," and someone else says, "No, this is the way." Then another says "No, that's not the way; go this way." After being jabbed again and again, you realize the information you've been given is not only unreliable, it's useless.

You don't necessarily need me to tell you which way to go, but you do need the lights turned on so you can see the paths for yourself. I'll turn on the lights for you with a bit of spoon-feeding for those who want it.

Computers are for all practitioners of the law. But computers, like shoes, come in different sizes and styles. One size doesn't fit all, nor does one style suit all. A shoe sized 9 person who tries to wear a size 12 shoe will stumble around and get nowhere. Some shoe salespersons will misfit customers just to make sales.

Most people know when a shoe misfits. But few people who are new to computers know when a computer doesn't fit. Many computer salespeople do misfit computers, for many different reasons. Some do it like the shoe salesperson, just to make a sale.

Most often, it's just a lack of knowledge as to what the customer really needs. In some cases, it's a lack of knowledge, period. They figure that if they use enough confusing computerese language, the customer won't know the difference.

I started computering long before lawyers generally were using computers. So, after stumbling around in the dark for years, I stumbled into learning all about computers and their programs.

After learning, and then unlearning, and then learning some more, I discovered some strange things. User manuals are useless. They are made for people who already know the subject matter.

Most legal programs are unsuitable for solo or small law firms because they require dedicated, skilled personnel. Programs useful to small firms are not only simple to use, they're simple to learn. Isn't that convenient?

Well, that should solve everything. Just ask for the program that's simple to use and to learn, and you've got it. Right? Wrong! Why wrong? It's simply that such programs are not perched on every dealer's shelf. Oh, they exist all right, but try to find them.

Why is this so? It's hard to believe, but the answer is easy-to-use and easy-to-learn programs are also inexpensive. That would be great if you could just pick them off dealers' shelves. Few of the distributor/dealers want to sell such products because there just isn't enough dollar profit in them.

So, the stalwart producers of these fine little programs must be content to market their own products with limited promotional, advertising budgets and short cash, production and inventories. So, you must just know where they are. I have set about to make that discovery a project.

No one else seemed to be doing this, probably because the big money was in the big, expensive programs. Early on, I spoke with the heads of several of the larger legal software firms about the lack of good, simple and inexpensive programs. No one disagreed with me, but no one did anything about it.

Finally, I had found some small producers with programs suitable for small law firms. Unfortunately, some of them, like Legal Tender, succumbed to a losing economic battle. Checks & Balances, AllDex, and others described in this book, are likewise now gone with Y2K or other phase-outs.

One of the larger producers, CompuLaw, saw the light and produced a billing program, CashFlow, for solos and small firms. Finally, someone saw the value in gearing a product to the growth potential of the small firms. The CompuLaw billing and accounting system, along with its diminutive CashFlow, has ridden off into the sunset. However, CompuLaw still puts out a terrific calendar system.

There are plenty of billing programs to take their places and more being born everyday. Is there one among them for you? Let's see.

ProLaw Software purports to have "One Office, *in a single solution.*" It boasts a Front Office, which provides a case and document management operation, and a Back Office, which is a billing and accounting program. More information about ProLaw is available by calling 1(800) 977-6529 or on its web site http://www.prolaw.com.

Gryphon99 offers what it states is "the new standard for case and practice management software." It consists of time & billing, case management, contact management, document management, telephone management, calendar management, conflicts checking, statute tracking and more. You can learn more and even get a "free" working demo or 60 day trial of the program by calling (800) 547-9746 or on its web site http://www.gryphonlaw.com.

The Tussman Program is still with us and has enhanced its functions. It claims "the easiest legal billing and accounting software to learn and use." Its "Windows Release 7.0" provides multi-tasking, trust accounting, a report writer and conflict checking at no extra cost." It makes a point of stating "Y2K compliant."

This program may be purchased for $295. If you wish the general ledger as well, an added cost of $295 is applied. $590 for the whole show could be a decent value. It isn't as elaborate as the ST Software package (below), but it could serve a solo or small office well.

[I wasn't able to look into the Tussman general ledger because the secret "code word" given to me didn't work. They ignored my requests for a working code, so I can't comment on its suitability.]

Information and a "full evaluation copy" may be had by calling (800) 228-6589 or web site http://www.tussman.com.

The ST Software Technology, Inc., ("STI") provides multiple software tracking with their time and billing program. They claim a Lawyers Weekly U.S. tribute as "Time & Billing Product of the Year."

The program is called "TABS III. The present version is 9. I find this program to be complete enough to satisfy the needs of a larger multi-lawyer firm. Whether it's adaptable to a solo or small firm depends on how conversant the user is to some complexities. The more adventurous solo may find it useful by limiting its scope somewhat. [See Chapter 11.]

Like most other billing and accounting programs, STI suffers from more than a little overkill. It takes some getting used to even in decisions as to which parts to exclude.

I'm not resorting to the humble bit in proclaiming my preference for simplicity. I've never had a knack for solving riddles, puzzles or undue complications. If it weren't for my passion for teaching, I'd find no virtue whatsoever in exploring new programs.

This should explain my persistence in staying with programs like WordStar, Legal Tender, Checks & Balances and others of similar simplicity well into the twilight of their marketability. I frankly didn't then, nor do I now, cotton to more complexity than needed to do the job.

Conversely, I am an incurable adventurer, trending beyond the horizon of the hardware leading edges. This comports with my background as an electronics engineer and electronics manufacturer.

TABS III is designed as a legal specific time accounting and billing system. The program client manager allows each attorney to use a pop-up timer and make their own entries, recap the day's activities, and review a client's account receivables without having to change the screen. Pre-bill tracking allows the bookkeeper to verify that all draft or reports are reviewed and approved for billing to the client.

Since the first task folder is customizable by each user, the system is reasonably adaptable. A solo can just use the basic programs on the first screen, i.e. client, fee entry, cost entry, payment entry, print statements and accounts receivable reports.

Larger firms can select different icons to customize the needs for each bookkeeper, attorney, or paralegal. The cost of this versatile program isn't bad, starting at only $295 for the billing system, $250 for the general ledger and $250 for the accounts payable. This will accommodate a two-timekeeper firm.

The new lawyer could possibly fill his/her accounting needs with just the billing system for $295. This will not print checks for you but you can use that system for everything else. As you grow you can augment your accounting with the other modules.

I was impressed with the accounts payable module's inclusion of 1099 form printing. If you can find the bucks, the whole system, costing about $800, could see you through for quite a while. That's a reasonable pop compared with the competition, function for function. For more information, call 1-800-487-7111-Ext. 372. Or, you can visit their web site at http://www.stilegal.com/cl.html.

I stress that STI is not my answer to the accounting illiterate solo lawyer's quest for a simple though efficient billing and accounting system. I still have a few accounting packages to sift through that may suffice. Unfortunately, my deadline won't permit inclusion of these until the next supplement.

In the meantime, using the basic programs such as TimeSlips or TreeBased, together with Money, Quicken or QuickBooks for both billing and accounting, can see you through during the first phases of your practice.

So, there it is. I will simply turn on the light. Well, maybe a bit more than that. I will offer some specifics on these programs and the computer hardware to fit them. But, in the main, after explaining the whats, whys, wheres, hows and whens, I will leave the particular selections to your own bent, style and tender mercies.

Previous *Solo* versions urged economy and simplicity in hardware as well as software. Back then, computers were divided into economical and astronomical versions. One either had to make do with limited facility or go bankrupt trying to pay for the monster models.

The difference in cost between these two groups was affordable and unaffordable. The cheaper computers, fit for solos, were in the $2,000 range. The top lines then cost between $10,000 and $50,000.

Today, the cheapest models suitable for law practice are priced at about $500. The top line models run about $1,500 to $2,500. These prices don't reflect any "rebate" reductions.

Since the computer virtually runs your entire practice, you can afford the best there is. Happily, that "best" can be had from the more active discount stores for under $2,000.

By a strange series of coincidences, my last several computers, each containing everything I considered desirable at the time, cost approximately $2,500 tax included.

I've done something revolutionary for me since I normally like to see what I'm getting and then drive it home. I contracted for a "custom to order" "CTO" Compaq Presario. If you're new to computer talk, read a bit further ahead for more complete definitions and explanations. For comparison's sake, my new Compaq is equipped as follows:

Model 5700T, with a 600Mhz, (megahertz) clock speed, RAM (Random Access Memory) 128MB (megabytes), 100Mhz syncDram, (more effective chips), 34GB UDMA (7200 RPM) drive, 10X-DVD drive, (ten speed) 56K Modem, 3D Blaster TNT2 Ultra w/DFP, CD-RW 4X 4X 24 Spd, (read and write CD recorder), 1 MBP's phone line Netw., with Diamond Rio MP3 Player, plus lots of software. The total price? You guessed it. $2,478 tax incl.

Of course, within a year, probably even when you read this, that unit will be grossly over-priced and under-powered. The cost of doing business, right?

A happy coincidence is that many of the new, broad spectrum programs demand computer functions that require about all that technology has developed. That, together with lightening speed of modern top of the line units, make computering a pleasure as well as a necessity. So, get the best.

§ 12:9 A first approach: Computers, hardware, software, peripherals, etc.

Here are some elementary points to use as a guide for certain decisions. Some are only rhetorical, such as why, whether or when to use a computer, etc. Obviously, the answer is "don't be silly."

The time is half-past now! In any event, these brief, cursory notes are only intended as preliminary to more detailed material which appears in this book and in the various manuals which will accompany your computer and programs.

Why doesn't every attorney use a computer?

A good question, to which there is absolutely no good answer. By "attorney," I mean a hands-on operation of the computer by the attorney, not a secretary.

In many cases, this avoidance is simply a lack of accurate information on computer use. More probably, it's just a case of inertia or just plain laziness. Laziness can't be the reason. There's no better way to indulge in laziness than to have a great computer doing most of the work for you.

So you think you're using a computer; look again.

Most attorneys' use of computers is secretarial. The secretary knocks out correspondence and pleadings, and that's it. Few lawyers are actually using computers anywhere near the extent of their value to their offices and practice.

Why have some tried and given it up? What went wrong?

Misinformation and inadequate instruction is usually at the heart of these failures. More than this, in most cases, those despairing lawyers simply did not appreciate the enormous help those machines can give them.

Why are some who are using it, using it wrong?

Again, misinformation and lousy instruction muddied the waters. Wrong use also stems from failure to use the computer for chores that they do so well. Misuse of a computer is like using a pure bred race horse to pull a milk wagon.

The "trained" computer operator myth.

The secretary who may be dynamite for churning out correspondence, routine documents and pleadings is not "trained" for the highest and best computer use to the attorney. Many legal programs are extensions of law practice.

Research, drafting, discovery indexing, and other legal programs are for lawyers, not secretaries. Who's to do it? A secretary isn't a lawyer. You're the lawyer. Right?

The upside and downside of computering.

In this computer competitive age, you must have a computer equivalent with your opposing lawyer's. You must assume that his/hers would be capable of state-of-the-art functions, capacity, speed and other functions.

You don't need his/her huge 21-inch monitor. Your 15-incher will do just fine. You don't need an ultra deluxe color printer. Your black & white printer is O.K., so long as it can spit out at least 12 to 15 pages per minute.

You don't need a high fidelity super dooper sound system for your computer. The little speakers that come with the computer will do the job. You don't need the highest quality, highest priced fax machine, you can get a good plain paper fax for about $100 that's just fine.

You don't need an equivalent office, secretary, support staff, automobile, mansion, yacht, or any of his/her trappings, but your computer must be his/her equal. He/she may have many shiny, nice office machines, gadgets, whatsises, or whatevers, but your computers and output characteristics must match.

I don't mean your accounting or billing program must be as sophisticated as his/hers or that you must have fanciness in your programs. But the basic operation must have up-to-the-minute capabilities of capacity, speed, access, memory and storage.

In all previous editions of *Solo*, I advocated extreme conservatism in your costs, expenses, and investments of your office furniture, supplies and equipment. I still do. But not where it concerns your computer output.

The "upside" of computering is to get on the computer bandwagon. Get serious. Get training and get state-of-the-art equipment. This doesn't mean learning how to be a computer expert. All you need is basic operation ability. That can be accomplished in a very few hours of relatively painless effort.

Please don't say you "can't" or "won't" without making a run at it. Until you actually get into it, you can't have any idea of its advantages to your law practice. Try it. You'll like it. No, you can't get by without it.

The downside (there is no "upside") of not computering.

You're on the "downside" if you are trying to run your office manually. If you are trying to operate with a computer that was designed even as recently as three or four years ago, you're not playing with a full deck. With good, modern equipment, decent information, and training, you won't fall behind. Without all of these, you will fall behind.

What the computer can do for you, if you'll let it.

A computer can literally run your entire office with minimal operator proctoring. Your computer can do the things you know about, like all secretarial functions, of course. When you read along further and see all the other computer wonders, you won't ask "What will a computer do for me?" Your computer will virtually run your office and your practice.

Each inch of computer output puts you miles ahead.

Unless you practice law on a mountain top, away from all other lawyers, you cannot compete in this modern, technical world without suitable modern, technical equipment.

Add another inch and then another.

As you learn about computer use, you learn more uses and more steps by which your computer can give you momentum. Then there are the marvelous things that haven't even yet been discovered about these marvels.

The secret of learning computering: Don't learn too much.

Your computer can, and will, do everything needed for your office and practice. This doesn't mean that you must be a computer programmer or engineer. Learn only enough to use Windows properly. Some lawyers have bigger learning appetites. Fine. Just do what you can do and it should be fine.

If you are a quick learner and are driven by curiosity, by all means, go for it. It's a fascinating subject and will serve as exciting a hobby as any other. But, if technologies confound you, or such understanding comes slowly to you, your time may be better devoted toward learning only the basic computer functions and toward the further development of your practice.

NEVER TOO SMALL OR TOO EARLY TO COMPUTERIZE.

Do not make the mistake of believing that you don't need a computer because your practice is small enough to manage manually. That rationale is toxically tenacious. Once you adopt it, you can be a prisoner of it forever.

The cost of computers and programs can be enough to put one off "until next week." Add to this, the inconvenience, such as it is, of the learning process, and "next week" never comes.

Advantages of starting early.

When your practice becomes big enough to offer problems keeping up manually, and that day will come sooner than you think, there'll be too much to do to start an expensive and time-consuming process. The result will be a start put off to an even less convenient time.

Do it now, while you can devote the time. You'll find the way to get it paid for, either through a payment plan, or whatever. The main thing is that you have the time now. You won't have the time later, but you'll be forced to do it anyway.

The secretary myth.

Don't fall into the "let the secretary do it" pit. A secretary can type but not draft. A secretary can prepare research memos but cannot do the research. A secretary cannot decide which documents to access for which particular purpose. These are decisions that go with case engineering. You are the case engineer.

If you have a secretary (by reason of "need" and not "want to need"), delegate those duties which are truly secretarial and not those which you just hate, or don't want, to do.

You should distinguish between office business and practice routines and practicing law. The former may be done by legal assistants and secretaries. The latter, you must do yourself.

Most of these legal procedures can, and should, be done on your computer. But done by YOU, not your assistants. So, you must be able to operate your computer. Don't fight it. Do it. Besides, you'll love it.

The computering solo lawyer is not really "solo."

Your computer has literally millions of little hands to help you with all of your chores, both simple and complex. No personnel help can provide the assistance of a good, competent computer and judiciously selected programs.

It's true that legal competition has forced this "stay even" push. While so much more needs to be done than in the past, the computer has eased your efforts. The real beneficiaries to all this are your clients. They get better, up-to-the-minute legal parity, higher polished work products and glitch free legal services.

The leverage factor.

When you start computering, you'll learn almost immediately about the computer leverage factor. You'll realize that even the clumsiest lawyer at the computer keys will outpace the fastest manual operator ten to one.

Time and effort saved; money earned.

Look around after using your computer for the myriad of tasks you've accomplished. What? Can the clock be wrong? How could you have done so much so fast? Add that time saved to your bank account. As you now know, time is money.

Horror stories you've heard about computers.

Forget the "crashes," the "glitches," the "viruses," the "lost data" and all the other horror stories you've heard about. They just don't happen.

When things happen, and things that do happen, happen very infrequently, you're prepared and you correct the problem with a few keystrokes. There are fright scenes like "a fatal error," "an illegal operation," or other signs of ultimate doom.

Why these terrorizing pronouncements were chosen to advise of simple problems I can't say. When you do see these ominous proclamations, you merely press "control, alt and delete" keys and select "end task" on the two subsequent windows. Then proceed with your work.

Nothing to fear from a computer but fear itself.

My advice in past editions has been to choose the computer with minimal specifications consistent with your application needs. I advised that your basic computer needs are accounting and word processing.

Since then, computers and software have developed to providing services that literally will run your practice. Then came the Internet and the thousands of applications to simplify your practice and your life.

All of this is at the cost of much more computer, computer memory and storage, which means more money. These developments are coming so fast that one cannot chose a dimension and bide time. This means we must buy the best there is and keep it up to date.

Everything you do in practice can be done on your computer, but better and faster. Besides your accounting and word processing, all of your research, document storage and retrieval, client profiles, and in fact every detail of your entire practice should be right in front of you, on your computer screen.

Basic needs in your practice: Software.

You'll need an accounting program. I've not found an accounting system with the simplicity of Checks & Balances but that's now history. Several choices were explored in Chapter 11. Whichever you choose will need some getting used to. Select one and stick to it.

Actually, my lamentations about the loss of C&B may be overdone. Being forced into learning a more complicated system had its compensations. Accounting systems like Microsoft Money, Intuit Quicken and QuickBooks, while more demanding in operation do automate your accounting.

As described in Chapter 11, QuickBooks Pro Legal can do both accounting and billing. Despite its generalizations, QuickBooks Pro Legal is specific enough for all your solo practice needs at least until you spread your wings way out there.

While I have mixed emotions about complications to ultimately simplify, I suppose the result somewhat justifies the means. The ease of C&B's operations to me seemed a better trade-off for a bit less automation.

You must have a billing program some of which we've also reviewed for you. Again, ease of use is not their strong suit. We'll index the simplest and you can take it from there.

An indexing program should also be on your list. AllDex is out now but many others have appeared not half bad. Pick one and most important, use it. Microsoft Works includes an indexing and client file. It's a bit cumbersome in needing to reset the alphabetical order after each entry but for the most part quite adequate. Obsolete though it may be, I still use my original AllDex version as a basic index for my clients and general phone directory.

Most of all, get a word processor. You've got to use word processing to do your correspondence, document drafting, pleading, etc. The word processor is the heart of your practice. My old standby WordStar is long gone. The two most popular word processors used by lawyers are WordPerfect and Microsoft Word. I use the latter. Why? A good reason.

Knowing WordStar's demise was imminent, I dabbled with a few, Word being one of them. Then, inertia took over and I've been using Word consistently since.

The advantages of a word processor—*any* word processor—over a manual typewriter are colossal. You can delete and words, phrases, paragraphs or whatever in a heartbeat. You can move words, sentences, paragraphs or whatever from anyplace to anyplace with a couple of mouse moves and clicks.

Revisions, deletions, amendments, alterations, additions or whatever you wish to do is done before its methods can even be explained. You can "cut and paste" or "copy and paste" from any part of any document to any part of any other document at any moment.

You can snip excerpts from programs such as Law Desk or Authority [see details of these programs ahead] or any other source material and paste them to whatever document you are preparing. The preparation of briefs, with all needed placement of authorities, commentaries or other applications, can be accomplished in a fraction of the time wasted in manual typing.

Spelling and grammatical errors are corrected as you type; forgotten capitalization as in first letters of sentences, are automatically inserted. A thesaurus is available to offer alternate or preferable word selections at the touch of a key.

Paragraphs can be reformed at the flick of a key. It's as though your thought processes can control the quality of your work. All of these marvelous work enhancers are part of all and any word processors.

I've been criticized by several lawyer friends for choosing Word over WordPerfect. Several demonstrations appear to establish WordPerfect's superiority. I have it loaded and have done some dry runs but nothing extensive.

The new (or I guess, newer) Word 2000, packaged in Office 2000, offers some distinct advantages over Word 7 in Office 97. A big one is the ability to cut or copy and paste in tandem segments instead of one paste at a time.

Now you can cut or copy as many parts as you wish and paste them within a single document or several different documents. In Word 7, on each cut or copy, the previous part was eliminated. Under pressure, it can be frustrating to return to copy or cut for each pasting.

Another step forward is Word 2000's display of the actual fonts when scrolling through looking for the font you need. These have been features of WordPerfect for some time.

WordPerfect's boosters will say that Word is finally trying to catch up to WordPerfect. Then a smirk, and "but it never will." Like anything else, we love what we're accustomed to.

My tenaciousness to Checks & Balances and WordStar through the years may best be justified that they were the first and best. They continued amply serving me after newer, better works came along. Perhaps this proves it may be just as well to bear with what serves you rather than hopscotch through a multitude of new offerings.

Each time you load a new program you can expect to spend hours becoming proficient enough to get your work out with the competence of the one you're discarding. Shakespeare said: "It is better to suffer the ills you have than fly to others that you know not of."

Whether or not that is the case, the advantages of moving forward are preferable to the stagnation of standing still. In the end, it's a balancing concept. What is the cost and what is the gain. If you're moving from working manually to computer automation, the gain is worth whatever the cost.

You should have a Pleading and Practice program. Prior to the advent of legal practice volumes and encyclopedia on CD-ROM, I used the Matthew Bender Pleading and Practice multi-volume set. Like all sets of this kind, the growth of law practice made them unmanageable in size, number and bulk.

The regular updating of looseleaf paging got to be a job in itself. At first, Lillian came to help. Soon this proved too much for her and my secretary. On these days, no time was left for our regular office routine. Fortunately, CD's came along in the nick of time. One could either select the pleading in entirety to customize or pick from the wide variety of paragraphs to constitute all of the desired causes of action, elements and issues of the whole document.

You'll want a legal research program of some sort. Many such programs are offered on CD but that can be laborious due to the constant need to update and re-integrate. The upside is economy. Cost isn't tracked to your use time since it's all done on the CD disks.

The most fluid and reliable method for research is on-line and on the Internet. Westlaw, by the West Group reviewed in *Solo-III* supplement, is astonishingly easy to use. I was given temporary use of Westlaw and I found it disarmingly usable and simple.

If you'll be doing any business work, you've got to have a comprehensive, reliable business agreements forms program. Don't try drafting a business contract without one.

Peter Siviglia has compiled a tightly drawn set of commercial agreements I've found very useful. No agreement text can cover all possibilities. The genius of any good text is its lending interpolations. This is where your own creativeness takes over.

Siviglia's work, **"COMMERCIAL AGREEMENTS, A Lawyer's Guide To Drafting And Negotiating,"** *(1999, West Group) includes: The ABC's of Drafting; The Promissory Note; The Guarantee; Pledge of Stock; Security Agreements; Employment Arrangements; Finders and Brokers Agreements; Partnership & Shareholders' Agreements; Limited Liability Companies; Licensing Agreements; Acquisitions; Letters of Credit; Purchase & Sale of Goods; Distributorship; Consignments; Equipment Leases; Settlement & Release and much more.*

Part Two of Siviglia's work, NEGOTIATING, presents a well rounded discourse on the "Elements of Negotiating."

It's a wonder that a source so sorely needed as a good business agreement text is so rare. There have been precious few and most of those have been a little less helpful than your cute three year-old's deathless utterings.

You shouldn't copy material directly from this book to complete any document. As the title states, a "GUIDE To Drafting." Siviglia provides a firm lead on the subjects but depends upon you for all relevant specifics and particulars. In that sense, this material is about as good as it gets.

Programs on CD, such as Am Jur Legal Forms 2d on Law Desk by West Group (and its companion Am Jur Pleading and Practice Forms), will provide basic legal documents of just about all descriptions. There are several varieties of leases. For instance, it contains multiples of land, homes, commercial, etc. leases that you can download. Am Jur Legal Forms 2d provides a command, "Go To Your Word Processor," which places the entire document in your word processor ready for customization.

Am Jur Legal Forms 2d not only contains about every general legal document you'd want, it also has a large array of federal tax forms. What is more impressive is its orderly indexing and contents accessing capability. See also a general tax analysis of legal forms and agreements.

Thumbing through Am Jur Legal Forms 2d forms, it'll seem there's no end to the number and diversity of titles. After about an hour of trying, I gave up the search for a form that wasn't included. In Annulment of Marriage alone, there are over 23 forms covering just property settlement agreements.

Wills are included among business documents. More surprising is Am Jur Legal Forms 2d's extensive selection of wills and a wide variety of will provisions one wouldn't expect to find among business forms.

It would be hard to visualize a commercial document that's not included in the Am Jur Legal Forms 2d panoply of document choices. Using a CD of this type beats any form of manual construction including scanning from a form book. (Look for more specifics in Chapter 9, "Law Practice Management.")

As you progress through your law practice, you'll become more and more conscious of the drafting cheats who simply copy forms and simply fill in the blanks. Don't be surprised to find many documents filed by your opponents, composed of as much as 75% of unrelated and irrelevant provisions.

None of these forms is intended to be copied and pasted in

whole as a virtually completed document. Copy the form to your word processor. Then, use the form to compose the document to conform to its intended meaning and purpose. Add to, amend and retain only those provisions that comport with that meaning and purpose, deleting the rest.

The choice of Pleading and Practice forms on CD is still Matthew Bender's "Authority" (previously known as "Search Master.") The version I'm reviewing is for California law, but Matthew Bender offers this same kind of program for many other states.

You've only to find the pleading form sought from the "Contents" of the disk and copy either the entire document or portion needed to your word processor and fill in the relevant material. It can all be done faster than it can be explained.

The Pleading set consists of three CD volumes, each covering a sizable number of topics. For example, California Codes, Rules, BAJI and CALJIC complete are contained in volume 3 of the set. This program is so huge, it'll take more time than I have before deadline to absorb it all.

I'm informed that the format is relatively similar for all other states serviced by Matthew Bender. Judging by the California set, it's hard to see how anyone can compete in a general law practice without the aid of this amazing group of programs. You'd be hard pressed to conceive of a form not included in this compact but comprehensive program. Any pleading form in Authority can be readily converted and customized, ready for filing, with just a flick of your fingers.

Microsoft Word 2000, as other word processors, has a customizable "Legal Pleading" provision to guide you through preparation of the form required in your state. Once that is done, your copy and paste buttons will paste the general "U.D." form from Authority directly to your prepared legal pleading form.

Amazing! Every word, every line appears in precisely the correct space and on the correct line number. Except for your customization of the pleading material, you have a complete product.

You'll need to add, delete and amend to complete the form to fit your case. Obviously there's more material on each form than fits your particular case. But the whole process shouldn't take more than a few minutes. It's an exercise in filling in the blanks that I'm sure you can do as well as any secretary. You'll find a pleading form in Authority for just about any kind of action that exists.

It should also be noted that the Pleading and Practice set links with Cases on Authority as well as Deerings California Annotated Codes. I'm informed that the same is true in the several other states serviced by this valuable program.

Another CD disk tool offered to California lawyers by West Group is the Civil Litigation Library Expanded Edition. This consists of just a single CD disk and included Civil Procedure Before Trial, Civil Trials and Evidence and Civil Appeals and Writs.

Check with your West Group representative for the possibility of a similar offering for your state. This program is updated semi-annually and contains just about everything you'd want in civil litigation.

Whichever you choose, go for the CD. It's not only simpler than printed works, it's more accurate and less prone to transitional errors. Civil Litigation Library Expanded Edition guides you along the route and generally makes your litigation life a bit easier.

Your scanner and your OCR.

Scanners come in all sizes and shapes as well as a full range of prices. There are flat scanners permitting you to lay down each sheet one at a time or with the use of an automatic feed as many as fifty at a time.

Your scanner will need an OCR to interpret the scanned text of which there's nothing better than OmniPage Pro 10.0. Your scanned document may be done automatically by pressing the button labeled, conveniently, "AUTO." Then the document can be edited through Omni's own proprietary editing system or directly through your word processor.

If there's a more efficient or accurate OCR than OmniPage Pro 10.0, you'll have to show it to me. It will work with just about any kind of document, faded, faxed, dot matrix, or whatever.

OmniPage 10.0 will scan in color as well as B&W and grayscale. A highly valuable feature of OmniPage 10.0 is the new addition of *voice read back* for aid in proof reading.

At the present time, OmniPage 10.0 retail price is $99.95. Although you may find a street price for less, that isn't a bad number for all this comprehensive program will do for you.

Basic needs in your practice: Hardware.

The leading computer brands are expanding their marketing to compete with mail-order houses. Until recently, mail-order firms like Gateway, Dell and others have been leaders in mail order customization. Two top brands, Compaq and Hewlett Packard, no less, are offering what they call "CTO's" or customized-to-order plans. This allows the customer to pick and choose as to which components and peripherals they prefer with their new computers.

The process is still "retail" in nature. The ordering is done at the retail store where Hewlett Packard and Compaq provide direct line computers. A basic model is selected by the customer from which choices of given specifications may be chosen.

The basic model may include peripherals, like a monitor, networking systems, speakers, or whatever, that the customer may upgrade, downgrade or delete. There are choices of hard drive types and sizes, memory, audio cards, video cards, etc.

You can "pick and choose" all right, so long as your choices are from those few options offered. The choices are limited to a very few alternatives. But it beats taking the package strictly as it sits on the dealer's showroom floor.

Another advantage of a CTO is the price. A stock top of the line Hewlett Packard which sells for about $2,300 can be customized with bigger and better components for about $200 less. There is a waiting period for the special assembly and delivery of about two to three weeks.

A downside is that many dealers will disavow any retailer's responsibility for customer service or tech support for CTO ordered merchandise. They treat such orders as though the purchase was from another company, not theirs.

Of course, the dealers will still offer the ever-present optional "extended warranty." If you're a gambler you may elect to go with the odds. If an insurer can profit from the warranty price, so can you. You should study whether you can best afford the premium or the expense of a serious breakdown.

Hewlett Packard offers a full year warranty with their top unit including on site service. Compaq's warranty suffers somewhat being only ninety days parts and labor. If you go for the extended warranty, these differences lose their meaning.

With these limitations and objections, these top brand manufacturers are coming close to the best there is in both quality and price, mail order or otherwise.

The best models offered by the brand named computers now are complete with most everything needed to serve the most demanding practice. My recommendations at this time are:

A Pentium III (or if out, the Pentium IV.) 600 - 1000Mhz.

128MB, or more, 100Mhz SyncDram Memory.

27GB - 50GB (7200RPM) hard drive (7200RPM, not 5400RPM).

Look for 2MB buffer and 9ns access or lower.

10X DVD-ROM drive.

56K V.90 modem.

512K level 2 cache.

32MB SyncGraphics video.

Audio PCI 64V sound card.

1MBP's Phone Line network card (Lets you use your phone lines to couple to all computers in your office).

Dual USB ports.

Some form of back-up. ZIP drive, CD burner or whatever (IOMEGA now offers a 250MB USB Zip).

Laser printer (HP preferred).

17-inch .25 Multimedia monitor (Maybe the flat screen 17-inch or 19-inch monitor will be available at a decent price when you read this).

Optional (but suggested) CD-RW (burner) drive (Prefer 4X Rec., 4X Re-rec. 24X speeds).

Canon copier (autodoc feeder) 250 sheet.

FAX laser type (Brother, HP, Panasonic or equal).

Ordinary supplied speakers (Premium Polk or equal).

Optional (but suggested) scanner (Canon or HP); should be USB (SCSI, if you have it). I would avoid parallel coupled.

No matter what they say, parallel is parallel, and parallel is about as fast as a turtle slipping on ice. Wherever available go with USB. Also USB is "hot connect" permitting connecting while computing. Parallel requires rebooting each time connected or disconnected.

All of the above features are available in a CTO customized computer by Compaq, or if you prefer, Hewlett Packard. As your practice grows, you'd want a notebook computer to keep your work current whenever and wherever your travels take you. Right now the preferred model is the Compaq 1685. Things you should look for in a notebook (that is, in November, 1999):

TFT active matrix 14.1-inch or 15-inch TFT XGA.

6.5GB-12GB hard drive.

64-128MB memory, 380-600Mhz.

6-10X (or faster) DVD drive.

56K V.90 modem, and all the trimmings.

Good stereo ported speaker system.

USB & PCMCIA ports.

Lithium or "Li-Ion" battery, heavy duty.

Scroller, Internet access, volume control.

Touch-plate mouse and myriad of "one-touch" adjustments.

The unit shouldn't weigh more than 7 to 7-1/2 lbs inclusive of battery with minimal dimensions all around. This should also include built-in floppy drive, CD-ROM, PCMCIA, modem and docking items for independent operation. Why both USB and PCM ports? Using a Zip drive would require a 120 volt source unless you have PCM host powered.

Experience has taught me as it will you that a dichotomy occurs when you have all you want in a notebook and try carrying it. A compromise must exist here as in most things. Unless it's a bit heavier than you'd like it to be, you'll be missing something you need or really want. Weight lifting may help in conditioning you for carrying it.

The notebook can also come in handy should your desktop model ever become indisposed. You can simply plug in your monitor, keyboard, mouse and printer and away you go. A docking station could make this a bit easier but not necessary.

Ease of operation should not concern you.

"EASY" DOESN'T ALWAYS KNOCK IT, AND HARD ISN'T THAT HARD. Don't be herded into the "easy way" by sales hype. Check for compatibility with the rest of your programs to make your office and practice management easier. Forget "easier to learn." You'll learn what you need to learn to make your practice better.

Price consideration; don't judge cost too quickly.

Hold your expenses down, but don't mistake that advice with anything said about buying the best computer you can afford. Your computer should be capable of handling all of the programs needed in your practice as fast as your competitor's.

Not so long ago, programs didn't need much speed or capacity. But then, they didn't do that much for you either. Now, programs are more extensive in their capabilities and require more speed and capacity in your equipment. Since your competitors will be availing themselves of those improvements, so must you.

Final considerations.

Use the specification information contained in this chapter, updated to keep pace with development. Then compare those characteristics with the genre marketed at the time you read this book. Get several valid opinions and select the setup that most closely tracks the characteristics listed, but considering the changes in the state of technologies.

§ 12:10 What you need to know about computer technology

Use the technical information given in this book as a rough idea of what you need. From this point, look for equipment with the specifications to do the job. Spend a few hours drifting around various computer dealers.

Look at stuff offered by the so-called computer "super markets." In the West, check out Fry's, CompUSA, Cosco, Circuit City, Best Buy, The Good Guys, Office Depot or other "biggies" in your area.

Analogy: Automobile technology and the driver's license.

You don't need an engineering degree to either drive a car or fly an airplane. You do not need to be a programmer to get full use of any program. You don't need to be a computer engineer to use any computer to its fullest capacities.

Bite off only what you can chew; leave the rest alone.

If it pleases you to know more, please do. If not, then be satisfied with knowing all that you need to know to use your computer and your programs properly.

We're not as dumb as "experts" would have us believe.

Computer experts are not all bad. It's just that most of them make it seem that they are. I never felt so inadequate as while trying to get information from the so-called computer "experts."

Don't let them do that to you. They're not as smart as they would like you to think they are. Nor are you as dumb as they would like you to believe you are.

The problem: Sifting out what you need to know.

It may be difficult at first, but after you learn some of the basic key words, computerese is not that confusing. Unless, of course, you go too far with it. At first, take it easy. Don't be afraid to ask for clarification. Just pay no attention to the stony stare you get.

"Legalese" and "computerese"; twin brothers.

We sometimes do the same thing to our clients as those computer "tyros" do to us. Reread some of the letters we send. How many of us wear our legal education on our sleeves?

We lawyers know what we're talking about and those computer dodos don't. You'll be quicker to cut through the B.S. haze than I was. When you do, cut to the chase and collect needed information for your ultimate purchases.

What you need to know is simple; forget the rest.

Once you get started with the terminologies, things will follow each other and before you know it, you'll be spouting the same garbage. After you get that out of your system, get your equipment and the software you need and get started.

§ 12:11 What are the choices and how to choose

Hardware: A handful of facts gets you the best for lots less.

From the number and variety of IBM copies, or "clones" seen in stores, it would appear that they exceed the number of IBM manufactured products. The term "clones," or more amiably "IBM compatibles," indicates they will work with all software workable in a genuine IBM computer.

You'd expect that true IBM computers would cost more than "100% IBM compatible" computers. That was the case until just a year or two ago. More recently, IBM machines have become lower in price and in fact, in some instances, at bargain prices over the "clones."

The manufacturer, such as IBM, makes the basic computer. The processor is made by another company. The Intel company makes the processor known as "Pentium." Operating systems such as DOS, Windows, etc. are made by those respective companies. An exception is Macintosh. That company, I'm told, makes everything.

Through the years, Intel's Pentium has been the leader in processors. As other firms developed better and faster processors, Intel has been the pacesetter in its constantly upward spiraling versions.

Where's all that competition?

Intel has proceeded on its merry way, developing higher and higher ratings, Pentium, Pentium II, Pentium III, enroute to IV, etc. and not looking back. Promises of other processors to compete with Pentium, such as MIPS R4000SC and MIPS T4400, have yet to be fulfilled.

Some computers in the $500 to $1,000 range have AMD K-6 processors. Then there was AMD K6-2. Now K6-3 is out. Soon there will be No. 4? K6-2 is no slouch, however.

In fact, its presence induced Intel to produce a competitive Celeron processor. I'm informed that the K6-2 blows the Celeron away and the new K6-3 may even surpass Pentium III in speed. My own tests will prove the point one way or the other.

Another new kid has moved into the neighborhood. This one's an economy brand called "CYRIX MII." It can be had in a computer street priced about $400 including a 4.3GB hard drive, 64MB RAM, a 32 speed CD-ROM drive, a 56K V.90 Modem, etc., etc.

The PowerPC is alive and well, but is still essentially for the Apple Macintosh. There is still some talk of adaptation to PC use. The PowerPC has been incorporated in Apple notebooks to give them top speed.

The "P6" is still a threat, but where or when remains a secret, at least from me. The world is still waiting for some hacker to break the X86 barrier. Should that occur, the lid will be off.

What about Microsoft? More and more good things are packed into its Windows and what's the result? The government's going after Microsoft for its alleged monopoly. I'll admit to some irritation at being herded into Microsoft's "MSN" Internet each time I try to update a program through Internet. I keep forgetting to start AOL first. Well, at my age what can you expect. What's your excuse?

Because of Windows being Microsoft, it's difficult to stick to a competitive host with MSN influences trying to carry you off under the pretext of "can't find your browser," or some such nonsense.

Microsoft's legal difficulties.

Microsoft's problems affect all of us in some ways. If the bottom line is a break up of all the "bundled" software in Windows, the revised operating system will present a whole new ballgame. If the phone company disassembly is an example, it may not be that great for the consumer.

Now that judge Thomas Penfield Jackson has issued findings that Microsoft is operating an illegal monopoly, the U.S. Attorney may revise his stand on settlement. Before that ruling, he extended the olive branch invitingly. Now it appears that Judge Jackson has been doing a bit of head knocking to get the parties together.

Even so, the odds at this time are that this case is going all the way. It looks now that the case will extend past publication date of this book. My prediction is that no order will be given for Microsoft's breakup. This not only would be an atrociously disproportionate penalty, but it's fallout could reach epidemic economic proportions.

The worst may not be whatever penalties, if any, are imposed upon Microsoft. There are many lawsuits pending against Microsoft and many more fresh cases posed. This powerful finding could give these litigators some explosive ammunition.

Since my roots and sympathies are in merchandising, I am annoyed that the governments (both state and federal) are piling it on Mr. Gates' back. It seems that Horatio Alger really, after all, was fiction.

This reads like good old fashion jealousy. How many big business tycoons can count $100 billion, (not million) dollars to use as spending money? And at, what, 45 years old or so. Let's hear it for the nerds. (But, Bill, there are other Internet hosts besides MSN you know.)

Who knows the founders' names of our nation's larger firms? Who started General Electric or General Motors? The Bill Gates story should be an inspiration for all young people. Here is a real live person who lived, and is living, the American Dream.

Instead, he is vilified by a government that professes equal opportunity for all its citizens. Unfair trade? Unlawful monopoly? Anti-trust? Why? Aren't these same opportunities available to all of Microsoft's competitors? Gates stated to the Associated Press:

"Microsoft competes vigorously and fairly . . . This lawsuit is fundamentally about one question: Can a successful American company continue to improve its products for the benefit of consumers? This is precisely what Microsoft did by developing new versions of Windows operating system with built-in support for the Internet."

The government would vigorously disagree with Bill's assessment of the "one question." It appears that the "question" is whether Microsoft's operation is "to improve its products for the benefit of consumers" or for the benefit of Microsoft.

Either way, I find it difficult to see how bundling programs with that product would constitute a wrongful act. Computer companies "bundle" components in their products, as do automobile manufacturers, etc.

My own new Compaq 5700T comes bundled with the peripherals selected by Compaq. You say I could eliminate them and buy my own? Not so easily done. I've been trying to use my Sony 20SE monitor with that Compaq but, to do it, I must use a Compaq driver with a much lower speed control.

I've seen no reports to indicate Microsoft's involvement in any conspiracy to thwart or prevent others from competing. If Windows is simply the best and other manufacturers just cannot present a more commercially attractive product, I'd say too bad for those other manufacturers.

Study hard and work hard so you can succeed. But don't succeed too much. That's against the law. If you race too far ahead, you must stop so the also rans can catch up.

Do I sound too cynical? Don't mean to. I believe in fairness, maybe to a fault. My older brother, Dave, once told me that I am too logical. He said, "Someday your sense of logic might be your undoing."

I shrugged that off then. Now, I don't know. Fairness could be a problem if "fairness" to one may be unfairness to another. Perhaps "fair" means just that—"fair," not "good." Perhaps the world expects Microsoft to slow down its competition from "vigorously" to languorously.

But that's too complicated for my simple philosophies.

What's this about Y2K?

Most everyone knows now whether their computers are working properly in 2000. If not, they'd have learned all about it when on January 1, 2000, their monitor greeting was "HAPPY NEW YEAR, 1900." By now it's old news for you. But, even so, is that all there is to it?

If you are considering a used computer that needs clock resetting, you can perform a Y2K test. Set the time and date. Choose Settings—Control Panel and then click on Date/Time. Or in Windows 95 or 98, right-click on the clock on the Taskbar. Set your computer clock to 11:59 P.M. Set the date to 12-31-1999. There's a reason for the four digits. "00" can mean 2000 or 1900. Your computer can't distinguish and that's the rub.

After it rolls over into 2000, make some test entries on your older programs to see if they respond. A first glance may not reveal the glitch. Many of the older programs used the two digit method for year designation. There may also be other causes for Y2K problems.

If you did have a Y2K failure, don't despair. Not right away anyway. The producer might have a patch fix. Check their web site, if any. Even with a date discrepancy, the program might be useful anyway so long as you keep that error in mind.

On the other hand, don't be too quick to conclude that no problem exists. Try a few operations in suspect programs and check the results. A "suspect" program might be an older DOS program, even if it happens to use four digits for the year. All the votes have not been counted for program roots.

In fact, the two digit disease isn't the only problem. Some programs will accommodate the *Leap Year* alteration of dates. Some won't. Other such glitches may not show up for several months after January 1, 2000.

Even Microsoft Office, no less, had a Y2K bug. Earlier versions used the two digit year method. To avoid problems in 2000, upgrade these programs. Actually, the problem is really one of convenience rather than necessity. If your work doesn't involve date tracking, the year transition will have minimum effect. It's nice to have your correspondence date automated, but not essential.

For further information you might access some Internet addresses for Y2K information. Try http://www.ticktickticks.com. Microsoft has launched a new web site to deal with its Year 2000 software glitch at http://www.microsoft.com/year2000. Microsoft admits that about two dozen of its products have Y2K glitches. However, indications are that all or most of these products will be updated through its web site downloads.

It seems that the hysteria caused by the indiscreet press will lead to more problems than any real hardware or software Y2K failures. People are being told to stock up on food, pharmaceuticals, water (I read one admonition to fill bathtubs with water) and other necessities to prepare for the Y2K disaster.

Shades of the 1950's flying saucers.

§ 12:12 Pentium II, Pentium III, Pentium IV, 333, 400, 500, 600, 1000: Then where?

Where are all the "new" "innovative" systems that were going to overtake and blow the Pentium system right out of the water? What's on the horizon now? All I see is more Pentium, and then more Pentium. The ink on my check for my Pentium III, 600 isn't even dry and they're touting the Pentium IV 1000 MHz.

The Pentium III board with a CPU processor at 600 MHz, MMX version, is just the start. A few months from now, that unit will be a comparative slug. Look for 1000 MHz right around the corner. Talk about "planned obsolescence."

Everything works, more or less, in tandem. There's Pentium II or Pentium III, at 500 MHz, 600 MHz, 1000MHz and up. Then you'll need more and more, and faster and faster RAM; 64MB, 128MB, 10ns, 8ns. But that's not enough, you'll have to change SIMM to DIMM. Now you start over. Is 64MB of DIMM fast enough? Depends on for what. Maybe not. So, move up to 128MB and so on.

What about Pentium IV? Strange kind of game, right? We lawyers don't make the rules but we're swept along with the rules they're making for us. We don't need higher and higher tech operating systems.

We could also live without higher and higher clock speed. But what have we got to say about it? We could just dig our toes in the dirt and say, "enough!" Shall we? Uh uh. We do make the rules. That is, OTHER lawyers do. They get bigger and faster stuff and we must follow suit or get left in the prop wash.

§ 12:13 Windows 2000. Will it cure all Windows' ills?

Time to upgrade? And upgrade? And upgrade???

Windows 98 was released in June 1998. "98" is oriented more for networks and Internet than its predecessor. To say that everything is headed in that direction wouldn't be much of an overstatement.

If you already have Windows 98, my opinion, at least now, is to stick with what you've got. If you're inclined toward Windows

2000, you should ask yourself the three important questions before upgrading:

Are you unhappy with Windows 98 in ways that can be materially improved upon in Windows 2000?

Are you happy with Windows 98 but, like me, always want the newest, best thing out?

Can you afford the upgrade?

Some authorities whom I respect say that the "Second Edition upgrade" of Windows 98 includes most of the important stuff in Windows 2000. I have that in my new Compaq 5700T. I haven't yet seen any earth shaking differences.

No one seems to be overly upset about it, or at least as has reached my ears. But just like Windows 98, Windows 2000 is glacier-like in booting. If you stare at the screen while it's booting, you'll start climbing the walls. This flaw, or so it seems to me, offers one more argument for not turning your computer off during your work day.

There are ways to minimize the boot-up time without courting the dangers of fussing around with the CMOS. Certain "Start-Up" items can be removed. This is done by pressing the "Start" button, then pressing "Run." Type in "msconfig." You'll see a window called "system configuration utility." Press the "Start-Up" tab and then uncheck all items that aren't absolutely necessary. I have unchecked them all. I've been told that certain ones are needed but, so far, I haven't found that to be the case.

One thing is certain, the more start-up items left checked, the slower the computer will respond. If you're concerned with virus infections, you might consider leaving the anti-virus items checked if you have an anti-virus program.

Upgrading to 95, or 98, or 2000, from 3.1.

If you have Windows 3.1, you should give a good, hard look at Windows 98 or 2000. Most important of all is the future of Windows 3.1. More and more programs are released that need Windows 98 and now 2000 for proper operation. Very soon now, Windows 3.1 will be a derelict much like DOS (as an operating system).

A possible headache for new Windows 98 and 2000 users is its incompatibility with some older hardware and software. Some of these problematic items can be squeezed in through persevering efforts, but know when to quit after you've tried everything and all fails.

Sometimes an update from the hardware or software manufacturer can solve the problem. I've found that careful re-installation of the original floppies can work when all other attempts seem hopeless.

Actually, the Y2K problem could in some instances be a blessing in disguise. You probably won't be bothered with many old programs. Not only are they tough to install, they even may be Y2K incompatible.

Windows 98's and 2000's "Plug and Play" automatically installs and configures most any added peripheral device. Most of us who've been confounded by software installation procedures can relate to that simplicity. This is especially advantageous when using peripherals with a notebook computer.

Upgrading to 98 or 2000 from 3.1 is a breeze. All of your programs are auto-detected and installed without your help. Not so, of course, if certain programs just aren't Windows compatible. Among the strange things that can happen, the program can just freeze.

It's important to use "PCI" cards wherever possible for installation of your added peripherals. Apparently, the older "ISA" cards, not truly "plug and play" circuits, give Windows fits. Some manufacturers either cannot or will not convert to the newer cards.

If you have a choice, you might save yourself a headache by insisting on devices that use the PCI cards. Windows likes PCI cards and will accommodate them by finding a correct usable "IRQ." Even if you have the installation done professionally, I'd recommend instructing the installer to use PCI. Problems could later arise if an ISA card is "forced" to an IRQ.

2000 is easier to use than 3.1. The "START" button offers access to all functions with a single mouse click. 98 and 2000 further make use of your right mouse button for lots of shortcuts.

You can forget combing through tools like Program Manager, File Manager, Print Manager, and Control Panel. No need for that with the "START" button. Windows 98 is minimally as fast as 3.1 in a Pentium with 16MB of RAM and considerably faster with more RAM and even faster with a Pentium II or III and especially so with 500Mhz or higher.

Remember that the lowest common denominator for speed is the hard drive access rate. The present edge is about 8ns. The transfer rate also dictates. Make a study of what the best ratings are. Consider also the size of the drive buffer. Most are 528KB. The better drives are 1MB or better yet, 2MB.

Lower prices being what they are now, I could not recommend buying anything less than a Pentium III with at least 64MB of RAM. We'll get into more specifics further along.

Windows, like an iceberg, shows only a small part of its capacity above the surface. The indexing feature of Windows appears to be what attracts many of its users. Clicking a mouse on one of Windows' cute Desktop icons to summon a program can keep a user intrigued for a while. You can customize those icons clicking on the right mouse button and making your selection.

Remember, when upgrading to Windows 98 or 2000 from 3.1, some of your older programs may not be compatible. There are usually some adaptation problems when zooming up to the newest, best and fastest systems. Contact the manufacturer for possible compatible driver updates or try, try again to get Windows to accept it.

Windows 98 or 2000 seems more complicated and difficult to use only because it has so much to offer. Although limiting your usage can greatly simplify Windows, don't fall into that bracket. If you do, you're giving away most of the dollars you've spent for the program. Don't be afraid to experiment. Read the manual if all else fails you. But take time to stretch your awareness of what Windows is all about.

If you're serious about using Windows to its optimum facilities, read the Windows manual carefully and do the suggested tutorial exercises. I hate to suggest that because of all the manual haters I head the list. But what's a body to do?

How about Windows NT?

By the time you get around to deciding whether you want Windows 98 or 2000 or Windows NT, you'll probably know enough about the systems to make that decision. The "NT" part of Windows NT basically refers to network operations.

Both NT and 98 are 32-bit systems. Their functions are directed to 32-bit programs. Still, you gain much even in using your present 16-bit items. Windows NT offers more functions than 98 but costs considerably more. It's also questionable whether those added functions will fill major needs in our law practices. NT is somewhat slower than 98 when using 16-bit programs. Further, it requires a "boot" selection on entry, directing operation to either Windows NT or DOS.

These aren't major objections but they can be a bit frustrating, especially if you aren't benefiting from the extra features of NT. Later editions of NT may be simplifying some of these complications.

Actually, if you're buying a new computer you'll get 98, maybe even Windows 2000 as a "throw-in." If it's 98, be sure to get the second edition. NT presently sells for anywhere from $200 to $300. It may even be extinct by April, 2000. Another cost is the hard drive space gobbled up by NT.

These days, a 20 gigabyte hard disk can cost considerably less than a 400 megabyte disk cost just a couple of years ago. NT is also RAM hungry, requiring at least 32MB, while 98 will work O.K. with just 16MB. Windows 2000 is expected to consume a bit more of each.

Windows 98, like NT, includes networking support as well as messaging and dial-up network access services. Windows 98 also supports a variety of inroads to Internet, such as TCP/IP, PPP (dial-in) and telnet. Seems like Windows 98 or 2000 would be the better choice at least for us lawyer folk.

Windows and DOS based programs.

Windows 98 has not been overly charitable towards DOS based programs, but with some care, and maybe a bit of trickery, you can still incorporate your old DOS favorites with Windows 98.

Actually, I had been rather successful in translating my old DOS programs like LawDex, Legal Tender, Checks & Balances, and a few more to Windows 98. Icons for these DOS programs can be placed on your desktop for easier access. But the programs lack facilities that make Windows what it is.

I still use LawDex, although the others are gone with Y2K. Sooner or later, hopefully later, all DOS programs will be completely phased out for newer, does-everything-better, Windows counterparts. Y2K may have taken care of some of that.

Although DOS programs can be operated through Windows, there is a decided difference between DOS-based and Windows-based system architecture. If Windows is used only when required by the program or for specific use, that difference will not be so apparent.

If that is your only use for Windows, you haven't grasped Windows' significance. You can switch DOS programs with Windows, but you can't really multi-task that way.

Windows-based programs are designed for use of a mouse to access icons within the program, as well as to open programs. Thus a consistency of rhythm is maintained. DOS programs may be used through Windows either by clicking on the "MS-DOS Prompt" icon and then following the conventional DOS method or by creating an icon for the DOS program.

Multi-tasking.

Those who use multi-tasking are within the main stream of Windows' usage. But if "multi-tasking" means to them only accessing diverse programs, the user is still far away from the real magic of Windows. This feature permits not only alternating a particular program with another program, but to flip to and from a series of applications, displaying and working with each program in separate windows while all are on screen.

For simultaneous window performance, each window should be reduced in dimensions to make room on your screen for as many other windows you want. You can size a window by placing the mouse arrow on any window corner and hold the button down while you drag the corner toward the window center. The frame will shrink as you move the mouse.

For convenience, you can copy icons of frequently used programs onto the Desk Top of your computer. Access whichever program you like by simply double clicking on its icon. Another program can be accessed for simultaneous operation by double clicking on that one.

You can do this for as many applications as you wish. When you exit a program, you'll be back in the previous one and then ultimately back to where you started. You can switch between programs by clicking that program's button on the Taskbar.

In a nutshell, you can slip into any program while working with other programs at any time. You never need to close or compromise the program you're using to access anything else in your system.

One can cut or copy and paste portions of files to apply to files in other programs at will. For instance, you can cut and snip parts of documents from here and there to assemble as a composite work in progress. Using material on a CD-ROM, as in Bookshelf, to get more sophisticated definitions, or some information pertinent to your document, is just a key stroke away.

Another use of multitasking is working your CD-ROM backup disk with hard drive programs. The CD operates just like another hard drive. You can access the CD, copy from and to the CD, and ultimately use it for backup and storage. All this can be done with the drag and drop, side-by-side method.

Windows reduces time and frustration to a tiny fraction to minimize error. In multi-tasking through any number of accesses, you flip from one to the next and to the next in an instant. When you flip from any number of files to your target work, you return to the precise position you left.

If you're not using an integrated billing and accounting program, a particular use of multi-tasking might be making counter entries between your separate accounting and billing programs. Each payment for fees would need to be entered in both programs.

By reducing the window size of both programs, you can make your entries and counter-entries back and forth while examining both simultaneously. Multi-tasking allows you to complete all of your accounting and billing in one, simple procedure.

Windows operates best with programs that are programmed for Windows. Quicken, QuickBooks, Money, TreeBased, Timeslips, etc., now offer only Windows versions and are each excellent. For instance, you might open Quicken and TimeSlips to enter a fee received from a client.

You'd make entries in both programs in appropriate accounts while viewing both windows side-by-side. (See also Chapter 11.)

The "cut and paste" facility seen in most Windows compatible word processors, lets you copy or remove portions of documents to paste in your work. Using "copy" instead of "cut" copies the information but leaves the document intact and then "paste" will transport it to the work.

Windows will allow you to keep the copied or cut material in its paste board until you're ready to use it. "Copy" is particularly useful if you want a heading retained in its original position but copied elsewhere. You need copy it only once but you can "paste" it repeatedly.

That scenario can be repeated by as many sources as you may require to assemble the data for your document. Each source appears as a separate window or may be layered one on top of the other. This way, you have each source available to either work with or review at any time. More of this, and in greater detail, will be discussed further along in this chapter.

Working with differing versions of documents is especially simple when using Word's "Versions." Labeling the documents as instructed permits you to have both documents on the screen as you page down to compare the provisions of each. You'll find "Versions" under "File."

Calendaring your events.

Microsoft Works Calendar works fine for me, and my guess is for you also. Like my old calendar, this new one shows a full screen for each month. Of course, you can expand that by any multiple to an entire year. Click on any day and a data box opens for descriptive entry for that day's activity.

The calendar box is spacious enough for your description instead of a truncated word signal. It's inexpensive, simple and efficient. The key word is "simple." Whichever calendar you use, use it. Make certain that every appointment, court date, special assignment, work project, whatever, is indicated on the calendar.

Works calendar has a reminder window that pops up in advance of the event date. You can set the reminder for a half-hour, hour, day or week in advance. Each time you power your computer, the reminder pops up showing you all of the events you've scheduled within the time periods you've selected. (See more of this and other features of Works Calendar in Chapter 9 and Chapter 11.)

If automated expedience appeals to you, use the "Start-Up" folder on the Programs menu accessed from your "Start" button. This permits the opening of programs in order of priorities of icon placement. For instance, if you would normally open your computer with your accounting program, you would place that icon first in the Start-Up folder. Your billing programs could follow directly in sequence.

I've found it more expedient to copy the program icons from the programs bar to the desktop. Scroll to the desired program and click the right key. A window will appear. Click on "create shortcut." A copy marked "2" will appear. Click on that icon and drag it to your desktop.

You can shortcut to exit Windows by pressing the Windows key on your keyboard. Then press the up arrow key to the first bar titled "Shut Down" and type "Enter." When the next window opens, it will be marked for shutting down. Press "Enter" again and you're done. This is simpler and faster than the several mouse clicks otherwise needed.

If you err and power off without touching the "Shut Down" bar and window, you'll face a "warning" screen the next time you power on. You'll be given some frightening words indicating that some terrible wrong occurred when you failed to terminate Windows properly.

There'll be some admonitions and consequences stating things like "lost data" and other dire penalties. The first dozen or so times you see these blasting paragraphs, you'll pray that you will see your work once more.

I've had this happen to me more times than I can count. I've never lost a syllable of work from this "catastrophic calamity." All that happens is a process showing Windows going through its tests, after which you're rebooted and all's fine.

§ 12:14 Pentiums for networks and global activity

"Pentium" is no longer a specific enough identity, even when qualified as to its clock speed, to produce the effect you want. There are the Pentium II, III and heralded Pentium IV. The MMX varieties further complicate your life.

Then frequency is component of speed. At present, the state of the art frequency is 650Mhz. When you read this, it may be 1000Mhz or higher. More and more, computer characteristics are designed to accommodate multimedia and the networking and Internet activities. To say these areas are developing is the year's understatement. They are exploding.

The demands of networking are endless as the functions become more automated and functional. There are multitudes of forms and documents related to the global contacts to further ease the lives of surfers and seekers but to complicate the lives of everyone else.

For those seriously involved in networking or in the Internet, a long and hard look at the newest versions of Windows NT rather than Windows 98 could be warranted. Not for me, though. Windows 2000 will accommodate much of what NT will do for networking.

§ 12:15 Computer prices falling despite advanced technologies

Prices.

Unlike the past, these advanced genre, high speed Pentium models are not being introduced at prices as astronomical as the fields they conquer. Here's an example of a "brand name" computer for $650 or less, as of this writing: Look for lower prices as of your reading this.

Pentium III, 400Mhz with MMX technology.

(No monitor).

64MB RAM.

6.5GB H/D.

56 Kbps, DSVD fax/data modem.

32x max speed CD-ROM, with access speed 80ms.

3D display graphics, 4MB EDO video card for high resolution graphics.

16 bit sound, telephone answering, voice mail, duplex speakerphone.

100MB Zip drive with two cartridges.

2 button mouse with scroll wheel.

If you tried to duplicate this setup with something custom made by your neighborhood shlepper, you'd probably pay lots more. I don't suggest limiting your computer to the above specifications. Set your sights on the specifications listed under. "**Basic Needs In Your Practice; Hardware**,"above.

Your computer monitor.

A good quality 15-inch monitor with .28 dot, non-interlaced, shouldn't cost much over $100. If you crave big screens, 17-inch integrated multimedia monitors are available now for about $175 to $350.

The newer flat screen, (about 3" thick) shows excellent qualities. It's certainly a boon so far as desk space is concerned. It can be moved about with no effort and looks good on your computer desk.

It's cost, however, is quite another matter. A 15-inch model runs around $800 and the larger 20-inch is up in the clouds at around $3,000. The 15-inch isn't bad when you consider the entire 15-inches is viewable. This closely approximates a CRT 17-inch.

Watch for these cuties to come tumbling in price as production and marketing grows. Competition sooner or later levels prices.

Your computer hard drive.

Hard drive capacities are increasing faster than I can type this script. It's no big thing these days to see hard drives of 30GB, 40GB, or more in packaged computers. Not so long ago I couldn't see the need for more than 20 megabytes. Well, I've learned, and so should you. "Too much" or "More than I need" are no longer fashionable terms.

Until recently, the Small Computer Systems Interface controller ("SCSI") was the system of choice. Its attraction was its highly flexible adapting capability. The external SCSI I/O permitted simple plug-in for any SCSI peripheral. If you wanted to back-up to an external hard drive, you simply plugged it into the external plug and away you'd go. It was, and probably still is, the fastest and best system around.

The Integrated Digital Electronics ("IDE") controller became very popular almost immediately upon its introduction simply because it was grossly cheaper than anything else. Its limitation was an inability to operate anything over a 250MB hard drive. In those days, that was enough for most users.

As demands grew in capacities, designs were improved to permit 500MB drives. IDE's kept pace below competition. Ultimately, the barriers were broken and IDE's could drive anything around. Now, most computers are designed around the IDE system. SCSI runs a poor second in numbers sold.

Supposedly the IDE drive is slower than SCSI. IDE is also reputed to be less durable than SCSI. I've not found either to be true thus far.

My new Compaq replacing my venerable old SCSI unit, described earlier, is 100% IDE. It comes complete with a 34GB, 7200RPM, UDMA drive that will rival SCSI in speed and beat it in price. There's enough equivocation in the IDE/SCSI debate to warrant some vacillation on my part.

Methods of speed control now determined by Windows.

Speed seems to be the leading goal among the lawyers with "turnoveritis." In the past, CPU clock speed was considered the criterion of computer speed. The CPU speed is limited by its base architecture and the mother board accommodation.

With the advent of 32-bit operation, those limits were pierced. Other innovations operate to increase computer speed more directly and effectively than through any of the above conventional methods. The "local bus" type board permits the controller and video cards to access CPU, memory and controller directly at 32-bit.

The mathematical rule of computers has historically been that upgrading of one component usually required upgrading of other components to gain full benefit overall. It did little good to install a hard drive with faster access speed in the face of a slow CPU or other limitations. The same is inversely true.

With Windows 95, the "plug-and-play" was born. Windows 98 and 2000 have extended that feature. This eliminates the old step-by-step process of Windows 3.1. In addition to automation, plug and play avoids many, but not all, of the conflict problems.

If you insist on installing peripherals that are not plug and play, this may possibly be done. Use the "Add/Remove Hardware" icon on your "Control Panel," accessed through "Settings" on your "Start" bar."

So long as Windows will accept the unit, everything will be O.K., both as to operation and memory. Once the unit is plugged in and its existence discovered by Windows, the installation is complete.

Another plus for Windows 98 is the allocation of interrupts (IRQ) and addresses. The stage will be set for address and interrupt applications through the "plug-and-play" automation. Everything should run smoothly as your computer finds all the hardware. That is, provided you use the compatible "PCI" driver cards.

Sometimes, happily not often, that automation gets us into a bit of trouble. A wrong interrupt is selected and maybe something fizzles. Then you've got to go into "Device Manager" to undo the conflict and reassign interrupts manually. This fix isn't for amateurs. Unless you know what you're doing, don't do it. This won't happen when using PCI cards.

Memory in the DOS sense is no longer our problem, it's Windows'. So, if we get impatient with Windows 98 because we can't do whatever we wish to do, bear in mind the problems we had with past systems which caused us confusions and interfered with our intentions. It was difficult for me to accept at first, but I soon got used to the strange ways of Windows 98.

Fast video cards can add substantially to the overall speed of your computer. Modern fast video cards come as standard with 16MB of SDRAM video memory. A stretch to 32MB is worthwhile.

Hopefully, this edition will remain in print for a few years as per the past three editions. Read the supplements for updates on solo law facts including computer technologies. If you're reading this book in 2003 and laughing your head off, remember I am saying that these numbers are only as rough guides for your practical interpolations.

§ 12:16 Research "on-line"

I've used Westlaw on-line for a brief period. I have used other on-line research host programs, but found them to be to costly due to difficulty in getting my queries understood, much less answered. Westlaw allows searches for cites using plain language, and I DO mean "plain."

I must say that I have had a good share of troubles searching for items on the Internet, legal research included. For some reason, I am dense where it comes to finding subjects for downloading. I found Westlaw to be a delightful exception.

I was asked to write a news article on the California vs. Indian Tribes gambling issue. I needed legal support for that article. My keywords were "Indian tribes gambling unlawful in California." A plethora of cites and encyclopedia information appeared on my screen instantly, all of it to the exact point and useful.

Each specimen set of keywords worked like a charm. I'm excited about that, mainly because I've never had that experience with any other research method or program. It's not an expensive setup for small or solo law offices. It's a lot cheaper and less all consuming than bound book sets.

Trusts and wills on CD-ROM.

I've also reviewed West's Wills and Trusts on CD-ROMs. I find these sets much more comprehensive and useful than the older C.E.B. sets and other sources. Of course, the keyword in that comparison is older.

The Trusts program is so versatile and simple to use that it could deceive you into the dangerous belief that you could simply boilerplate your way through developing a trust for a client. Don't do it. It's a great program but it's not a "plug 'n play and get paid" deal. You still need to know something about what you're doing. There are some good MCLE courses on Trusts.

The Wills set is a bit different. Most lawyers presumably know the basics in will drafting. Whether you're competent to draft the particular wills assigned to you is your call. This program will save you tons of time and effort. Everything is laid out for you. You can do simple wills without drawing a deep breath.

More complicated wills are also simplified in their separate clauses organization. Using your word processor's "cut and paste" copy method, you can compose a complex fifty page document almost as fast as you can type it.

Proportional use prompts most publishers to issue their software in WordPerfect. Happily, Word will convert WordPerfect while it loads the program. This is true of most other word processors as well.

§ 12:17 Shhh—There are legal research programs out there for free

Check out FindLaw (http://www.findlaw.com) for your research projects. FindLaw was originated by two Stanford University graduate students and posted on a web page as "shareware." FindLaw is not simple to use and is not a "plain language" seeker like Westlaw. However, it's O.K. if you've got lots of time to find what you need. If you do have that much extra time, shame on you. But, anyway, the price is right.

Apparently, this project is funded through book sales and MCLE courses. In any event, you can take advantage of the enormous range of legal authorities to be found in FindLaw. There are encyclopedia topics, legal news, and many other sources of information as well as appellate and higher court decisions of various states.

A free Internet program that I find fascinating is "Yahoo." Call for it as "Yahoo.com." You'll find almost anything you want on its lists. I've even used its travel atlas for routes and distances to places by auto. It's accurate as well as informative.

§ 12:18 Networking

Can a network help a small practitioner?

The newest network innovation is the telephone line home network. This permits the networking of any number of computers so long as they're located within the same home or office. The only requirement is that each computer be equipped with a home networking card at a cost of about $35 each. Then, simply plug each computer into an available phone jack.

If a phone jack is inconvenient, you can use one of several available types of radio transmitted terminals. These are also relatively inexpensive and simple to install.

Networks are getting more popular by the minute. Even the smallest firms are finding bonuses in networking. Being able to draw from common storage pools can help ease the burden on a busy office even though a small one.

This technique also avoids errors because of multiple data input at different PC's. If two persons are working on the same project or operating from the same data source, although located on their separate respective machines, gaps can occur on the final version, supposedly a composite of both inputs.

Obviously, if both inputs are conjoined into a single data bank, there can be no such omission or confusing duplication. Networking can prevent such errors. Actually, a competent network is neither expensive nor complicated.

When you upgrade your computer, instead of discarding the present unit, use it for the network server. It needn't have the specifications you'd want in a PC station. The only problem you may have is finding office space for an extra computer. Setting it up is reasonably simple.

Another good use for the old unit, even if networking isn't yet in the cards for you, is as a great backup device. Using the hard disk as a backup is faster, more reliable and more versatile than any other form of backup.

All you need do for this purpose is to connect your new computer to the old one with a parallel input/input cable. This type of cable is generally provided with transfer programs such as LapLink. The rest is simply following the menu directions.

You can either transfer certain prioritized files or dump in the whole enchilada. Whichever, the entire process is fast and requires little or no expertise. If your old unit has limited storage space, you can compress the transfer through the use of the "PKZip" or some other similar compression program.

How does networking benefit a solo lawyer? Certainly a two member firm will gain more from a network's capabilities than a solo attorney. However, busy computers have caused many solos to sit thumb twiddling waiting to continue his/her work.

While you are printing out a large file, or scanning a huge stack of documents, or optimizing your hard disk, backing up data, sending or receiving modem communications, or whatever, wouldn't you enjoy continuing your work simultaneously? Sure, you would.

Networking allows you to disregard any of those activities and go right on computing. It's the nature of a networking system to separate those functions from the business of keyboard input.

Local area networks (LAN).

Local Area Networks ("LANs") have come of age. LAN hardware and software costs have been shaved down to a level that solo lawyers can afford. One such LAN system is LANtastic. All that is needed are two network cards and suitable cable lengths and software. The entire package was, when I last looked, about $200. This is only one of a number of similar type systems, but quite good, especially for the price.

A LAN makes possible multiple users of your multi-use programs, situated on a single computer (the "server") without interference. This means that two or more persons can input, say, some accounting or billing entries simultaneously, with each set of entries being treated separately by the accounting program.

My information is that the SMC EtherCard Elite Ultra adapter uses something called "UltraChip" which makes it extremely fast. I'm also told that the SMC people will provide a "special evaluation kit," consisting of two adapters and a demo disk at a low, low price. Might be worth investigating.

Many of the newer offices and even homes are now being equipped with computer lines in the walls like power and telephone jacks.

§ 12:19 The Internet: A marketing tool for you?

If you want the Internet to repay some of the dollars you're paying to Microsoft, AOL or whichever host you select, think about using the Internet to bring you some business. Web sites have now been established as another vista for marketing. Some businesses report that the bulk of their action comes from the Internet.

If you get the word out that you have a web site, clients, and potential clients will tune you in. This gives you an opportunity to do some promotion. If you're handy with graphics, you can do some fancy stuff yourself. Or services such as FirmSite (http://www.wld.com, a West Group service) will provide expert help in designing your web site.

What can you do with a web site? If you have some imagination, you can be a web pace setter for lawyers. You can provide your clients and prospective clients with a valuable service on the web. You can garner lots of law business from your web site if you refrain from overt advertising.

Advertising will almost invariably lead to some form of misrepresentation. As Amos of Amos 'n' Andy said, "the big print gives it to you and the small print takes it away." If one is ultra-prudent, some mild forms of advertising can be done without any form of "switch-pitching" or "bait and switch" kinds of offers.

A woman set up a web site to sell her home and it worked. Others have used their sites for investment services. Attorneys may use a web site to provide a resume which may be continuously updated, and include areas of practice, office locations, and descriptions of representative cases successfully handled.

You can prove expertise by posting or providing links to articles you have written, or to seminars where you're scheduled to speak. The big effort is getting the message out that you have a web site. We can explore some ideas.

The biggest complaint about using the Internet is the time factor. Logging on and downloading require saintly patience. Whatever your patience quota, kicking your computer won't make it go faster.

You want speed, big time? You got it. But for big bucks.

DSL. THE REALLY, REALLY FAST WAY TO INTERNET.

DSL means Digital Subscriber Lines. This is a way around the delay, but it's a bit pricey. The "DSL" transmission method increases speeds up to 100 times. Depending on where you're located, you can contract for DSL starting at about $49.50 per month.

That's a lot of loot but it's bargain basement compared to the top line stuff. Telepacific Communications offers DSL at about $120 per month. To add to the confusion, there are two kinds of DSL. The regular kind that runs about $50 per month is ADSL or Asymmetrical Digital Subscriber Lines.

The more expensive kind is SDSL or Symmetrical Digital Subscriber Lines. Symmetrical is better. It's faster and offers more features. Most people I know who have DSL have the Asymmetrical type. They advertise it's about 100 times the speed of modem internet. That's not ADSL, it's SDSL, the symmetrical system.

FlashCom is another service offering asymmetrical DSL at $49.50. Some services will install free on a two year contract. Otherwise, installation runs about $150. Call FlashCom at 1(877) FlashCom. Services may, or may not, extend to your location.

At present, most will serve only locations within a given distance from a "switching station." In some instances, that means about three miles. Whether that includes you can be determined by calling the DSL servers in your area. Don't be discouraged by the lower speed of ADSL. It should still beat the modem system by about sixty or seventy times.

While even $49.50 isn't cheap, there are some economic offsets. Internet use through DSL doesn't consume a phone line. Because of its method of transmission, your phone is in full service for regular calls while you're on-line. You don't need a special Internet line.

The DSL fee covers your access on an "all you can eat" basis. So, knock off the $20 or so you regularly pay plus another $15 or $20 for a dedicated line. This would sift the price down to about

$10 or $15 to get the faster DSL speed. That makes it look more attractive.

Look to http://www.telepacific.com for more information. They offer first month free service, free installation and equipment, fax to e-mail number and web-hosting. They also brag they "will beat any competitor's price." Of course, that's on the SDSL scale.

A call to Telepacific could be worth your time even if paying $120 per month isn't in your cards. They are very congenial and informative.

Electronic legal directories.

West's Legal Directory provides a listing of every practicing lawyer in the U.S., including even me. It is available on the web (http://www.wld.com), on CD-ROM, or on-line on Westlaw. You can also heavy-up your listing with more self-aggrandizing material if you wish, at some extra cost. Is it worth some bucks to list all of your noble enterprises, such as which charities you've supported, plaques received for civic efforts, citations for this and that? Not of my money.

Bear in mind that this listing (at least on the CD-ROM or Westlaw) is for lawyers, not for potential clients. Lawyers are not going to be overly impressed with your cascade of lofty deeds. They'll want information only about your legal qualifications.

This on-line research method permits spot listing of lawyers sought in the desired geographic location as well as having all preferred practice qualities. Certainly, advocates of hard bound volumes can argue their preference, with compelling persuasion, but try this CD-ROM method and decide for yourself.

§ 12:20 Sound cards: Why not?

Sound cards have been steadily improving, to keep pace with faster CD-ROM's and computers in general. Now you can record narrations on your hard drive to dramatize documents and memos. Producers are using sound more innovatively to enhance their programs.

Originally these cards were used only to enhance computer games with Sis, Boom, Bah, explosions, sirens, hoots and hollers, along with symbol crashes, rim shots and other special effects suitably accompanied with appropriate musical tracks.

Sound cards now come with stereo inputs and outputs. If you intend to dictate to your computer rather than resort to the keyboard, or use voice on the Internet, your card must have a microphone input. Your talk program will require other soundboard functions.

Remember that "cards" are electronic circuit boards and need to be inserted in one of the card slots in the CPU.

To operate a sound card, speakers or headphones are needed. Not all sound cards will drive speakers directly. Some require an amplifier or speakers containing an amplifier. Adequate amplified speakers are available anywhere from $5 or $10 to upwards of $50 or $60 for the higher quality selections.

If you really dig sound for your computer, take a listen to Microsoft's digital speaker system. The set is composed of subwoofer, (amplifier built in) two satellite speakers, (one with power switch, bass and volume control) and cables. It's attractive and petite. What's more, it's price won't frighten you. Some discounters offer the set for $99 with a (you guessed it) *rebate* of $50 leaving a cost of $49, if you ever collect the rebate.

But rebate, shmebate, it's a great sounding system. It's so good you might want one for your stereo or TV set. The bass will shock you. If the price shocks you too, don't. You don't need to spend even that much for sound unless you either enjoy it that much or have good uses for it.

Computers you can talk to.

If someone sees you talking to your computer, you might be talking to some guys in white coats. However, if you're swearing at the box nobody will think twice about that. Sure, voice activation for computers has been around for a few years but now it's for real. The newer systems can actually be used for daily dictation. Dragon Systems, Inc., produces voice programs ranging from $149 (DragonDictate) to $695 (NaturallySpeaking, Deluxe Ed).

The lower priced DragonDictate is usable but requires slight pauses between each word. NaturallySpeaking uses continuous speech technology to permit speaking in phrases. Modules are offered to allow special vocabularies such as in legal terminology. If you're interested, check the discount houses for lowest street prices. Make sure that you have a reasonable time period for a try before you buy option.

Your computer must have a really fast processor to accommodate such voice activation if you want a practical, workable program. The requirement for RAM is equally demanding. Forget your 32MB whether SIMM or DIMM. Reach farther into the ranges of 64MB or even 128MB. I'd suggest Pentium III at 500Mhz or higher if it doesn't give you a nose bleed.

This doesn't mean that less prodigious programs may not work for you if you're agreeable to extra time correcting the work. If your intent is to dictate to your computer as you would a live secretary, you shouldn't even try to "get by" with the advertised models.

As with most other newer, complicated wonder programs, more effort is required on your part. You'll find that the installation processes on any of these voice programs are not simple. You can expect to contribute hours in getting up to speed. Then the business of relearning to talk will be a thrilling experience. But, when all the smoke clears away, you should have a real "talk to" secretary.

At this writing, you should expect to spend around $100 for a program that will allow dictation at about 100 words per minute. You can see a printout of your words so any needed corrections can be made before you print

So it shouldn't be a total loss, you'll be encountering other newer programs with equal or even greater appetites. Look to your hard drive size. Voice programs are greedy. But that won't be unique in the vanguard of extravagant programs.

Don't even think about getting into voice operation if your computer has marginal memory and speed characteristics. Voice recognition, discrimination as to minute sound variations, intonations, etc., all are involved in your spoken words resolving into formation of written words. These attributes are all functions of memory and speed.

Before you leap, consider that memory and speed relate to many aspects of your computer design. Getting those spoken words up on the screen with accurate typography requires just about the best of everything in the computer chain. You'll pay a big price for the convenience of having an automated secretary.

I don't go for that fancy stuff and my advice is to stay away from it. If you're not satisfied with the way you type, learn how to type better. But no matter how slowly, your typing should do you quite well. On the "talking computer" bit, remember that OmniPage Pro 10.0 has a nice sounding voice helping you to proof read your work.

§ 12:21 DVD or CD-ROM: Not an option, a necessity

Almost everything you need in your law practice is on CD-ROM, making things easier, faster and cheaper. The problem is that too many time diversions are offered on this fun filled medium. Games are supposed to be for kids? Apparently no.

Each time I see the mind boggling graphics of a hi-tech game on a lawyer's screen, I gawk. Lawyers playing games? But then, why not? Aren't we the world's most accomplished game players.

There's so much out there on CD to make your practice simpler and more lucrative, playing games on your computer, hi-tech or not, seems ultra-expensive. Besides, doing your work is more fun than playing games if you relax with it.

There's some controversy regarding computer eye strain. I don't believe that any permanent damage is done, but I do feel some eye irritation after a few hours in front of the screen.

I've been computering for about twenty years and my eyes are still correctable to 20/20. Between all of my law work and all the extra writing I do, including this book, I probably have been spending more computer time than you do or will, and my eyes are still O.K.

Still, I might suggest that you refrain from non-essentials, like games. You'll have all the hours you should handle in just doing your work. Make it a practice to get up about each hour or so. Walk around the office, look out the window (if you have a window), and take a couple of deep breaths.

Your chair should be a good posture type supporting your back. The seat part shouldn't extend far beyond your buttocks so that your thighs aren't being compressed against the seat. The seat should be firm but not hard.

The keyboard should be placed so that your arms are roughly parallel to the floor and your palms resting on the keyboard front panel. The monitor center should approximate eye level. Your mouse should be at a comfortable reach.

Convenience of CD-ROM.

Almost all programs now come packed with CD's instead of floppies. Without a CD drive, you're out in left field. Not only would it take a truck load of floppies to load these programs, the CD is faster and much more reliable.

CD's have made the costly, laborious job of filling the extensive book sets with supplements a thing of the past. Your research has been reduced to a flick of the keyboard. With disk cost reduced to less than 10 cents, monthly issues are now the rule rather than the old quarterly or even yearly, supplements.

What information can I get on DVD or CD-ROM?

Virtually all legal texts, encyclopedias, cases, codes, digests, you name it, have been rendered on CD-ROM. There's no need to store the endless volumes of legal forms, practice and procedure forms, law digests, summaries of the laws of this or that state, federal laws and digests or any other formerly "must have" sets. It's getting so lawyers don't know what to put on those empty shelves.

It's a close race, virtually neck and neck, between publishing companies to cover newer, better legal research applications. The battle is fierce. Quality and speed of access and research ascends inversely proportional to price reductions. The spigot continues to churn out an unending supply of great stuff.

West Group has been adding steadily to its CD-ROM research tools as have Lexis, Matthew Bender and other publishers. ALR and Am Jur sets are complete and are valuable additions to your CD-ROM library, both in LawDesk® (using Folio® software) and Premise® formats. West also offers a full set of federal appellate cases dating back to 1880 in full paginated text. The whole set consists of about 20 discs, organized by a single "Table of Cases" identifying all cases from 1880 to the present. Also recorded on that same disc are "Slip Opinions."

Each disc is labeled according to the group of volumes it covers, i.e. Vol. 726-880, etc. The table of cases refers to the particular disc containing the volume reporting the case sought. A change to that disc quickly brings up the sought disc. Just as in library research, cases may be invoked through pertinent words or phrases.

West may have missed something in not identifying the dates on each disc just as they do their bound case volumes. This would make disc selection a lot simpler. I've passed that suggestion along so maybe future issues will have that convenience. As noted, above, even legal directories are on CD-ROM.

Which came first, the chicken, or CD-ROM?

Statistics are confused as to which came first; the increased buyers' interest or the advances in CD-ROM speed. The newer generation 100 speed, 60ms drive, and faster, has taken the laziness out of CD-ROM. Actually, the original reputation of CD-ROM as a "slug" made it necessary for the medium to advance in speed as well as usefulness.

Disk access and transfer rate are so improved that they come close to approximating hard drive ratings not so long ago.

Writeable CD-ROM. For everyone; anyone.

They used to call them "worm drives." They were cumbersome and expensive, up in the thousands. Not anymore. You can write on CD's. In fact, you can re-write on CD's over and over. Some say re-writes are limited. But even that "limited" re-write capability will no doubt exceed any reasonable expectation.

These jewels are colloquially referred to as "burners." You can record data, music and even some forms of video on your writeable CD-ROM disks. You might want to use the burner to compile some music. You can transfer your music tapes onto disks. They're much more durable and simpler to use.

Prices for burners have fallen to below $125 and expected to go lower before you read this. The CD-RW in my new Compaq stores my data fast and copies CD's just fine. It records music, both analog and digital from any source to the disk. It's rated at 4x read, 4x read RW and 24X CD read. I don't know what more any brand can do.

The software I use for that purpose came with the package and is called "Just Burn" by CeQuadrat. Another burn software that I've used and found excellent is Easy Creator Deluxe. Plug in your LP, tape or whatever, press the button and sit back. You can also copy CD's or program them to select only the tunes you like. That's not practicing law but fun's important too, if you don't overdo it.

For backup purposes, the recording CD beats all other systems I've seen. At less than a buck a disk, it's cheaper than ZIP drives and certainly more reliable than tape. If you wish, I don't, you can make your regular backups on re-write recording disks. Most machines will now record on both re-write and single write disks.

DVD: Time waste? Movies? No, No, No. What's it got??

Sure, you can run movies on your computer DVD the same as the DVD you bought, (or will buy) for your TV. But your eyes and time are too precious to waste watching movies on your computer. That's for work. Or so you try to convince everyone.

DVDs are replacing the CD-ROM. The reason: Unlike the CD, maximum space, 650MB, the DVD holds several gigabytes. Plus the unit is susceptive of greater compression plus a method of stacking. Right now, the DVD can contain an entire movie. Eventually, the disk will hold multiple movies. Translate that into computer flexibility and downloading capacity.

Even now, some programs require two, three and more CD's to be installed on your hard drive. In some instances, the space needed is so immense that either your drive won't hold it all or you just don't want to use up that much space. So what do you do? You sit there and feed disks. "Insert disk No. 3," and so on. Who needs it?

A DVD disk can hold anything that exists now and whatever they may conjure up in the future. Then there's the disk storage thing. Remember what it was like to store all those floppies? They were everywhere. But try to find the one, or ones, you need. Now it's getting to be that way with CD-ROM disks.

As you improve one thing, you invariably need to improve another. DVD wants a higher quality video card. Then you'll want a wider spectrum sound card. See, one thing leads to another.

The keyboard.

The keyboard should have a comfortable "feel" for you. Some

people like a definite key "click" and others prefer the silent response. Keyboards have plunged in cost, so that the very best boards are now within just a few dollars of the cheapest kind. Some things important to me are large rectangular backspace and enter keys. Smaller keyboards are more difficult for me to use. I find myself touching the wrong keys almost invariably when using that kind of keyboard.

Most newer keyboards come with the Windows keys making it simpler to access the start bar and your e-mail. This is also handy when you elect the shortcut shutdown method earlier described.

An irritating fact regarding Microsoft keyboards, which I must say are among the best, is that the Internet keys tend to signal MSN and ignore other choices of hosts. I have been using AOL (America Online) and I cannot get through using any of those keyboard "one touch" keys.

Most programs provide a simple method of upgrading their products. An "upgrade" key appears upon accessing the program. If you subscribe to MSN, everything is hotsy totsy. If you are an AOL (or other) subscriber, you'll be given a merry chase to find your "password" isn't correct.

The only way to bypass this catch-22 is to open AOL first and then press the "upgrade" button. That will let you sneak through the MSN barricade.

Card slots and peripherals bays for your computer.

The circuit cards for some of the peripherals included in your computer are installed in provided slots. Your computer should have at least eight card slots to for these plus other things you may want later. You'll want a CD burner somewhere along the line if one isn't factory installed. That will require a driver card and a slot to fit it in.

Your computer should have a total of five bays to hold peripherals already installed plus those you'll want added like CD-ROM drives, Drive back-up units, a CD Burner, etc. Make sure the machine has one or two vacant bays for things you'll want in the future.

These tiny little half-pint "mini-tower" computers hold more stuff than you'd believe. How they do it confounds me. Anyway, you should count bays and slots to make sure you have enough for future wants.

§ 12:22 Office 2000. Like Office 97, it may be more than you want, but get it. It'll grow on you

Every generation of computer hardware and software brings something to the table. It's got to or it will die on the vine. Office

2000 offers many improvements over 97. "Office," being a Microsoft program, was made to fit like a Siamese Twin with Windows and in particular Windows 98. Now that Office 2000 has been released, consider getting that version if you want the newest in Microsoft "Word."

Office 2000 is still very pricey, costing about $125 to $175 for the standard upgrade version and more than $300 to upgrade to the "Pro" version. Then there is a "Premium" version. But perhaps you don't want to pay about $800 for that, do you?

Look hard, deal sharp and haggle all the way and you can save lots of bucks. As with its predecessor, Office 97, lots of great programs accompany the 2000 "Pro" version. If you can afford the difference, look closely at Office Pro 2000.

These, and other, functions are bundled, so don't panic if you think some of them have been left out. In fact, more have been added. As with 97, the new Office automatically converts data to read in the new language. Even data from Office 97 must be converted to read in Office 2000.

Office 97 has a neat calendar in its Outlook. More than just a calendar, Outlook handles addresses and even serves as a control center for just about all of your computer functions. It's a powerful scheduler, phone book, journal, e-mail and fax center, and work product timer. I prefer the Works Calendar.

§ 12:23 Notebook computers: Your office away from your office

Just when you thought it was safe to buy a notebook. Hah! Like the monster you thought was so little, cuddly and cute, notebooks are growing and growing. There's nothing you can get in a desk top that can't be had in a notebook. I have recommended that every lawyer should have a notebook for the convenience of portability.

If you do any work away from your office, as you should, a portable computer is a necessity. Selecting a notebook lightweight as possible, consistent with essentials of a good computer, would be conducive to more frequent use.

My notebook computer is a Compaq Presario, AMD K6-2, 380 MHz, 6.5GB hard drive, 64MB RAM with DVD drive and an active matrix TFT 14.1 inch screen. That unit comes with a plethora of software. Its battery is lithium-ion with an operating time of about 1 to 2 hours, though they claim up to 5 hours.

My investigation reveals that notebooks of speeds beyond 166 MHz, 24 or more RAM, and active matrix screens, will zap conventional Nicad battery life in less than an hour. Make sure you get the lithium-ion battery.

It's PCMCIA port supports both the type II and type III cards. Again, my damnable impatience caused me to pay about $2,300 plus tax. Now, the same unit can be had for under $2,000 total. I find no inconvenience in its smallness of keyboard or screen. The monitor, active matrix color, is as attractive as my desktop screen and just as sharp at least to my old eyes.

Another advantage to the matrix, rather than dual scan, screen is the visibility of the mouse arrow. Although improvements have been made in the general quality of the dual scan type screen, they haven't done much about the disappearing arrow. It can be mighty frustrating trying to follow that frenetic, illusive arrow to where you want it.

The dual scan suffers also from narrow viewing angle. You must be almost directly in front of the screen for good visibility. It also is limited in the colors it will reproduce.

My son, Alan, who practices law in Seattle, said he has a dual scan notebook because he prefers it to active matrix. His reasoning is interesting. He feels more secure using it around others because they can't see what he's doing from alongside. Anyone want to trade a dual scan notebook for a slightly used active matrix kind?

Yes, but how big is the screen? My active matrix screen is 14.1 inches. Now they have 16.1" beauties. Then, to confuse us more, they break the active matrix into many sub categories. Which is better and why? I don't know.

It's a bit confusing with the way notebook promotions and advertisements have been drifting. I thought the reason for introducing the notebook was to make its reduced dimensions and weight more conducive to portability. Now it seems that stacking everything that's available in the little jewel has brought the size and weight even greater than the previous models.

Of course, it's nice to have your CD-ROM, sound card, speakers, PCMCIA adapters, and everything else with you as you go. It's even nicer when everything is all built in. It's also nice to have a multi-gigabyte hard drive, 64 MB of RAM or so, 400 MHz, maybe even the Pentium III variety with enough cards to drive a Sherman tank, and whatever else may cross your mind. And, if you want both a floppy drive and built-in DVD drive, one or the other needs to be included in your handy little (not so little anymore) carry case.

But, what happened to the idea of grabbing your little 3 or 4 pound wonder in one hand, your briefcase in the other and dashing out for wherever. Of course, those little lightweights didn't have all those marvelous things built in. You had to select from among them to decide which ones you absolutely had to bring along.

I've been advising use of a portable computer since before portable computers were really portable. I went through the prehistoric models, including the 14 pounders, the "gas plasmas," and the entire gamut of so-called "portables." They're still basically designed for Arnold Schwartzenegger, but better to have and lug one than to not have one at all.

My present "notebook" weighs in at about 7.4 pounds, with everything installed. 7.4 pounds may not seem much but add that, along with the accessories, to your brief case with files, reference materials, etc., and you're a weight lifter. To me, shaving off a few pounds even at the expense of some extra whatever, is a good tradeoff.

Aha. There is such a super miniature model. Sony and Toshiba both offer a notebook weighing less than 3 lbs. But, of course, you must carry the floppy drive, CD drive and anything else you want separately along with you.

I value lighter weight and more compact size, but not at the expense of inconvenient plugging and unplugging of the peripherals. I must say though, both of these little units are mighty attractive. Take a look. Maybe you might prefer them.

Notebook components and peripherals. Careful! Many are proprietary.

Notebooks, unlike desktop computers, are hardware proprietary. The so-called desktop "clones" exist solely because IBM was unable to establish protection for its basic hardware and architectural designs. Dozens of computer manufacturers hopped on the gravy train, building exact copies of the basic IBM desktop, which dates back almost fifteen years.

All computer circuit cards and boards are directly interchangeable between all desktops, other than the Apple Macintosh units. This universality resulted in competitive discount pricing throughout the industry.

Not so with laptops and notebooks. Each of the notebook manufacturers has maintained its own configuration and adaptation of its components, cards and boards. So far as I've seen, few notebooks, whether under "brand" names or "private labels," have parts which fit in other brands.

Each notebook has its own look and functionality. Some things, like "touch plate" modems, have been picked up by competing brands, but by and large, each has its own distinctive design.

If you want a larger hard drive for your notebook, chances are that you'll need to get one from the manufacturer of your notebook. Naturally, there being no competitive after-market source, the price will be high. The same would be true of video cards, internal modems, internal CD-ROMS, batteries and most other peripherals.

This is a good reason to get all you think you may need in the next foreseeable future when you buy the notebook. That's when you can make your best deal. You can get lots of stuff thrown in when they sit you down to make the deal. If not thrown in, the price will certainly be much cheaper than if you come back, even the next week or so, to add something.

I haven't investigated this yet, but I will for next time. It seems there are some notebook peripherals that qualify as "standard industry." This is not to the degree of the desk top standards but at least there is some compatibility. If this is as described, it could be an advantage to consider notebooks that would adapt to such standards.

PCMCIA may save the day for you.

All may not be lost. PCMCIA ports are universal to all notebooks having that feature. Many of the "extras" you want are adaptable to the PCMCIA port. External drives, modems, CD-ROMS, and other peripherals, will work with your notebook, provided you have the size PCMCIA port to fit.

I recommend that you buy a notebook with a PCM port that will fit both the II and III sizes. It's true that one port for both sizes will be limited to one device at a time. That could possibly be inconvenient when you need two devices operating at the same time. But how often can that happen?

PCM components are not seen by the notebook computer as "externals." They respond with the same speed as internal equipment. This is the reason that you should prefer PCM items rather than those which connect to the parallel port.

Another big advantage is that PCM connections can be made at any time. You don't need to reboot as you must with parallel connections. That is also true of USB devices.

PCM stuff is a bit more costly than parallel port externals. This is mainly because of the miniaturized size. But the overall benefits are worth the extra dollars. Besides, as with everything else, the cost of PCMs is decreasing every day. Much of the foregoing is rendered moot by the inclusion of a USB port. To the extent usable, the USB would be the selection of choice.

Removable hard drives.

Notebook hard drives are especially flexible since they are removable. While the cost may be higher, the ease of replacing the drive is a great feature. Having the ability to segregate drives to specific uses can be an advantage, if your capacity demands warrant that method. This could also be a benefit in the unlikely event of a hard drive failure.

CD-ROM and your notebook portable computer.

If your notebook doesn't have a built-in CD or a CD module, you'll be stuck with a portable CD-ROM. You must have a CD-ROM If it's detached, the notebook size and weight is reduced. This is a trade-off of posi-negative proportions.

A portable CD drive may be adaptable to either your parallel, USB or PCMCIA ports. Whichever you have, plug it in, insert a CD-ROM disk and away you go. Imagine, having your West Group, Lexis or whatever CD-ROM libraries right with you in court, along with your trusty notebook computer, to challenge any case or code law thrown at you.

Extending the capacity of your notebook computer with an external hard drive.

Actually, notebook drives now have as much storage as many desktop drives. Mine is 6.5GB. Other notebook drives are as large as 10GB and more.

The PCMCIA slot can also accommodate use of an external hard drive for added capacity or back-up. So many things formerly relegated to the PCMCIA slot are now included in notebooks, modem, network, (both external and local) CD and other peripherals, that this little accommodation has lost much of its former attraction.

But don't count that slot out entirely. Remember what was said about "proprietary peripherals." When your built-in CD or your modem becomes obsolete due to size, speed or whatever, your PCMCIA slot saves the day. You can buy an updated slot device and go right on with your work.

ZIP drives are now 250MB. They can be internal or can attach to either your parallel or USB ports. As stated, if you have a PCM to USB card, your ZIP drive won't even need to be power connected since the card is host powered.

You won't always be carrying the extra stuff with you. You'll organize your sub-notebook hard drive with the stuff you mostly use. When the occasion arises, and it will quite frequently, you'll slip the extra drive, or whatever, in your handy carry bag. How that bag seems to always accept one more thing after it's loaded to the hilt still surprises me.

§ 12:24 DANGER, WARNING: Caution when loading programs in Windows 98 or 2000

Make sure that the program you intend to load through the

"Settings: Control Panel" of Windows 98 or 2000 is compatible with Windows. There are some programs which are mismarked as being O.K. with Windows 98, but which are in fact NOT compatible with, and even hostile to, Windows 98. It could be even worse using 2000.

Look for the Windows logo on the product for compatibility. If you don't see that and you proceed to download it, you could possibly be headed for some bad trouble. A true Windows 98 synchronous program will integrate with the Windows files.

This makes the program more fluid and workable under the Windows aegis. If the program attempts Windows integration but lacks the necessary coordination, the program could fail and you'll see the dreaded, "FATAL ERROR." This notice is usually innocuous but sometimes presages trouble.

The worst of this trouble is the horrendous difficulty you face trying to remove the offending program. Even re-installing Windows may not cure the problem because the "ERROR" intrusions may survive the re-installation. What to do?

There are solutions but none of them are fun things to do. The worst would be to reformat the hard drive. If you've kept your drive backed up, at least to a relatively recent date, that wouldn't be the worst fate for you.

If you intend to install a program that you're not certain is compatible, BACK UP THE HARD DRIVE FIRST. Whether you use a tape back-up or an external hard drive, do this before you proceed with the loading process. Then, if you experience such problems, format your hard drive and reload from the back up resource.

§ 12:25 Some observations about hardware and software prices, upgrading problems, and local purchases

If you're looking for a plateau in computers, forget it. There's no end in sight and there never will be. Clock speeds will go up, up, up, and away. Hard drives will get bigger and bigger. 20GB, 30GB, 100GB and more and more gigabytes are in the definite, and near, very near, future.

External modems will get faster and faster, smaller and smaller. They're so small even now that you can swallow one like a pill. Although phone lines are still the bottleneck, modems are being standardized at 56K. You can expect that to remain status quo for a while because most phone lines cannot transmit data faster than 28.8K.

Can that stop or even slow progress? Hah! The new high speed access to the Internet has appeared. Right now, it's pretty expensive, but look for prices to drop in your lap by the time you read this.

RAM is increasing even as we watch. When was it that 16MB seemed like all there is and all we would ever want. Now, 64MB is a more or less standard amount. 128MB is preferable. Soon that will be obsolete. Does this mean to wait? Wait for what? Buy the best you can afford and expect to replace it like automobile tires.

If your board isn't too old, you may be able to use the "DIMM" memory rather than "SIMM." The difference is speed. DIMM can clock at 10ns, considerably faster than SIMM at 60 or 70ns.

If extra RAM is important to your particular uses, check out DIMM for its extra efficient qualities. Bear in mind that several variations of DIMM do exist. Investigate before you invest. It's possible that certain of those varieties could work better for your computer and applications. Make certain that the RAM you prefer will be compatible with your outfit.

Right now the PC100 DIMM chips are the fastest. If your motherboard isn't built for it, you won't be able to use the PC100 chips. Look for that label to fade out. What's next? You'll have the answers before the supplement.

Prices for computers and accessories are generally more attractive in the larger cities' supermarket computer giants than in the usual neighborhood computer shops. Such discount operations as Fry's, Best Buy, Circuit City, The Good Guys, Office Max, Office Depot, Cosco, CompUSA, etc., can overwhelm smaller stores with buying power. Even more compelling than price, these magnamarkets stock just about everything you might need. They have the space and big bucks to keep and manage gigantic inventories.

What they lack, however, is the personal "one-on-one" attention that the smaller shops can give to you. Unless you are both computer literate and experienced with computer assembly and circuit technologies, that personal attention is not only appealing, it's essential. Just about every town has its local computer shop.

The bigger cities are also dotted with computer stores and shops of varying capacities. I have found a few of the more enterprising of the so-called local store operators to offer some compensation in service if not competitive with the supermarkets. Right now, price may be more important to you than treatment.

Follow the recommended procedure laid out further along to shop for your best quotes. There are disadvantages to buying at discount stores. Transactions are coldly impersonal. Also, you could get stung dealing at a disreputable discount dealer. It's just as true that a "genuine franchise dealer," "fully authorized and franchised" by a well-known company, can screw you just as royally.

So, check the places out before you buy. You're a lawyer presumed to know your way around. Read the following material and use your head. Then, get the best, most competent setup you can afford.

Peripherals: Some good stuff for great things, but watch out!

Lots of the peripheral devices that you will be using, and deriving tons of high leverage results from, will ripen for you later. Right now, you can get along without some of those things. A scanner, for instance, will nearly save your life when you get into voluminous contractual negotiations.

Accessories: A few gadgets are O.K., but don't clutter up

There are many, many, more and other kinds of jim gigs to use with your computer, without even mentioning the games. Hold it down. Get only the things that can help you practice law.

The revolt of the brand name computers.

Until very recently, the generic computers could be had for far less, sometimes as little as half, of the big name computers. Now, names like Compaq, Hewlett Packard, Sony and others have reduced their prices to below the open market competitive line.

The so-called "custom built" computer put together by your friendly neighborhood computer "specialist," is the worst choice of all. Now that the biggies are in the picture, those little guys don't have a look in.

This is another instance of the sum of the parts far exceeding the whole. If you price all of the components included in a leading brand's top of the line, the total would equal at least twice the list price of that unit.

To make matters worse for the custom builders, manufacturers like Compaq are offering to customize their products. You can literally select which components you want (within reason) included and excluded and come up with an even cheaper price than the retail version with lesser quality components.

Hopefully, by the time this book is published, that same offer, or better, will exist. One HP model is offered at about $1800 including a Pentium III processor, 600MHZ, 28GB HD, 128MB RAM, 8MB Video 3D graphics, an 8X max DVD drive, CD-RW burner, 56K V90 Modem, 512K level 2 cache, premium speakers, digital camera port, 10/100 BaseT network, HP color printer **PLUS** a 17-inch HP .28 dot monitor.

Perhaps, by publish date, that price may be even lowered with specifications improved. Who says there's an inflation. For this, as well as many other reasons, the independent computer business is not so well off these days.

The same is true now for peripherals. Printers, copiers, fax machines, are offered by Hewlett Packard, Canon, Panasonic, Brother etc. at prices so low, it's hard to imagine any real off-brand competition.

This is not to say that the market will remain that way. Maybe when you're reading this you might be wondering what brand of scotch I've been drinking.

Is it ever smart to buy mail order? When yes, when no.

The world is getting smaller and smaller every day. That fact, together with the U.S. Postal Authority getting bigger and bigger, has made the mail-order dealer "guarantee" a bit more valuable. Watch the mail order ads. The older, more consistent advertiser may be reasonably reliable.

When to buy mail order? Only when it is a very specific item, brand and model number that you have thoroughly checked out, and know all facts and the full price range. When you know that you are saving at least 30% to 40% by mail over a local purchase, and you are somewhat familiar with the dealer, that would be my choice.

Don't fall for the item that you don't know all about. Then think some more about before you buy. You can sometimes save some sales tax along with the retail price break. However, shipping costs can be more than the saved sales tax.

Watch the mail order purchase rules. Watch the calendar and make sure you're getting delivery according to the terms and the law. Know the deal, of course. But know the law too.

A few specific pointers. What about a scanner? Should you have one?

The best way to track your documents is through either a document management and retrieval program or one of several other lower cost "file finder" methods. To use your computer for this purpose requires a scanner. Most any scanner will do for because the process is simply copying. After the paper is scanned, your scan program will ask where you want it saved. You select an appropriate folder.

For any more sophisticated work, your scanner quality should be a level or two above entry. By "sophisticated," I mean doing any editing such as in pleading, contracts, etc. If you do any business law, you'll absolutely need this device.

Transactional work (contracts, negotiations, etc.), such as that involved in entertainment law, etc., will require a good quality scanner to keep abreast. If you don't have a SCSI controller card, the next best variety for speed in the USB input model.

I would stay away from parallel port models. They're not only slower but they offer problems that could interfere with printer operation. They also require rebooting on reconnect unlike USB. SCSI is fastest and best. Then comes USB and finally, bringing up the far back rear is the parallel port devices.

Should you have a fax card or a fax machine?

To start with, you must, absolutely must, have a fax. In fact, you just can't practice law anymore without one. A fax card in your computer can be a great aid, but it won't replace a fax machine. You can't fax an existing document from your computer, although your computer fax card can receive faxed data.

If you have a scanner, you can use that to transmit your document through the computer Fax card. This method will do in a pinch, but it's cumbersome and not always reliable.

You must have a fax machine, and a good one. These days laser faxes abound at prices unbelievable just a year ago. Thermal paper faxes are just not in the running. Don't consider one.

The laser fax machines are now priced so low the customarily advertised "plain paper fax" just can't cut it. Cost of copies rendered by the engines plus a price so close to the laser models won't justify those so-called equivalents.

What's coming down the pike? What's in store for you?

So many marvelous things are yet to come, I hate to leave. I'm jealous of your youth. You will see things that will make present electronics seem like wooden ox carts.

Does this mean you should wait? Of course not. There will never be a day when whatever you buy won't be stale tomorrow. Does obsolescence mean useless? Don't be ridiculous!

You don't always have to be in the vanguard of perfection. Keep and use what you have until the competition says move on. Then, if you don't move on, you're just as ridiculous.

§ 12:26 How to buy, rent or lease a computer and peripherals

First, you decide whether to buy, rent or lease your computer. The economical choice is, of course, to buy whether cash or payment plan. Some discount operations offer a bank finance plan. This somewhat restricts your ability to get the best price.

The way around this restriction is to arrange for a short term loan at a bank. Bankers around the general Los Angeles area have convinced me that most new lawyers can get approval of a time loan if for no more than $5,000. You can cover everything you need for substantially less than that.

Bargain prices are still subject to competitive pricing by dealers.

When you are told "You can't buy it for less than "$xxxxx.xx," that's your cue to find it for less, much less. How you do that depends upon your thoroughness in stating what you want. What you want is the most you can possibly get for your money, or your ability to pay on time.

It's O.K. to negotiate with mail-order firms but hold off ordering until you've determined precisely the model, size, shape, color etc. of the product. Then when you order, make certain that it is received *exactly* as you've described it.

Most reputable mail-order houses will permit exchanges if mistakes are made but returning any mail order product is complicated. You can normally find by mail anything you can find locally. Financing by mail order won't fly. Make a list of the qualities you want in your computer and the peripherals, item by item.

§ 12:27 Warranties, service, technical support and other hand-holding

You'll be told by the small operator that "Price isn't everything, we service what we sell." That's a bit like the "It isn't the money, it's the principle of the thing," bit. That's double talk for "It's the money." The small dealer is trying to condition you to pay him more than you'd pay elsewhere.

All computers, as well as all peripheral devices, are guaranteed by their respective manufacturers. Most all components follow the same basic designs. The computer consists of an assortment of plug in circuit boards. The hard drives, floppy drives, CD-ROM drives, etc., all slide in place, plug in and are "plug-and-play."

The big manufacturers like Compaq, Hewlett Packard, Sony, Toshiba, etc., all guarantee their products. Some warranties even PROVIDE "on-site" service in your office or home. Some offer this service for an entire year and some for three months. All will provide an extended on-site service warranty for two or three added years for about $200.

All manufacturers will provide a "tech support" phone number offering "walk through" technical advice free during the warranty period. Most problems are solved this way after a short phone conversation. Some phone numbers are not toll-free but the phone charges are not usurious.

Most all problems are software related and are corrected with simple phone information on re-installation around the problem areas. Should the problem be more involved or a hardware failure, a technician will be dispatched to your office or home, usually within a day or two. No two-bit dealer can offer more.

Chapter 13

Salesmanship in Solo Law Practice

§ 13:1 Generally

In every phase of law practice, as in business; SALESMANSHIP.

You've been more or less indoctrinated to the first level of understanding salesmanship as a professional term. Bits and pieces of selling information have been interspersed throughout the pages of this book. You should now realize that salesmanship incorporates more than the business of selling things.

This chapter is designed to regulate that information into more definable and usable terms. Unless you've been previously trained in selling, reading all of the material on salesmanship in this book should have changed your prospective on the subject completely.

If you still view salesmanship in the same light as before reading this book, either you haven't fully concentrated on what was said or some of the pages have stuck together. It is highly unlikely that you were aware of the elements of the sales interview before reading this book.

This chapter should bring what has been said before into focus. It's important that you not only understand this subject but that you also can see how different salesmanship is from what you earlier believed it was.

Perhaps you may already see how important using salesmanship is in succeeding as a solo lawyer. If you do, you will have gained a giant step in your development as a solo attorney.

Your practice will thrive and blossom into a satisfying and important money maker to the extent that you know about and can use salesmanship. Virtually everything you do in practicing law is selling.

When you're soliciting work from other lawyers, you're selling.

When you're interviewing new clients, you're selling.

When you're negotiating to settle cases, you're selling.

When you are discussing your case with an opposing lawyer, you're selling.

When you are discussing your case with your own client;

When you are trying to get a favorable ruling from a judge;

When you're eliciting evidence from witnesses whether in a court or jury trial;

When you are demonstrating, arguing, or simply speaking to a judge or jury in whatever framework; you are *selling*.

In fact everything you do in law and indeed in life, involves selling. Getting what you want wherever, whenever or however, is, to one degree or another, selling.

Salesmanship is silent and unseen.

This should be understood from the onset. Salesmanship, in the true sense of the word, is silent and unseen. When you hear or see something that sounds or appears to be salesmanship, it is not. The mechanism of selling must be both inaudible and invisible to be effective salesmanship.

A recent article in a legal publication on law office marketing, or more specifically, "rainmaking," made the categorical statement that an effective superstar lawyer, must never appear to be selling.

It went on to state that superstar lawyers avoid selling-based marketing which casts them in the role of a salesperson because it undermines their credibility. That statement marks the author as knowing nothing whatever about salesmanship. Selling, whether by a lawyer or especially by a professional salesman, should never be an identifiable component of the interview.

Marketing is nothing other than selling in various forms. There is no way to market a product, any product, without selling, whether by printed or spoken form. It's not surprising that the author of that article made such a statement.

What is surprising is that so few people, even among successful professional salesmen, comprehend the anatomy of the selling process. You'll understand why this is so as you read along.

The position you take, whether right or wrong, doesn't mean a damned thing if you can't sell it.

Before we get into the use of salesmanship in your solo law practice, let's examine that word so we don't get hung up on terms.

What is "salesmanship?"

Few people who use the word have even have a clue as to its meaning. In fact, most people who earn their living selling really aren't salesmen, although they do sell things.

Clerks in department stores sell things, but they are not salesmen. Salesmanship is not just the selling of things. It is something far more involved and requires some learning.

Let us agree on this:

"Salesmanship" is the developed ability to cause a person to decide either to do or not do some particular thing which decision would not have made had that person not been sold.

Someone shopping for a certain item is not "sold" that item by the store clerk because the purchase would have been made regardless of who had waited on him/her.

Oftentimes the clerk is more successful in dissuading rather than in persuading the buyer. Stores need clerks for simple mechanical jobs like ringing up sales and wrapping goods, etc. For this reason, you see more and more self-service stores every day. Store owners know that most clerks simply get in the way of sales.

Now, you may not have thought about this, but sales are never made as a result of superior argument. One may argue another down or even have incontrovertible supporting logic. But rarely, if ever, does this tactic end in a sale.

There is an old saying:

"One convinced against one's will is of the same opinion still."

Thus, you may overwhelm another by your dazzling oratory and the other person may be forced to grant your conclusions. But you will not sell that person anything.

The mechanics of salesmanship are simple to explain and would be simple to execute except for one thing. The simplicity of it defies belief.

This book promises that you won't miss a meal if you follow its simple instructions. But not missing meals alone is not what you bargained for in attending law school. You want to be eminently successful as an attorney.

What does it take to be enough of a salesman to reach that degree of success? One cannot read a paragraph or two on selling and be a competent salesman even though written by the best authority on this subject.

There are many pages on salesmanship in this book. The information is there. Assiduous personal application to the task is a good beginning. The first approach is to recognize the importance of learning this skill.

Most people, including lawyers, believe that selling is not an acquired skill but simply the natural ability to talk to people. You've learned this much: those people are wrong.

If a violin were described to you, never having played one before, and you were shown how to hold it, how to draw the bow across the strings and where you press your fingers against those strings to get different notes, and then the instrument were handed to you with a command "play it," could you?

Perhaps you could play that violin if you were a prodigy. Some people do have a natural inborn negotiative sense. One is about as rare as the other. For the rest of us, the learning process is excruciatingly slow. Some people just cannot, or maybe will not, apply this much effort. Is it worth that effort to you? Of course it is.

Selling ability doesn't come with your Bar card. Many top-notch students fail in this subject as attorneys. You cannot be assured of developing sufficient sales talent to earn top dollar as a professional sales person by reading the material in this book. But it will give you more than enough to reach the upper income regions as a lawyer.

Let me repeat what has been said in various places in this book:

Salesmanship is the giving of information of value to the listener.

A simple idea, yes. Why then so little understood? The confusion stems from diversities in what information the *listener* values. It's in the nature of people who try to sell that the listener ought to be interested in the *seller's* proposed ideas.

§ 13:2 An example of unintended salesmanship

You have just seen a house which you believe is exactly the kind of house your friend is looking for. You mention this to your friend. You know that your friend knows that your only purpose in telling him about the house is to give him some information that he will value.

The essence of this information's effectiveness is its reliability. In other circumstances, your friend would be incredulous. He or she would resist being told "this looks like just the house you are looking for," because it would be considered "sales talk." But, coming from you, it is not sales talk, but sincere reporting of observed facts.

You will understand what is meant by the fact that the simplicity of it defies belief. Imagine a real estate salesman trying to assume that same note of sincerity.

You can now see the difficult dilemma the real estate salesman faces. To attempt convincing someone that a salesman's interest is purely that of giving valuable information possesses some problems.

The difficulty is in the knowledge shared about the salesman's true motive. We know that the salesman wants to sell the house to earn a commission. The negative to selling is that the salesman's own interests will dominate the customer's interests.

But, despite all this, salesmen do sell houses to people who wouldn't have bought had it not been for that particular salesman. There are salesmen who have learned their craft.

Whenever a sale of that nature has taken place, it was due to the giving of information based upon certain facts indicating that the prospective customer valued that information.

In many, if not most, cases, sales are completed despite, rather than because of, the "salesman's" efforts. The buyer is so taken with the house fortuitously shown, the transaction occurs for that reason alone.

But in some instances sales are made through information given by knowledgeable qualified salespeople. The salesman has been trained to get all pertinent facts from the buyer to determine the buyer's points of interest.

The professional salesman also assembles information as to when and how that prospect intends to make a purchase. This, in sales parlance, is "qualifying the prospect."

For instance, in an approach to negotiating with opposing counsel to settle a case, you must know, in addition to other facts, what the opponent's interests are in settlement. It isn't necessary to know at this juncture what it will take to settle the case only that both parties are interested in settling.

The salesman assembles those points to formulate the information satisfying that interest. In giving the buyer that information and demonstrating how the buyer's needs and desires are fulfilled, the sale may be consummated.

In order to perfect your talent as a solo law practitioner, you should know some of the elements of salesmanship. If you can accept the information in this chapter without reservation, you will be well on your way.

Salesmanship does not require any of the things you probably believe it does. You needn't be glib, charming, personable, witty, or any of the other things so often believed necessary.

§ 13:3 Salesmanship is a body of knowledge

Salesmanship is a body of knowledge as is the entire subject of entering solo practice. This information is all that is needed to equip you with that extra punch for success as a lawyer.

Salesmanship can be learned from data, whether written or oral, as a body of knowledge, just as bookkeeping or mathematics, and the study of law itself, are bodies of knowledge and may be so learned.

Everyone knows that you have to learn how to be a bookkeeper, mathematician, or lawyer. For some reason, most people think that, to be a salesman, you only need to put your best foot forward, be charming, and talk well.

People without the least understanding of salesmanship will conclude after listening to another person talk impressively, "You certainly are a good salesman." This is often said derogatorally. In any case, it's an unfortunate characterization.

One would never peer over the shoulder of a bookkeeper at work and make such a comment unless trained in accounting. The difference is that the confusion of numbers can baffle but words don't seem to.

I've said that "salesmanship" is simply the giving of valued information and it is just that. This isn't to say, however, that the giving of such information is always a simple thing.

In some circumstances, like in the selling of a home by a real estate salesman, it can be quite difficult to master. But this difficulty is not in the subject matter. It is in the nature of the circumstances that causes the salesman to "sell" too much and inform too little.

The major confusion regarding giving information stems from a lack of understanding of what information is valued and how to obtain that information. You may believe the information you are giving should be of interest to the listener. What makes you think so?

The most reliable test of valued information is that requested by the listener. How does the real estate salesman discover which facts are so valued? The answer is so simple it escapes most people, amateur and professional.

Most salesmen are so imbued with the idea that their own appraisal of a home's attributes must impress any prospect that they fail to explore other facts. What does the listener want? What would impress the listener? Where does he or she want to live? How big a house is wanted? What style? What else.?

Assume that the real estate salesman has found just the house that the prospect is interested in. Now, transform that salesman, in your mind, into the "friend" that we spoke of a while ago.

The friend knows the prospect's wants and needs. This is the reason the friend's advice is so valued. The salesman may **think** he or she knows, but why does he or she think so?

If, somehow, the salesman could succeed in giving the same information to the prospect with the same objectivity as did the "friend," the stage would be set for a completed sale.

So, the first problem in selling is to eliminate "selling" completely and only give information. This doesn't seem hard to do, does it? Of course, we spoke of a "body of information" which requires some learning, so you might guess that there must be more to it than that.

As we have just learned, there is the business of finding out what "information" would be valued by the customer. There is also the means by which the sales interview is terminated. The latter, in selling parlance, is called the "close."

There are professional salesmen who specialize in terminating sales interviews. These are called "closers." These are the rarest and highest paid among professional salespeople. You'll see the reason for this, and you may wonder why it is so.

The reason for their scarcity, and their premium worth, may seem at first overstated. It is that they have learned to do something that is probably the most difficult thing for any salesman, or lawyer, to do: stop talking and write the order.

More lawyers have talked themselves out of winning a case than have ever talked their way into a win. Most judges would agree that a lawyer's trouble is in not knowing when to stop talking and sit down.

Some of the most potent poisons may be rendered virtually harmless if diluted sufficiently. Similarly, some very good arguments can be dulled by verbosity.

§ 13:4 Salesmanship in the practice of law

Suppose an attorney could really assume the posture of the purist "officer of the court." Consider the effect of being before the court, not as an advocate, not as a representative of a partisan litigant, but merely as one who has information as to the legal positions of the parties.

Assume that the lawyer has no interest whatever in the case outcome or debating the correctness or incorrectness of the legal authority cited. Once the lawyer has given the desired information, he or she will stop talking and sit down. The job is done.

Suppose that the judge suggests to this purist lawyer an approach contrary to the principle the lawyer had taken. The lawyer then says: "I see." No further statement is made.

The tone of voice, attitude, demeanor, and concern of the lawyer clearly show that all information that should be of interest has been given. There is nothing further to be said.

The lawyer has stated the facts or the law of the case simply. The lawyer has made it clear that if he or she is in error, nothing further need be added to the point.

Now, in contrast, consider the polemicist who will beleaguer the court with persistent and repetitive arguments. He or she hurls the verbal gauntlet in the judge's face, provoking useless, self-defeating debate. Lacking is the calm assurance of the fact giver. In its place is the smoking atmosphere of challenge.

Which will "sell" the court? The polemicist will sweep away what could have been a devastating stroke with a deluge of anticlimax. The point is lost.

The quiet authoritativeness of the calm lawyer, conversely, will thunder, leaving a stunning aftermath of silent pensiveness.

The exercise in self-confusion will be left to the other side. It is the opposition that will rant and rave and, like the fabled tiger, turn itself into melted butter through its own pointless centrifugal force.

And, this is the essence of salesmanship. The giver of valued information will have the ear of the listener.

Not so with the spinner of embroidered oration.

But that information must be "valued." In order to find that value, some facts must be learned by the salesman. The sale consists of four phases:

Getting information;
Giving information;
The demonstration; and
The close.

In commercial sales, the relevant information concerns the kind of product that is of interest to the prospective customer. What kind of television set is the customer looking for? What color cabinet? What size? What make? What model? When does he or she intend to make a purchase? How much money does he or she intend to spend? Who will use the set? Etc.

It is the salesman's job to elicit all of the information possible, so that the job of giving information about certain selected products can be simplified. Too often, the salesman will overwhelm the prospect with information that is not in keeping with need or desire.

Similarly, the lawyer will supply a wealth of information that might be interesting but not tailored to fill any need or desire. Such a lawyer has not taken the time or effort to determine what information is needed or desired.

You will normally be given some indication as to what argument the court wants. In some courts, there are "notes" provided for the attorneys to limit the time and scope of the issues to be argued. Where this is not done, the judge will usually start the proceedings by telling the lawyers what points need to be resolved.

One way or another, the court will let you know what it needs to know. Sometimes, the indications are quite subtle. Hence, you must attune yourself to the signals from the bench. This takes a certain sensitivity that is not difficult to acquire.

In these instances, you must "feel" what needs to be stressed in argument. Oftentimes, this "sensitivity" is nothing more than restraining your anxieties a bit. Your innate intelligence will do the rest. Your ability to do this separates you from the losers.

What puts you in the win column is your knowledge that the judge really does want information. You are not just whaling away, but taking careful aim. The other attorney doesn't know this. He or she thinks winning is a quotient of sheer word power.

§ 13:5 Phase one: Information-seeking

As we have seen, the "information-seeking" phase is perhaps the least understood and most neglected part of the sales interview. This is coupled with the speaker's anxiousness to start selling. Of course, there can be no "selling" without having valued information to be transmitted to the listener.

Most often enthusiasm prompts the speaker to jump the gun. It is his or her conviction that the product to be sold has great value. That conclusion is of no value whatsoever. It may seem strange to hear that the seller's belief in the quality of the product has no part in the sales interview.

In fact, it is often that very enthusiasm which defeats the would-be salesman. The more rapturously the sales delivery, the greater would usually be the listener's resistance. Recall what was said about the salesman's motive.

More of this later. At this point, we must start with an overview of the sales interview. Keep in mind that each of the selling phases must be kept separate from the others.

There are two things to remember in this first phase, which we have labeled the "information-seeking phase." First, you must not let your nerves or anxieties stampede you into blurting out unproductive talk. Reserve your comments for application to the areas of "value."

Second, you must distinguish valued from meaningless material. The way you make this distinction is through a developed sensitivity that will aid you in listening to what is being said to you, and attuning yourself to the signals.

This listening process must be employed in every phase of your law practice, including client interviews, court arguments, trial, settlement, communication with associates and employees, preparing witnesses, and every other part.

Of course "listening" involves more than just "hearing." Although you may hear what is said, you may not be listening to what is meant. For example, when you are asked a question by a judge, you're not being asking for a retort as a general rule. Most often, the asking of a question is an expression of disagreement (or even possibly agreement). If this is so, you will get little or nothing by attempting to parry the question.

Give yourself a moment to analyze the question, and the demeanor of the judge in phrasing it. You can especially harm yourself if the judge's question is helpful to your case and you argue it.

Remember the truism:

"One convinced against one's will is of the same opinion still."

Don't be hasty in trying to score your point. Your point may not be the court's point. Remember, the judge may not always be right, but the judge is always the judge.

In asking the question, the judge may or may not have indicated disagreement with your point. You will usually find somewhere within the question a responsive sensitivity. Your job is to find this sensitivity, and address yourself to it. Reserve your statements to satisfy interest.

In a sense, you learned a part of this technique in taking the bar exam. You learned to avoid the irrelevant traps present in most questions, and to devote your time frugally to expressing the information demanded by the question. You did this because it was the rule of the game, and you were trained with such rules.

Regrettably, law schools do not teach salesmanship or *savoir faire*. This is the main difference between law school and the problems in your law practice. It is the blatancy of the former and the subtlety of the latter.

Although you learned to spot "issues" for the bar exam, no one taught you the subtleties of persuasion where issues are vague. What do you do when all of those hard hours of research and preparation fade in the thunder of the court's question from left field?

If the judge meant only to finally disagree with you and nothing more in asking the question, it would probably not have been asked. Though the judge may not be asking for the answer framed by the question, he/she might be tossing you a lifeboat. Don't cast it aside. Think of how it may aid your side and use that aid.

An example of masked "information."

Your case facts almost square with the facts of a precedent decided against your position. Your trial judge went with the precedent, and against you. You perceive the facts as being in your favor, and consonant with the law. The trial judge was wrong, and the precedent case was wrongly decided.

The question: "Counsel, how do you distinguish this case from the facts in Coleman v. Epstein?" You are all prepared to argue the inequities of that case and the strength of your legal position here. The judge is decidedly not asking for your critique of the Coleman case or for further embellishment on the law as you had briefed it.

Nevertheless, you do have the tribunal's ear at this juncture, and the coordinate opportunity to make a sales pitch. The court would not normally be predisposed toward your undoing of *stare decisis*. The court does not need your permission to reject a precedent, nor would it ask for your assistance in doing so.

Stop for a few seconds before responding. All right, so, you haven't come prepared to argue your way around the point. Your facts are different from those in Coleman. No two cases are precisely alike. Consider the positive connotation in the court's question. Is it that the court does not like the Coleman case and would like to rule in opposition?

You cannot know the court's thoughts. But you can and you must grapple with the probabilities. Assume that the question would not have arisen if the court were not disposed, if not toward your position, at least not diametrically against it.

Perhaps other thoughts expressed by the court during the session offer a clue. Perhaps they were likewise enveloped in nebulosity. Was there some vague suggestion of a point that could somehow relate to a fact or an issue in the case?

Why must you play such crazy games? If the court wants to find for you, why not just do it and stop this word game silliness. Aside from the fact that the system must be preserved, there is the same kind of consternation in the minds of the judges that you suffer. The decision-making process is strenuous and perplexing.

This is not much different from the "salesman/customer" adversary situation. The customer doesn't give the salesman straight information to ease the sales making processes, either.

But the ordinary customer doesn't have a million dollar training in the adversarial sciences. So getting pertinent information in the usual commercial setting doesn't often involve such subtleties.

Most judges are masters in deceptive questioning. That comes from the advantage of having no spine prickles from the case. It's also a legacy derived from folklore of the bench brethren.

Sometimes, deception is necessary to avoid betrayal of the spirit of *stare decisis*, if not its letter. Sometimes, it is a technique to prevent a dissent from becoming the majority decision. A judge who may be on your side might be trying to divert an adverse judge.

The ultimate test of the trial and appellate advocate is his or her degree of imperturbability. The same test applies to just about everything encountered in your day-to-day practice of law.

Although the emotions are different in settlement negotiations from arguments at court, the resulting loss of objectivity is common to both, when one fails to "listen" and responds to adrenaline instead.

The silent response.

You hear nothing, but should feel it.

It is most frustrating to making a point when the prospect offers no responsive comment. No argument is offered. No word of assent. Nothing. The result is increasing nervousness. Then, a steady loss of objectivity leading to even more nervousness.

Nervousness: The deadly attack.

Strangely enough, nerves alone are not necessarily the culprit. One can be the nervous type and still capable of retaining objectivity. So the antidote to nervousness is confidence. That's possible? You can be nervous and yet confident? How's that done?

Most actors are pathologically nervous just before their stage entrance or stepping before the camera. Some shake visibly. Some feel faint. Some even vomit. I've never known an actor who claimed immunity to nervousness. How then can some of these nervous wrecks give such marvelous performances? Confidence.

How can that be? How can they, on the one hand be so nervous and on the other, be serenely confident? The answer is that they know their job. The have learned their craft and are confident they will rise to the occasion. But they'll still be nervous.

You've done your homework and know your job. Don't let silence rob you of that self-assurance. You've learned that attitude is the key ingredient to selling. Words spoken with differing attitudes have correspondingly different meanings.

Controlling nervousness is essential, but that alone won't make the sale. You've still got to transmit information of value to your listener whether or not that listener is silent. But if the listener doesn't tell us what information interests him or her, how can we know what to say?

In a two-way conversation we ask questions and the answers will tell us what we want to know. Even with taciturn people we have learned how to probe enough to get what we need. However, there are some circumstances where such probing is either impossible or forbidden. What do we do then?

How do we get information from a listener who is silent?

A jury, for instance, doesn't often tell you what particular information is of interest. In fact, the law forbids us from holding question and answer sessions with juries, other than voir dire. Still, you must know what particular information is of most interest to the jury in order to get a desired verdict. So, how do we proceed?

§ 13:6 Information giving

Giving of "facts" may not be giving valued information regardless of how correct or "on point" those "facts" may be.

Juries are supposed to be impartial and unprejudiced. They are not. Even as you and I, most jurors have their prejudices despite our attempt at combing out the prejudiced ones during voir dire.

As an example, consider the trial of an accused child rapist and murderer. Could you panel a jury of twelve totally unprejudiced jurors? Perhaps so, in the next world, not in this one. You'll have twelve fair, equitable and open minded jurors who will be seeking only one fair and just result: Hang the son-of-a-bitch!

Will the basic tenet of American Jurisprudence, "Not Guilty Until Proven Guilty" control? In theory, perhaps, but don't look for it. If you can show the prosecution's failure and you've produced enough evidence to spike its case to boot, don't be surprised if you lose. Those things alone are not enough.

Remember, that salesmanship depends upon the giving of information which is of value to the listener. You may have piled the weight of your case heavy and miles high. But all your evidence and all your arguments against the prosecutor's evidence may not constitute that particular information of sufficient value to the jury to respond in your favor.

You must somehow find the resonant chords in those twelve (or however many) people through which your favorable information may be effectively transmitted. Objectivity in such a case depends upon creating the atmosphere which places you within the same group as the jurors.

When you speak of the prosecutor, the judge, the law enforcement agencies AND the jury, you must refer to that whole group, INCLUDING YOU!, as "Us." "We, you, the jury, and all of us, do not want child rapists and killers to run loose."

Everything must be prefaced with words, intimations, and innuendo to show a thread of common interest. This is crucial to avoid being placed in the "seller" category.

Is this chicanery? Not at all. Before you can adequately represent your client, you must remove unfair barriers, the worst of which is prejudice.

Sometimes the chords may be siphoned to and through one particular juror. Look them over. There is always one member who is more communicative with you than the others through expression, gesture, or whatever.

Once you've found that person, direct your comments, off and on, to him or her. If you note signs of interest, glance around to the others to see possible sparks of concurrence. Whichever tactic you use, use it to zero in on their body, eye, or whatever, language you are receiving.

A recent California case ended with the conviction of the defendant charged with the kidnap, rape and murder of a nine year-old school girl. The jury recommended death. The defense was "not guilty by reason of insanity."

Put aside our natural repugnance at the thought of a child

molester/killer for this academic exercise. Our job, if we choose criminal defense, is to defend, not condemn. So, how might the jury be sold that defense to so ugly a crime. In that case, several jurors polled agreed that the defendant had suffered some mental illness.

Still, all concluded that defendant's attorney had failed to convince the jury that illness, not malice, was the culprit. The jury foreman said, "We felt that there may have been some underlying illness that he (the defendant) had, but the defense . . . did not pinpoint (how that illness) related to the crime."

The defense attorney reacted angrily to the jurors' statements. He stated, "We had more than 10 experts testifying about (Defendant's) illness, his inability to control his rage. There was a chain-link fence that showed how his sickness was linked to his action. I don't know how many more experts we have to bring in to show that he was, and is, a very sick man." [Case as reported in the Los Angeles Times.]

The attorney's angry reaction might tip us off to a possible selling failure. The salesman may not have been giving valued information. Perhaps he was beleaguering the jury with his own personally evaluated viewpoint. Did he watch for all telltale expression changes on jurors' faces as testimony unfolded?

In the example of "unintended salesmanship," we differentiate between the interests of the salesman and the prospect. The prospect's interest is in finding the product he/she wants or needs. The salesman's interest is in selling and earning a commission.

Certainly the prospect understands that the salesman's business is selling. He/she knows that the underlying motive is making the sale. Still, it can be that the information given will be of value to the prospect.

If enough selling creeps through to contaminate the business of giving information, the prospect's facts receptors will slam shut and the sale is lost. One cannot block off all selfish indicia. It's sufficient to maintain a preponderance of objective information over the seller's personal interests.

Juries, judges, opposing lawyers, clients, everyone knows that lawyers have two basic personal interests. One is to win and the other to make money. Once the lawyer's position becomes too heavily laden with either of these two points of interest, the listener's attention will be diverted and lost.

The defense counsel's position in our murder trial obviously became too personal and not informative enough. He failed to reach the jury with information separated from argument.

Did he take pains to identify himself with society's forces that protect children? Did he thoroughly show how his "experts" would clarify his client's sickness and reach the jury's susceptibility toward finding the proper verdict?

This could have been a classical case of too much client loyalty. That attorney might well have oversold himself rather than to concentrate on selling the jury. Recall what was said in the book about the salesman who falls in love with the product. He forgets to give valued information and instead beleaguers his prospect with his own conclusions.

Of course, it's much easier to learn about the needed or desired particulars after the trial when questions are answered. But, those same unanswered particulars were present during the trial and unheeded by counsel. The so-common problem with lawyers who lack salesmanship training is too much preparation and too little resonance with the flow of evidence at trial.

The jurors' remarks expressed their unsatisfied quest for specific information. Certainly it's difficult to ferret that out from twelve silent people. Difficult, but not impossible. Most people get signals when being a bore. Nobody says, "stop talking, you're boring me." The expressions of boredom are unmistakable. All one needs to do is look.

Jurors are silent only as to words. They transmit signals as unmistakable as the bored listener. Look for them. Note the pursed lips, the squinty eyes, the yawns, the folded arms of disbelief, the nodding heads, either of drowsiness or affirmation. Jurors are people. They react to information just like anyone else. Look for those reactions.

Keep yourself flexible instead of rigidly tracked to your prepared script. If you detect some deflection of your given "information" by unimpressed jurors, switch channels and give them a different twist.

Your job is not to trumpet your prepared program of stunning data, however formidable you believed it to be. Your job is to only give information of value to the jury, your listeners.

§ 13:7 The final phase: The "close"

The last phase, which we have called the "close," is merely your recognition that you have made your point, and that it's time to shut up and sit down. If you think there's something more to say but can't bring it to mind, don't bother. Sit down. Sit down, anyway.

Do not risk undermining the scores you've made by babbling. Don't worry about the lost pearls of wisdom. They are far better left unsaid than offered to adulterate your clean argument.

Besides, it may only be your anxiety gnawing at you rather than an elusive unspoken point.

More fools are trapped by their inability to find a closing line than any other failing. Be happy when that occurs to you. The only downside to that failing is having the accompanying inability to quit talking without one.

Unlike a freeway, you don't need an "off-ramp" to get out of a sales pitch. You only need to stop. It is important to note that a summation should be both "underplayed" and "brief." This is in keeping with the idea that you are merely "giving information" and not trying to convince anyone of anything.

If you're intent on going offstage with a flourish, you will undo all that you have done. You would be far better just to stop dead, in the middle of a sentence, than to end with a meaningless dramatic triumph.

A well-worn technique for closing in an embarrassing lapse is to stop abruptly and request a trade for some added minutes in your response or rebuttal. This glosses the roughness somewhat.

Of course, the essence of salesmanship, the mere "giving of information of value," abhors repetition. There should be no repetition, ever. If you believe that the point you have struck is so beautiful that it bears repeating, don't.

Judges, like everyone else, will appreciate your brevity. Your information, if valuable, will have its greatest value in its economy of words to make the point. Sometimes, you will have occasion to ponder whether you should offer any argument at all. If so, offer none. There will be times when the judge will address all of his questions to your opponent.

In such instances, tune your radar to each of the areas of concern. If your "listening processes" tell you that the judge is not searching for anything from you, it simply means that you are out in front, at least as to that issue. To stay there, remain seated and buttoned up.

Most lawyers lack the ability to stop talking at the crucial point. Some don't know when not to talk at all. There are times when, if you permit, the judge will win your case for you.

Give the judge that opportunity, and the courtesy of your silence. Remember that the entire point in argument is to give "information." If none is needed, give none.

You will be tempted to jump up to counter an argument offered by your opponent. This is because you will have forgotten the purpose of your argument. You will be confused into thinking that you are engaged in a duel with the other lawyer instead of serving as an advocate to the court for your client.

Now that you know something of basic salesmanship skills, you understand the absurdity of two lawyers, standing toe-to-toe, snapping at each other, while the judge glowers at both of them. You will immediately recognize what a lawyer, trained in sales technique, could do to either of them, or both at one time.

To say that you cannot convince a person against his or her will is really understating the point. More precisely, you cannot convince anyone of anything, if there is a quest for information unfulfilled. However persuasive you may be, you will not succeed in substituting valuable information with irrelevant oratory, regardless of its rhetorical effect.

Just as you may be proud of your silver tongue, the listener may be even prouder of his/her own beliefs. Just as you may be the irresistible force, so may the listener be the immovable object.

There are perhaps more people broadly called "salespeople" than in any other work class designation. Yet, the ratio of expert to unqualified is probably higher than in any other profession. Why is this so?

Most people who can talk with reasonable fluency believe that they can sell for a living. This rationale is based upon the common misbelief that the art of selling is related to the drawing room talent of persuasive debate.

Almost everyone harbors a secret belief in his/her superior powers of persuasion. Why not? Haven't they held their own in downing others in argument? If Smith can best Jones, time and again, in their running political harangue, why shouldn't he be able to persuade a customer to buy something?

This simple logic sounds correct. But like other sophistries, it lacks the element of factual sufficiency. It is one thing to run a neighbor down to exhaustion through persistent argument. It is quite another thing to cause someone to do something which he/she would not have done but for your given information.

In running up a white flag after a beleaguering argument, your neighbor may simply be saying, "I've had enough." His or her retirement from argument is not necessarily an indication that he or she is convinced. It is most usually an opposite sign.

Getting a favorable court order, a signed attorney/client contract, or a satisfactory settlement, as a direct result of your words, represents the fruits of salesmanship.

Salesmanship is the art of causing another to do or not do a particular thing because of information you give when otherwise it would not have happened that way.

If your position in court is so strong that the ruling must be in your favor, you needn't be concerned with salesmanship. Such a position, however, is quite rare.

In most instances, even though you may have a decided edge, the matter could still go against you. Your strength is not as you perceive it but as the judge does. For you to have so cinchy a hand that it cannot be beat, you must have all of the cards not just most of them.

Now, look at the other side. Your hand is weaker than your opponent's. Is all lost? Not so long as you remember your salesmanship. You'll note the odds against my client, DMJM, at the hands of the Iranian delegation, as described in Chapter 18. I do not recall ever having approached a task with so little reason for optimism.

There were more than 900 claimants who failed, each with a solid belief in the right of their cause. You'll read of two claimants whom I interviewed. They not only failed, but each flatly declared that the settlement conferences were trumped-up propagandist platforms. They each predicted that no one could gain anything from the settlement conferences. They even warned of grave personal danger to me. Selling would be required just to get out alive.

The unquestionable difference that won the day was the sales approach to that meeting with an adequately prepared program. The executed plan was not to beard the lions in their den, as did my predecessors, but to make a "sale."

You must maintain your posture of listening for needed and valued information. You must limit your presentation to the giving of that information. This technique can win for you if the scales are tipable. If you succumb to the trap of desperation, whining, panic and pawing at the dirt, as some attorneys do, you will probably lose.

Your old monster friend, embarrassment, can be of great help to you. For instance, you are interviewing a new client. The time has come to ask for the retainer. Time was when this would prove too embarrassing for you and you couldn't do it.

Now, you know that the moment you ask for the retainer, the monster will leave your side and trot over to the side of the prospective client. Now, the embarrassment prevents further resistance. The client pulls out the checkbook, and the deed is done. Where embarrassment kept you from even asking for your fee, it now acts to help you get it from the client.

When you contemplate going through the distasteful processes of asking lawyers for work assignments, what looms as the most distasteful part? Lots of answers come to mind.

You feel it demeaning to ask for money. You believe it might suggest untrustworthiness. You think it might be viewed as gauche. You intend to bill him or her later, etc., etc.

What keeps you from zeroing in on the truth? Why all these silly, phony reasons? You know the truth. You know, now that you've learned a few facts about the great obstacle.

Embarrassment, right? But now you know that you must shift the monster to the other lawyer's side. He or she won't know what to do with it, because he or she hasn't read this book. You win again.

This brings us back to your interview with a prospective assignor attorney. You're there to get some work assignment from that lawyer. How do you use the monster in this instance.

You've said, "Well, Mr. Singer, I know how busy you are. I'm here to help you relieve some of your work congestion. I can take care of any small job you have that needs doing. Since I'm here, I'm ready to do it right now. I can have it done for you in a jiffy."

You could say lots more but why? You've made the intended point quickly and with the least number of words needed. You've stated the reason for brevity.

You have said what you're able and willing to do. Most important, you've given that lawyer information which you believe to be of value to him/her. Your statement, "I'm ready to do it right now," can be an effective "close."

Now the embarrassment has moved to my side. It works on me to give you the job rather than to find ways to avoid it. Besides, why do I want to avoid it? Aren't you doing me a favor by your willingness to help? Embarrassment is really everybody's friend.

See how many examples you can think of where embarrassment, our friendly monster, can help you in your general practice of law. If you put your mind to it, you could fill a book with such ideas. Don't do it though. That's my job.

While the "grabber" you use to get the work could be called a "close," there is something more to the sale. We need more work than just this one assignment. How do we accomplish that?

We demonstrate our product. Remember, we have another word for demonstration. It's called "the show." We take that first assignment and put our all into it, whatever it is. Most important, we show that lawyer how fast we do our work.

This means we pull out all the stops to do this. The first assignment for each of the lawyers we've added to our roster is always the most important one. Once we've given that "show," the other jobs that come along aren't that vital. This doesn't mean to give any of them short shrift. But the first one is always our very best effort.

§ 13:8 Salesmanship to a jury

The use of salesmanship to a jury involves a slightly different twist. The major elements must be observed, but absent the dialogue. You speak, and the jury listens. That is, you hope they listen.

One of the problems in selling a jury is selectively getting the information to them. So much goes on during a trial that the jury often gets bogged down with trivia and irrelevancies, not just from the other side, but from your side as well.

Even the points you consider highly material can confuse and divert the jury from your really important points. They hear the evidence, and they are instructed on the law by the judge. But, keeping all of that in order can overwhelm them.

Opening and closing statements are supremely important in sorting out the information you must get to them in order to sell the jury on your case. Far too often such opportunities are thrown away by lawyers intent on arguing rather than selling.

Remember that selling is simply the "giving of information that is valued by the listener." This is information that will mean something to them, not rhapsodic speeches that may seem impressive to you.

The jury knows that you want them to be swayed your way. All of your gesticulations and marvelous orations, which might be equal to an Academy Award performance, may entertain them, or even cause them to react with the emotions you wanted, but will not sell them.

Many juries have found defendants guilty with tears in their eyes. Feeling sorry for the defendant will not often detour jurors from their charged duty.

In making the opening statement, after a very brief synopsis of the facts, you should outline what you propose that the evidence will show. Do this in a very matter of fact, step-by-step style and tone of voice.

Then, state your predictions as to what the other side will attempt to show, and the reasons that they will fail. Look at each juror, in a panoramic scan, as you talk. Try hard to keep excessive voice modulation out of your delivery.

Remember the natural resistance that most people have to being argued into submission. Pausing from time to time, and pacing your delivery, can carry all of the urging that you need. Think of this: in a very quiet room, late at night, a whisper can be jolting.

Look for the opportunity to drop your voice to just above a whisper. You'll be amazed at the impact. Do this only when the courtroom is very quiet, and when you are looking directly into the eyes of each juror, one by one. Don't overdo this, however. Use it once per session at trial.

Stand behind the lectern. Do not wander around the area of the jury box. This is not only bad decorum, and will probably irritate the judge, but it will also distract the jury from properly receiving your information. Try to avoid manual gesticulations. Keep your hands clasped to the sides of the lectern.

During the course of trial, find ways of emphasizing bits of testimony, where possible. Where something very important has been said, particularly from an opposing witness, you might ask for the witness to repeat the statement. Again, do not overdo this.

Your case stands or falls on the persuasiveness of the evidence. Arguments that do not track the evidence will turn the jury off and antagonize the judge. Trying to elevate the weight of evidence with vocal emphasis will often do the opposite with a jury and a judge.

Just as you've shown the jury what the evidence will prove during your opening statement, so you must show them what the evidence did in fact show in your summation.

You hear the term "closing argument," and this leads to the wrong characterization of that process. Judges will tell you that certain matters brought up during trial are for "argument." These references could set the tone of that last crucial stage. Don't let it.

What you are, in fact, doing in your "closing argument" is summing up all of the powerful evidence you've presented. This means only a recapitulation of what "the evidence has shown." It is in this process that you are sorting out what evidence you're asking the jury to consider.

You don't need to rant and rave about these points. Your process of simply giving valued information will do all of the emphasizing you need.

Remember what was said about being cool, and simply giving information to the judge on a legal point? Recall we agreed that maintaining an attitude of virtual indifference to whether the listener is convinced is the winning way? This cool, calm, almost indifferent manner is even more important in your closing presentation to a jury.

Recall the example of telling your friend about a house that might interest him? Remember that, as a friend, you are not trying to persuade, but only to inform. Recall the power of that understatement of penetrating information. This is the targeted method of getting information to a jury.

Point out to the jury each crucial fact that was revealed by each testifying witness. Name the witness, and try even to index when that testimony was given. What you want to accomplish is to present, and group, all of these facts under the umbrella of the judge's instructions.

Never ever lose sight of the need to reassess the jurors' reactions to the information you've been giving. Look at each of them individually. Note their expressions, their demeanors, little betraying body moves that can convey to you their quotient of interest.

Let the other lawyer argue his or her head off. Don't be concerned with the unfurled flags and trumpets blowing. Salesmanship, not theatrics, will win your case.

§ 13:9 Embarrassment: The biggest monster

The next problem offers a much more potent challenge. This one goes to a sort of phobia found in most people. I have referred to this particular "villain" as the **monster**," because it haunts almost everyone. This monster is often solely responsible for people being denied things that they often want most in life.

Many who have tried their hands at salesmanship, and failed, are puzzled by their failure. They learned their craft, made the right moves and did their homework. Why couldn't they make the sale?

Any journeyman professional salesman could explain it. They failed because they lacked the ability to fight the monster. When the time came to enter the "close" phase of the sales interview, they were too embarrassed to do what was needed.

One method of effecting the "close" is simply to begin writing a delivery slip and invoice. But, embarrassment consumes the "salesman" and stupefies him or her.

Instead of doing what he or she knows should be done, the embarrassed "salesman" will continue talking. He or she hopes that somehow the prospect will alleviate that discomfiture by saying "I'll take it."

Why not? Surely, this expert salesman has demonstrated a whole bag of tricks. He or she has gotten information, given information, and done a dazzling job of demonstrating the product. Why doesn't this dumb prospect say something?

He or she has been taught that a good salesman bears down at this point and simply starts writing. But fear steps in, and resolve dissolves. Our salesman anticipates the prospect saying something like: "Wait a minute. What are you writing there? Say, you've got your nerve! I didn't tell you to do that!"

So passes the moment of truth, and the talking continues. Ultimately, the prospect yawns, looks at his watch, and yawns again. The prospect may have been sold, and quite ready for the "close," but with no one there to close the sale, it just didn't happen.

The prospective client is sitting across the desk from you. He has told his story. You know what the matter is all about. Time now to get a substantial retainer fee. You know that this case easily merits a retainer of $6,000.

You avoid the request, and talk more about the case. You talk, and talk, and talk. The prospect finally gets up, looks at his watch, yawns and says: "I'll think about it and be back." He won't come back. They never do.

Some other lawyer who has read this book found this prospect used the monster embarrassment as an ally instead of an enemy, and has gotten a $6,000 retainer and the attorney/client agreement signed. Does this ring a bell?

Think of this. Your embarrassment is your obstacle. You are blinded by it. You cannot seem to get out of its way. You are doomed. What if it were the other way around? What if, somehow, you could shift that burden to the other side, while at the same time relieving yourself of its pangs. Interesting?

It can be done. Remember the prospective customer who so embarrassed the salesman that he just kept talking and couldn't close? Suppose you acted like the pro. Suppose you reached for the delivery slip and invoice with pen poised.

Suppose you then started writing, name, address, phone, etc. Then you say something like, "then we'll have the RCA model 544 in walnut, the one you like, delivered first thing tomorrow morning." You shove the completed order form over to him/her along with a pen. "You sign right there, where I've made that little x."

What has happened to embarrassment? Notice, it's gone from your side, and has slipped over to the customer's side. Now, it's not you who is the embarrassed one. It's the customer. He/she is now too embarrassed to stop you from writing and merely sits back to accept the inevitable.

This is a difficult concept. Your embarrassment is so deep that you cannot contemplate such a shift. You are so afraid that if you start writing, the prospect will growl: "What are you doing there? Who told you to write that!" Your embarrassment is so great that it wouldn't occur to you that to start the writing would shift the embarrassment.

What you cannot realize is that the prospect is just as susceptible to the pangs of embarrassment as are you. You think that the other side is free of all the frustrations that plague you.

Why do you think this way? The only difference between you and the other side is that you are holding the ball at the moment.

The moment you start to write, you have pitched the ball to the other side. Now, it's the other side who holds it. You are merely doing your job, writing. Now it's the job of the other side to defeat the monster, not yours.

Silly, isn't it? So simple and tiny a thing. Just a matter of tossing a ball, and you're out of the spell of embarrassment. And so few can do it. But you can because you see how silly the whole thing of embarrassment is and how simple it is to reverse it.

If you've done your job, the listener is sold. It's just that some clean-up work needs to be done. Remember to close the sale.

You must perform some little task like writing up the order, asking for the retainer, asking for the court's ruling in your favor, asking the jury for its verdict in your client's favor, or whatever you're selling.

The most important message in this chapter is that in selling we create neither a desire nor a need. So that you won't misunderstand this, we create nothing of the kind.

If the listener doesn't want our product, doesn't need it, we cannot put either that want or need there. If we've been pushing something neither wanted nor needed, we've been wasting everybody's time.

Our sole purpose is to discover from the listener what his or her need or desire is. We do this by asking for information and then for more, and more, and even more information.

It's only when we have explored and searched diligently and completely and we are sure we have all facts concerning the listener's interests that we start giving information.

We are thereby providing the material upon which the listener may react in the manner that we understand as being sold. We recognize this state by all signs that signal the listener's complete attention.

§ 13:10 Lawyer advertising: A form of selling

Actually, advertising could, and perhaps should, be treated under a separate chapter heading. But it's really a part of the selling process. So much of what is done in advertising is an extension of sales principles that it translates better if thought of that way.

An ad, to be effective, must be drawn as a sales presentation. Yet, the sale is a separate bundle of operations. This occurs after the consumer has read the ad and has appeared to partake of the offer.

Once that happens, the advertiser must employ the whole array of sales tactics to close the sale. So the transaction is twofold. The first step is to "sell" the customer into doing something he or she would not have done had it not been for the advertisement. Doesn't that fall within our agreed definition of salesmanship?

So we now undertake to examine the anatomy of an advertisement that will operate to bring clients into the lawyer's office. Some background information on advertising in general will be helpful by way of introduction to this very important subject.

In a retail business that promotes consumer products or services, advertising is usually the lifeline upon which success or failure hinges. My business firm was no exception.

Our retail operation, including that of our franchises, needed a constant flow of advertising, like heartbeats, without which we could not survive for long. It wasn't enough to just advertise. The ads had to be fresh attention-getters, with magnet-like qualities to literally pull the customers into our stores and the stores of our franchisees. Writing those ads was like writing songs or screenplays. Some hit, some missed. Some were like skyrockets, and some were duds.

The skyrockets, happily, came along often enough to offset the duds, and the hits made up for the misses. Through it all, business moved along. The trick was to keep the sales volume at least somewhere near consistency. A neat trick if you can do it.

§ 13:11 Two kinds of advertisements: Institutional and promotional

There are two kinds of ads. One kind is called institutional. This is the kind of advertisement that utility corporations or huge raw material suppliers might sponsor. Such ads do not appear to actually present or urge the purchase of any product. The ostensible purpose of such ads is often merely to keep the firm's identity vividly in the public mind.

Some of these institutional advertisers are so big and powerful that they don't even need that kind of publicity. Still, they run such ads. The purpose involves hugely complex public interrelations. They are so intertwined with the political scene that public service ads are necessary to swing sentiment to their side of political issues.

These sometimes appear in television as half-hour, or hour, "infomercials." The messages do not appear to have any kind of commercial content. This is the subtle, often insidious, motivating ingredient.

The other kind of advertising is called promotional. Such ads are designed to apply consumer pressure to buy a product. The more pressure, the more promotional the ad. The pressure is at its highest in aggressive, so called "fast-floor" retail stores. The mission is to get customers into the stores immediately, or the ad dies.

The task of the advertiser is compounded by the limiting factor of economics: the cost of advertising. An ad failure will not only result in a dead sales floor, but a hefty ad cost. Another unkind cut.

Metropolitan newspaper advertising is expensive. A full page ad in a metropolitan newspaper can cost as much as $35,000, or more, in its Sunday edition. Depending upon the product, in the average retail floor business, the cost of a reasonably successful ad might represent anywhere from 3% to 10% of the gross revenue which it generates. If the product is sold by mail order, the ad cost can constitute a much higher portion of the sale proceeds, amounting to 50% or more, and still be called successful.

This should not be misconstrued. Business ads of the promotional kind are basically deceptive. The advertisers modulate the copy to literally hide the negative information.

The use of asterisks will sometimes permit the appearance of cheaper prices, better and more expensive models, or other enhancements, when the facts, subdued by asterisk indexing, will reveal that the model pictured, or the price set forth, will not apply to the item offered.

The use of emphasizing through print size is designed to deceive. The language, which blatantly states that the price is the "lowest anywhere," is often belied by another ad offering the same product for less on the very next page.

Pictured products often give the impression that many accessories are included at no additional cost, when in fact they are not included in the sales price. Again, an asterisk is often the culprit that disguises the truth.

Recall the "rebate" scam. The words were all there but in such vast distinctions of size, fonts and placement that the commanding price less the rebate controlled. The ad reader was led to believe that the total price was the loudly proclaimed one instead of the "in-store price." Or, as deceptively, that the so-called "rebate" would be sent promptly with little done other than the purchase.

The plethora of full-page ads, the blistering competition for the readers as customers, and the advent of more and more discount supermarts have just about eliminated any value to the straight and truthful retail ad.

The trick in retail advertising is to lure the customer into the advertiser's store with the promise of more for less. Since most stores offer the same or similar products, acquired at or near the same cost, one store is hard-pressed to boast with strict honesty superior merchandise or pricing.

So, the advertising war wages on, with retail stores hovering near, or even below, the lines of legitimacy. It's a constant struggle to state what is needed to bring in the trade, while skirting actual fraud.

Then, there is the "switch-pitch." This is the deplorable practice of luring the customer into the store, or worse, getting the salesman into the customer's home, with a promise of something for virtually nothing.

§ 13:12 A brief history of "hype" in advertising

Some years ago, this practice was honed in a field called the "Sew-Vac Biz." Every big town spawned clusters of opportunistic predators who advertised impossibly low-priced sewing machines and vacuum cleaners.

The competition, even in this cesspool of an operation, was fierce. The usual formula went something like this. Ads in newspapers, and on the radio, blared out offerings of state-of-the-art sewing machines and powerful vacuum cleaners for "$9.95, full price."

The ads featured phone numbers rather than addresses. Phone rooms, called "boiler rooms," were set up to monitor the calls, referred to as "leads." Leads were then distributed to sharpshooters, whose talents were closer to those of con artists than salesmen. These vultures then descended upon unsuspecting, lower-income victims, naive enough to believe the ads.

The pitchman would then shower dirt all over the living room carpet, and whip out the $9.95 little wonder. Of course, that rigged item couldn't make a dent in the mess. The pitchman babbled on, while the bewildered housewife stared at her besmirched floor.

She would love to have a vacuum cleaner, and could ill afford even the $9.95 special. But, she needed something to pick dirt up, not just to lay there and sniff at it. The viper then just happened to have a new, modern Zippity Do-Dah mighty canister model in his car. He had promised it to his Aunt Susie, because it was one of those once-in-a-lifetime special price deals.

Well, of course that particular unit is not for sale. It was faithfully promised to Aunt Susie. Still, you really ought to show the customer how a top of the line model works. Why not just bring it in, and show what it will do?

Of course, it picked up all of that messy stuff just fine. And, of course, it cost $279.95, not $9.95. Oh heck. Aunt Susie's a great old gal. She'd be willing to wait the ten or twelve weeks for another unit like this.

After all, this customer has some rights too. But, don't worry, he assured the quivering housewife, it can be purchased on real easy time payments. Just sign right here.

See the monster embarrassment slipping over to further the housewife's discomfiture.

Those ads were aimed at a certain class of customers, whose lack of sophistication made them susceptible to this dodge. The percentage of sales to leads was astounding. Most of these bloodsuckers closed as many as 8 or 9 sales out of 10 prospective leads.

Well, that kind of scheme is all but extinguished by more aggressive consumer fraud policing operations almost everywhere. But the "victims," with that same innocence, are still out there in abundance.

The advocates of "loss leaders, bait advertising," and other nefarious activities are still in full bloom, but with a bit more cleverness in diverting attention to their activities.

§ 13:13 Attorney advertising is essentially retail advertising

An ad placed in a general circulation newspaper offering the services of a lawyer is a retail ad. The lawyer is offering to sell his or her services directly to the consumer. The heavy competition among advertising lawyers has placed those practicing such promotion in the ticklish position of having to shape their ads to meet that competition.

I'm not sure that attorney advertising was even honestly intended to be the blessing for the lower middle class, as touted. I have seen the present crop of lawyer ads, and I fail to see much of a difference between most of them and the "switch-pitch" of yore.

I see ads touting, "Divorce for $45 plus costs." Now, how many of those divorce clients who respond to such ads do you believe are signed up at that price? I see ads which read, "Incorporate for just $50 plus costs." Is there anyone among us who believes that the advertising lawyer will confine his corporation practice to these offers?

Ads for "Wills at $25" do not state clearly, in big bold type, that such wills are not what will be suggested when push comes to shove. The more usual, family-type will, with testamentary trust and other more involved provisions, will be suggested, you can be sure, and at prices more consistent with the promotional intent of the advertiser.

But, the point is that people who respond to this guff are deceived. That they may ultimately get what they should get is not a redemption of the scam. Moreover, they are quite likely further conned into spending more for the "better model" will than a reputable lawyer would charge.

What about the immigration ads that promise "green cards for everyone" at prices like $30. Who do these ads attract? Are these people really capable of discerning a bait ad from a legitimate one?

For those who claim that their bargain-priced operations are legitimate, are their clients well served? Is a client who responds, and is actually given a $45 divorce, properly served? Can the attorney give proper service to all divorce clients for that price?

Are facts that would require more extensive investigation properly explored? Can such an operation devote the time and attention to each case, to assure that all cases are given due consideration and service?

If such operations are run like the mills that their prices would indicate, are they the blessing for the lower middle class that their proponents would argue? Or, are they the same self-interested opportunists who lurked in the now discredited "switch-pitch" operations?

There is nothing wrong with offering divorce services at low prices, where the facts warrant nothing more by way of time than is price-consistent. If one is involved in legal aid activity, such services might be subsidized in one way or another.

But such ads are not directed solely to candidates specifically tailor-made for the advertised services. Some people, whose situations are much more complicated, are also attracted by the bargain price ads. When such prospects respond, do the advertising lawyers provide their services at the advertised rates regardless? One would doubt that.

§ 13:14 Attorney ads can be honest and yet productive

If ads are used to introduce new clients to the office, with no purpose of upgrading or switching the particular service offered, they can be both effective and forthright.

As an example, an ad offering wills at reduced prices might bring in new clients, even though the service advertised could be a loss. This kind of "loss leader" would be a reputable offer, if the advertiser were, in fact, willing and able to do any and all wills at the advertised price.

Another fringe benefit to this program is the building of a will file, and the ultimate probability of probating estates in your later practice. Why not come right out with your motive. Tell it like it is.

§ 13:15 Examples of attorney ads

An inexpensive ad in the classified section of your local newspaper could read something like:

LET ME DRAW YOUR WILL,
ANY KIND - - - ANY LENGTH
ONLY $50.00,
FULL AND COMPLETE PRICE.
This offer is made so we can
get acquainted. I'd like to be
your family lawyer.
Please call me at (333) 333-3333
GERALD M. SINGER, Lawyer.

It may seem silly to be so up-front in advertising, but it could be refreshingly disarming. At least the readers will see your "ulterior motive" in the ad. Many people have become fearful of unexplained "bargain-priced" sales items.

But in the advertisement suggested, you don't have to use a ploy. You are saying: "I want something from you, and I'm willing to give you something in exchange. I want you to get to know me and my attorney services. So I'm willing to give you an introductory service, at a bargain price, for your time spent in looking me over." A fair exchange?

It's true that you could get stuck drafting a 50-page trust will for $50. But consider the upside gain from that downside risk. The caliber of client who would need such a will might be worth grooming, even with a loss-leader of this magnitude.

You could use services other than wills, but most people either have no will or could use an updated one. Other kinds of services may not be so universally appealing.

If radio time in your town is not cost-prohibitive, you might try the personal appearance method. A thirty-second radio spot could go something like this:

> "Hello. I'm Jerry Singer, your neighborhood lawyer. I'd like very much for us to get acquainted so you can see my office and

the kind of lawyer work I do. So, if you'll call me, I will make you a will or re-do your old one to bring it legally up-to-date for the full price of only $50, regardless of size or type. This even includes lengthy trust provisions or whatever you may need. Call me, Jerry Singer, at (333) 333-3333, please. Why not do it now, so we can get to know each other, and have a new will for only $50. That's Attorney Jerry Singer at (333) 333-3333. Thanks for listening."

Television, in most areas, is usually quite expensive. But sometimes stations offer time at very low rates, if you're not too choosy about time slots. Even if you're not the Robert Redford type, your appearance on screen can add much credibility to your offer.

Back in the early fifties, I made several appearances on television advertising our products. The very amateurishness of my delivery is what made those ads effective. Some of our later ads, done professionally, were not nearly as productive per dollar of cost.

Car dealers have found that their personal work in front of the cameras produces the best results. Nothing beats a face-to-face offer. You can use the same kind of script as suggested for radio. You might have the scene done on remote in your office, standing, not sitting, next to your desk.

Another idea I like is the two-minute "Legal Chat" theme. The scenario is to present yourself sort of like the "Green Grocer" of lawyerdom. Each segment is designed to give a mini-lecture on rights and liabilities in situations that interest most people.

You can give brief talks on divorce rights, such as deferred sales of the family residence, or joint custody, or whatever. You can capsulize some of the important bits of bankruptcy information. Probate is a good subject which would be of interest to many people. Or, you might acquaint your listeners with how to approach small claims actions.

This kind of program is more in the nature of the institutional ad previously referred to. You don't promote any specific service, but you are obviously selling yourself as a knowledgeable attorney. If the TV deal is good enough, and you can afford some missionary work of this type, it ain't bad.

You can cap off your little speech with: "I'm Jerry Singer, attorney, and I'll be happy to answer any questions if you call me at (333) 333-3333 any time between 9:00 A.M. and 5:00 P.M. If I'm in court, please leave your name and number so that I can return your call."

While the air time is expensive, even at cheap prices, a well-paced and informative show of this kind could produce dramatic results. Also, because of its public interest value, the station might be persuaded to make you an extra special deal. Don't overlook the public service stations, if you have them in your area. Cable TV, a burgeoning vista for talky "infomercials," is another possibility.

This kind of low-keyed, institutional gig can develop as much, or even more, business than the hard-sell promotional variety. Moreover, the class of clientele it draws could be more satisfying and lucrative for you in the end.

Advertising for lawyers can be both productive and contributive, if done honestly and with common sense. But don't fall into the trap of the high-flying promo artist. While the law has flexed a bit on this subject, there are still laws against fraud everywhere.

Caveat! Research local laws on advertising.

Before you embark on any kind of advertising program, thoroughly research your local laws and bar rules on advertising. Lawyers' advertising has historically been prohibited in any form. It is only recently that any kind of advertising has been allowed in some states. Other states still take a very dim view of lawyer ads.

The suggestions given in this book for certain kinds of advertising are not meant to advocate the disregard of local restraints. I, personally, have never advertised my wares as an attorney, despite my background, training and experience in the advertising field. I don't think it's necessary. I only treat the subject for those who wish to indulge in that method of stimulating clientele enhancement.

§ 13:16 Other means of "marketing" yourself

The terms "marketing" and "business development" are relatively new to lawyering. In fact, it hasn't been so many years since they were considered dirty words in the legal profession. Lawyers have traditionally viewed themselves as being above mundane merchandising tactics.

We were taught to disdain the notion that lawyers are tradespeople or business persons. Commitment of service to our clients, and to the law, has historically been accepted as paramount.

Now, attorneys have learned that it is no betrayal to the profession to equate the idea of income with that of service. Even though dedicated to the ideals of meaningful contributions to society, a lawyer soon learns that he or she must live too.

Then came the dawn of the advertising lawyer. Like long hair, beards, jeans, and open-necked shirts, the legal profession learned to co-exist with the "hype" generation. After the thunderous shock of the advertising lawyer echoed and faded, the movement toward marketing and business development techniques hardly created a ripple.

Marketing and business development have become specialty fields proctored by promoters whose targets are the more affluent, multi-lawyer firms. Still, there's room in the movement for the progressive solo lawyer.

If you can restrain your adrenaline long enough to let your practice get up to speed, you might then adopt some of the following suggestions for your own private program of marketing and business development. Remember though, the first order of business is to get your practice going well enough to create some momentum. There will be time enough then to shift to a higher gear.

§ 13:17 Some thoughts on marketing methods

You can let your clients know how appreciative of their support you can be. Each time a client refers a new client to you, send the client a letter expressing your appreciation, and perhaps some little token of your thanks.

You might have a store of pens, note pads, calendars, or other little somethings that couldn't be confused with "payola." It might still be enough to register your sincere gratitude.

Follow this routine even if the referral fails to materialize. Let your client know that you appreciate the thoughtfulness and not just the economic returns to you. This might stimulate future efforts. Just as in the case of the referral by an assigning lawyer, never let your client know that the referral was a dud.

Add your clients' birthdates to their file information. When you do this on your computer list program, an occasional printout will remind you to send out birthday cards.

The same should be done for wedding anniversaries and other occasions. The more often you make contact with each client, the more you might stimulate referral efforts.

If you have other sources of referrals besides clients, add their names to the list, and follow the same procedures for each such source. Bear in mind the limits of such conduct, and do not exceed the limits of ethical standards.

A brochure, if tastefully prepared, can enlighten your clients, other attorneys, and others, as to the various services for which you are especially qualified. Even a regular newsletter could be welcomed and perhaps even productive.

No need to reserve those open house cocktail parties to Christmas or New Years only. In fact, no special occasion is even needed. It wouldn't hurt to select any date for such an event. Send out announcements of your open house for the simple reason that you value your clients and referring lawyers and wish to show your appreciation.

It might be productive to do this as many as four or five times a year. If you must be sticky about it, limit the guest list to those who've been somewhat active in generating clients.

If you feel you have too many clients to invite them all, you can probably afford to invite them all. Whatever you do or however you select your guests, do it right. Make each affair one to remember. If you stint on the trimmings, you will have wasted your money.

Every once in a while, schedule a breakfast or a coffee for a seminar on developments within your area of practice. If it's in taxation, keep your guests abreast of tax problems and certain areas of tax law that could provide advantages. Do this as often as would be prudent.

This is especially workable if your practice is in a relatively small city or town. An intimate "chit chat" talk show could be the hit of your local radio or television station. You could take viewer or listener calls and respond to their legal troubles.

Your comments would be prefaced with the generalities of such interplay, and that you are by no means "advising" on any subject. Still, the subject matter could be of widespread interest.

Such an enterprise, though not directly for advertising purposes, could result in an avalanche of business for your office. If holding public office is your eventual goal, such a background could work well for you at election time.

While you should not, and perhaps could not, inter-mix any reference to your own office within the program, and should not even think of sponsorship, you can be sure that interested persons will find you.

Wherever talk shows on subjects relating to your specialties are scheduled, call the program director and offer to appear either as a moderator or an advocate. Such exposure can be very productive as well as personally stimulating.

Whenever you spot a newspaper or magazine article that relates to the interests of a client, clip it and send it on, marked "for your interest." Let your client know that you're interested in his or her concerns.

There are many publications of the various organizations in our profession. Each bar association publishes some sort of news bulletin. Each is usually hungry for contributors. Be a contributor. The more notoriety you can get for your activities in your specialties, the more exposure and probability of case referrals.

And—you never can tell—you might be giving vent to a bit of Hemmingway in you. Other publishers, even your town newspaper, would probably welcome your contributions. With a bit of ingenuity, you might even establish a regular newspaper column on facts of interest in your legal specialties. Some columns of this kind have found their way into syndication, and have reached levels of national interest.

Despite my admonition against being a "joiner," you can indulge rather lavishly in participating in community and civic betterment efforts. Wherever you can speak on subjects related to your legal specialties, grab the opportunity. These are usually scheduled for evenings or weekends so they should not interfere with your regular workdays.

The positive exposure from activities devoted to the enhancement of your community can only produce good results for you. But beware of any such activity of a controversial nature. I would avoid all political exposure except when your participation is low-keyed, such as when your efforts are directed toward a possible judgeship. You certainly do not want to estrange any opposition party potential clients.

None of the above is meant to modify what was previously said about refraining from being a news hound. Your efforts at article contributions should never in any way be connected with your cases or constitute an attempt, however veiled, to gain personal publicity.

All of the foregoing plans will blossom for you best when approached, and delivered, without any tinge of personal aggrandizement. In fact, to the extent that you let any promotional intent creep into your program, the plan will fail. You must just have faith that, in these efforts, the most sterilized altruism will be your best chance for commercial success.

§ 13:18 Be considerate to other lawyers and to judges!

You've heard a lot about the "attorney/client" relationship and the privileges, duties, and rights involved. You have been taught to beware of conflicts of interest, betrayal of confidentiality, unprofessional conduct, and the many "no no's" involved in your representation of clients.

Your attorney/attorney relationship.

This may seem a strange subject under the salesmanship heading, but it's not. Little has been said about the protocol, decorum, or standards of behavior between attorneys. The lack of a fiduciary duty toward opposing counsel doesn't justify treating her or him like a leper.

On the contrary, there are good reasons for you to be greatly concerned with the quality of your relations with other attorneys. This is particularly important if you practice in a smaller community where the likelihood of repetitive contact is great. Even in larger cities, you never know when paths will cross again.

In fact, the rapport existing between attorneys can even affect the promptness and size of settlements. In the overwhelming majority of cases, the attorney has great persuasiveness in both the decision to settle and the amount to be paid.

The opposing attorney is your only contact with the ear of the other side. You must assume that the client will be influenced by the attorney's advice on settlement. In many cases, this influence approaches dominance.

If you play your cards right, you can convert this influence to an asset for your side. Sometimes, the effect is quite subtle. You don't get your way in the case simply because you have not been a pain to your opposing lawyer. But, you can, by keeping the lines of communication open, get information exchanged which could auger well for the settlement effort.

Consider the lawyer who, right from the start, has established and maintained an objectively professional attitude. He/she is never unduly critical of the other lawyer. He/she never imposes harsh ultimatums or terms upon him.

He/she avoids personality duels, and all forms of polemics. He/she makes it clear to the opponent that he/she would always prefer to sidestep confrontations, if in doing so he/she can still adequately represent his/her client.

Such a demeanor, if maintained, must eventually result in a softening of the other fellow's belligerence. Most of the difficulties existing between lawyers stem from attitudes of challenge, which, if not active, are at least passively present. The fact that only one may be the aggressor does not necessarily exonerate the other.

It will usually take more than a pacifistic manner to quell the zeal of jousting blood. In fact, it is not even pacifism that is required. You needn't talk of peace when there is no awareness of war.

I've heard attorneys brag about the fact that they "never stipulate to nothin' no how." This rustic approach has a lot to be said for it, upon first blush. At trial, such rigidity imposes the obligation upon the opponent to lay foundations and prove up each point of evidence.

Aside from making life tougher for the other person, this offers the possibility of "winning odds." What is hoped for is the chance that, somewhere, the other side will fail on an important evidentiary matter, and the issue will go by "default."

Whether in chess, checkers, or law practice, the practice of "trading men" does not often prove positive. You can never be sure of your future vulnerability.

The world turns, and the people who were on top get switched with those who were on the bottom. Stipulation requests should be carefully considered and usually granted where no detriment is seen.

What very often happens is that, at some point along the way, your situation will gain by an agreement from your opponent. If you've been cooperative, you may very well be grateful for your farsightedness.

Although you must always view such requests from an overall position, considering what you are being asked for, what you have to lose, and what can be gained, you should assume a positive and friendly attitude. As much as you can, and wherever possible, you should be gracious and affirmative.

If it costs you nothing, be "generous." Quite often, the stipulation requested is to avoid having to go through mere formalities. If you know that saying "no" will only result in making a bit more trouble which in the end won't constitute a measurable gain, then you might consider an alternative: be overwhelmingly gracious.

Being pleasant and cooperative not only makes for a more enjoyable courtroom experience, it also plants the seeds for a harvest you may later be able to reap. You gave something that cost you nothing. The next time around, it may be that you want a stipulation that could otherwise be very troublesome for you.

Even if this doesn't happen, and you aren't able to profit in any direct way, have faith that somewhere along the route you will gain from this attitude.

Another situation where you can "give" what amounts to nothing involves the time limit for an answer to be filed by the other side. You get a call from the attorney for defendant asking for an extension of time to file and serve the answer.

What if you refuse? This means you intend to take a default. Perhaps, in some jurisdictions, this could mean a serious problem for the defendant. But in most jurisdictions, it only means a slight bit of trouble in making a motion to set aside the default on grounds such as inadvertence or mistake.

In many jurisdictions, "inadvertent mistake" includes everything but the most flagrant disregard. Hence, no matter what the reason is for failing to file a timely answer, there is virtually no likelihood of making a default stick. But, if you practice in a jurisdiction in which courts look for cracks to drop cases into, let that be your guide.

Of course, unless you are a real idiot, you will not refuse the extension point blank. The question is how much of an extension you will give, and how graciously you will give it.

I suggest that you say something like: "Sure, just tell me what you want." Don't be stinting or grudging on stipulations to extend time, since there would be little or nothing you could do about preventing it anyway.

Not only can the defendant successfully move to set aside a default, but he can prevent the default by getting the judge to grant an extension. And there's little, if anything, you can do to prevent it.

So, knowing that the extension is inevitable, one way or another, as Confucius say, "Relax and enjoy it." As long as you know you're going to grant the request in the end, don't just give in. Make a sort of ceremony of it. Be almost sickening in your attitude. In other words, make a positive thing out of it, instead of a useless negative thing.

The same thing applies to extensions of time to file responses to written interrogatories. Sure, there are variations in the consequences of failing to respond to interrogatories within the statutory time period from state to state, but rarely is there a serious penalty for taking a bit longer than the law permits in any state.

Usually, unless there is a demonstrably willful failure to comply, the most that can be expected on a motion to compel is that the court will so compel and will give time for compliance. When the time for the motion is added to the time given by the court, more time will probably be given than had been asked for.

The net result is a gain to your opponent, with the aftertaste of your not having been very nice. Moreover, you will have expended considerable time in resisting the motion, and trying to explain to your client why he should pay you for this exercise in futility.

Remember a basic tenet of the law, that the "law abhors a forfeiture." So, if you've got some kind of advantage thought out, which is built on forfeiture of any kind, forget it.

Develop the reputation in the legal community as a nice person. And, as long as you are going to be a nice person, be a really nice person. Don't be chintzy, give your adversary all he or she wants, and then some. Kill him or her with kindness.

This same routine applies to times set for depositions, inspections of documents, or any other such thing. Incidentally, unless you are in a very unique situation, it's a good rule never to notice a deposition or inspection without first calling the other lawyer to clear an acceptable date.

Some courts even insist on it. Once you have agreed on a date, then notice the proceedings. Doing it the other way around not only causes extra and needless trouble, since you have to reset the date anyway, but causes an initial antagonism in the other lawyer that may never be cured.

On the other hand, even though you have agreed upon a date, do not treat the agreement as a "stipulation." Although the distinction is a subtle one, the far-reaching effects of the distinction are important.

For example, if there is a willful default in a "stipulated" deposition, you are powerless in most states to get any kind of remedy. However, in a "noticed" deposition, you will have much greater power and control over the situation.

Be sure, therefore, to file and serve the notice of deposition after you have arranged for a mutually satisfactory date. Don't make the mistake that is frequently made in such situations.

Do not state in your "notice" that the deposition is set upon "stipulation." Merely notice the proceeding for a particular date just as though no conversation had existed between you and the other attorney. All you have done is to agree upon a date. Nothing else was "stipulated."

In your discussions with your opponent about dates and such, be as gracious as possible. You will occasionally run into a wise guy who will make your life difficult with calendar problems, etc., but try, where you can, to be the nice guy and let him have the pleasure of being a jerk.

Distinguish, where you can, between your feeling of frustration and anger over your adversary's attitude and a genuine imposition upon you as a result of his unreasonableness. If it is the former, try to rise above it, and continue in your congenial tone and attitude. If it truly is the latter, and there is no way of controlling his weight upon you, try to terminate the conversation on as positive a note as possible.

Quite often there is an attitude in certain types of people that can be overcome with a persistently kind and reasonable treatment. Do what you can to determine whether such may not be the case before you chuck your efforts. Remember, you can gain a lot if there is any possibility of maintaining a good rapport.

Of course, niceness is not always merely its own reward. Sometimes, if the request is something more than a formality, you can parlay giving into getting a concession that can put you ahead of the game.

Litigation is a game of jockeying for position. As in the game of Monopoly, you can "trade" into a favorable position. In that game, litigation trades depend upon your ability to disguise the significance of what it is that you are requesting. In most facets of trial technique, you can tell the amateurs from the pros by the way they handle themselves in such negotiations.

There is no stereotype for "trading" conduct. You will be faced with a new kind of situation each time the occasion arises for making a trade. I can give only very generalized advice in this region: don't be "cute."

You would look very foolish in pretending that what you want means nothing to you when it is obviously quite important. On the other hand, don't get hysterical.

A straightforward and objective approach is always best in this situation. Very often, a "matter of fact" demeanor will distract from the urgency of what you are asking. This might result in more attention being directed toward what you are giving.

The success in trading for such stipulations often depends upon your coolness in walking a balanced path. Just as you mustn't try to overplay the importance of what you offer, so must you not try to underplay the value of what you are asking.

As in general salesmanship, you should eliminate all apparent "selling" in your attitude. In any situation, selling is an art completely dependent upon the impression that you are merely "giving information." Any overt signs given by you that you are trying to persuade will turn your pipeline off.

Remember at all times to keep your "cool." No matter what turn your negotiations take, maintain a free and easy channel of communication. Even though things don't work out for you in this deal, there will be other trades to make and other things to discuss. You cannot afford a breakdown in communications. Never mind that you're both in the same boat and that the responsibility is shared by both.

You can succeed in keeping good relations with the other attorney only if you are willing to bear 100% of the load. It will be no consolation to you whose fault it was if the result of the collapse was a loss to you.

On the other hand, if as a result of your efforts, the lines are kept open, and somewhere along the way, you gain a strategic advantage, what difference does it make that you carried the whole thing on your own shoulders.

The thing to remember is that it cost you nothing to be nice.

The worst thing that can happen is that being nice didn't gain you anything other than being known as a nice person.

It's not always easy to get along with other lawyers. Some lawyers think that, to be a good attorney, you must be a stinker. Other lawyers don't even think about it. They were stinkers at birth.

You'll find attorneys who sincerely believe that, unless they are difficult, they will be accused of not protecting their client's interests. Other lawyers maintain a nasty disposition because it pleases them to create turmoil. It seems that a larger number of the latter kind are turning to the legal profession.

But, you have the jump on all of them. You now know that it will behoove you to be nice. And in case you think you will be lonely, in a world of sadists and stinkers, don't you believe it. Most lawyers are really fine human beings, regardless of what you read in the newspapers.

If I were asked to identify the most prominent and troublesome fault or defect in lawyers, I would have to say it is an overdose of loyalty. Lawyers, by and large, are loyal to a fault.

It is probably this characteristic that gets us into most of our troubles. We are, too often, too quick to commit ourselves to the service of clients, and too slow to realize where that commitment will lead us.

The average lawyer in general practice sometimes acts on behalf of a client in a way which, if analyzed, would be embarrassing. If thought out carefully before hand, the lawyer wouldn't do it. But, lawyers are modern day squires, oftentimes with too much zeal for their client's position and too little restraint.

It is this characteristic which is often the lawyer's undoing. Few attorneys are able to leave their client's troubles in the office. Tossing and turning during sleepless nights is another of the lawyer's syndromes. Next time you're in a courtroom, notice whose expression shows more reaction to unfavorable rulings, the attorney's or the client's.

Try to remain as objective as you can about the cases you handle. Don't take the case personally to your heart or your home. Your spouse will tell you this too. You may not realize it, but your family bears some of the brunt when you come home ashen-faced after a bad judgment.

While you may not succeed in ridding yourself of this fault, you can at least be conscious of its side effects. The paradox of client loyalty can be most obstructive when dealing with other lawyers.

Carrying your client's pendant on your sleeve is perhaps the most serious obstacle to negotiation with the opposition. If you can create the illusion of being pro-settlement, you will encourage negotiation, and thereby win the last point for your client.

In corresponding with your opponent, try to make your letters as personal and friendly as possible. Address him by his first name, and sign your letters with your first name. Try to avoid starchy formalism in your style, and try to import a free and easy format. It is incongruous for two lawyers to be using friendly informality in their personal conversations, and then the most formalistic structure in their correspondence.

All of these things tend to make discussions easier, and to pave the way to earlier and more productive settlement efforts. You will find generally that the thing standing in the way of settlement or other agreement is an inability to communicate. Often this is a lack of understanding of what is said in this section.

What is said here is not reserved for lawyers on the other side of your cases. Almost any attorney that you come across could be an opponent in the future, or worse, a judge in a case you are handling.

You can never be sure how, or in what way, the person you confront can someday control your situation. All judges, and many statesmen and politicians, are ex-attorneys. You may never need to face a judge or statesman with whom you've had dealings in the past as lawyers, but, if you do, you'll fare much better if your relationship was pleasant then.

Later on, you'll look back and be amazed at how many lawyers you've known, and classmates from law school, have become judges and big shot politicians. You'll wish that you had treated them kinder and with more respect. It's better to do it, and not to have to wish you had.

It usually takes more energy and effort to be nasty than to be nice. Observe, as you go through the years of your practice, most bad fellows really have to go out of their way to be that way. In most instances, it's easier to say "yes" than to say "no." Most of the time, you are saving more energy and time in giving what is asked than in opposing it. Think about this.

Your "attorney/judge" relationship.

You can "judge a book by its cover" much more accurately than you can judge a judge by attire or apparent behavior. Judges, just like all kinds of people, quite often like to give the impression that they are "hip" or "with it."

A judge may let his hair grow a bit longer, or use an "in" word or phrase now and then, but this does not necessarily indicate an extensive tolerance or permissiveness in courtroom decorum, or even in thought processes.

A school teacher may crack a joke, now and then, but this does not mean that audience participation is invited from the class. Army officers often are labeled as "chicken," because of a misconstrued inconsistency in attitude. On the one hand, there is an apparent laxity in joking with the men, but then, all at once, a sternness takes over, and those who attempted to participate in the joviality suffer the brunt of the change.

The officer wants to be "accepted" by his troops, but he does not want a breakdown in discipline. The problem with this schizoid behavior is that it is difficult to manage. The officer, who truly wants to be just "one of the boys," doesn't present a challenge either to his men or himself.

More often, however, the desire is not at all to be "one of the boys," but merely to get credit for that illusion. The officer whose temperament is consistently harsh has fewer problems. Everyone knows what must be done, and what to expect.

The same high percentage of individuals who want the accolade of liberality, without being intruded upon, exists with judges as with army officers. They want their jokes appreciated, but do not appreciate yours.

This very fine line is difficult to find, and even more difficult to maintain. Most people who are given authority are totally incapable of finding it, much less maintaining it. For this reason, it is rare to find a working executive who at once is both popular and capable.

It is said that General George Patton was greatly envious of General Omar Bradley because the latter had such enormous popularity with the men, whereas Patton failed in this area. Patton made attempts, from time to time, to generate some camaraderie with the men, but never quite succeeded.

Like many people holding authority, Patton may have overestimated his own sense of humor. The rare commodity, which is called a sense of humor, does not relate to how well one can tell a joke. It depends more upon how well one can accept one's own foibles or being the brunt of a joke.

It is probable that Patton would have fared better on the popularity scale had he made no such attempts, and had he remained aloof. At least there would have been less opportunity for the confrontations with which the general became so infamously identified.

Of course, it is illogically inconsistent that one should behave in a particular way and yet resent such behavior in another. Yet, it is said that "we have most predominantly in ourselves that which we can tolerate least in others."

Such baffling inconsistency is greatly multiplied when one is placed in a position of power over others. When applied to the courtroom, the effect of this personalities game is even more far-reaching.

The lawyer who becomes "victimized" by his own inability to "psyche out" the judge is not only himself injured, but carries with him the injury to his client.

Presume that whatever the judge says or does, or whatever his/her conduct, he/she is only trying to convey an impression and not an invitation. Even if wrong, that presumption cannot hurt you. But the other conclusion can. Whatever the judge does, or doesn't do, the courtroom is no place for you to unleash your "cute" personality.

Regardless of how informal a judge appears to be, or how informally he/she seems to operate the courtroom, it is a rare judge who won't appreciate the formal courtesies observed by a lawyer. Even though when you ask, "May I approach the witness, your honor," his/her response is "Certainly, certainly," and he/she waives you on with a shrug, this does not mean that he/she doesn't expect that courtesy.

If you don't lose track of the fact that the judge doesn't want to be thought of as starch and procrustean, but as one who is humanly flexible, you will realize that your treatment of him/her in a very respectful and formal way will not in any way frustrate his purpose.

When one responds to a "thank you" with a "don't mention it," this doesn't mean that the "thank you" was not only appreciated but expected. Think about this. The last time you did a big favor for a friend, and you were mildly embarrassed by his thanks, how would you have felt if he had merely taken the favor and said nothing at all? Chances are that you would have been very resentful of his brass at taking without expressing some form of gratitude.

Of course, there are always exceptions to this situation, just as there are to all points which I have raised throughout this book. But, in the main, the following are some rules which I believe should be followed in court appearances and in dealing with judges, that is, if you want the odds with you.

Some suggested guidelines on courtroom demeanor:

(1) **Dress as conservatively as your wardrobe will permit.**

Of course, the touchstone for conservative wardrobe has changed dramatically within the past twenty or so years and is undergoing more changes as I write this paragraph. Still, my observations are that a conventional dark suit with white dress shirt and tie offers the greatest safety.

Women are advised to avoid frilly dresses and slacks. The safest bet is still business suits and conservative simple dresses.

You can taunt fate if you wish by following the vanguards of trend, but without some guaranteed advance information, you are running a bit of a risk. In my view, a courtroom is no place to demonstrate fashion bravery.

(2) **For men, remain either clean-shaven or have only a mature beard.**

Unless you have already developed a mature beard or mustache, be clean-shaven. If you are growing a beard or mustache, be sure that you are not scheduled for any court appearance, until the whiskers are far enough advanced that the judge will not mistake the stubble for unkemptness. I haven't seen much change along this line. A stubble is a stubble. The whiskers do not broadcast their ultimate purpose.

Make-up for women should be low-key and subtle. Heavy eyeliners or shadow might still be sources of potential irritation. If the judge perceives that you care as little about your case as your grooming indicates, you are likely to get a result commensurate with that registration.

(3) **Be well-groomed and manicured.**

Even though the counsel table may be far away from the bench, and the judge's eyes are no longer as young as they once were, they may still be acute enough to encounter your dirty fingernails, unshined shoes, grimy hands, etc. Besides, you may be asked to come to the bench, or to chambers. So, make sure you are also freshly bathed. Women wearing scents might consider toning down the quantity or even switching to a less provocative brand for court.

(4) **Be prompt in all court appointments.**

Come to court on time. If you are late, the least that will happen is that the matter will be put on "second call." You will not only be subject to a squeeze for the lunch adjournment, but you will be viewed as a villain for being late.

More and more, courts are leaning toward punitive sanctions for tardiness. In some instances, substantial monetary sanctions have been applied. Not so long ago, I witnessed a judge offer a lawyer the option of either paying a **$500** fine or contributing **$600** to the court law library fund.

That lawyer was less than ten minutes late. He attempted to explain his lateness, but the judge refused to permit that. That happened in the United States District Court, Central District of California, but such instances are not limited to that court, or even the Federal courts.

Sanctions are bad enough, but you are also putting your client's cause on the line. I can hear you complain that your conduct should not result in punishment to your client. So, what else is new?

(5) **Address the judge as "your honor" at all times.**

Always address the judge as "your honor," and never as "you" or "judge." Whether or not judges will admit this, more than a little of a judge's judicial compensation is the homage paid in being addressed with the title, "your honor." As many times a day as this salutation is mouthed, and for as many years as the judge sits on the bench, the gloss of pride in that tribute never seems to tarnish.

(6) **Never, but never, interrupt the judge.**

Never interrupt the judge even though you know that he/she has made an error in his/her commentary. Wait until he is finished, and then be careful of what you want to say concerning any believed "error." It's not enough to say "never interrupt," because it takes extra patience to know that you're not interrupting.

Some judges have a halting manner of speech. They think while speaking instead of before speaking. The fact that there's a lull in the judge's phrasing that may indicate the full thought has been expressed is no guarantee. Impatience will try to overtake your discretion.

You want to start talking again before your opposing counsel gets his or her licks in. Cool it! You won't be cut short. You won't be, that is, if you've curried the judge's favor with your courteous behavior.

A most perplexing paradox is the fact that the attorney who pushes for first will often be shoved into last by the judge. You get the feeling that this is an impatient and irritable judge. You think that if you do not speak up fast, the judge will move the matter on, and you'll have lost your "next."

This is not a likely occurrence. Judges, by and large, like, and favor, courteous attorneys. The attorney who fights for the place in line will set the tone for the irritations and impatience anticipated.

That attorney is his/her own executioner. He/She is positively convinced that this kind of judge requires a quick draw. That attorney's own improvidence will probably prevent realization of the vicious cycle he/she has created.

(7) **Never interrupt opposing counsel.**

Never interrupt opposing counsel to make a correction, or to interpose any statement, no matter how innocuous the interruption may be compared to the value which you believe the statement will have.

Discourtesy is discourtesy. You will be tagged as discourteous, regardless of the target of your conduct. You are not exculpated because opposing counsel had interrupted you several times.

Can you recall in your grade school and high school days being chastised for acts that others had been doing as well? Were you miffed at the unfairness of being singled out? Did you call the teacher's attention to the non-exclusivity of your conduct? Did that help? Does that answer your question?

(8) **Make a point of standing when you address the court.**

Always stand when you address the court. Do this even though the judge invites you to remain seated. It's like the "don't mention it" thing: the reply to your "thank you" with a "don't mention it" does not mean you were wrong in saying "thank you."

Stand up when you address the court, when you are making an objection or opposing one, or at any time when making a courtroom statement. Do this, even though your opposing counsel prefers to accept the judge's invitation to remain seated. It's also a good idea to stand when the judge enters the courtroom even though the judge's habit is to motion all to remain seated.

(9) **Address all comments to the bench even when meant for others.**

Always address your comments to the judge, and never to opposing counsel, no matter how obvious it is that the remark is directed you will indicate to the judge that you have great concern for the case in general, and for courtroom decorum.

§ 13:19 Salesmanship through every crack and crevice of the practice of law

Everything you do, every conversation you have, every letter, brief or pleading you draft, in fact, everything but using the bathroom, once you step into your office, is either salesmanship or a failure. You don't know it yet. And, you probably won't really understand it for quite a while. Some may never understand it. Salesmanship is at the root of your practice. It spells success or failure. You cannot avoid the test.

Argument, whether in the courtroom, at a deposition, on the phone or anywhere, any place you happen to be, can NEVER EVER win a point, any point. You cannot "argue" anyone into anything. You can NOT "persuade" anyone to do or not do anything. You CAN, however, give information which is valued by the listener, and which will cause the listener to either do or not do what you wish to be done or not done.

Listen carefully to what information may be valued. Then confine your salesmanship to giving that information and NOTHING ELSE. Watch the opposition crumble.

You will have much trouble doing that for quite a while. Lawyers are taught, unfortunately, to argue. That is a glitch in the study of law which I hope will someday be corrected. Argument will fail; giving information will succeed. Observe and see this for yourself.

If you think about it, there's really no place in litigation for actual "argument." The proper term is "summation." If you're doing your job, you are summing up your points. The more you can sound like an adding machine, reconciling your points with the issues, the more effective you will be.

You will be far ahead of the game if you can keep this one thought in mind. Everything you do in your law practice must be done with salesmanship. Even if you think not, rethink it.

Even if you're right by some mysterious happenstance, and you do score through argument, the point is nonetheless lost. Your "victory" will have had nothing whatever to do with your overpowering persuasion.

Think of the clerk waiting on a customer who gives the customer a hard time. Still, the customer buys and walks out of the store grumbling. The fact that the clerk's surly behavior did not dissuade the customer was only incidental to the "sale." The "sale" could have been made by Scrooge.

Your adversary also may have had little option but to buy your argument. You'll never know about that, but you'll reaffirm a fallacious belief. Don't.

Whomever you may be talking with, give information. I don't mean give the store away. Give the information necessary to cause the effect you would hope to have happen. Before you do or say anything, think. The point will come to mind. Then, sell.

§ 13:20 The "papermill" syndrome

Falling further out of fashion with judges each day is the technique known as "paper milling," practiced by unethical larger firms. When this happens to you, it might cause some frustration and even panic. Don't despair, you can handle anything they throw at you.

In fact, this is often an indication of frustration on their part. They may be more worried about your position than they will admit. Hence they will fall back on the tactic of smothering you with paper, hoping that you and your client will cave in.

You have two things going for you. First, the computer age has done much to level the advantage disparity. In the typewriter age, their secretarial staff held the high cards. Now, your computer can turn out a credibly impressive counterattack despite the help advantage they've got.

You can compensate for quantity with quality. When you receive that twelve pound package of guff, you won't need to open it to know that it's full of sand-in-the-wind, water, and good old B-- S--. Your well-written half pound gem will rip theirs open at the jugular.

That will be the time to review your SALESMANSHIP IN WRITING technique. First, glance through their garbage, underlining and annotating all the irrelevancies and obviously prejudicial material. Then note the authorities that you can see superficially will not score any meaningful points.

After you've narrowed their stuff down to legitimate issues, you'll see that what's left is not so thick or frightening any more. Then, you can start your research toward countering inapposite citations, points, issues and conclusions.

Take a few of the more offensive points, with outlandishly inappropriate "authorities," and mark them for strategic insertion into your responsive document. It's not necessary for you to negative each and every impropriety on their part. Judges don't need it, nor will they appreciate the waste of their, and your, time.

Then, devote the bulk of your time, effort and thought to launching a direct attack against those few salient points which need addressing. Make sure that your citations are valid, centrally relevant and precise.

Then, remember the essences of salesmanship in law practice, whether in speaking or writing. Put your paper together bearing in mind the signal lessons in selling sentences. Get attention fast, keep it, and make your point as early as possible.

The fault that appears most often in written material is the same as that found in oral presentation. Little thought is given to what might be of interest to the reader. This is no time for you to demonstrate your entire portfolio of academic proficiencies.

Your brief will be one of dozens. Don't deceive yourself that the judge is going to put all else aside and give your prose his or her attentive admiration. Your document will be only one of many others that will need to be glanced at before court convenes.

Thick briefs often cause obscurity rather than clarity. The problem with the full-scaled broadside literary assault is that it tends to obscure the point. I don't mean that you shouldn't dot every "i" and cross every "t." Nor do I mean that you need to write in the style of "see the pretty brown cow."

Do your job, but don't overdo it.

Do your homework. Cite authorities for all your points. State fully what you mean to say. But after you've done all that, get off it. Forget the minutiae. If your major points won't make it, the small stuff won't help.

Pity the poor judge who must read all of the tons of guff that lawyers dream up. If you want something from the judge, make it easy for the judge to find what you want.

You don't need to match briefs, thick for thick.

Too often, lawyers who are responding to a ten-ton brief will respond in kind. The judge won't necessarily find against you merely because you've let a few fragments of the moving brief slip by. In most instances, the judge will be grateful for your succinctness.

My experience in grading test papers and in sitting as a superior court arbitrator and as a judge pro tem has been confusion in reading papers rather than edification. Confusion, though, is less harmful than wrong conclusions. When the judge misunderstands your points, you may not get an opportunity to set the record straight.

Don't write briefs like you wrote bar exam papers.

Someone, I forget who, once said, "dying is easy, comedy is hard." Dying is a tag line everyone understands. Tagging a laugh line is not always that easy.

The great comedian, Jack Benny, developed the talent of the unspoken tag to a shiny finish. His response to an obvious straight line was either a "Hmmmmm," or folded arms and a stare sideways. Was he afraid that the audience wouldn't get the drift?

I believe that embarrassment drives some comedians to overplay their routines. They're afraid that if a tag is left unexplained, the audience won't respond. The prospect of being up there with silence instead of laughter is their constant nightmare.

Have you ever found yourself laughing at a joke you honestly did not understand? Sure you have. Know why? You were too embarrassed to show your ignorance in not laughing. Right? The comedian shifted embarrassment over to your side. Getting the point of a joke isn't so different from seeing a legal point.

Put yourself in the judge's seat.

Before you've reduced your thoughts to the written pages, think for a moment. What points would impress you? Those are the points you should write about. Forget the rest. Then, do your job thoroughly. Support your arguments with sound legal authorities and trust that the judge will be as smart as Jack Benny's audiences.

Use the computer's strength and edit out superfluities.

A nice thing about doing your drafting on the computer is that you can very easily delete as many words, sentences and even whole paragraphs as you need to sharpen up your work. Trying to do that with a typewriter, dictating machine or yellow tablet isn't that easy.

§ 13:21 What do you say to your client when you lose?

THE ULTIMATE EMBARRASSMENT.

The verdict is in. The judgment is for your opponent. Your first reaction: contemplation of suicide. Your better judgment prevails. Still, life holds little joy for you. You have suffered the humiliation of defeat. You look at your client, and your client looks at you. His or her quizzical expression tells you that your client does not know what happened.

What can you possibly say to your client? Like an enormous aftershock to a gigantic earthquake, you now face an almost equally devastating trauma. You must now translate for your client. But how? What can you say? How can you justify your client's faith and all the money paid to you in fees?

You know, and the whole legal world knows, that lawyers do not win or lose cases. Facts win or lose cases. You didn't manufacture the facts. Or, at least I hope that you didn't. You had to do the best possible job with the facts that you were dealt.

So, what do you say to your client?

Defiance begins to creep into your forethought. No, this is no time for your defense mechanism to take over. But isn't it the natural thing to beat back blame by shifting it away, preferably to the accuser? Wouldn't this be a good time to call up our old friend the embarrassment monster?

There's some confusion here. Isn't the monster a player in the salesmanship scenario? We don't use our friend to escape our responsibilities as a lawyer. Shifting embarrassment in this case will accomplish nothing. You would like to keep your client, and you certainly do not want a disgruntled client as an enemy.

O.K. So what do you say to your client when you lose?

Before we get to the core of this problem. Let me fortify you with a basic fact of legal life.

You never, never lose a case. Any case.

You're are a good lawyer, even a great lawyer. So, how can a lawyer like you lose a case? A simple answer: it doesn't happen.

Well, how did this thing happen then? How did that jury come back against you? Why? A good lawyer like you. Where is the silver lining to this black, ugly cloud? Well, of course it wasn't your fault, was it? You did your job.

So, what do you say to your client? You've had a judgment against your client for $15,000. The prayer in the plaintiff's complaint stated damages in the amount of $100,000. A $15,000 judgment in not a loss; it's a win!

You are having trouble with that logic? Well, let's look at a different picture. Your client is the plaintiff, suing for $100,000 which your client truly believes should be the judgment. The judgment is for $15,000. Did you win? Would your client think so? Probably not. Well, if you didn't win, did you lose?

If you lost, what happened on the other side? Both sides don't lose, do they? To answer this question, we need to dip into our salesmanship well. If we've done our job in the course of this case, we've learned many things about our client and his or her thoughts about the case.

Remember, in the earliest interview, your client telling you that the suit wasn't about money, it was for the "principle of the thing?" Now, of course, you have a result which admittedly was light on profit. Your fees were in excess of $25,000. Costs mounted substantially. Your client is out some other monies having to do with the case. And the verdict was for $15,000, not the $100,000 sued for.

But, your client wanted to prove a point, right? Principle was served, wasn't it? We won, didn't we? Sure, the whole thing may have cost your client a bob or two, but what's that compared to the noble purpose of "principle"?

And look at the other benefits derived. Your client wanted to teach the defendant a lesson, right? Well, winning certainly accomplished that, didn't it? O.K. So winning a $15,000 judgment is a win, nothing less.

Now, you are the defense attorney, facing a $15,000 loss. Heck, that's a win, no question about it. Your client was also consumed with the need to score a principle win. His opponent didn't get the $100,000 sued for, right? Also, look at all the money spent on fees, costs and other things. The lesson taught, just as your defendant client set out to teach it.

Once again, principle was served. We win, whether plaintiff or defendant. We just don't lose. That's fine. **But what do you say to your client?**

Remember, salesmanship is the giving of information valued by the listener. What you say to your client must be enveloped in words having such value.

First, resist the defeatist expression that is trying to overwhelm your facial muscles. You are happy. And, why shouldn't you be. You won, didn't you? So, you turn to your client exhibiting a happy countenance. You report the terrific news that the plaintiff failed to win the $100,000 sued for and only gets a measly $15,000.

There's more good news, of course. You tell all about the enormous fees and costs expended by the plaintiff. And don't forget the time and inconvenience. For what? Nothing but a puny $15,000.

Winning or losing is just a matter of point of view. Does a country win a war in which thousands of persons have been killed or wounded and untold property losses were sustained? Is it the criterion that the other side lost even more in people and property? It seems so.

Your job in explaining the result to your client is to put the relationship of facts and events in proper perspective. It is not for you to lie, but to interpret things in the light of what functions an attorney can or cannot perform. And, within that scope, you've done a superlative job.

What you have done, and all that any attorney, regardless of talent and experience, possibly could have done, is to manage the facts and circumstances in the best possible manner.

So often, we lawyers berate ourselves for our losses or meager wins. We think of the famous legal giants, winners of important civil rights cases, abortion rights cases, gender and other sex discrimination suits, sex harassment and date-rape cases.

We lament our bad luck at missing out on national moments, such as the lawyers who handled Miranda and other landmark escape hatches. Why have such comets escaped us? What's wrong with us?

Nothing. All that stands between us and national prominence is chance. None of those cases were won because of superior legal skills. The most important civil rights cases were won not by the legal advocate but by the Supreme Court composition at the time the cases were selected for review.

Earl Warren, Chief Justice of the United States Supreme Court, was a dedicated Republican as Governor of the State of California. When he was seated on the Court, his true biases and prejudices surfaced. He was a Republican only nominally. His true point of view was that of a liberal Democrat. This much is clearly seen in his written opinions.

When were the "blacklist" defendants exonerated? Their days in the sun came only after Senator McCarthy and his group were run out of power. The climate changed in the courts when it became politically fashionable for that change.

Any lawyer, you or I or any other lawyer, facing the courts at those crucial times would have won these startling victories. Sure, one needs the basic skills. We have those. But it's not the craftsmanship or rhetoric that brings those results about. It's the time and the place and the event searching for the lucky lawyer to herald the cause. The rest is in the bank.

Sometimes we need more than simple, superficial reasoning to give our client. Sometimes, after the smoke clears away and emotions subside, a secondary plan of attack is warranted.

"We wuz robbed."

Breathes there a loser with soul so dead, who never to himself hath said, "We wuz robbed." An adverse judgment is a bitter pill for both the litigant and counsel to swallow, regardless of the above rationale.

After a hard fought trial, knowing all the while that the facts, or the law, or both, are on your side, it is difficult for you to accept anything less than a sterling result.

There is an old photographers' adage which goes: "If the picture looks bad, blow it up. If it still looks bad, soften it. If it still looks bad, tint it. If it still looks bad, use an ornate frame. If it still looks bad, offer it as a work of contemporary art."

The "lawyers' lament" may be similarly expressed: "If a trial is lost, move for a new trial. If this is denied, appeal. If the judgment is affirmed, petition for rehearing. If this is denied, petition to the next highest court for hearing. If this is denied, petition even further for a stay of execution or for a remittitur. If these are denied, apply to the United States Supreme Court for a writ of certiorari. If all is denied, write a law review article on the injustices in our judiciary system and the need for reform."

All of the above may be condensed into the venerable military defiance, "Surrender? Hell!" The creaking "remedy route" after judgment is jammed with sore losers whose only virtue is stubborn tenacity. A stubborn lawyer finds it difficult enough to admit failure to himself, much less to a client. Napoleon's admonition, loosely translated as "discretion is the better part of valor," is not within the portfolio of the stubborn lawyer.

Appeal.

Sometimes, however, the opposite may be true. It may be that a "prudent advance" is the path of choice, even though it is directly into discouraging odds. There are occasions when the steep uphill appellate climb must be taken, even when hope of reversal may be slight.

These are options which may, or may not, be open for selection. Those decisions transcend the scope of this book. For when you've advanced for enough to be cogitating on such extreme remedies, you'll be past finding your answers within these pages.

Chapter 14

Ethics Traps and Pitfalls for Solo Lawyers

§ 14:1 Generally

I have never figured this out. Law students generally dislike Legal Ethics to the point of supplanting class studies and assignments with canned materials. Just as mysteriously, many law schools appear to grade more liberally in this subject than in others.

My information also is that more bar candidates score lower in Legal Ethics questions than in other parts of the bar exam. Why are these things so?

If there is any bar subject more worthy of full study and learning than Legal Ethics I don't know what it is. The subject matter isn't just common sense or logic. Nor is it the kind of material that can be successfully learned from canned briefs.

Successful bar candidates aren't told of the various grades received in their papers. This may be a disservice to the public as well as to the candidate. He/She is admitted to the practice of law in many instances with a toxic deficiency in a highly important subject.

This is not "blissful ignorance." It is an appalling condition that sometimes results in severe harm to both lawyer and client.

The fault lies mostly with the law schools that fail not only in giving this subject the credit deserved but in perpetuating the short shrift given it by students.

You should be alerted to certain ethics issues that apply especially to solo attorneys. Forewarned is forearmed, but don't confuse forewarning with foreboding. None of those things need alarm you, but they should concern you.

Think of this subject as a sort of honor test. Consider ethics as a barricade. No one is there in control. It's just a road block on a lonely, semi-deserted road. It's easy to go around or hop over. Chances are you won't be seen doing it.

You have the power to commingle, or even misappropriate clients' funds or violate any of the hundreds of rules on ethics. No one will punish you unless your conduct is reported. Will the offending conduct be reported?

A marked tendency toward exposure appears these days in most legislatures and courts. Your client has an indeterminate time period in which to complain in many jurisdictions.

Legal ethics often involves a weighing process. On one side, the best interests of the client. On the other side, the lawyer's self-interests. When and where does that division become an ethics violation?

Self-justification often obscures the weight shift. Sometimes it results from the lawyer's ignorance of legal ethics. A significant number of violations occur simply because of the lawyer's indifference or belief in immunity from detection.

There is no way for any attorney to practice law and avoid all of the pitfalls and traps. Sooner or later, each lawyer finds himself or herself face-to-face with their own private moment of truth. The weighing process measures not just the challenge, but the lawyer's fiber and mettle as well.

§ 14:2 Fees: A hotspot for ethics violations and discipline

There's an old joke (not so funny) about a lawyer entering heaven. He was immediately surrounded by awestruck angels. Intrigued by this special attention, he asked St. Peter the reason for it. St. Peter said, "Why Mr. Jones, it's your age. You are the oldest person ever to pass the Pearly Gates."

Jones looked perplexed. "My age? There must be some mistake, I was only 65." "Nonsense," exclaimed St. Peter. "You were older than Methuselah. We know this because we checked your time sheets."

Lawyers traditionally have believed that the size of their fees was within their own discretion and cannot be subject to review.

Whatever an attorney chooses to charge per hour is indeed left to his or her own judgment. However, as in the case of Lawyer Jones, one cannot charge for more than 24 hours in a day regardless of the amount charged per hour.

A San Francisco attorney was disbarred for charging for more than 24 hours on some days and for more than 100 hours per day "on a substantial number of days." He had also billed for unperformed work. Adding to this attorney's discomfiture, he was sued civilly, losing a verdict of $286,024 plus $41,000 in costs.

It's difficult to know what time periods may be reasonably expended to accomplish specific tasks. Each attorney has his or her own method of research and extrapolating material needed for particular project. Unless the charge suffers from outrageous comparative disproportion, the Courts will usually not go behind the attorney's contentions of time spent.

But there are objective factors to reveal false charges. In the San Francisco case, that attorney's own time sheets betrayed him. While Lawyer Jones' time sheets may have been a joke, there is the proverbial truth spoken in jest.

These are obvious evidentiary facts leading to discipline. But don't be overly sanguine about being impervious to indictments for less overt overcharging claims. Charge what you like per hour but give a fair accounting of your work and charge only for work you do.

§ 14:3 Particular ethics concerns for solo lawyers

There is a disproportionately high percentage of solo lawyers included in "Discipline Reports." More than ever, you recognize names, maybe law school buddies or lawyer colleagues, among those chastised. Some of them are suspended from practice or even disbarred.

Why is this? Are there greater pressures on solo lawyers due to increasing competition? Is the practice developing faster than the capabilities of the lawyer to cope? Frustrations can develop out of a greater work load with less net income because of organizational incompatibility.

These problems, plus others, can be attributed to the lack of management and/or ethics training. Not always. Sometimes the problem is not a deficiency in course material but the level of understanding that each professor hopes will be radiated to every student.

§ 14:4 Some probable precursors of ethics problems

My observations in teaching law school classes have convinced me that most law students view law practice as a means of doing something worthwhile. This differs somewhat from my observations of practicing lawyers.

Disillusionment with the courts, clients and other attorneys, as well as with the realities of making a living from the practice, dims the noble enterprise. Expedience and need gradually displaces altruism. To a large extent, this is natural and indeed even laudatory. We cannot live in a dream world while trying to function in real life.

I have found that only limited success may be achieved in teaching Legal Ethics as a law school class. Law students are simply not ready to accept the idea that temptations can alter their convictions. Theoretical exercises just cannot simulate a real-life scenario of challenge, temptation, trepidation, and the thousand natural shocks that the lawyer is heir to.

The same may be said for law office and management courses. It is not just happenstance that law schools cannot adequately prepare the student for the rocky roads ahead. What do poets and theorists care about the mundanities of paying bills, profits and losses?

The best legal education and practical training cannot duplicate the conditions and challenges of actual practice necessary as a foundational training ground.

Former President Richard Nixon could have gotten an "A" in Legal Ethics. However he may have excelled in that course would have no bearing on conduct in the real world.

Everyone, including Mr. Nixon, finally understands the difference between ethical and unethical behavior after having finally been taken to task. Everyone believes he or she knows the difference between right and wrong. Very few lawyers would wish to do wrong. Still, wrongs are committed by otherwise ethical attorneys every minute of every day.

Alas, even a thorough understanding of that difference cannot protect lawyers from the ethics traps sprinkled throughout law practice. We all need that understanding, plus specific knowledge of the Rules of Professional Conduct, AND persistence of that rigid determination to follow the rules that we held as law students.

Does our innate understanding of right and wrong protect us from commingling clients' funds? You say "yes"? Well, how about depositing an insurance company draft for a P.I. settlement into our general account, with good-faith distribution to the doctors, hospitals, ambulance company and our correctly-computed fee to ourselves?

Oh, you know that's wrong. How did you know that? Did your teaching in Legal Ethics have anything to do with that knowledge? Is there anything fundamental about the keeping of a client trust account?

What's "wrong" with joining a client in an investment, or investing time or money in a client's business? Why is it "wrong" if it is, to include in an Attorney-Client Agreement, an exculpatory clause covering your negligence in representing the client?

Is it fundamentally "wrong" to represent two opposing parties when all you wish to accomplish is a fair result for both parties? These rules of ethics are black letter. Still, would we have an inkling of them without the fortuitous learning in preparation for the bar exam?

Still, one wonders, what of those few hundred other rules that we haven't learned or haven't been included in law school test or bar review courses. Few law students, let alone lawyers, could pass a comprehensive exam in Legal Ethics, covering all rules.

Then, there are hundreds of other rules which have not been inculcated into our mental inventories that lurk in the practice peripheries to trap us. What is our protection from those? The obvious answer is training and education, of course.

Training and education, yes. But remember Richard Nixon's "A" in Legal Ethics.

Dishonesty in lawyers and judges.

It's easy to recognize dishonesty in one who takes money or things in exchange for violating a legal oath. Lawyers and judges are sworn to uphold the law, as well as the canons of ethics.

A lawyer or judge who receives money or thing of value to disregard that oath is not only guilty of an ethics violation but also a number of statutory crimes. That is not a difficult concept, and most lawyers and judges understand the principle, whether or not it guides them.

What may not always be recognized as an ethics violation is an act in response to persuasions other than direct reward. Certain influences, under special circumstances, can produce forces in some people causing confusion and corruption of their judgmental processes.

For instance, desire to please another can motivate unethical conduct. Other situations could lead to conduct beyond one's normal behavioral restraints.

It's easy for the remote observer to say: "What an awful thing to do. I would never have done such a dastardly thing." These thoughts, I'm sure, were shared by a great many people reviewing the actions of the White House Watergate group.

Yet, how can one be certain that they would not do things in service to the President of the United States that they otherwise wouldn't do? Most people could sincerely make such a declaration. Easy to say if one is not in that situation.

Who knows what you might, or might not, do when thrust into unique and compelling circumstances. It is important to know that as an inexperienced person one cannot fully appreciate all potential possibilities.

Hypothetical information may be fun for parlor room debates. But unless you've been there and felt the forces, how can any decision really be an informed one. What acts might we commit for the safety of a loved one, for instance?

The solo lawyer is the solo guardian of his or her conscience. The employee has superiors and others in the office to keep the guidelines. It's easy to drift out of line. It's quite difficult to find one's way back.

These thoughts are expressed merely to alert you to some suggestions that may not, and probably would not, have occurred to you. I have found that very few solo lawyers subjected to discipline would have placed themselves in such positions had it not been for such unforeseen forces.

§ 14:5 The solo lawyer has a special vulnerability

Being a solo or small office practitioner, you have a special problem. You don't have the necessary help to operate a personnel system to avoid violation of rules. You can and should have an effective, automated rules protection system. But you must set it up, you must operate it, and you must proctor it. We'll go further into that in just a bit.

Is a fee split expected when a case is referred to you?

Normally, when a case is referred, the referring attorney expects a percentage of the proceeds. There are two usual exceptions: when the referring attorney expressly waives participation, and when the referrer is your regular assigning lawyer. This doesn't mean that he or she would not be entitled to participate in the proceeds.

This isn't documented, nor can the percentage of demands for fee splits even be approximated. During the years since I first taught this subject in 1973, my research and interviews have revealed only rare instances of such demands. Normally, this happens when the new lawyer has been practicing for awhile and appears to be in reasonably solid financial shape.

For a number of reasons, you hold a preferential position. The assigning lawyer wants your loyalty. You are doing some important work for him or her at substandard fees. There is a reciprocity that comes with this relationship. The referrals are given as part of that operational cycle. Perhaps more to the point is that the new lawyers are, more or less, "mother henned" by the veteran attorneys.

Are fee splits legal even if the referring lawyer does no work?

Ethics rules vary in the states, but generally, and in California, the answer is yes. This is based upon the built-in liability of the referrer for "negligent referral." Since the referring lawyer bears that burden, the fee split is warranted, even though that lawyer does nothing but refer the client.

There's more to consider. The client must be totally informed, and must approve, of the fee division and the fee must not be increased as a result of the fee split. Other requirements must be met and anyone considering such an arrangement should review the professional responsibility laws of your state.

Are large firms disciplined less than solos because of "special privilege"?

Are large firms less likely to be disciplined than solo or smaller firms because of some "special privilege"? This kind of claim is not new but it appears to have gathered more steam recently. This is possibly the result of greater activity by the disciplinary bodies responding to the accelerated public antipathy toward lawyers in general.

The claimants cite a disproportionately larger number of solos being disciplined than lawyers in large firms. The charge is that fewer large firm members are disciplined because of a "special privilege" shared by the larger firms. The rationale is that the large firms contribute more money to bar associations. It's also claimed that complexities of larger firm complaints would be too expensive and time consuming to administer.

A summary investigation of the ratios of large and small firms and respective disciplinary proceedings does not reveal any unexplained substantial disproportion. Even had the investigation revealed such disproportion, this would not necessarily support a charge of favoritism.

There are multifarious reasons for a larger number of solo lawyers being investigated over members of large firms. It matters little that others may enjoy some advantages over you. We never say "never" but sheer favoritism is rarely the case.

The important thing is that your practice be protected and well maintained. Those who point the finger somewhere else when they bear the guilt are sufferers from a form of paranoia. No one but you is responsible for your problems.

§ 14:6 More common causes of unethical conduct: PREJUDICE!

An educated guess, because of the lack of any controlled studies, is that an average of at least 30% of attorneys' efficiency is wasted because of the intrusion of various forms of prejudice. Not all kinds of prejudices are so harmful, but certain harmful ones do seep through our defenses to cause disruption of our thought processes and conduct.

To deny that one is prejudiced is like an alcoholic denying that affliction. We all suffer from our own prejudices of various kinds and degrees. Some are relatively innocuous, as in political, religious, foods, fads and other such tenacious beliefs. Other forms of prejudice range from inconvenient to downright virulent.

We cannot make our prejudices go away by simply denying their existence. The first step in combating this disease is to accept that we are infected. The second step is to deal with those prejudices that interfere with our career progress and even our personal happiness.

Some male lawyers, usually insecure in their own competence, will find any target for blame. Women are often singled out. No matter what kind, or how appropriate the proceeding, the frustrated male will often divert the process toward personal confrontations.

There are female lawyers who suffer from similar prejudices. She will view most male lawyers as "chauvinists." Regardless of the nature of her opponent's position, whatever is said or done may be taken as directed toward her sex rather than any other possible motivation.

Some men will view female judges as their enemies upon entering the courtroom. When the issue is decided in his favor, he will congratulate himself upon his "superior" handling of the matter. The immovably prejudiced male will not recognize the female as a fair and impartial jurist.

The embittered, acerbic male lawyer will accuse a governor who appoints a woman to the bench of being a "panderer" to votes, totally disregarding the candidate's outstanding legal qualifications. The term "lady lawyer," although used less and less frequently, is an ill-disguised epithet of prejudice.

The same unreasoning bigotry applies to African-American lawyers, Mexican-American lawyers, Jewish lawyers and lawyers of other extractions. Sometimes the bigoted comments are voiced in paradoxical complimentary guises, such as, Jewish attorneys are "clever," or black lawyers are best for cases against black opponents.

Such stereotypical attitudes are more widespread than might be believed of educated professionals. Even more confounding is the wide range of age, cultures, education, and even supposed wisdom of the offenders. Prejudices know no bounds.

The backhanded "compliments" may not seem particularly hurtful to the stereotyped lawyer. But these generalizations are in fact toxic. They feed the noxious prejudices, ultimately hurtful to everyone, including the speaker. Prejudices clutter up the mind with nonproductive exercises.

Solo lawyers, especially new solo lawyers, cannot afford unproductive efforts. Time wasted on concern for the race, gender, religion or other classification of an opposing attorney, judge, or litigant can dilute the lawyer's effectiveness.

When something is said or done by your opponent that seems typical of his or her race, religion or gender, tear that thought from your mind. Rip it out! Not only is it false, it is destructive to your case to think this way.

Try to maintain your sense of humor at all times. Remember what was said of a sense of humor in the book. The test of a sense of humor is not whether you understand jokes, but whether you can laugh at a joke on you. A better test is whether you can treat an affront as a joke and laugh at that.

Most female lawyers are simply trying their best to do their job, and not out to prove they're better attorneys than men are. The male lawyer who entertains such prejudices loses the point. The opposing female lawyer won't need to prove anything. She is the better lawyer. Most lawyers, male and female, generally do not accept nor react to these stereotypes. Governors, in raising the appointment percentages of minority judges, have been accused by some vitriolic, prejudiced lawyers, of political chicanery, and even of attempting to scuttle the judiciary.

Judges are appointed (or elected), have always been appointed, and always will be appointed for many reasons other than being the best qualified to occupy the bench. I do not believe that judges give bench seats to undermine the courts. To be sure, there are judges who have won their appointments because of political favoritism. My research hasn't shown a preponderance of minority appointees in this category.

It is necessary to integrate the judiciary, just as with all sectors of population, to better effectuate equal protection and representation. It would be just as toxic to raise the level of judicial incompetence as to systematically suppress judicial appointments to members of any race, religion or sex. It should be presumed that all appointments are made of qualified candidates even though certain groups are given priorities to rectify past inequalities.

When you appear in court, try to wipe your mind of thoughts that are not helpful to your case. Lamentations of any kind whether directed to, or concerning, the judge, your opposing counsel or any other invariable, cannot help your case.

The practice of law, like the practice of life itself, is to work with the luck of the draw. In as many cases as not, you'll find your luck will hold. Assume the posture of color blindness, asexuality, secularism, and total aloofness to everything but the law and relevant facts of the matter.

Our main concern is your legal professionalism and career success. However, you would profit even more to carry this anti-prejudice philosophy into your personal life as well. Prejudices can corrupt the mind, diminishing its ability to think productively in social activities as well as in business.

It isn't necessary, or reasonable, to expect that you will accept the wrongfulness of your prejudices, harmful or otherwise. Try rather to contain them. Isn't it your main purpose to realize your highest law practice potential? Though I suspect that once you adopt this philosophy you'll see the virtues in focusing on goals without untoward diversions of any kind.

§ 14:7 Zealous representation vs. unethical conduct

A perplexing dilemma: when does zealous representation of a client cross over and become a violation of the Rules of Professional Conduct? Too often, lawyers mistake malfeasance for diligent effort.

Sometimes the crossover is not so praiseworthy. The adversarial instinct to win may overwhelm the rectitude of conscience. Even more egregious is the trade of ethics for money.

Motive isn't an issue. It may be a given that the questionable conduct was pursued through client loyalty. Only the innermost core of conscience will know the core reason for violation. How far will client zeal take a lawyer in Bar Disciplinary proceedings? Excessive client concern covers a multitude of sins, but far short of exculpation when a rule is willfully and intentionally violated.

The Eric and Lyle Menendez, Beverly Hills, California case demonstrates an interesting ethics issue. A psychiatrist's notes taken while interviewing Eric were used in his testimony as an expert. Those notes differed materially from the copy of notes provided to the prosecution. When confronted by the prosecutor, the expert stated that he was instructed by Eric's attorney to omit some note entries. Some of those deleted statements appeared to indicate premeditation in the murders of the Menendez parents. Eric's attorney denied the accusation but refused to discuss details. If true, would this have been a case of zeal for the client or for the love of winning?

It could be that it's all a big mistake. However, the scenario makes for an interesting study project. Tampering with evidence, subornation of perjury, fraud upon the court, and a number of other potential charges could possibly be filed against a lawyer whose conduct crosses into such territory.

§ 14:8 The three strikes rule: A fertile opportunity or a sand trap?

At first glance, the idea that a prospective client, second or third striker, faces life imprisonment seems like a fee bonanza. That client will be forced to defend in court, since a cop-out would be a forfeiture to a life sentence. Hence, the case which would otherwise be for a minor felony, now takes on the parameters of a capital offense defense.

Does this augur for a big fee? Perhaps, provided your client is O.J. Simpson or otherwise handy with money. Alas! That's not the bedraggled, pathetic creature who waltzes into your office. Time was that Criminal Defense Appointment Panels in many states would cover fees for your time at livable, if not royal compensation.

Not now. Most states, with strapped county treasuries, are too pressed with other financial drains to give you such a blank check, even at those older, marginal rates. For many reasons, including the over-burgeoning prison populations, there has been increasing resistance to the three strikes rule.

You've taken the case. This time around, the charge is a relatively minor one but one that counts as a "third strike." Can you punt? You could be on for the duration. What's more, you'd better not fumble. The consequence, and your responsibility, are multiplied by its third place position.

Such forces are not always from outside influences. An act or reaction motivated by prejudice or some personal concern can be as unethical as one which is compensated with some form of payment. The only difference is the available proof of motivation. State of mind or emotion is not visible as is receiving money or money's worth.

Unethical conduct, whether through bias, prejudice, religious faith, race, gender, social standing, sex or sexual orientation, or whatever, can be as serious a violation as taking money to accomplish that end.

A judge who may act prejudiciously because of tendencies toward business, or labor, or plaintiffs or defendants, or any other ideas, is just as guilty of violating that oath as the judge who takes money for the court's ruling.

I was once privy to a judge's declaration, concerning a certain business association, that, "if it wasn't right the (blank) business association wouldn't have done it." Having said that to "justify the order," the judge ruled for the association.

§ 14:9 Alcohol, drug abuse and ethical failures

Somewhere near the top of the list of things we know so little about is whether we, each of us, is a candidate for alcohol or drug abuse. Who but a self-resolved alcoholic, or a recovered drug addict, will admit that he or she cannot control alcohol or drug use?

How many who have been involved in alcohol or drug related incidents, causing arrest, injury or even death, were aware of intoxication at that time? How many ascribe the incident to happenstance, bad luck, overzealous police action, or some force other than that person's fault?

Consider the following situation: You're at a party and have had some drinks, but no more than you can handle. You feel perfectly able to drive your car, though you recognize that you're "feeling good."

You get behind the wheel and note that you are fully aware of the speedometer and all other instruments. You take stock of yourself and your reflexes. You conclude that you are in complete control. You start your drive home.

Oh, oh! You see the red light behind you. Well, you don't know what you did, but you know it has nothing to do with being drunk. The police officer calls your attention to the boulevard stop you drove through.

You remember that stop sign. You've driven through it before, several times when you've had nothing to drink. That sign is partially covered by shrubs. You explain that to the officer. He calls your attention to the prior sign warning of the stop.

The officer detects some odor of alcohol. He asks you to step out of the car. After a field sobriety test, the officer concludes that you should blow. You do and your blood alcohol hovers just around the minimum legal reading for intoxication.

You were correct about your ability to operate your car. You were fully aware of all your actions and your reflexes at all times. You were certainly not an unsafe driver. Yet, you are going to be prosecuted for drunk driving.

You know that the same thing could have happened to you without having had a single drink. In fact, it has happened at that very intersection.

After you have been bailed out of jail, you return to that intersection and start preparations for your defense. You take pictures of the shrubbery and the other approach problems. You prepare a full scale exhibit book for your trial defense. You are confident that you will win. The lawyer you've retained agrees with you.

You lose. You are convicted of drunk driving.

You know all about the difference between self-appraisal of intoxication and the physical impairment to reflexes and perception caused by alcohol. But you are certain that you were able to drive your car competently that night.

You don't care about the volumes of scientific support for such impairment at the legal reading limit. You know that despite that reading, you were not drunk. You paid your fine and did your penance, whatever the judge imposed, because you were found legally intoxicated. But, you know you were not drunk.

Now, relate the above set of facts to your law practice. You take a few drinks at lunch, not every day, but from time to time. During court days, you always do. Who doesn't? After all, you've got to have something to smooth out the ripples.

You may, perhaps, take a hit or two on a joint. Well, why not? There's no hard evidence that grass ever really harms anyone. They even use it medicinally, don't they?

You have tried a line or two of coke here and there. You know that could be a problem if you don't watch it. You're too clever for that. Besides, you only do that on very rare occasions.

You'll never know that your "few drinks," or "hit or two" or "line or two," affected your judgment and may have contributed to the loss of that court case. The failure to timely object, the document that somehow did not get offered into evidence, and other things that just may have slipped your mind, didn't help.

You'll never know, because you won't let yourself know. Being a solo lawyer, you have no one in your office to offer any suggestions about your capacity. You're your own boss. You can do, drink, pop, smoke or snort anything you wish, anytime.

A law practice is a pressure job. The responsibilities you assume with each case can cumulatively build up and create great stress in some people.

This can result in emotional problems with a wide variety of syndromes. If you are the type to buckle under to this kind of pressure, you should give much thought to some other field of work.

This is a very complex subject, and I am neither a psychiatrist nor psychologist. However, I have followed several students and readers of my books into and through their practices. I have also had many occasions to observe other young lawyers in their battles with these pressures.

I do not pretend to know which of these young people will collapse under practice strain. But I have seen early signs of incapabilities which would lead to such troubles.

Not the least of such incapabilities relates to a poorly-organized law office and practice. Put another way, I have never seen an attorney in serious trouble, either with substance abuse or ethics violations, whose office and practice are well organized.

Nor have I seen a lawyer who starts with an orderly office and practice later become disorganized and fall into such serious trouble. I suppose there are types who are so susceptible to booze and drugs and other failings that no amount of order and organization to the office and practice can save them. But I don't believe that.

In my opinion, someone who cannot control alcohol or narcotics would never get organized in the first place. This is because proper organization of a law office and practice is not a spontaneous act; it is an ongoing duty. To set up your shop properly and then let it fall to pieces is not to organize it.

Just like alcoholism and drug abuse are diseases, so is management and organization a disease. Once you are a chronic manager and organizer, you are as hooked with that burden just as the drunk and junkie are with theirs. You must just decide which of these is your poison.

This chapter will tip you off to some of the practice pitfalls which dog the progress of many solo practitioners. But, it isn't an automated mechanism toward good law practice management. You are the mechanizer. You must institute scrupulous office and practice management systems.

Whether or not practice follies and foibles will lead to bar discipline, they are likely to contribute to a lawyer's frustrations, self-doubts and possible alcoholism, or worse, if they are not controlled.

I want you to succeed as a solo lawyer, but not at the expense of your mental, emotional or physical well-being. Anxieties, confusions, depression, and other emotional disturbances arising from inadequate practice control, can, and often will, degenerate into even more toxic syndromes that can ultimately lead to one or another form of escapism.

Alcoholism and drug abuse are not uncommon results of

escalating practice problems. My research in such matters has led to examples of serious physical disorders and even suicide attempts. Very few attorneys can view the problems of their clients objectively.

Most of us, whether consciously or otherwise, assume part of the emotional distress of our clients when faced with difficult legal pressures. In some instances, our suffering may even be greater than that of our clients. Perhaps that is the *simpatico* which makes for a better all-around attorney.

Some will say to leave your problems and your clients' problems at the office. That is easy to say but, for some of us, very hard to do. Some believe that to feel the pain stimulates the fibers for better advocacy.

Feeling for your client is fine, so long as that feeling is mobilized into meaningful and ethical action, and so long as the feeling is kept within reasonable bounds. How is that done? To start with, the ability to take action from the pain depends upon a developed competence to keep your pathways open toward that action.

If none of these caveats have meaning for you, it may be due to your impregnable moral fiber. Or, it may be that you just haven't grappled with the concept.

It just can't happen to you? How can you really know what you would, or would not, do when placed in a predicament that you may never have even contemplated?

Think about some of these scenarios:

Perhaps you've smoked cigarettes, or other funny things, but you'd disdain narcotics?

Perhaps you do take some wine, beer or other form of alcohol now and then, but you'd never become an alcoholic?

Perhaps you might enjoy being asked to serve in some capacity at the behest of the United States President, but you could never be influenced by the President to act in any way unethically?

Perhaps you've never had all the money it takes for everything you want, but you'd never let money lure you into an ethics trap?

Perhaps you can appreciate the loyalty of a friend, but no obligation of that kind could detour you from the straight and narrow ethical path?

Doing a favor for a relative or friend is just not your style if it means even the tiniest ethics breach, right?

No matter what the compulsion, be it love, hate, sympathy, altruism, or whatever, you are made of iron. Aren't you?

§ 14:10 Keep your clients informed

If you read the Discipline Reports, usually distributed by your bar association, you will notice an oft repeated condemnation cited, "failed to keep clients informed." Of the many variations of lawyers' offenses, this seems to find its way into most of the reports.

Although this is not the transgression which triggered the charge, it is usually at the core, or the seed, of the ultimate malfeasance.

No one likes to admit mistakes, particularly when it involves a failure in discharging a duty. So, if a mistake is made, after having ignored the client for a lengthy time, the misdeed is magnified.

The worst scenario is to cover up a mistake and then have it compounded with the series of errors which will usually follow. Most people are understanding of human foibles. And, contrary to the belief of some lawyers, clients are people.

In any event, start the ritualistic process of making an extra copy of anything and everything that goes through your office concerning each of your clients. Mailing or faxing each of those copies to the client will dispel a multitude of possible ills.

If you want to show double faith, mail the copy after having faxed it (I don't always go that far for every client, but it's a good idea). If you do not mail a follow-up, type the words, in bold caps, **SENT BY FAX** at the head of the letter, and type the date and time of transmission.

That is a great start, but it's not enough. You must also write an "update" letter to each client explaining what is happening. In fact, where you fax or mail something that may not be self-explanatory, you should send a cover letter explaining it.

Doing these things will so ingratiate yourself with your client that when, as and if some error does occur, you can rely upon some bit of sympathy from him or her, if not complete absolution. This is not a guarantee, but the statistics are on your side. Regardless, it is something you should do, and your case files will look better to any tribunal considering the matter.

§ 14:11 Why me, the solo practitioner?

I have been asked many times for the reason that so many solo lawyers are disciplined, sometimes even disbarred. The fundamental reasons for these calamities are:

1. **Solos are often not properly trained in office and case management.**

2. **Priorities of solos are sometimes misscheduled or vague.**

3. **Solos sometimes fail to recognize their time limitations and are overworked.**

4. **Some lawyers (both employees and solos) cannot judge when a job is done.**

5. **The solo may just not be solo material.**

Sometimes, all of the above.

DOES IT HAVE TO HAPPEN TO YOU? NO! IT DOES NOT AND SHOULD NOT.

All you need are a few basic facts that are easy to understand and just as easy to put into operation.

I am proud of the many thousands of new lawyers who were introduced to solo practice through my books, classes, lectures and general advice. I am proud of their fine records of success, but mostly of their avoidance of the ethics pitfalls. I am just as proud, even more so, when I meet some of them in court and they pin my ears back. Well, they had a good teacher.

Some lawyers were born for trouble.

There are some people, and unfortunately a few of them become lawyers, who can't stay straight. You find them in practically every field, business and profession.

Even the loftiest position isn't enough for these rebels. Presidents, Supreme Court Justices, Congressmen, Senators, you name it, utilize their gilded offices to corrupt their sacred trusts.

Millionaires, yes, even billionaires, still find it necessary to cheat, steal, falsify and otherwise defraud gullible victims. They go to jail, pay huge fines and are publicly disgraced. One would expect that these examples might enlighten others on the price of such folly. Not at all.

Still they come. Younger, "smarter" politicians, CEO's, and yes, lawyers, believing they can beat the odds. They never learn. I would even doubt that those who were caught and paid the price really learned much of anything.

I believe that such persons are never really sorry for what they've done, but I'm sure they're very sorry to be in jail. I don't think they even mind paying the millions of dollars in fines. I believe they are convinced they can make it all back when they get out of jail by repeating their crimes.

Obviously, for such lawyers, solo practice would be like catnip to a cat. In employment, those attorneys would at least have some restraint through the company hierarchy. This wouldn't stop them from their mischief, but it would slow them down a bit.

I have nothing to say to persons with such bents. The only advice I can give regarding those scumbags is that you take all pains to avoid them. The material in this book on solo practice ethics is directed only to attorneys, like yourself, who want to practice law honestly and ethically.

§ 14:12 Patience is, among other things, a virtue

I guess this comes under the heading, "don't do as I do, do as I say." I've never had much patience. Back in my business days, I could never tolerate an employee's indifference to quickly responding to a ringing telephone.

If a phone rang three times, the one closest to the phone had some explaining to do. I did not want to hear that third ring. I always assumed that the customer was also impatient. I think you should assume the same of your clients.

That aside, patience is a valuable commodity in touching all bases in your practice. This includes the dry, boring details of law office management, as well as the more exciting parts of your practice.

I've never been the subject of a bar association disciplinary report, let alone a malpractice claim. Of course, I'm knocking on wood as I say that. Such a thing can happen to anyone at any time, regardless of the care taken.

There lurks a client out there just waiting to make a claim against me, and you too. It doesn't matter that you and I do nothing wrong. Some clients view anything that, doesn't go their way as malpractice.

But I do take my chores seriously. So should you. I screen my clients carefully and recommend that you do likewise. One can usually tell a troublemaker by the manner in which the case facts are recited to you. A paranoid client will usually spell problems.

I know it's easy for me to say, since my practice is established and yours isn't. It's hard to turn a prospective client away when cash is involved. But, like anything else, tomorrow's problems are best avoided by today's prudence.

Another troublesome area is taking an inadequate fee because the dollars look bigger when your need is greater. You must always keep a watchful eye on the bargained for exchange. The bank deposit may comfort you today, but the morning after can be pretty dismal.

You cannot run your practice on a "bargain day" philosophy. "Distress sales" are fine for retailers. They can even get away with fudging the truth to some extent, but you and I cannot. You must be adequately paid for your work at all times, regardless of when the work is due.

Don't be lured into false comfort because you're being paid now for work that needn't be done for some weeks or even months. Judgment day will come, and you won't like it if you haven't been fully paid. More disturbing is when you have accepted a small fee for something even bigger than you knew.

If you have a sum commensurate with the job in your trust account, your payment (from the trust account into your general account) will be proper compensation. If not, you will be unhappy, or even incapable of retaining the help you need to do the job, for lack of proper funding.

§ 14:13 Practice pressures, inadequate management controls and time

Again, this is a weighing process. On the one side is the amount of practice pressure. On the other side is the adequacy of management controls and available time to do the work.

What are the variables? What is "adequacy" of management controls? What amount of time is "adequate?"

In some cases, the lawyer is a better craftsman at soliciting work and clients than he or she is at doing the work. Sometimes the ability to get work transcends any lawyer's ability to do the work.

Who is the judge of whether the management controls are "adequate?" Of course, you are, but what do you know about law office management as compared with the increasing weight of work load? When do you reach the point of needing help with the work? Here we must add another factor to the scale, "profit."

We agreed that solo practice offers the great opportunity of keeping the fruits of your efforts instead of giving it to some unworthy employer. But, like almost everything else, that opportunity has its limits. Paramount is the need to get the job done for your clients.

This chapter is written for those who might slip off the path for lack of information to prevent it. I have nothing to say to those who know better and will knowingly step into problems.

I no longer am surprised at the ilk of lawyer who finds and courts trouble along the way. Bright young men and women, scholars at law school, high achievers, constitute not a small percentage of the transgressors.

It always surprises me because it makes no sense at all. Why do these highly intelligent, immensely capable people, with everything good in life within their grasps, intentionally pick the road to disaster? "Intentionally," because their intellects would certainly make the choice clear to them.

I do not have the answer, but I know it happens because I see it repeatedly. Is it that their brilliance blinds them to the reality that their conduct is not invisible? Or, is it a game in which the stakes must be high enough to kindle excitement in the face of constant boredom?

Whatever it is, I have no solution to that kind of malevolence. These super-intellects do not need me to point out the silliness of their ways. They've been told by experts, perhaps throughout their lives.

Well, jolly good luck to them for whatever thrills they may find in tweaking the noses of convention and propriety. This is not your way, or you wouldn't be reading this book.

Chapter 15

Professional Liability Insurance

§ 15:1 Generally

Almost from the start, another dilemma hits you. To be insured or not to be insured. That is certainly a question, the answer to which isn't simple. (But I think you know what it is.)

The complications lie in the understanding of errors and omissions. The terms, "malpractice" or "misfeasance," or "errors or omissions," imply carelessness. If one is careful about one's work, why is there a need for insurance?

Every trained airplane pilot knows the importance of a "checklist." Before the props are turned, every detail of the craft is checked in accord with the checklist.

Every move in flight executed by the careful pilot is done according to formal aerodynamic principles. This method leaves virtually no realistic probability of failure.

The airplane pilot is gambling with his/her life. We lawyers are gambling with our personal fortune, reputation and the fortunes, reputation and sometimes even the lives of our clients. Which is the greater gamble?

The pilot has a "checklist." The potential sources of failure in flying are within reason calculable. We lawyers have no such formal list.

Every day malpractice lawsuits occur, charging lawyers with unpredictable errors or omissions. What "t" was uncrossed, what "i" was undotted? How could the lawyer have had foreknowledge of an event that was beyond his/her ken?

The answer is not what you might have predicted but what

actually occurred. The danger is not in what or where the error or omission but what was perceived by the aggrieved client. Serendipity often controls the lawyer's fate, not caution, preparedness or any kind of "checklist."

If no one ever complains about your legal work, the lack of E&O insurance coverage won't hurt you. To some, any insurance is valuable only if the event insured against occurs. To others, the value of insurance is in its peace of mind.

This offers yet another but different kind of dilemma. How much insurance do I need and which ones? Insurance brokers will argue the point, but it's possible to become insurance poor.

So how can I select the right coverage for my particular situation at costs I can afford? This isn't simple to equate. Every person presents different parts of the equation. What are the assets? How far back do the possible events extend? What is the nature of the practice?

There are many other issues, too many to list. One may apply the factor of probabilities to offset premium costs. This permits either lower limits or greater deductibles.

In olden days, when I started practice, insurance premiums were not much of an issue. Premium rates were low and coverage was needed for only a fraction of what is customary now.

During the intervening years, the malpractice insurance picture underwent many changes. The cost of writing insurance by carriers accelerated drastically. Many carriers were not able to handle the claims reserves and had to resort to "re-insurance," meaning to sell off a part of their insured inventory to other carriers.

You don't need to be an attorney to be aware of our present litigious society. The attitude of sue thy neighbor has been with us for several years. What's worse is the unpredictable and uniqueness of modern case theories. Some of these novel ideas were discussed in the preface. More are surfacing daily.

One could never be sure of invulnerability to a malpractice claim even in those less contentious days. Today, an attempt at self-protection through a cautious approach to legal work is about as silly as avoiding auto insurance through "careful" driving.

The only way one can be safe practicing law without insurance is to have no assets to attach. That's only a temporary measure because a judgment is good for ten years. Dedicating your life to being unsuccessful seems a dreary prospect.

For many reasons, including a surge of malpractice claims, the Errors and Omission's (E&O) field became less and less attractive to insurers, and many of them withdrew such coverage. Those companies left offering professional responsibility insurance had to raise premium costs to stay in that business.

Added to the increased costs of claims was a diminution of carriers willing to "re-insure," and a resulting increase in reinsurance costs. The effect of all of this was a dizzying upward spiral in the cost of E & O coverage for lawyers.

The solo lawyer was hit particularly hard, having no basis for spreading coverage costs. Whereas in the early 1970's, adequate coverage premiums were in the low hundreds range, the prices zoomed up to many thousands of dollars for that same coverage. This caused many solo lawyers to simply shrug and go "bare." In many cases, this wasn't an election; it was a financial necessity.

For reasons of their own, the carriers did not see fit to fully disclose the facts causing the premium increases to the legal community. The natural result was a general belief among lawyers that the insurance firms were unduly opportunistic in the rates being charged.

In retrospect, it seems unrealistic that so many insurance companies left a field in which "opportunistic" rates could be charged as a "windfall." But, at that time, most lawyers were not thinking charitably about companies charging those "outrageously high" premiums.

Then, like a knight on a white horse, a new California company was formed. It was hailed as an antidote to the "ogres" which had been "victimizing" the lawyers. It was described as a "lawyers' insurance company." Whether or not it's promotional theme was "lower premiums," that is the purpose believed by many lawyers to be its theme.

That lawyers' insurance company was then generally understood to be a sort of "lawyers' own" insurance company. Its innovation was supposed to be in opposition to the "black-hatted" commercial malpractice insurers.

The idea accepted by the lawyers' community at that time was that soon no coverage would be available at all. Thus, the founding of "our own insurance carrier" engendered an almost patriotic fervor of support.

Had the thinking then been straight, we would have realized that such a foundation could not prove to be a panacea. Ultimately, as should have been predicted, its rates rose to meet, and in some instances, exceed, competition levels.

It wasn't long before that "lawyers" insurance company was viewed by many lawyers as "one of *them*," not one of us, as had been supposed. Profits, losses and other business demands dictate prices, not altruistic ideologies.

Those compulsions forced that company into a posture similar to the "big companies," resulting in higher rates, more stringent controls, seemingly hair-triggered cancellations, and multiple exclusionary provisions.

Beginning in about 1993 to the present, it appears that the pressure has been steadily diminishing. Rates have declined somewhat, and coverage is as easy to get as one may be willing to pay premiums. The correlative of fewer controls, exclusions and cancellations has begun to spread among the carriers, including the "lawyers" insurance company.

Today, a ballpark premium for $100,000/$300,000 coverage with a $2,500 or even less deductible may be had for somewhere between $1,500 and $3,000 annually, depending upon the kind of practice and claims history. This "ballpark," as with all estimates, quotes and approximations in this book, will vary with time, geography, economies and insurers' experiences.

Is this adequate coverage? That is the $64,000 question. What is the claims likelihood? What is the amount of your assets to be covered? Being underinsured can be tantamount to being uninsured. If you have $1,000,000 in assets and only $100,000 in insurance, a $1,000,000 judgment against you could ruin your whole day.

§ 15:2 The "bare" attorney

Many states now require attorneys to disclose whether or not they have E&O coverage in all attorney/client contracts. If your state has such a requirement, check it out thoroughly. This has resulted in some lawyers obtaining insurance at inadequate coverage sums with ridiculously high deductibles just for technical compliance.

Many attorneys are nonetheless going "bare." Some have taken this route imprudently. If the "bare" lawyer has much in personal assets, the exposure can be chilling. There is no real assurance of protection in practice precautions.

Attorney victims of malpractice suits will tell you that calamities are not always telegraphed. They can, and often do, sneak up on you. In most of the instances I have researched, the error or omission was an "out-of-the-blue" surprise to the lawyer.

Claims can, and do, arise from the least anticipated sources and from the most unsuspected clients. I have not seen many cases in which the prospect of a claim would have been that apparent even to the most careful lawyer.

Juries are not overly sympathetic to lawyers accused of client abuses. Neither are many of our judges. Strange, since judges were once lawyers and many will again practice law when retired from the bench.

One reason for the dearth of insurance firms willing to tackle malpractice claims is the sharp rise in lawsuits. People have become litigation-prone. The word spreads. Has anyone offended you? Sue the bastard! Who do we blame? Don't look around, look in the mirror.

New lawyers, with bar card print still wet, will grab the first malpractice case that rears its head. Well, didn't I say to take any case that's offered? So I guess I'm to blame as well. The word "cannibalism" comes to mind. Isn't that where one devours its own species?

But what's wrong with that? The misused client is entitled to a remedy. A difficult point to argue. What's wrong then? If claims are being paid, it must follow that wrongs are being perpetrated.

Still, there are, and always will be, attorneys who strain for "gray" cases. It's difficult to see the motive. In most instances, such cases do not provide paid fees. Scholars and altruistic observers applaud these legal "pioneers" as champions of the downtrodden.

Often the "downtrodden" become the predators spawned by six-figure verdicts, and new "victims" are carved from the groups who used to be labeled "villains." It's getting to be that you have difficulty distinguishing the "victims" from the "villains" these days.

That's the price we pay to maintain the elasticity of the law. New torts are fashioned almost every day. Certain acts that used to be accepted, more or less, as "traits" or the "nature of the beast," are now grievous civil wrongs for which payment must be made. And, the pay is pretty good.

Not so many years ago, a "fender-bender" auto accident was often resolved with a handshake. In some instances $25 or $50 may have changed hands right there at the accident scene, and that was that.

A lawsuit was a last resort, and even then only in very substantial matters. In those days, doctors weren't afraid to stop and help injured persons.

We never carried a key to our house. I wouldn't know what to do with one anyway since our door was never locked. Yet, there were few, if any, burglaries.

Well, that's enough of such reminiscences. I only point these things out to illustrate that the blame can't be focused on one cause only. You cannot cure the problem by refusing to take malpractice claims any more than preventing burglaries by leaving doors unlocked.

While we continue to look for answers and cures, we must protect ourselves. I don't know of any substitute for professional responsibility insurance coverage. Nor can I retread the formulas that I included in this book's prior edition.

The old preferred coverage of the "occurrence" kind is a thing of the past. What used to be the second-class type of insurance, which required that you be covered at the time of the incident as well as at the time of the claim, is now prevalent, at least in California.

Now, the "chip" to bargain for is the "tail" or coverage that persists after policy termination. Some companies will offer this extended coverage only upon retirement. Of course, if you continue in practice, you'll continue to need coverage. The only question is whether you'll want to continue with that same company.

Obviously, the cost of the "tail," as well as its terms, will vary with companies. You'll still see ads offering "money-saving" plans and "new and unique" ones. The trick is to find good coverage with extended protection that will still let you pay your rent and feed the kiddies.

Of course, if you have no assets, and never expect to have any, you won't need to be bothered with such problems. You are a perfect candidate for going "bare." The nasty side of this is that your best-laid plans can often go awry. (CHECK YOUR STATE BAR REQUIREMENTS.)

The worst of all situations is making a premature assessment of your dismal financial holdings. You scoff at the high coverage premiums, and smirk at the fools who pay them. Then, insidiously, like your age, and almost unnoticed, your hard work pays off, and your assets grow and mature.

Funny thing about having financial substance. Before you had it, you didn't need it. You ridiculed the eager beavers who sought it. But once acquired, like dope, you become addicted.

The thought of having to do without all those nice things—your Mercedes, home in the suburbs, country club membership, stock portfolio, antique collection, etc.—is more horrible than any other prospect.

Millionaires have leapt from tall buildings for the loss of the bulk of their fortunes. What was left would probably satisfy you or me. We haven't become accustomed to luxuries at the highest level. They had.

What could be worse than such a thought? Reality. Some little case you'd almost forgotten has surfaced to threaten your comfortable little corner. You are covered now, of course. Heaven forbid, being "bare" with all these luxuries.

That forgotten matter happened before you developed this new concern for financial security. Oh, you were careful back then, but careful wasn't enough then, just as you know it's not now when you're so rich. Well, you know the rest.

So, the question: is there ever a time when you can be absolutely certain that being insured is not necessary? The answer is: certainly, so long as the thing insured against doesn't happen while you're not insured. So, the secret word is clairvoyance.

An inescapable fact is that the practice of law is fraught with hazards. The shortsighted lawyers who sell their services cheap undervalue not only their merchandise but also their contingent responsibilities. Few lawyers really give much thought to setting their fees. $100 per hour sounds good, so that's what they charge.

How many actually analyze the cost breakdown? What percentage of the projected monthly, quarterly, or yearly income, based upon $100 per hour is allocated to the many and varied costs of operating a law office?

What percentage of that projected income would cover the premium cost of a $500,000 professional responsibility insurance policy? Would the cost of doing business be excessive if it included insurance against fees of $100 per hour?

These questions would bewilder many veteran attorneys, so don't feel chagrined if you can't answer them. The answers are dependent upon the volume of business being done.

If your practice consists of ten hours per month at $100 per hour, the answers would reveal that you couldn't afford an office, much less any of the other items which comprise "costs of business."

Most private practitioners simply started doing business without giving any of the logistics much thought. Then, like Topsy, they just "growed."

Items like rent, secretarial, process services, library, office supplies, etc., are unquestioningly understood as unavoidable expenses. But, other items sometimes offer perplexity as to their importance and are often disdained as "needless."

In some instances, these determinations are prudent. But, there are times when decisions are the product of inexperience or even ignorance. It is understandable that a business cost not immediately translatable into dollars earned might be viewed as an unredeeming negative.

It is then that experience, or special insight, might need to be called upon for sound business judgment. When, just a few years ago, professional liability insurance costs went through the roof, the resulting wave of elections to go uninsured was understandable. Understandable, but wrong.

Professional responsibility insurance coverage is as much a legitimate cost of doing business as is rent or any other expense. More so. It is a duty of every lawyer to protect every client with such insurance as well as to protect himself or herself.

Back in the days when the old blanket coverage was available, it was not such a disaster to go unprotected for a period of time. Then, after the attorney had accrued financial assets, such coverage was seen as warranted.

That was a sensible delay because belated coverage could have been obtained with full protection. All that was then necessary was an affidavit that any pre-covered period did not present any potential claims.

Now however, such coverage is available only in very few states. In most states, only the "claims made" type of policies are offered (i.e., only claims that are made during the period of coverage are insured).

The decision to go unprotected at any time can result in deep trouble later on. One can never tell when an event may surface, especially at a vulnerable time, which is rooted in those past, uncovered days. Hence, the decision seemingly sound at that time, might (and almost predictably will) prove less judicious later on.

Whether, when and why are questions intelligently asked. Not everyone needs life insurance. Those who they have no dependents, are wealthy enough to self-insure their dependents, or just don't care about them, don't need life insurance. Auto insurance isn't needed unless you drive a car.

Whether, when and why you should, or should not, be concerned with professional responsibility insurance will be discussed. What kind of policy? How much will it cost? Is it O.K. to go with a "nonadmitted" issuer or insist on one that is fully licensed to transact insurance business within your state?

You know what you want in an automobile, a stereo, a refrigerator, or whatever. These are things you can appreciate. You know what they will do for you and how to evaluate them.

Insurance is another matter. Not really, though. You can easily understand the importance of life insurance if you have a family dependent upon your support. You know how devastating it would be to have a serious auto accident without full auto insurance coverage.

Why is errors and omissions insurance different? Many lawyers eschew the need because they believe themselves to be careful and able to avoid malpractice situations. Others simply do not wish to pay the escalating E & O premiums. Some just don't give it a thought. There are those attorneys who are able, they believe, to be "self-insured."

So, who among lawyers would be justified to "go bare?" Can a "careful" lawyer truly avoid any and all such missteps? Is the "self-insured" lawyer sufficiently informed on the subject?

Are E & O premium payments an intelligent exclusion from operational costs? Should all lawyers give malpractice insurance coverage lots of "thought"?

A preliminary evaluation might be to weigh the potential and probable claims by all clients in your office. Perhaps adding up the total of all such possible claims could be a way to determine whether you can "self-insure." Is that logical? Of course it's logical, but not realistic.

Unless the lawyer is foolish enough to act as his or her own defense attorney, the cost of defense must be integrated into those calculations. How does one evaluate that factor? I don't know how to do that. The way things are these days, the strategy of plaintiffs' lawyers in malpractice cases is unpredictable.

Some lawyers, far too many, behave as though they consider themselves immune from personal liability. This breed seems to consider a bar card as a license to victimize merchants and others who bargain with them in good faith. Why pay the bill when they can avoid it by intimidation.

This same illogical logic is applied to professional liability. There is minimal fear of a malpractice suit for the very reason that the "bare" lawyer is bare. Why would any malpractice attorney attack an uninsured lawyer?

Good thinking? Wrong! Bad, very bad, thinking. More than that, it is converse. A "bare" attorney is a sitting duck. An insured lawyer is not the lush target supposed. Insurance companies have become more and more niggardly and tenaciously defensive.

Any seasoned malpractice litigator will agree that a "pro se" attorney defendant is cold meat before a jury. A lawyer defendant has a two-strike call to start with. Add to this a dramatized version of the lawyer's malfeasance and a hapless, abused client, and you can build the gallows.

Does it matter that there is no "deep pockets" insurance company? Not much. Judgments are good for a long time, and a lawyer's future, however marginal now, has got to be pretty good. To be sure, those lawyers know lots of tricks. Skilled plaintiffs' attorneys know some too.

Besides, who needs perpetually cyclical debtor's examinations and other aggravations. Bankruptcy is an even bigger nuisance, and a bore. It's definitely not a good alternative to E & O coverage.

Even though it's painful to pay substantial sums each year for protection that you may never need, you should have it. Besides, "never need" is really a side-door oxymoron. You need that protection for its own sake.

I promise you that you will find yourself staring at the ceiling all night, many nights, contemplating disaster, if you go without coverage. Get covered and sleep.

§ 15:3 How to obtain E & O coverage without a rich uncle

First, try to include coverage participation in your "time-for-space" agreement. Certainly, you should be covered for assignment work done. Negotiate for coverage extension to your other work to make certain of this.

Canvass all of the agents for available E & O carriers. Your local bar associations will have recommendations, and many have affiliations with such carriers. You'll find a surprisingly large variation in premiums among the companies.

§ 15:4 Enter the "nonadmitted" carrier

One of the prominent reasons for lower prices will be "nonadmitted" carriers. What does that mean? It simply means that the insurance company has either not applied for or has not been accepted by the state insurance administrative agency which proctors insurance practices.

Does that mean that the company is no good and will not properly insure you? Not at all. There are a variety of reasons, many of them political, that an "offshore" insurance firm may, or may not, wish to write policies within a given state as an "admitted carrier." To be sure, a reason for noncompliance could relate to its unreliability.

Whether a company is admitted or nonadmitted to your state should not be the sole deciding factor in your selection. However, you should investigate the reasons for its not being admitted carefully. Is it a failure to meet substantive requirements or a matter of superficial noncompliance?

The significant element in a substantive problem is the company's inability to meet the state's capital minimum. If that is the problem, look elsewhere.

Even if the carrier does meet that requisite, you should look into what kind of assets are pledged. If it consists only of real property, you should investigate its other assets. You must be sure of adequate financing to meet all reasonable potential losses.

Being admitted is no guarantee that the company will be financially able to cover losses. You should also know something of that company's track record in handling claims.

§ 15:5 Are there still some of those "off-shore," E & O, "nonadmitted" carriers out there?

Is there still a choice for either nonadmitted vs. admitted carriers?

There are more changes in California, and in certain other states, involving the "bargain" E & O nonadmitted insurance carriers. All of those changes have increased the negatives against non-CIGA companies. More and more, attorneys seeking protection from client threats for misfeasance, nonfeasance or other claims, real or imaginary, find instead evaporated ex-E & O carriers.

Unlike any other product or commodity, you get nothing for the purchase price from an insurance firm unless you need it. With many of the so-called "surplus line insurers," having bitten the dust, scores of attorneys have been left to their own devices for protection.

The only offshore firms of any real visibility are within the so-called "London Group." These include ZURICH Re (UK) Ltd., and Lloyds of London. Zurich Re is related to, but not the same as Zurich America. The latter is admitted in California, the former is not. Exactly why Zurich maintains the offshore firm as a namesake company is not easily gathered information. Likewise, no one has given me convincing information as to the reason for Lloyds remaining nonadmitted.

Some states have no special provisions with regard to local vs. foreign insurance providers. In these states, where there are set standards, all companies must conform to the same requirements. In other states where there are distinctions, the requirements may be only fiscal.

Other states have no requirements whatever. In such states, apparently any company with, or without, minimal financial or other abilities, can, and does, carry on business unhampered by state interference. Presumably, in these states, brokers must carry the burden of investigating and imparting information and advice to their clients.

In California, the difference between admitted and nonadmitted is substantial. The biggest advantage to going with an admitted carrier in California is a guarantee of coverage and defense in the event of the carrier failure. "CIGA" meaning, California Insurance Guarantee Fund, will pay any proved claim, including defense costs, if the admitted carrier becomes financially disabled.

Nonadmitted carriers, termed "Surplus Line companies," are not provided with such a guarantee. If the company goes belly up, the result will be a "bare" attorney with egg on his or her face.

This is not meant to absolutely avoid nonadmitted carriers but to be very circumspect in considering them. If you choose this method of saving bucks, then spend the necessary time and effort of investigation and research to satisfy yourself that you'll be protected.

Go with the admitted carrier if premium dollars are no object. Before you leap in this direction, examine the premium differences. Certain nonadmitted insurance firms will charge fees greatly in excess of other nonadmitted carriers. This difference is seen usually in larger, higher profile companies. Lloyds of London, for example, though not admitted in California, commands premiums substantially higher than do other nonadmitted companies.

Don't be overly impressed with the company magnitude. Corporate conglomerates will insulate their subsidiaries from each other, just as a corporation will insulate its shareholders from corporate debts. Thus, the mere fact that a nonadmitted corporation bears a name whose parent company is familiar does not mean that the parent will be subject to your claim if the nonadmitted "name" firm fails to protect you.

Some companies were able to meet state standards for admittance awhile back and nonetheless choose to remain nonadmitted. At that time, the reasons could be certain advantages such as lower taxes assessed against foreign companies not admitted than as against admitted firms. There were also logistical advantages in not being subject to all the complicated yearly filings with the Department of Insurance.

These advantages no longer apply. The filing requirements are now the same for both. There is no longer any tax difference between them. If there is any advantage in remaining nonadmitted, aside from the right to charge lower premiums, it escapes me.

Hence, the only reason for continued nonadmittance seems to be an inability, for one or another reason, to gain admittance. It could now be fairly interpreted that a nonadmitted carrier should be placed in the "suspect" category.

Some of the carriers who've not previously been admitted have applied for admission. In some instances those applications could be granted. If you had chosen a nonadmitted carrier wisely, you could be a winner.

The process for granting or denying admittance is complicated and lengthy. There could be a considerable time span during which a carrier might be awaiting a decision from the Department of Insurance. Much of this has become moot. Most of the offshore companies are now gone.

Are the remaining firms responsible and safe? It seems that their names and company sizes would indicate strength. The question mark is placed on their choice to remain nonadmitted. Besides that question, there is the omission of CIGA, to protect us in the event of failure. Where is the net to break the fall?

Their argument appears to be solely premiums related. Once admitted, a CIGA company would have to adhere to dictated premium structure. Being nonadmitted, the firms can charge whatever premiums they wish. Is that answer enough? They argue further that each of these giant companies already have admitted carriers within their corporate structure. Does that help?

You save lots of premium dough. That adds to the balance. But, do you save enough to warrant the risk? Easy to say, but what happens if things go wrong and you're left bare? How far will you stretch your luck to save a buck?

Can we still save a buck by opting for those "good" but offshore firms?

Yes. Zurich Re (UK) Ltd., offers coverage for lower premiums than counterpart admitted firms. Can you find an admitted company with lower premiums? Maybe, if you shake the bag hard enough and long enough.

Is this a good idea?

Choosing an "offshore," or nonadmitted carrier is a delicate, perhaps dangerous, cost conservation exercise. The nonadmitted carriers exist only because they offer equal coverage for less money. One wonders how premiums can be so much less for the same insurance dollars.

Risk of insurer insolvency alone cannot be the answer. If a company is stable and will be there when needed, what other factors are present that permit prices at one-half, or less, than admitted competition? Interesting question?

Before you think of ways and means to reduce premium cost, decide whether or not you need the product. All insurance, per se, is not required for all people. You don't need automobile insurance if you have no car. You don't need life insurance if you have no dependents.

Do you need E & O insurance if you are extremely careful in your law practice? After all, if you never make a mistake, why be insured against mistakes? Do you need E & O coverage if you have no assets to protect?

What can they get from you if you have nothing? What about having a clause in your attorney-client agreements that states you are not insured and clients agree to hold you harmless from any possible legal faux pas?

Well, you may not have a car but you do practice law. As a lawyer, you do have dependents, although perhaps not blood kin. Your clients are your dependents. Malpractice insurance is not a substitute for care and caution in your practice. Mistakes are unintentional and cannot be guarded against by exercising caution regardless of how stringently it's done.

Having assets, or not, may influence your personal concerns regarding insurance, but it doesn't satisfy your Bar Association, or the courts of your state. Your clients must be protected from your folly regardless of how well intended on your part.

My information is that most, if not all, states require some form of errors and omissions coverage, whether by demonstration of personal holdings or insurance protection. In fact, there is presently some pressure in California to legislate mandatory E & O coverage for all practicing lawyers.

Besides, you can't know what your personal wealth will be, say in two, three, or maybe five or ten years from now. "OK," you say, "I'll get the coverage when, as and if I ever get rich." That won't knock it. If you practice for a while before getting a policy, you won't qualify for "prior acts" coverage.

This means that anything you had done before being insured will not be covered. Thus, if a claim arises for conduct occurring a few years back (before your having hit it big), you are a sitting duck. A bare duck, I mean.

So, you can't save a buck by avoiding coverage until you develop some assets. How else can you save on E & O insurance? You can get less coverage amounts. Premiums for a policy for $100,000/200,000 would cost less than for a $500,000/1,000,000 policy. That's O.K. if it adequately protects both you and your client.

E & O coverage is much like automobile insurance. If your assets and income are insignificant, minimal coverage may be sufficient. Even if the incident creates a major loss, the plaintiff will usually accept the "tossed in" policy limit. Beware, though, if you have some good investments, a nice home, cars, etc., your

$100,000 policy limit will just be a part of the judgment along with your personal assets.

If you are thinking of tiered elevation of coverage, inquire as to whether an increase in coverage later will carry an equal sum with respect to prior acts. I don't think so.

Probably the most logical savings in customizing your policy would be in requesting a higher deductible amount. Instead of the usual $2,000 or so deductible, try for $10,000 and see how much that reduces your premium. If you have a few bucks and can afford to self-insure for the deductible, that's a reasonable solution for premium conservation. There's a stumbling block to this option also. Many companies won't insure with deductibles over $5,000.

The selection of a nonadmitted carrier is the ultimate savings tool. No matter what else you do, using an "offshore" company will plunge your premium rate down like nothing else will. Everything you do to limit your yearly premium will create corresponding risks. The offshore risk is obvious.

No matter what you do, you must consider carefully how you will be affected by the savings method you select. No contemplation on your part will be helpful to you without adequate research in every aspect of how the parameters of insurance protection will fit your individual situation.

If you under-insure, your coverage may be eaten up in attorney's fees, leaving nothing for possible judgment liability. Don't suffer under the delusion that the claim fragility will limit the defense cost. These days, any legal defense can be disastrous financially.

Just because you can't get big litigation fees, don't believe that malpractice defense fees are comparable. $100,000 can be eaten up by insurance defense lawyers in a heartbeat.

If your deductible is escalated beyond your personal financial underwriting capability, you could have problems there. You must balance the risk, however determined, with the relative savings.

§ 15:6 Is mandatory E & O insurance an equitable method of protecting clients?

Once again, the California legislators are struggling with the age old issue of how to protect clients from us attorneys. If the client loses something because of our error or omission, and we lack the funds to compensate the client, what remedy is there? There it is. Our clients are our dependents.

We can go bare on life insurance and our families suffer. That's up to us. Is it also up to us to let our clients suffer? Some say no. But is the imposition of mandatory E & O insurance a fair, just and equitable solution? Not in my view.

§ 15:7 Getting the best price

Thirty new carriers now willing to write E & O insurance policies in California: Does this mean a premium price drop?

Almost overnight, new carriers, admitted carriers, no less, are deluging into California. In fact, at the last count, over thirty carriers, some name companies that used to offer legal Error & Omissions coverage, are back in business in California.

Does this mean a drop in premiums? Certainly, that seems likely as with any business competition. However, greed dies hard. So far, the companies are soliciting business like the pestilence, but no big bargains are offered.

An even bigger problem is making contact with the various companies to get quotes. E & O brokers have always been few and far between. That hasn't changed. None I've contacted will divulge information on how to find companies who might offer better pricing structures.

If you can divert your attention away from the price for a moment, the new competitive situation spells something, I believe, much more important than premium cost. The willingness of these companies, some of which had been death on E & O coverage not so long ago, to engage in that field now, poses an interesting question: Has the jeopardy for California lawyers been reduced?

For the past several years, the major threat in legal E & O coverage has been legal defense cost. In the old days, a $100,000/$300,000 policy limit was sufficient for the average attorney. That would hardly cover even defense fees. That's the situation even in cases where the claim is shaky. $250,000/$500,000 is marginal enough.

For a "product" that you can't touch, smell, feel or otherwise enjoy, the vendors are pretty cocky not only about what they charge, but to whom they'll even sell.

Companies will insure your life for less money and with less pain. The applications are still as complex and companies are as finicky about every blank being filled in, as ever.

The reason for this influx of new carriers has remained a mystery to me after interviewing several people in the business. No one will admit that fewer claims are being made, or that defense costs are less.

I hear cryptic statements like "maybe they think this is a profitable business." It's hard to imagine that hard headed insurance firms would flock to cover a risk that isn't profitable. And, if it's profitable, it's axiomatic that competition will lower prices. Can you go bare until then?

Actually, there have been some premium changes of late, although it may be too soon to judge them as reflective of lowering rates. The California Bar has sponsored special coverage for part-time lawyers. This kind of policy hasn't been seen for several years.

There are some rather stringent provisos to qualify for such coverage. For instance, the applicant cannot have practiced full time for at least ten years. If you do qualify, however, the premium would be dramatically lower than what one in that category would otherwise pay.

The word on the street is that premiums are buckling. Some agents appear optimistic about locating admitted carriers who will issue more competitive policies. I have asked a few agents to follow up on these rumors but so far any price differences haven't been that impressive.

Part-time lawyer coverage available (at least in California).

New, at least in California, is the offer to insure part-time attorneys at a reduced rate. My information is that other states are also getting in this act. The offer extends only to practices which are confined to a certain number of hours per month. In some instances, that limited practice would have had to not been exceeded for some prior period.

At any rate, the premium cost is dramatically lower than anything else available, onshore or offshore. The policies are severely restricted and it's a no fooling kind of restriction. If you qualify and you aren't expecting an expansion for quite a while, it bears considering.

Well, prices do vary among all carriers, even the hoity-toitiest. One criterion of premium calculation is the type of practice you have. Certain practices are death to carriers, such as a securities practice. Their premiums are out of sight.

In the lower echelons of high premiums is criminal practice. Some of these fields change from time to time depending upon loss experiences of carriers.

The best approach to this problem is to solve it head-on. I suggested going to the professional within the profession and discipline of your concern? Well, the same solution applies here. Ask your E & O insurance agent about the high risk, high premium parts of law practice.

I don't advocate deception. It wouldn't do you any good anyway. Your policy coverage is predicated upon the truth of your application statements.

Oftentimes, the lawyer will be uncertain about the practice apportionment. As a new practitioner, you would very likely not even know what you will be concentrating upon.

Talk with the agent candidly. Together, you can set up a schedule for your application that will satisfy the carrier, bring in a rate that won't choke you, and permit you to get your mind off of goblins and onto your practice where it belongs.

Chapter 16

Tax and Investment Considerations for the Solo Practitioner

§ 16:1 Generally

Never too soon to plan.

It may seem a bit premature to discuss such things as tax shelters, investments, retirement preparations and other things related to the maturation of your practice when you're just beginning. The truth is it's never too soon for such thoughts.

When I was your age, I never thought about things older people were concerned with. Vulnerability, apprehension, fears and doubts, ailing health, financial instability, were things that rarely, if ever, crossed my mind. I was healthy, full of ideas and ambition and raring to go. Maybe you're smarter than I was. You may be contemplating your older age. You may be, but I doubt it.

Older people tend to consider the gap between youth and aged as pretty narrow. In the early years, every day has its hills, valleys, twists and turns of good, bad, worry, excitement, and variations of all kinds.

Later on, your life follows a kind of sorting out process. It takes much more to cause worry, excitement or other concerns. You've been there and your attitude becomes "What can they do to you?"

It takes more, yes. But one thing does greatly concern you later on. Have you adequately prepared for your retirement?

So many older people I know have expressed anxiety about outliving their investment income. Not so many years ago, a reasonably adequate retirement "next egg" was $50,000 to $100,000. Today that wouldn't last a year. Who can say what your future will foretell?

Would I have done differently had I known at your age what I know now? So many things it's hard to say which would head the list.

The reason it's so difficult for older folks to relate to young people is those hills, valleys, twist and turns. Looking back, one cannot see into those irregularities. All that one sees looking back are the "major" variations. That's the rub. What is a major variation? What is a minor variation?

Living through those "minor variations," life is a long journey. Looking back over those "major variations," life is short. What was important, even earth shaking, to me at your age is of small moment to me now.

The suggestions in this section, as elsewhere throughout this book, are subject to the whims of the economy and other fiscal influences. Hence, you cannot take any particular suggestion or recommendation given under this subject heading without adequate independent consideration as well as professional counsel.

Take the soul of the idea and then go to work investigating, studying and contemplating these thoughts, just as you would your own thoughts in all matters. After getting all of the facts, prognostications and evaluations concerning any intended venture, and only upon your best counsel, go for it.

There are certain benefits to be derived from the income tax laws for the solo practitioner. There are also certain investment opportunities. These suggestions are to some extent applicable to employees as well, but they may not be as practical for them as for the solo as a business person.

§ 16:2 Tax advantages of solo practice

As you'll see, there are many ways you can control taxes in a business operation not available to a salaried employee.

I don't propose to instruct anyone on the intricacies of taxation. Your accountant is far more capable of getting you into tax troubles than I am. These suggestions are not intended as "cute tricks" or manipulations of the tax laws, but are offered merely to call attention to certain tax facts in the business world.

With each federal administration, ideas regarding taxes, tax benefits and deductions will reflect that administration's platform and policies. Some administrations are pro-business, some pro-labor and some are pro-taxing everyone and everything imaginable.

Most people don't like taxes unless they fall on someone else. Persons of modest means are not particularly disturbed when higher income groups are taxed heavier or their deductions are curtailed. Attitudes change when tax benefits and consequences change.

Tradition will more or less prevail in certain areas of the tax laws and regulations. Percentages will vary here and there, and sometimes the Congress or the White House will tamper with some sacred cows.

Recently, the capital gains structure was completely overhauled, removing many of those benefits from the investor's portfolio. That has been one of the "sacred cows." The proposal of a reduced capital gains tax finally came about.

Still, removing benefits has always been looked upon by politicians as a way of gaining favor with constituents who are not investors. Tax benefits are seen by many as ploys of the rich. New solo practitioners are not, as a class, rich, but would certainly enjoy some tax benefits.

Part of your profit in solo practice will be whatever avoidance of taxes you can manage by lawful means. There are some ways you might explore toward that end. But be aware of the cyclical advent of tax benefit tampering in Washington.

Your law office at home.

For instance, if you are a workaholic, as you should be for a year or two, you will be working at home after office hours. You will need a dedicated part of your home for such activities.

A recent Supreme Court ruling indicates that to qualify for tax benefits you must show that you use your home office for the major part of your total work output. Convenience alone will not justify a tax deduction.

You can expect further intrusions into business tax deductions in keeping with efforts to chip away at our enormous national debt. Also, be reminded of the limits and restrictions regarding your office at home.

That particular part of your home must not be used for family functions but only for your law work. You must keep a diary of work done at that location. Further, you should show a valid reason for it's impracticability to complete such work at your office. Paperwork, such as bookkeeping and billing, alone will not suffice.

The depreciation schedule of that percentage of house area should be proportionate to the totality of the improved property, and this should be based upon the property's tax base. As you know, bare land is not depreciable, only the improved parts are.

Thus, you would take depreciation against a capital asset in much the same manner as applied to a curve for conventional commercial property. For specific details on how the particulars apply to your situation, you will need to consult your accountant.

Just as in any business, you should also be entitled to write off that same portion of all of the house costs, such as utilities, phone, etc., as business tax deductions. All of these tax benefits are applicable if, and only if, you are actually using the depreciated part of your house for your business, and only for your business.

Entertaining your clients.

To a certain extent, you should also be entitled to deduct the cost of entertaining your clients. This means taking them out to dinner, etc. Occasional client parties held in your home, or wherever, are likewise subject to deductibility.

These activities, while primarily done for business development, will provide entertainment value for you as well. These advantages, while to some extent shared by employees, are not as widely available to them as to the business person.

Call the IRS, at (800) TAX-1040, for information, and at (800) TAX-FORM to receive Publication 587, "Business Use Of Home."

In order to qualify as a tax deduction, the purpose of entertainment must be business development related. If you are entertaining one who is a client of your employer's office, and you are on salary, the business development concept might be ruled as too remote.

Such a situation may be challenged as an expense of your employer and not yours. In that framework, you'd be entitled to reimbursement under an expense account but not to a tax deduction.

You'll want to take vacations from time to time. You will plan carefully on when and where you will want to go. Why not put that planning to more strategically valuable use?

Use your valuable time away from the office for educational or practice enhancement exercises. Let tax deductions help pay for these important participations, while you coordinate them with vacation excursions.

As a lawyer/business person, you are entitled to write off a portion of any expenses incurred in the advancement of your education or of the profitability of your practice.

Travel for education (with a bit of fun).

For instance, the Minimum Continuing Legal Education ("MCLE") programs are required courses for all lawyers in many states. Some of them are held in places away from home. In some instances, the locations might be enjoyable places to visit. These necessary experiences can be sources of valuable education and, coincidentally, enjoyable vacation sojourns.

Wherever travel can be done in connection with any legal service, it can be subject to tax deductions. If you still have an eye out for potential employment, though ensconced in your solo practice, job interviews could qualify for deduction, even though they may take you to far off places.

Business seminars are traditionally tax deductible. This is no less true in law practice. For instance, the regularly scheduled bar conventions are usually considered legitimate tax write-offs.

The American Bar Association holds its annual conventions in places that are interesting to see. Is this merely coincidental? A portion of the 2000 convention takes place in London, England.

Would it be a terrible chore to travel to England to attend this important and highly informative legal seminar? Why not coordinate such a trip with your vacation plans?

True, you would not have time to luxuriate in the sun during seminar sessions, but you should find enough time for fun. And, you'd be helping to build your competence and practice the rest of the time.

Some items which you might like to own, but which you are putting off because of the cost, might seem more attractive if you could defray a part of the cost though tax deductions. For instance, a video cassette recorder could be very constructively used in your practice.

There are some very informative and helpful video cassettes produced by various legal seminar operators. The purchase of a video cassette recorder when used for such educational and informative purposes could be subject to tax deduction.

You might also find it profitable for you to use a video camera along with your recorder to record depositions and scenes of accidents or other events in connection with your cases. It would certainly be an advantage in your practice to have recorded interviews with witnesses in your cases, wouldn't it? Undeniably true.

Of course, some of these and other acquisitions could be tax deductible if made by an employee. But how much opportunity would you have to utilize them? Then, there is the same question of remoteness of the purchase to your own business development as an employee.

As your own boss, you decide where and when you want to travel, and what and when you think it would be advantageous to purchase as aids in your education or office profitability. Many of tax advantages open to solo practitioners are not generally available to employees.

Fiscal control of income and expenses.

Operating your own law practice offers yet another tax advantage over salaried employment. Being in charge of the fiscal functions, you can control the timing of receipts and disbursements.

The "cash basis" for accounting means that your income is determined upon receipt of *payment* for your fees. Similarly, your expenses are registered upon disbursement of your checks to your creditors.

The "accrual basis" means that your income is based upon the debt *owed* to you by your clients and entered into your accounts receivable control, even though you have not yet received payment. Likewise, your expenses will accrue upon billing to you by your creditors and incorporation of the debts into your accounts payable register.

The former system, the "cash basis," offers a bit more fine tuning of your tax situation. Obviously, you can control the input of cash received and payments actually made a bit better than the timing of accounts receivable and payable.

My understanding of this fiscal choice is that you are not required to meet any kind of timetable for either of these functions. Even though you are exercising some arbitrary options in early bill payment and delayed fees billing, my information is that you are not violating any Internal Revenue Code sections or rulings of the IRS.

Certainly, you shouldn't write off prepaid expenses which have not yet accrued nor liabilities not yet ripe. You don't deduct all of next year's office month-to-month rental in December of the previous year.

But you can prepay a portion of next year's month-to-month rental in advance. Two or three prepaid months should not arch too many IRS eyebrows.

If you have a lease, you are at liberty to prepay any or all of the lease at any time. The difference is you owe for all the months of the lease. You don't owe anything on a month-to-month rental agreement other than the forthcoming month.

You are certainly at liberty to pay bills for which you are indebted. This would include billing arrangements which would permit later payment. So long as the debt is established, it may be paid at any time even before billing.

Keeping an eye on the accumulating year's gross income, you can opt to bill for January of the coming year instead of December of the current year. This way you can defer some income into next year to prevent a bumper crop year from defeating itself through taxation.

Conversely, you can anticipate purchases intended for next year by writing the checks in late December. If the investment credit concept is with us at publication, you can make equipment purchases as late as December 31st and still qualify for the investment credit.

As head of your own firm, you can save thousands in tax dollars by hiring members of your own family. So long as the employment is bona fide, you can shift a goodly part of your income to family at far lower tax bracket rates than yours. Many other tax advantages are available in family hiring.

If your spouse actually does help in the office, either as a part-time secretary, filing clerk, or whatever, you can add to your retirement quotient to some extent by including your spouse, at least for IRA investment purposes. You will need to examine the full spectrum of your tax matters for the advisability of doing this. Check with your tax accountant.

§ 16:3 Attorney, incorporate thyself

I cannot explain why, but I've never gotten around to incorporating my law practice. It may, or may not, be true that law firms which incorporate enjoy more tax benefits than do those of us who choose not to. The present political trend is toward heavier taxes on close corporations. What will happen in the years to come is anyone's guess.

My understanding is that many, perhaps most, of these advantages have been abrogated along the way. It used to be, maybe still is, that all medical expenses are deductible and not just those exceeding the minimal percentage requirements.

Further, as your corporation's employee, personal income tax is paid on your salary and not on the corporation's earnings. This may offer a means to control taxable income with some fine-tuning.

The mechanics of creating a professional corporation are much more complicated and exacting than the simple commercial corporation. If you need help, the fees for setting yourself up are considerably larger than those to set up the ordinary business corporation.

There are also certain nuisances that must be addressed regularly, such as corporate returns and minimal franchise tax payments. These could be minor when compared to the gross tax savings, if there are such.

Being a professional, you cannot take advantage of the liability insulation. Your most fearful business liabilities would be client claims. Ordinarily, a compelling reason for small businesses to consider incorporating would be such insulation. But perhaps there are other compensating benefits.

§ 16:4 It's never too early to start your retirement plan

If you are solo in support of your family, as well as in your law office, you should cast some thoughts to retirement. Though with somewhat less pressure, this subject should occupy a priority even if your spouse shares in breadwinning.

Retirement can be either a wonderful time of life or a nightmare. One significant difference is the presence or absence of proper planning. Proper planning involves timing as well as substance.

This is an exercise that should concern you from the very first day of your practice. That same discipline, applied to law school tribulations, the bar exam and into your solo practice adventure, could be employed in preparing for those inevitable days.

Consider a portion of your earnings contributed to your retirement plan as simply another cost of doing business. Look at it as a "rent" addition. It won't hurt that much, and it is an important disbursement.

This issue focuses also on the advantages to being quite alone in your practice. Most of the desirable plans require certain employee participation. This means that whatever you do for yourself might also be required for your employees.

Selfishness is not a trait to be admired. But think of it this way: you are all alone in your practice. It will be solely up to you to provide for the time when you can no longer practice. You owe it to yourself and to your family.

Those who wish the umbilical cord of having someone else contolling your future will find that security in employment. Not for you! When you are "solo," you are solo!

If you contract for your help, as needed, you have no employee obligations. Thus, whatever provisions you make for your retirement will only require your participation.

This exclusivity opens doorways to all kinds of ideas which will make your investment plans exciting and highly productive. And, you will find that the contributions will not be as traumatic as you think.

A good piece of the contribution will actually be provided by your two silent partners, Uncle Sam and the governor.

Whatever you spend for your living and pleasure costs is taken only from the residue after taxes have been paid. But dollars paid toward your retirement programs are taken before taxes. Therefore, depending upon your tax bracket, Uncle Sam is paying a good part of the freight.

You can use the fiction of the "necessary expense," but don't be deluded into the idea that these payments are expenses. What is more important, that set of golf clubs or your future? Those contribution dollars will be your key to true independence. The golf clubs are only potential rust.

There are so many places to go, things to see and do, beautiful treasures to buy, and the Joneses to keep up with. What's left over for your retirement program? Well, maybe next year. Big mistake!

In the first place, your retirement investment is your best buy. Every dollar you put into that purpose is tax-deferrable. Each dollar invested only costs you a certain percentage, depending on your tax bracket. Every dollar you spend for your pleasures costs you not just that dollar but the taxes paid to earn it.

As a solo practitioner, you can call the tune. There are two basic retirement plan schedules for your consideration. One is called the "Defined Contributions Plan." This plan permits a very limited dollar percentage to be deducted from your earned income.

If you're a bit older starting out, as I was, you should be thinking of the other plan. This is the "Defined Benefits Plan." This plan is computed to your projected retirement fund as anticipated to the year of your retirement.

The advantage of the latter is that you can take a much larger amount from your earned income and invest it free of income tax. The earnings of that plan, whether interest or other yield, are also tax deferred.

One other point concerning the "Defined Benefits Plan" form of retirement program is attractive. You are named in the trust plan as your own trustee. Unlike the other plan, which requires an appointed trustee, such as a bank, this plan permits your own appointment. This means that you can select whatever kind of approved investment you choose for your retirement.

It's true that you will have less money to spend. But the amount not invested for retirement will be whittled away by taxes. Uncle Sam wants you to save at his expense to lighten the impact of the increasingly geriatric American population.

Figure it out with pencil and paper (or better still, with your computer budget program). It's too expensive to ignore. Before you conclude that you can't afford it, see if you can afford to do without it.

§ 16:5 Tax-exempt investments

Municipal bonds have carried a curse which, for the most part, has really been undeserved. If you don't go out of your way to find troublesome bonds, you'll be reasonably safe with most bond purchases.

If you are interested in long-term investment at the highest yield consistent with safety, demand "AAA" insured tax-free municipal bonds. Make certain that the bonds are tax-exempt.

At this writing, AAA insured bonds with late maturity dates are available at about 4% to 6% interest, tax-free. If you're in the higher tax bracket, that means an actuarial income equivalent of about 8.70% to 9.85%. Not bad.

Your portfolio should have some municipal bonds. Consider something like a 10% investment of this kind. Of course, the value of municipal bonds, especially municipal bond trusts and funds, will fluctuate with the money market.

Naturally, if interest rates increase, the fixed bonds will devaluate. The picture would need to change enormously for the bonds' values to become really bad. Tax-free interest yielding relative 7% to 10% values would appear to be reasonably prudent in most predictable times.

If you are skittish and worry about such things, you might be too nervous for this kind of investment. But if you can just put the bonds away and forget equivalent values, and just enjoy the tax-free income, you'll love 'em. I do.

A complicated, but effective, tax-free plan can also be accomplished through life insurance trust plans. These are plans under which you purchase policies and borrow against them. The borrowing is not in actuality a debt. It is a plan whereby the payments to you, being under a loan, are not taxable.

These plans appear to be quite widely used and seem to be IRS-approved. They pay considerably more return on your dollar investment than municipal bonds. The problem with these investments is the kind of "protection" offered.

Each insurance company issuer is insured by another insurance company. Thus, the quality of protection is the quality of the insuring company, as well as the issuing company.

If the larger interest numbers impress you, it would be prudent for you to take steps to investigate both insurance firms, the issuer and insurer, before you invest. If the insuring company is solidly reliable, the issuer is not that important. At the moment, I do not personally have any insurance annuity investments.

There are other programs that you should be thinking about. Some are tax-deductible, or deferrable, and some are not. But you should be concerned with putting at least a part of your income into some form of an investment program.

All of these tax saving thoughts are for more than just retirement. You'll get much more satisfaction from your practice if it's subsidized with some investment bucks. Think of the pleasure of saying "no" to a client instead of taking cases and clients you hate because you need the money. Money isn't everything. There is . . . uh, ah . . . ah . . ..

§ 16:6 Other investment opportunities for the solo practitioner

Real estate has long been considered one of the safest and most productive of all long term investments. The short term real estate investor is usually a speculator who buys, refurbishes and resells properties. This takes considerable skills and knowledge of the real estate market and has obvious risks.

I favor commercial over residential real estate as an investment opportunity. Business tenants give you fewer headaches than residential tenants. Also, the laws so favor residential tenants in many states that, aside from financial considerations, there could be substantial statutory problems for the property owner.

If you lack enough cash to get into a real property purchase on your own, consider a partnership or syndication. There's nothing wrong with starting small and growing. Small store buildings can be had for small down payments in many areas.

Certainly, you must investigate the area and the particular offer carefully before you take any plunges. But, generally speaking, dollar for dollar, real estate investments are your best bets. Interest payments are also tax-deductible.

For example, a small retail store property selling for $100,000 might be available for $10,000 down. Chances are such a sale would require the seller to take back a second deed and note. It's also likely that the property will not give you any positive cash flow. You haven't enough of your own money invested. But, that $10,000 investment would give you leverage to depreciate maybe $60,000 or even $75,000, depending on the appropriate ratio of land to improvement value.

When you've reached the upper tax brackets, that depreciation could net you a fairly decent return on your money. Moreover, the pay down will yield a growing equity for you.

Economies cycle and real property, as with many other kinds of properties, can have reverses. But, historically and prospectively, carefully selected real property can be your most valuable investment.

Contrary to the tax concept of realty depreciation, the fact is that real estate has appreciated, and will undeniably continue its curve of appreciation through the years.

If things continue to hold as history dictates, your $100,000 building could be worth as much as $150,000 or even $200,000 in just a few years. Of course, this is not always the case in every situation.

History has not always been kind to real estate in catastrophic economic crises as in the late 1980's. There is a strange truism concerning real property. Real estate is like the tail end of a whip. It is the last to react to both boom and bust.

Real property values linger at price levels longer than do personal property values. Food and energy prices fluctuate almost wildly with economic changes. On the other hand, prices of homes die hard in recessions. Happily, they are not as slow to revitalize when times improve.

There are compensations with real property investments not present in other kinds. With rare exceptions, you can usually count on the relative value of your real estate regardless of the economic indices.

Whether during inflation or deflation, prosperity or depression, your real estate will continue to have a relative value which is more or less commensurate with the totality of the economy.

While other kinds of property can virtually go into the toilet during really hard times, realty located in choice locations will usually hold its relative value.

With a reasonable amount of investigation, you can find some decent property in good, substantial geographic areas that would show some promise of holding value in shaky times. Then, if, as some predict, times become "better than ever," you've got a real winner.

Enormous profits have been made in real estate. That is true of the stock market also. But the volatility of the latter kind of investment has always frightened me. I've steadfastly shied from highest leverage, problem properties.

Commercial real estate is normally bought and sold on an 8 to 10 times gross basis. This means if the property grosses $100,000 per year in rentals, the selling price should hover at about $800,000 to $1,000,000. That rule of thumb is not always one to follow nor one always offered.

In some areas, properties are offered at less than 8 times gross. That is because the rentals are possibly undesirable or there are other problems. In other areas, such as what are called "100% block" business buildings, more than 10 times gross is demanded. These are areas in which more reliable tenants are available

Since the capital gains smoke has cleared away, real property should somewhat stabilize. I am not an advocate of speculation in any arena, including real estate. If you buy prudently and not for quick profits, time will be your, and your property's, friend.

If you are an astute analyzer of real property, you might be able to spot a good buy on what appears to be a depressed property. Sometimes the property goes begging for lack of decent management or some other superficial cause.

If you don't know that business, stay clear of bad properties with "reasons" for the depression. An uneducated buyer can easily be fooled by an expert seller with logical reasons for the failures.

There have been enormous losses virtually overnight in the stock market. You usually have plenty of warning before sustaining any enormous kind of loss in realty.

U.S. Government bonds are not federally tax exempt, but they are protected by the United States, and they traditionally pay somewhat better interest and are safer than many other bonds. Once again, they have the market place volatility.

There are many other choices (including stocks) besides those I've mentioned for your collateral income program. Set one up soon. You have chosen to practice law as a solo mainly to gain independence. Increase the quotient of independence by assuring that your practice won't need to be your (and your family's) sole support.

It's more fun to be a solo practitioner than to be tied down to a workaday job. But it's even more fun to be a solo when you're not under economic pressures.

A substantial collateral income program can not only relieve you of money anxieties, but can permit you to practice the kind of law that you enjoy most and are best equipped to handle. So, it follows that your early investment prudence can make you a better lawyer.

Take your choice. Pick the kind of investments you understand and like. Carve out a part of your income (15%-20%?), regardless of how small it may be, for your long-range investment program.

Even though it's only a few bucks, it serves a good purpose. It starts you on the program. From there, you will build on it and, before you know it, you'll be fixed for your retirement down the road.

Chapter 17

Expanding Your Solo Practice

§ 17:1 Generally

An exasperating part of business, any kind of business, is in trying to expand its income while maintaining a solid profit base. A law office is no exception. Marketing specialists abound claiming to have a successful formula for increasing a client base.

In other instances, the business, like Topsy, just grows by itself. It can be difficult to manage in either case. Some lawyers enjoy a compact practice permitting them to run it with the least effort. Others aspire to continual growth.

Merchandising businesses use loss leaders to entice customers into their stores hoping for enough profitable sales to offset the losses. Law offices can't do that ethically. Other tactics are used by lawyers, but getting more business isn't the complete answer.

The expanding practice; Point of diminishing returns. There is, in every business curve, a point at which one more dollar in business volume will cost several more dollars in operating expenses. This is called the point of diminishing returns.

Simply put, there comes a time when, in order to handle the business increase, you must hire more help and, in other ways, increase your scope of administration to a degree that less will be expended than will be realized in increased income.

The greater the volume of paperwork, the more secretaries and clerks you will need. The more clients and court appearances, the more attorneys in your firm will be required to handle the flow. No matter how industrious and capable you may be, there's a limit to your capacity.

There may come a time in your practice when you just can't stem the tide. Like a snowball rolling down the mountain, it multiplies rapidly and, even though it may be your preference to keep your operation trimmed, you can't do anything about it.

Your expenses will be more diversified and extensive, and your bookkeeping procedures may even need to be more sophisticated than the simple system we started you on to keep astride of these changes. The number of entries in your daily log will multiply, and each process in your office will increase proportionately. Don't be too quick to act on that one, though.

When you started out in your practice, you were worried about how you were going to get business. You were limited in ways to obtain clients. You couldn't employ agents to solicit, or proselytize, for clients in any way. You had no idea how your clients would come, and you were surprised to find that, like Topsy, your practice just "grew."

Just as getting business then required extra effort, you may face the problem of how to turn it off. You may reach the point where you just don't want to expand any further.

You can't handle the business you are getting, and yet you haven't enough to warrant enlarging your operation. Don't laugh. This can be a much bigger problem than you faced in starting your practice.

The bigger you get, the further removed you become from your administration. Instead of making your own daily book entries, you now have bookkeepers to do this. Instead of doing your own filing, you find that you must have filing clerks for this crucial job (this is one job that I would personally always supervise). You may even get so big that you find it expedient to delegate authority to sign checks (Whoops!).

One fine day, you find yourself in the midst of a full fledged "organization." Everything must now be done by "remote control."

As you grow larger and larger, you find another strange thing happening. The length of the curve to each point of diminishing returns gets shorter and shorter.

This is simply because you are farther from the controls. The more remote an administrative activity from your control, the less efficient that activity is.

When you handled everything directly, or at least indirectly supervised its operation, you saw to it that things were done, right now! Your one or two employees were under your constant observation, and wanted your approval, just as they were fearful of your displeasure.

But now, you are too busy to be concerned with each detail on a daily, much less an hourly, basis. Even though you pay more for help than before, you are not buying the same qualities that you got then. This is not anomalous. It is mathematically predictable. It costs more per unit of operation to run a large concern than a small one.

Logic says that when there were just you and one or two others, each job assigned would need to be more complex. Just the opposite is true. The smaller the scope of each assigned task, and the more people involved in the operation, the more complex each part must be.

This is because each member of a small group is familiar with all of the parts involved. But each employee in a large concern is isolated, so to speak, from the other employees. The systems must be set up in a way that will merge with the whole, even though the "left hand doesn't know what the right hand is doing."

You didn't, then, need a fancy identification system to ascertain in which file a particular document belonged. You were the file clerk, and you knew each paper like the palm of your hand. Later, when you needed secretarial and clerical help, your secretary did your filing. But, even then, there was a closeness to each client and client's files.

When you got bigger and needed filing clerks, you found a need for automation so that no errors would be made. To simplify the method to prevent clerical mistakes, the file system had to be complicated. Silly, isn't it? Of course, this kind of complication has to be injected into each category.

So, you can see that when the operation is closest to your vest, you get maximum productivity from the minimum number of employees. You will be able to handle a respectably large practice volume all by yourself.

Even if you are quite industrious, the chances are that, when you hire your first secretary, you will not have reached a point where you are unable to go further without that help. Sometimes confusion more than common sense dictates. When you believe you need secretarial help, cool it! It's no doubt too soon.

The profit and loss changing reference line.

Once you go the help routine, you move into a whole new profit (or loss) perspective. As you have now learned, it costs much more to hire help than small business owners may realize. The one-way door into bigger business may be easy to enter, but difficult, sometimes impossible, to exit.

The first part of your operational curve is during the stages of your true "soloship." You are all alone. Not even a secretary is present to disturb your solitude.

If you operate as I have suggested, you will be able to gross well in excess of $250,000 per year. Because your operating expenses are so low, your percentage of profit will be quite substantial. I know many lawyers who've moved into the "big business" picture. More than a few will admit that solo practice is where they made most of their money.

§ 17:2 Hiring a secretary

Your first big personnel expense will be your secretary if you find you can't get along without one. This engagement will, theoretically, permit you to accommodate a larger gross volume of business. But there is considerable question as to whether you will be able to utilize a secretary to actually expand your volume of business.

Many lawyers have found that their volume of practice has actually diminished after hiring a secretary. Surprising? After hiring a secretary, a lawyer will often merely find more time to play golf or sleep later in the mornings.

Even though you've seen the problems involved in employing help, and you believe you can handle them, you may be fooling yourself. You can waste more time dealing with secretarial help than you might net from their services. Even if you are able to use help efficiently, you still might be surprised at the result.

Few lawyers know what to do with the freedom that sometimes comes with having a secretary. More often than not, a new secretary will work at chores that could be better expedited by the lawyer, or by a secretarial service.

Let's assume that you have an average overhead expense of $1,000 per month. You are working alone. You have now reached what you believe is the time to hire a secretary.

Let's say that you have decided to hire your own full-time secretary. Assume you can find a competent secretary at a salary of only $1,500 per month. Your expenses are now $2,500 a month, plus the insidious added costs of employment which few employers fully apprehend.

Prior to hiring the secretary, your gross volume was about $80,000 per year, or about $6,600 per month. Your net profit was about $68,000 per year.

Without bothering about such things as employee contributions, payroll taxes, workers' compensation insurance premiums, and other such costs attached to hiring employees, you will need to gross at least $3,000 per month more to pay for this added employee.

It is a reasonably accurate rule of thumb to figure about two times the direct cost of employment as the true cost of each employee. Of course, the "direct" cost would include all of the extras that I said we wouldn't bother about in this computation.

As you've already learned, the double-up theory is a conservative computation. Hence, you will need to increase your gross by about $36,000 per year, just to pay for the secretary, without yielding one cent to you. Now, you are doing $116,000 per year, and you haven't yet left square one.

Assume that you are blessed with that certain kind of business acumen that enables you to glean value from employees. You have increased your gross commensurate with the added cost of your first employee. But, we didn't take on the additional responsibility and complication of personnel to gain an insignificant increase.

We expect a substantial return for our tycoonship. We must add an additional multiple of the direct cost to our increase in volume. In addition to the $3,000 per month needed to pay for employee cost, there must be an increase of $1,500, or a total increase of $4,500 per month more than we were doing prior to hiring the secretary.

This now means that the total gross volume must now rise an additional $18,000 in annual dollars, or a total of $154,000 per year.

Prior to hiring the secretary, you netted about 80% of your gross volume. After hiring your secretary, your profit dipped to less than 60%, even though your gross income almost doubled. Even this dismal picture presupposes an unlikely ability to use an employee to advantage.

It may seem that what I say is inapposite to growth. Not at all. My heartiest wish for you is that you become the General Motors of the legal profession. The point intended is that growth in law business depends as much upon foundational development as in any other business venture.

Growth is not accomplished simply by hiring help. The hiring of help should occur as a result of the need to accomplish the increased business load. You are a good attorney and will work hard. You will therefore develop an ever-increasing clientele. Eventually, this pattern will burgeon into growth of proportions which demand help.

I have said that you have what it takes to succeed as a solo lawyer. I've given you my reasons for saying this. But those reasons should not be misconstrued. This doesn't mean that you have that very special capability needed to run a large business.

Once you extend yourself into the areas of management and capital, you are in a whole different arena. That is where I leave you. No one, but no one, can tell another how to succeed in big business, whether by really trying or otherwise. Do not equate opening a solo practice with becoming a big business person.

Being in private practice is being in business, true enough. But this doesn't qualify you as a bona fide "business person." You are a lawyer, a poet, even a bit of a scientist, if you will. But a business tycoon? No. A lawyer's standard equipment should be business competence, not business genius.

Give both of us a break, and recognize the difference between running your law office and operating a business organization. If you have that natural organizational talent that is in the portfolio of the inherent business person, you will not need me to advise you on that point.

When the time comes for departure from your solo practice into something more enterprising, your innate abilities will tell you which road to take. Until that time arrives, don't pace yourself at too great a trot. And, if that time never comes, be happy with your $150,000 or $250,000 a year. You're still better off than being an employee.

You hear stories of the "jewel" of a secretary who "literally runs the office." Such stories are born of two sources. The first is the lawyer whose eyes are closed to the secretary's true value, and the second is the lawyer who is in the upper income echelons and can afford to pay a secretary a bigger salary than you are earning in your practice. Even in the latter case, the value of this "jewel" is usually an inflated figment of the storyteller's wishful thinking.

After you have chased this rainbow for a few years, you will learn that the elusive "jewel" is hiding somewhere between the proverbial pot o' gold and that million dollar case you've heard tell about.

It is true that many secretaries do "run the office." But they often run it into the ground. I hope that you will subscribe to the same inviolate rule that I do. I run my office, and I always will run my office. As a lawyer, you should run your office, now and always.

In lieu of your own set of criteria, you might find the following suggestions useful:

Possession of minimal basic skills, at least.

The applicant must be able to spell well and, most importantly, must recognize the need to look up words. Sometimes, paradoxically, the lack of spelling ability, together with the knowledge of that lack, is preferable to good spelling ability with an accompanying super-ego on the subject.

I've seen good spellers misspell due to an inability to allow for the possibility of mistake! If a person recognizes a problem in this area, there may be a greater tendency to check on the word before using it. The applicant must have basic skill with a typewriter or the computer keyboard.

Every decent word processor program has an accompanying spell-check program. Both Word and WordPerfect have rather large dictionaries and thesauri. It only takes a very few moments to let those programs do their jobs.

These word processors both have automated spell checkers and basic grammar aids. Even that assumes the operator knows what steps to take to correct either spelling or grammar.

Would you believe the number of secretaries who won't take that time and trouble. This is not usually forgetfulness. This is an outgrowth of the "I'm a good speller" syndrome. Some of these people are so convinced of their spelling prowess they simply will not allow for possible mistakes.

Accuracy is a must.

You cannot tolerate an applicant who is mistake-prone. Don't you make the mistake of believing that this tendency will be corrected with experience. The applicant who makes mistakes because of "nervousness" will continue to make mistakes long after the reason for nervousness has passed.

Look for the applicant who will adjust speed to the circumstances, and not make any mistakes. A bit of slowness may be justified because of newness and nervousness, but not mistakes. A secretary who makes mistakes will neglect to calendar a court date, misfile a document, or do or neglect to do other things which will cause more harm than the good such a person could possibly do.

Personalities must mesh.

No matter what other attributes the applicant may have, you will be done no good if the two of you cannot get along. Look for signs and vibrations which will indicate that there could be a personality clash or worse, a constant undertone of disharmony and abrasion.

When I hired people for my business, I was not concerned with whether or not I personally liked them. That is, unless I was hiring a secretary for me. I could tolerate people I disliked on a production line, or in sales, or advertising, merchandising, or whatever, but not in my secretary. The relationship is far too close for any kind of personality dissension.

Prepare a little test for the applicants to take which will demonstrate bits of the above categories. Then, be resolute in your adherence to whatever criteria you set. If you compromise in any material way, you'll be sorry.

§ 17:3 Your very own law clerk

There may come a time, whether because of your desire for more leisure time or because of an encroaching, insurmountable work load, when you will want or need some legal assistance. At this point, you probably won't need a full-fledged attorney, but you may be able to use the services of a bright law student.

Through proper administration and supervision of a talented amateur, you can relieve much of the pressure in your office. In the beginning of this stage of your growth, it is important that you make the right selection and then set the right tone in your use of this new employee.

Since you have big, broad shoulders, and can handle more work than you think you can, there's no big fat rush about hiring a law clerk. Your first step will be to send out letters, or make calls, to the various law schools in your area, asking that interviews be set up to select candidates for your job.

Make it clear in your offer that you want part-time help only, but that, if the person selected works out, the job can become full-time. Remember, you are not hiring a lawyer, but only a law student. Therefore, it is not necessary that you pay a plumber's salary.

Contrary to your humble beginnings, you will expect your student law clerk to be satisfied mainly with experience, and the extreme satisfaction of being permitted to work with such a fine attorney as yourself. Hence, don't let embarrassment compel you to offer more than the most minuscule rate per hour. Recall your uphill battle when you were interviewing for work.

Explain to the candidates the varied experiences to be gained, both in the courtroom and elsewhere, while in your employ. After all, this is as much a part of their legal education as classes and case briefing.

A number one priority is to keep the law clerk busy all the time. Though this point was explored previously, it bears repeating. As overloaded with work as you may be, you may find it difficult to apportion and delegate work to your clerk.

Strange as it seems, this is not easy to do. It is a talent not commonly possessed to utilize help properly and efficiently. It may seem simple at first glance, but I promise you that this is one of the most difficult parts of being in business for yourself.

You must remember that it is as important to keep your law clerk busy as it is to keep your secretary busy. Help is like a finely tuned, high-compression engine. Unless you keep up the "Rpm's" sluggishness sets in, and a fine edge becomes dulled.

The most industrious, competent, and ambitious employee will become slovenly, difficult, and indolent, if allowed to mildew on the job. Even an "exercise in futility" is better than idleness.

If you analyze the problem of keeping help busy, it will boil down to the fact that you are being imposed upon by having to break the work down into basic parts to accommodate what you believe is a limited capacity for understanding.

Well, you may be right or wrong about the limit of capacity, but you are certainly wrong about your need to be concerned with that issue. You not only don't need to indulge in spoon-feeding your employee, but that is exactly the wrong thing to do.

Assign the projects to your clerk without the slightest regard for whether the clerk fully understands what is supposed to be done. If the clerk stumbles over the problem, two things will have been accomplished. One, the clerk will be forced to expand his or her capacities to rise to the new challenge, and, two, the clerk will be kept busy with minimal effort on your part.

Even with inflated salaries, should there be an inflationary economy, law students should not be that expensive to hire. So, even though your clerk takes three times too long to do the job, the multiple of three should not make the help outrageously expensive.

As your practice gets healthier, and you get handier with money, you can increase the time schedule and even hire more and more people. If it is your desire ultimately to become the head of a large law office, this is the tack you must take.

The trick, in getting to be big, is to be able to delegate work and even authority. Take my word for it, this is much, much easier said than done. It is because this is so difficult that there are so few at the top.

Whether a secretary, a law clerk, a paralegal or any other kind of employee, there is something else that is a must. When you say something to the employee, there must be a rather immediate display of understanding by the employee.

During the interview, send out some test instructions and ask the candidate to explain what was meant. If there is trouble at that point, you can be sure of later trouble in paradise. You don't have the time to explain things repeatedly or with too much detail. Look for someone who doesn't need a diagram with each instruction.

§ 17:4 Taking on a partner

The most successful partnerships are not planned. They merely happen. Many of the partnerships that start out to be partnerships end up like many marriages, i.e., in dissolution. This is because ideal partnerships are not creatures of design, but of growth and development.

Very often, partnerships mature from practice associations, or from an employee/employer relationship. The typical embryo partnership that springs from law school associations fails simply for want of a reciprocal need. It's no good having a partner merely because you get on well, or because you respect each other's abilities.

The catalyst, forming the adhesion of a partnership, is a quality that is very difficult to assess going into the start of it. It is quite nearly impossible even for the veteran lawyer to predict the potential of another lawyer as a partner, let alone a new lawyer fresh out of the box.

A successful partnership consists of members who have a need for each other, so far as the overall practice is concerned. All too often, that need has nothing to do with what one initially sees, or thinks is seen, in a new partner.

Since need is often treated as a failing or weakness, it is usually overlooked. This usually leaves the wrong factors to be counted as the crucial assets in the successful partnership.

Play it cool and don't force the issue. When the time comes, if it does, that a partner is right for you, a partnership will emerge, pretty much the way all other aspects of your practice take shape. There is no virtue in a partnership per se.

If you have a reasonably successful practice, you will not be terribly anxious to hire a lawyer at a salary equal to half your income. Yet, taking on a partner amounts to that, and even more. If your practice is not so successful, taking on a partner is like a poor family with ten kids adopting an eleventh one. You have another mouth to feed.

There are many different ways of setting up and operating partnerships at law. The conventional business partnership is comparatively simple. Each partner shares in the profits in direct proportion to his or her interest in the partnership. Normally, "interest" is directly related to the amount of capital investment compared to amounts invested by the other partners.

Of course, profit shares are computed after certain expenses are deducted. Usually, the salaries of the working partners are included within the deductible expenses. Hence, the productive partners, as a rule, will receive a total greater share than those who participate less in the business operation.

Although it is typical that each partner thinks that the other contributes very little to the success of the business, and that he or she is the prime motivating force that keeps the business afloat, there is, under normal circumstances, a split down the middle between them, both as to salary and profits.

It is virtually impossible to ascertain the exact quantum of productivity of each participating partner. It is quite probable that a substantial disparity may exist in many instances of equal partners. At least this may be so insofar as their work values are concerned.

Happily, it is not essential in most cases to make such an assessment. The successful partnership is one in which each partner does his/her job, and respects the value of his partner's efforts.

In fact, to ensure success, each partner must be willing to accept the usual presumption that the other is not producing as much, and yet is entitled to a fair and equal share of the proceeds. This is doubtlessly another point that you will find difficult to accept.

As you may imagine, it is not always the complainer who is the superior producer. It isn't uncommon to hear such complaints from both partners. Obviously, one of them or perhaps both are wrong.

A partner may be willing to share with another on the basis, for instance, of the other's honesty, or his or her dependability, or whatever. There may be situations where having someone on hand who can reliably "mind the store" is more important than the amount of business produced. But be careful of this possibly circumventing fiction.

This is generally not a good basis for a partnership. The best partnerships are founded on need, and the values bargained for are not always visible to outsiders. But be certain that it's genuinely visible at least to you.

Rifts in partnerships occur when one partner forgets what was bargained for and becomes unhappy because the other partner cannot contribute something else. Or, one partner may outgrow the other, and no longer needs what originally was the goal.

Too often in partnerships, as in marriages, little thought is really given to the *quid pro quo*. Too often, the unimportant things are emphasized, and the important things are completely overlooked. Then, there comes a day when the partners come face-to-face with what is important.

Make certain that you have fully considered what you need from a partner before you start thinking seriously about a partnership. When you are convinced that you know what you need, you must then ask yourself whether you are willing to give to the partnership more than you may get.

Even if it isn't true that you will get the short end of the stick, you will believe that it's true. Prepare yourself for this feeling, and if you are content with it, you may have a chance of succeeding with a partnership. That is, of course, if your partner feels the same way.

The nature of law practice, being essentially a personal service, is such that customized partnership arrangements are often appropriate. Too, considerations of ethics, client relationships, bar association rules, and other extrinsic factors affect the position of the partners.

In the ordinary business partnership, an irreconcilable break is remediable through a conventional dissolution and liquidation of assets. Obviously, this cannot be done in a law partnership.

In the ordinary business partnership, there can be a division of the operation according to some prior agreement or contract. In law, we have a duty to our clients, and we are bound to discharge that duty regardless of any contrary contractual provisions. It may be natural, then, for the duty load to be apportioned in a different fashion from the right to income.

It is commonplace for law partners to retain their own clients and remain committed to them independently, even though the income therefrom is subject to division among the partners. In some cases, only a portion of the fee income is thrown into the hotchpot for division and the rest retained by the servicing partner.

In other cases, an incoming partner must contribute all of the fee income to the partnership. Yet in others, each partner is entitled to a percentage of each new client he or she brings to the partnership.

The rest becomes partnership property.

As you would imagine, there is little actual capital investment in a law partnership. The main "assets" of the partnership are the clients. Thus, the ratio of clientele value is often the determining factor in how the partnership interests are divided.

You should be forewarned, though, that this is far from a reliable measuring stick. You cannot always equate the value of a clientele with the fee income it engenders.

A personal injury clientele may be worth hundreds of thousands of dollars if you base it upon the fees it may bring in. However, such clients are normally one-shot deals. How many accidents can a personal injury client get into?

That type of clientele is only as valuable as the personal injury lawyer is capable of continuing to generate new business. It is his or her ability you must then assess, and not the clientele.

Often the growth and development of profits from a personal injury practice depends on the methodology of the lawyer who gets the business. The mainstay of this process is in the contacts made and sustained.

On the other hand, a solid business or corporate clientele is more likely to be self-perpetuating. Even a trial lawyer may offer something of a more predictable, valued clientele, since much of his work comes from other lawyers.

An historical analysis might indicate his continued potential. Although certainly variable, his income is not as uncertain as in the case of the volatile personal injury practice.

One of the greatest fictions of all is the oft-repeated reason for partnerizing, i.e., that you can get some relief at the helm. This is not only an extremely extravagant way of handling a very simple problem, but it doesn't even offer an adequate solution.

In the first place, a productive partner is one who practices in a totally different area of the law from your practice. This is the point. You don't need duplication.

By amalgamating distinctive kinds of practices, you cover a much broader scope in the field. If you do it this way, and you should, you would not have a competent lawyer to service your clients in your absence. Other than very perfunctory services, his or her expertise would be out of phase with yours.

Still, most kinds of practice fields don't usually require unpredictable attention. Things that arise during your absence could probably be handled by any lawyer.

A much better solution to your "relief" problem is to stay "single." Work out a reciprocal arrangement with one of your neighbor lawyers who does the same kind of work you do. You can work this out on a reasonable and mutually satisfactory basis. It will cost you nothing but reciprocation, and you are spared the complications of partnership.

You simply make an agreement with your neighbor to cover for you during your absence. In return, you will cover for him when he wishes to be relieved. This is no big deal for either of you, and there's no great imposition or cost to either. After your vacation, or whatever, is finished, you go back to your regular routine.

Partnership does not deserve a prominent place in this book. This is not only because this book's theme is "solo" practice, but because the formation of a partnership is sort of a spontaneous combustion.

There is really no reliable way to advise lawyers on how to find and cultivate a good partnership,. Neither can one advise another on how to find and cultivate a good marriage. I have been consistently poor at predicting both lasting marriages and lasting partnerships.

This is simply because I cannot see what the other person might see in an intended partner or spouse. I never expected my own marriage to last when Lillian and I married over fifty years ago. Lillian recently confided that she harbored the same doubts. Now she says: "Leave him, never. Kill him, yes!"

I have outlined the various bases for partnerships. If you are afraid of the dark and need company, be my guest. Find another lonely soul who will be amenable to any of the suggestions I have outlined above. The two (or even three or more) of you can do your thing for as long as it lasts, which shouldn't be too long.

§ 17:5 Looking to a judgeship

Can you buy a judge seat for "X" dollars? I've heard the same stories you've heard. Oh sure, there are deals made in the offices of some public servants. I am not naive. Such deals are made by hardheaded, inveterate politicos who know their way around political structures, not by amateurs like you and me.

Oh, I know that you've heard many stories about this judge or that judge and how such appointments were made. But, do you really know? Were you there? Did you see? Chances are, no. It's so easy to malign a person who holds a position so coveted by the seeker.

You know the usual derision: "Judge so-an'-so. The only way he could have gotten the appointment was to pay for it." How many judges are there who could pass muster in the eyes of envy? Count them. Then you'll understand the reason for these myths. It's such an easy logic to sell.

O.K., does this mean that all appointments are made regardless of the most qualified judicial material? Of course not. I said that I am not naive. To see the answer to this question, survey the number of judicial appointments made to members of parties other than that of the governor's.

Loyalties do persuade. Of that there is no doubt. There is valid justification for this remnant of the "spoils" system. There is ample qualified judicial material in both major parties. It's not then unreasonable for appointments given from the "in" party?

Be a loyal hard working supporter of your party's gubernatorial candidate, and you could get your appointment, if he or she wins, if you're qualified, and if you're lucky.

Disregarding the variables from state to state, governor to governor, party to party, and circumstance to circumstance, there are some oft-quoted basics that appear to have some logical basis.

If recent events have taught us little else, we have learned that lawyers abound among those politics. Lawyers are usually in the vanguard of the campaigns.

If only from fear of change in customs and habits, candidates for office will first curry favor with prominent attorney political activists. These are also the last people that the vote-conscious politician will want to antagonize.

The quality of the governor's judicial appointments is therefore an important part of his or her political sway. The judges who are appointed by the governors whom lawyers have helped to elect serve more often as a barometer of the governor's future political success than of his or her other official acts.

Here is a rare case of experts being graded by experts. If in the main, the appointments are of good and competent jurists, this record will count for much on the governor's political scoreboard. A few tested criteria regarding appointments are:

(a) Some government agency background;

(b) Some pro bono experience;

(c) "Belongingness";

(d) A good, clean practice record; and

(e) Some token opposition selections.

Thus, in order best to ensure some degree of competence, the governor will often look to tried, tested, and true criteria. Elaboration on some of the preceding points follows:

(a) Some background and experience in governmental or public agency work. For example, a few years in the district attorney's office couldn't hurt.

(b) Some work in pro bono publico organized agencies. Legal Aid work for some extended period counts for a few merit points.

(c) "Belongingness." Contrary to what I said regarding getting "other business," your affiliation with certain clubs, institutions, and legal fraternities can play a big part in your being considered for the bench.

(d) A good, clean practice record. The absence of a blemish on your practice escutcheon isn't so much to assure your purity of behavior on the bench as it is to assure no embarrassment to his or her Excellency later on. Sadly, it is mostly for that reason that "the black robe will not fit over a dirty shirt."

(e) Naturally, his or her Excellency will look for such pedigrees within his or her own party first.

True, there will usually be a few token appointments from the other party just to show he or she is fair, but if you are in the wrong party, don't be overly optimistic. Wait your party's turn and then roll up your sleeves and work like a beaver to get your leader elected.

In order to best orient your political work toward recognition for later consideration, you must start early. Late comers are rarely given much credit. Sure, you want to see which way the wind is blowing before you commit yourself to too much effort, but so does everybody.

If you are one of many, you'll be forgotten quickly after the victory celebration. But, if you are one of the few who had "foresight" at the beginning of the campaign, you will be a charter member, and in the front line for appreciation.

The process of finding and choosing the person within the campaign to act as your "sponsor" is a critical and delicately balanced one. The officers in the upper echelons are very often highly ambitious and crafty people.

Many of them are the type who would use your efforts and talent to their own ends. You could very well be working under an affable, charming person who, while encouraging you in your aspirations, will take full credit for all of your ideas and work, while you get no recognition at all.

On the other hand, you might find yourself shackled to a dolt with neither opportunity nor influence. If he or she has the governor's ear, he or she will usually use his or her position for whatever purposes serve him or her, not you.

Once in a while, however, you do run into a rare bird who really does want only to help his or her candidate win, and wants no favor for himself or herself. If, after great scrutiny, you are convinced of this, go like a rocket.

Naturally, the closer you get to the candidate, the more likely your accomplishments will come to his/her attention or the attention of his/her upper level staff. The problem, of course, is that unless you have some very special entree or sorely needed ability, you will get relegated to the minor leagues. It's very difficult to command any attention for having done a great job putting posters in windows.

If you have a flair for writing speeches, you stand a good chance of moving into the front lines. If you are the gregarious type and have many influential friends, you might be involved in helping to set up the candidate's stumping itinerary.

Your writing talents may not be along speechmaking lines and yet could be useful for white paper work. In this area, you'll have a chance to put both your literary and research abilities to work.

Sometimes, an ability that you would least suspect could be

valuable may be just the thing that could put you way out in front. Search your repertoire for anything that you can say you know all that there is to know about. Even if you don't know positively "all" there is to know, you might fudge a bit and claim "all."

In a political campaign, anything could be important, and you might just strike it lucky. If you find such an expertise within your unused and forgotten bag of accruals, shout it to the skies. Someone might hear and take heed.

Contribute some money. Keep it to a modest amount, even if you can afford a bundle. Everyone is skittish about large contributions these days. If your contribution is a big one, you may get passed over because of fear that your appointment was bought and paid for. Besides, at present, the election fund rules limit contributions to $1,000, and then only $100 of it is tax deductible.

This doesn't gainsay the occurrences of appointments made upon large monetary contributions. It happens, of course. Most of these events relate more to who one knows rather than how much.

Circumstances alter cases, of course, and amounts will vary with the circumstances. But no matter what else you do, you would probably profit by the giving of some moderate amount.

Again, the contribution, like your other participation, must be done early in the game. The trick here, as with anything else, is to be a good prognosticator of the outcome of elections. If you guess right, you are at least in the position of possibilities.

As you must surely know, there are no guarantees. You may have worked like a Trojan, and have contributed the most valuable pluses to the campaign, with only a hearty handshake and the most heartfelt gratitude expressed, but no appointment. That's the way it goes, sometimes. To add insult to injury, you may have even contributed some money to the bum.

Now, if you are an able fundraiser, that's a different story. Giving a few thousand dollars won't help you much. But raising a few thousand might just do it for you. The combination of getting much needed campaign funds, and having worked to do it, is an attention getter.

Besides, fundraisers are quickly introduced to all the important party people, and are siphoned into the inner circle almost immediately.

Don't be bashful. To avoid the agonizing frustrations of oversight, make it clear to all that you feel that you could best serve the legal profession from the bench. Never put it in barter terms.

But, just as your candidate has declared that he or she would be of greatest value to your state as governor, you must make the same kind of declaration.

Make it clear that you only want to serve your community, your state, and your party. The best way you know of doing this is to call upon your natural and trained abilities. You were born to be a judge, and adequately trained for the job.

For the most part, state judicial posts are for a limited term, unlike federal lifetime judgeships. But the term is, with rare exceptions, also in reality a lifetime. The only real difference between state and federal posts is that the state judge must go through the formalities, occasionally, of standing for election.

In normal times, only once in a blue, blue moon is an incumbent judge not re-elected. However, we are now passing through (hopefully) some abnormal times. At present, there is great suspicion of the incumbency.

If you are an incurable optimist, find yourself an influential party worker who will spend the time and attention in spreading your gospel around the community, arranging for neighborhood "coffees," promoting newspaper and radio space, and in general paving the way toward your election. This is the hard way, but if you lack the other combinations for appointment, it is the only way.

The bar associations, in many states, are clamoring for selective processes by elite committees. In California, such a committee already exists, but has little or no control over the selection of judges.

The governor has no obligation even to consider the recommendations of the committee. Still, the committee goes on recommending, and it is hoped that someday there will be a requirement that the governor make his/her selections from the committee's eligibility list.

In some foreign countries, judges are selected from lists of candidates who were successful in competitive examinations, after completing prescribed judicial training courses. Although such a system does not foreclose all political favoritism, there is at least some assurance that the appointees will be competent and qualified.

If you do your job as a solo lawyer and develop a successful practice, in the true meaning of the term "success," you won't need to gravitate off to other pastures like the bench. You'll spend your forty or fifty years serving your clientele, your profession and your society, and retire with the satisfaction that you've done something constructive.

What more can anyone ask from life?

Chapter 18

Some Selected Specific Aspects of Solo Practice

§ 18:1 Generally

If you have some definite ideas about the kind of law you want to practice, you're about average. If you eventually do find your way to that kind of law, you're a rare bird.

Unless you've had some serious exposure to specialized practice, your ideas about any particular specialty would be only a romantic notion. I'd heard comments from students like "I want to work for personal rights not property rights. I want only to practice criminal law."

Such students hadn't yet confronted child molesters, rapists, wife beaters and drug dealers, not to mention inveterate drunks, gang bangers, petty grifters and other such species of humanity. Oh, you may ultimately meet that singular "innocent" defendant being browbeaten by the law because of prejudice or some other irrelevant factor, but most likely your "clientele" will be the former.

This isn't to say that protecting personal rights doesn't include those of a child molester, rapist or whatever. But it's questionable whether most students expressing such thoughts had considered the subject fully.

The practice of law offers a huge variety of vistas. A great benefit to following the route to solo practice is the exposure you receive to the full legal panorama. Give yourself a break. Taste of all the flavors before you commit yourself to any one particular part.

Somewhere along the way you may drift into one or another particular field of law. This can happen subtly or suddenly. Whether or not this happens, you should expand your legal horizons to survey what's out there.

If you find one or another such legal area attractive, you might find yourself, willingly or unwillingly, a specialist in that field.

Oft-times, a specialty develops from a spectacular win in a particular case. Personal injury offers such possibilities. Criminal law, such as it is, is another pregnant field.

Sometimes a case that just drops in out of the blue can have this kind of magic. You score a big victory and then the line forms to the right. This happened to me after a successful defense in a film copyright infringement matter. Thereafter, every so-called "film pirate" camped on my door step.

I was, and continued to be through most of my law practice, an entertainment attorney. Suddenly I was the darling of the film pirates. When I caught my breath, I realized I didn't want that kind of "fame."

Had I felt otherwise, I could have made my bed amongst the unlicensed film vendors. It was a lucrative business, and could have grown much larger. I just didn't want that.

Advice cannot be given on the basis of potential financial rewards. You must make your decisions on your practice direction based upon your own criteria. Sometimes fate plays a hand and you're steered toward a field whether with, or against, your will.

No doubt you will have experienced touches of some of the fields listed below as part of your work project experiences. Others will sooner or later come your way.

No single book, or multi-volume set of books, can include every molecule of information on how one should approach the practice of law, much less instruct on the myriad of legal specialties into which the law is divided.

Law schools leave much for the new lawyer to fathom through the practical routes. I am confident that you will not need more than being pointed in the right direction. The preceding chapters should have given you all you need to start and manage your solo law office and practice.

The rest is the actual practice of law. Your internship will be adequately completed under the capable tutelage of your various assigning lawyers. It is not intended that this book go further.

However, there are some perspectives in certain areas of the law that you might need to deal with in the beginning of your solo practice. Here are a few.

§ 18:2 Personal injury practice

The personal injury, or negligence, practice is one with which you'll probably have some initial contact. You may find the following of some help when that happens.

An exception to the admonition to avoid contingency fee arrangements is the client who was injured in or by an automobile that was driven by a negligent, insured driver.

Other kinds of personal injury matters should be considered carefully before acceptance on a contingency basis. Automobile cases are especially suited to contingency fees, whereas other matters do not have those built in advantages.

The purpose of the contingency fee arrangement is not to give vent to your sporting blood instincts. This is an arrangement that will usually serve as a convenience to both you and your client.

Lawsuits are expensive, far too expensive for the average person adequately to finance. As a lawyer, you cannot, and should not, gamble on issues of liability or the collectability of judgments.

Although these issues may be present in automobile injury

cases, they are, more or less, resolvable at a point somewhat near the beginning of the case. A look at the police report of the accident can usually place the liability one way or the other.

Even the facts, as related by your client, can often establish the probability of liability to a sufficient degree to permit you to conclude on this issue, at least for the purpose of deciding on the feasibility of a contingency fee.

It is possible that your state either has, or will have, some form of "no fault" insurance law in effect regarding personal injuries. If so, much of what appears in this section will be of academic interest only.

Assuming that such is not the case, it is important that you have a contract with your client setting forth the terms of your representation. Naturally, terms will vary according to applicable law from state to state, but the following specimen contracts will at least give you some ideas to draw from.

[CAVEAT!! Be certain to review your local laws and bar rules regulating the content of attorney/client agreements. Many states now require statements regarding professional responsibility insurance to be included. There are also mandatory changes related to which advanced fees must be placed in trust accounts as opposed to so-called "true retainers" which may, under narrowly controlled circumstances, be commingled with general funds.]

ATTORNEY-CLIENT RETAINER AGREEMENT

Los Angeles, California, Dated ________, ("Client") retains GERALD M. SINGER, attorney at law, ("Attorney") as Client's attorney to represent Client in enforcing and protecting Client's rights and interests pertaining to that dispute and/or cause of action arising out of ________.

Attorney accepts this employment under the following terms and conditions:

1. Client empowers Attorney to take all steps in the matter deemed by Attorney to be appropriate, namely, to effect a compromise, settle the case, institute any and all legal proceedings and to take any and all other steps considered by Attorney to be advisable.

2. Client shall pay to Attorney for his services in this matter, a fee of $________ and a sum equal to ________% of any amounts received or recovered by Client in the matter by way of settlement, judgment or otherwise, if such receipts or recovery are realized prior to the filing of the complaint in the matter, or a sum equal to ________%, if received or recovered thereafter.

3. Client shall advance and pay to Attorney all costs and disbursements in connection with the matter, and shall reimburse Attorney immediately for any such costs and/or expenses which Attorney may, for convenience, advance on Client's behalf.

4. Client grants to Attorney a lien on the cause of action, and any related proceeds and judgment, to the extent of the share and sums above mentioned, as Attorney's fees and disbursements, and Client empowers Attorney to retain the share and sums out of any amounts received in settlement, judgment or otherwise, in full, for services and disbursements furnished by Attorney.

5. Client bears all responsibility, obligation and liability for all medical, pharmaceutical, hospital and other such charges rendered to, or for the benefit of, Client and all of such charges will be paid by Client.

6. Client shall not discuss Client's case with anyone unless under Attorney's express permission.

7. Client shall heed and follow all instructions given Client by Attorney in connection with the conduct of the case.

8. CLIENT ACKNOWLEDGES AND AGREES THAT ATTORNEY HAS MADE NO REPRESENTATION OF ANY NATURE AS TO THE OUTCOME OF THE CASE, OR OF ANY AMOUNTS WHICH MAY BE RECOVERED BY CLIENT UPON TERMINATION OF THE CASE, OR THAT ANY AMOUNT AT ALL MAY BE RECOVERED.

9. In the event that no recovery is realized at all, Attorney shall not be entitled to any fee other than provided above. However, Client shall be responsible for and obligated for the payment of all costs and expenses as above described, whether there be any recovery or not.

HAVING READ THE FOREGOING, ATTORNEY AND CLIENT SIGN THEIR NAMES HERE, AGREEING TO THE ABOVE TERMS AND CONDITIONS.

[Signature of Attorney]
[Signature of Client]

ATTORNEY'S RETAINER AGREEMENT

(Another Form)

THIS AGREEMENT, made on ________ *[date]*, at ________ California, by ________, Client, and ________, "Attorney," provides as follows:

Client retains Attorney to represent ______ as ______ *[his or her]* attorney at law in a cause of action against regarding ______ and empowers him to effect a compromise in the matter, or to institute such legal action as may be advisable in his judgment, and agrees to pay him for his services ______% of the amount recovered, if settled without suit, or ______% of the amount recovered after suit is instituted.

Costs and necessary disbursements are to be advanced by ______.

Attorney is given a lien on the the claim or cause of action, and on any sum recovered by way of settlement or judgment, for the sum and share mentioned above, as his fee; and it is further agreed that Attorney shall have all general, possessory, or retaining liens, and all special or charging liens known to the common law.

It is agreed that Attorney may retain his share out of the amount finally collected by suit or settlement or judgment in full of his services.

Client agrees that he will make no settlement except in the presence of Attorney and with his approval, and should he do so in violation of this agreement he agrees to pay Attorney the sum and share above indicated.

Client agrees not to substitute attorneys without the consent of Attorney, except for misconduct or incapacity of the Attorney to act; and if substitution is effected, Attorney shall be entitled to the full share and fee stated above.

It is agreed that Attorney has made no guarantees regarding the successful termination of the cause of action, and all expressions are matters of his opinion only.

Attorney accepts the retainer on the conditions enumerated above. In witness, the parties have set their hands the date first above mentioned.

[Signature of Client]
[Signature of Attorney]

In some instances, you may agree to take the case partly on contingency and partly on advanced fee. In this event, use a part of the contract applying to the retainer in conjunction with that part applying to contingency fees. If you take the case on straight contingency, merely strike out the part pertaining to the retainer fee.

You may wish to have a "sliding scale" type retainer fee. For example, you may agree to take 33-$^{1}/_{3}$% if the case settles prior to the filing a complaint, and 40% after a complaint is filed.

If the case is particularly speculative, and you have decided to ignore my admonitions about taking speculative cases on contingency, you may wish to up the percentage all across the board. Or, you may want to increase your percentage if the case goes to trial. All of these things are matters of negotiation between you and your client.

On the other hand, if the case is a good one, and it augurs well for a big pay day, you may be agreeable to accepting a much smaller cut, perhaps to as low as 25% or so.

Good, conservative personal injury cases taken on contingency can be bread and butter to your practice. But, unless you are a personal injury specialist and handle cases of this nature on a "production line" basis, you won't get rich in that line of work. Still, they can pay your overhead and maybe a bit more.

I have a different view of contingency fee matters from most personal injury lawyers with whom I've discussed this subject. I see a sort of conflict of interest.

You have an interest in keeping your case load moving, and getting your fees as quickly as possible to pay the rent, etc. Your client has an interest in getting the most possible from the case. That may not seem like a "conflict" at first blush, but look a bit closer.

This is not a "business" with your client. But what is it with you? Although you are a professional, your practice is a business. You have many cases; this is the circumstance for your client.

You're not dying to try the case. You know that a good settlement is usually better than going all the way to judgment. You know about the complications of trials, appeals, and even the tenuousness of judgment execution.

So, you'd rather take the money and run. Also, consider this: if you can settle for $5,000 right now, and get $2,000 on a 40% retainer agreement, or try the case and maybe get a verdict for $6,000 or even $7,000, how would you feel about urging settlement? Think about that.

Suppose you went all the way to a jury verdict and got the $6,000. You would net $400 more after spending, what, two days and maybe more, in preparation and trial. Then, you will wait the statutory period for motions or appeals from the other side. Finally, you get your reward for tenacity: the additional $400. Let's even say, $800 more for the route.

On the other hand, you negotiate settlement, get the $2,000, net to you without sweat. No monkey business, no problems of any kind. Since it's a settlement, the money changes hands within a few days.

But what about your client? The client's cut is an extra $600. Or, if the verdict was $7,000, the client gets an extra $1,200. The trial is your baby, not the client's.

You do all the preparation, not the client. True, you both must wait, but the client's livelihood doesn't depend on it. This is not the client's business. It's yours.

So, in whose principal interest is it to get the case settled? If you were to ask your client whether he or she wanted you to do all that extra work so that he or she could get an extra $600 or $1,200, what do you think would be the reply? That's right. But you don't put it exactly that way, do you?

You talk about the risks of losing the case and getting nothing. Or you emphasize the horrors of having to take the witness stand. Suddenly, you are not quite as confident of the client's persuasive abilities as you were when you first discussed the case with him.

Of course, these thoughts are not conscious ploys on your part to shortchange your client. You want the best for all of your clients. But there it is. Think about it. Maybe, that's not the scenario you'd present. Maybe, you'd put it squarely on the line.

Maybe, you'd say something like:

"This trial will be a rather simple one. Liability is well established. It's just a question of how much money the jury will give us. We've got a settlement offer of $5,000. 1 think that the case is worth $6,000, maybe $7,000, and I believe the jury will think so too.

Trial should last maybe two days, and my preparation will take the better part of another day, but so what. With that much increase, you stand to gain an additional $600 or even $1,200, after my 40% fee deduction. Sure, it's a lot of extra work for me, and I'll have to wait a few months for my fee, but what the heck."

Well, what is a "conflict of interest" anyway? If all lawyers were so ethical, would there be such a thing? Isn't a conflict of interest only a situation in which there is a possibility, even the appearance, of subordinating your client's position to some other objective?

Doesn't that apply here? Is it necessary that you be consciously trying to gain some advantage at your client's expense? Isn't a "possibility" that you are profiting at your client's expense all that's required?

You have a case where you could get a large reward. I mean a possibly very large one. You are looking at a possible $100,000, maybe more, case. You've been negotiating a settlement. You've nursed the offers from $7,500 up to $35,000. You have some insight into where things are, and you figure a top of maybe $50,000.

You know that you can't even explore that level, unless you are ready to talk "deal." You've got to talk to your client, and present the situation to him, fairly and honestly. You know that if you settle for $50,000, you'll come away with the biggest single payday you've ever had, and maybe ever will have.

If you pass on this offer, you believe that there'll not be another one. You'll have to go to trial. This is not the simple little $6,000 or $7,000 case that you can figure to the penny. You know that, in these biggies, many things can happen. You also know the percentages on appeal increase almost to the square of anything over $50,000.

You also know that a trial of this magnitude could take many days, maybe even weeks. The insurance company is not going to assign this case to Herman Shlizipsky who practices with his father down the street. This one goes to the big league firm. You're going to be paper-milled to death.

Well, you've got your computer and printer and you can do a bit of "milling" yourself. But all that time, effort, and risk. And for what! Here you have $20,000 net cash, in your pocket. That lump sum would turn this year into a banner one, right? Yep.

This is not the same situation as the $5,000 settlement versus the $6,000 or $7,000 trial verdict. A new something has been added: Fear! Have you ever been to Las Vegas, and watched the high rollers plunk down five or six hundred on this number, and five or six hundred there, and another there? Did it make you dizzy? One lousy seven, and it's all down the drain.

This is a whole new experience for schoolboys who have never really been far from the school yard until they opened their cozy little solo practice offices. All right, so that's not you.

You've been around some. You're not Little Lord Fauntleroy. Still, how many times have you held decisions like that in your trembling fingers?

O.K., so maybe you've got a fix on that kind of situation. You'd tell them to shove it, and go the route. But, what if it was a $75,000 offer? Then what? Shove it? How about $80,000? See the point? At some crossing, you've got to decide something. You cannot, or at least you should not, balk and go for trial all the time.

Can you be positively certain that your decision is based on what's best for your client? Can you be sure that your own interest, or your own trepidation, isn't the pivotal point? Well, so much for conflict of interest. Maybe you'll be lucky, and not get the real big ones to test your fiber.

If there are any risks in the case regarding liability or

collectability, I insist on the usual hourly fee basis. In that way, if there is a big win, the client can't complain, since he or she gets all the marbles, less my pittance.

If the defendant is self-insured, you can bet the matter will be tried, unless you take pennies in settlement. So be prepared to go all the way. Then, there's the question of whether the bum is collectible after you win.

It's enough to risk the normal hazards of trial, without doubling the risk on issues of liability and the defendant's collectability. In case you are ever criticized for refusing to play a "sure thing," you can quote some accurate statistics on the number of "sure thing" cases that have gone to defendants by jury verdict.

You may have raised an eyebrow on the provision for absolute right to negotiate and complete a settlement without your client's permission or even knowledge. Naturally, this clause is not enforceable, probably in any jurisdiction. However, it does add a bit of strength to your "negotiations" with your own client in getting him to come down to earth on demands.

Sometimes, clients have a tendency to over evaluate their own damages, but most often attorneys themselves set the tone for this exaggeration. In their zeal to get the matter, some attorneys will overstate the case value.

If the case comes to filing a complaint, there could be a bit of a problem stemming from the amount stated in your prayer. You are asking for damages of $150,000, which you know is grossly overstated.

An offer is presented by $3,500 in full settlement. Your client has some difficulty with the discrepancy. You try to explain, but everything you say sounds like you don't know what you're doing.

The case is actually not worth more than $3,500, but you can't convince the client of that. You set the stage for that confusion in the prayer, but what can you do about it now? The only antidote is salesmanship. Salesmanship is a mighty tool, but why go out of the way just to use it?

The best way to handle this sort of thing is to acquaint your client with the "hype" of complaints and prayers right from the start. Tell your client that we're suing for $150,000 as a matter of strategy only. Don't let the client get sold on these figures. If you do, he or she will be deciding whether to winter in Florence or Monte Carlo with the $150,000.

The "prayer" sum may not be a problem in your state. In California, tort general damages can't be stated in a specific sum. The prayer can state only "as adduced by the evidence," or "according to proof," or such language.

Your rapport with your client throughout all stages is vitally important in this kind of case. Getting the client to sign a contract giving you 40%, 50%, or even 60% is no trick. But convincing the client to accept the amount offered at settlement time is quite another matter. Whatever your contract may say, the client still has the last word on his or her case.

You cannot deny your client his or her rights. But you can exercise what is called "attorney control." This does not mean that when you say "jump," your client asks, "how high?" It does mean, though, that in strategic matters your words are valued and soberly evaluated. Consider the fact that you must at least be able to control the general direction of your cases.

Much is written on "client control." Some favor the use of psychology, while others speak of mastery of voice tone. Actually, neither of those techniques means anything, unless you have one of those special skills.

There is a trick to client control, of course, which like everything else about solo practice, you can learn. The trick, mainly, is to take only clients that you can control.

Sometimes your opposition goes way off in evaluating the case. You get an offer of $50,000 for a case that you wouldn't buy for $5,000. You would have to pull a jury from Aesop's Fables to score anywhere near such a verdict.

You even stand a good chance of losing the case altogether. Your client purses his or her lips and says "No." What is in his or her mind? You remember: "For even the devil himself knoweth not the mind of a man."

The client could really be saying "no" to the contract split, but he'll never admit this to you. This could be the client's cute little way of pressuring you into taking less than the percentage agreed upon. To prevent this kind of sandbagging, you must get and retain the upper hand at all times.

The words that you have included in the agreement, giving you full power in making decisions about settlement, are golden words in such a predicament. You may succeed in persuading the client to accept this sensational offer, keep your end of the split intact, and maintain the good relationship between you and your client to the last.

This is not to say that you may minimize the paramount duty you owe to your client to preserve, enforce, and protect his or her interest to the fullest at all times. But you will find, to your consternation, that some people are their own worst enemies in this regard.

Clients have been known, sometimes, to stubbornly refuse a

generous offer without regard to the division between client and lawyer. You try patiently to explain all of the factors which go into the computations of the value of a case.

You try the horror tactic. You suggest a real possibility of losing the case and getting nothing at all. The client just sticks his or her toes in the dirt, juts his or her jaw out toward your nose and says, "I'll just have to take that chance."

Don't waste your time trying to convince such a client through superior argument. Don't panic. Remember the power of salesmanship. Use it. Getting information here means discovering the real reason for the refusal. Then, give information upon which your client may agree.

Without salesmanship, you are stuck with two choices. Either go toward trial, hoping that the client will relent at some point with the offer still open, or invoke your contractual clause to withdraw as counsel. This will preserve your right to a fair division of the offer at that time.

Depending on the laws of your state, you may, or may not, be entitled to your contracted percentage, but whatever the percentage, it will be calculated upon the $50,000 offer. Your successor lawyer will share only in what remains.

The very best way to handle situations like these is not to get into them in the first place. You can generally estimate a client of this type within the first few minutes of the interview.

They usually begin by telling you how to run the case. They will also tell you of four or five cases which they know of where each litigant got enough to retire on. They will explain that the ways to such huge judgments are simple, and they will show you how. Take another look at your calendar, and find that you don't have time for this case after all.

§ 18:3 Some tips on evaluating a case

There are some very good books on the subject of evaluating and settling personal injury cases, and this book is not meant to be included among them. There are some general facts, though, that you should acquaint yourself with on this subject.

You'll be getting some of your own cases and clients much faster than you would believe possible. Before you know it, you'll be called upon to throw out a figure into the settlement ring. Believe it or not, you may find use for this information even while accepting work assignments.

Don't be surprised if an assigning lawyer expresses some interest in your opinion as to the value of a case. There is some science to case evaluation, but only just so much.

He or she may not hang on your every word, but don't minimize its input value. If you have been working the case more than the assignor, you may have some valuable insight.

Unless you have some high influence with a good swami, you're going to need some basic information to help you to evaluate damages. You should at least know enough to be able to bluff the insurance company's adjuster.

As you have learned in law school, all cases are broken down into two basic components: liability and damages. If your client was rear-ended while stopped at a traffic signal, you generally have no problem with liability.

If this same client suffered a broken pelvis, compound fracture of the femur or collar bone, and was hospitalized for six months, during which time he or she was treated for related shock, cardiac failure, and a ruptured spleen, you can relax on the subject of damages.

Fortunately, or unfortunately, depending upon your point of view, this will not be the average case that will come your way. For some strange and exotic reason, such cases always seem to come to your colleagues down the hall.

Oh yes, you will hear all about such cases from your co-tenants. You will be entertained, by the hour, with graphic accounts of the gory cases which they have handled.

You will have word pictures vividly portrayed of maimed and twisted bodies. There will be fractured skulls, internal bleeding, amputations, and other delightful opportunities for six-figure judgments. So many happy clients in casts and traction will be described in gory details of those who shared in your colleague's good fortune.

You will hear strange, exotic, and thrilling terms like "permanent and stationery" and "objective injuries," along with enthralling words like "totally and permanently disabled."

But such thoughts as these are not for you to contemplate. Your clients will have mundanities like "whiplash" or "sacrolumbar sprain," and not one single little bone fracture in the lot. These are "soft tissue injuries." The "pains" which result from such "injuries" are called "subjective symptoms."

This is a euphemism to describe a condition where no one in the whole world, except your client, knows exactly where it hurts. And, sometimes even your client can't recall the spot he or she pointed to yesterday.

But "objective injuries." Well, now, these are entirely different. Here you have broken bones, clearly revealed on X-rays. You may also have an assortment of open wounds, skin hemorrhages, massive contusions, abrasions, and other magnificently portrayable and provable hurts.

These are called "objective," because anyone who looks at the greenish mass of tortured flesh in the color photograph, or at the X-rays of the compound fractures, will be able to see at a glance where and how much it hurts.

You won't need to be bothered with such things as X-rays, nor will you have to learn to love the sight of mangled bodies, because your clients will have only the much disparaged "subjective symptoms and injuries."

Liability and damages are separate elements to be treated separately and developed with distinction in your lawsuit. Still, they interact upon each other in very definite ways.

For example, your client complains of severe whiplash pain in the cervical or neck area. You are limited to proof of subjective pain only. It would be of great help if you can show a more flagrant negligence on the part of the defendant.

You aren't seeking punitive damages, nor could you do so in the usual auto accident case. Nonetheless, the jury will have an underlying desire to "punish" the wayward defendant. Without resort to punitive or exemplary damages, how can this be done?

You will learn that the law is one thing, and human nature is quite another. You will either learn to live with such paradoxes, or spend your whole life fighting windmills. There are no black and white legal precedents for elevating a damage award because of the "extent" of liability. A defendant is either liable for vehicular negligence or not.

Then, there's the other side: damages. If you can show a severe impact, you are going to be much more successful in convincing a jury of the credibility of painful subjective injuries. The degree of damage done to an automobile does not properly relate to personal injury.

This is more properly within the property damages part. Still, there is no doubt that proof of extensive property damage to the car will indicate a heavy crash, which in turn will support the claim of a chain of violence carried through to the body, thereby causing the injuries complained of.

It would be far more difficult for you to persuade the jury that your client should be awarded $10,000, if the total repair bill for his or her car was only $225.87, than if you could show repairs in the amount of $2,500.

There is a relationship between dollars spent to repair a car, and the dollars awarded to compensate for your client's pain and suffering. This might seem a tenuous one, but experience will show an indisputable connection.

Naturally, such evidence would not follow in the order of proof for personal injury as a matter of procedure. But, jurors are human, and they will react to a humanly logical deduction.

It is not impossible for a person to receive horrific injuries in an accident that caused only minor property damage. Extreme injuries would probably be taken as unlikely, unless proof could be shown by objective standards. Thus, the element of "impact" will to some extent control acceptance by the jury of how hurt your client really was.

The contrary is just as true. If there is a borderline question on the fault of the defendant, the heartrending sight of your mangled and crippled plaintiff will do much to tip the jury toward finding the defendant negligent.

Even though we are dealing with civil not criminal law there is the flavor of "letting the punishment fit the crime." These are not facts of law; they are facts of life.

It is wise first to assess your position with regard to the quotient of liability before stipulating or accepting a stipulation as to liability. Let's say the defendant was driving while drunk, exceeding the speed limit, ran three red lights, and rear-ended your "sitting duck" client.

Defendant's attorney offers to stipulate as to liability. You will politely refuse your opponent's kind offer to stipulate as to liability. Thank your opponent for his or her noble attempt to save the court's valuable time, but say "No, thank you."

Tell your opponent that you prefer to try the issue. Then, lower all of the booms to show what a dastardly villain the defendant is. Show his or her utter disregard for the law, and for the rights of others. The more unsavory an individual you can make the defendant, the bigger the verdict may be for your client.

Absent a stipulation, you will be obliged to prove the defendant's negligence. You will need to show, in the most gruesome detail, the horrendous manner in which the defendant operated his or her vehicle.

As the evidence unfolds, the jury will come to realize, more and more, what a despicable person the defendant is. They will decide, without need for your persuasion, that the defendant certainly should be taken to task for such ignobility.

There is no need now to remind the jury that this hateful person should not be entitled to the slightest sympathy in their assessment of damages. Then, in your summation, you will once again let the trumpets sound, the drums roll, and the castigation be reprised, but with even more histrionics.

Should you give all this up in a stipulation? Bite your tongue.

It goes without saying, on the other hand, that if the issue of liability is in doubt or uninspiring, and you are made an offer to stipulate as to liability, grab it fast.

But enough of trial technique, since this is not a trial manual. Further, there is every likelihood that your case will settle long before trial. This is another fact of life. Most cases settle even before the complaint is filed. Your time is, therefore, better spent learning to develop a practical approach to settlement.

§ 18:4 Other "contingent fee" matters

Contingency fee arrangements were probably invented by the same fellow who first sold the Brooklyn Bridge to a wide-eyed tourist. You can quickly build up an inventory of cases on contingency that will be almost as valuable as a trunk full of Confederate money.

Except for the few kinds of cases dealt with in this book which work reasonably well on contingency, say "no." The woods are filled with people with "great cases" who want your services for no money up front. Pass them on to the nice deserving lawyer down the hall. You know, the one who's always bragging to you about his fantastic cases.

§ 18:5 Where there's a will, there's a way to probate

Ask each client about the state of his or her will. This inquiry can not only produce fees for you but will be doing your clients a big favor. Most people either have no will or their will is woefully outdated.

What has happened since the last will was executed? Is there a new baby? Has there been a wedding or a divorce? Have finances among intended beneficiaries shifted such to warrant a review of the distribution?

Perhaps only minor changes have occurred. A codicil may serve the purpose. Whatever is needed, you will have performed a valuable service by simply calling the matter to your client's attention.

Sure, your fee for this service won't be monumental, but think of the general effect on your practice. You will be building a will inventory which can be a source of substantial fees later on. Many of the wills which you draft will someday be probated during the term of your practice.

Some of these wills may be redone by other alert attorneys, with the probate going elsewhere. But some of them will come your way. Use this inquiry as a means of keeping contact with all of your clients. You should draft a generalized letter something like the following:

Dear Client:

In reviewing your file, I noted that some time has passed since we prepared your will. Perhaps there have been some changes in your circumstances or those of your family which might warrant revision of your will. Also, some changes have occurred in the law involving taxation and estates in general. These and perhaps other personal factors could alter the direction of your estate away from your intended goals.

You may also wish to consider a living trust. As you know, such a trust could result in very substantial tax savings and some considerable reduction of inconvenience to your family.

After you have thought about this, you might call me so we can discuss this subject in detail.

Sincerely,

GERALD M. SINGER

As often as not, an office conference brought about by this letter could produce other legal business. Some other little problem may have been disturbing your client but maybe not enough to stimulate a call to you. This conference would be a good opportunity to flush out such things.

Such contact shows concern for your client's welfare and will be appreciated. Lengthy pauses in activity of the attorney-client relationship can sometimes cause rust and straying by the client to other legal pastures.

If you've never drawn a will for a particular client, your letter should read something like this:

Dear Client:

In reviewing your file, I don't find a will for you. My indexing system is designed to keep tabs on these important personal documents. I would appreciate your calling me to let me know whether you have a will and that somehow this has escaped our indexing.

Many important changes have recently transpired concerning taxation and other estate laws. You may wish to have me review your will so you can be assured that it will accurately reflect your desires. Such a review would not obligate you for any fee. Call me at your convenience so we may discuss this as well as any other circumstance changes which could affect you and your family. You may, for example, wish to consider a living trust which, as you may have heard, can save your family substantial taxes and possible inconvenience.

Sincerely,

GERALD M. SINGER

Another positive factor in drafting or revising a will is the selection of the executor. If a bank or other commercial executor is nominated, there would usually be an automatic appointment of the drafting attorney to represent the executor.

Often a client will prefer a commercial executor to either a spouse or other member of the family. Bereavement often displaces concern for practicalities. Explaining the functions of professional services of this kind to the client can justify the moderate statutory fees payable. Often the savings in lower property appraisals, more likely approved by the IRS for a bank, can more than equal the executor's fee.

§ 18:6 Consider advising incorporation

Explaining the advantages of corporate personal liability insulation to a client operating a partnership or sole proprietorship can sometimes result in a fee for you and a good turn for your client. If the business isn't large enough to warrant the intricacies of corporate taxation, taking the option of the IRC Subchapter "S" provision can permit taxing your client as a partnership or sole proprietor, as the case may be.

Partnerships can be sticky in disputes even if the interests are equal. Corporate interests can avoid such entanglements. Proportionate stock distribution will better define the respective interests as well as provide the senior investor with appropriate business control.

§ 18:7 New limited liability company

A newer idea recently implemented in California and in many other states, is the limited liability company. This allows a partnership or sole proprietorship to remain private and still reap the advantages of liability insulation of a corporation.

The LLC has no formal ongoing procedural requisites such as minutes, nor is it necessary to keep personal transactions separate from the company's as with corporations. The company is run and managed in the same manner as though no such election had been made other than the name being identified as limited. The term "LTD' may be used to convey that information.

There is an initial filing document called "Articles of Organization," which is arranged about as simply as a basic "Articles Of Incorporation." The organizational structure can be amended at any time through the filing of a document conveniently called a "Certificate Of Amendment."

There are some aspects to the LLC that still need to be ironed out, mainly with the IRS as to parity with a corporation. Recent indications are that these will be ultimately determined as on par with corporations.

There are pros and cons to both systems. There isn't much savings in franchise taxes between the two, but a great deal less inconvenience in avoiding corporation procedures. Another possible downside for some businesses is that the franchise fee for LLC'S, at least in California, can accelerate based upon the amount of business being done by the company.

§ 18:8 Employment contracts

Your smaller business clients should be aware of the many pitfalls in contracting with employees. However, many rights are given to employees statutorily that can be circumvented contractually. Wrongful termination is a creature that has been with us almost forever but has blown up considerably in recent years. Careful contracting can minimize much of the risk.

You should also keep your business client informed about the dangers of engaging workers as "Independent Contractors." Most states are touchy about the term when, in fact, the worker is an employee in independent contractor's clothing. In California, the penalty for misapplying that term can be very expensive.

The idea is that the employee gets away without paying the employment taxes, withholding, etc. and the employer escapes its contributions. What often happens is that the employee tries to seek unemployment or workers' compensation only to "learn" of his or her lack of coverage. (Of course, he or she knew it all the time.) Who gets it in the neck? Your client, of course.

Who was at fault? Well, the employee didn't want any payroll deductions, but neither did our client, the employer, want to make his or her employer's contribution. So greed was the culprit, as it almost always is.

Keeping your client advised as to flux in the employment picture can be of great benefit to him or her and engender fees for you.

§ 18:9 Debt collection cases

Debt collection practice is another area in which contingency fees have been prevalent. I am not an advocate of the contingency fee arrangement at best, and I like it in debt collection cases even less.

Those who argue the merit of the contingency basis have probably never really checked the hours they spend on those cases. I have logged time on all of my cases, as I suggest you also do. I have found, as will you, that the contingency fee case is often no bargain for the lawyer.

The only argument that I can really accept for taking contingency fees is that the case would not otherwise be available to you. If you could choose on which basis you will take each case, contingency or straight fee, I would urge you to take the $100 per hour and never look back.

Oh sure, you hear stories about the $1,000,000 case that was the "making" of some lawyer. These are the same kinds of stories you hear at the race tracks about longshot horses, or from that lawyer down the hall.

You very well may be taking contingency fee debt collection cases at first. This is simply because most lawyers don't like them. So you'll be the happy beneficiary of such cases through auspices of the "overflow" system.

You'll be handling a lot of collections and, even though the money per case quotient won't thrill you, the volume of cases can be large. The procedures in processing these cases are relatively simple, and, as a rule, the percentage of success is high.

Your contingency fee structure should be something like the following: 33-$^{1}/_{3}$% of gross collected after the demand letter; 40% after filing the complaint; and 50% upon commencement of any legal procedure.

Costs are paid separately, off the top, just as with personal injury cases.

Spend a little time developing a good style of writing your demand letters. The difference between a good and profitable debt collection practice and an ineffective one is in the style of the demand. The following is a sample of an effective demand letter:

Sample debt collection demand letter:

Dear Mr. Jones:

We represent the Schmoehawk Co. with regard to the 75 Gadfoys you purchased and failed to pay the $760 as agreed.

You've broken your promise. Now it is our job to sue you for that amount, plus all court costs and our attorney's fees.

Our instructions are to proceed with suit.

Your debt will be increased substantially by fees and costs, in addition to your inconvenience by a court trial.

Despite our instructions, we are giving you a short time to reconsider this matter.

If we receive the full payment from you of $760, to the penny, no later than seven (7) days from this date, we will accept that payment and withhold suit.

Your payment must be received no later than on our opening of the morning mail, on Wednesday, October 5, 2000, or a complaint will be filed against you then and there, without further notice to you.

You must know it is only a question of time before we will collect the full amount plus our fees and all other costs. It is up to you as to whether you want this matter resolved the easy or the hard way.

GERALD M. SINGER

In certain circumstances, a phone call may be productive. Facts may indicate that a failure of communication existed between your client and the debtor leading to the debt delinquency. Refusal to pay a bill may sometimes be nothing more than stubbornness arising from a personality conflict.

Remember the first phase of salesmanship: getting information. Let the debtor tell his or her story without interruption. You may get facts to get the matter settled right then and there on the phone.

Being too lawyer-like can often be more destructive than constructive. You can always play the lawyer. After you've learned the reasons for delinquency, you start the second phase, giving information. Keep criticism out of your delivery. Let the debtor expand on his or her side of the story. Try even to see the debtor's point of view.

If the thorn in the debtor's side is related to a collateral matter, you might even agree with him or her. Suggest the possibility that your client may not have acted entirely blamelessly.

Then, try to show the debtor that continued refusal to pay the debt is no way to try to teach your client a lesson. The debtor will have to pay the debt in the end, plus the possibility of additional costs.

Get the debtor to see this eventuality, but do not ignore his or her rancor. Tell the debtor that you will relay what he or she has said to your client. Impress upon him or her that the debt and the other dispute are not related and payment must be made without delay.

Quite often, the only thing that the recalcitrant debtor wants is the satisfaction of having his or her "say." You will have served this purpose.

When venom is flowing on both sides, don't threaten lawsuits. When the conversation has ebbed a bit and the volatility subsides, point out that the debtor did, after all, receive the merchandise and, aside from anything else, he or she must pay for what was received.

§ 18:10 Class actions

A decidedly different kind of "contingency" case is the class action. Not only different in its fee methodology, the class action is different in almost every respect from other kinds of cases. The rules will, as with all suits, vary from state to state.

In the past, the class action suit has been a favorite among adventurous and speculating lawyers. Lately, however, such actions have been fraught with hazards.

If you are fresh from law school, you are probably well informed of the case law and legislative trends which have been given class action lawyers big headaches.

Under some court rules, the class action must be tested for merit on a variety of elements. It must be established that the action is one deserving of that status. Such tests are determined in court hearings, usually several, upon motion of either or both of the parties, or on the court's own motion.

Once it is established that the action is proper to pursue in the class procedure, the court takes the case "under its wing," so to speak, and the parties no longer have full control. The term "parties" in a class action includes all of the class members for whose benefit the action is being prosecuted. All of the class members are being represented by the fiduciary party, or parties, having actively taken part in the suit.

The plaintiffs' champion or champions (the actual people who have instigated the suit) can no longer make unilateral decisions as to certain things usually taken for granted by plaintiffs.

For example, in the usual lawsuit, the plaintiff may dismiss at anytime, unilaterally, with or without prejudice. In the class action, this is not an option open to those bringing the suit.

In an ordinary suit, the plaintiff and defendant can get together at any time and agree upon a settlement, thus ending the matter. In the class action, this is not the way it works.

All class action settlements must be approved by the court after, and only after, a very complicated procedure of notices to the class and court-approval hearings has been fully satisfied and thoroughly exhausted.

If the judge decides that the settlement figure is not duly compensatory to the class members, the judge will deny the settlement and send the parties back out, either to work out a new settlement or to proceed to trial.

It is also during these hearings that the judge will approve or disapprove the amount entered as attorney's fees. So, regardless of any agreement that may or may not have existed between you and your "clients," with or without the concurrence of the defendants, the court has the final say on your fee.

You must set forth a detailed accounting of your services with a justification of your hourly rate, in a sworn declaration presented to the court in support of your request for an award of fees. It will be necessary for you to document and support your request for fees, both thoroughly and persuasively in most instances.

That still may, or may not, be enough. The court may have ideas of its own. This is another area of court discretion that won't be disturbed on appeal. It's not enough that your well-documented accounts and fees schedule may be independently impressive. If the court rejects your presentation, that's it!

If you like the thought of class actions, and if you have a valid class action case, have at it. After you have analyzed the situation from every angle, and educated yourself thoroughly on all of the class action methodologies, by all means, jump right in.

The pay can be exceptional, if the action has real merit. And the bona fide class action case can be jolly good fun as well. As in most personal injury cases, if you can put up a good show along the way, the settlement can be quite substantial.

Whether or not you've actually decided to file a class action, if the facts are susceptible of one, you should include its mention in your demand letter.

Sometimes, the mere mention of "class action" can cause a vulnerable defendant to swallow his teeth. Caveat! Know and understand the local laws on unlawful coercion, etc.

Where there is any likelihood that the defendant may have caused the same injury to others as well as to your client, you might suggest the possibility of such a broadside attack. An indication that it might be appropriate to take steps to protect the interests of the public from possible misconduct could produce interesting results.

For example, your adversary might just come running over with his or her checkbook, pen, and shaking hand. Be wary of the ethical bounds of this, or any other kind of pressure that might be considered irregular.

There are sundry other kinds of cases which for various reasons lend themselves to contingency fees, but as I have said, don't be lured by the charming chant of the Lorelei. Take your hundred bucks an hour, and say thank you.

§ 18:11 Expert testimony in small cases

A big problem in small cases is money for things like investigation and experts. Some cases, large or small, require the input of experts. If the case is so small that the expense cannot be justified, you could be in a no-win situation.

Experts have become more and more commonplace in larger cases, and increasingly so, marginal matters. Courts have progressively looked to experts to establish facts that were once considered self-evident.

For example, a court award of attorneys' fees. Don't try to prove attorney's fees by your own testimony in most jurisdictions. Time was that legal fees could be proved by your own simple testimony.

What is your hourly fee? Is that fee reasonably commensurate with your background, expertise and experience? How much time was spent on the matter? Was each time segment reasonable for the work accomplished? Was the work reasonably necessary to the case? Judges had, and still have, the expertise needed to rule on the sufficiency of the answers. But they won't.

To prove reasonable legal fees these days, it's not enough that you take the stand to answer these questions yourself. You need another lawyer, almost any lawyer familiar with the particular area of law to testify. That "expert" may mouth the exact same testimony that you could give yourself, but the expert is at least ostensibly independent. You are not.

Few cases, large or small, would not be benefited by expert testimony. How is this accomplished under a limited budget? Well, there are experts and then there are experts.

In intersection collision cases, left turners are always wrong, it seems. For example, your client was hit during a left turn. He insists that he was stopped and the other guy sped through the intersection against the red signal. Your client's leg was severely injured and his car was totaled.

No witness, and no pictures were taken. According to your client, no attempt was made by the other driver to stop. How can you establish fault by the other side?

The car damage shows no lateral trenching of metal. This could indicate no cross motion by your client's car. Also, the extent of inward displacement of metal and the springing open of the hood and trunk lid are indications of excessive speed by the other car.

Your client could testify to all of that, but argument from the other side could muddy the picture and lose the day. Most judges would be predisposed to a defense position in left turn situations.

An expert could testify that these conditions prove that your client was stopped. The expert could further show that the other driver's speed was such to unlawfully cover a distance that would have otherwise offered safety for your client to proceed with the turn.

The expert shouldn't be too expensive. An experienced body shop person could demonstrate relative impact points and traces to establish the movements of the vehicles and speed of the oncoming car within reasonable limits. The cost for such testimony should be relatively nominal.

Is that testimony irrefutable? Of course not. But it would cause the other side the need to disprove a logical condition. In any event, the presence of an expert could help your settlement position.

Take another case. Your client was leaving on vacation. He realized at the last moment that his business was underinsured. He called his broker to increase the coverage. The broker assured your client that the amount would be increased as requested.

While your client was away, the carrier notified the broker that the increase was denied. As luck would have it, a fire destroyed the business. The existing insurance amount didn't come near compensating for the damage. A broker's acceptance binds only until the carrier issues or rejects the endorsement.

The appropriate question is: What is the custom of insurance practice regarding notification of rejection? In some areas, the notice must be copied to the insured, not just sent to the broker. Thus, if the carrier failed in its notification by merely notifying the broker, this should be proved up by an expert. Assuming expenses to your client are an issue, what can you do?

An independent insurance broker could testify on the custom and practices within the insurance industry. It could be difficult for the opposition to prove otherwise.

§ 18:12 Ethical considerations regarding use of experts

It's not just advisable to use experts where appropriate, it can be a serious problem if you fail to do so in some instances. The loss of a case for lack of expert testimony can, in certain circumstances, subject you to possible malpractice action and even perhaps Bar charges.

It may not be a viable defense to argue the lack of your client's finances. You can count on your client protesting "Why didn't you ask me? I would have paid for the expert." Of course, he couldn't pay for your fees or other costs, but somehow when it's all over, money would have been no object.

When you see the reasonable need for experts and your client can't or won't pay, you must send a letter, registered, to the client explaining the necessity and the costs involved. If you get either an unsatisfactory response, or none at all, request substitution. If all else fails and the client refuses substitution, move the court for relief.

As a lawyer, you may be stuck for lots of things when clients can't pay, but being a bank isn't among your obligations. Even the cheap way to supply experts may backfire. Your judgment must tell you when experts are necessary and what kind would be appropriate.

§ 18:13 Settlement: How and when

Tons of books are in print on how to settle cases. Most books on this subject suffer from the same malady as those on solo practice. If there is one single book available offering a practical understanding of the psychology of settlement, I have failed to find it.

With as many areas as this book attempts to cover, it should not be expected that great profundity would be given to each particular point. Keep in mind the real purpose of this book.

There are many more things that I have to say about law practice which could be of interest to you. But, you don't want to spend the rest of your life reading about them. I do propose, and I will expect, that you will hold your own in settling cases after reading this book, to an extent that few lawyers are able to do.

If you have substantial objective injuries to work with, the lid is off on the issue of damages. Each case involving such damages must be considered unique. Before you can enter into any settlement talk, you must have first done much research and investigation on the subject.

These are not the cases that will probably come your way. Most of what is said on this subject will be confined to the usual case, involving subjective or "soft tissue" injuries.

There are a few rules of thumb on settlement which are recognized by most insurance adjusters. In soft tissue injuries cases, the first approach to settlement is from the position of the quality and quantity of the medical "specials."

Medical specials, as you remember, are damages related to actual expenses for such things as physicians' fees, therapy, hospitals, orthopedic devices, pharmaceuticals, etc. The approach toward settlement from the position of medical specials is relatively simple.

You must have all of the medical and pharmaceutical bills in your file, and all medical treatment must be completed. The point of the "medical specials game" is to win the highest number possible to use as a multiplier of the total amount of specials, to arrive at the settlement figure. The average range of such a multiplier is from 3 to 5. This means that you will multiply the total of all of the medical bills anywhere from 3 to 5 times, depending upon the quality of your case.

We are talking about the garden variety of soft tissue case. These would not include any cases involving demonstrable or objective injuries or other unusual injuries or circumstances.

Conventionally, the "specials" figure used in this multiplication game is confined only to medical diagnostics, ambulance, treatment, pharmaceuticals, and orthopedic devices. With a little arm-twisting on a friendly adjuster, you might squeeze in some "special shoes, mattresses, chairs, etc.," anything which may logically be classified as therapy-connected.

Try the claim that your client has had to buy some expensive "corrective" shoes to remedy his or her foot injuries as a result of the accident. If you have a physician's prescription, you'll win that point. If no "script," a friendly adjuster might go along with it anyway.

The "mattress" thing is not so far-fetched. A bad back may well require a special orthopedic mattress for therapeutic comfort. Again, see if your client can get the "script" from the doctor.

With a little ingenuity, you may succeed in expanding the list. Bear in mind that every dollar added to this list means three, four, or even five dollars in the ultimate settlement. Hence, a $60 pair of shoes can mean an added $200 to $300 to the settlement figure.

Don't be shocked if the adjuster balks. You may be told that the shoes are O.K. for medicals, but not to compute general damages. In fact, many, if not most, adjusters won't even acknowledge the multiplication method.

When your client calls up to complain that the doctor insists on treatment three times per week which interferes with his or her tennis game, remind him or her: (a) tennis is bad for his or her back; (b) a more consistent and lengthier history of medical treatment is better for his or her case; and (c) to expect to see herself or himself in the movies, playing tennis, during the trial.

It is difficult to classify, with any degree of accuracy, the category of a case. The sooner medical treatment is started, the more consistent the treatment, the greater the automobile impact, the more susceptible the plaintiff to injury, the better the doctor's report, and a couple of dozen other considerations, the higher the multiplication factor.

It is also generally true that the more the specials, the higher you may multiply them. Of course, like most other things, there are a million exceptions. There have been cases where the medicals were only a few dollars, and the judgment was up into the many thousands.

But, these were cases where it was evident that the treatment served as no indication of the credibility of the injury. This is especially true in the case of objective injuries. For example, if an eye was put out in the injury, the cost of medical treatment would be totally irrelevant.

If you have a case where the evidence can unequivocally establish the extent of injury, you can forget all about any ratios to medical costs. The medical ratio is only important to serve as some measuring mechanism for the injury evaluation.

It has been traditionally established that people hate going to the doctor so much that the only impetus to do so is pain and suffering. Hence, the more treatment, the more the pain and suffering.

As with almost every other detail concerning dollars and cents, judgment sums will vary from place to place. Not just from state to state, but from city to city, even sometimes from district to district, juries will tend to give more or less for the same kind of injury.

Factors which influence are the general economy, the liberality of the populace, the attitude of the judiciary, and inscrutable notions which just seem to permeate the place.

In most states, books are available showing the listings of jury verdicts over a past given span of time. There are usually enough descriptions of the cases to give you an idea of where your case might lie.

Even more valuable would be consultation with other personal injury lawyers in your suite. Check around, and then integrate all information gleaned to strike an average. That should be your target for the adjuster.

At this writing (which, like everything else, is subject to momentary changes), the average number for settlement in the simple garden variety whiplash case hovers somewhere between $2,500 and $7,500 in the general Los Angeles area.

Your simple case will probably average around $700 to $1,500 in medical specials. Sans anything unique or special about the case, this should result in a settlement within the general range given.

These rules of thumb have a rather low saturation point. Running up a larger doctor bill will not follow the ratio, unless there are facts in the case to support it.

For instance, if you have that ordinary and everyday kind of case with a $2,000 doctor bill, your client is in trouble. The chances are that the award won't be much more than just the medicals. Remember, the theory of settlement is that everyone wants to save the time and expense of trial. No one is deathly afraid of it.

If the adjuster believes that the case won't support your demand, and you insist on that demand, you'll find yourself in court. The ratio concept is valid only if it follows the usual relative figures, and your case holds some water.

Some cases involve very complicated medical diagnostics and therapy, even though only subjective injuries and symptoms are present. For example, where there is a diagnosed "discogenic" trauma, there are some important subtleties which could hike up the jackpot.

These are cases where the spine has been deteriorating, as a result of either anomalous bone patterns or advanced age. Your claim is that the accident has aggravated a preexisting condition of susceptibility. This would be a case which typically involves an arthritic spine or some vertebra previously damaged by accident.

The value of this theory depends upon your showing that the pre-existing condition had existed for a substantial time period prior to the present accident. Your client must persuasively testify that he or she had not suffered any pain or discomfort from the past problem for at least a year or so. Very important, you must establish this situation right at the start of your case.

If you slip up, or fail to bring these facts out on direct examination, you can bet that the other side will zing it in by way of impeachment. Even worse, if you have not prepared your client for this testimony very carefully, he or she will fall into a thousand pieces as soon as defense counsel mentions the old accident.

Your client will react as though trapped, and will look to the jury like the kid who was caught with a hand in the cookie jar. Thus, your unprepared client will turn what could have been an advantage into a debacle.

A properly prepared client will speak of the old accident in an even and forthright manner, with the same emphasis used in describing his or her present injuries. You will then build upon this pedestal to show the likelihood of a high ratio of pain created by the most moderate impact. A jury can be led to see how the site of an old injury could be more easily flared into pain than one which was healthy and more resistive.

Naturally, the success of this tactic will depend completely upon your client's candor with you. It would be natural for your client to try to hide his or her past problems from you. The expected thought is that you would be disenchanted with the case if you knew he or she had had previous accidents.

This is a difficult concept for many new lawyers to understand. In order to pry such past experiences from the client, you must make it clear that the presence of any previous injuries is a plus. You must explain to your client that past injury occurrences will add value to the case. You must, in effect, lure these admissions out of him or her.

Try this on your client after being told of no past accidents: "Well, that's too bad. If you'd had any auto injuries before, we could use them to get you some more money." Watch your client scratch his or her head and cogitate: "Oh yes. Now I recall. There were some accidents." The list will spew out like ketchup from a warm bottle.

You must, then, unfold his or her past history before the jury, using the same positive attitude as in presenting any other advantageous evidence. It can be a positive only if you present it correctly with the help of medical experts. You must show how this accident impacted upon a pre-sensitized lumbar, cervical, or whatever, area. That impact created more pain than if there had been no pre-condition.

Where the impact was slight, this technique is vitally valuable. If there was a heavy smashup, the importance of preexisting susceptibility will be neutralized. But even then, the jury will better understand a disproportionate pain claim involving a sick back than with a healthy one.

One of the problems with preexisting conditions is proving that there was any aggravation at all. Most jurors, being of a more mature age, will have some idea of what arthritis is all about. Some of them might relate your client's condition to their own plaguing backaches.

The defense will be strenuously arguing for apportionment at the very least. You will press for the theory: "take your plaintiff where you find your plaintiff." Who is the defendant to minimize the pain caused to the plaintiff? Well, that's the game plan.

There are other means by which subjective injuries may be corroborated by evidence. In certain instances, a manifestation, such as limited mobility, may be established through demonstrative tests that will defy cross-examination.

Of course, the virtue of such tests lies in the practical inability to counterfeit the results obtained. Thus, where a successful demonstration is produced, you have what is close, but not equal, to objective injuries.

As the proof of the pudding is in the eating, so is the last analysis of damages in the jury verdict. The subjective injury case must go to the jury before you can predict its value with any degree of certainty. Too much depends upon variables to permit you to count your fee ahead of time.

Tests or no tests, you are still dealing with your client's statements and conduct to illustrate the existence of pain or movement limitation. Objective injuries, on the other hand, may be shown incontrovertibly.

There is also the unpredictable inconsistency of nature. On a good day, your client can do handsprings. Let it rain, and your client is crippled. This could partly explain away the defendant's movies of the plaintiff playing golf.

Your client has the wonderful good fortune of feeling just fine, and as flexible as a teenager, on the very day that he is to testify at the trial. But a broken bone is a broken bone is a broken bone. The X-ray picture is there to prove it, rain or shine.

But whether provable subjectives or good old reliable objectives, you must develop your file with meticulous care to command a big-time verdict. No matter how beautifully banged up your client may be, your verdict will be cut down to size if you don't touch every base at trial.

Not the least important is the witness quality of your client. The ability to testify is important, even for settlement purposes. You will never score a big-league settlement until after depositions have been taken.

Too often, lawyers give short shrift to deposition preparation of clients. "What the heck's a deposition? We're saving our efforts for the big show." If this is your attitude, you will need to save your efforts, because you won't get the settlement amount you want.

Prepare your client for testimony at deposition as fully as though it were for trial. Your client's performance will show the other side what kind of witness he or she will make at trial.

If your client does well, and the case stacks up in the other departments, the opposition will meet your demand for an amount that they believe they could lose at trial. That amount obviously will be as substantial as the testimony warrants.

If your client fails to demonstrate credibility, or is easily confused and diverted, the opposition may well offer nothing at all or only a nuisance amount. They will play the odds on your losing the verdict altogether, or on a jury coming in with far less than the case would otherwise be worth. So, work with your client until he or she performs like a star.

Don't just give your client the file, with instructions to study it. Go over his or her interrogatory answers carefully, emphasizing the areas of trouble. Do the same with the complaint. Use the blackboard constantly.

There's no better way to demonstrate things than to draw pictures on a board. Draw an intersection, reconstructing the respective positions of both cars.

Review the geography of the area. What buildings were on which corners? How many lanes in each street? Where were the traffic signals? How wide are the streets, the intersection, the lanes? Describe the traffic on that day. Where was the defendant? Where was your client? How far back? Etc., etc.

After you have thoroughly reviewed each and every point which could in any way be raised at trial, do it all over again. In these phases, repetition is not only warranted but mandatory.

§ 18:14 How to handle the insurance adjuster

The best thing you can do in dealing with the adjuster is to forget that you are a lawyer, completely. Forget the meaning of the word "adversary." Don't be cute with the adjuster. He or she is not a lawyer, but deals with lawyers all day long.

You can't impress an adjuster with your finest legalese. You can turn him or her off with it, though. The adjuster's got legal terms, including those in Latin, coming out of his or her ears.

Get on a first name basis with the adjuster just as soon as you can. Then, remember the first phase of salesmanship: "getting information!" Well then, get information. Ask questions. Ask more questions. After awhile, you'll have enough information to start giving some.

Don't jump the gun. If you can't find a thread to start with, ask more questions. Don't be too anxious to dive into the money part. Many adjusters will start right off with asking for your demand. Don't take the bait too soon.

When the time ripens to talk money, let it be known you're not all that tough. Agree as much as possible with his or her position. If you've played your salesmanship cards right, you'll be given sufficient material to start the settlement ball rolling.

When the adjuster mentions weaknesses in the case, don't argue the points raised. Trust in the fact that all of your arguments have been heard before.

At some point, "soft tissue" will be mentioned. You should agree with this in principle. But then, at the right moment, you can say something like, "I know we have no broken bones here. But the tests do show a severe injury." Don't elaborate; it's not necessary.

Then, talk about your own back and how painful it is, even though you know that no X-ray or anything could prove it. Don't argue generalities. Agree that soft tissue injuries lack the objective tests.

You're not going to win your case on the telephone with the adjuster. Don't try. But you're not talking about soft tissue, objective, subjective, or bonkus of the conkus. You are speaking of your client, Mr. John Jones.

One thing you do know about Mr. John Jones is: "He is hurtin'. You've seen the police accident report. You know who caused the accident. I know that Mr. Jones is hurtin', because I can feel his hurt in my own bones. Now tell me what you want to give me." But remember, keep smiling all the while you are talking.

When the adjuster makes the offer, it will be far too little. Don't laugh or be derisive. Simply say: "I know that you know that I know that the offer is not enough. But I'll tell you what. Let's talk about a figure that we both can agree Mr. Jones might possibly consider. The guy is hurting. Give me an offer that I can at least take back to him."

Tell the adjuster that you are not fighting him or her. Say: "You know I can't get one single dime out of this case until I get it settled, or the case goes to judgment. I'm as interested in settling this darned thing as you are."

"Look, Jones wants at least $10,000. You don't have to tell me that you're going to give that much. I think I can make him see more reason than that. But if I take your offer of $1,500 back to him, the whole thing will blow up. You are as far out of line as he is, and you know it."

"Make me a decent offer, and maybe I can help get rid of this thing for both of us. I'll tell you what. Let me try him out on $8,000. I can't promise anything, but let's see what I can do. O.K.?"

Of course, he won't offer $8,000. But your attitude of confidentiality will help to melt the ice between you. Adjusters nearly all operate in the same way. They have progressive levels of authority.

After the first level, the adjuster must go back at various stages of the matter to get more authority to increase the offer. The adjuster is rarely bound by the approach level, which is what he or she is authorized to offer on your first meeting.

Of course, the adjuster's authority is almost always much greater than the amount he or she reveals to you. But don't push too hard on this first go-round. If you come on too strong, you will only accomplish his or her crawling back into a defensive shell, and that will be that.

Save some of your strength for later. This doesn't mean just argument. You must also have a trump card or two left in your hand, like a good witness whom you forgot to mention, or whatever.

Later on, after your negotiations develop and the adjuster obtains secondary authority, you start to increase the pressure. As the adjuster eases up from his or her original figure, you whine that Jones is just the most stubborn fellow you have ever dealt with.

If it wasn't for the fact that you know how much he is hurting, well, it would just be a different thing. But, you tell him, Jones just won't budge. But you do really believe that if you could go to him with a bona fide offer of $7,000, you could get him to give it real consideration.

While it is true that the adjuster has a dollar ceiling authority, you will rarely, if ever, know what that is. The trick is to get as close as possible to that sum. You are not interested in trying to get the last buck.

Are you surprised? Don't be. Adjusters can only keep their standing if they can go back to their superiors and show that they saved the company a few dollars.

Settlement, like many other kinds of negotiation, is a business of "live and let live." If you can get close to the "top authority" and let the adjuster have a little bit of glory too, you can go around with him or her again successfully the next time. This is not charity. This is common sense. The odds are that you could not strip the adjuster naked anyway. So, it just doesn't make any sense to try.

It is probable that if you push past the crucial point, the adjuster will fold up, and report that you won't settle. The case will then be processed for trial. The opposition will take the position that the next ploy will take place on the "courthouse steps." This stand will cost you more time and money.

The one thing you must never believe is that the adjuster can really be intimidated. True, the adjuster's job is to settle cases, but only so many get settled, and a certain number must be tried. If you are too feisty, you get put into the trial bin.

The whole business is really just a big game. The political structure is very complicated, and the total mechanical scheme is confusing, even to the adjuster. He or she is given dollars, much as the Monopoly player is given certificates, to play with.

Just as you can antagonize a Monopoly player into throwing in his or her hand and quitting the game, so can you cause your adjuster to "disconnect." You must bear in mind that you are not dealing one-to-one with someone who has a measured ratio of interest in the outcome.

You know that you will personally get a fixed percentage of the amount that you finally agree upon. The adjuster has no such interest to protect. So, be assured that you have very little clout insofar as the power of your hand against the adjuster's is concerned. I am convinced that the "buddy-buddy" attitude will go much farther than the "Sherman Tank" technique.

In the above little scenario, the following is usually what you find in the last act. You know that your client would be tickled pink with a $2,500 gross offer. After insisting that $5,000 is positively, absolutely, the rock bottom level, you finally accept $4,375, and everyone is ecstatic.

The next time you draw the same adjuster, and you can bet it's bound to happen, you are old buddy pals, and it works even better.

§ 18:15 Arbitration as an alternative to trial: Hero or villain?

The courts in virtually every state are spilling over with logjamming cases. Several alternatives to trials, primarily arbitration, have evolved to help relieve the congestion. Most of these have received judicial endorsement. However, the zeal with which these alternatives have been embraced by the courts has produced certain untoward side effects.

§ 18:16 Commercial or contract arbitration

Contract arbitration is a predetermination of the means of settling contract disputes by virtue of a clause in the contract. The language which prescribes such a method must be clear and unequivocal.

Where such language is present, the parties are legally bound to arbitration as the means of dispute resolution, unless all parties agree to waive the requirement. If one party is recalcitrant, the other party may petition the court for an order compelling arbitration.

In most states, such an order will most certainly issue, unless (a) the right to compel arbitration has been waived by the petitioner, or (b) grounds exist for revocation of the agreement.

There is no requirement that the arbitrator be a judge, or even an attorney. In fact, in many instances, the arbitrator is selected from the members of the profession or occupation, and sometimes even the particular discipline, of the contract subject matter.

For instance, if the contract subject is building construction, the arbitrator will often be a building contractor or an architect. The theory is that a respected member of the parties' own field can best settle such disputes.

Arbitrators needn't follow the strict rules of either legal procedure or evidence. A happy choice, since lay arbitrators would hardly be equipped with sufficient training or knowledge of these subjects.

Most courts will enforce arbitration awards, without concern for either the evidentiary or factual support. Depending upon the side of legal weight one's client is on, this could be a delight or a disaster.

If your client is on all-fours with the law, heavily weighted with supporting facts and equities, it might be a cinch in court. But since an arbitrator needn't bother with such "niceties," your client could lose in arbitration.

An arbitrator needn't even state a rationale for the award and often does not. The rendering of the award can even be totally and completely contrary to all that was brought to the tribunal. No findings of any kind are required to support an award. The court which enforces it will have no concern for the reasons.

So what do you do? Appeal, right? Wrong! You do not appeal from an award. Your first level for redress is to resist the motion, by the winner, to reduce the award to judgment. Or, conversely, you can move to vacate the award if you are the loser.

The courts and the legislators are so in love with arbitration, in practically every state, that little is left for the unhappy party to get sympathy or succor. This is what you'll be facing when you move to vacate.

§ 18:17 Grounds for vacating award

Grounds for attacking a commercial arbitrator's award are found mostly in your dreams. Those that do exist are strictly statutory in most states. Now that you know how enamored the judicial system is of arbitration, you can guess how liberal those statutory grounds are. Look an example of them over:

(a) The award was procured by corruption, fraud or other undue means;

(b) There was corruption in any of the arbitrators;

(c) The rights of a party were substantially prejudiced by misconduct of a neutral arbitrator;

(d) The arbitrators exceeded their powers and the award cannot be corrected without affecting the merits of the decision upon the controversy submitted; or

(e) The rights of a party were substantially prejudiced by the refusal of the arbitrators to postpone the hearing on sufficient cause or by the refusal of the arbitrators to hear evidence material to the controversy or by other conduct of the arbitrators contrary to the provisions of this title.

So, you can see that if the arbitrator provides sufficient time for each party to produce and present evidence, and attentively hears all of that evidence, the statute has been given due service. Fine. Then, the arbitrator rules for the side whose evidence was shallower, thinner, and less persuasive than the other.

You move to vacate, arguing that the arbitrator has defied the spirit of the law, if not the letter. Of what use is the opportunity to present evidence if the preponderance of evidence has no effect on the award? The arbitrator followed the statute. All of the evidence was heard or seen. Next case.

Since the courts, as well as the legislators, love arbitration, they will do nothing to frustrate it. You'll not even find a sympathetic ear. Your motion will be summarily denied.

Appeal? Save your time, and save your client's money. You will have no grounds. The unkindest cut will be the court granting sanctions to the other side for your frivolous appeal.

There are various kinds of arbitration tribunals, many held under the auspices of the professions and the arts. For example, the Screen Actors Guild, The American Federation of Musicians, and other associations in the entertainment fields, require arbitration of all disputes under their respective auspices.

In the ordinary contract, a provision for arbitration must be spelled out within the contract itself. However, in these association matters, the criterion for arbitration is contained within the master charter or bargaining agreement to which all members subscribe.

Not only are the members compelled to adhere to this arrangement, but the forum itself is often before a select board. There are, in some instances, appellate procedures. These too, however, are restricted to particular circumstances, mainly having nothing to do with legal authority or weight.

The point is that all of your lawyer training will serve you naught if the arbitrator is bent toward the other side. To a more evil mind than mine, this could spell potential corruption.

§ 18:18 Scrutinizing the arbitrator

We hear stories about dishonest judges. But, a court is confined to legalities, so a judge can corrupt the judicial process just so far. Tough as the appellate route may be, you can still be assured of justice, if the respondent has not the slightest basis for judgment. The judge is bound by the law and the rules of evidence.

Not so with an arbitrator. If an arbitrator can rule any way he or she wishes, without the slightest regard for evidence or the law, what is there to stop bias or bribery? You say the arbitration statutes forbid this. That is true. But how does one prove bias or bribery?

The laws and the rules of professional ethics are at least to some extent constraining to lawyers and judges. But what of the lay arbitrators? They don't even have a Bar card to cancel.

Bribery aside, bias alone can boggle the mind. Who knows what prejudices lurk in the minds of men and women? When an arbitrator is appointed, your client is at his or her mercy. Once the arbitration begins, the fat, so to speak, is in the fire. The arbitrator's bias or prejudice may then become very apparent. But, it's too late.

§ 18:19 Arbitrator selection can mean winning or losing

In the conventional court matter, you protect your client through adequate preparation. You must prepare your case in arbitration also. But, the bulk of your preparation is in the arbitrator selection process.

In the first stage of arbitration, you are permitted a sort of reverse form of selection. Under most arbitration rules, you are given a list of potential arbitrators. The American Arbitration Association (AAA) has a policy of providing lists of certain arbitrators who were selected in conformity with the case nature.

If the matter involves building construction, the proposed candidates will usually be contractors or architects. There will also be some lawyers included, who've perhaps had some experience litigating construction disputes.

You are permitted to reject any or all of the names submitted. The other side is also given this privilege. If, after a couple of go-rounds, the parties cannot agree on at least one candidate, the AAA will arbitrarily appoint one.

A substantial portion of your total preparation time should be applied to investigation of the candidates. You should set up a multi-level investigation program. In the event the proposed arbitrators are lawyers or retired judges, the initial approach might be checking such superficial publications as Martindale-Hubbell listings or local judicial profiles.

The former listing will identify the college and law school of the candidate. You might then get a line on such affiliations as legal fraternities or other associations. Each state has its own form of such expositories. Follow through on every such source until you have exhausted all of them.

These preliminary checks could reveal something about the person, and his or her political or sociological bents or other predispositions. In the case of retired judges, local profiles can reveal much about the person.

Naturally, the information you get along this line will require something of an analytical ability on your part as the investigator. You must be able to translate that information into meaningful indications of what biases or prejudices may be involved.

§ 18:20 All arbitrators are biased or prejudiced

Even as you and I are biased and prejudiced, don't make the mistake of believing that you can find an unbiased or unprejudiced arbitrator. One cannot attain mature status in our society without having points of view. A point of view differs from an opinion, or even from an attitude. Points of view are preconceived, usually inflexible patterns.

Most mature adults develop abiding political party preferences. Are you a Republican, Democrat, or of some other political persuasion? Is this just your "point of view"? Is it your expression of a bias or prejudice?

"Bias" exists when one political persuasion is favored over the others. "Prejudice" exists because one may cling to a certain political party out of fear or hatred of the others. Which is your "point of view"?

Not infrequently, points of view are shaped from familial indoctrination. In some instances, the bent is the result of lifestyle or business involvement. Certain classes of business people tout the idea that "what's good for business is good for the country." They believe that legislation which aids business will result in business prosperity, which results in more hiring and higher salaries for employees. These so-called "trickle down" proponents usually would disdain any political philosophy which would promote platforms other than those pro-business. Are you convinced that your political preference should be that of everyone?

Another point of view argues that "what's good for labor is good for the country." Their belief is that higher wages and fewer working hours will require more hiring and more spending power, and hence, prosperity.

Then, there are those who believe that business, as it exists in a capitalistic society, is a toxin, and should be completely overhauled. This point of view sees business as a function of government. Even with the toppling of many Communist governments, some people hold fast to this "point of view."

What is remarkable about each of these points of view is that it excludes all others as reasonable or workable. It doesn't matter that there are those within each of these diametrically opposed political philosophies with equal intellectual and analytical quotients. Each is convinced that the country cannot survive if lead by forces other than those which they espouse.

What is even more perplexing is the permeation of these beliefs and views into the variety of thoughts and actions which seemingly have nothing to do with politics.

§ 18:21 Compute whether that bias or prejudice can win for you

To utilize knowledge of the bents of judges and arbitrators, one must be left to one's own analytical powers to predict the manner in which such bents would affect the decision-making process. In some instances, these factors alone would be sufficient to form some reasonable prognostications.

There is, of course, much more to learn about the potential arbitrator candidates. Many such beliefs and views are biases and prejudices that can, and often do, affect day-to-day judgment.

One cannot help but modulate opinion with such preconceptions. Many of us truly believe that we can surmount these overriding orientations and render completely impartial decisions. But is this realistic?

Mr. Justice Brandeis called these ideas "fighting faiths." While he expressed the belief that these ideas could be subject to change by "testing them in the marketplace," changes of views so closely proximal to basic personality would seem unlikely.

The modern concept is to deny such symbolisms as stereotypes. These days, we prefer to think that each person is an individual. We would hope that each can develop thought independently of dogmatic background.

Perhaps this is so, but some attention to underlying motivations can be helpful in finding a threshold of approach to a person's receptiveness.

Differing opinions may exist in persons who share similar points of view. Two persons who identify themselves as "Republicans" may have sharply divided opinions on candidates for office. They may both share an identical political goal, but not agree on the particular person who can attain that goal.

Self-interest is a forceful motive in shaping points of view. Looking for such stereotypes can be helpful, preliminarily, in finding points of view of arbitrator candidates. However, these are only valuable as initial evaluations.

Some stereotypes evolve from residential districts. In California, Orange County, just outside of Los Angeles County, has long been stereotyped as mostly housing Republicans. Using such a broad brush can be helpful, if one bears in mind that nothing conclusive may be determined at this level.

This process of picking the arbitrator is not a game. In most instances, it amounts to winning or losing the arbitration. Remember, the arbitrator can rule as absolutely as the arbitrator wishes to.

This would be denied by most of the arbitration associations, and by the arbitrator candidates themselves. Few individuals, or organizations, would admit that bias or prejudice would control their functions.

This doesn't mean that an arbitrator cannot rule impartially. The question is, can you rely upon such impartiality when there is no objective way of assuring it?

It's been said that nobody knows anything about anybody, not excluding oneself. You won't be in practice very long before you see some logic in that idea. "How can a person do a thing like that?!" You can ask that question ten times before breakfast while reading the morning paper. Explanations don't help.

If the arbitrator candidate is a lay person, such as an accountant, try to get some localized input. Confer with your own accountant, or perhaps an accountant among your clientele. Try to find as much information as possible from anyone who knows anything about the person.

Check with the local professional organizations to which that person might belong. If he or she is a contractor, check with the local Contractors' Licensing Board to see if any information might be gained.

If the case merits the expense, you might consider engaging an investigation service. The result could prove to be well worth the expense. Go as far along the investigatory curve as the case will justify. You simply cannot know too much about the person holding an unfettered prerogative to make what might be an unsupported and arbitrary award.

Knowing everything there is to know about the candidate will do you no good, if you haven't formed some idea of how bias or prejudice might help or hurt your case.

Some of the factors which could be up for grabs are your client's race, characteristics, attitude, behavioral patterns, and the nature of your client's cause. Suppose the case concerns an employment contract dispute, and your client is the president of the large and successful employer corporation. You would probably want a pro-business arbitrator.

It might be difficult to get that exact picture, but putting all of the facts you've learned together, they might just add up to an assessable conclusion. The process is similar, in some ways, to analyzing prospective jurors' voir dire responses. In the case of jurors, you've usually got only minutes to accept or reject the candidate.

In the case of an arbitrator, you will usually have days, weeks, or even months in which to collect and sort out the needed facts.

A jury consists of several members, and a mistake in the selection of one member may not be fatal. An arbitrator has the sole and unchallengable right to decide your client's case. A wrong selection can end the ball game, disastrously for you. So, you can see the need for much greater scrutiny of a much larger set of facts.

§ 18:22 How to avoid arbitration: Don't contract for it

The time to make the decision on the forum for settling disputes is when you draft the contract. So many lawyers, new and old, use canned contract forms as guides to draft contracts. Many of these include arbitration provisions as standard clauses.

If you include a provision for arbitration, make certain that this is what you really want. You and I have been trained as lawyers. We know our business. We know what we can do before a judge or jury. I suggest to you that neither of us can really be sure of what we can do before an arbitrator.

My personal feeling is that I do not wish to waive my abilities as a lawyer. This is precisely what you do when you elect to arbitrate. All of our training can amount to zero, if the arbitrator determines the award on factors other than the evidence and our case presentation.

§ 18:23 Salesmanship in the arbitration process

If one is to presume that evidence will not control, but that the arbitrator will nonetheless maintain an attitude of relative impartiality, then salesmanship may well prove the deciding factor.

It is reasonable to presume that the arbitrator will admit as "evidence" just about everything but the relative golf handicaps of the parties. This presumption is based on the admonition, in most arbitration practice, that the more grievous sin is to exclude rather than admit evidence.

If your analysis of the arbitrator's profile is that neither bias nor prejudice will be negative factors, you can look to salesmanship as your most useful tool.

If you try to conduct the proceedings under legal constraints, you will probably be submerged in floods of hearsay, supposition, conjecture, conclusions, and most every other form of "objectionable" material.

Since you are a skilled lawyer, you will be above that sort of thing. Do not expect the same professionalism from your opponent. Do not expect it from the arbitrator either.

It could be productive to ask for a stipulation, from opposing counsel, to conduct the proceedings under the rules of evidence. If the arbitrator is willing, and knows enough about the game to conform to those rules, and everybody agrees, you could have what amounts to a judicial hearing. The entire arbitration principle is one of contract. Whatever the parties agree upon will set the course rules.

Such developments are rare, but it happens. With such full stipulations, you could have some appellate protection against the possibility of the arbitrator's reversible error.

Despite the reassurance by the American Arbitration Association and other arbitration services of impartial rulings on the facts presented, I am not convinced. My natural skepticism rises up where no objective measures are present to ensure that impartiality.

I, invariably, advise my clients to avoid contractual provisions for arbitration, and to cast their lots with our court system. Defective and frustrating as it may be, I have great confidence in the system. I find no comparable substitute in arbitration or any other "alternative."

§ 18:24 Another myth: The economy of arbitration

These days arbitration is often not the more economical route. Some of the arbitration associations use a sliding scale for setting arbitration fees. These depend upon the amount of the award sought. Check on this scale. You may be shocked at how high those filing fees zoom in more substantial cases.

Also, arbitrators are often permitted to set their own fees. Retired judges, for instance, will often require much higher daily fees than other arbitrators. Before you rejoice in a judge selection, review his or her fees.

There is a general belief that selection of a retired judge, as arbitrator, will assure better adherence to legal principles and rules of evidence. It's true that lay arbitrators usually know little about the law. Judges usually know the law, but will the judge apply the law?

In the general Los Angeles area, retired judges will command, and get, about $1,500 or more per day for their arbitration services. What's more, they demand payment of their fee before each daily session begins.

This means that each side must share that daily expense. Each party must present the judge with their one-half payment, equaling $750, or more, before each day's proceedings begin.

Now, $1,500 per day is no fortune for a lawyer running a law office. But, to one who is retired with nothing else to do to occupy time or earn money, it can be a veritable bonanza.

It's an unpopular suggestion, but consider the polarities of expediting a case versus permitting it to drag on, and maybe even on and on. The $1,500 per day, while a case is in progress, is better than nothing a day while waiting for the next assignment.

Judges still active in the court system receive no more while hearing a case than while idly waiting for a trial assignment. In fact, getting rid of a case may permit the judge to spend a bit more time on the boat or golf course. Meanwhile, the income continues.

In California, there is a trap for judges who continue to work past their retirement time. Their retirement compensation diminishes as they remain on the bench beyond retirement age. It becomes a problem of diminishing returns. Retirement, with their pensions and "picking up time" as arbitrators, can be much more lucrative than staying on the bench and watching the retirement benefits shrink.

I, personally, do not believe that most retired judges would act unfairly in the arbitration setting. I think that a reputable retired judge would give full measure, consciously. But, being a natural cynic, I just have trouble with scenarios which lack the basic protections of the law. I also have a certain amount of trouble with the differences between the conscious and subconscious mechanisms.

I hope that I'll be forgiven for these thoughts I share with you. But, I am much more comfortable with the atmosphere of a courtroom and the rules of law and evidence, with full appellate protection.

There's no question that an arbitration can be much faster than a trial. But, this is no guarantee. Most arbitrators have other jobs or demands on their time.

Arbitrators are usually much more subject to the "checkerboard" calendar than are judges in the court system. They usually are agreeable to multiple recesses and continuances to accommodate conflicting schedules of parties and counsel.

Quite often, the arbitrator will announce a continuance to serve his or her own private interests. Many active judges will not brook these interruptions in court.

Most modern state arbitration statutes will provide the same pretrial and discovery rights as are incident to court trials. This means that the time needed for these proceedings is being pushed farther and farther ahead.

Arbitrators are being enabled, more and more, to emulate the functions of judges. In California, arbitrators can issue injunctions, grant both partial and total summary awards, and institute contempt and other provisional orders.

Because the courts are so enamored of arbitration, they are prone to compel arbitration in the most tenuous of situations. Even in cases where arbitration is claimed to have been "orally assigned," a court will usually find the "assignment" sufficient. The ruling will usually be to order the matter out to an arbitrator for a ruling on the authenticity of the "oral assignment."

On the one hand is court congestion and the so-called arbitration "expedience." On the other hand is the right to a trial on the merits. This conflict will often result in at least one of the parties being "victimized."

§ 18:25 International arbitration

It could be several years before you find yourself confronting an opponent in an international forum. Or, it may happen sooner than you think. More and more companies doing business on an international plane are turning to contractual arbitration as the means of settling their differences.

Even the American Arbitration Association has expanded its perimeters to worldwide boundaries. Its institute in New York City, the World Arbitration Institute, now caters to a variety of cases on the international scene.

In many cases, this is not an "alternative," as with domestic arbitration. Quite often, it is offered as the only game in town. This is so, particularly between countries which do not share treaties guaranteeing litigation rights.

The arbitration "alternative" is not selected, but imposed. Such was the case in the claims by American firms against the Islamic Republic of Iran. This arbitration "alternative" was mandated by President Reagan, as an adjunct to negotiations with Iran for the release of the American hostages taken by the alleged Iranian "students."

I have a twofold reason for retelling of an experience which was included in the previous edition of this book. It isn't my thought to occupy your time or these pages with lawyers' "war stories" just for their romance.

It serves some purpose in explaining the international arbitration function. More pointedly, it demonstrates how salesmanship, together with careful thought, patience, and planned strategy, can succeed where perhaps nothing else can.

This is an especially appropriate example, because it combines most of the elements of salesmanship in legal practice. It also suggests a sort of blueprint for conduct in arbitration proceedings, where selling is often the only force which can possibly work for you.

I represented a firm, Daniel, Mann, Johnson & Mendenhall ("DMJM"), a California corporation, against The Imperial Iranian Navy in an action which was commenced in the United States District Court, Central District of California. The suit was for sums due under a contract between DMJM and the Iranian Navy.

As a result of the taking of American hostages by Iranian terrorists, then President Carter (followed by President Reagan) bargained away the litigation rights of these plaintiffs, and confined them to the newly established "IRAN/US CLAIMS TRIBUNAL," at the World Peace Palace in The Hague, Netherlands.

The mandate was respected by all judges in whose courts these cases were pending. Eventually, all of the cases were "suspended," pending a determination as to which of the nine hundred and some cases would be relegated to that tribunal or some other form of "remedy."

Our case was one of those permitted to petition to the claims tribunal. In the interim, a few claimants were invited to ostensible "settlement" meetings with Iranian representatives in the Iranian Embassy in Vienna, Austria. DMJM was one of them. As DMJM's lawyer, I was scheduled to attend.

I contacted two claimants who had already had their "settlement meetings," hoping to learn something of their experiences. Both were in architectural engineering fields and disciplines similar to DMJM's.

The impression given by these parties, and their counsel, was that the meetings were designed strictly as a terrorists' propaganda forum. They related their experiences as a series of tirades denigrating American firms which had done business with the Shah as "war mongers and frauds."

One of these parties told horror stories of being led through corridors, lined with teenage girls holding automatic rifles at the ready. He said that throughout the entire meeting, he endured nonstop accusations and threats. Both parties and their attorneys stated that not one word was ever said about paying anyone anything.

Though apprehensive, I believed that attending the meeting offered the best hope in my lifetime of collecting the money due DMJM. I also knew that this would be a supreme test of salesmanship.

Next, I interviewed as many persons as I could find who knew anything of the Iranian people and their culture. I read the scant available material about the revolutionaries then in power. Much of it was contradictory. None of it offered me any comfort.

Armed with this information, I prepared a full sales portfolio, with charts, diagrams, pictures, and full paraphernalia, concerning DMJM's wide range of world-wide service operations. I included as much about DMJM's non-military operations as I could accumulate.

I arrived in Vienna during thunderstorms, which did not add to my peace of mind. There was some difficulty in getting into the Iranian embassy. I was ushered through some dark and cold corridors right enough, but no teenaged, machinegun-holding girls were there to greet me. There was, however, a portrait on a wall of a young girl holding some kind of automatic weapon.

Our claim was against the Iranian Navy, so the representatives consisted of two Iranian naval officers and one ex-Iranian attorney; "ex" because the Iranian Bar had been abolished by the Islamic government. I was told that this was done because lawyers are immoral and can't be trusted. (Sigh!)

The meeting lasted for three days. The morning of the first day was devoted entirely to the castigating of Americans in general, and my client, DMJM, in particular. We were cast as "war mongers," because DMJM had done the architectural and engineering work on the Chabahar Naval Base for the Shah's Imperial Government of Iran.

I knew that any argument against the war mongering label would be useless, as would be any confrontation. Instead, I chose to weather the storm. It wasn't until late afternoon of the first day that I was finally permitted to talk.

I started by agreeing that war, and the business of war services or materials, were despicable. I withheld comment about our work on Chabahar. I set up my charts on a rack, and flipped pasteboards showing the schools, churches, city bus and other transportation services, dormitories, public buildings, apartment houses, bridges, and other civic works done by DMJM in the Mideast.

I then demonstrated, with an intra-corporational breakdown, that DMJM was entirely employee-owned. I emphasized that DMJM's orientation was toward peacetime architecture, engineering, and construction.

Then, during the afternoon of the second day, when I felt that I had seen some positive response from at least one of the officers, I cautiously tiptoed into the Chabahar complex. I used my pasteboards to show the civilian portion of the base.

Page after page demonstrated living quarters, transit programs, schools, churches, and other civilian functions, and that the military parts of the project were not DMJM's main concern.

I felt that I needed even more to convince them. The signs indicated that I was making some inroads, but I needed some kind of backup. I thought that my chances would improve if I could inject the idea that DMJM could be of future use to Iran.

Judging from what had happened to those two other claimants, and many others that I'd heard of, I suspected that these people wouldn't give a dime to anyone who would be of no further value to them.

I repeated, as often as I felt my words were not boring, that the new order in Iran needed some Western contributions. I said that DMJM would like to participate in the Islamic Republic's efforts in accomplishing these goals.

Then, when I felt the circumstances were right, I volunteered the statement that DMJM was the world's leading operational authority on aircraft fueling systems. From the looks on the faces of the two officers, I knew that I had made a big point. The ex-lawyer was superfluous.

On the morning of the third day, we began talking of DMJM's Chabahar services, and the validity of the presented statements and invoices. There was much quibbling and arguing about dollars. I was not dealing with children.

Captain Vahdat, the apparent leader of the group, suggested drawing the agreement outline. I realized that they had no secretaries. I told them that I would type the agreement if a typewriter was available. That was a remarkable statement.

"You can type?" There was disbelief. All of my legal training, my superb presentation, my electronic background, my fantastic golf swing, nothing was nearly as impressive as the declaration that I could use a typewriter.

The rest was a fish-shoot in a barrel. This wasn't just an

"outline" for an agreement. This was to be, in fact, the "Memorandum of Understanding" between Iran and DMJM.

The settlement agreement called for a sum equal to better than $.87 on the dollar. After signatures of the three representatives were executed, it was necessary for counter-signatures by other officials in Tehran.

Still, being the cynic and skeptic that I am, I flew from Vienna to The Hague, and filed our Petition for Hearing, along with the M.O.U. for ratification. As it developed, the last day of the meeting in Vienna was the day before the first date for filing before the claims tribunal. I wanted to be the first in line. This was a precaution to back up the M.O.U. in case the Iranians defaulted in the settlement payment.

Although it took the better part of three months to jell, the actual draft was ultimately received for the full sum agreed upon, and the case was closed.

Subsequent facts more than substantiated the value of salesmanship in the transaction. DMJM was the second firm among all claimants to receive money, either directly from Iran or through the tribunal. The first company to receive its claim money was the Goodrich Company.

Long after DMJM had been paid, only four or five firms had received any money at all. My understanding is that most of the claimants had received nothing at all, and that, among those who had any chance of getting anything, the majority are still waiting for payment.

An epilogue to the story. After getting the M.O.U. signed, I started to leave the embassy, and Captain Vahdat and his aide accompanied me through the halls. They were both very friendly, and the captain asked if I would remain in Vienna for a few days to be entertained by their delegation. This invitation capped my success. The perfect "sale" should leave the buyer content.

Of course, I had to decline the invitation, since I had to be in The Hague the next day. But it was flattering. These two representatives of a culture so removed from mine, and from my comprehension, appeared to have a genuinely high regard for me, and wanted more of my company.

The point to this story, if you haven't already seen it, is that the Iranians were not receptive to a contest of right and wrong. They couldn't have been less interested in our superior and inferior positions. There would be no issue of whether or not DMJM had done its job, and was entitled to the money.

Remember what I said about salesmanship being the giving of information of value to the listener. I learned many useful facts from my pre-trip research and interviews. The rest of the needed information was derived from that first day's verbal onslaught by the Iranians.

I knew that the only chance I had to get to the money part was to give the delegation information of some value to them. I had to do this while avoiding the traps that others had fallen into. After finding the pathways, I could wend my way into the core of our case.

I had learned that the Islamic followers were unbending on the idea of workers sharing in the proceeds of communal efforts. Thus, I stressed the "employee-owned" aspects of DMJM. I knew also that, while these people professed belief in altruism, their underlying motivation was anything but.

Despite the characteristic hostility of the Iranians, I recognized their need for the play-acting on concern for humanity. The Iranians live with guns, and yet do not want to discuss guns.

They were intently interested in the information I had given them concerning DMJM's work in laying out and planning entire cities, and in the general area of civic development.

I knew that even though the Iranians were involved in a war with Iraq, they would insist on assuming the role of a people philosophically opposed to the idea of war and militarism. It is not necessary to understand the things you learn about people to use that information in selling.

I will never understand the Iranians. Yet, I learned enough about them to know what to avoid, and what would impress. Iran needed military assistance, obviously, particularly in the field of aircraft support. This is the reason for my finding the opportunity to point out DMJM's expertise in aircraft fueling systems.

Then, after having gotten past the barriers which apparently had stopped the two claimants with whom I had conversed, I could get to the subject of Chabahar and our claim for work done on this military project.

I had learned the penchant of the Iranians for setting up negotiating defenses even before starting negotiations. What my informants apparently did not realize was that a frontal attack against these defenses would result in accelerating those defenses, with nothing accomplished.

Had I immediately broached the subject of Chabahar and our claim, the Iranian officers would have intensified their attack. The conference would have ended just as those other two had ended, with humiliation and wasted efforts.

§ 18:26 Judicial arbitration

Another "alternative" to conventional court proceedings is

"judicial arbitration." Most states have innovated one form or another of this convenient vehicle for aid in relieving snowballing court congestion.

In California, the state legislators have declared: "It is the intent of the Legislature that:

(1) Arbitration hearings held pursuant to this chapter shall provide parties with a simplified and economical procedure for obtaining prompt and equitable resolution of their disputes.

(2) Arbitration hearings shall be as informal and private as possible and shall provide the parties themselves maximum opportunity to participate directly in the resolution of their disputes, and shall be held during nonjudicial hours whenever possible.

(3) Members of the State Bar selected to serve as arbitrators should have experience with cases of the type under dispute and are urged to volunteer their services with out compensation whenever possible."

These arbitration sessions differ from those of commercial or contractual arbitration in several ways. First, they are held under judicial auspices and are not contractual in nature. Since the courts may order cases to such proceedings without the concurrence of the parties, it would defeat due process to deny at least minimal judicial safeguards, including the right of appeal.

In California, as in many other states, either party may request a trial de novo if displeased with the arbitrator's award. Then, as with conventional trials, the ultimate judgment is appealable. However, there is one little clinker along the due process pathway.

This process would lack the substance sought by the legislatures and the courts if it were merely a parallel to regular court proceedings. The twist that makes the difference may not be readily apparent, but the effect is sufficient as a deterrent to the trial de novo route.

Once again, the courts' romance with arbitration will cause many judges to look hard at cases that have been subjected to arbitration, although reference thereto is prohibited.

Trial de novo must be requested within 20 days after the arbitrator files the award. Another restriction is the prohibition of discovery after issuance of the arbitrator's award.

For these reasons, as well as others, very few trials de novo actually take place. Of course, the proceedings must be presided over by attorneys who have attained statutory status, or by retired judges. The rules of evidence do apply in these proceedings, and, though informal, the methodology is not unlike conventional court hearings.

Some selective efforts are possible. While parties aren't normally given selection rights from lists of candidates, either party has the option of "disqualification." The California statute speaks of this process as a privilege rather than a right. The language is, "any party may request the disqualification of the arbitrator . . .." This request must also be filed within five days of the naming of the arbitrator.

It is recommended that you carefully examine such information as is available on the arbitrator named. Reference to the listings in Martindale-Hubbell will, at the very least, reveal the academic background of the proposed arbitrator.

Some attorneys are given greater biographical coverage in the Martindale listings. Naturally, with the presence of the post-award remedies, such as they are, the width and breadth of investigation is not as compelling as in commercial arbitration.

Your attention is called to the statutory requisites, in the conduct of judicial arbitration, for the presentation of evidence. Some lawyers or judges serving in an arbitrational capacity are more strict in statutory observance than others. Don't assume that the informality of the hearing will necessarily mean informality all the way.

Prepare your case as fully for these hearings as you would for a full-scale court action. Oftentimes, attorneys give short shrift to preparation simply because the entire matter takes place in the office of the lawyer-arbitrator.

If this is your opponent's style, you will have an opportunity to make big points with a fully prepared case. Remember, the arbitrator is an attorney or a retired judge. Your meticulous preparation will be appreciated and respected.

§ 18:27 "Rent-a-judge" proceedings

Another "alternative" to court trials is the more recently innovated, "Rent-A-Judge " proceeding. This is strictly a stipulated meeting. These sessions are organized under the auspices of commercial organizations, normally not unlike those which administer contract arbitrations. The difference is that this alternative is normally elected after the dispute has arisen, perhaps after an action has been filed in court.

There are no concrete rules such as in commercial or judicial arbitration. Hence, the course rules are what the parties say they are. Most of the officers are retired judges. In electing this alternative, the parties' gain will be expedience.

As with all organized means of settling disputes, the vast majority of plaintiffs want expedience, and the vast majority of defendants want delay. As one might appreciate, this program will usually be of appeal only where both sides want the matter disposed of quickly. With this selection, as with commercial arbitration, the costs may be greater than with conventional court proceedings.

§ 18:28 Mediation proceedings

Mediation is a plan where both sides approach a sort of ombudsman, whose sole purpose is to settle the dispute. For some reason, this program has more or less predominated in the marital dispute area. Many courts sponsor such programs within their own jurisdictions. The procedure is free to participants, and lawyers' services are often discouraged.

This plan is probably the most sensible of all the trial "alternatives," since it is, very often, free of cost, and does offer true expedience. Marital disputes are not adversarial in the strictest sense, particularly where they involve children.

A marriage break-up, as sad and emotional an experience as it may be, does not usually start out belligerently. As often as not, the hostility starts when lawyers square off against each other. Mediation, if done properly, can circumvent the fusillade and ameliorate the hostility.

Very often, the most pressing parts of the matter are emotional. Thus, a lawyer well-trained in family law can perform valuable services for couples who have lost the ability to communicate with each other.

This remedy depends upon the willingness of both parties to bend toward a negotiative stance. Even more essential is a lawyer/mediator who is skilled both in the specific area of the law and the art of finding the common points upon which the parties can achieve some communication.

I strongly suggest that you spend some time serving as pro tem judge and/or arbitrator. This experience will be a great teacher of litigational and arbitrational technique and decorum.

The best way to learn a judge's or arbitrator's reaction to an approach is to have had the experience of receiving such an approach yourself. Besides, in many states you are compensated, though sparingly, for such services.

I am hopeful that these few tips on some of the more prevalent parts of the general law practice may be helpful. At least they may give you some thoughts on how the practicalities of legal practice function. The main thought I hope you have gained is to look behind the obvious to find ways to get a leg up.

§ 18:29 Court appointments

Attorneys are routinely appointed by courts to represent indigent defendants in criminal cases when there may be some conflict with the public defender's office. Keeping in close touch with the courts can produce a goodly number of such appointments. The fee isn't enormous, but it can be interesting work and a good learning experience.

Each state has its own criteria for qualification and representation as well as payment. The requirements can't be too stringent since well established lawyers would not be likely candidates.

The Superior Court of Los Angeles County has an experimental program called P.A.C.E., Professional Appointed Court Experts, which includes attorneys as expert witnesses in criminal and civil cases involving indigent parties. Claims by attending attorneys are filed under this program and fees are paid based upon the prescribed terms and conditions.

This source of business should not be overlooked, at least during the first phase of your solo practice development. You should investigate your local jurisdiction to determine whether it has a similar program.

§ 18:30 A stranger among them

Only a new lawyer would walk into an out-of-town court with an assured stride and brief case swinging confidently. You may have already learned about engaging local counsel in a foreign court appearance. The idea is to create the impression with the court that one of the "good ol' boys" is on the case.

That's better than nothing, but often still not good enough. "Local counsel" by itself doesn't always knock it. He or she needs to be familiar with the laws involved as well as knowing all about the local procedures, including everything about the judge.

You've flown into town expecting to be heard, dispose of the matter and be on the afternoon flight back home. That could happen. You could also win the lottery. Often though, the court will insist that you meet with the opposing attorney, work out the details and settle. This usually means to give the local guy or gal his or her way.

If you indicate either an unwillingness or inability to settle, you may be placed on the back of the docket for a hearing at 5:00 P.M. You may return to court to find that four other matters have intervened and your case is continued to the next day. Can that treatment go on for several days? Maybe not in Utopia.

This is called being "home-towned." Such practices have been censured by the appellate courts, but do they go on, anyway? Well, there's also Shangri-La. So, what to do?

Select your local attorney with the care and scrutiny that you'd select a commercial arbitrator. After you've reduced your list of potentials to three or four, phone each of them for further input.

You don't want to send his or her kids through college, so you negotiate a bare fee for appearance, but you make it clear that he or she must participate in argument so the judge knows he or she is there and has an interest in the case. Better still, settle the case if you can.

§ 18:31 Look for possible law specialties if you don't want general practice

You will be in general practice at first, whether or not you like it. Since you are receptive to any and all case and client referrals for at least the first few weeks and months of your practice, you'll have little chance to specialize. But, as time goes by, opportunities to branch into specialties will be yours if you want them and are alert to them.

Some of these opportunities may not be heralded with unfurled banners and blaring trumpets. Recall the instance referred to in the book concerning a former student in my class and subscriber to this book. He had the opportunity of defending a claim against a smaller title insurance company. He was successful in this defense. This led him to research the field of title insurance, and the dearth of available qualified defense lawyers for that field. In rather short order, he became known throughout the title insurance business as a specialist and was sought after by many of those companies. Thereafter, he was identified as the primary T.I. defense attorney and has held that position through rapid growth of that area of law.

When I learned of this young fellow's climb up that legal ladder, I was amazed, no, shocked, to learn that so few attorneys had made a mark in that area. My investigation informed me that other success stories concerning a wide variety of disciplines had developed in pretty much the same way. In each such instance, it was simply a matter of seeing the opportunity and grabbing it.

It wasn't so long ago that living trusts were only an adjunct to the probate field. Now, there are many lawyers commanding huge fees specializing in living trusts. It had been there, bold as you please, since long before you were born, but it took just a handful of enterprising attorneys to forge trusts into a lucrative legal specialty.

If you're into trust and/or wills, give the West Group CD-ROMs a try. They aren't voracious speed and memory guzzlers and don't occupy much hard drive space but are about as complete as you'll need. (See Chapter 12.)

Lawyers are specializing in child abuse, sex harassment, stock broker fraud and other relatively "new" areas, and getting big fees simply because they saw the opportunities and dived in. There's really very little new in legal areas for specialty; there is only a lack of ingenuity and industry by shortsighted attorneys.

Don't be overly concerned with prognostications of doom regarding any field of law. At present, personal injury attorneys are about ready to hold a funeral for their specialty. It's true that the insurance industry's lobbies have successfully instigated the California initiative limiting pain and suffering judgments against uninsured driver plaintiffs. But that law has been ruled unconstitutional in a recent trial court decision.

How that ruling will ultimately resolve can only be guessed. Either way, it doesn't spell doom for P.I. practitioners. It just means that those lawyers will need to shift gears. Not every P.I. plaintiff will be uninsured. Besides, as you've learned, or soon will, there's always an approach to every brick wall that takes you around, or through it.

Too many attorneys are prone to cling to past patterns, like elephants, each hanging to the next one, treading through the forest. Unlike elephants, lawyers are individuals and should think like individuals. Don't fear treading off to your own horizon and to your own drummer. There is something out there that will be just for you. Look for it and then, go for it!

Nothing is forever and nothing is perfect. Your practice, like the law itself, is dynamic. Change in itself is neither bad nor good; it's only different. I've learned to shift with the changing tides. You'll learn to do that too. When the dust settles, you'll find, as I've found, tomorrow is always better than yesterday.

§ 18:32 Internet for FUN and PROFIT—A new marketing tool

You can have a web site for free if you are a member of AOL. This offer includes up to 10MB of space. That would encompass quite a bit of material. That's perhaps the deal with other hosts as well. AOL also has an inexpensive rental plan for sites if something more elaborate is desired. What you do with the site depends on either your ingenuity and skill with graphics or your willingness to spend some money getting it professionally done.

There are many things you can do that can attract attention and maybe get you some new clients or build on your existing clientele. A newsletter, for instance, can be a vehicle to let you bring some of your special services out front. Discuss new trends in the law within your scope of practice. Or you can do this with ordinary windows such as you see in many commercial offerings.

Why not consider a column-type feature, like "Ask Your Lawyer," or "What's New In The Law," or maybe "It's The Law!" Here you can discuss kinds of things related to your practice that might be of general interest. If done well, you can develop an extensive regular readership.

The trick in getting business from the Internet is no different from any other form of advertising. You must get readership. You can mail brochures directly to homes on your mailing list. The quantity of mailings will be your maximum readership. Newspaper circulation determines readership probabilities for your ads. With television and radio, the transmission coverage of the stations will control the number of persons who might see your commercial.

Internet requires ingenuity on your part. You must design the method by which people may know of your web site. But that knowledge alone isn't the answer. You must also devise a "gimmick" or "bait." The question to be answered is "why should anyone want to seek your web site?

Although some browsers subscribe to an "all you can eat" deal, such as Microsoft, AOL and other hosts offer at $20 per month, others opt out for a lower monthly and a time charge arrangement. In order to grab maximum readership, you've got to make it attractive to everyone.

Design your "gimmick" with the idea that everyone must pay a fee per minute to see your show. There are thousands and thousands of web sites on the "net." Nobody's going to just "flip" to your site, even by accident.

If you have a phone directory advertisement, include your "hook" somewhere prominently within that ad. Make your site address as simple as possible and as closely related to your firm name as possible.

All World Wide Web site addresses start with "http://" and include the letters "www". However, when distributing the name of your web site, you can usually ignore the "http://" prefix, since most web users know to add that (and also because most web browser programs now add that prefix automatically when an address with "www." is entered in the address box).

Obviously, you cannot use an address that's already occupied by someone else. Check with your host to find a clear name but persist in trying for a name that would ring a bell. People don't retain thoughts in their memories just for your convenience. You've got to jog that memory with a mind bender. Your address must be short, sweet and provocative. It's your game so you name it.

Graphics are important also. When your site is reached there should be something on your first page to grab attention. If you're doing P.I., perhaps a picture of an injured party with a caption, "What do I do now?" Or, perhaps an accident scene with a caption, "Don't let this ever happen to you. But if, Heaven forbid, it does . . .." Then, your name, address and phone number only.

You don't like those ideas? I didn't think you would, but you get the point, right? You work it out. I never agreed with lawyer advertising anyway. Stay more institutional with your illustrations and copy and you'll probably get as much business as with the "punchy" hard sell.

Concentrate on getting readership. If you can get people to punch in your address, you've got the problem three quarters licked. Do the newsletter. If you can keep your articles punchy and short you'll keep your readers. If your articles are changed often and kept fresh, the readers will keep coming back to your site. Eventually, your phone will ring.

"Letters To The Lawyer," or "Ask The Lawyer" kind of thing are always attention getters. You know, "Mr. Ralph Gondorff asks, 'I'm in serious trouble financially. I owe over $25,000 and my total yearly income is only $15,000. I need every cent to support my wife and five kids. What can I do?'" A nice little dissertation on working things out with creditors, or a composition, or maybe even a bankruptcy has good readership appeal.

Or, the question may be raised, "My wife and I have separated and friends have told me that the woman always gets every dime as well as the house, the car and the kids in divorces. How will I live?" Your response will perk up lots of ears from both sexes if done nicely and briefly.

I'm just tossing the ball to you. Catch it and run with it. The point is to make the information catchy and simple. Keep it changed often so readers will keep coming back.

Try to cover as many areas of law that you service in these things. Have enough variety so there will be something for everyone. Arrange for a "comment" provision so readers can write questions for you. If you can accomplish that, you've got a built-in clientele.

Be sure to include both your email address and web site address in all your office references, such as business cards, phone directory listings, stationary, memos, etc. Get your clients used to checking your Internet activities often. A newsletter can develop into a regularly sought after publication. You can get lots of readership without having to pay printing or mailing costs. Give this some thought.

You can also use your Internet "email" address for another route for your clients to reach you. This can save some frayed tempers if, for instance, you're in court, on vacation or otherwise involved. Wherever you are, if you drag your laptop with you, you can read the email and respond.

EPILOGUE

Congratulations!

You have just completed phase one of your new adventure into the practice of law. For some, this phase is the easier part. For others, it's the harder part.

Some people will find the book material difficult. It's always difficult to shed erroneous positive beliefs. Those who are convinced that it takes lots of money and many years to earn a living in a solo practice must exert great effort to unlearn that.

Once convinced of the truth, those doubting people might find the doing of the tasks much easier than learning about them.

I won't claim that this work is worthy of the Nobel prize for literature but, if someone wants to nominate me, I won't object. I don't expect you to be entranced by my writing style. My purpose in writing this book was not to win any literary honors. I won't be dismayed if I'm passed over for literary prizes. (Still, it would be nice.)

I have claimed title as the world's leading authority on how to open, manage, and succeed as a solo lawyer. I've also claimed unequaled expertise in the field of salesmanship training for lawyers. Both of those claims are indisputably true.

You've not seen a trace of a claim that my work will live forever. It may not even live half that long. Even if I'd wanted to charm you with clever turns of phrases or fancy verbal embroideries, I wouldn't know how.

What I had to say had to be said straight out. I wanted to be sure that you would understand my meaning without any attempted stylized literary tricks. The subject matter is far too important to risk having you miss any of the points.

If you forced your way through the rustic prose, misuses of grammar and countless repetitive phrases, you will have scored high on the chart of potentially successful solo practitioners.

Is there more to say on solo practice? Of course. I could easily write two or three more volumes with more good stuff. Is it necessary? No. This book and its regular supplements will be all you'll need. If you must be guided on training wheels through your practice, you won't make it.

What you've read in this book is all you'll need to inform you on the subject. The doctor spanks the new baby, and the baby screams with life. The spank was the jump start, but the baby had to do the rest.

Being informed is an indispensable precursor to success. But knowing how to do things and doing things are miles apart. Ask any schoolteacher.

You know how to do it. **Now do it!**

My twelve years as an adjunct law professor at Loyola Law School convinced me that many law students harbor erroneous beliefs concerning the practicalities of opening and operating a solo law practice. That problem has been treated in depth in this book, so there is no need to dwell further upon that.

I do hope that you did not bypass any topic based upon such prejudice. If you did, I really must urge you to go back and read each of these skipped topics. Of course, if you're a CPA, you wouldn't need to scrutinize the subject of bookkeeping. Still, even as an experienced accountant, you might find the peculiarities of law office accounting interesting if not edifying.

The most important thing to remember, and the greatest demand that will be placed upon you, is the need to hit the trail every day in canvassing the other lawyers for work assignments. If you sit and wait in your office for business to come, the only one who will come will be your landlord to collect the rent.

It's a drag, particularly in the beginning, to keep going, hour after hour, day after day, but this routine is essential in getting started. You've got to remember that the only reason for your getting the work, instead of someone else, is the fact that you were there and nagged for it. So, be there and nag for it.

If this is discouraging, think about how it will be in just a few months when you no longer have to ask anyone for anything. This book was written for you, because you don't have the money to set up a plush office and support yourself for months, perhaps years, before the clients start coming in.

You must also avoid falling into the rut of hitting the same lawyers over and over again because the ice has been broken and it's easier to go to them than to new people. Don't get too comfortable too early with a handful of lawyers who give you a few deals now and then. You will not only severely restrict your income, but you will delay the development of your own clientele indefinitely.

Don't rely on your telephone. It's too easy to be put off when you are only calling on the phone. Make personal visits. To be sure, you should augment your efforts by phone use and letter writing, but the mainstay of your plan must include personal appearances.

Remember what was said about "embarrassment" and how it can work for you as an ally instead of an enemy. Don't you be embarrassed; let the other person struggle with that problem.

Above all, keep going. Keep going. Put in a full eight hour day, every day, every week. But do first things first. Spend whatever time is necessary on the outside calling on your colleagues to get the work. Push yourself. You'll need to push yourself.

Don't think about the drudgery. Think about what you have gone through to get your education and its purpose. Think how nice it will be finally to have a full-fledged practice with your own clients.

You can't have everything. You want a practice of your own, and you ought to have it. You don't have a bankroll or a bank angel. This is the only alternative.

Even if you were rich, this would still be the best way, because having money won't buy you a practice. You've got to start somewhere, and even if you could afford to sit and wait, that will not get you a practice.

If you responded to the self-analysis test honestly and decided that you were cut out to be a solo practitioner, you need have no fear. If, on reflection, you reserved doubts, the doubts must be resolved before deciding one way or the other.

There is no shame in the recognition that you are just not cut out for solo practice. On the contrary, "Discretion is the better part of valor." We can't all be solo practitioners. Otherwise, who would we solo practitioners hire to help us when we expand?

If you are the stuff that the solo lawyer is made of, then go gung ho. There are some intelligent reasons for fearing to tread into solo practice. Fear alone is not one of them. I expect that this book will have shown you the senselessness of groundless fear.

If you have a doubt about your ability to make your way, and that doubt is the only obstacle in your path, I say to you, have no doubt.

If, on the other hand, your doubt suggests to you that you are the type who would better function in an employment atmosphere, then that is another matter. Consider that possibility thoroughly and at length.

A round hole is still strictly for round pegs. If you interpreted anything said here to the contrary, re-read that part. You have misunderstood.

It's not my intention to induce readers to disregard their natural bent and try to become something they are not. I don't wish to persuade anyone unsuited to attempt solo practice.

I do believe, however, that many so called "natural bents" can be re-bent. If one has the will to do a thing, that thing can usually be done. The power of the will is a gigantic force. I believe with all my heart that, you are what you believe you are, if you truly believe it.

I said that almost anyone with the brains and perspicacity to survive the rigors of law school and the bar exam has what it takes to go directly into the solo practice of law from law school. That is so, even if one lacks the financial staying power.

The fact that your trepidation, anxieties or other personality conflicts tell you that this is not for you doesn't change that statement. You can change, but why should you? Going into solo practice is not meant as a game or emotional therapy.

As a practical matter, however, I don't believe that any trained lawyer would make such a mistake. I am confident that after reading this book, you will be convinced one way or another. Your reactions and instincts will dictate whether you should go forward or not.

Of course, you won't like the canvassing part of starting your practice. Who said you would? This is the gateway that separates those who are going to be successful solo practitioners from those who are going to just fade out of the picture. You know the importance of this phase. The next person does not.

You also understand that this phase, like other things, will pass. You know that after you have used this part of the program to the full extent of its purpose, you will go on to bigger and better parts, so you don't mind the imposition upon your pride.

You have learned that the way to a successful law practice is charted just as surely and as scientifically as a point on a navigational chart. You also know that the greatest distaste and basis for fear, is lack of confidence in purpose and the prospect of eventual success.

The other person suffers from such distaste and fear, not you. This is why he or she will either get discouraged and quit or not even start at all, and why you will go on toward a nice comfortable and lucrative solo practice.

There is a sort of law of compensation. At first, you will find excitement and interest in virtually every kind of case. You will, to some extent, be carried by this excitement and interest through the worst part of the garbage stage.

As someone once said about show business, "There are no small parts; there are only lousy actors." This could be paraphrased for the law business, "There are no small cases; there are only lousy lawyers."

Every case, every client, every single thing to be done involving the law, ought to have some challenge and some attraction for a lawyer. It's only when you become so blasé because of the diversity and scope of your practice that you will really deserve to scoff at the so-called "garbage case."

As you look around, everyone you see seems to be in the legal profession. This is not true. It still takes a pretty special kind of a person to make the grade as a lawyer. Not everyone can get into a law school. Not everyone can pass the bar exam. Not everyone has what it takes to even attempt these challenges.

You have, and you succeeded. You have that special, certain something. You are special. You have also shown your extreme good taste in books. Be thankful for this, and don't ever allow yourself to complain when you are foraging through this beginning stage.

I am always interested in quandaries that may serve as input for future supplements. If you have such material, you may reach me at my e-mail gmsinger2@aol.com or my office address: 38-180 Del Webb Boulevard, NPO 271 Palm Desert, CA 92211 (or through West Group), and I will do my best to respond. Phone calls are expensive and not usually very productive.

Good luck.

See you in court.